Aerial view of the Theatre, the excavations and adjacent areas. (*Copyright J. K. St. Joseph*)

Reports of the Research Committee
of the
Society of Antiquaries of London
No. XXVIII

Verulamium Excavations

Vol. I

By

Sheppard Frere, M.A., F.B.A., F.S.A.

With sections by
I. W. Cornwall, R. Goodburn, B. R. Hartley, K. F. Hartley, W. H. Manning,
H. Waugh, and M. G. Wilson

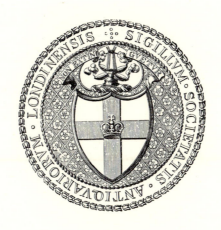

OXFORD
Printed at the University Press by Vivian Ridler for
The Society of Antiquaries
Burlington House, London
1972

PRINTED IN GREAT BRITAIN

PREFACE

VERULAMIUM, which came to extend over 200 acres (80 ha.), was one of the largest cities of Roman Britain. Its site, today empty and reverted to park and agricultural land except for the church of the parish of St. Michael's and its surrounding buildings, lies west of St. Albans, facing the city across the small river named the Ver. In ancient times the Roman city lay on the Watling Street, some 20 miles from the Thames at Westminster, at the point where it intersected roads leading east to Colchester, south-west to Silchester, and westwards to Alchester and Cirencester. But in reality the city owed its position not to these roads but to the pre-existing Belgic stronghold already styled VERLAMIO on the coinage of king Tasciovanus.[1] This was the capital oppidum of the Catuvellauni and the seat of its kings until Cunobelin obtained possession of Camulodunum.

In Roman times a short-lived military post appears to have been the first occupation of the valley floor, but in or soon after 49 a regular city was laid out. There is cumulative though not quite conclusive evidence that it was a *municipium iuris Latini*.[2] Despite destruction in the rebellion of Boudicca (A.D. 60–1) the new city flourished and expanded. In 79, as its inscription shows us, the forum was dedicated in the governorship of Agricola.[3] By the reign of Hadrian the original defensive earthwork had become obsolete and was filled in, to be crossed by streets and houses. A further serious fire took place *c*. 155–60, but was a benefit rather than otherwise to the expanding town, for in the later Antonine period large town houses for the first time appeared, the theatre was built, and the reconstructed forum was adorned with new temples.

Towards the end of the century, and probably under Clodius Albinus, fresh earthwork defences were begun on the line of the bank and ditch known as the Fosse, but were apparently left unfinished. The new line aimed at enclosing 225 acres (90 ha.) an increase to almost double the area enclosed by the original defensive earthwork (the '1955 Ditch'). The area of this had been 119 acres (47·6 ha.). Before the middle of the third century the defences had been remodelled and realigned as a bank with town wall; the area enclosed was reduced to 200 acres (80 ha.). The famous theory that Verulamium *c*. 275 'must have borne some resemblance to a bombarded city' due to the decay of its public and private buildings[4] and the lack of any constructional activity during the third century is now known to be a myth: it will be shown below that a long frontage of shops on the *cardo maximus* was built in stone at precisely this time (*c*. 275). During the fourth century prosperity was maintained; town houses were being built and provided with mosaics down to the end of the century, and during the fifth several phases of structural activity have been identified.

This brief history of the site will serve to introduce it. A fuller assessment will be provided in Volume II of this report as a final statement of conclusions when all the evidence has

[1] R. P. Mack, *The Coinage of Ancient Britain* (London, 1953 and 1964), no. 172.

[2] The evidence is set out in *Bulletin of the London University Institute of Archaeology*, iv (1964), 79–80.

[3] R. P. Wright, *Antiq. Journ.* xxxvi (1956), 8–10; D. Atkinson, ibid. xxxvii (1957), 216–17; S. S. Frere, *Britannia* (London, 1967), 202.

[4] R. E. M. and T. V. Wheeler, *Verulamium, A Belgic and Two Roman Cities* (Oxford, 1936), 28; cf. R. G. Collingwood in *Roman Britain and the English Settlements* (Oxford, 1936), 202.

been collated. Meanwhile lengthy and still mainly valid mutually complementary accounts will be found in *Antiquity*, xxxviii (1964), 103–12, and in the *Bulletin* of the (University of London) Institute of Archaeology, iv (1964), 61–82, these being interim statements.

Modern excavations at Verulamium began in 1930 with the opening of the five-season campaign directed by Dr. R. E. M. (now Sir Mortimer) and Mrs. T. V. Wheeler. The work was published for them as the eleventh Report of the Research Committee by this Society, under the title *Verulamium, A Belgic and Two Roman Cities* (Oxford, 1936). The excavation of the Theatre, part of the same campaign, was published separately by its excavator, Dr. Kathleen Kenyon, in *Archaeologia*, lxxxiv (1935), 213–61, and a public building facing it across Watling Street in Insula XVII, apparently a *macellum* or shopping-precinct, was excavated by Miss K. M. Richardson in 1938 and published in *Archaeologia*, xc (1944), 81–126.

Meanwhile the inauguration of the Verulamium Museum near St. Michael's Church in 1939 and the fortunate fact that its first two curators should be Dr. Philip Corder and Mrs. Audrey Williams (now Grimes) ensured that first-class professional ability has been applied to all subsequent finds. Finally, before the present series of excavations began in 1955, came the 1949 excavations of Sir Mortimer Wheeler and Mrs. M. A. Cotton, when Building C, the most north-westerly of the temples at the south-west end of the forum was explored and somewhat summarily published, and part of a building in Insula XIII was excavated as a training scheme for students of archaeology.[1]

[1] *Transactions of St. Albans and Hertfordshire Architectural and Archaeological Society*, 1953, 13–97.

CONTENTS

LIST OF PLATES

LIST OF FIGURES IN THE TEXT

ABBREVIATIONS AND BIBLIOGRAPHY

Antiq. Journ.	*The Antiquaries Journal*, Society of Antiquaries of London
Arch. Ael.[4]	*Archaeologia Aeliana*, 4th series, Society of Antiquaries of Newcastle upon Tyne
Arch. Camb.	*Archaeologia Cambrensis*, Cambrian Archaeological Association
Arch. Journ.	*The Archaeological Journal*, Royal Archaeological Institute
Bar Hill	Macdonald, G., and Park, A., *The Roman Forts on the Bar Hill, Dumbarton-shire* (*P.S.A.S.* xl, 403 ff.)
Ber. R.G.K.	*Bericht der Römisch-Germanischen Kommission*, Frankfurt
Brampton Hoard	Manning, W. H., 'A Hoard of Romano-British Ironwork from Brampton, Cumberland'. *C. &. W.* lxvi (1966), 1 ff.
Camulodunum	Hawkes, C. F. C., and Hull, M. R., *Camulodunum*. Society of Antiquaries Research Report XIV. Oxford, 1947
Cranborne Chase	Pitt-Rivers, A. H. L., *Excavations in Cranborne Chase*, i–iv (1887–1905) (privately printed)
C. & W.	*Transactions of the Cumberland and Westmorland Antiquarian and Archaeological Society*, new series. Kendal.
Dark Age Britain	Harden, D. B. (ed.), *Dark Age Britain, Studies presented to E. T. Leeds*. London, 1956
Devizes Museum Catalogue, ii	Cunnington, M. E., and Goddard, E. H., *Catalogue of the Antiquities in the Museum of the Wiltshire Archaeological and Natural History Society at Devizes*, Part ii (1934)
Eburacum	Royal Commission on Historical Monuments, England, *Eburacum, Roman York*, 1962
Espérandieu	Espérandieu, E., *Recueil général des bas-reliefs, statues et bustes de la Gaule romaine*, i–xii (1907 ff.)
Glastonbury	Bulleid, A., and Gray, H. St. G., *The Glastonbury Lake Village*, i–ii, Glastonbury Antiquarian Society, 1911–17
Great Chesterford	Neville, R. C., 'Description of a Remarkable Deposit of Roman Antiquities of Iron, discovered at Great Chesterford, Essex, in 1854'. *Arch. Journ.* xiii (1856), 1 ff.
Hod Hill, i	Brailsford, J. W., *Antiquities from Hod Hill in the Durden Collection*. British Museum, 1962
Hod Hill, ii	Richmond, Sir Ian, *Excavations carried out between 1951 and 1958*. British Museum, 1968
ILS	Dessau, H., *Inscriptiones Latinae Selectae*
Jewry Wall	Kenyon, K. M., *Excavations at the Jewry Wall Site, Leicester*. Society of Antiquaries Research Report XV. Oxford, 1948
J.R.S.	*Journal of Roman Studies*, Society for the Promotion of Roman Studies, London
Liverpool Annals	*The Annals of Archaeology and Anthropology*. Liverpool University Press
Liversidge	Liversidge, Joan, *Furniture in Roman Britain*. London, 1955

Lydney	Wheeler, R. E. M., and Wheeler, T. V., *Report on the Excavation of the Pre-historic, Roman and Post-Roman Site in Lydney Park, Gloucestershire.* Reports of the Research Committee of the Society of Antiquaries of London IX. Oxford, 1932
Lysons	Lysons, S., *Reliquiae Britannico-Romanae,* i–iii (1813–17)
Maiden Castle	Wheeler, R. E. M., *Maiden Castle, Dorset.* Reports of the Research Committee of the Society of Antiquaries of London XII. Oxford, 1943
Newstead	Curle, J., *A Roman Frontier Post and its People: The Fort of Newstead in the Parish of Melrose.* Glasgow, 1911
Num. Chron.	*The Numismatic Chronicle.* Royal Numismatic Society, London
O.R.L.	*Der Obergermanisch-Raetische Limes des Römerreiches,* Lieferung 15, Kastell Dambach (Band I B, Nr. 7); Lieferung 32, Kastell Zugmantel (Band II B, Nr. 8)
Proc. Soc. Ant. Lond.	*Proceedings of the Society of Antiquaries of London,* 2nd series
P.S.A.S.	*Proceedings of the Society of Antiquaries of Scotland.* Edinburgh
Richborough II–IV	Bushe-Fox, J. P., *Second, Third and Fourth Reports on the Excavations of the Roman Fort at Richborough, Kent.* Reports of the Research Committee of the Society of Antiquaries of London ii, no. VII, iii, no. X, iv, no. XVI. Oxford, 1928, 1932, 1949
Richborough V	Cunliffe, B. W. (ed.), *Fifth Report on the Excavations of the Roman Fort at Richborough, Kent,* Reports of the Research Committee of the Society of Antiquaries of London XXIII. Oxford, 1968
Roman Colchester	Hull, M. R., *Roman Colchester.* Reports of the Research Committee of the Society of Antiquaries of London XX. Oxford, 1958
R.I.B.	Collingwood, R. G., and Wright, R. P., *The Roman Inscriptions of Britain,* i. Oxford, 1965
Sandy Hoard	Manning, W. H., 'A Roman Hoard of Ironwork from Sandy, Bedfordshire'. *Bedfordshire Archaeological Journal,* ii (1964), 50 ff.
Three Hoards	Piggott, S., 'Three Metalwork Hoards of the Roman Period from Southern Scotland', *P.S.A.S.* lxxxvii (1953), 1 ff.
Trans. Birmingham A.S.	*Transactions of the Birmingham Archaeological Society*
Trans. Bristol and Glouc. A.S.	*Transactions of the Bristol and Gloucestershire Archaeological Society*
Trans. Dumfries and Galloway N.H. and A.S.	*Transactions of the Dumfriesshire and Galloway Natural History and Antiquarian Society*
Trans. London and Middlesex A.S.	*Transactions of the London and Middlesex Archaeological Society,* new series
Verulamium	Wheeler, R. E. M., and Wheeler, T. V., *Verulamium, a Belgic and Two Roman Cities.* Reports of the Research Committee of the Society of Antiquaries of London XI. Oxford, 1936
Wedlake, *Camerton*	Wedlake, W. J., *Excavations at Camerton, Somerset.* Camerton Excavation Club, 1958
Wheeler,	Wheeler, R. E. M., *London in Roman Times.* London Museum, 1930
Wheeler, *Verulamium*	See *Verulamium*
Wroxeter, i, ii	Bushe-Fox, J. P., *First and Second Reports on the Excavations on the Site of the Roman Town at Wroxeter, Shropshire 1913 and 1914.* Reports of the Research Committee of the Society of Antiquaries of London I and II. Oxford 1913 and 1914
V.C.H.	*The Victoria County History.* London

DARK or BLACK SOIL		OPUS SIGNINUM	
BURNT DAUB & DEBRIS		CONCRETE	
DISTURBED BURNT DAUB		CHALK	
ORANGE CLAY		FLINTS	
BRICKEARTH		TILES	
GRAVEL		PLASTER	
BURNT CLAY		CHARRED WOOD	
OCCUPATION SOIL		CHARCOAL & ASH	
SAND or MORTAR		TRAMPLED DIRT	
BRONZE~WORKING 'BOX'			

FIG. 1. Key to sections. Note: the positions of published sections are shown on fig. 26 (p. 111).

INTRODUCTION

IT WAS in 1954, on the receipt of news that a wide new modern highway was to replace the narrow lane which then climbed Bluehouse Hill carrying the main road from St. Albans to Hemel Hempstead, that the Verulamium Excavation Committee was reconstituted by the Society of Antiquaries, and the present writer was invited to become director of excavations. The lane, deeply worn down by the traffic of centuries, bisected the Roman city of Verulamium, since its course approximately coincided with that of the street between the Forum and Insula XXVII. It was clear that any widening would involve much cutting back on either side with consequent destruction of Roman levels; and since the new road was to be extended north-east from the old right-angled corner in the vicinity of the church, so as to cross the river Ver and make contact with the A5 road beyond it, what amounted to a gigantic section of the complete town along its central north-east–south-west axis would be cut away (Frontispiece).

Archaeological excavation in advance of this threat was imperative, and was begun in the summer of 1955. As the result we had three clear seasons of excavation, and by rigidly confining work to within the boundaries of the threatened zone almost all that could be hoped for was achieved. Only in Insula XIV did the unexpected depth and complexity of the structures prevent total excavation: this was an area previously devoted to the cultivation of allotment gardens, access to which was impossible until 1957. By 1958 road-widening was in full swing; thereafter it remained to complete the excavation of structures previously partly revealed and already destroyed, by following them back on either side of the road.

In this way seven seasons of work were achieved, and the excavations ceased at the end of 1961. Each year digging was undertaken for between seven and eight weeks in July and August, except in 1955 when work started in mid-June and continued for nine weeks, and in 1960 and 1961 when only 5 weeks' work was done. The area to be explored was divided into a number of sites each controlled by a supervisor; the actual digging was done partly by paid labourers and partly by volunteers. After the first season the labourers hired were always students on vacation, who proved to be a sturdy, reliable, and intelligent band. In the fullest years it was normal to have over a hundred people at work daily. Under such pressures we found it impossible to prolong the seasons beyond about eight weeks, even if time had been available from other duties; but much was achieved in the period. That this was so was largely due to the skilled excavators who gave their services as supervisors: through them standards were created and maintained and they kept the detailed records of the work. I myself exercised a general control and measured and drew the building-plans. An incalculable debt is also owed to members of the Excavation Committee who helped with the organization. In this connection tribute must be paid to James Brabazon Grimston, fifth Earl of Verulam, chairman of the committee and also owner of much of the land, who took the keenest interest in the work and furthered it by far-sighted skilful management. Mrs. M. Aylwin Cotton was Hon. Secretary, and indefatigable in the help she gave. We were privileged to have the support of James Broad, F.S.A., as Hon. Treasurer until his untimely death in 1957, when his place was taken by Mr. H. J. M. Petty who with his wife gave the keenest full-time service to every aspect of the organization. Without these various friends my own task would have been impossible. Thanks are also gratefully expressed to the officials of the Borough of St. Albans, especially to Mr. W. B. Murgatroyd the Town Clerk, and Mr. A. S. Moody the Engineer, through whose active interest the support of the Corporation

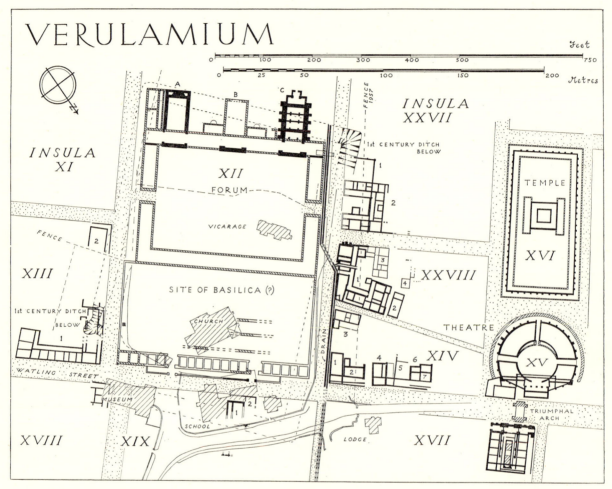

FIG. 2. Plan of the central part of Verulamium showing the position of Insula XIV.

was maintained; much help in kind was made available by Mr. S. F. Tomkins, Superintendent of the Highways Department. Finally Mr. J. Lunn and Dr. Ilid Anthony, successive Directors of the Verulamium Museum, were unceasingly generous in their support and in the provision of facilities.

It is one of the characteristics of the organization of British archaeology that much keenness and devotion go to the raising of funds and the contemplation of large-scale programmes, but at the end the Director is left with fifty or a hundred chests of material and no resources for their disposal. Whatever plans may have been made to lay aside funds for aftercare are all too often nullified by the needs of the excavation in progress, and by constantly rising costs. I have been particularly fortunate, therefore, in having enjoyed the services of Miss M. G. Wilson, F.S.A., who for nine years has drawn and classified the coarse pottery in return for the small pittance which was all that could be paid to her; and I am grateful to the Craven Fund of the University of Oxford for grants of £100 in 1968 and 1969 to the excavation fund when this was all but exhausted at a premature stage. That it lasted so long is due to the skill of the present Hon. Treasurer, Mr. G. B. Dannell.

Miss Wilson has also drawn much of the decorated samian, the rest of which was undertaken by Miss G. Adams and Mr. B. R. Hartley, as well as most of the glass and a good deal else. Other finds have been drawn by various artists as available, and this has resulted in some variation in style. In a large enterprise such a result, however regrettable, is really inevitable, at least until those who have the administration of funds establish a central institute for the processing of excavation finds. For the cleaning of corroded metal work I was fortunate in being able to persuade my colleagues Miss Ione Gedye and Mr. Henry Hodges to have this done in their laboratory at the Institute of Archaeology of London University.

The site photographs of 1955 were the work of Miss Nancy Lord; in all subsequent seasons they were taken by Mr. M. B. Cookson, whose cheerful presence throughout the dig was a constant support; thanks are also expressed to Mrs. M. Conlon for her prints and for certain studio photographs. Mr. R. L. Wilkins has also photographed objects at the Oxford Institute of Archaeology.[1]

It soon became clear that the report on the excavations would extend to more than one volume. The present book deals with the finds made along the north-east side of Insula XIV in the excavations of 1957–60. The reason for publishing this area first is not merely the great interest of the structures, but also the more practical consideration that the close stratification observed here has yielded a very large mass of finely dated pottery, at least for the period down to 175, the publication of which is fundamental to the chronology of the rest of the sites investigated. It is a regrettable fact that Wheeler's five-year excavation in the city, 1930–4, resulted in the publication of only seventy-nine pieces of Roman pottery, including five plain but no decorated samian vessels: indeed most of the material still remains unpublished in the Museum. There exists thus a lacuna in our knowledge of local coarse-pottery chronology, an essential tool of research, which is only partly filled by the small groups published by Miss K. M. Richardson in *Archaeologia*, xc, and by Mrs. M. A. Cotton in *Trans. St. Albans and Herts. Archit. and Archaeological Society*, 1953. Hence the necessity to lay the foundations firmly in the present volume.

[1] My gratitude is due to Miss E. M. Grisdale and especially to Miss A. M. Welch, successive secretaries to the Oxford Institute, for their work on the typescript.

PART I

INSULA XIV

I T WAS in 1957 that work reached Insula XIV (Frontispiece). In that summer excavation was continued to its east side below the course of the new road; but the interest of the discoveries made there, and the great depth of surviving stratification (pls. VI, VII), amounting to almost 6 ft., persuaded us, once the urgent work elsewhere had been done, to continue excavation in this Insula. The site had previously been used for allotment gardens, and it had not proved possible to dispossess the holders until road-building became imminent. The unfortunate result of this was that the relevant portions of Insulae XXVII, XXVIII, and XIV had all to be dealt with in a single season, the summer of 1957; as a consequence the plan of this part of the present site (i.e. south-east of the '1957 fence' marked on figs. 8, 10, 11, etc.) is not as fully recovered as is desirable.

During the years 1958–60 a length of some 210 by 96 ft. was explored along the south-west frontage of Watling Street.[1] The result was the recovery of three principal periods of building: (i) the original pre-Boudiccan layout of timber-framed shops: (ii) timber-framed shops of the post-Boudiccan period, at intervals renewed and expanded until they were destroyed by a conflagration in the Antonine period: (iii) masonry shops of the later third century (pl. I).

The method of construction used in Periods I and II, involving horizontal sleeper-beams set in the soil, meant that frequent renewals were necessary. In Period II no less than four successive reconstructions were identified within the years c. A.D. 75–150, and within each of these phases there were often two, sometimes three, renewals of flooring. The demolition of half-timbered structures, whose framework was packed with daub, resulted in a rapid build-up of clay or, rather, brick-earth layers, so that the surface rose some 2 ft. 6 in. during the course of seventy-five years. In archaeological terms this meant that, in addition to a series of plans illustrating the growth of the Insula in great detail, we were able to recover a sequence of pottery and other objects closely stratified and well dated, often to within 5–10 years. Because of the importance of the dated succession, the evidence has been fully set out in tables below. After Period II A it might have been sufficient to list only the critical pieces of samian; however, the full list is given for each period, as this throws interesting light on the problems of rubbish-survival. There is an obvious time-lag in the coin-lists also.

The site was not occupied from c. 155 to 275, and above the floors, or even the make-up levels beneath the floors, of the late third-century buildings agricultural disturbance had destroyed the stratification.

At first the method of excavation was to dig comparatively small trenches some 10–14 ft. square, separated by 3-ft. barrowing balks; but great difficulty was experienced in correlating

---

[1] The supervisors responsible for the work recorded in this volume were Miss M. G. Wilson, Miss Charmian Phillips (now Mrs. P. Woodfield), Dr. Alison Ravetz, Mr. R. Hope Simpson, and Dr. W. A. Cummins. I gladly acknowledge my debt to them.

the timber buildings because the layers were found to vary enormously from trench to trench. In subsequent seasons, therefore, efforts were made to open up much wider areas. This meant some sacrifice of sections, which was amply compensated by more complete plans. It turned out that the stone buildings of the latest period had been extensively robbed north-west of XIV, 2; and even where this had not occurred their foundations had been sunk right through all earlier levels down to natural soil. The method consequently evolved was to excavate the interior of these buildings, leaving a thin section against the robber-trenches for later drawing. Only in the cellar of XIV, 4 were no earlier deposits left, but the area of this was sufficiently small to allow reasonably certain restoration of destroyed wall lines.

The early buildings were excavated below XIV, 1–5; north-west of this only XIV, 6–7 and the burnt Antonine buildings below them were exposed, leaving the earlier levels untouched. It was intended in this way to lay out the plan of all these periods for permanent exhibition in such a way as to illustrate their respective levels; but the regretted and premature death of the fifth earl of Verulam, our chairman and land-owner, interrupted the implementation of this plan when only the buildings of Period I had been treated.

Methods of construction

The masonry buildings, built of flint and mortar, rested as stated on deep footings. In XIV, 1 the foundations were of flints and concrete filling the trenches dug to receive them, and this was probably true also of XIV, 4 where even the footings had been robbed away: the remaining walls of Period III, apart from those of the cellar and interior partitions in XIV, 5, rested on foundations of chalk flung into the trenches and packed tight. Robbing had not affected these footings (pl. IV and fig. 25).

In Periods I and II, however, the buildings were half-timbered, and good evidence for their form of construction survived in the walls burnt in the Antonine fire. Careful dissection was carried out in the north-west, north-east, and south-east walls of Room 23 and the north-east wall of Room 55 (figs. 3, 4; pl. XXIII) where the structure was especially well preserved because the lowest 12–18 in. had been baked *in situ* within the enveloping hot daub collapsed from the higher parts. The internal partition walls (23/24, 23/17, 55/56) were all only *c.* 8 in. thick, though the supporting sleeper-beams were sometimes rather wider, up to 12 inches. The north-west wall of Room 23, an external wall, was 1 ft. thick. Wall 23/24 was built of clay packed against each side of what appeared from the baked impressions to be a framework of wattle hurdling whose twigs ran horizontally (pl. XXIIIc). Only two intermediate uprights were identified. The remaining walls, however, had a framework of a more substantial type, consisting of squared posts evenly spaced at vertical and horizontal intervals, between which much thinner laths were keyed into the sleeper-beams below and forced alternately in front and behind the higher horizontal members (pl. XXIIId; fig. 4). In this way a core of almost continuous wood was created, to be packed with clay and then plastered if required. Before plaster was applied, the surface of the clay was keyed to receive it, sometimes by means of trowel cuts but often by the use of some kind of roller or stamp incised with a chevron pattern. The effect of the latter was a much more regular, deeper pattern with rounded edges; considerable pressure must have been applied to the clay while it was still surprisingly plastic. The trowel cuts, on the other hand, were sometimes random, but sometimes carefully executed to form a chevron pattern; they were sharp and shallow. It seemed that occasionally the surface was rouletted and then not subsequently plastered: this if true would make a dusty surface and one attractive to spiders, and it is more likely that the intention was to key a second application of clay which has become detached in the burning. See pp. 160–2 and pls. LIV–LX for a description of some of the fragments.

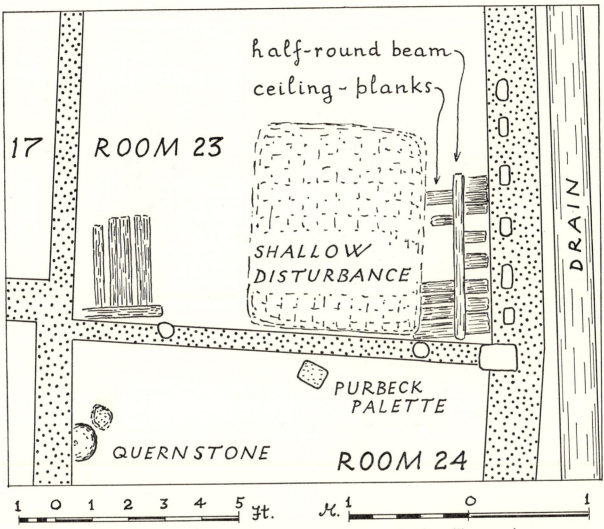

FIG. 3. Period II D, Rooms 23, 24: plan of detail from fig. 19. For the ceiling remains see p. 75.

In the north-west wall of Room 23 the main uprights, set at 14-in. intervals, were rect-angular timbers measuring 6 by 3 in. (fig. 3); their longer sides were placed along the axis of the wall so that the sockets for the horizontals when cut in them would not unduly weaken the upright.[1] In wall 55/56 the uprights were 4 in. square and set at intervals of 1 ft. 10 in.

[1] See Richmond, *Hod Hill*, ii, 76; Van Giffen, Valkenburg, *Jaarverslag van de Vereeniging voor Terpenonderzoek*, xxv–xxviii, Afb. 43.

in an oak sleeper-beam which was $2\frac{1}{2}$ in. thick when excavated, though its remains may have shrunk (fig. 4). A horizontal timber was set 8 in. above the sleeper; it measured 3 in. high by 1 in. wide. The mortice hole for its tenon in the vertical members at each end would still be supported, accordingly, by $1\frac{1}{2}$ in. of sound wood each side of it, and by a core of perhaps 2 in. between it and the opposite socket. The first application of clay to this wall was reinforced

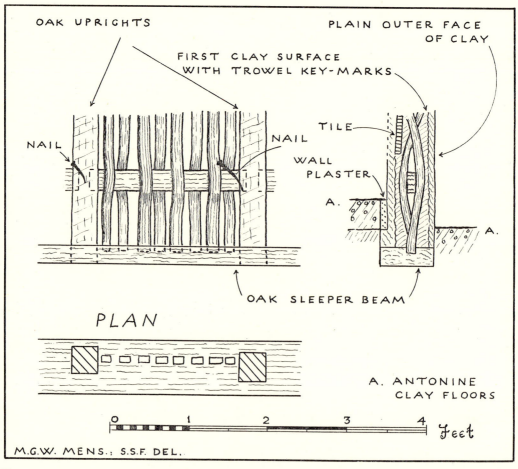

Fig. 4. Diagram illustrating the construction of a timber-framed wall: Period II D, Wall 55/56.

with sizeable tile fragments and sherds, and its surface was keyed with trowel cuts to take a second clay surface 1 in. thick; the south-west face of the wall had an inch of plaster in front of this again, which only survived where protected by a later floor. There were no keying marks for it on the surviving outer face of the clay (which, however, only stood 6 in.); the plaster accordingly may be a later refinement, added with the secondary floor. The laths measured *c.* 2 by 1 in. and had been anchored in sockets cut in the surface of the sleeper-beam. No nails were used in the structure except at the junction of main upright and horizontal beams, where one nail at each joint occurred: the two nails recovered measured 3 and $5\frac{1}{2}$ in. long.

The south-east external wall of Rooms 55 and 56 was *c*. 8 in. wide and though less well preserved it retained traces of uprights *c*. 4–5 in. across at 1 ft. 6 in. intervals centre to centre (pl. XXVII*a*). It was not clear whether these posts had been squared or not.

Further details of structure are given below in the detailed description of the buildings, including the evidence for wooden floors (pp. 74–5). Here enough has been said to establish the character of construction. Except at certain points on the plan of Period II D there were few deep-set posts: sleeper-beam construction was uniform. But in some walls of the reconstruction of *c*. A.D. 150 (Period II D), where the line chosen coincided with deep cleavages due to the soft filling of lower foundation trenches on the same line below, posts had been driven deeply into the ground to keep the walls upright, and had sometimes been packed with large flints (pls. VIII, XXII*b*). It is unlikely that sleeper-beams were used at these places, though their use could be proved in other walls of this phase. Very occasionally stone packing was found in Period II C (pl. XVI*a*).

It remains to show that the character of this timber framing based on sleeper-beams, so well preserved by the Antonine fire, was typical also of the predecessors of the structures of Period II D. Buildings of Periods II A–C, underlying II D, not having been burnt, were not well preserved. They had been demolished in the course of successive reconstructions. The walls for the most part were marked only by slots between the floors (pl. XIV*b*), though the quick build-up of brick-earth layers showed that the demolished walls had been packed with this material. In only one wall (pl. XIII*b*) did the decayed remains of the sleeper-beam survive. The buildings of Period I, however, had been destroyed by fire in the Boudiccan rebellion. Unfortunately even here little remained *in situ*, for the whole bed of burnt daub was much shallower than the one above, and it seemed to us that much had been carted away and the rest raked over by survivors seeking their valuables or for the dead. Here and there, however, burnt oak sleeper-beams remained *in situ* (pls. V*b*; X; XIII*a*), and the daub itself retained impressions of timber-framing analogous to that already described. But while the impressions of prepared laths were indeed present, the impressions of wattles were more common in the debris of the first-century fire. South-west of the main range of burnt buildings faint traces of other structures were found, which had not been burnt (p. 14). These usually revealed themselves as rows, single or in one case double, of stakeholes of a size to hold the withies or wattles of hurdled framework. The double row (pl. XII*b*) was *c*. 8 in. apart, too wide to represent the separation of the sticks of a single hurdle round a nearby horizontal. Rather it is to be interpreted as a clay wall faced on each side with wattle work for the purpose of keying plaster.[1] It must not be forgotten, also, that impressive remains of a Period I building, showing an upright 8 by 6 in. morticed into a sleeper-beam and supporting a wattle frame, were found on the other side of Watling Street in 1938 in Insula XVII.[2] Thus it seems evident that basically the same techniques of half-timbered construction were used from the beginning of Period I, *c*. A.D. 49, down to Period II D, *c*. 150.

A very noticeable feature of the samian lists published below is the enormous proportion of residual sherds yielded by deposits of successive periods. Normally the presence of such material on a site is accounted for by such processes as 'the digging of pits and of deep

---

[1] See I. A. Richmond in E. M. Jope, *Studies in Building History* (London, 1961), 23: *Arch. Ael.*[4] xxx (1952), 242; ibid. xxxi (1953), 210.   [2] *Archaeologia*, xc, pl. xv, c.

foundation-trenches'.[1] Here, however, there were as yet no stone walls requiring deep foundations, nor were contemporary pits anything but infrequent within the buildings. How, then, can the survival of such quantities of early sherds be explained, or the distribution of pieces of a single vessel over parts of the site widely separated both spatially and chronologically (as could sometimes be established)?

It may be suggested that the explanation lies in the incorporation of sherds, sometimes intentionally, sometimes by chance (depending on their size) within the brick-earth daub which was applied to the timber framework of the walls. It is probable that daub for reconstructed walls was puddled on the spot and was largely derived from surplus material obtained from the demolition of standing buildings. A simple calculation shows that (if we omit the colonnade from consideration) the plan of Phase II B (fig. 11, p. 52) contains 1,027 linear feet of wall over a total area of 7,408 sq. ft. Assuming a height of 10 ft. and an effective thickness of clay of c. 6 in., the walls would have contained c. 5135 cu. ft. of clay. On demolition such a quantity would have covered the whole area to a uniform depth of 8·32 in. In fact, however, no layer of make-up or primary floor in Phase II C is much more than 4 in. thick. The surplus has presumably been built back into the walls, together with fresh brick-earth specially introduced. See pp. 28 and 338, no. 1011.

The final plans here published are not exactly identical with those published previously in interim reports, for they have been corrected here and there when further study of the note-books and sections rendered it necessary.

The architectural tradition

A comparison of the plan of Period I (fig. 8, p. 22) with that of any pre-Roman complex in Britain is sufficient to indicate how great an innovation was the architecture involved. In the Iron Age the Britons lived in huts which for the most part were circular. In the Belgic period, while circular or oval huts still continued popular,[2] at Canterbury a sub-rectangular hut, recessed some 3 ft. 6 in. into the surface of the soil, has been excavated;[3] it was inhabited from c. A.D. 5 to 60. At Park Street there were indications of further sub-rectangular Belgic huts[4] not recessed. But these, both in their form (detached individual huts without clear shape) and in the manner of their building (sustained by posts set in postholes or by banks of turf), are totally different from the structures seen on fig. 8. These are a row of shops planned and roofed as a unit. In plan it recalls a military barrack-block, even to the extent of possessing rather larger quarters at the end, though the stark simplicity of the plan may have been over-emphasized owing to the difficulty of tracing the unburnt appendages to the rear. The military flavour suggested by the plan is probably not, however, illusory, for it is intensified by the evident military origin of the wall structure. No pre-Roman building in Britain exhibits timber framework of such complexity: but the style is immediately recognizable at the Roman fort of Claudian date at Valkenburg Z.H., close to Leiden near the mouth of th

[1] C.B.A. Research Report No. 6, *Romano-British Coarse Pottery* (1964), 3.

[2] e.g. Camulodunum, C. F. C. Hawkes and M. R. Hull, *Camulodunum* (Oxford, 1947), 66 and pl. CVI; Lockleys,

Welwyn, *Antiq. Journ.* xviii (1938), pl. LXX.

[3] S. S. Frere, *Roman Canterbury* (3rd edn., 1962), fig. 14.

[4] *Arch. Journ.* cii (1945), 23–5, fig. 2.

Old Rhine in Holland,[1] and is found again in later military buildings at Corbridge.[2] Remembering its early date, we cannot doubt that military architects and craftsmen were lent or sent to aid the construction of the new city. Indeed, in view of the government's need to expedite its programme of urbanization in the new province with all speed, it seems likely that military supplies of seasoned timber may have been made available: even in the small area explored it can be calculated that over 3,300 yds. of squared beams would be required for the wall-frames, without taking account of the roofs.[3] At the date suggested only army stockpiles are likely to have had ready timber in such quantity. By the time that the buildings came to be reconstructed in Period IIA, it can probably be assumed that local builders had mastered the technique. Indeed this conclusion is forced on us by the dating: the time for army aid was in the period 61–8 under the governors Petronius Turpilianus and Trebellius Maximus when the province was at peace; but it will be shown that reconstruction was delayed until *c.* A.D. 75, in the time of Vespasian, whose whole reign saw the army of Britain fully engaged on further conquest.

The function of the buildings

There is no difficulty in recognizing the range of buildings of Period I as a row of shops. From the comparative simplicity of this original plan the sequence of development to the complexity of Period IID is continuous. The utilitarian function of the buildings is further demonstrated by the absence of tessellation and the rarity of painted plaster. Even *opus signinum* is absent until late in Period IIB, when it was laid down in four rooms *c.* A.D. 120–5.

It is certain, however, that many of the premises were not simple retail shops in the modern sense of that term, but workshops of manufacturing metal-smiths, mainly in bronze, who sold and repaired goods manufactured by themselves on the spot. As early as Period I small 'boxes' appear in the floors, apparently for trapping waste material from the lathe-turning of bronze vessels (p. 18), and these recur from time to time until the end of Period IIB, *c.* A.D. 130. Noteworthy also is the thick fragment of bronze drapery from IIA, Room 4 (p. 144, no. 160): this suggests the resmelting of metal from a statue overthrown in the Boudiccan revolt. Much evidence in the form of scrap and crucibles is noted in the description of individual rooms and in the reports on the finds; but no actual moulds were found. However, in this context attention should be drawn to fig. 49, no. 157, a faultily cast leg from a statuette which had probably been rejected, before sale, when it was found that an air-bubble had formed at the knee. This piece was almost certainly residual in its late third-century context. A large number, indeed, of the metal finds give the impression that they were collected for reworking or were the by-products of manufacture; this is especially true of the large group of finds in the cellar of Period III.

[1] See van Giffen in *Jaarverslag van de Vereeniging voor Terpenonderzoek*, xxv–xxviii, Afb. 38 and 43; also Richmond in E. M. Jope, *Studies in Building History* (London, 1961), p. 21, fig. 3.

[2] See note 1, p. 9. Sleeper-beams in fact are rare in military contexts in Britain. Their use seems to have been soon given up by the army in Britain in favour of trenches in which the uprights were set directly on the trench bottom.

For their occasional use at Flavian Pen Llystyn see *Arch. Journ.* cxxv (1968), 127: cf. *Richborough V*, 17.

[3] Fig. 8 shows *c.* 922 ft. of wall, and it is assumed for the calculation that uprights occurred at 1 ft. 6 in. intervals and that they were on average 15 ft. high. The actual reconstruction (fig. 5) is discussed on p. 15. The roof would call for at least another 1,050 yds. of scantling.

Iron-working is attested not only by the sets and punches and other tools recovered, but also by the blacksmith's scale found in Room 26 of Period II B. And bone-carving as an activity carried out here is suggested by Mr. Goodburn's comments on fig. 54, no. 187, from Period II D, Room 55: this room also yielded goldsmith's equipment. Commercial activity of a more general kind may be deduced from the three weights found in II B, Room 33 (p. 124, nos. 88, 89), while the large quantity of oyster-shells from the portico in front of Room 4 suggests the refuse of an eating-house.

Social implications

It is shown on pp. 15–16 below that the plan of the building of Period I demands a communal roof with ridge running parallel to Watling Street. The same is true of those of Periods II A and II B. It probably follows from this that the building was in single ownership and the shops in it hired out to tenants. If we are right in suggesting that the building of Period I shows unmistakable evidence of official assistance (p. 11), it would be possible to suppose public ownership, whether by the government or by the municipal authority, on the ground that the land was acquired for the purpose. It is perhaps more likely, however, that the landlord was either one of the Catuvellaunian nobility whose plot it already was, or else perhaps even an immigrant speculator in land who paid for the assistance rendered, in expectation of profit to come.

Shops of this sort in the classical world were often let out to freedmen,[1] but in Britain at this date it is perhaps unlikely that the Roman social system had had time to take root so thoroughly, and we may rather suppose that the tenants were free craftsmen and labourers, though even these might have had correspondingly close traditional or legal ties with their Celtic patrons. However, in the later periods we should not rule out the presence of freedmen,[2] and even in Period I they could have been installed if the landlord were an immigrant speculator.

The plan of Period II B (c. A.D. 105) shows the beginnings of an interesting expansion of the premises to the rear, linked with the provision of small lanes or footpaths for access. The plan presents problems of roofing which were solved by setting the subsidiary ridges at right angles to the main roof, which must still have been parallel with the street. By the beginning of Period II C (c. A.D. 130) the expansion of the rear has made necessary a radical replanning, and this frontage is no longer roofed continuously as before: instead the gaps for drainage between blocks show that the complex is now composed of a series of buildings running back from the street, though still masked by the continuous portico in front. It is noteworthy that the sleeper-trench of the front wall of the buildings can be shown to have crossed the gaps; this probably implies a door through the rear wall of the portico at these points. The processes of individual development have proceeded still further by Period II D (c. A.D. 150). We may conclude, as at Cirencester in the same period, where a block of half-timbered shops was being converted piecemeal into stone,[3] that by about the reign of Hadrian tenurial arrangements were changing. Individual tenants had sufficiently enriched themselves

---

[1] Cf. R. Meiggs, *Roman Ostia* (1960), 224.   [3] *Antiq. Journ.* xlii (1962), fig. 4.
[2] See *RIB*, 1065, for a Catuvellaunian *liberta*.

to acquire their own and perhaps neighbouring premises and to rebuild them in individual fashion, behind the portico which was doubtless still under town-planning control.[1] Indeed, it can be shown that in Period II D a whole block (Rooms 17–24) was in single possession (p. 78).

PERIOD I, *c.* A.D. 43–60

(a) Pre-building occupation, c. A.D. 43–9

The buildings planned on fig. 8 appear to be the first on the site but the earliest metalling of Watling Street predates them: the road was laid on the subsoil after removal of the humus (fig. 26, sections B–B[1], M–M[1]). Here and there below the buildings 'floors' and occupation-material appeared, lying above the old plough-soil; but no foundation trenches were identified nor even any alignments of substantial postholes. The old plough-soil itself produced Belgic sherds, the rim of a Gallo-Belgic plate (fig. 100, 26), pieces of Terra Rubra beaker and two sherds of samian, f. 18 (?) ('probably Claudian') and 29, Claudian. Between Room 6 and the adjacent part of the colonnade the burnt wall was only faintly recognizable in patches, because here the sleeper-beam had been placed on the surface of floor T II 39 (in fig. 26, section B–B[1], right half, it occupies the slight hollow below the figure 36 in the circle). It follows that layers T II 42–4 are certainly pre-building. Layer 44 was a gravelly floor on the natural brick-earth; it was associated with a hearth of chalk. It was sealed by 43, a floor of clay and pebbles in which was a mass of small stakeholes forming no recognizable pattern; above this was a layer of occupation material containing much charcoal (42). The status of layer 40 is less certainly previous: its relationship with the south-east wall of Room 6 was such that it was probably contemporary and formed the original floor of the room. Indeed, a large posthole was found in the appropriate position in this layer to indicate the front of the original room (see plan, fig. 8): in that case it would seem to follow that the shop lacked a front wall at first, and was closed merely by shutters.

Below Room 2 there was no pre-building occupation; below Room 4 was a stony floor with an occupation level on it (fig. 23, section C–C[1], layers 40 and 39). Below Room 8 rather similar occupation occurred—a thin gravel floor over old plough soil and sealed by occupation material (fig. 9 (p. 27), section Y–Z, layers 38–41): layer 38, however, might be thought of as the original floor of the building of Period I if we assume that its sleeper-beam was laid *on* the floor. Beneath Rooms 26 and 27 there was a fairly substantial floor of gravel, up to 4 in. thick, which underlay the sleeper-beam (fig. 27, section M–M[1], layer 41 C): but one cannot disregard the possibility that here again the beam was laid *on* the floor instead of being sunk into it, and that both are contemporary. Likewise the front wall of the room appeared to be laid on the surface of 43 A, the original metalling of Watling Street. Below Room 30 a brick-earth floor with hearth occurred, and in the occupation layer (B IV 42 S) over it was found a brooch of Hod Hill type (fig. 30, 16). It is probable that this floor is primary in the original Room 30–1 (for the wall 30/31 appeared to be secondary) and is not

[1] *ILS*, 6085, 68; 6087, 78. The first, from the *Lex Julia municipalis* of 44 B.C., forbids building on, obstructing, or gaining ownership of, public areas and porticos in Rome which are under the jurisdiction of magistrates. The second, the Charter of Urso of the same date, enacts 'Respecting public roads or footpaths within the area of the *colonia*, all such thoroughfares, roads and paths that do, shall or have existed in the said area shall be public property.'

an indication of pre-building activity. There was no samian. Thus, definite evidence for occupation earlier than *c.* A.D. 49 is confined to the south-east end of the building below Rooms 3–8.

As for contexts for this early occupation, it is known that features of the Belgic period occur in the vicinity, and the area of Insula XIV lies also within the probable perimeter of the early Roman fort (p. iii). The dating evidence is tabulated[1] as follows:

BELOW ROOM	LAYER	COINS	SAMIAN (all South Gaulish)
4	Z I 40, stony floor		15/17, pre-Flavian
	Z I 39, occupation on 40		15/17 (three), pre-Flavian
			18, probably Neronian
6	T VI 40, floor		27, Claudian
			18, 33, pre-Flavian or Flavian
	T VI 39, occupation on 40		15/17, Claudian
			29, pre-Flavian
	T II 43, floor (fig. 26, B–B¹)		29, Tiberio-Claudian
	T II 42, occupation on 43		29, 15/17, pre-Flavian
	T II 40, ? primary floor of building		27, probably Claudian
			15/17, pre-Flavian
8	T XX 40 (fig. 9 Y–Z)		15/17, pre-Flavian
	T XX 38, ? primary floor of building	Claudius I dup. *RIC* 67d	29, *c.* A.D. 45–55
			29, Claudian
		Augustus, *RIC* 351	15/17, 18, pre-Flavian

(*b*) *The buildings, c.* A.D. 49–60. See fig. 8 (p. 22)

The buildings of Period I were destroyed by fire all along the frontage of Watling Street. But south-west of this range there were faint traces of out-buildings (Rooms 21 and 22) which had not been burnt, and of which little could be traced because of much later disturbance in this area. The absence of burnt deposits suggests that at the time of the Boudiccan sack the wind was south-westerly and that Insula XIV was fired from Watling Street.

Bordering the street-metalling, which was identified in four places, was a continuous sleeper-trench bounding 18, an undivided side-walk or portico *c.* 11 ft. wide. Beyond this was a double range of rooms 14–16 ft. wide, whose back rooms were occasionally subdivided. These may be taken for a series of shops and work-shops. They were not all exactly regular. The corner premises, less fully explored than the others, appeared to be exceptionally large, contained in a block 40 ft. instead of 32–4 ft. deep; Room 6, the corner shop, was 24 ft. wide,[2]

---

[1] The dating is that of Mr. B. R. Hartley, who kindly listed the large amount of samian, much of it small scraps, with his comments, before a detailed study of the stratification had been undertaken.

[2] It seems unlikely that the wall between 3 and 5 extended to divide 6, since this would result in two shops narrower than all the others with a width of only 11 ft. 6 in.

and Room 3 was 20 ft. The remaining premises in this corner block (8 and 11) had front rooms of normal size (14 ft. 6 in. wide by 19 ft. deep) and back rooms respectively 19 ft. 6 in. and 18 ft. 6 in. deep. Room 13 was only 9 ft. by 10 ft. 6 in. Next came a regular series of four in which the front room was 19 ft. and the back 12 ft. deep.[1] At Room 30 a new series began, in the first of which the front as well as the back was eventually divided, though at first 30 and 31 seem to have been one room.

It is clear that all these shops were under a single roof since there are no gaps for drainage; the roof-ridge must have been parallel with the street. A reconstruction is offered in fig. 5. The height is governed by the colonnade and by the need to insert windows above it if the shops were not to be unduly dark. The colonnade is restored at 7 ft. high, which seems to be a minimum figure. If it merely consisted of a series of spaced posts, postholes would perhaps have been more economical. The presence of a sleeper-beam has been taken to imply a balustrade as well (but see p. 77). The side-walk is 11 ft. 6 in. wide: its roof with an angle of only 19 degrees touches the front wall of the building at a height of 12 ft. Five feet have been allowed above this for windows (closed by shutters), making the front wall 17 ft. high. With a roof-slope of 30 degrees the apex comes at 30 ft. above the ground.[2] This would allow space for a loft for storage. Alternatively with a single roof-slope of 30 degrees from apex to colonnade the front wall would still be 15 ft. high and the apex 27 ft. The omission of windows, accordingly, does not afford much saving. Scattered traces of what was probably a similar building with colonnade were found on the opposite side of the street by Miss K. M. Richardson in 1938.[3] It is evident that an attempt was being made to provide the town with the amenities of a classical city, if only in timber.

The colonnade is assumed to have turned the corner (Room 1) since no street-metal accompanied the outside of the south-east wall of Rooms 2 and 3. Its external foundation trench was not looked for since its position was later occupied by a sewer, subsequently robbed, running from the forum (fig. 2).

Some rooms received renewals of flooring, and this led to a difference in level between adjacent rooms. Room 3 had a shallow, saucer-shaped pit, 1 ft. deep and lined with clay, near its north-east wall: this pit had later been sealed by a floor. The tiled hearth in Room 6 was later sealed by a secondary floor (fig. 26, section B–B¹). As already mentioned (p. 13) the front wall of this room was an afterthought, lying as it did on the surface of a secondary floor: the large posthole seen on the plan marks the position of a shutter in the first phase (fig. 27, section B–B¹, trench T II, layer 40). In the west corner of Room 6 was a circular hollow 2 ft. 8 in. in diameter with curving, saucer-shaped base sinking in the centre to 6 in. below floor level (fig. 6). It was filled with fallen burnt daub, and represented the emplacement of some wooden feature such as a barrel. The concave character of the floor of the pit could perhaps be explained as due to wear caused by continual tipping. Alternatively the pit may have housed a basket with rounded bottom. The tub had been in position when the fire occurred, for its sides could be made out rising c. 5 in. through the burnt daub enveloping it; but the fire had destroyed it too thoroughly for any definite

[1] The wall between 19/20 and 23/24 was not found owing to the deep robber-trench of Building XIV, 4.
[2] This would seem a minimum angle; see, however, p. 162, no. 16, for a piece of daub from Period II D, which retains the imprint of timbering suggesting an angle of 50 degrees. This would extend the height.
[3] *Archaeologia*, xc, pl. xxi.

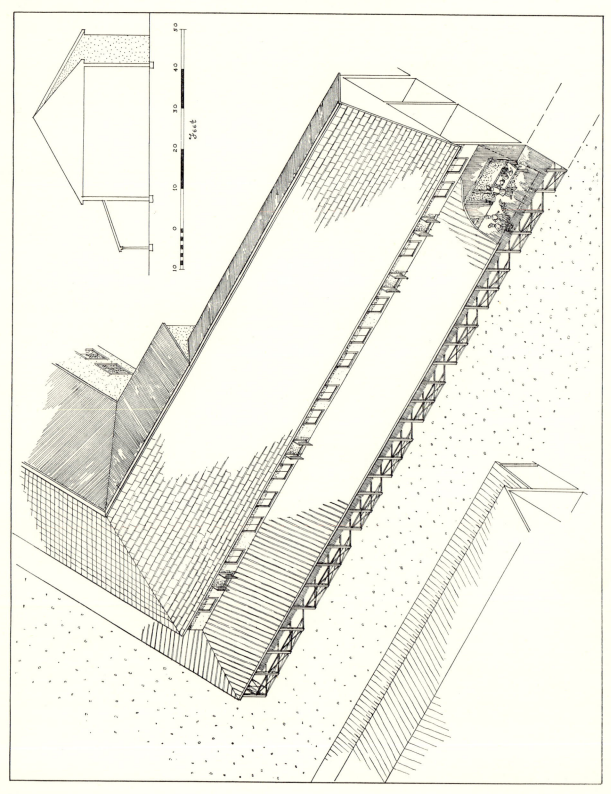

Fig. 5. Reconstruction of the Period I buildings (*drawn by J. C. Frere*).

conclusions to be drawn about its character. A tub for drinking-water is perhaps the best explanation; if it had contained anything such as oysters or material stores it is hard to see how they came to be rescued in the emergency. By a curious coincidence an analogous feature was found in Room 10 of Period II D almost directly above (p. 76). Four feet further north was a rather less regular pit beside the wall (fig. 9, section Y–Z). It was filled with a mixture of clean yellow clay, burnt clay, and charcoal and was perhaps the stokehole of an oven beyond the section-face.

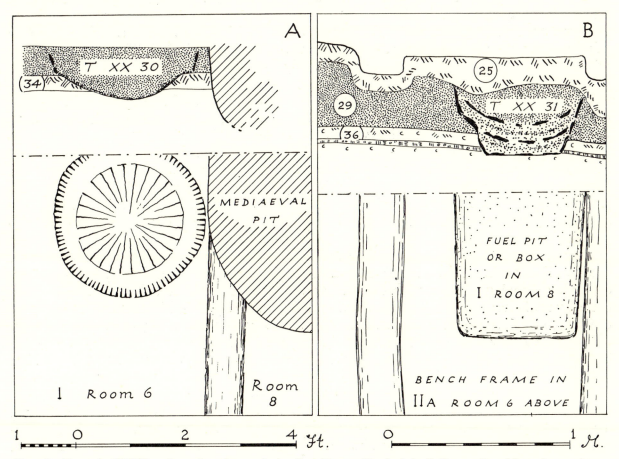

FIG. 6. Trench T XX: plan showing tub in I,   FIG. 7. Fuel pit in I, Room 8 and bench-emplace-
Room 6.   ment in II A, Room 6 (see also pl. IX*a*).

In Room 8 the edge of an oven showed in the side of the trench; it consisted of six courses of tiles. Nearby was a rectangular pit (fig. 7) with sloping sides; it had held a wooden container whose charred remains rose 9 in. through the fallen daub. The box had been empty at the time of the fire, but it can be explained as a fuel-box for the oven on the analogy of a parallel in Room 8 of Period II C (p. 55). It produced some fragments of crucibles.

In the south corner of Room 15 two whole jars were buried up to their lips in the fallen daub; one was a polished grey vessel with barbotine dots (fig. 101, no. 64), the other a coarse-ware jar (no. 79). They had probably been standing on the floor, for if on a shelf they would have broken as they fell (p. 80). The same room had a shallow rectangular pit cut against its north-west wall, measuring 6 by 4 ft., and some 1 ft. 6 in. deep (pl. XI*b*). It had been open at the time of the fire, and was full of burnt daub; but at its base, and especially along the sides, lay pieces of coke-like organic material which had melted as it carbonized. As it burnt it had given off a viscous material, and is now devoid of any uncarbonized matter. Dr. I. W. Cornwall examined a sample; he decided that it was not bread as had originally been thought by us, but was perhaps wool or hair. The pit perhaps contained a chest for storing clothing.[1]

Room 20 contained many traces of burnt planks, which were taken at the time to be fallen roofing, but are more likely to have been traces of flooring (p. 74). They lay at the base of the layer of burnt daub, though not completely in register like those shown in pl. XXIX, but their disarray might be explained by the collapse of joists.

Room 27 was a bronze-smith's work-shop. In the east corner lay a large hearth. At a distance of *c.* 2 ft. 6 in. from the front wall three rectangular emplacements were found on the floor (pl. XIII*a*). They were 22–24 in. square and about 2–3 in. thick, with level bases. Two more, 17 by 13 in. and 16 by at least 26 in., were found in the rear premises of the next shop, against the north-east wall of Room 25. The contents rose proud of the room floors on which they lay (fig. 27, section N–N[1], 32) and thus seemed to have been resting in shallow wooden trays though no trace of these could otherwise be recognized. The contents consisted of fine sandy earth interleaved with much bronze powder and tiny lumps of this metal, so much so that the whole deposit was tinged green. Some contained a little iron as well. When closely examined the material seemed to be very fine and densely stratified as if deposited by water. It seems likely that we have here an apparatus for trapping the waste from lathe-turning, engraving, or filing bronzes, with the intention of resmelting it later.[2] It would follow that the trays lay below a bench on which the work took place, and that dripping water conducted the dust to the tray below: the trays were too shallow for more than a drip of water to be used, unless indeed they were actually substantial boxes of which only the bases survive to the height filled with deposit. No postholes were found either here or elsewhere in association with these trays which could be certainly interpreted as supports for benches: in Room 27 there were some random stakeholes in no regular pattern; in Room 25 there was a short length of wood 20 by 6 in. set in the floor between the two trays and possibly a second might have been present beyond the section-face to north-west. Nearby was a charred, approximately rectangular upright, 10 by 12 in., set 4 in. in the floor, and beyond this remains of a hearth or oven.

It is interesting to record that a further tray of the kind described was found in the front of Room 20 of Period II A (fig. 10) which lay immediately above the three trays in Room 27, and three others occurred in Room 22 of that period which roughly overlies the present Room 30. But whether this means that the same tradesmen survived to return to the sites of their former premises must be considered doubtful in view of the long delay before the rebuilding of these shops was undertaken (p. 40). Two more trays were found elsewhere in

---

[1] As a parallel the chest, containing armour, cloth, and other material, found buried in the floor of a building at Corbridge in 1964 may be cited: *J.R.S.* lv (1965), 203;

Arch. Ael. xlvi (1968), 115–26.
[2] See p. 382, no. 1.

the building of Period II A (Room 9) and one in that of II B (Room 13), but none later (fig. 23, section D–D¹). This means that after *c.* 120 this method of manufacture, as far as the evidence goes, became obsolete at Verulamium.

In Room 9 of Period II A the two emplacements were successive, and neither survived to the end of the Period (p. 27). The later of the two itself seemed to have two phases, the upper being *c.* 1 ft. 6 in. square, the lower being only 1 ft. wide. The upper one had a piece of lead embedded in it, the lower a piece of iron.

In Room 13 of Period II B, immediately above, another similar emplacement occupied the corner of the room. It was 1 ft. 11 in. wide by more than 10 in. long, and 0·5 in. deep. At the bottom was what appeared to be powdered iron lying on a thin layer of white clay, which may have been the remains of the wooden container. There was much powdered bronze, and also a larger fragment *c.* 0·5 in. long.

At the time of discovery no parallel to these collection-trays could be traced; but in 1959 Mr. J. S. Wacher discovered exactly similar, and in one case rather better preserved, features at Catterick. One lay below Building III, 4 there and belonged to the Flavian-Trajanic period. Two others were found in Building VII, 2, one of which was *c.* 21 in. square and retained traces of timber round the edges. A third in the same building was different, the material being contained in a small pit dug in the floor (*c.* 18 in. square by 12 in. deep) with no sign of lining. The date of these three examples is no earlier than late Antonine.[1]

In the front of Room 30 a semicircular hearth of burnt clay over chalk, surrounded by a kerb of flints, lay against the north-west wall; but it was probably earlier than this wall, since there were indications that the partition between Rooms 30 and 31 was secondary, whereas this hearth was sealed by a secondary floor. The hearth in Room 27 and the oven in Room 8, however, and probably those in Rooms 6 and 19, seem to have been placed with no trepidation against the neighbouring timber-framed walls.

(c) Dating evidence, Period I buildings

The *terminus post quem* provided by the presence of pre-building layers containing Claudian pottery has already been mentioned (p. 13); moreover the earliest floors of the building contain pottery and coins of this date, and the building itself occupies a secondary relationship with Watling Street, its colonnade being placed over the silted-up side ditch (fig. 26, section B–B¹). Thus time has to be allowed between A.D. 43 and the construction of the building, a gap which can be accounted for at least in part by the original military occupation (p. iii). On the other hand, the building itself had been erected sufficiently before A.D. 60 for lengthy occupation often involving two layers of floor to occur. The date A.D. 49/50 is accordingly suggested. This fits the general historical picture in Britain sufficiently well,[2] and if Verulamium can be accepted as a Claudian *municipium*, its foundation is unlikely to be earlier than, but might well be contemporary with, that of the *colonia* at Camulodunum. The latter, as Tacitus records, was founded for both military and civil purposes, and the urbanizing part of the policy could well have been extended by the establishment of a city at Verulamium also.

---

[1] I am grateful to Mr. J. S. Wacher for this information.　　　　[2] See S. S. Frere, *Britannia* (London, 1967), 82.

The dating evidence for Period I can be tabulated as follows:

Note: **D1, S2,** etc. in col. 4 refer to *Decorated* vessels and *Stamps* illustrated on pp. 218–62

ROOM	LAYER	COINS	SAMIAN (all South Gaulish)
1 portico	T III 34, primary floor		29, Claudian
	T III 33, trample on 34		29, 18, pre-Flavian 27, Claudian
	T VII 50, primary floor		15/17, 18, pre-Flavian
	T VII 49, trample on 50		15/17, 18, 27, pre-Flavian
	T VII 47, secondary floor		29, 30, Claudian 29, c. A.D. 55–65 15/17, 18, 27, pre-Flavian
	T VI 37, trample on floor		29, probably Neronian 15/17, pre-Flavian
18 portico	T I 22, primary silt of Watling St. ditch below colonnade (fig. 27)		29, Claudian
	T I 19, burnt sleeper-trench in front of Room 6		18 R, Ritterling 8, pre-Flavian
	B IV 40A, occupation below secondary floor		27, probably pre-Flavian
	A IX 5, burnt debris on Watling St.		29 (four), c. A.D. 50–65 (**D 1**) 29 (five), c. A.D. 55–75 ⎫ 30 (three), c. A.D. 50–65 ⎬(**D 2–D 8**) 30 (three), c. A.D. 55–65 ⎭ 29 base stamped ME⊕ILLVS (**S 2**), c. A.D. 60–85 Ritterling 8, 15/17 (three), 18R (two), 18 (two), 24/25 (three), 27 (eight) including stamp OF PRIM (**S 4**), all pre-Flavian.
2	T III 35, primary occupation		18, stamped OF MVRRAN (**S 3**), Claudio-Neronian 17, Claudian
	T III 32, secondary floor		15/17, 24/25, pre-Flavian
	T III 31, burnt daub		30, 24/25, Neronian 18R, pre-Flavian
3	T VII 51, occupation patch below 48		15/17, 24/25, 29, pre-Flavian
	T VII 48, primary floor		29, pre-Flavian

ROOM	LAYER	COINS	SAMIAN (all South Gaulish)
	T VII 46, secondary floor		29, 27, pre-Flavian
	T VII 41, burnt daub		15/17, probably Claudian
			29, Ritterling 8, pre-Flavian
			15/17, Ritterling 12, probably pre-Flavian
4	Z I 37, occupation on primary floor	Claudius, As, *RIC* 66	29, pre-Flavian
	Z I 35, occupation on secondary floor	M. Agrippa, As, *RIC* (Tib.) 32	29, *c* A.D. 55–65
			15/17, 24/25, pre-Flavian
		Claudius As, *RIC* 66	
	Z I 34, burnt daub		15/17, 18R, pre-Flavian
	Z I 36, burnt wall-trench		15/17, pre-Flavian
6	T II 40, primary floor (fig. 27, B–B¹)		27, probably Claudian
			15/17, pre-Flavian
	T II 39, secondary floor	Claudius, As, *RIC* 66	29, Claudian
			18, pre-Flavian
		Claudius, *RIC* 69	18, 27, 29, probably pre-Flavian
	T XX 34, secondary floor (fig. 9, Y–Z)		29, Claudian
	T VI 34, secondary floor		29, *c*. A.D. 50–65
			18, probably Claudian
			15/17, 18, stamped OF PRIM (S 5)
			27, pre-Flavian
	T VI, 29, burnt daub		15/17, 18, pre-Flavian
8	T XX 35, occupation on 37 (fig. 9, Y–Z)		15/17, pre-Flavian
	T XX 33, occupation on 36		29 (two), first cent.
			18, pre-Flavian
	T XX 29, burnt daub		27, pre-Flavian
10	A XI, 24, burnt daub		15/17, *c*. A.D. 55–70
			18, pre-Flavian
	A XI, 26, burnt wall-trench		29, Claudian (D 9)
14	A IV 41, burnt daub		29, burnt, Neronian (D 10)
			27, pre-Flavian
15–16	A I 40, burnt daub	Claudius, As, provincial issue, *RIC* 66	29, Claudio-Neronian
			15/17, 27, pre-Flavian
		Uncertain denarius, prob. Republican	

ROOM	LAYER	COINS	SAMIAN (all South Gaulish)
20	A X 22, burnt daub		29, *c.* A.D. 55–65 18 (two), 24/25 (two), 18, pre-Flavian 15/17 (two), probably Neronian
	A VII 44, burnt daub		15/17, 18R(?), pre-Flavian
21	A II 66, early occupation		29, Claudian (?) 15/17, 18 pre-Flavian
	A II 65, secondary floor		29, Neronian
	A II 64, burnt daub		29, probably pre-Flavian 27, pre-Flavian
Interspace 21/22	B I 51, floor		29, stamped [OF•CRE]STIO (**S 1**), *c.* A.D. 55–70 18, 24/25, 27 (three), pre-Flavian
	B I 50E (?destruction deposit)		15/17 (two), 27 (two), pre-Flavian 24/25, probably pre-Flavian
22	B II 42, primary floor		29, *c.* A.D. 55–70 27 (two), Neronian 18, Ritterling 12, probably Flavi an
	B II 41, secondary floor	Claudius, As	29, Claudian 15/17, Neronian 18 (two), Ritterling 12, Neronian/ Flavian 18R, first cent. 27 (*c.* eight), Claudian to Flavian 29, *c.* A.D. 65–80 37, *c.* A.D. 75–85 (*It is evident that this deposit is somehow contaminated and perhaps layer 42 as well*)
	B II 40, tertiary floor	Claudius, As, prov. copy (cf. *RIC* 66)	30, *c.* A.D. 55–65 (**D 14**) 29, *c.* A.D. 55–65 15/17, probably Neronian 18, pre-Flavian
25	B IV 35, floor	Claudius, As, poor copy (cf. *RIC* 66)	27 (two), Neronian 15/17, pre-Flavian
26	B IV 41D, primary floor		24/25, pre-Flavian
	B IV 37D, secondary floor	Claudius, As, copy	27, 29, pre-Flavian (**D 11**)

ROOM	LAYER	COINS	SAMIAN (all South Gaulish)
27	B IV 40B, primary floor		18, pre-Flavian Ritterling 9, Claudian
	B IV 40C, primary floor		15/17, 24/25, pre-Flavian
	B IV 37C, secondary floor		27, pre-Flavian, Curle 15(?), probably pre-Flavian
26–7	B II 38, burnt daub		30, Neronian 15/17, Neronian 18, 18R, 27, Neronian/Flavian
30	B IV 41L, primary floor		29, c. A.D. 45–60 (**D 12**) 15/17, pre-Flavian
	B IV 41S, primary floor		29, c. A.D. 50–65 (**D 13**) 15/17, pre-Flavian
	B IV 40L, occupation on 41L		15, Claudian 15, Claudio-Neronian
	B IV 40S, occupation on 41S		15/17, 27, pre-Flavian
	B IV 37S, secondary floor		24/25, probably Claudian 18, 27, pre-Flavian 29, first cent.
26–31	B IV 36, burnt daub		29, Claudian 15/17, 18, 27, pre-Flavian

PERIOD II A, c. A.D. 60–105

(a) *Pre-building activity, c.* A.D. 60–75

A consideration of the dating-evidence tabulated on pp. 28–39 shows that there was a delay of some fifteen years before the rebuilding of this insula. During these years a number of pits, some of them deep, were dug on the site: their fillings were not properly consolidated before rebuilding, and gradual sinkage played strange tricks with subsequent stratification (pl. X*b*). Only one of the deep pits was fully excavated by us (Pit 7 in trench B I, fig. 23, section F–F¹); it produced contents consistently datable to the period *c.* A.D. 60–75/80. Other shallower pits could be more easily assigned to these years by their position in the stratified sequence: in the deep pits sinkage was usually so great as to sever the stratification. Pits 1, 3, and 4 were probably dug at this time but were not fully excavated. Pit 7 was sub-rectangular, 8 ft. by 7 ft., and was 12 ft. 6 in. deep from its contemporary surface; it may have been intended as a well. Mr. Hartley notes that there is sufficient wear on the footrings of the samian vessels in it to show that the deposit does not derive from a pottery-shop. The pit also produced a number of crucibles and some window-glass.

PIT	DESCRIPTION	COINS	SAMIAN
6	B I, Pit 6, small, rect-angular pit between Pits 1 and 7: not marked on fig. 10		29, 27, probably Neronian
7	B I, Pit 7 (see above)		(All South Gaulish): for the decorated ware see **D 15–50** 29, probably Neronian 29 (at least two), prob. Vespasianic 30, *c.* A.D. 60–75 37 (at least four), *c.* A.D. 75–90 27 (five), one stamped OMOM (**S 17**), Flavian 35, probably Flavian 18 (at least four), Flavian 29, stamped OF CRE2T[I] retro. (**S 9**), *c.* A.D. 65–80 15/17, Neronian/Flavian 22, probably Flavian 67 15/17 35/36 24/25 The following stamps: 15/17, OF. RVFNI (**S 22**), *c.* A.D. 65–80 18, OF PONTI (**S 20**), *c.* A.D. 65–90 18, MASCVLVS (**S 14**), *c.* A.D. 55–70 18R, OF PRIMI (**S 21**), *c.* A.D. 50–65 18, OFRONTI (**S 10**), *c.* A.D. 70–90 27, OF. MACCAR (**S 13**), *c.* A.D. 40–60 18, OF. PATRICI (**S 19**), *c.* A.D. 70–90
	Pit 7, layer 63 layer 64 layer 65 layer 66 layer 67		18, Flavian 27, *c.* A.D. 60–80 36, Flavian 30, *c.* A.D. 70–85 18, stamped OF MONTANI (**S 18**), *c.* A.D. 65–80 27, stamped CV[or CA[retro. (**S 23**), Flavian 35/42, probably pre-Flavian 29, stamped [OF]CREST[IO] (**S 8**), *c.* A.D. 50–65 (**D 15**)

PIT	DESCRIPTION	COINS	SAMIAN
	layer 69		18, stamped OFIV[CVN] (**S 12**), c. A.D. 65–80
			27, stamped OF̑ALBAN̑I (**S 6**), c. A.D. 65–80
	layer 70		27, stamped OF CALVI (**S 7**), c. A.D. 65–85
			Ritt. 12, c. A.D. 60–85
			27, stamped MȆMO (**S 15**), c. A.D. 65–80
			27, [O]FMOI (**S 16**), c. A.D. 55–75
			29, GERM̑ANIOF (**S 11**), c. A.D. 65–75 (**D 16**)
			30, c. A.D. 65–85
			35, 27, Flavian
8	A II 56, 2ft. long, 10 in. deep		18(?), ? pre-Flavian
			29, pre-Flavian
			27, pre-Flavian
10	B IV Pit 10, diam. c. 3 ft. depth c. 18 in.		15/17 (two), one stamped PRIMVLI (**S 24**), c. A.D. 70–85
			27, 18, Flavian
11	B II Pit 11, oval pit c. 4 ft. 6 in. by 2 ft. 10 in.; depth 8 in.		15/17, probably Neronian
			Ritt. 8(?), Neronian
12	A VI 38		18, pre-Flavian

(*b*) *The Flavian rebuilding c.* A.D. *75–105* (fig. 10, p. 38)

Eventually (*c.* A.D. 75 or soon after, see below p. 40) the Watling Street frontage of Insula XIV was rebuilt in half-timber as before; the plan shows that a continuous row of shops once again occupied the site. A covered walk 11–12 ft. wide was provided beside the street. The premises behind this, however, were now less rigidly planned. Room 4 at the corner was at least 14 (and perhaps as much as 17) ft. wide and 14 ft. long, if it has been correctly divided from Room 3 by a wall beneath the unexcavated balk: this is supported by the dimensions as well as by a difference in the floors in the two trenches. These rooms are best understood as part of a range facing south-east on to the other street, for wall 3/4 is certainly not an extension of the rear wall of Rooms 8–10. Nor was the rear wall of Room 7 found extended to bound the back of Room 5 (fig. 23, section C–C¹), so that shop 6 seems to have had an exceptionally large rear room. But it must be admitted that shortage of time due to the unexpected depth of deposits prevented the lower levels of this part of the site being fully explored in the summer of 1957 before the new road covered them, and the plan is correspondingly more conjectural here than elsewhere.

From Room 8 north-westwards there appear to be two attached blocks, 8–10 and 11–23. Room 10 was 15 ft. 6 in. wide, but 8 and 9 were 13 ft. each, and all three were connected behind by Room 7 which was 9 ft. wide and contained an oven. Room 14 was 11 ft. wide and 17 ft. 9 in. deep with a rear room, 13, equally wide and 9 ft. 3 in. deep. The remaining front rooms, with the combined depth of Rooms 13 and 14 were 28 ft. long: Room 20 was 17 ft. 6 in. wide. Room 16, at 22 ft. 6 in., is exceptionally wide, but it might have been divided by a continuation of the wall 15/18 towards the front: such a wall would have been totally destroyed by the third-century cellar except for a few feet at the front which were not looked for beneath a balk. On the other hand, wall 20/22 is rather narrow and might perhaps more properly be regarded as a partition- than a party-wall: if so, shop 20–2 would be 26 ft. wide.

Further irregularity can be seen in the way in which the rear Rooms 12–19 overlap the premises in front in a manner inconsistent with the strict delimitation of tenements. This may be due to their being later additions to the structure. Though the faint traces of rear buildings in Period I perhaps also point to communal arrangements for storage or to inequality in the divisions of the rear area, the shops themselves in that period were regularly laid out in a series of easily recognizable front and back rooms. That regularity is patently absent in Period II A, though it was to be to some extent restored in subsequent rebuildings. It would appear that we may see here the play of free enterprise in the rebuilding, in contrast to what may have been a plan imposed by government architects at the start of Period I: in the first setting-out of a whole city the requirements of individual clients may well have received scant attention. Nevertheless it is impossible yet to suggest that tenements are individually built and owned: that stage does not appear until Period II C. The necessity still in this phase to restore a common roof with ridge parallel to the street, at a height sufficient to allow lean-to roofs for the portico in front and Rooms 12–19 behind, shows that the whole is still in single ownership and that individual shops are still let out to tenants, whether these were freedmen or free craftsmen.

Room 1 in an early phase of this period had a tile oven or hearth in it, but this was later destroyed and sealed by two subsequent floors before the end of II A. Room 2 had a hearth of clay near its corner. Room 4 may have been a bronze-worker's shop since in layer T VI 25, the make-up for Period II B Room 4 above it, was found a group of bronze scrap and discarded objects (pl. XLVIc) which may have been intended for the melting-pot. A notable find in this Room (T VI 28) was a bronze fragment evidently from the drapery of a life-size statue, no doubt intended for the melting-pot (fig. 49, 160). A discarded and broken statue at this early date (A.D. 75–85) strongly suggests destruction in the Boudiccan revolt, though the fall of Nero in 68 might have occasioned the overthrow of a statue of that emperor. In either case the fragment is valuable evidence for a pre-Flavian public monument at Verulamium. Room 6 contained an interesting emplacement consisting of two shallow parallel slots, 3 ft. 3 in. apart, set 3–4 in. in its floor near the middle of its north-west wall and at right angles to it. Lengths of 6 ft. 7 in. of these bearers were exposed, and they could have been up to 8 ft. long (fig. 7). That they had carried something exceptionally heavy was clear from the fact that the floor beneath them had been fractured and caused to sink c. 5 in. by compression of the burnt daub below (fig. 9, section Y–Z, layer 25). There were, however, no indications from small finds or other discoveries of what was the function of these premises. As Room 6 is the front room, the emplacement is not likely to represent a large cupboard in such a position, and if it represents a normal counter, the absence of such features elsewhere is striking: more likely therefore it supported a stout work-bench on which the repeated hammering of the cobbler or the smith eventually caused its bearers to sink. No hearth was found for a smith's forge, but layer 24, covering the contemporary clay floor, was a dense deposit of black charcoal an inch thick, which might suggest that one lay just outside the area excavated.

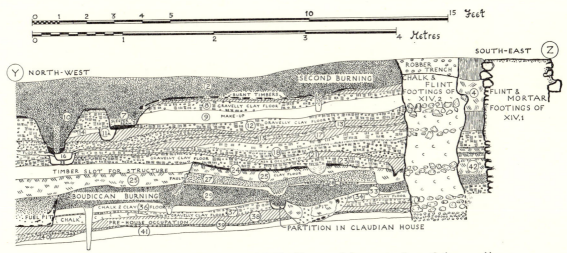

FIG. 9. Trench T XX, section Y–Z. (For position, see fig. 26 (p. 111)).

Room 8 had a small circular pit in its north corner, 5 in. deep with sloping sides, and filled with burnt and unburnt clay and charcoal. Room 9 was certainly the premises of a bronze-smith, for two of the rectangular catchment boxes, already described (p. 19), were found adjacent to its front wall, as if they had lain beneath a work-bench in this position (fig. 23, section D–D¹). These were successively in use, the one in the corner being the earlier. They were succeeded by a late floor of Period IIA in which lay a pit for a fuel-box, 5 in. deep by 1 ft. 10 in. wide, full of charcoal. Other bronze-smiths worked in Rooms 20 and 22; in the former the 'green box' lay almost directly above its pre-Boudiccan predecessors in Room 27 of Period I (pl. XIIIa); but, as has already been noted, the length of interval between the two occupations is against any direct continuity of tenancy: the preservation of very detailed plans and records would otherwise have to be invoked. Further south-west a shallow pit only 10 in. deep was cut in the floor of Room 20; it contained nothing but a filling rich in charcoal. In the floor itself was a small group of nineteen pieces of bronze scrap and fragmentary objects (pl. XLVb), and an iron T-shaped lift key (fig. 68, 74).

Room 23 also seemed to have been a smith's shop. The floor was covered by a 4-in. layer of occupation-earth which was black with charcoal, and in the corner was a shallow rectangular pit which probably contained a fuel-box. It was filled with yellow brick-earth, but some charcoal remained down its sides and at the bottom. The north-west part of Room 19, to rear of this, had similar indications: its floor was covered by a thick layer of occupation-material (B IV 31) containing much charcoal, small burnt fragments of bronze and some iron slag.

By some curiosity of dampness the sleeper-beam of wall 17/18 survived in perceptible form despite not having been burnt (pl. XIII*b*). Outside Room 17, Pit 9 appeared to be a demolition pit of *c.* A.D. 105. It was cut through B II 32G, the deposit contemporary with Room 17 to its south-west, and was sealed by 30G, the new floor of Period II B Room 23, above. It had a loose charcoaly filling, containing a large group of pottery. Pit 2 also appears to have been dug at this date; later floors had subsided into its filling. In a contemporary accumulation of rubbish outside Room 17 was found (fig. 59, 237) part of a large column-base of Bath stone; it is perhaps a broken fragment brought from the construction of the Forum nearby, as was the larger fragment found below Insula XXVIII Building 1 (*Antiq. Journ.* xxxviii (1958), 11).

Room 16 was probably a pottery shop, selling samian ware. A large group of broken but virtually complete vessels, all consistently late Vespasianic or early Domitianic in date and with a high proportion of decorated ware, was found in trench A VII. A curious feature was the wide distribution of the sherds throughout the stratification. The earliest occurrences were in A VII 40, the floor of Room 16, and in the trampled dirt (A VII 39) lying on it (fig. 24, section J–J¹); sherds were also found in the latest layers of trampled dirt in the portico of Period II A opposite Room 14. But many sherds of substantial size were also distributed through Period II B levels above, in the clay floors of II B Rooms 22 and 17, and in various contemporary layers in the portico. It is hard to account for this. Clearly, a consignment of samian was smashed early in Period II A, perhaps *c.* A.D. 80, and sherds were trampled into the floor. For large pieces to remain on the spot for a further 30–40 years, and to survive a rebuilding, it is probably necessary to suppose that they were used in a repair of the half-timbered wall, being incorporated in the clay as reinforcement. It is certain that tiles and sherds were used in this way (pp. 8, 10). Perhaps the pottery was broken because the shelves supporting it collapsed, bringing part of the wall down with them, and the wall was then repaired, the broken vessels being used to reinforce the patch. Then, when these walls were demolished for the Period II B reconstruction the sherds would find themselves in the new floor.

(c) Dating evidence for Period II A

Note: **D 53, S 40**, etc. in col. 4 refer to *Decorated* vessels and *Stamps* illustrated on pp. 218–62

ROOM	LAYER	COINS	SAMIAN (all South Gaulish unless otherwise stated)
1	T VI 32, primary floor		29, *c.* A.D. 50–65
			27, first cent.
	T VII 43, primary floor		29, *c.* 50–65
			27, Claudian
	T III 28, primary floor		29, probably pre-Flavian
	T VI 30, secondary floor		27, prob. pre-Flavian
	T III 27, intermediate floor		29 (two), pre-Flavian, one stamped [ME⊕I]LLVS (**S 40**)
			37 (two), 27, Flavian
			18, pre-Flavian

ROOM	LAYER	COINS	SAMIAN (all South Gaulish unless otherwise stated)
	T VII 30, late floor		30, 18, pre-Flavian
	T VII 38, late floor		29, c. A.D. 70–85
			18 (two), Flavian
			18, pre-Flavian
			Curle 15, pre-Flavian
2	T III 26, primary floor	Vespasian, As, *RIC* 757*b* (A.D. 77–8)	29, Neronian
			30, c. A.D. 70–85
			18, Flavian
			15/17, first cent.
			27 (four), two pre-Flavian, two Flavian
	T III 25, occupation on 26		30, 37, Flavian
			Curle 11, 27 (two), Flavian
			15/17, first cent.
			18 (three), one pre-Flavian, two Flavian
3	T VII 39, primary floor		29, 27, 30, pre-Flavian
	T VII 36, secondary floor		29, c. A.D. 55–70
			18 (three), two pre-Flavian, one Claudian
			27, pre-Flavian
			18R, stamped MESILLVS[FI] (S 41), c. A.D. 60–80
	T VII 35, occupation on 36		15/17, pre-Flavian
	T VII 29, later floor	Nero, As, *RIC* 329r	18 (three), two pre-Flavian, one (?) Flavian.
4	T II 37, floor		29(?), pre-Flavian
	T II 33, late floor		27(?), Flavian
	T VI 28		29, Neronian
5	Z I 30, primary floor	Claudius, As (barbarous), *RIC* 66	29, pre-Flavian
	Z I 27, occupation on 30	Vespasian, dupondius, *RIC* 473 or 739 (A.D. 71–3)	18 (two), pre-Flavian
			37, Flavian
			30, probably Flavian
	Z I 29, occupation on 30		29, c. A.D. 60–75; 15/17, pre-Flavian
	Z I 26, secondary floor	Domitian, As, *RIC* 237 (A.D. 81)	37, Flavian
			18 (two), 27 (two), Flavian
	Z I 25, occupation on 26	Claudius, As (barbarous), *RIC* 66	18, pre-Flavian

ROOM	LAYER	COINS	SAMIAN (all South Gaulish unless otherwise stated)
6	T XX 27, make-up for first floor		27, pre-Flavian
	T XX 25, primary floor		30, *c.* A.D. 70–90 29, Flavian 27, probably Flavian
	T XX 42, primary floor	Claudius, As (barbarous), *RIC* 66	
	T XX 24, occupation on 25		27, pre-Flavian 35, first cent.
7	A XI 22, make-up below primary floor		15/17, 24/25 (two), pre-Flavian 18, 18R, *c.* A.D. 60–80 27, *Central-Gaulish*, Trajanic (an intruder)
	A IV 39, make-up below primary floor	Tiberius, As (barbarous), *RIC* (Aug.) 370 Republican denarius L. Plautius Plancus, Syd. 959 (*c.* 47 B.C.) Claudius, As, *RIC* 66 Vespasian, As (*fair*), *RIC* 497 (4) or 747 (A.D. 71–3)	29, Neronian 24/25, pre-Flavian 27, Neronian/Vespasianic Ritt. 12, pre-Flavian
	A XI 23B, make-up below primary oven	Nero, As, *RIC* 329r Vespasian, denarius (*good*), *RIC* 16 (A.D. 69–71) Vespasian, As	
	A IV 38, primary floor		27, stamped OF SEV[ERI] (S 53), *c.* A.D. 65–80 27, Claudian/Neronian 15/17, Ritt. 8, pre-Flavian
	A XI 23A, primary floor and oven		27, pre-Flavian 27 (two), Flavian
	A XI 20, floor sealing oven		15/17, Claudian 18 (two), Curle 11, Flavian
	A XI 18 (=20)		27, *c.* A.D. 60–80 27, Flavian 18, probably Flavian
	A XI 16, occupation on 18		27, *c.* A.D. 60–80 27 (two), Flavian

ROOM	LAYER	COINS	SAMIAN (all South Gaulish unless otherwise stated)
			18, ? Flavian
	A XI 19, floor over 20		27, Flavian
	A IV 33, secondary floor		29 (two), pre-Flavian
			18 (two), Neronian/Vespasianic
			27 (three), two Claudian/Neronian, one Neronian/Vespasianic
	A IV 34, occupation on 33		37(?), Flavian
			27, pre-Flavian
	A IV 26, occupation on 33		29, Vespasianic
Rubbish accumula- tion out- side (SW. of) Room 7	A IV 40		29, pre-Flavian
			29 (two), Flavian
			37, Flavian
			30, c. A.D. 85–105
			37, Trajanic
			15/17 (two), pre-Flavian
			18, ? Flavian
			27 (three), Flavian
			Ritt. 9(?), pre-Flavian
			15/17 or 18 stamped [O]FNIGR (S 47), c. A.D. 45–65
	A IV 42		37, Flavian
			37, c. A.D. 75–90
			37, Trajanic
			27, stamped MIO retro. (S 42), Flavian
			15/17 (three), one Neronian, two Neronian/Flavian
			24/25 (two), one pre-Flavian, one Neronian/Vespasianic
			18 (five), Neronian/Vespasianic
9	A XII 27, primary floor		29, pre-Flavian
10	A VI 33, early floor	Nero, As, *RIC* 329*l*	30, c. A.D. 70–85
			37, c. A.D. 70–85
			15/17, probably Flavian
		Nero, As, *RIC* 321*l*	18, Neronian/Flavian
			27 (two), one pre-Flavian, one Flavian
	A VI 36, above 33		30, pre-Flavian
	A VI 32, upper floor	Nero, As, *RIC* 176	
	A VI 31, above 32		30, Flavian
			29, probably Neronian
			27, Neronian

ROOM	LAYER	COINS	SAMIAN (all South Gaulish unless otherwise stated)
			27, stamped OF ALBAN (**S 25**), Neronian/Flavian
			27, stamped OF CRE2TI retro (**S 34**), Flavian
			15/17, probably Flavian
			18 (four), one stamped OF AQVITAN (**S 26**), one pre-Flavian, one Neronian, two Flavian
			Ritt. 12, Neronian/Flavian, 36, first cent.
11	T I 14, wall-trench of portico at SE. end		29, probably pre-Flavian
			15/17 (two), 18, pre-Flavian
			18, ? Flavian
	A XII 26, primary floor	Nero, dupondius, *RIC* 286*l*	
		Vespasian, dupondius, *RIC* 744 (A.D. 72–3)	
	A VI 35, primary floor	Claudius, As (barbarous), *RIC* 66	29, burnt, Claudian
			29, Neronian
			27, pre-Flavian
			18R, first cent.
	A VI 25, secondary floor above 35		29, ? Flavian
			37 (two), Flavian
			27, Neronian
			18, probably Flavian
	A VI 24, above 25		37, *c.* A.D. 75–90
			Curle 11, Flavian
	T XXI 24, secondary occupation		18, pre-Flavian
			18, Flavian
			35, first cent.
			?27, probably Trajanic
	T II 31, occupation on primary floor		?37, Flavian
12	A I 33, floor		37, *c.* A.D. 85–105
			27, Flavian
			18, probably pre-Flavian
Rubbish accumulations SW. of Rooms 12 and 15	A II 62		30, ? Neronian
			Ritt. 9, pre-Flavian
			27, ? pre-Flavian
	A II 61, above 62	Nero, dupondius, *RIC* 308*r*	

ROOM	LAYER	COINS	SAMIAN (all South Gaulish unless otherwise stated)
	A II 47		29, Flavian Curle 11, 18R, 18 (three), Flavian 18, Claudian/Neronian
	A II 42	Domitian, As (new), *RIC* 356f (A.D. 87)	29 (four), one Neronian, one *c.* A.D. 60–75, two *c.* A.D. 70–85 37, Vespasianic 37, *c.* A.D. 80–100 37, C.G., Trajanic Curle 11, 27, Flavian 27, stamped OF NGR (**S 48**), Neronian 27, stamped OFBASSIC (**S 31**), Neronian/Vespasianic 15/17 (five), Neronian/Vespasianic 18 (two), pre-Flavian 18 (six), Flavian
	A II 59, below 58		30, Neronian 15/17, Neronian 18, stamped FELIXS·FEC (**S 36**), Claudian 18, stamped [OF·L]ABIO (**S 38**), *c.* A.D. 50–70
	A II 58		29 (two), before A.D. 85 67, 15/17, Neronian, 18 (three), Neronian/Vespasianic 27, pre-Flavian
	A II 46, above 58	Vespasian, As (fair), *RIC* 763(?) (A.D. 77–8)	
14	A I 39, floor	Claudius, As (barbarous), Domitian, As	29, stamped OF[NI]GRI (**S 46**), *c.* A.D. 50–70 29, *c.* A.D. 65–80 29 (four), Neronian 30, probably Neronian 15/17 (several), Neronian and Flavian 67, probably Flavian 36 (two), 24/25, Neronian Ritt. 8, probably Neronian
16	A X 21, primary floor	Vespasian, dupondius (good), *RIC* 740 (A.D. 72–3)	29, *c.* A.D. 65–80 18, Neronian 27, stamped OSABI (**S 51**), Neronian

ROOM	LAYER	COINS	SAMIAN (South Gaulish unless otherwise stated)
	A X 70, primary floor		27, first cent.
	A X 19, secondary floor		37, 18, 67, Flavian
	A X 68, secondary floor		37, c. A.D. 75–95
	A VII 40, floor		Some of the large Vespasianic group of broken whole vessels, see p. 28
	A VII 39, occupation on 40		As for A VII 40 above
	A I 37, late floor		29 (two), Flavian
			30, c. A.D. 60–75
			37, c. A.D. 85–105
			37, C.G., Ranto group, Trajanic
			27, probably Neronian
			15/17 (two), prob. Vespasianic
			18, Neronian
17	B I 49, make-up	Nero, As, *RIC* 329*r*	15/17, Ritt. 12, pre-Flavian, probably Neronian
	B II 32F, floor		37 (two), c. A.D. 80–100
			27, Flavian
			18 (two), one with stamp VIR[THV] (S 57), Flavian and Neronian
			15/17, Curle 15, first cent.
Accumulation outside (SW. of) 17	B II 32G		29, c. A.D. 65–80
			37 (two), c. A.D. 85–105
			27 (two), Flavian
			18 (two), Flavian
			18R, Trajanic
			33, Trajanic or Hadrianic
	Pit 9, cut in 32G (p. 28)		33a, C.G., stamped VIDVCOS F, Trajanic, footring heavily worn (S 54)
			18/31, C.G., Trajanic/Hadrianic
			37, C.G., c. A.D. 100–30
			27, 29, 15/17, Flavian
			24/25, pre-Flavian
	B I 48		29, probably Neronian
			Ritt. 12, probably Neronian
			15/17, Ritt. 8, 18, 30, 27 (two), pre-Flavian
			18, probably Flavian
	B I 45, above 48		29 (two), c. A.D. 60–70
			27 (two), one Flavian (?), one pre-Flavian

ROOM	LAYER	COINS	SAMIAN (South Gaulish unless otherwise stated)
	B I 38, above 45	Claudius, As, barbarous	29 (three), *c.* A.D. 65–75, one stamped GERMANIF (**S 37**) 30, *c.* A.D. 65–75 18 (two), Neronian/Flavian 29, Claudian/Neronian (**D 53**) 29 (two), Vespasianic 29, [OF.P]ASSIEN (**S 49**), Neronian 30, Flavian (**D 52**) 37 (four), *c.* A.D. 75–90 35/36 (three), first cent. Ritt. 8, probably Neronian 33, Curle 11 (two), Curle 15, 15/17, Flavian 15, probably Claudian 27 (at least 8), including stamp ATRI (**S 27**); one pre-Flavian, seven Flavian 18R, probably Flavian 18 (two), 24/25, 27 (two), pre-Flavian 18 (at least seven), Flavian 18, stamped VIRTH[VS FECIT] (**S 56**), *c.* A.D. 50–65 18 (two), stamps OF.BASSI (**S 29**), [OF B]ASSI (**S 30**), Neronian 18, stamped CARB[ONISM] (**S 32**), *c.* A.D. 65–85 33a, C.G., stamped DOMII retro. (**S 35**), *c.* A.D. 100–20
	B I 43E, above 45		30 (two), Flavian 37, *c.* A.D. 75–85 27 (three), probably Neronian 15/17, first cent. 18, Flavian 22, probably Flavian
19	B IV 32, primary floor		29, probably Vespasianic 37, 30, Flavian 24/25, 15/17, Neronian/Flavian 36, probably Flavian 27 (two), 18 (two), Flavian

ROOM	LAYER	COINS	SAMIAN (all South Gaulish unless otherwise stated)
	B IV 31, occupation on 32		37, c. A.D. 75–95
			37, Flavian
			35, probably Flavian
			18, 27, Flavian
			27, Claudian/Neronian
	B II 32D, floor	Claudius, As, *RIC* 66	29, Vespasianic
			37, c. A.D. 75–90
			37, c. A.D. 75–95
			27, 35, Flavian
			18 (two), Neronian or Flavian
			18/31, V]+ΛLISMSF (**S 58**), C.G., Trajanic
Accumulation outside (W. of) 19	B II 37E		29, probably Claudian
			29 (two), Neronian, one C.G.
			29, c. A.D. 60–75
			29, 30, 37 (two), Flavian
			30, Neronian
			29 (two), 37 (two), c. A.D. 70–85 (**D 62**)
			18, Neronian
			18 (two), Flavian
			15/17 two, 24/25 (two), Neronian/Flavian
			36, probably Flavian
			27 (five), two Neronian/Flavian, three Flavian
			33, probably Trajanic
			18, 27, Ritt. 12, pre-Flavian
			27, probably Claudian
			15/17 or 18, [OF M]ODES (**S 43**), Neronian
			18R, 37, 27, 15/17, 18 (two), Flavian
	B II 36E, over 37E		29, c. A.D. 65–80
			37 (two), c. A.D. 85–105
			27, [OM]OM (**S 45**), Vespasianic
			Curle 15, 27 (two), 18 (two), Flavian
	B II 32E, gravel floor over 37E		29 (two), Claudian (**D 55**)
			29 (two), Flavian (**D 54**)
			37 (three), Flavian (**D 56, D 57, D 59, D 60**)
			37 (two), c. A.D. 80–100 (**D 58, D 61**)

ROOM	LAYER	COINS	SAMIAN (South Gaulish unless otherwise stated)
			37, styles of Igocatus, Ioenalis. C.G., *c.* A.D. 100–20
			30, C.G., probably by Donnaucus, *c.* A.D. 100–25
			Curle 11, Flavian
			33a, VIDVCOSF (**S 55**), C.G., Trajanic or Hadrianic
			27 (several), Flavian and Trajanic
			18 (several), Flavian and Trajanic
			15/17 (two), 18R, Curle 15, probably Flavian
	B II 31E, occupation on 32E		29, Neronian
			37 (two), Flavian (**D 61**)
			27 (two), Flavian
			27, C.G., Trajanic or Hadrianic
			18 (four), three Flavian, one probably Trajanic and C.G.
	Pit 2, early filling		37 (two), Flavian
			Curle 15, probably second cent.
			18R, Flavian
	B IV 33, with oven	Plated denarius	29, *c.* A.D. 60–70
			37, Flavian
			Ritt. 9, Neronian
			27, probably Flavian
			18 (two), Curle 11, Flavian
			18, stamped ΛVINII (**S 28**), Flavian
	B IV 25J, above 33; some sherds confused with 23J above, of Period II B		30, *c.* A.D. 65–80
			15/17, probably Neronian
			27, pre-Flavian
			27, Flavian
			18 or 18/31, Trajanic
	B IV 23F	Domitian, As (*new*), *RIC* 353a (A.D. 87)	
20	B II 35, make-up below primary floor		15/17, Claudian or Neronian
			18, 37, Flavian
			36, first century
	B II 37B, make-up below 36B		18, 27, Flavian
	B II 36B, make-up	Vespasian, As (*very fair*), *RIC* 502 (A.D. 71)	Curle 11, Flavian
			18, probably Flavian
			Ritt. 8, Neronian

ROOM	LAYER	COINS	SAMIAN (all South Gaulish unless otherwise stated)
	B II 34, make-up above 36B	Republican denarius of M. Lepidus, *Syd.* 830*a* (*c.* 66 B.C.) Nero, As, *RIC* 342*l* Nero, sestertius, *RIC* 149*z*	29, probably Neronian 37 *c.* A.D. 70–80 27, 18, probably Vespasianic
	B II 30B, floor		37, *c.* A.D. 80–100 37, *c.* A.D. 75–95 18 (two), 27, Flavian
	B II 30C, floor	Vespasian, As (*good*), *RIC* 763 (A.D. 77–8)	29, Neronian 37, style of L. Cosius, *c.* A.D. 80–100 18, Neronian 27 (two), pre-Flavian 36, Flavian Ritt. 8, stamp OF PRIM (**S 50**), pre-Flavian 27, C.G., stamped [CAT]VLLINVS (**S 33**), *c.* A.D. 100–25
21	A VII 43, make-up for primary floor		29, *c.* A.D. 50–65 15/17, probably Neronian 18, Claudian/Neronian
	A VII 42, ash patch on floor		37, *c.* A.D. 75–95 (**D 51**) 24/25, stamped [S]ENICI[O] (**S 52**), *c.* A.D. 55–65 27, stamped [O]MOM (**S 44**)
	A VII 34, late floor		Some of the large Vespasianic group of broken whole vessels, see p. 28
	B I 44, make-up for primary floor B I 42, make-up for primary floor B I 41A, primary floor B I 36A, late floor		29, Neronian 15/17, 27, pre-Flavian 29, 18R, Claudian or Neronian 15, 18, 24/25, 27 Neronian 15/17, pre-Flavian 29, Flavian 30, *c.* A.D. 70–75 37 (two), *c.* A.D. 75–90 18 (two), 67, Curle 11, Flavian 15/17, probably Neronian 27, Neronian
	B II 36A, make-up below primary floor B IV 29A, primary floor		37, *c.* A.D. 70–80 18, Curle 11, Flavian 29/37, *c.* A.D. 70–85 (**D 63**)

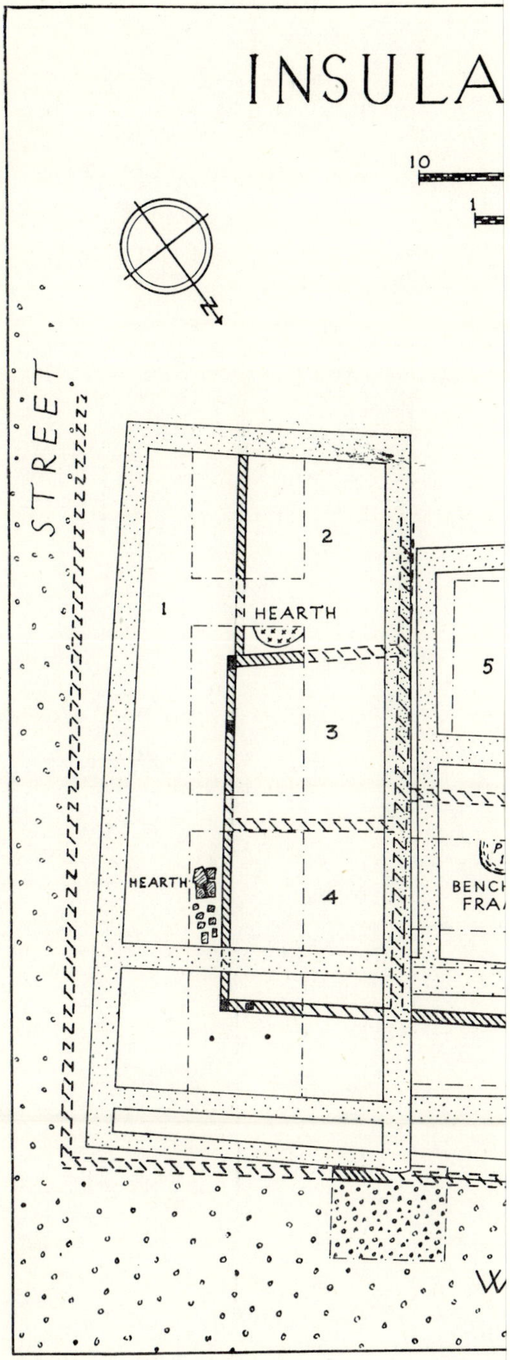

INSULA

STREET

10

HEARTH

1

2

3

4

5

HEARTH

BENCH
FRA

W

Fig. 19. Plan of the Period II A buildings, c. A.D. 75–105.

ROOM	LAYER	COINS	SAMIAN (all South Gaulish unless otherwise stated)
			37, *c.* A.D. 75–85
			37 (two), *c.* A.D. 75–95
			Ritt. 12, probably Neronian
			29, 18, Neronian
			27 (four), Flavian
			18, pre-Flavian
22	B IV 28D, make-up below 29D	Vespasian, As (*good*), A.D. 71–2	
	B IV 29D, primary floor		15/17, 18, pre-Flavian
Wall-trench 22/23		Vespasian, dupondius (*fair*), *RIC* 740 (A.D. 72)	
23	B IV 34, make-up for primary floor		29, *c.* A.D. 50–75
			29, *c.* A.D. 50–65
			29, *c.* A.D. 55–70
			37, *c.* A.D. 70–80
			67, *c.* A.D. 70–80
			24/25, probably Neronian
			18, Neronian
			Ritt. 9, pre-Flavian
			27, 33, probably pre-Flavian
	B IV 29L, make-up	Vespasian, As (*good*), *RIC* 494 (4) (A.D. 71)	
	B IV 29B, primary floor		18, Curle 11, Flavian
	B IV 23B, occupation on 29B	Nero, dupondius, *RIC* 304r	29, ? Neronian
			37 (two), Flavian
			18 (three), 27, Flavian
	B IV 23D, occupation on primary floor	Vespasian, dupondius (*v. good*), *RIC* 753*b* (A.D. 77–8)	
	B IV Pit 9, fuel-box in Room 23		15/17, pre-Flavian
			18, *c.* A.D. 60–80

Summary of dating evidence, Period II A

From a study of this table and of the relevant sections it emerges that in some rooms, e.g. 14, 19 and 20, there was recognized only a single rather thick floor of brick-earth; such floors contain pottery or coins covering the whole date-range (*c.* A.D. 75–105) suggested for Period II A, and it is clear that sherds were trodden into the brick-earth, or that original floors were patched in a way which was not recognized by us. But other rooms have a sequence of floor-deposits, sometimes with a layer of earthy burnt daub as a make-up below. This burnt daub was distinguishable from the clean red daub of the undisturbed Boudiccan levels below.

It is an important point for the dating of Period II A that such make-up levels in Rooms 7, 22, and 23 contained coins of Vespasian minted between 69 and 73, and that primary floors later sealed within the period by secondary ones also contained coins of Vespasian in good or very fair condition: Room 5 (A.D. 71–3); Room 11 (A.D. 72–3); Room 16 (A.D. 72–3); Room 20 (A.D. 71); for what it is worth as evidence, an As of Vespasian of A.D. 72 was in the wall-trench 22/23.

The latest coin in a sealed primary floor was that of A.D. 77–8 in Room 2. It is evident that though the latter may have been trodden in during the life of the building (and there was another of identical date on the floor of Room 23), there is nevertheless a heavy weight of coin-evidence to suggest that the floors of Period II A were not laid down before c. A.D. 75. This is confirmed by the samian. Primary floors contained the following well-dated decorated pieces:

Room	Form	
2	30	c. A.D. 70–85
6	30	c. A.D. 70–90
	29	Flavian
10	30	c. A.D. 70–85
	37	c. A.D. 70–85
16	29	c. A.D. 65–80
21	29/37	c. A.D. 70–85
	37	c. A.D. 75–85
	37	(two) c. A.D. 75–95

Primary floors also produced sufficient Flavian plain pieces to confirm a date not earlier than c. A.D. 75. On the other hand, the virtual absence of anything but pre-Flavian samian in the make-up levels, where present beneath the floors, suggests that it was not appreciably later.[1]

The date thus archaeologically arrived at agrees very closely with that indicated epigraphically for the adjacent Forum: this is shown by its inscription to have been dedicated in A.D. 79, and we may assume that work started on its site some 2–5 years previously.

End of Period II A. The latest coins in deposits of Period II A are four of Domitian: one not further identified, one of A.D. 81 and two dated 87 and lost in new condition. There are, however, several pieces of Flavian/Trajanic and Trajanic samian mainly with terminal dates of c. 100–5, but a few with date-ranges extending later than this. Eight of the nine latest are a form 37 (c. A.D. 100–20) and a form 30 (c. A.D. 100–25) which together with a 33 (VIDVCOS F), dated Trajanic or Hadrianic, and a 27 with the same range, were found in layers outside (west of) Room 19, and a form 37 (A.D. 100–30) which together with a form 33 again stamped VIDVCOSF, another stamped DOMII, and an 18/31 (Trajanic or Hadrianic) was found in similar relationship with Room 17. Though these layers do not date the II A

---

[1] In Room 23 the earthy burnt-daub make-up produced two pieces dated c. A.D. 70–80 and that in Room 20 one piece: make-up in 21, the portico, also produced one piece with this date-range.

structure itself, they were sealed by floors of the II B building which succeeded it, and which extended further over this part of the site. The ninth, a form 27 stamped by Catullinus, was in a floor of Room 20. Mr. Hartley writes that no stamps of Viducos have been found on Hadrian's Wall and only one in deposits of the second London fire; both our stamps are from the same die and one is on an early variety of form 33. There is no reason why he should not have started work by 105. A terminal date of *c.* A.D. 105 therefore is suggested for Period II A both because of the rarity of these late sherds, and because a life-time of thirty years seems ample for timber-framed buildings resting on sleeper-beams in damp soil. An extension of life after 105, moreover, would unduly strain the dating-evidence for the spans of Periods II B and II C which succeeded it.

PERIOD II B, *c.* A.D. 105–30 (fig. 11, p. 52)

Soon after the beginning of the second century the whole block was reconstructed. It has already been pointed out that the method of construction used meant that the structural timbers could have only a limited life, and they were by now about thirty years old. Indeed, since this was the first time that the necessity of reconstruction occurred spontaneously, it may be that they were left standing unduly long: the following two reconstructions seem to have been undertaken after only about twenty and twenty-five years respectively.

The new shops of Period II B once again opened on to a covered walk or portico still 11 ft. 6 in. wide beside Watling Street, but the corresponding timber colonnade on the south-east side of the insula appears now to have been abolished or curtailed. A timber-framed wall found in a trench at the extreme south corner of the plan (fig. 11), below the later stone drain, seems to mark the building line on the south-east side at this time. Rooms 1 and 2 accordingly will have opened directly on to the street. Room 3 perhaps represents a short return of the portico round the corner, or may have been a shop some 13 ft. wide with an open front.

The main novelty on the new plan was the full occupation of the rearward areas. The space behind Rooms 7–13 was unfortunately little explored: but 10 is a gravelled path, of the type better illustrated by 18, approaching the premises from the rear. Rooms 9 and 14 presumably therefore are roofed buildings as certainly are also Rooms 19–29. It seems clear that the ridge of the main roof was still parallel with Watling Street and continuous, and that its span covered the area of Rooms 4–8–22–34, with the portico attached as a pentice in front and Rooms 11–32 behind. The remaining structures further to the rear must have had roofs at right angles to these, draining off into 10 and 18 and presumably also into the unmetalled space 28. But a hint of developments to come is provided by 22 A, where a metalled alley-way seems to be partitioned off from 22, giving access to the chalk-floored lobby 21, which in turn opened on to the path 18. For the present, however, this through-passage was contained beneath the main roof.

For the first time also we have evidence for the use of *opus signinum* (Rooms 29–32) in this sequence of structures. Its use is very rare at Verulamium before the early second century, but is attested once in Building B beneath Wheeler's house III, 2, a building apparently erected in Flavian times, corresponding to Period II A here.[1] Here the floors belong to the

---

[1] Wheeler, *Verulamium*, p. 94.

later phases of Period II B: Room 30 originally had a floor of chalk, like the secondary one in Room 33. We also see (Room 16) the first appearance of a better-built circular oven standing on its own rectangular tile-and-mortar plinth. Normally these ovens were badly preserved, as is inevitable in the circumstances of successive reconstruction; but fine examples were buried in the debris of the Antonine fire (pp. 78, 80 and pl. XVI*b*, XXVIII*b*).

The front premises were 28 ft. deep and of varying width. Rooms 4 and 7 were *c.* 14 ft. 6 in. wide, Room 8 was 17 ft. 9 in., and Room 13 *c.* 25 ft. 6 in. Room 7 originally contained a hearth of baked clay (now partially destroyed by the medieval pit 13) surrounded by a wide area of black ash (fig. 9 (p. 27), section Y–Z, layer 21); against the south-west wall were the remains of an oven. At a later stage a clay floor (section Y–Z, 18) sealed these features, and a new oven was constructed on the north edge of Pit 13. This oven itself had later been destroyed and was represented by an oval hole, 5 in. deep, filled with burnt clay and tile fragments from its robbing. Contemporary with it was a small emplacement consisting of a rectangular hollow 2 ft. 9 in. by 1 ft. 1 in., sunk 2 in. into the floor. Presumably it held a wooden container, perhaps a fuel-box; but it produced no clue to its purpose. Room 4 was certainly a metal-worker's premises. A group of bronze scrap ready for smelting (pl. XLVI*c*) was found in its make-up or primary floor (T VI 25), and there was much charcoal on its secondary floor (T VI 22); the make-up levels of the II C floor above (T VI 21) contained bronze fragments, charcoal, and burnt clay (fig. 26, section B–B¹).

In the portico, Room 5, a stone base made of flints and broken tile was placed in front of Room 7, and three postholes 3–4 in. in diameter and *c.* 1 ft. deep were found. It is possible that there was a partition extending the line of wall 7/8 across the portico, for in the following Period II C a foundation trench is found on this line, as also in II D; it was uncertain whether these trenches contained walls or drains, but though the floor continued uniform each side of the postholes of II B, there was a slight change in II C, consistent with two rooms. In II D, however, the floor was continuous, and the plan makes the case for a drain much more cogent in that phase (p. 74 and fig. 19).

Room 13 was a bronze-smith's work-shop. It had one of the 'green boxes' in its east corner (p. 18) as well as two hearths and a circular oven, and Room 12 produced two small crucibles; further crucible-fragments occurred in the make-up for the II C floor above. It is interesting to note the concentration of 'unguent-jars' (fig. 113, nos. 476–9) in this area; two occurred in Room 14 and one each in Rooms 12 and 13. Only one other, in Room 5, was found in the entire range in this period. They seem to be connected with metal-working.

Room 15 may perhaps have been a store-room: it produced a bow-saw blade, a hipposandal, and a hub-lining with hub-rim, all of iron (figs. 61–4, nos. 13, 24, 32). Room 22 contained an oven, as did 16 and 17. It is not easy to be sure whether, or which of, these served for bread-baking rather than for metal-working. In Room 16 the skeleton of a baby was found buried below the oven. Room 24 had access to path 18 by means of a door in its south-east wall which was marked by an extra threshold, perhaps serving to support a shallow porch. From this room came the iron leg or foot of a box (fig. 71, 146). Room 33 had an oval clay hearth in its east corner and a central hearth of tiles 2½ in. thick, both contemporary with an early flooring of chalk; near its north-west wall an oven of horse-shoe shape similar to that in Room 27 went with a later reflooring in brick-earth. It is probable that 33 was also a smith's work-shop. The earlier floor levels in the portico outside Rooms 33 and 34 contained much debris from metal-working including bronze fragments and much iron-slag and iron-pan formation presumably induced by trampling.[1] Room 34 itself in its early floor had much charcoal and burnt clay interleaved with levelling layers of yellow brick-earth (fig. 27, section N–N[1]), and a late occupation layer yielded a small lump of molten bronze waste. Against the south-east wall a hoard of fifty denarii (the equivalent of two aurei) had been buried in the primary floor BIV 21D (pl. XVa). The hoard, which has been published by Dr. C. M. Kraay in the *Numismatic Chronicle*,[2] contained twenty-one Republican denarii running from the second century B.C. down to five base legionary issues of Mark Antony, and twenty-nine imperial ones, the majority being of Flavian date. The series ended with two of Nerva and six of Trajan; one of the latter was a plated forgery of anomalous type, four were minted between 98 and 102, and there was one coin minted between 112 and 117. It seems clear that the date of deposit must lie within a few years of 115 to allow time for the secondary floor and occupation which sealed it. The evidence derived from the stratification points to a date some years before *c*. A.D. 130 (below p. 73), the date when the buildings were demolished.

Dating evidence for Period IIB

Note: **D 82**, **S 68**, etc. in col. 4 refer to *Decorated* vessels and *Stamps* illustrated on pp. 218–62

ROOM	LAYER	COINS	SAMIAN (all South Gaulish unless otherwise stated)
1	T III 23, primary floor	Domitian, As, *RIC* 354*b*	29 (two), *c*. A.D. 70–85 18, 27, Flavian
	T III 22, occupation on 23		37, *c*. A.D. 70–80 33, Flavian
2	T VII 28, primary floor		29, pre-Flavian 37, *c*. A.D. 70–85 18, 27, 33, Flavian 15/17, Claudian/Neronian
	T III 24, secondary floor		29, *c*. A.D. 70–85 18 (two), Flavian 15/17, Neronian
3	T VII 24, occupation on floor 25		18, 27, pre-Flavian
	T VI 27, secondary floor		29, first cent. 18, pre-Flavian
4	T VII 26, make-up	Vespasian, As, *RIC* 764	67, Flavian 29, pre-Flavian 37, *c*. A.D. 75–90 27, Flavian 18 (three), including stamp COTTON retro. (**S 68**), Flavian/Trajanic

[1] See Appendix, p. 382.　　　　　[2] Num. Chron. (sixth series), xx (1960), 271–3.

ROOM	LAYER	COINS	SAMIAN (all South Gaulish unless otherwise stated)
	T VI 25, make-up	M. Agrippa, As, *RIC* (Tiberius) 32 Nero, As, *RIC* 338	29, *c.* A.D. 50–65 18, 27, pre-Flavian 35, first-cent. Lezoux ware, **Fig. 80**
5	T II 26, primary floor		29, *c.* A.D. 60–75 37, *c.* A.D. 70–80 18, Flavian
	T XXI 25, primary floor		37, *c.* A.D. 75–95 37, Flavian
	T XXI 18, secondary floor	Barbarous, *Fel. Temp. Reparatio* (intrusive)	30, *c.* A.D. 75–90
	A XII 25, primary floor		29, first cent.
	A XII 23A, late floor		37 (with handle), *c.* A.D. 75–95 (**D 82**)
	A XII 12, late floor		37, *c.* A.D. 75–100 18 (two), Curle 11, Flavian
	A VI 23, primary floor	Vespasian, As, *RIC* 762	29, Neronian 29 (two), probably Vespasianic 29 (two), *c.* A.D. 75–85 37 (four), Flavian 27 (two), 35/36 (three), Curle 11 (four), Flavian 15/17 (two), one Neronian/ Vespasianic, one Neronian 27, stamp illiterate, Flavian 18, stamp OF PATRICI (**S 82**), Flavian 18 (ten), including stamp OFVIRIL (**S 89**), Flavian 27, C.G., stamped [PĀT]ERNVLI (**S 81**)
	A VI 15, secondary floor on 23		29, Vespasianic 30, first cent. 18 (two), 27, Curle 11, Flavian
	A VI 28, early floor		29, Flavian 18 (two), Flavian 27, probably Flavian
6	Z I 20, primary floor		37, Flavian 18, 27, Flavian
	Z I 18, secondary floor		27, C.G., Trajanic/Hadrianic

ROOM	LAYER	COINS	SAMIAN (all South Gaulish unless otherwise stated)
			18 stamped OF CLGEMME (S 67), Flavian/Trajanic
7	T XX 23, primary floor		29, *c.* A.D. 70–85
			37 (two), *c.* A.D. 75–95
			27 (four), two pre-Flavian, two Flavian
			15/17, Neronian/Flavian
			18 (three), incl. stamp LORI•R (S 76), ? pre-Flavian
			36, Flavian
	T XX 21, occupation on 23		29, *c.* A.D. 65–75
			15/17, Neronian
			27, probably Flavian
	T XX 18, secondary floor		37, stamped [GERMA]NI (S 74, D 83), *c.* A.D. 70–85
			37 (two), *c.* A.D. 75–95
			30, *c.* A.D. 60–75
			29, *c.* A.D. 60–75
			27 (burnt), C.G., first cent.
			27, OF MVRANI (S 79), *c.* A.D. 60–75
			27, probably Flavian
			15/17, Neronian
			18 (about five), 36, Flavian
			18 (three), 36, pre-Flavian
	T XX 17, occupation on 18		27, Neronian
			18, probably Flavian
	T XX 22, wall-trench 7/8		37 (two), Flavian
8	T XXI 20A, primary floor		37, Flavian
			Curle 11, C.G., probably Trajanic
	T XX 19, occupation on floor	Titus (under Vespasian), denarius, *RIC* (Vesp.) 218*d*	
	A XI 13A and B, floor	Claudius, As, copy, *RIC* 66	18/31, Flavian
			18, pre-Flavian
			27, Claudian
9	A II 41, floor		37, C.G., style of Ioenalis, *c.* A.D. 100–20
10	A II 39, make-up below 37		29 (two), Vespasianic
			37, Trajanic or Hadrianic

ROOM	LAYER	COINS	SAMIAN (all South Gaulish unless otherwise stated)
			37(?), unusual decoration, ? early second cent.
			27, SVLPICI· (**S 87**), Flavian
			27, Neronian/Flavian
			27, Trajanic/Hadrianic
			18 (three), Flavian
			18/31, Trajanic
	A II 37, gravel over 39		18 or 18/31, ? Flavian
11	A IV 28, primary floor	Domitian, As, *RIC* 333 (A.D. 86)	29, *c.* A.D. 75–85
			18, Curle 11, Flavian
	A XIII 8, primary floor		18, Flavian
			37, C.G., *c.* A.D. 100–20 (**D 84**)
			37, C.G., Trajanic or Hadrianic (**D 85**)
	A XIII 6, occupation on 8		29, *c.* A.D. 45–60
			30, *c.* A.D. 70–90 (**D 86**)
			27 (two), *c.* A.D. 60–80
12	A IV 32, primary floor		29, Neronian
			Ritt. 12, pre-Flavian
	A XI 14, primary floor		27, probably pre-Flavian
	A XI 13, secondary floor on 14	Tiberius, As, *RIC* 40	27, 15/17, Flavian
			33, C.G., Trajanic or Hadrianic
			27, C.G., GII∧[, uncertain potter, (**S 73**), Trajanic?
	A XI 11, secondary floor		35/36, Flavian
	A XI 11A, wall-trench 8/12		37, Flavian
13	A XI 17, primary floor		37, *c.* A.D. 75–95
	A XII 17, secondary floor		37, *c.* A.D. 75–95
			18, Flavian
	A XII 16, floor above 17		27, pre-Flavian
14	A II 52, floor	Nero, As, *RIC* 277*l*	29 (two), first cent.
			18, stamped [OF]MO[VΛ[(**S 77**), Flavian
			27, OF PATRIC (**S 83**), Vespasianic
	A II 53, hearth on 52		37, Vespasianic
	A II 51, occupation on 52		37, Flavian (**D 87**)
			15, 18, Neronian/Flavian
			35, first cent.

ROOM	LAYER	COINS	SAMIAN (all South Gaulish unless otherwise stated)
15	A II 48, floor A I 26, floor		27, Flavian 37 (three), *c.* A.D. 80–105 18, Flavian or Trajanic 15/17, Vespasianic
16	A I 38, primary floor	Republican de- narius, C. Con- sidius Pactus, *Syd.* 990–1, (*c.* 45 B.C.)	29, Flavian 24/25, *c.* A.D. 60–75 15/17, 27 (two), Flavian 18 (three), probably all Flavian Ritt. 9(?), Neronian/Flavian
	A I 27, secondary floor	Titus (under Ves- pasian), As, *RIC* (Vesp.) 789*a* Domitian, As	29, 37, Flavian 27 (two), Neronian and Flavian 35/36 (two), probably Flavian 18, 18/31 (several), Flavian
	A I 21, latest occupation	Domitian, As	27 (two), 18/31 (two), C.G., pro- bably Trajanic
16/17 wall- trench		Domitian, As, *RIC* 353*a* (A.D. 87)	
17	A I 31, floor		29, Vespasianic 37 (three), one Vespasianic, two *c.* A.D. 85–105 27, 33, Flavian 27, 15/17, Neronian/Flavian (**S 111**) 18, probably Flavian
	A VII 28, floor		Some of the large Vespasianic group of broken whole vessels, see p. 28 (**D 64–D 81**; **S 59–S 63**) 37, C.G., early second cent.
	A VII 19, occupation on 28	Domitian, As Republican de- narius, *Syd.* 705– 7 (87–86 B.C.) Trajan, As (*new*), *RIC* 562 (A.D. 103–11)	37, C.G., *c.* A.D. 100–20 36, C.G., second cent.
18	A II 44, make-up for gravel path		29 (two), *c.* A.D. 75–85 37 (two), Flavian 37, *c.* A.D. 85–105 18 (three), 27, 67, Flavian 27, ? Trajanic

ROOM	LAYER	COINS	SAMIAN (all South Gaulish unless otherwise stated)
	A II 40, gravel		29, Flavian 37, c. A.D. 75–95 27, Flavian 35/36, probably Flavian
19	B I 38E, primary floor		29, Flavian 37 (three), c. A.D. 80–100 15/17, probably Vespasianic 18, 27 (two), Flavian 33, TITVRONIS (S 88) C.G., Antonine ⎫ strays 38, Lud. Tg/Tx, C.G., Antonine ⎭ from Pit 7, upper filling
	B I 37E, secondary floor		18R, Flavian 35, probably Flavian
	B I 32X, late floor		37, Flavian 18 (at least three), including stamp LOGI[RN] (S 75), Flavian 18R, OF VITALI (S 90), Flavian 33, [DA]GOMARVSF (S 71), Trajanic/Hadrianic 27 (two), one Flavian, one Trajanic 18/31, stamped BIGA•FEC (S 65), C.G., Trajanic/Hadrianic
20	B I 37D, primary floor		29(?), Vespasianic 18 (three), Flavian 27, probably Flavian
	B I 32Y, secondary floor		37, c. A.D. 85–105 18/31, 33, probably Trajanic
22a	A I 29, make-up		29, first cent. 29/37, c. A.D. 70–85, probably the same vessel as in IIA, room 21 (B IV 29A); see also Room 26 below (D 63) 18 (two), 37, Flavian 67, etc., barbotine, probably Flavian 37, prob. early second cent. 18, marbled, c. A.D. 60–75
	A I 28, gravel over 29		15/17, Vespasianic 27, first cent.

ROOM	LAYER	COINS	SAMIAN (all South Gaulish unless otherwise stated)
22	A VII 27, floor		Some of the large Vespasianic group of broken whole vessels; see p. 28 (**D 64–D81; S 59–S 63**)
	A X 15, secondary occupation		29, Flavian 37 (two), Vespasianic 18, 27, 36, Flavian
23	B I 37F, primary floor		37, c. A.D. 70–85 27, Flavian
	B II 30G and H, primary floor		37 (four), 29, 18 (three), Flavian 29, probably Neronian 18/31, C.G., DAGOMARVS·F (**S 72**), c. A.D. 100–15 18/31, 33, C.G., Trajanic or Hadrianic
	B I 32F, secondary floor on 37F		18 and 18R, 27 (two), Flavian
	B II 29G, secondary floor on 30G		27 (two), Flavian
24	B I 37G, primary floor		29, Claudian or Neronian 29, c. A.D. 65–75 29, Flavian 37, style of Germanus, c. A.D. 70–80 37 (two), Flavian 15/17, 27, pre-Flavian 18 (three), 27 (four), Curle 11, Flavian
	B II 30F, primary floor		37, C.G., second cent. 27, Flavian
	B I 47, primary floor		29, Claudian 30, Neronian or Vespasianic 18, Neronian 27 (two), pre-Flavian 24/25, stamped CRESTIO (**S 70**), c. A.D. 55–65
	B I 32G, secondary floor on 37G		29, Claudian 37, Flavian 37, c. A.D. 85–105 37, C.G., Trajanic 18 (two), 27 (three), Curle 11, Flavian 15/17, Neronian

ROOM	LAYER	COINS	SAMIAN (all South Gaulish unless otherwise stated)
	B I 31C, secondary floor on 32C		37 (at least two), Flavian 18 (two), 27, Flavian
26	A VII 33, primary floor		Some of the large Vespasianic group of broken whole vessels; see p. 28 (**D 64–D81; S 59–S 63**)
	A VII 32, secondary floor	Titus (under Vespasian), dupondius, *RIC* (Vesp.) 775*b*	Some of the large Vespasianic group of broken whole vessels; see p. 28 (**D 64–D 81; S 59–S 63**)
	A VII 23, occupation on 32		27, Claudian or Neronian
	A VII 29, late floor		As VII 32 and 33 above
	B I 35A, primary floor		37, *c.* A.D. 70–80 18, 27, 67, Flavian
	B II 29A, primary floor		29/37, *c.* A.D. 70–85 (**D 63**) Probably same vessel as in II A Room 21 (B IV 29A); see also Room 22A above 29, Flavian 27, Flavian 18/31 or 31, probably Trajanic
	B II 28A, secondary floor on 29A		29, *c.* A.D. 65–85 37 (three), Vespasianic 37/29, see above, II 29A 15/17, Neronian 27 (three), 18 (three), Flavian 27, stamped OF NI (**S 80**), *c.* A.D. 40–65 36, probably Flavian
	B IV 21A, primary floor		29, ANTIGR[V] (**S 64**), C.G., ? Neronian 29, Flavian 37 (two), Flavian 37, *c.* A.D. 85–105 37, C.G., style of Igocatus, *c.* A.D. 100–20 18, pre-Flavian 18, 27 (two), Flavian 18, probably Trajanic 24/25, Neronian 35/36, first cent.
	B IV 19Z, late occupation		18, 30, 67, Flavian

ROOM	LAYER	COINS	SAMIAN (all South Gaulish unless otherwise stated)
	B IV 19A, late occupation on 19Z		18/31, 27, C.G., Trajanic 46, C.G., Trajanic or Hadrianic 37 (rim), C.G., probably Hadrianic 37, Flavian 37, Trajanic 18, Flavian 18/31, Curle 11, C.G., Trajanic/ Hadrianic
27	B IV 25M, make-up B II 30E, floor	Nero, As	29, 37, Flavian 18, 35, Flavian
29	B IV 23J, make-up		29 (two), c. A.D. 70–85 29 (two), Neronian 37 (two), c. A.D. 70–85 37 (three), c. A.D. 85–105 29 base stamped [O]F MONTI·CR (S 78), c. A.D. 65–80 15/17 (four), Neronian and Vespasianic 33, Flavian 24/25, 36, Neronian 18 (five), Flavian 27 (seven), two stamps, BIO FECIT retro. (S 66) and OFIPR (S 84), two pre-Flavian, five Flavian 37/29, c. A.D. 70–85 37R, C.G., Trajanic or Hadrianic
	B IV 21J, primary floor on 23J		29, Neronian 37 (three), Flavian 37, c. A.D. 80–100 30, probably Trajanic 18, 18R, 27, Flavian 35, probably second cent.
30	B IV 21F, primary floor		37 (two), Flavian 15/17, probably Vespasianic 27 (two), one Neronian, one Flavian 18, Neronian
	B IV 20P, secondary floor on 21F		37, c. A.D. 85–105 Curle 15, probably Trajanic/ Hadrianic 18, Flavian

ROOM	LAYER	COINS	SAMIAN (all South Gaulish unless otherwise stated)
33	B IV 21E, primary floor	Vespasian, As, *RIC* 746	29, Flavian 37, graffito (*post coct.*) SABINA, *c.* A.D. 80–100 (**D 88**) 18, Curle 11, 67, Flavian
	B IV 21Y, primary floor	Trajan, dupondius (*new*), *RIC* 505 (A.D. 103–11)	
	B IV 20E, secondary floor on 21E	Titus (under Vespasian), sestertius, *RIC* (Vesp.) 772 Domitian, denarius (*v. good*), *RIC* 18 Domitian, As (*fair*), *RIC* 335 (A.D. 86)	29 (two), Vespasianic 37, Vespasianic 37, *c.* A.D. 80–100 15/17, 18 (four), 27 (two), Flavian 35/36, first cent. 24/25, Neronian/Vespasianic 27, stamped ꙅEꞜVND (**S 85**), *c.* A.D. 60–85
	B IV 20Y, secondary floor of chalk on 21Y	Vespasian, As, *RIC* 746 Trajan, As (*good*), *RIC* 395 or similar (A.D. 98–9)	
	B II 29C, secondary floor		33, C.G., probably Hadrianic 27, C.G., Trajanic 15/17, pre-Flavian 29, 30, 37, 27 (two), 15/17, 35, Flavian 18 (three), two pre-Flavian, one Flavian
	B II 29B, secondary floor	Hoard of three: Vespasian, As, *RIC* 500 (3): Vespasian, As: Titus, dupondius, *RIC* 111*a*	18 (two), 27, Flavian
	B II 28B, occupation on 29B		27, Flavian
34	B IV 21B, primary floor B IV 20L, secondary floor on 21B B IV 21D and 21, floors	Vespasian, As Vespasian, As, *RIC* 747	37, Flavian 27, Flavian 35, probably Flavian 29, Neronian (**D 89**) 29, Vespasianic 37, probably Trajanic

ROOM	LAYER	COINS	SAMIAN (all South Gaulish unless otherwise stated)
		Hoard of 50 denarii ending with Trajan, *RIC* 252 (A.D. 112–17); see p. 43	18 (two), Flavian 27, Neronian 35, probably Flavian 27(?), illiterate stamp, Flavian
	B IV 20D, floor above 21D		33, probably Trajanic/Hadrianic
	B IV 20Z, occupation on 20D		37, probably early second cent. 18/31, Trajanic or Hadrianic
	B IV 23L, secondary floor		29, Vespasianic 37 (three), Flavian 18 (four), one Neronian/Flavian, three Flavian 27 (two), Flavian 35, first cent.
	B IV 21L, occupation on 23L		29, Neronian 18, probably Flavian 27, 35, Flavian 18, OFSEV[ER+] (S 86), Flavian
Watling Street	T I 12		27 (two), Claudian and Flavian 27, stamped CRACVNA•F (S 69), probably Hadrianic/Antonine 18/31, Trajanic or Hadrianic

Summary of dating evidence, Period II B

It has already been shown that samian of Trajanic date exists below the levels of Period II B. From these levels themselves, apart from seven coins of Domitian, come three coins of Trajan and a hoard of denarii of *c.* 112–17; one of the coins, minted between 103 and 111, came from a primary floor in Room 33.

Of the samian from these levels the percentage of residual material is remarkable. But a number of rooms produced a little Trajanic or Trajanic/Hadrianic material, some of it from primary floors (that is, floors which were sealed by later floors of II B). There were three decorated pieces dated *c.* A.D. 100–20 as well as a 37 (rim) and a form 33 dated probably Hadrianic. These are the latest certainly dated pieces. On this basis a terminal date of *c.* A.D. 130 is suggested for the occupation of Period II B. It can hardly be extended much later if time be allowed thereafter for Periods II C and II D before the Antonine fire of *c.* 150–60: a slightly earlier date of *c.* A.D. 125 would have been possible on the II B evidence considered in isolation; but it will be seen below (p. 73) that 130 is the earliest date possible for the start of Period II C. This conclusion is to some extent supported by a 'probably

Hadrianic-Antonine' stamp CRACVNA•F which was found in a layer of Watling Street metalling (T I 12, fig. 27, section B–B¹). The layer could not be related stratigraphically to walls, but it is immediately sealed by a 2 in. layer of clay which is best attributed to the demolitions at the end of Period II B.

PERIOD IIC, *c.* A.D. 130–50

In the middle of Hadrian's reign the building was reconstructed (fig. 15). The evidence for this date is discussed on p. 73. In this period the level of Watling Street was raised about 3 ft. by successive deposits of gravel. The portico seems to have been about 12 ft. wide, though its front wall was not certainly identified owing to later disturbance at the points examined. In this period it did not turn the corner, for the continuation of the north-east wall showed Room 3 to be enclosed on this side. The main lines of Period II B were reproduced along the frontage, both the front and back walls of the row of Rooms 3–45 being set in the same position as the similar walls of the previous period. But this time the continuous roof was abandoned. Instead, a series of blocks was constructed, each separated from its neighbour by a narrow gap sufficient to collect drainage from the roofs. Two of these gaps (12/16 and 16/20) had plank-lined drains down their lengths; at others a drain across the portico apparently sufficed. The effect of such an arrangement, masked though it was by the continuous portico in front, was to allow roof-ridges at right angles to the street, and thus to facilitate full exploitation of the space to the rear without the need either for ridge-junctions or for subsidiary roofs at lower levels with all the problems of lighting that these undoubtedly created. Unified planning was giving way to individual initiative, as is demonstrated by the replacement of the multiple block by the narrow strip-shops which are such a well-known feature of Romano-British towns, and which by this date had already appeared at Wroxeter in half-timbered form. It is no long leap in logic to deduce that private ownership by individual craftsmen was replacing the tenant-landlord relationship. It also follows that now for the first time piecemeal rebuilding is theoretically possible: in fact, however, there is nothing to suggest that the whole frontage of Periods II C, and of II D after it, was not rebuilt at one time as before, or as nearly at one time as makes no difference to the dating evidence.

One must regret that the position of the main dump of soil from the excavation, immediately to the south-west of the trenches on the plan, where it is still in position today as a view-point for the public, prevented further excavation in that direction. The full extent of the buildings is thus unknown. Access from the rear was provided as in Period II B by two gravel paths, one, 26, being immediately above its predecessor, the other, 21, being moved some 10 ft. further north-west. The latter carried a central plank-lined drain.[1]

Wall 3/4 was for most of its length a normal beam-trench, but for a length of 4 ft. in T VI it was packed with large flints apparently consolidating an upright (pl. XVI*a*): the wall was in the same position as its predecessor, and the filling was loose. Room 4 contained a mortar-spread or apron (fig. 27, section B–B¹, T VII 14) as indicated on the plan, and just below this in an earlier floor was one of pebbles set in clay (T VII 20); these presumably related to ovens further north-west, just beyond the trench. About 1 ft. behind the front wall

---

[1] See p. 75 for more details of such drains.

was a row of small postholes which perhaps supported a counter; these were seen in T II 18 (fig. 27, section B–B¹). This room also produced a large pudding-stone block over 2 ft. square by 1 ft. thick in T VII 21. In the portico in front of Room 4 the equivalent of two buckets-full of oysters was recovered from the primary floor T II 20, and more in 19 above it. This suggests that Room 4 was an oyster bar.

A notable find from Room 7 was the upper part of a sword (fig. 73, 163). Such weapons would be out of place in a civilian commercial environment; another, however, was found in the cellar of Period III. Room 9 had a hearth near its south corner, the baked clay base of which was sunk 2 in. into the floor, the hollow being filled with ash and charcoal. Floor T XX 13 (fig. 9 (p. 27), section Y–Z) produced two clay lamps. The plan shows that this room had two north-west walls little more than 1 ft. apart. It is a question whether the inner one once carried some kind of built-in cupboard, or whether it was really the outer wall of this block as suggested by the position of the (?) drain across Room 13. If so, this wall might have been expected to continue through Rooms 8–6. It has not been so depicted on the plan because in the same area of Building II D, above, the Wall 8/10 was found continuing across the gap. The rest of trench T XXII was very disturbed by robbing, and it was not excavated down to II C levels. The situation in II D strongly suggests a cupboard, and by implication in II C as well.

Room 8 contained the remains of a circular oven next its north-east wall, and nearby a small rectangular pit, 31 in. wide and 10 in. deep with vertical sides. It was entirely filled with charcoal, yet the sides of the pit were unburnt. The interpretation as a fuel-pit, or pit containing a box full of charcoal for the adjacent oven, seems clear, and it provides a key to similar pits in other levels which did not so clearly proclaim their function. Yet parallels elsewhere in Roman Britain do not appear to have been recognized.

For the possible partition on the Portico, 13, see pp. 42, 74. The occupation layer on its primary floor in front of Room 4 yielded two large balls (c. 30 mm. in diameter) of blue material, which microscopic examination showed to be Egyptian blue.[1] Room 15 had a demolished tile oven and Room 16 a clay hearth closely adjacent to their north-west walls. Between these rooms and Rooms 11 and 12 ran a plank drain set in a trench of rectangular section, 5–6 in. deep and 12–13 in. wide (fig. 23, section D–D¹); in trench A XI there was 1 in. of grey clay on the bottom, probably representing the original plank, for traces of nails survived in it. Better-preserved examples of such drains survived from Period II D (p. 75).

Rooms 17–20 formed the beginning of a new block; their outside (south-east) wall-trench was exceptionally wide at 2 ft. 2 in. and probably contained a plank drain as well as the wall foundation; this suggestion is supported by a narrower extension north-east where presumably the drain ran on unaccompanied across the portico. At the north-east end of Room 17 was a very narrow trench only 4–6 in. wide and lying only 2 ft. from the south-west wall of 18. It is impossible to suppose that such a space can have been a room, and if it were a cupboard the question of access to Room 17 arises. We may accordingly suggest that the narrow trench indicates a floor-joist others of which were not seen. It will be shown below that floor-joists do not seem to have been regularly set in the earth like wall foundation trenches;[2] they were originally laid on the surface of the ground, but sometimes thereafter sank if the supporting soil was soft, and thus created their own slots. In Room 19 was an

_____
[1] Thanks are due to the British Museum Laboratory for undertaking this work.　　　[2] Pp. 74–5.

ash-filled hollow which was probably the stoke-pit of an oven: nearby was a circular ash-filled hollow containing eleven small stakeholes, similarly filled.

Room 23 had a floor of weak yellow concrete (fig. 24, section G–G¹, layer 23). Room 24, despite an oven centrally placed against its back wall, had a floor of good *opus signinum*. This was its latest floor. As first built the room had had another *opus signinum* floor lower down; this had been replaced by a clay one on which was an oven surrounded by ash. The top *opus signinum* floor sealed these levels. In this latest floor were the bones of the incomplete skeleton of an infant. It had not been buried in a hole cut in the floor, but seemed rather to have been incorporated in the aggregate. Another infant burial was found in the floor of Room 19; two more occurred on the edge of the path 26; and a fifth against the north-east wall of Room 22. Inside Room 22 Pit 5, which contained a large group of pottery, appeared to have been dug at the end of Period II C for the disposal of rubbish. Pit 16, a shallow scoop dug in B IV 18E, the floor of Room 45, also contained pottery and oyster-shells.

Room 28 seems to have been connected with metal-smithing, for it contained a good deal of bronze scrap together with pieces of lead and iron, and also produced a cast bronze dolphin (fig. 41, 133). The iron objects included part of a hipposandal, three linch-pins, and two pole-tips (figs. 63–4, nos. 29, 33–5, 37–8). Room 27 had a large oven on its primary floor (pl. XVI*b*). This was later sealed by a new clay floor on which accumulated occupation-soil with much ash and charcoal and a large quantity of bones.

Outside Room 35 the portico 36 had been floored locally with chalk in which were some foundation trenches and postholes. The wide one in the middle, containing postholes, was *c*. 6 in. deep but the others had a depth of only 2–3 in.; presumably they carried benches or counters extending the shop and blocking the portico. Room 33 had traces of painted plaster coloured red and yellow on its south-east wall. Its south-west wall still survived to a height of 1 ft. above the floor, with a 2-in. plaster-facing painted white. The core of the wall was 7 in. of daub, and below it was a row of postholes 5 in. deep representing the frame of wall 23/24 of Period II B below.

In Room 31 part of a rectangular vertical-sided pit (fig. 15, Pit 15) survived the destruction of most of it by Pit 4. In shape Pit 15 resembled the fuel-pits already described (see above, Room 8), but it had been filled with packed chalk presumably at the time of the reflooring in chalk of this area at the beginning of Period II D. The chalk filling suggested to us at the time of excavation that it was a latrine pit, but this is perhaps unlikely in a room containing the *aediculae* described below, and the chalk can be explained as Period II D levelling.

Room 37 had an *opus signinum* floor in its latest phase (fig. 28, section L–L¹). In the east corner of this room a narrow partition enclosed a small closet rather less than 4 ft. wide and *c*. 6 ft. long in which the *opus signinum* was missing. Instead there was a shallow and somewhat irregular hollow 6–9 in. deep full of animal horns, bones, oyster-shells and pottery. Room 39 had an oven on B IV 18J, a secondary gravel floor, on which much dirt, charcoal, iron-slag, and animal bones had accumulated. It had been roughly refloored several times. The latest occupation layer in this room, B IV 17K, produced a very large amount of coarse pottery, seventy-seven vessels being listed.

Rooms 41 and 42, originally separate, were merged during the period, and two successive floors passed over the demolished partition (fig. 28, section L–L¹). The change was probably brought about by the wall being found to be inconveniently close to the oven in 42. Room 45 had one, and Room 44 two, horseshoe-shaped ovens. The former had no tiles in its structure, being built only of clay. Its floor was sunk in B IV 18D to a depth of 1 ft. 4 in., and the hollow was filled with ash and charcoal. The surface of the floor was burnt outside the mouth of the oven. Near it was a shallow irregular scoop in the floor (Pit 16), full of occupation material, oysters and much pottery. The section (fig. 27, section M–M¹, layer 18E) close to the south-east wall of Room 45 shows a small beam trench 6 in. wide and 3 in. deep, parallel with wall 45/44 and 1 ft. 3 in. from it. This was not planned, but presumably represents a cupboard or set of shelves against the wall. In Room 40 there was a dog's skeleton buried in the latest floor (pl. XV*b*), and in Room 46 an infant burial accompanied by a small used crucible.

The aediculae (figs. 12–14 and pls. XVII–XIX)

Room 31 contained a small tile-built structure against its north-west wall: a second structure had been placed beside it later in Period II C, and in Period II D both were altered or perhaps abandoned. These were the sole masonry structures (apart from ovens) found in any of the timber periods and they clearly represent something unusual. They are interpreted here as *lararia* or domestic shrines.

The first, A, resembled a cupboard, open to the front, with tile walls 7–8 in. thick on three sides and resting on a solid base. Shrine A was contemporary with B III 22, a gravelly floor of Room 31 which sealed a mortar-spread at the base of the structure. Above the occupation on this floor was a thin local layer containing fallen wall-plaster (21), which probably came from the stripping and redecoration of the walls of A when shrine B was added. This layer was sealed by B III 20, a floor similar to 22 in which was buried, just on the north-east side of A, a carinated beaker in fine grey ware (fig. 116, 581) of second-century type, containing a worn As of Vespasian (reverse type probably *Aequitas*). Shrine B was added at this stage. A wall with tile quoins front and back, but of flint and mortar laced with tiles in between, was built parallel with A, and a rough foundation of flints and mortar (*a* on fig. 12A) was thrown in to the intervening space giving to Shrine B a floor *c.* 6 in. lower than that of A. At the same time, the timber-framed wall 31/37 behind was removed for the required 3 ft., and its foundation trench filled in. Floor 20 was laid against the new wall of B. Both floors (20 and 22) produced samian of 'probably Hadrianic' date, consistent with their attribution on grounds of stratigraphy to Period II C.

Both shrines, but particularly B, were in a very bad state of repair when excavated owing to subsidence into surrounding underlying pits, the cause of much confusion to the stratification. As can be appreciated in pl. XVII, the back wall was missing when the photographs were taken; it had been exposed in 1958 in the edge of a trench and taken to belong to the buildings of Period III: it did not survive the winter. Parts of A survived to a height of 3 ft. 4 in. above the floor. It is probable that both shrines reached to ceiling height, perhaps *c.* 10 ft., for otherwise it is difficult to account for the absence of a room-wall behind them.

The base of A had surviving pink marbled wall-plaster on all but its rear side: inside the niche the side walls were predominantly white with borders as shown in fig. 14. The floor, too, was plastered, and a narrow portion of this survived at the back: there was a narrow band of black bordering red. Some white plaster also survived on the outside of the south-west wall of A above the level of the base. It was not clear whether this represented the original exterior decoration of A or the later interior decoration of shrine B.

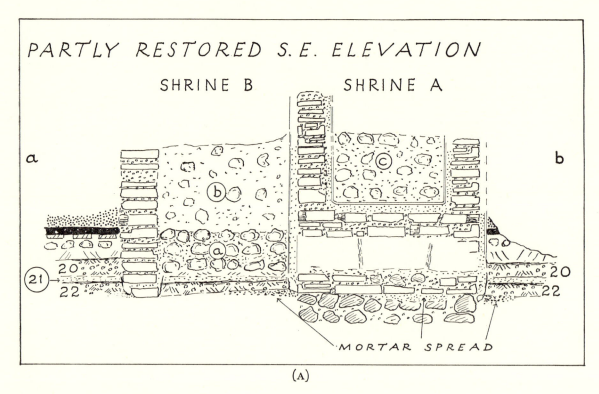

(A)

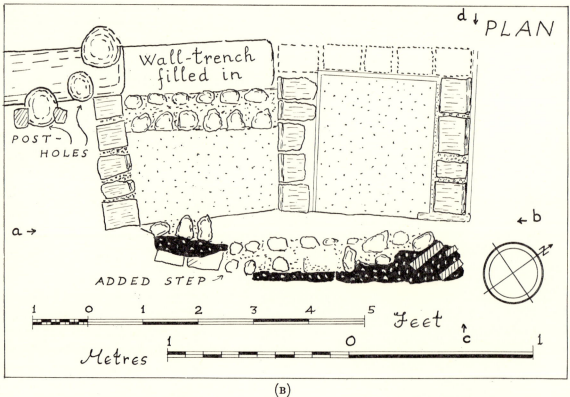

(B)

FIG. 12A. The *aediculae*: elevation.   FIG. 12B. The *aediculae*: plan.

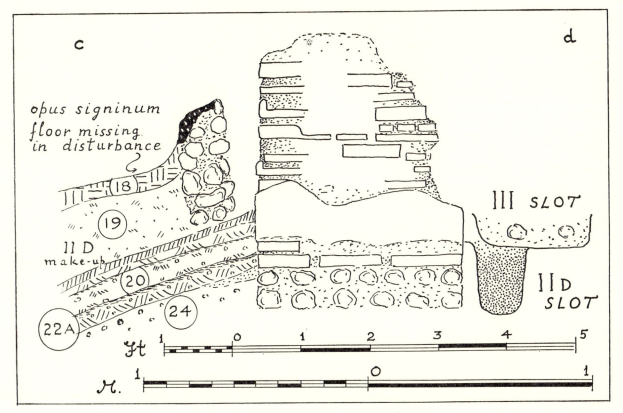

FIG. 13. The *aediculae*: cross-section.

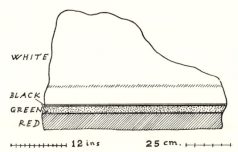

FIG. 14. Detail of wall-plaster from
the inner face of *aedicula* A.

In Period IID it might seem that the *aediculae* were disused since they were filled with
rubble masonry to their surviving tops (*b* and *c*, fig. 12A). It is more likely, however, that the
purpose of this was only to provide a higher floor to each shrine rather than to obliterate
them, for if this had been intended it would have been easier and preferable to demolish them
entirely. That they did continue in use in Period IID is suggested by the remains of a narrow
wall 1 ft. 3 in. wide carried across the front of both shrines (pl. XVII*a*). This was probably
the remains of a step: it certainly belongs to Period IID, being founded on floor 20 and

supported by make-up (19) and a clay layer 18 which were put in to carry the new *opus signinum* floor; and traces of the *opus signinum* were found attached to some of its tiles. Thus the raising of the shrines and the provision of a step go together; and they remedy the rather inconveniently low level of the original shrines which were little more than 1 ft. above the floor of Room 31.

The religious purpose of these structures is confirmed by the votive pot (pl. XVIII*a*) and coin, and reference may be made to not dissimilar *lararia* at Pompeii. In Britain domestic shrines of comparable character are less easy to find. But at Silchester in Building XIV, 1 a small structure 6 ft. 6 in. square with a step in front of it was found, though situated in the open air of the courtyard; while in XIV, 2 a very similar though free-standing example of about the same size was found in a room specially devoted to it.[1]

Dating evidence for Period II C.

Note: **D 90, S 105**, etc. in col. 4 refer to *Decorated* vessels and *Stamps* illustrated on pp. 218–62

ROOM	LAYER	COINS	SAMIAN (all South Gaulish unless otherwise stated)
1	T III 21, primary floor		29, *c.* A.D. 75–85
	T III 20, secondary floor		37, *c.* A.D. 70–85
			30, C.G., Trajanic/Hadrianic
			18/31, C.G., Trajanic/Hadrianic
			18 (two), Flavian
	T III 17, later floor		36, Flavian
2	T VII 21, primary floor		37, *c.* A.D. 75–85
			18, 67, Flavian
	T III 18, primary floor		27, stamped VITALIS[F] (**S 107**), Flavian
			15/17 or 18, stamped [ROPP]VS•FEC (**S 105**), *c.* A.D. 60–80
	T III 16, secondary floor		27(?), Flavian
3	T VI 20, primary floor		29, first cent.
			37, *c.* A.D. 70–85
			Curle 11, 18, Flavian
			15/17, probably Flavian
	T VII 12, secondary occupation		29, *c.* A.D. 70–85
			18 (two), 27 (two), Flavian
			18R, first cent.
	T VII 17, secondary occupation		18 (burnt), Neronian
			18, pre-Flavian
4	T VI 19, make-up		37, *c.* A.D. 75–85

[1] For XIV, 1 see *Archaeologia*, lv, 223–4 (= Silchester 1895, 9–10); for XIV, 2, ibid. 237 = offprint p. 23. Cf. G. C. Boon, *Roman Silchester* (1957), 124. For Pompeii: A. Mau, *Pompeii, its Life and Art* (1899), 262 ff.

ROOM	LAYER	COINS	SAMIAN (all South Gaulish unless otherwise stated)
	T VI 21, make-up		18, 27, pre-Flavian 18R, first cent.
	T VI 18, primary floor		29, probably Flavian 18, pre-Flavian 35, first cent. 27, probably pre-Flavian
	T VI 17, occupation on 18		18 (two), Flavian 15/17, first cent. Curle 15, probably Flavian 37, Flavian
	T VI 14, late floor		37, C.G., probably Antonine
	T VI 11, late occupation		37, Flavian 27, C.G., probably Hadrianic
	T II 24, primary make-up		29, probably Claudian 29, c. A.D. 55–65 18, 27, pre-Flavian
	T VII 19, secondary floor		29, pre-Flavian Stanfield unusual form 42, first cent. 18, probably pre-Flavian
	T VII 11, late floor		27, Flavian 18/31, probably C.G., ? early second cent.
	T II 16, late floor		37, c. A.D. 85–105
7	Z I 12, occupation		27, C.G., Trajanic 18/31, C.G., Trajanic/Hadrianic
8	Z I 22, primary occupation		Curle 11, 18R, 27, Flavian 18/31, C.G., probably Trajanic
	Z I 17, secondary occupation	Domitian (under Vespasian), As, *RIC* (Vesp.) 791*a*	Stanfield unusual form 12(?) 81, C.G., Trajanic/Hadrianic
9	T XX 15, primary floor		37, style of Germanus, c. A.D. 70–85 30, 37, Flavian 18 (two), 27, 35, Flavian
	T XX 13, occupation on secondary floor	Vespasian, As, *RIC* 747 Vespasian, As, *RIC* 500	30, probably Claudian 37 (two), Flavian Curle 11, 18, Flavian 31(?), burnt, Antonine (stray from Antonine fire)
	T XXI 16A, floor		31, C.G., Antonine

ROOM	LAYER	COINS	SAMIAN (all South Gaulish unless otherwise stated)
	T XX 14, occupation in cupboard		37, *c.* A.D. 75–95 36, Flavian
12	T XX 14A, floor		37, *c.* A.D. 80–100
12/16 interspace	A XII 13A, beside drain		27, probably Flavian
13	T II 19, occupation on primary floor		29 (two), *c.* A.D. 70–85 37 (two), *c.* A.D. 70–85 Ritt. 8, Neronian 15/17 (two), Neronian/Vespasianic 27 (four), one Claudian, three Flavian 18 (four), including stamp [OF C]RE2TI retro. (**S 96**) (*c.* A.D. 65–80), one pre-Flavian, three Flavian
	T II 14, late occupation		27 (two), C.G., Trajanic or Hadrianic 18/31, C.G., Hadrianic/Antonine
	T II 13, demolition above 14		27, 18/31, C.G., probably Trajanic or Hadrianic
	T XXI 16, primary floor		29, Flavian 37, C.G., probably Hadrianic 27, 33, C.G., Trajanic/Hadrianic 18/31, C.G., PATER•F (**S 101**), *c.* A.D. 130–50
	T XXI 13, secondary floor	Hadrian, As, *RIC* 577*a* (A.D. 119–38)	
	T XXI 14, occupation on secondary floor		37, 18, Flavian 18/31, C.G., probably Trajanic 15/17, 27, first cent.
	A XII 11, primary floor		Curle 11, Flavian
	A XII 12A, occupation on 11		29, probably Flavian
	A VI 7, early floor		37, late Flavian
15	A XI 12, primary floor		37, *c.* A.D. 85–105 18, Flavian Curle 15, Curle 11, 18/31, C.G., Trajanic
	A XI 8, secondary floor		37, *c.* A.D. 80–100 18 (two), 27, Flavian

ROOM	LAYER	COINS	SAMIAN (all South Gaulish unless otherwise stated)
16	A XI 10, floor		18/31, 27, C.G., Hadrianic 33, C.G., Hadrianic/Antonine Curle 23, C.G., probably Antonine
16/20 inter-space	A VI 22, early level		18/31, C.G., with illiterate stamp (**S 108**), Hadrianic/Antonine Curle 11, 27, Flavian
14/17 inter-space	A IV 18, early level		37, C.G. (two), Trajanic 27, C.G., Hadrianic
17	A IV 21, occupation on primary floor		18, Neronian 27, probably Neronian Curle 11, Flavian
18	A IV 22, secondary floor		37, ? second cent.
19	A VI 9, primary floor	Vespasian, As, *RIC* 500	37, *c.* A.D. 75–90 18 (two), Flavian
	A VI 19, occupation on 9		37, Vespasianic 37, probably Trajanic/Hadrianic 15/17, 18, Flavian 35, ? second cent.
	A VI 10, ash in oven		30, first cent. 18, Flavian
20 SE. wall-trench	A VI 14	Vespasian, As, *RIC* 497 (4) or 747 Hadrian, As (*good*), *RIC* 578 (A.D. 119–22)	37, C.G., Trajanic/Hadrianic 27, C.G., Trajanic/Hadrianic 35/36, Flavian
21	A IV 20, make-up for path		Curle 15, second cent. 18, 27, Flavian 27, C.G., probably Hadrianic 33, C.G., Trajanic/Hadrianic 18, Flavian 18/31 (two), C.G., Trajanic/Hadrianic
	A II 23, make-up		33, C.G., stamped MATIIRIINIF (**S 100**), Hadrianic or early Antonine 18/31, C.G., Hadrianic 36, C.G., second cent.

ROOM	LAYER	COINS	SAMIAN (all South Gaulish unless otherwise stated)
22	A II 27, floor		29, Flavian
			29/37, C.G., Trajanic
			30, Rosette Potter, Trajanic
			37 (three), C.G., Trajanic
			33, late Flavian
			27 (two), one Flavian, one C.G., Trajanic/Hadrianic
			18 (two), Flavian
			35, probably Flavian
	A II 26, occupation on 27		37, *c.* A.D. 85–105
			37, *c.* A.D. 75–95
			37, C.G., Drusus I, *c.* A.D. 100–20
			18 (two), one Flavian, one probably Trajanic
			27 (three), one pre-Flavian, one Flavian, one C.G., Trajanic/Hadrianic
			15, pre-Flavian
	A II 36 = Pit 5, demolition pit.		37, C.G., style of Acaunissa, *c.* A.D. 125–50
			18/31, C.G., Trajanic/Hadrianic
			18, C.G., Trajanic/Hadrianic
23	A II 22, floor		27 (three), two Flavian, one C.G., Trajanic/Hadrianic
			18/31, C.G., probably Trajanic
			35, C.G., Trajanic/Hadrianic
	A I 22, occupation		24/25, Lezoux first-cent. ware
24	A I 20, first *op. sig.* floor	Trajan, sestertius, *RIC* 560 (A.D. 103–11)	29, Claudian/Neronian
			37, C.G., Trajanic
	A I 18, clay on 20		37, C.G., Trajanic
			18/31 or 31, C.G., probably pre-Antonine
			18R, stamped Ⓕ SE[VERI] (S 106), *c.* A.D. 65–85
			33, C.G., Trajanic
			35, C.G., Trajanic/Hadrianic
	A I 17, occupation on 18		18/31 or 31, C.G., probably Hadrianic
	A I 15, floor-patch on 17		29, Flavian
			Curle 11, C.G., Trajanic/Hadrianic
			18/31 and 31 (at least five), all C.G. and pre-Antonine

ROOM	LAYER	COINS	SAMIAN (all South Gaulish unless otherwise stated)
	A I 13, top *op. sig.* floor		27 (two), C.G., probably Antonine 33, C.G., Trajanic/Hadrianic 27, C.G., probably Antonine 37, C.G., probably Hadrianic 18, stamp PA[TRI] (**S 103**), Flavian
24/25 wall-trench		Trajan, As, *RIC* 417 (A.D. 99–100)	
25	A I 25, occupation		29, Flavian 37 (two), *c.* A.D. 85–105 37, C.G., Antonine 27 (two), Flavian and Trajanic 22/23, Flavian 35 (two), C.G., Trajanic/Hadrianic 67, etc. with barbotine, probably Flavian 18, 18/31, C.G., early second cent.
26	A II 24, primary gravel		37, C.G., style of Ranto, Trajanic (probably same vessel as in IIA Room 16) 37, *c.* A.D. 80–100 37, C.G., Trajanic 37, C.G., style of Acaunissa, *c.* A.D. 125–50 36, C.G., second cent. 18, Flavian 18/31, C.G., early second cent. 27, C.G., :·BONOXV[SE··] (**S 93**), Trajanic/Hadrianic
	AII 19, secondary gravel		37, C.G., second cent. 37, C.G., second cent. 18/31, 31 (two), C.G., probably Hadrianic 27 (three), including illiterate stamp (**S 110**), one Flavian, two C.G., Trajanic/Hadrianic
27	B I 32A, secondary floor		36, C.G., probably Antonine 33, 35, Neronian/Flavian
	B I 31A, occupation on 32A		18/31, 33, 36, C.G., Hadrianic/Antonine

ROOM	LAYER	COINS	SAMIAN (all South Gaulish unless otherwise stated)
	B I 31E, occupation on floor sealing oven		37, C.G., Trajanic 27, C.G., Trajanic or Hadrianic
28	A II 30, primary floor		37, C.G., Trajanic/Hadrianic 18/31, 27 (two), C.G., Trajanic/ Hadrianic 33, C.G., probably Trajanic/ Hadrianic 36, C.G., second cent.
	A II 29, occupation on 30		27, Flavian 18/31, C.G., Trajanic 33, C.G., C·INNΛMV retro. (S 95), c. A.D. 140–55
	A X 66, primary floor		37, c. A.D. 75–95 18, 33, Flavian 36, C.G., second cent. 27, 18/31, C.G., Trajanic or Hadrianic
	A X 65, secondary floor		31, C.G., Hadrianic
	A X 63, late floor		27, C.G., ? Hadrianic/Antonine
	B I 32D, make-up	Hadrian, denarius (new), RIC 202d (A.D. 125–8)	18, 37, Flavian
	B I 31D, secondary floor		37, C.G., style of Sacer(?), c. A.D. 140–60 27, C.G., Hadrianic 33, C.G., Antonine 18/31 (two), C.G., probably Hadrianic/Antonine 18/31, C.G., ΛVVVIOF (S 91), probably Antonine
29	A X 14, floor	Uncertain As, first cent.	
30	A VII 25, primary floor	Trajan, As	
	A VII 21, late floor		18/31, C.G., probably Trajanic/ Hadrianic
31	B II 27H, floor		37, style of Drusus I, c. A.D. 100–20 18, Flavian
	B III 24, make-up below 22		37, c. A.D. 80–100 18 (two), Flavian
	B III 22, primary floor round aediculae		29, c. A.D. 75–85 30 (two), Flavian

ROOM	LAYER	COINS	SAMIAN (all South Gaulish unless otherwise stated)
			24/25, *c.* A.D. 60–80
			31, C.G., probably Hadrianic
	B III 21A, fallen plaster over 22		33, C.G., probably Hadrianic
	B III 20, secondary floor over 21A	Vespasian, As	30, *c.* A.D. 65–80
			37, C.G., *c.* A.D. 110–40
			18/31, C.G., probably Hadrianic
			35, Flavian
			Ritt. 12, pre-Flavian
32	B I 31G, floor		37, *c.* A.D. 85–105
			18, 27, Flavian
	B II 28G, floor		29, Claudian
			29, 37, Vespasianic
			37, C.G., Trajanic
			33, Flavian
33	B I 32C, floor		37, C.G., Trajanic or Hadrianic
			18/31, Curle 11, C.G., Trajanic or Hadrianic
			18, Flavian
	B II 28F, floor		37, style of Drusus I, *c.* A.D. 100–20
			37, Flavian
			37, C.G., Hadrianic
			18, 27, first cent.
			18/31, C.G., Trajanic or Hadrianic
	B II 27F, occupation on 28F		37, C.G., style of Drusus I, *c.* A.D. 100–20
			37, C.G., *c.* A.D. 100–20
			37 (three), 30, Flavian
			29, Claudian
			18/31, probably Flavian
			33, Flavian
			Curle 11, C.G., Trajanic
35	B I 28B, secondary floor	Nerva, denarius, *RIC* 14	
36	A VII 9, late floor		37 (two), Flavian
			31, C.G., Hadrianic or Antonine
			27, C.G., pre-Antonine
	A VII 10, late floor		30, Claudian/Neronian
	B II 27Y, occupation on primary floor		18/31, 18/31R, 27, C.G., probably Trajanic/Hadrianic

ROOM	LAYER	COINS	SAMIAN (all South Gaulish unless otherwise stated)
	B II 27A, late occupation		31, 33, C.G., Hadrianic or Antonine
	B I 29A, late occupation		30, C.G., c. A.D. 115–35
	B IV 18A, occupation on primary floor		37 (two), Flavian
			37, C.G., Hadrianic/Antonine
			30, C.G., rouletted, probably pre-Antonine
			27 (two), one Flavian, one C.G., Hadrianic
			18/31 (two), C.G., one Trajanic, one Hadrianic/Antonine
			33, Curle 15, C.G., Hadrianic/Antonine
			36, C.G., probably Hadrianic
	B IV 17A, secondary floor on 18A		29, 37, Flavian
			18/31, C.G., Trajanic/Hadrianic
37	B II 29E, primary floor		37, style of Drusus I, c. A.D. 100–20
			30, pre-Flavian
			37, 67, Flavian
			80, Antonine (perhaps intrusive from pit or trodden in)
	B IV 21X, primary floor (= II 29 E)		29, c. A.D. 75–85
			37, c. A.D. 85–105
			37 (two), 18, 36, 27, Flavian
			37, C.G., style of Ioenalis, c. A.D. 100–20
			37, C.G., Donnaucus-Sacer, c. A.D. 110–30
			18 (two), Flavian
			31, C.G., probably Hadrianic
			42, C.G., second cent.
	B IV 21M, occupation on 21X		37 (two), c. A.D. 85–105
	B IV 20M, make-up for op. sig. floor		27, C.G., probably Trajanic
			30, Neronian or Flavian
	B II 28E (= IV 20M)		35, first cent.
			37, Flavian (**D 90**)
			37, c. A.D. 85–105
			18/31 (two), C.G., Hadrianic
			33, C.G., probably Hadrianic
			18, C.G., probably Trajanic
			18/31 or 31, illiterate stamp (**S 109**), Hadrianic/Antonine
	B IV 19M, op. sig. floor		27, pre-Flavian

ROOM	LAYER	COINS	SAMIAN (all South Gaulish unless otherwise stated)
			37, Flavian
			38, C.G., Antonine
39	B IV 19J, primary floor		37, C.G., probably Hadrianic
			27, C.G., probably Hadrianic
	B IV 18J, secondary floor on 19J	Vespasian, As, *RIC* 497 (4)	37 (two), Flavian
			37, C.G., Hadrianic
			37, C.G., *c.* A.D. 130–50
		Trajan, sestertius (*good*), *RIC* 390 (A.D. 98–9)	37, 37R, Hadrianic
			31 (two), 33 (two), 38, C.G., Antonine
			18/31, C.G., [AT]TIVS•FE (**S 92**), Hadrianic/Antonine
			31 (two), Curle 15, C.G., Hadrianic/Antonine
			18/31R stamped PRYD.IC.L.I. (**S 104**), Hadrianic/Antonine
			18/31 (two), C.G., Hadrianic
			Curle 11 (two), one Flavian, one C.G., Hadrianic
			27, Flavian
	B IV 17R, late floor		29, Flavian
			37 (two), *c.* A.D. 85–105
			18/31 (two), C.G., probably Hadrianic
			18/31 or 31, C.G., probably Antonine
	B IV 17J, late floor (= 17R)	Aelius, denarius, cf. *RIC* 444 (A.D. 137)	37, C.G., Trajanic
			37 (two), C.G., Hadrianic
			37, late Montans ware (**D 91**)
			Curle 15, 36, C.G., probably Trajanic or Hadrianic
			18, 27, Flavian
			18/31 (three), 33 (two), C.G., Hadrianic/Antonine
			18/31R or 31R, C.G., second cent.
			33 (two), C.G., one stamped CAVPIRRA (**S 94**), Antonine (intrusive?)
			27 (two), C.G., Trajanic/Hadrianic
			18/31, C.G., probably Hadrianic
	B IV 17K, occupation on 18J	Uncertain As, first cent.	29, Neronian
			37 (two), C.G., Antonine

ROOM	LAYER	COINS	SAMIAN (all South Gaulish unless otherwise stated)
			38, C.G., Antonine
			36 (two), C.G., second cent.
			27, 18, Flavian
			27 (two), C.G., probably Hadrianic
			27, C.G., Hadrianic/Antonine
			33 (four), C.G., one stamped [DI]VICATVS (**S 97**), Antonine
			18/31 and 31 (three), Hadrianic/ Antonine
			Curle 15, C.G., Hadrianic/Antonine
40	B IV 18H, primary floor	Titus (under Vespasian), As, *RIC* (Vesp.) 786	37, C.G., *c.* A.D. 150–80 (probably intrusive via Antonine wall-trench)
			37, C.G., probably Hadrianic/ Antonine
			38, C.G., Antonine
			27, Flavian
			35, C.G., second cent.
	B IV 18G, primary floor		37, C.G., probably Hadrianic/ Antonine
	B IV 18F, secondary floor		37, C.G., style of Sacer(?), *c.* A.D. 125–50
			81, C.G., probably Antonine
			27, C.G., Hadrianic
			38, stamp LVPIN[(**S 99**), C.G., Antonine
	B IV 17G, secondary floor on 18G		37, Flavian
			18, 33, C.G., second cent.
	B IV 17F, occupation on 18F		18/31, Curle 15, C.G., Trajanic/ Hadrianic
			18/31R, C.G., probably Hadrianic
			33, C.G., Hadrianic/Antonine
	B V 12 (= IV 17F)		37, C.G., style of Acaunissa, *c.* A.D. 125–45 (**D 92**)
			33, C.G., stamped GRANIO (**S 98**), *c.* A.D. 130–50
	B II 27D, secondary floor		37, C.G., style of Igocatus, *c.* A.D. 100–20
			37, C.G., style of Birrantus, Hadrianic
			37, C.G., potter X–5, *c.* A.D. 125–45
			27, C.G., Trajanic or Hadrianic
			18/31R, C.G., probably Hadrianic

ROOM	LAYER	COINS	SAMIAN (all South Gaulish unless otherwise stated)
			15/17, 18, 27, 29, Flavian 33, Curle 15, C.G., second cent.
41	B II 28C, primary floor		18 (two), 27, Flavian 18/31 or 31, C.G., probably Antonine 79, C.G., Antonine
	B II 27Z, secondary floor		37, C.G., style of Igocatus, c. A.D. 100–20 27, probably Trajanic 30, Flavian 18/31 or 31 (two), second cent.
	B II 27C, late floor		33, C.G., Trajanic or Hadrianic
43	B II 27X, primary floor		37, C.G., probably Hadrianic 27, C.G., Trajanic
44	B IV 18B, primary floor		37, C.G., Hadrianic 37, C.G., style of Igocatus, c. A.D. 100–20 (**D 93**) 18/31, C.G., Hadrianic or Antonine 35, C.G., probably Antonine 27, 35, Flavian
	B IV 17B, occupation on 18B	Barbarous, *Fel. Temp. Reparatio* (intrusive)	29, 37, Flavian 37, C.G., Ranto group, c. A.D. 110–30 37, C.G., rouletted, probably Hadrianic 37, C.G., ? Antonine 18/31, C.G., Trajanic 27 (two), C.G., Trajanic/Hadrianic 33, C.G., Hadrianic/Antonine
44/36 wall-trench	B IV 22		27, C.G., probably Trajanic or Hadrianic
45	B IV 18E, primary floor	Tiberius, denarius, *RIC* 3	
	B IV 19D, primary occupation		27, 33, Curle 15, C.G., Trajanic/Hadrianic 18/31, 35, ?46, C.G., Hadrianic 18, 35, 37, Flavian 29, pre-Flavian

ROOM	LAYER	COINS	SAMIAN (all South Gaulish unless otherwise stated)
	B IV 18D, secondary floor		31, 33, C.G., Hadrianic/Antonine
	B IV 17D, occupation on 18D		18/31 (two), C.G., Hadrianic/Antonine
			36, C.G., probably Antonine
			27, C.G., Trajanic
	B IV 17E, late occupation		37, C.G., c. A.D. 130–60 (**D 94**)
			Curle 11, C.G., Antonine
			18/31, Curle 15, C.G., Hadrianic/Antonine
			Curle 11, C.G., Hadrianic
			27, Flavian
	B IV Pit 16, in 18E		18/31 (two), C.G., Hadrianic/Antonine
			31, C.G., Antonine
			31R, C.G., Antonine
			36, C.G., probably Antonine
46	B IV 19C, primary floor		18, Flavian
			27, C.G., Hadrianic
	B IV 18C, secondary floor		27 (two), C.G., Trajanic/Hadrianic
			18/31, C.G., Hadrianic/Antonine
			33, C.G., probably Antonine
	B IV 17C, occupation on 18C		37, C.G., style of Ranto, Trajanic
			Curle 15, probably Hadrianic/Antonine
Watling Street	T I 7, first deposit of metalling		Curle 11, Flavian
			31, C.G., probably Antonine
	T I 5, later metalling		27, C.G., Hadrianic/Antonine
			31 (two), C.G., Antonine
			33, C.G., Antonine

Summary of dating evidence, Period IIC

It is in levels of this period that coins of Hadrian first appear, though few in number. There were four of these (including the denarius of Aelius): one came from a primary level—a denarius of 125–8 in new condition in the make-up below Room 28. An As of 119–22 lay in the south-east wall-trench of Room 20, but, as the latter also contained an open plank drain, this coin cannot be used with complete confidence to date construction. There were also four coins of Trajan, two of them in primary floors and one in a wall-trench.

The proportion of residual samian going back to Flavian and even to Claudian times is still a remarkable feature of the list, but at least from Room 16 north-westwards there is a distinct indication that Trajanic wares are now present in significant quantity.

It was suggested above (p. 53) that Period II B ended *c.* A.D. 130, though the evidence for this mainly depended on the opening date of II C. In the primary floors of Period II C (that is, floors which were sealed by later floors of this same period) material of Trajanic or 'probably Trajanic' date was not uncommon. The following rooms produced Trajanic/ Hadrianic or 'probably Hadrianic' samian in primary positions: 21, 26, 28, 31, 37, 39, 40, 43, 46. The latest of these pieces is a form 37 by Acaunissa (*c.* A.D. 125–50), which with the denarius of 125–8 shows that the opening date cannot be earlier than *c.* A.D. 130. It should not be much later, however, if we are to allow time for the decay of the building before its reconstruction *c.* A.D. 150.

It will have been noted that similar primary levels in a few rooms produced even later sherds. Room 40 produced a form 37 of *c.* 150–80 and also a form 38 of Antonine date; Room 41 produced an 18/31 or 31 dated 'probably Antonine' and an Antonine form 79, while Room 37 yielded a form 80, Antonine, and Room 46 a form 35, 'probably Antonine'. This group might suggest a later starting date for Period II C of 140–50. However, the weight of the evidence is against this, not least the *terminus post quem* provided by the Antonine fire of *c.* A.D. 155–60 at the end of the succeeding Period II D. It is not without significance that, apart from Room 46 where the form 35 is not a serious impediment (for single sherds may be trodden into earlier floors, and the date itself is not completely certain), the difficulties are centred on three deposits only, each of which has yielded an obviously intrusive piece of full Antonine date. The chance of this happening occasionally in the large-scale excavation of a site where postholes, wall-trenches, and pits pierce earlier levels is obviously to be taken into account. More remarkable is the rarity of such intrusions in earlier levels; those of Period II C are only just below the final floors of Period II D in which there was a much greater number of disturbances than occurred lower down. The material coherence of the dating evidence as a whole is impressive.

As for the end of the period, there are no coins later than Hadrian (though coins are less common now). The samian, however, extends later than the coins. There is much Trajanic/ Hadrianic and 'probably Hadrianic' material, and there are forty-four Hadrianic/Antonine sherds with another three 'probable'. In addition there are fifteen 'probably Antonine' and thirty-one Antonine sherds, not counting decorated pieces of form 37 which are assigned dates as follows: 110–40 (one); 125–50 (three); 125–45 (one); 130–50 (one); 130–60 (one); and 140–60 (one). It is clear from this evidence that Period II C extends some years after 140. Previous rebuilding had occurred after *c.* thirty-five years and *c.* twenty-five years; if Period II C lasted twenty-five years the terminal date would be 155, a date not inconsistent with the samian evidence. But this would not leave sufficient span for Period II D before the Antonine fire. It is therefore suggested that Period II C ended *c.* A.D. 150, after only twenty years.

PERIOD II D, *c.* A.D. 150–155/60

The final rebuilding of the half-timbered shops took place about the middle of the century (fig. 19). Not long afterwards the whole area, and much else of the city as well, was destroyed by fire; a thick blanket of burnt daub covered the remains of the buildings, and had the effect of preserving a good deal of structural evidence as well as a very large amount of pottery and other objects. The dating evidence for the beginning of Period II D and for the conflagration is summarized below, pp. 97, 256, 262.

In this period the portico was increased in width to 18 ft. 6 in., save that in front of Rooms
12 and 14 there seems to have been an inset. Between 25A and 25B it is crossed by a trench
of which the probable explanation is that it contained a plank drain leading rain-water off
from the interspace 10–12. This channel first appeared in Period II C when a difference in
the floor material each side of it, together with the presence of postholes in the Period II B
levels along this line, suggested a partition (pp. 42, 55). But in Period II D the floor was
uniform and a drain is more likely: yet it leads off awkwardly from the corner of Room 10,
more as a wall would do. Between 25C and 25 there was a distinct change in floor material;
in the former it was greenish brick-earth, in 25 gravel. To account for this a possible extension
of wall 18/24 is dotted on the plan. In fact, however, it is very unlikely that the portico was
divided, and a precedent for an abrupt change of floor material has already been noted in
Room 36 of Period II C. Very probably the explanation lies in the responsibility of individual
householders for maintaining lengths of portico.

From it the buildings run back in a series of blocks 9–10, 12–14, 18–24, 30, 35–42, 49–50,
and 54–9, each separated from its neighbour by an interspace which often contains a plank-
lined drain running on beneath the portico to the main sewer below Watling Street;[1] some
blocks are further subdivided at the rear by gravelled approach paths. The arrangement of
rooms is far more complicated and confusing than at any time previously, and the straight
continuous alignment of rear wall to the front rooms, which survived as late as Period II C,
is no longer seen. Each building has attained complete independence (fig. 18, p. 79).

The presence of large deep postholes is a noticeable feature; these frequently occur singly
or in pairs in the wall-trenches (e.g. 10/25, 13/14, 30/25, or 46/51) and can be accounted for
by the deep soft cavities created by successive wall-trenches on the same lines. Others appear
beside the walls rather than in them (see especially Room 46). We should probably assume
shelving rather than an attempt to prop up crumbling walls, since the length of Period II D
was cut short by the fire. Another notable row of postholes appears in the portico outside
Rooms 35 and 42. These were driven very deeply into the underlying deposits (fig. 28,
section K–K[1]) and traces survived even in the blanket of burnt daub; their regular plan
suggests a well-built counter. It is stratigraphically possible, indeed, that they are really
structurally later than the fire, and date from some point in the period 160–270: layer B I 16
which seals them is make-up for the building of Period III.

Some wall-trenches, as 36/37 or 10/25, lay at the base of shallow U-shaped trenches up to
3 ft. wide and 10 in. deep (fig. 27, section M–M[1]; pls. V*b*; XX*a, b*; XXI*b*), which were
filled, like the wall-trenches at their base, with burnt daub from the fire which terminated
the period. It is evident, therefore, that they were still open and empty when the fire occurred
and must have been concealed beneath timber floors. They were probably dug in the
search for firmer levels on which to lay the beam.

Plank floors

There was further and surer evidence for timber floors towards the north-west end of the
site. In Rooms 45 and 46 there were a number of transverse slots (pls. XXIX*a*, XXX*a*) too
close together to make sense as wall foundations: the narrowest 'room' would have been

---

[1] This sewer was not found at Insula XIV, but it was seen traversing the foundation of the North Monumental
Arch: *Antiq. Journ.* xlii (1962), 154–5.

1 ft. 3 in. wide. It was clearly a case of floor-joists, and confirming this traces of three parallel planks were found, one of which slightly overlapped a joist. The joists ran north-west–south-east across the width of the room, whereas the planks ran down its length.

Room 49 also provided evidence. Here (pl. XXIX*b*) the sleeper beam 48/49 survived as charcoal, and in its surface were visible remains of mortice holes in which the wall framework had once been fixed (p. 6). Parallel with the wall and 2 ft. 4 in. away were remains of a joist, while at right angles lay three parallel planks which had evidently once been supported by the lip of the sleeper-beam though now fractured under pressure at the critical point. The floor-boards were 8–11 in. wide and 1–2 in. thick. In Room 50 also there were similar traces of planks running north-east–south-west, while below them and running in the same direction were some very narrow channels. It is not easy to see what these were, since floor-joists should be at right angles to the planks, and in any case Room 50 is only 3 ft. wide and joists unnecessary (p. 80).

Floor-boards but no joists were found in Room 55, while in Room 56 there were faint traces of planks aligned north-east–south-west and a short length of joist running transversely. These traces occurred only in the south-west half of the room, and it seems likely that the area round the oven in the north-east end was not floored in this way.

The irregular occurrence of joists made it clear that they were not normally placed in a dug channel: in any case this would have vitiated their purpose which was to support the floor-boards *above* the level of the damp soil. They may, indeed, have been jointed into the sleeper-beams of the walls they touched, but, unfortunately, we did not find evidence of this surviving. Alternatively they may just have been placed on the surface of the earth. That they could be traced by occasional channels is due to sinkage into a soft underlying ground: where it was hard they had left no trace, unless as in Room 49 the charred beam itself survived on the surface.

An interesting illustration of all this was provided by the large timber hut lent us by the Ministry of Public Building and Works as an excavation headquarters (pl. III*a*). This hut was erected on the site seen in pl. III in the early summer of 1957. The joists of its floor were laid directly on the grass. Thereafter for four seasons some 100 people a day made use of it. At the end of the season of 1960, being dilapidated beyond recovery, it was burnt down with Ministry permission. Pl. III*b* shows the site, where the fortuitous creation of joist-slots in the earth is obvious.

In Room 23 somewhat similar remains were found (fig. 3) where they were partly cut away by a shallow pit of Period III (not marked on the main plan, fig. 19). The remains consisted of parallel planks running north-west–south-east and a beam north-east–south-west. Here however, not only was the burnt timber lying directly on an *opus signinum* floor, but the half-round beam appeared to be on top of the planks. This, then, was a fallen ceiling.

Plank drains

Very early in the 1958 season three parallel 'foundation' trenches appeared on the north-west side of Room 24, within an over-all width of 4 ft. 6 in.; all were filled with burnt daub, but it was clear that they could not all be contemporary walls (fig. 24, section G–G¹; 23, section H–H¹). Later the central one was found continuing across the portico and it became clear that it was a gutter draining the space between two buildings; it had been open to the surface since it was full of burnt daub, but it contained $\frac{1}{2}$ in. of greenish silt on its flat bottom, and here and there traces of the lining planks were visible.

Another well-preserved example was found running round two sides of Rooms 55–7; it lay at a distance of 1 ft. 6 in. from the south-east wall, which probably indicates the width of the eaves (pl. XXVIIa); on the south-west side of the building, which was doubtless a gable-end, it did not maintain this relationship. The channel was 1 ft. wide in the yard and narrowed to 9 in. on entering the interspace 51/56. It ceased to be visible on the surface just short of the doorway into Room 54, but continued underground below this room, where it was found in a trial trench on its course to the street-sewer: the general excavation was not taken below the Period II D floors in this area. Outside the building the channel was 6–8 in. deep and had been open, as it was full of burnt daub: at its base was charred wood which also lined the sides up to the top in places. There were nails in the filling but not at significant points. The gravel metal of the yard and interspace extended on both sides of the drain.

Room details

Room 1 had a gravelly floor and Room 2 one of the rare *opus signinum* floors of this phase. The plan of this area was not sufficiently worked out in the emergency of 1957 (p. 5); there was also much disturbance by pits of a later date. Room 4, which was L-shaped like Room 1, had in its rear section a tiled hearth (pl. XXVb) near which was a patch of clay on the gravelly floor. Here and in Rooms 7 and 25A there was evidence of the extreme ferocity of the conflagration in the form of molten glass, and even pieces of bronze fused to stone.

In Room 10 the plan of Period II C Room 9, which underlay it, was repeated. The outer north-west wall-trench was 1 ft. 6 in. wide and contained two postholes. The inner wall, only 1 ft. 6 in. away and parallel, was $c.$ 9 in. wide at floor level: it yielded a great number of much smaller postholes which descended to a sleeper-beam, the charcoal remains of which were found in the bottom of the slot (fig. 9, section Y–Z). The junction of this wall with the south-west wall 8/10 was explored in trench T XXII. There was much disturbance from the robbing of the Period III wall, but it was clear that wall 8/10 continued north-west to join the main outer wall: there was thus no question of the 18-in. space being an interspace between blocks, and the south-east wall of 12 has accordingly been restored to create one. The 18-in. space must represent built-in furniture such as a cupboard, with perhaps shelves above—the sort of equipment seen in several reliefs of commercial life in Gaul.[1]

In the east corner of the room was part of an emplacement resembling that in Room 6 of Period I, almost directly below; about half of it had been destroyed by the footings of Period III. What remained was the segment of a circular flat-bottomed hole, 4 ft. in diameter and 9 in. deep below floor level (fig. 17; pl. XXVIIIa). It had charred wood on bottom and sides and was filled with burnt daub. Its floor consisted of a layer of fine yellow sand 1–2 in. thick. This presumably had been supplied to facilitate a level bedding and perhaps to prevent adhesion; for the likely explanation of the emplacement is that it held a barrel. This had been empty (of anything but water) at the time of the fire.

Wall 10/25A was supported by pairs of postholes driven deeply into the underlying sleeper cavity; the more north-easterly row seemed to be later additions to an original single row.

[1] Cf. E. Espérandieu, *Recueil général des bas-reliefs, statues et bustes de la Gaule romaine*, nos. 3097 (Lillebonne), 3608 (Til-Châtel), 3469 (Dijon), 3317 (Langres), and 7795 (Simpelveld).

Collapsed on to the surface of Watling Street just beside the outer wall of the portico in trench T I opposite Rooms 7–10 were some sizeable chunks of burnt daub with rouletted pattern on the south-west side (pl. XXX*b*); one large piece in particular seemed to be *in situ* but subsided out of the vertical with part of its timber frame behind it (fig. 27, section B–B[1]). This seems to indicate that at this point at least the portico had a solid wall (of whatever height) dividing it from the street, and not merely a timber balustrade as shown in the reconstruction (fig. 18). In front of Room 14 the floor level of portico 25B had been raised

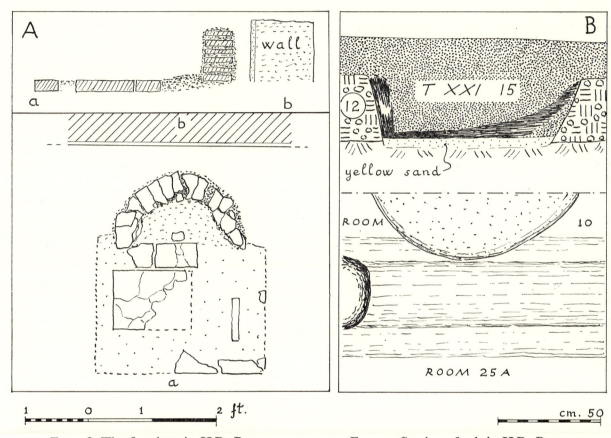

FIG. 16. The fireplace in IID, Room 17.   FIG. 17. Section of tub in IID, Room 10.

about 1 ft. with a layer of flints capped with gravel at the beginning of Period IID. This appears to be one of those local treatments of the portico which have already been alluded to (p. 74). The north-west wall of Room 14 and the south-east wall of Room 18 both projected into the portico, the latter for some 6 ft. before ending abruptly. The former was interrupted by some Period III foundations at this point. There was a space of *c.* 4 ft. between these walls. It is not easy to see the reason for this arrangement unless these wing-walls gave shelter to projecting counters in front of the shops. Evidence for continued bronze-working in this area was provided by a small piece of molten bronze waste on the floor of Room 13.

Rooms 15, 20, 21, and 23 all had floors of *opus signinum*. Perhaps 15 and 20 were living rooms but 23, like 17 beside it, contained a substantial hearth. Room 15 was largely destroyed by pits. In a burnt deposit subsiding into pit 21, and probably therefore belonging to the debris of the Antonine fire, was a little hoard of 108 lead roundels resembling coins but blank; they may have been intended as weights (p. 146, no. 185; pl. XLVII*b*).

In Room 22 a very thin charcoal line was seen in the floor parallel to, and 2 ft. 3 in. from, its north-west wall; it was perhaps a floor-joist. In Room 20 the *opus signinum* floor had a quarter-round moulding against wall 19/20 and 20/22; its south-east wall was painted red.

The south-east wall of Room 17 was stepped back from that of 18, whose line was continued alongside that of 17 by a second trench 6 in. away from it, which must be taken as a drain. The character of the hearth in Room 17 is best appreciated in pl. XXVIII*b* and fig. 16. The back was built of broken tiles including *tegulae* and stood to a maximum of six courses; inside was a baked-clay floor and in front lay a tile apron, broken by heat, but more or less intact, measuring 2 ft. 8 in. by 1 ft. 11 in. This is perhaps better defined as a hearth with raised fire-back to protect the wall than as an oven. On it cooking could take place, or even smithing with the aid of bellows. The hearth was set up against wall 16/17, which still stood to a height of 1 ft. above the floor. Nearby was a dish of grey-ware (fig. 128, 973) and a 'flower-vase' of three small vessels set on a circular ring (fig. 125, 886) from which they had become detached, and in the vicinity several other almost whole bowls and a mortarium stamped by Sarrius (fig. 130, 1031). There was also a small slab of Purbeck marble, lying on the floor (p. 156, no. 232, pl. XLVIII*b*); the room also produced an iron paring-chisel, an iron spoon, and (from a wall-trench) a punch and the case of a tumbler lock (figs. 60–67, nos. 10, 4, 66, 46). Two large flagons (nos. 807, 821) came from Room 16. In Room 23 a fine long-handled shovel of iron (fig. 60, 6) was found beside the north-west wall, and had doubt-less been used in connection with the similar hearth there (pl. XXVII*b*). This room also yielded an ox-goad, a drop-hinge and staple, and several other objects of iron (figs. 62–72, nos. 21, 58, 83, 123, 138, 140, 153). Another interesting collection of iron objects came from Room 18. They included a hand-saw, a hipposandal, a knife, a lock-case, a U-shaped wall-hook, and two pieces of binding (figs. 61–70, nos. 12, 28, 43, 67, 87, 134, 135).

The fire in this area had been very intense. The interesting structural details yielded by the still-standing walls of Room 23 have already been described (p. 6). One problem posed by their survival was that of access. It has normally been assumed that the rear rooms were living quarters accessible from the shops in front. But wall 23/24 was standing to a height varying between 1 and 2 ft. for its entire length; there was no doorway (pl. XXV*a*). Access from 24 to 23 must have been via Rooms 18 and 17; wall 17/23 still stood for much of its length, but there was space for a doorway towards its north-east end. This fact proves that the whole block was in single possession, rather than two separate premises, with interesting social corollaries (p. 12).

Room 24 had a very hard compact floor of sandy gravel. There were many fragments of bronze in this room including strips about $\frac{1}{4}$ to $\frac{1}{2}$ in. wide which had been folded up and later crushed flat. These seem to be clippings from manufacture. In the west corner were several pieces of waste lead sheet. There was also an iron set (fig. 60, no. 3) and two whetstones (pp. 156 f., nos. 238, 243). Near wall 24/18 a large portion of a quern (p. 158, no. 252) was set in the floor and close to it lay a pounding-stone; near wall 23/24 lay a slab of Purbeck marble (pl. XXIV*b*). Several of these slabs have been found in contexts which show that they are

FIG. 18. Reconstruction of the Period IID buildings (*drawn by J. C. Frere*).

not wall or floor decoration; they are presumably palettes or perhaps hard working-surfaces for jewellers and the like.

The drain between Rooms 24 and 30 and the deep, wide character of the foundation trench 25/30 can be seen in pl. XXI*b*; in the background is the corner of a rectangular fuel-box pit belonging to Room 30 (fig. 24, section J–J¹). It had vertical sides and was 1 ft. 3 in. deep; it seems to have been almost empty at the time of the fire, and the chalk packing connected with Period III had compressed its filling of debris. In the burnt daub covering the portico (Room 25) in front of Room 24 were several sherds to which a pink material adhered. X-ray diffraction analysis carried out at the British Museum Laboratory showed this pink material to be composed chiefly of calcite (calcium carbonate); the pink colour is probably due to the presence of iron compounds.

Wall 32/33 was not rebuilt at the beginning of Period IID; the wall 32/33 of the Period IIC plan (p. 70) continued in use with new floors abutting it, but no painted plaster survived at IID level. In Room 32 the north-east face of wall 32/31 was painted white.

This was a new wall of Period II D. In Room 33 was a small rectangular pit with vertical sides close to a hearth. This and the fact that its lower contents included charcoal and burnt clay suggested that it was a fuel container. On the other hand, it was over 4 ft. deep, much deeper than its parallels, and its upper filling was chalky. These facts might suggest a latrine pit, but its proximity to the hearth makes this unlikely.

Room 31 had an *opus signinum* floor, and the *aediculae* which had survived from Period II C were now filled with rubble-masonry: however, as explained above (p. 59), this probably only means that their interior level was being raised. For simultaneously a rough step was added in front (see detailed plan and sections, figs. 12, 13).

In the north-west half of Room 42 (pl. XX*b*) sleeper-beam 42/41 lay at the bottom of a U-shaped trench, but part of the floor level had been made up with rough lumps of chalk and flint which were much burnt on top (pl. XXI*a*). It seems improbable that this rough surface could ever have been the floor, and a covering of floor-boards should undoubtedly be restored. The sleeper-beam itself survived in a charred condition; it was of oak, 1 ft. wide, 5–6 in. thick, and at least 12 ft. long.

In the north corner of Room 43 was a tile oven with its wall still standing four courses in places. This 'room' was a large chalk-floored area which is perhaps best taken as a yard. In its north-west wall was an 11 ft. gap perhaps giving access to one of the narrow back lanes. The gravel of this lane, however, was covered with a good deal of rubbish containing large fragments of pots. Such gaps for doors or gates are unusual. The only other identified is in wall 53/54 of this same period. North-west of Rooms 39–42 there was a passage-way (42A) which instead of lying between blocks had been embraced within the outer wall of the premises; the true interspace lay north of this boundary wall and contained a plank drain.

The wooden floors in Rooms 45, 46, 49, 50, 55, and 56 have already been described (p. 74). Room 40 contained a number of postholes the purpose of which is uncertain. It is always possible that some belong to Period III and were not noticed in the burnt daub above the floor. The north end of the foundation trench of wall 46/51 was plugged with flint and mortar (pl. XXX*a*), as was a short length of the back wall of the portico between Rooms 50 and 54. These seemed to be contemporary, and not later intrusions; their purpose may have been to prevent water from the interspace entering the foundation trenches. Room 50 is only 3 ft. 3 in. wide at its maximum, and it is probably best to regard wall 49/50 as either a floor-joist or at best as the back wall of a counter. The room produced a number of bronze fragments. Between Rooms 46 and 55 lay a gravelled courtyard; the drain shows that it was open to the sky. Pit 14 in its middle was of later date, as was Pit 19 in all probability (p. 101).

Room 48 did not have a timber floor; instead it had one of 'opus signinum substitute', consisting of pounded tile set in puddled chalk. In Room 44 the attempt to produce the same thing was less successful since the chalk had not been puddled. Room 55 was the terminal room of its suite, as shown by the drain. The plank floor has already been mentioned (p. 75). Above this was a thick deposit of burnt daub which enveloped a large quantity of objects, mostly near the south-west and north-west walls (pl. XXXI*a, b*). Certain of these were pieces of iron work, some perhaps from the walls themselves; others were broken vessels which had presumably crashed down when their shelves collapsed. There were three coarse-ware lamps (fig. 142, nos. 6–8); a glass vessel containing purple pigment and two facet-cut glass beakers (fig. 77, nos. 41, 42); a Purbeck marble palette, and two large and two small flagons (figs. 121–2, nos. 802, 807, 809, 820); a vessel of black Lezoux samian (a variant of form 74) decorated with appliqué masks (fig. 96, 112, pl. LI); a bone hinge-component (fig. 54, 186); a triple vase (fig. 125, 887); part of a wooden vessel with bronze mountings; a bronze chain, two hones, two fragments of antler; many pieces of iron including a bench-anvil (fig. 60, 1), a punch (fig. 60, 5), pieces of (?) two bowls (fig. 65, 47–8), a hanging lamp (fig. 65, 52), and a narrow iron ferrule (fig. 69, 122); and some twelve small crucibles (pl. LIIa), some still showing minute globules of gold in their interiors. It is clear that these were the premises of a goldsmith or jeweller, and that Room 55 was his store-room.[1]

Painted wall plaster

Though the impression was gained that not many of the rooms of earlier periods had possessed decorated wall plaster, this may be misleading because of the thorough nature of replacement. There were certainly considerable though fragmentary remains from the buildings of Period II D. From wall 7/25 came a fragment with red and white panels or bands. In the burnt debris of Room 15 were fragments showing a 1½ in. red band on white, a thick white band on red, and two thin, parallel red bands with a third at an oblique angle. The south-east wall of Room 20 has been mentioned as being white with splashes of red as was the south-west wall of Room 30 (pl. XXIVc), and in Room 23 the lower parts of the north-east and north-west walls were painted white (pl. XXVIIb), though discoloured by the fire, as was the south-west wall of Room 17 (pl. XXIVa). Room 44 had white plaster, Room 45 red, and 46 red with a darker red stripe. Room 49/50 produced pieces with the following scheme: a red panel or band adjoining a broad white band divided in two by a grey stripe, and itself separated by a dark red stripe from an area or band of olive-green. This was applied to a single thin coat of plaster covering the daub. There was also some pink marbling. Room 55 produced pieces painted plain red, red and white, and plain white, and also some pink marbled with dark red and white spots. Room 57 produced a piece with a yellowish-green stripe on a white background with narrow borders in red painted over the green; and another in red with a white band, bordered by a broader black stripe. In Room 56 were pieces with red and white bands of the same type, and some yellow.

Dating evidence for Period II D

The evidence falls into two parts, (a) that relating to the construction and occupation of the buildings, and (b) the material from the destruction-deposit caused by the Antonine fire. They are listed separately below.

A. Floors and occupation deposits

Note: **D 98**, **S 120**, etc. in col. 4 refer to *Decorated* vessels and *Stamps* illustrated on pp. 218–62

ROOM	LAYER	COINS	SAMIAN (all Central Gaulish except as stated)
I	V XXXI 10, floor T III 15, floor		37, *c.* A.D. 125–45 (**D 95**) 18, S.G., Flavian 27, 35, Hadrianic

[1] A goldsmith employing slave-labour is attested at Norton near Malton, Yorkshire, in *RIB* 712.

ROOM	LAYER	COINS	SAMIAN (all Central Gaulish except as stated)
2a	V XXXIII 6, 7, make-up		29, S.G., Flavian
			33, 81, Curle 15, Hadrianic / Antonine
			33, probably Antonine
			33, MOSSI•MAN (S 120), c. A.D. 155–75
	V XXXIII 11, make-up		31, 31R (several), Antonine
			37, 27, S.G., Flavian
			37, c. A.D. 100–25
			37, Quintilianus Group, c. A.D. 125–50 (D 96)
			31, Antonine
	V XXXIII 5, floor over 7		35/36, probably Hadrianic
			37, signature C R (S 114), c. A.D. 135–75 (D 98)
			37, c. A.D. 140–70
			37, Attianus?, c. A.D. 125–50 (D 97)
			31, Antonine
			44/81, Antonine
			18R, S.G., Flavian
3a	Z II 9, floor		31, PATER (S 121), c. A.D. 130–50
8	Z I 6, oven		37, S.G., c. A.D. 90–110
			36, (?)
	Z I 5, floor		Curle 11, Trajanic
			18/31 (two), probably Hadrianic
			27, Hadrianic/Antonine
			31, ΛNNIV[SF] (S 112), Hadrianic/ Antonine
			18, [I]ABVSFE (S 117), Neronian
10	T XX 9, make-up		37, style of Drusus I, c. A.D. 100–20
			27, Trajanic/Hadrianic
			18, S.G., Flavian
	T XX 8, floor		29, S.G., c. A.D. 55–70
			30, 18/31, c. A.D. 100–20
			18/31, probably Hadrianic
			27 (two), S.G., Flavian
	T XX 8a, floor of cupboard		29, S.G., c. A.D. 55–70
			37, S.G., c. A.D. 85–105
	T XXI 12a, floor of cupboard		18/31, Hadrianic/Antonine

ROOM	LAYER	COINS	SAMIAN (all Central Gaulish except as stated)
13	A XI 7, make-up		37 (two), c. A.D. 100–20 37, c. A.D. 130–50 27, 33, Hadrianic/Antonine
14	A XII 7, floor		27, S.G., Flavian Curle 23, probably pre-Antonine
15	A IV 19, make-up for floor		33, SEVERI·M·I (S 124), c. A.D. 130–60
15–20 inter-space	A II 15, gravel path		27, Trajanic/Hadrianic
16	A IV 14, floor		37, style of Cinnamus, Antonine 33, Hadrianic/Antonine 18/31, Hadrianic 31, Antonine 35, probably pre-Antonine
17	A IV 13, floor	Trajan, As, RIC 395 (?)	27, S.G., first cent.
	A IV 12, occupation on 13		29, S.G., Flavian 37, style of Igocatus, c. A.D. 100–20 37, Docilis, c. A.D. 130–55 (D 101) 33, probably Trajanic 18/31 or 31, probably pre-Antonine 36, second cent.
18	A VI 4, floor		29, S.G., pre-Flavian 27, S.G., Flavian 37, S.G., c. A.D. 80–100 Curle 11, Trajanic 18/31 (two), Trajanic/Hadrianic 18/31 or 31, Hadrianic/Antonine
	A VI 3, occupation on 4	Titus under Vespasian, As, RIC (Vesp.) 786	
19	A II 16, occupation on floor		37, S.G., Flavian 37 (rim), Trajanic/Hadrianic Curle 11, S.G., Flavian 27 (two), Trajanic/Hadrianic and S.G., Flavian 18, S.G., Flavian

ROOM	LAYER	COINS	SAMIAN (all Central Gaulish except as stated)
			18/31 or 31, Trajanic/Hadrianic 33 (three), probably mid-second cent. 33, S.G., Flavian
20	A II 20, *opus signinum* floor		37, style of Drusus I, *c.* A.D. 100–20 15/17, S.G., probably Vespasianic
20–27 inter-space	A II 13, 14, gravel path		18/31, BⱯLBI[NVS.I:] (S 113), Hadrianic 33, Hadrianic/Antonine 37 (two), Flavian, S.G., and (?) Antonine 27 (two), Trajanic or Hadrianic Curle 11, 30(?), S.G., Flavian 18/31, 31 (three vessels), probably mid-second cent. Stanfield unusual form 29/34
23	A I 11, *opus signinum* floor A I 10, occupation on 11 A I 7, occupation on 11 A I 30, in clay of NW. wall		18/31, Hadrianic/Antonine 18/31, probably Hadrianic 27, Trajanic/Hadrianic 18/31, ERIC[VM] retro. (S 116), Hadrianic/Antonine Inkwell, S.G., probably Flavian 36, S.G., Flavian 31, 36, Antonine 27, Hadrianic/Antonine 37, free-style, probably pre-Antonine
Drain 23/29	A I 14, silt		33, E.G., Antonine 27, Hadrianic/Antonine 27, S.G., Flavian 31, stamp [SEC]VNDINI (S 123), Hadrianic/Antonine
24	A I 12, floor		37 (two), style of Igocatus, *c.* A.D. 100–20 37 (scraps), probably Hadrianic 37, probably mid-second cent. (D 102) 38, Antonine 18/31 and 31, many fragments, Hadrianic and early Antonine 27, Hadrianic 33, 35/36, probably Hadrianic/Antonine

ROOM	LAYER	COINS	SAMIAN (all Central Gaulish except as stated)
	A I 9, occupation on 12		37, Cinnamus—Cerialis Group, c. A.D. 145–70 (**D 104**)
			37, Hadrianic/Antonine (**D 103**)
			35, mid-second cent.
			18, probably Trajanic
	A VII 5, floor		37, c. A.D. 115–35
			37, S.G., c. A.D. 75–95
			Curle 11, Curle 15, Trajanic or Hadrianic
			27, 35/36, probably Hadrianic
			Stanfield form 32, C.G., (?) second cent.
25a	T I 9, make-up below beam of front portico wall		31, Antonine
			31, probably Antonine
	T XXI 12, floor		37, S.G., Flavian
			15/17, S.G., pre-Flavian
			27, second cent.
			18/31R, 27, Trajanic/Hadrianic
25b	T XXI 10, floor		27 (?), S.G., Flavian
	A XII 10, stone make-up		18, S.G., Flavian
			27, Trajanic or Hadrianic
25	A VII 7, floor		37 (?), S.G., ? Flavian
	B II 26A		30, rouletted, second cent.
			37, Hadrianic/Antonine
			33, Hadrianic/Antonine
			31, probably Hadrianic
			15/17, 18, S.G., first cent.
	B IV 9A, floor		37, Potter X–6, c. A.D. 125–50 (**D 105**)
			27 (three), one Trajanic/Hadrianic, two Hadrianic/Antonine
			31, 33, probably Hadrianic
			18/31, Hadrianic/Antonine
26	B I 27E, occupation on floor		37, probably Hadrianic
	B I 27X, occupation on floor		27, PRISCINVS FC (**S 122**), Hadrianic
			18/31, Trajanic or Hadrianic
			36, second cent.

ROOM	LAYER	COINS	SAMIAN (all Central Gaulish except as stated)
27	A II 33, floor		37, style of Igocatus, *c.* A.D. 100–20
			37, Donnaucus–Sacer, *c.* A.D. 115–35
	B I 30X, floor		37, probably Trajanic
			Curle 15, Hadrianic
			31, Hadrianic/Antonine
	B I 27B, occupation on 30X		Curle 11, probably Hadrianic
			18/31, Trajanic or Hadrianic
28	B I 27D, occupation on floor		18, S.G., Flavian
29	A X 7, floor		18, 35, S.G., Flavian
			18/31, S.G., probably Flavian
	A X 3, occupation on 7		18/31 (two), 27, probably Hadrianic
			35, second cent.
			36, probably Antonine
30	A VII 11, occupation on floor		27, SILVAN[I], *c.* A.D. 130–50 (**S 125**)
			64(?), probably Hadrianic
31	B I 30H, make-up		37, S.G., *c.* A.D. 80–100
			18, S.G., Flavian
			37, probably Hadrianic/Antonine
			42, probably Trajanic or Hadrianic
			18/31, 27, probably Hadrianic
			33, mid-second cent.
			79, Antonine
31	B III 19, make up		18/31, S.G., *c.* A.D. 75–85
			36, S.G., Trajanic or Hadrianic
	B III 12, occupation on floor		18, S.G., Flavian
33	B I 30C, floor		37 (two), S.G., Flavian
			31, Lud.Tx., Antonine
	B I 28C		18 (two), S.G., Flavian
			33, S.G., Flavian/Trajanic
	B II 26F, secondary floor		27, S.G., Flavian
			42, second cent.
			Jar form with beaded rim, second cent.
36	B II 26D, floor		33, 36, second cent.
			37, S.G., *c.* A.D. 75–95
			27, Trajanic or Hadrianic
			36, probably Trajanic or Hadrianic

ROOM	LAYER	COINS	SAMIAN (all Central Gaulish except as stated)
38	B IV 9G, floor		37, probably Hadrianic (**D 132**)
39	B IV 9F, floor		37, Trajanic 37, *c.* A.D. 130–50 27, Trajanic/Hadrianic Curle 15, probably Hadrianic 18/31, Trajanic or Hadrianic
40	B IV 9D, floor	Greek imperial: ? Hadrian	31, probably Antonine Curle 11, Hadrianic
	B IV 7, occupation on floor		37, Trajanic 37, style of Sissus II, *c.* A.D. 135–65 (**D 106**) 37, Antonine (**D 107**) 33, probably Antonine 27, Trajanic or Hadrianic
42	B II 26B, floor		37, style of Igocatus, *c.* A.D. 100–20 18, S.G., Flavian 27 (two), one Trajanic, one Hadrianic 18/31, probably Hadrianic 31, Hadrianic or Antonine
	B II 17, occupation on 26B		18, S.G., Neronian 37, *c.* A.D. 130–50 Curle 15, Hadrianic/Antonine 31, 33, 38, Antonine
	B IV 9B, floor		37, *c.* A.D. 130–50 18/31R, Hadrianic 27, Hadrianic/Antonine
43	B II 27E, make-up		37 (three including **D 108**), 18, 35, S.G., Flavian 27, probably Hadrianic 18/31, Hadrianic/Antonine 33, Trajanic/Hadrianic 33 (two), Antonine (**S 118**) 37, probably style of Albucius, Antonine 37, late Montans ware (= II C Room 39, **D 91**)
	B IV 9J, floor		29, S.G., Claudian 37, *c.* A.D. 130–60 (**D 94**) Curle 11, S.G., Flavian 27, Trajanic

ROOM	LAYER	COINS	SAMIAN (all Central Gaulish except as stated)
	B V 26, make-up		37 (two), Hadrianic/Antonine (**D 110, D 111**)
			31 (several), 33, Hadrianic/Antonine
			27, 33, Trajanic
			29, 15/17, S.G., Flavian
	B V 25A, make-up		35/36, Trajanic or Hadrianic
	B V 23A, make-up		31, early Antonine
			80, DVPPIVSF (**S 115**), early Antonine
	B V 32, occupation on floor		33, Trajanic
			31, Hadrianic/Antonine
Interspace NW. of 43	B V 23, occupation on gravel		27, Hadrianic
			27, 31 (two), Hadrianic/Antonine
			33 (two), 79, Antonine
44	B XI 17, make-up below 16		37, style of Acaunissa, *c.* A.D. 125–45 (**D 92**)
	B XI 16, chalk floor		33, Hadrianic/Antonine
50	B XIV 14, floor		37, *c.* A.D. 110–30: part of same vessel in burnt debris above (B XIV 9A)
Yard SW. of 51	B VI 5, gravel floor		31, Antonine
53	B VIII 6, occupation on floor		33, Hadrianic/Antonine
54	B IX 5, occupation on floor	Vespasian, As, *RIC* 500	
55	B XV 11, occupation on floor		18/31R, IAXXVXI[(**S 126**), *c.* A.D. 150–80
			31 (two), 38 (rim trimmed off), Antonine
			33, Trajanic
	B XV 11A (same)		33, MA·SV·ETI (**S 119**), Antonine
	B XV 4 (same)		27, Trajanic
			33, probably Trajanic
			74, variant, black-glazed (**D 112**, pl. LI)
Wall 55/56	B VI 11, clay of standing wall		36, probably Antonine

B. Destruction levels of Antonine fire

ROOM	LAYER	COINS	SAMIAN (all Central Gaulish except as stated)
1	V XXXIV 6 T X 5		33 (two), Antonine 31, Antonine 37, Hadrianic or Antonine (**D 113**)
2	V XXXII 7		Jar ('cut glass'), Antonine 37, *c*. A.D. 110–40 (**D 114**) 33, pre-Antonine
2a	V XXXIII 4		33, Antonine
3a	Z II 5		18/31, S.G., CREƧTI retro. (**S 138**), Flavian 18, S.G., Flavian
	Z II 6		Curle 11, probably Hadrianic
Wall-trench 3a/5	Z II 7		31 (two), Antonine 33, probably Antonine

4	T III 11		30, style of Cinnamus, *c*. A.D. 150–
			    80 (**D 115**)
			37, style of Docilis, *c*. A.D. 130–55
			    (**D 116**)
			37, Hadrianic
			37 (two), style of Cinnamus, *c*. A.D.
			    150–80
			44 (two), one stamped CΛV•PIRI•ΛM
			    (**S 132**), Antonine
			31R, 38, Antonine
			27 (two), one S.G., Flavian, one
			    Trajanic/Hadrianic
			33, Trajanic/Hadrianic
			33 (about four), one stamped
			    TRICIVS F (**S 148**), Antonine
			33, BVTVRO✹ (**S 131**), Antonine
			18/31 (two), Hadrianic

Wall-trench 1/4	T III 12		37, style of Secundus, *c*. A.D. 150–80
			    (**D 117**)
			33, 44, Antonine
			27 (two), one Trajanic/Hadrianic,
			    one Hadrianic

ROOM	LAYER	COINS	SAMIAN (all Central Gaulish except as stated)
7	T VI 9	Antoninus Pius (A.D. 139) Faustina II (A.D. 145/146)	29, 18R, S.G., Flavian 27, 33, probably Hadrianic 31, Antonine 37, Trajanic 27 (two), S.G., Flavian 18/31, Trajanic or Hadrianic 35, second cent.
Wall-trench 7/25a	T II 11		37, S.G., c. A.D. 85–105 37, c. A.D. 160–80 27 (two), Hadrianic/Antonine 18/31, Trajanic or Hadrianic
Wall-trench 10/25a	T XXI 7		Ritt. 8, S.G., pre-Flavian 31, Antonine
Wall-trench 5/11	Z III 4		33, probably Trajanic
8	Z I 2		29, S.G., Flavian 30, 37, Trajanic 32, Curle 23, 33, 36, Antonine 35, probably Antonine Curle 11, 18, S.G., Flavian
	T XXII 2		31, Antonine 29 (burnt), S.G., c. A.D. 70–85
Wall-trench 8/10	T XXII 5		33, Hadrianic/Antonine
10	T XX 2		29, S.G., pre-Flavian 30, S.G., c. A.D. 70–85 18, S.G., Flavian 31 (two), ? Stanfield 32, Antonine 36, probably Antonine 33, second cent.
Wall-trench: NW. wall of 10	T XX 10 T XXI 8		18, S.G., Flavian 18/31, Trajanic/Hadrianic 37, probably Antonine
Wall-trench 13/14	A XI 9B A XI 4A	Domitian, denarius, RIC 144	18, S.G., Flavian

ROOM	LAYER	COINS	SAMIAN (all Central Gaulish except as stated)
14	A XI 4		27, pre-Antonine
	A XII 3		18, S.G., Flavian
			31R, 33, Antonine
15	A IV 11		31R, M͡ARC[ELLINI] (**S 143**), Antonine
			27, Hadrianic
			31, Antonine
	A IV 6A, collapsed clay wall		31 (two), heavily burnt, Antonine
	A V 4		Inkwell, probably Antonine
			Jar with 'cut-glass' facets, Antonine
	A V 6		33, mid-second cent.
	A V 12		Curle 21(?), Antonine
			27, pre-Antonine
	A V 13		31, 33, Antonine
17	A IV 8		18, probably Flavian
			37, probably by Bassus, c. A.D. 125–45 (**D 100**)
18	A IV 2		37, Antonine
			27 (two), one first cent., S.G., one probably Antonine
			31Sa (three), 33 (two), 36 (two), Antonine
			18/31, Hadrianic/Antonine
			31Sb, Antonine
	A VI 2		31, 33, Antonine
	A VI 1, burnt daub, *disturbed*		18/31, Hadrianic/Antonine
			27, 33 (two), Antonine
20	A II 7		33, [BVTT]VRRI (**S 129**), Antonine
			33 (two), Antonine
			31 (two), Lud. Tg, Antonine
	A II 6, collapsed wall		31, 33 (burnt), Antonine
23	A I 2		37 (burnt), Cerialis–Cinnamus, etc. c. A.D. 145–70 (**D 118**)
			37, c. A.D. 145–70 (**D 119**)
			37, style of Attianus, c. A.D. 130–50 (**D 120**)
			31, Antonine
			33 (burnt), PATRICIVS F (**S 147**), Antonine

ROOM	LAYER	COINS	SAMIAN (all Central Gaulish except as stated)
			33 (burnt), HABILIS F (**S 139**), Antonine
			33 (burnt), Hadrianic/Antonine
			33, 31 (several) (burnt), Antonine
			18/31, Hadrianic
			18/31 (three), 27, 33, Hadrianic/ Antonine
			27, 46 (burnt), Hadrianic/Antonine
			18 or 18/31, ? Flavian
			27, S.G., ALBVSF[E] (**S 127**), Neronian

Trench of
   25a front
   wall
	T I 4		37, S.G., Flavian
			31, Antonine
			33, REGINI·M͡A (**S 154**), Antonine

	T XXIII 3		33, Antonine Footring, Antonine
25a	T II 8		29, S.G., c. A.D. 50–70 37, S.G., c. A.D. 75–95 37, style of Sacer or Attianus, c. A.D. 125–50 (**D 121**) 33, Antonine 35, probably Antonine
25b	T XXI 5		18, S.G., Flavian 37, Hadrianic 33, probably Antonine 18/31, Trajanic/Hadrianic
25	A VII 3		37, S.G., Flavian 27 (three), one Trajanic, two Hadrianic/Antonine 31(Sa), Antonine 46, probably Hadrianic
	B XIV 6		33, S.G., Flavian/Trajanic 31, Antonine
	B XIV 5, burnt daub, *disturbed*		27, S.G., Flavian/Trajanic

25 and 35	B I 18		37, style of Sacer, c. A.D. 140–70
			37, style of Acaunissa (**D 92**), c. A.D.
			   125–45
			Curle 15 and Curle 15 with strap-
			   handle, Antonine

ROOM	LAYER	COINS	SAMIAN (all Central Gaulish except as stated)
			27, Flavian
			35/36 (two), probably Antonine
			18, OF COELI (S 137), Flavian
			31R (three)
			18/31R, MARCE·LLI·M (S 144), Antonine
			31 (seven), Antonine
			18/31, probably Hadrianic
			33 (five), stamps COCVRO·F (S 136), [PE]CVL////RI·SF (S 150), one probably Hadrianic, four Antonine
	B I 15, burnt daub, *disturbed*		37, rim-stamp [CINTVS]MVSF (S 135), c. A.D. 150–80 (D 122)
			33, Hadrianic/Antonine
28	B I 21, burnt daub, *disturbed*		27, S.G., Flavian
			37, c. A.D. 115–35 (D 123)
			37, Antonine (D 124)
			33, Hadrianic/Antonine
			31, Antonine
29	A X 2		37, c. A.D. 130–50 (D 125)
			31R, 31 (two), Antonine
			18/31 or 31, Hadrianic or Antonine
			33, 35/36, probably Hadrianic
			38(?), Antonine
31	B III 11		33 (three), Hadrianic/Antonine
			37, Blickweiler ware (D 126)
33	B II 14A		31, MALLEDV (S 141), Antonine
			42, MARC·IILLIN (S 142), Hadrianic
32–42	B II 14, general burnt deposit		33 (two), Antonine
			36, probably Antonine
			18/31 and 31 (three), Hadrianic/ Antonine
			33, stamped REBVRRIⲰOF (S 151)
	B II 13, as 14, (*disturbed*)		37, S.G., Flavian
			37, Hadrianic/Antonine (D 127)
			33 (two), one probably Hadrianic, one Antonine
			27, Curle 15, Trajanic or Hadrianic

ROOM	LAYER	COINS	SAMIAN (all Central Gaulish except as stated)
			38, Antonine
			18/31 and 31 (several), Hadrianic and Antonine
	B II 2, as 13		18/31, Hadrianic/Antonine
			31R, Antonine
Wall-trench 36/37	B IV 10	Hadrian, As, *RIC* 669	27, S.G., Flavian
38–42	B IV 3, general burnt deposit	Trajan, sestertius, *RIC* 663	37, S.G., Flavian ~~XIV...~~
			~~37 (two), *c.* A.D. 130–50 (**D 128**)~~
		Barbarous radiate (? stray from 3A)	~~37, *c.* A.D. 150–80~~
			37, Antonine (**D 129**)
			37, rim stamp CINT[VSMVSF] (**S 135**), Antonine (**D 122**)
			36, probably Antonine
			27, Hadrianic/Antonine
			27, PAVLI (**S 149**), Hadrianic/ Antonine
			Curle 11, S.G., Flavian
			Curle 11 (two), Trajanic/Hadrianic
			38 (two), Curle 15, 33 (four), Antonine
			46 (with barbotine leaves), Hadrianic
			37 (two), Hadrianic/Antonine (**D 130, D 131**)
	B IV 3A, burnt daub, *disturbed*	Gallienus, *RIC* 164	37, *c.* A.D. 130–50 (**D 128**)
		Tetricus I, *RIC* 90	37 (two), Hadrianic/Antonine (**D 132, D 133**)
			37 (two), Antonine (**D 122**)
		Tetricus II, barbarous	37, S.G., Flavian
			33 (about four), one Trajanic/ Hadrianic, three Antonine
		Victorinus, *RIC* 118	18 (two), S.G., Flavian
		Claudius II, *RIC* 168	18/31 (three), Trajanic or Hadrianic
		Constans Aug.	18/31 and 31, Antonine
			18/31R, REBV[RRIωOF] (**S 152**), Antonine
			15/31, Antonine
			37, style of Cinnamus, *c.* A.D. 150–80
	B IV 2, burnt daub, *disturbed*		33, BVTTVRRI (**S 130**), Antonine
			31 (three), 31R, Antonine
			46, Hadrianic/Antonine

Latin fortificationum ex cuius [handwritten marginal note]

ROOM	LAYER	COINS	SAMIAN (all Central Gaulish except as stated)
43	B IV 3C		30, probably Trajanic Curle 15, Hadrianic or Antonine
	B IV 3B, burnt daub, *disturbed*		42, probably Hadrianic/Antonine
	B V 21		18/31, Hadrianic 37, *c*. A.D. 130–50 (**D 128**)
Interspace NW. of 43	B V 22 B XI 11		31, Antonine 33, MAXIMI (**S 145**)
Wall-trench 44/45	B V 30		Curle 11, Trajanic or Hadrianic
45	B V 7a		31R, Antonine
45 trench of SE. Wall	B V 9		37, Antonine 37 (burnt), Hadrianic (**D 134**) 31 (three), 33, Antonine
41–8	B V 7	Trajan, dupondius	37, Cinnamus style (**D 136**), *c*. A.D. 150–75 37, *c*. A.D. 140–70 (**D 135**) 31, 33, 38, Antonine 18/31(?R), Hadrianic/Antonine
	B V 5, burnt daub, *disturbed*	Constans Aug.	37, S.G., *c*. A.D. 80–100 Curle 11, S.G., Flavian 31R, Antonine
46	B XI 7A B XI 14A B XI 15		33, Antonine 37, S.G., probably Vespasianic 33, second cent.
48, SE. wall-trench	B XIII 9		18, S.G., Flavian 31, Antonine
	B XIII 12		27, S.G., Flavian 31 (two), Hadrianic/Antonine 31, Antonine
49	B XIII 7		37, 18, S.G., Flavian 36, second cent. 31, probably Antonine
	B XIII 4, burnt daub, *disturbed*		Ritt. 8, S.G., pre-Flavian 46 or Curle 15, Hadrianic 31, 31R, 18/31, 33, 79/80, Antonine 'Cut-glass' jar, Hadrianic/Antonine

ROOM	LAYER	COINS	SAMIAN (all Central Gaulish except as stated)
50	B XIV 9 (*disturbed*)		27, OF·PATRI (**S 146**), S.G., Flavian/Trajanic
	B XIV 9A (*disturbed*)		18/31R, Hadrianic
			37, *c.* A.D. 110–30
	B XIV 15 (*disturbed*)		31, 33, Antonine
	B XIV 16 (*disturbed*)		15/17, S.G., pre-Flavian
			37, style of Igocatus (**D 138**), *c.* A.D. 100–20
50, NW. wall-trench	B XIV 13		37, 27, S.G., *c.* A.D. 85–105
Wall-trench 50/25	B XIV 10		46, Hadrianic
	B XIV 7		18/31, Hadrianic
			46, Trajanic or Hadrianic
51	B VI 8, wall-trenches		31, 38, Antonine
52	B VII 4	Nerva, sestertius, *RIC* 93 or 104	18, S.G., Flavian
			33, REBVRRIꙍ OF (**S 153**), early Antonine
			33 (several), Antonine
			31, 31R, Antonine
		Barbarous copy of Constantinian Æ	33, Trajanic
53	B VIII 8, wall-trenches		18, S.G., Flavian
			31, Antonine
54	B IX 4	M. Antony, legionary denarius	33, Antonine
			18/31, Hadrianic/Antonine
			Curle 11, Hadrianic
55	B XV 3		18, S.G., Flavian
			31R, Antonine
	B XV 10		27 S.G., probably Claudian
Drain outside 55	B VI 10		37, *c.* A.D. 130–50 (**D 137**)
			Curle 11, Hadrianic/Antonine
			18/31, 27, Hadrianic
			31, Antonine
	B XV 12		27, S.G., pre-Flavian
			37, probably Hadrianic
56	B VI 4		30, S.G., Flavian
			18/31R, early Antonine

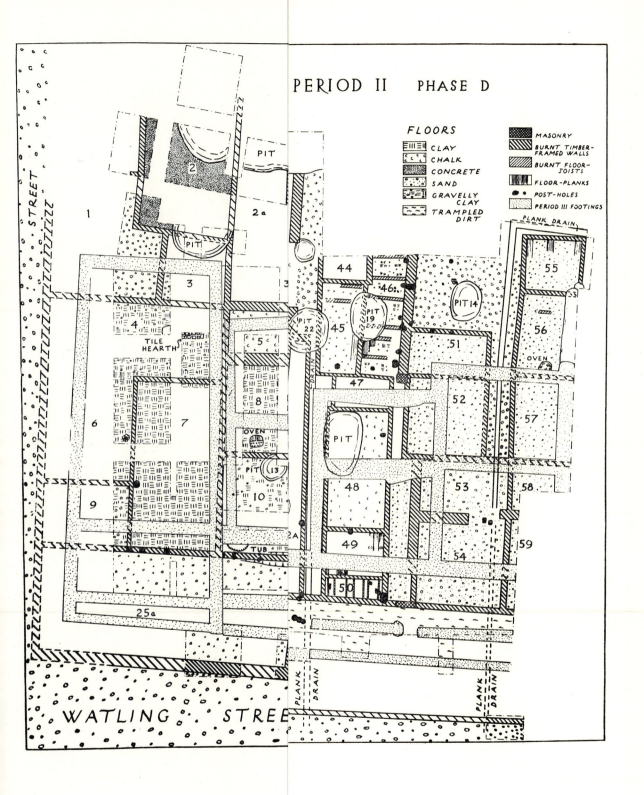

PERIOD II   PHASE D

FLOORS

≡≣≣ CLAY
⊂⊂⊂ CHALK
CONCRETE
SAND
GRAVELLY CLAY
TRAMPLED DIRT

MASONRY
BURNT TIMBER-FRAMED WALLS
BURNT FLOOR-JOISTS
FLOOR-PLANKS
POST-HOLES
PERIOD III FOOTINGS

Fig. 19. Plan of the Period II D building

ROOM	LAYER	COINS	SAMIAN
			(all Central Gaulish except as stated)
	B XV 5	Faustina II, As	
	B XV 7		38, Antonine
	B XV 3A (*disturbed*)		27, S.G., pre-Flavian
			33, 38, Antonine
57	B XVI 3		33, Trajanic or Hadrianic
	B XVI 4 (*disturbed*)		37, 33, Trajanic
			27, Hadrianic/Antonine
	B XVI 6		33, Hadrianic/Antonine

Summary of dating evidence, Period II D

In these tables the contents of some secondary deposits of burnt daub from the fire have been included. These layers, indicated as *disturbed* in the lists, were apparently churned up during subsequent building operations in Period III; some of them have produced third- and fourth-century coins as listed, but the samian appears to belong to the Antonine fire, and therefore to be worth including: none of it can be dated later than that from the fire deposits, and some of it is burnt.

The coins listed from these deposits should be neglected in the present context. Of firmly stratified coins it is noticeable that the numbers have greatly decreased: this is partly a sign of the times and partly due to the short life of the buildings. The latest coin in any floor of Period II D is one of Hadrian, but there are two of Faustina II in the destruction deposit.

For the beginning of the period, therefore, we have to depend upon the samian in or under the floors. In levels interpreted as make-up levels below the floors there are three vessels of f. 37 dated *c.* 125–50, 125–45 and 130–50; a f. 33 dated *c.* 130–60 and another dated mid-second century; together with a f. 80 stamped by Duppius and dated as early Antonine. In addition a f. 33 stamped by Mossius and dated *c.* A.D. 155–75 came from a make-up layer in Room 2A; but since this layer was partly exposed at the base of a shallow pit of later date, no great reliance should be placed on its evidence, for the sherd cannot be regarded as properly sealed. From the floors themselves came a f. 31 and two vessels of f. 37 dated *c.* 130–50; a f. 37 dated *c.* 130–60; another dated *c.* 135–75 and a third of *c.* 140–70. In the occupation levels on the floors were found one f. 37 dated *c.* A.D. 135–65 and another dated *c.* A.D. 145–70, together with an 18/31R stamped IAXXVXI, dated *c.* 150–80. On this evidence, and taking into account the dating of the preceding Period II C, it is suggested that Period II D began *c.* A.D. 150.

The dating of its termination depends upon an estimate of the date of the fire. As mentioned above, two coins of Faustina II were found in the burnt deposits. These are generally thought to have been minted *c.* A.D. 145–6 after her marriage with Marcus Aurelius. One was lost in very good condition; the other was too much damaged by fire and corrosion for its condition to be clear. As an indication of the brevity of the period it must be mentioned that out of a total of fifty-nine rooms examined, only two produced evidence of renewed (or secondary) flooring. One was the portico at 25b in front of Room 14 where a foot of flints had been placed as make-up for a gravel surface, and this surface had subsequently been covered by 8–9 in. of greenish, gritty, sandy material. However, the section suggested that the original flint make-up had been placed in a shallow excavation in the Period II C levels, and the gritty material may possibly represent a fairly rapid accumulation on the original gravel surface. The other was Room 33, where the original chalk floor was covered with thick ash from the hearth, and this was patchily sealed by a thin layer of brick-earth, which in turn soon accumulated a thick covering of ash (fig. 28, section K–K¹). It is true that other rooms in this period had timber floors, but by no means all. It does not appear that more than 5–10 years are likely to have passed, to judge by the frequency of re-flooring in the twenty years of Period II C.

The final analysis, however, depends upon a study of the evidence provided by the large group of samian in the burnt deposits, and this is undertaken in detail below by Mr. B. R. Hartley. His conclusion is that the fire which terminated Period II D and destroyed much else in Verulamium can be dated c. A.D. 155–60 (see pp. 256, 262).

PERIOD III

For over a century after the fire this area of Insula XIV lay empty. It will be shown in Volume II that as part of the reconstruction of the town after the disaster a new street was made to run obliquely from the Forum to the new theatre; this bisected Insula XIV, and the detached south-west portion is numbered as Insula XXVIII. It may be that the reduced area of Insula XIV was at first reserved for some public building in the new plans: at this date it seems improbable that rebuilding was inhibited by purely economic difficulties.

The question arises whether this open space was not meanwhile utilized, for instance for market stalls of a temporary nature, from time to time. Certain signs of activity were indeed noted, such as the digging of pits (p. 101); but the absence of coin-finds, and of trampled layers of dirt, seems to preclude much pedestrian traffic. What intermediate layers there were intervening between Periods II and III are best taken as the lowest levels of make-up preparatory to Period III construction: on some of these there had been traffic sufficient to compact the surface, but little if any accumulation of occupation. On the whole it seems likely that the whole area was enclosed by hoardings and kept empty for a century after the fire.

At the end of the third quarter of the third century the Watling Street frontage was rebuilt as a row of shops, this time of masonry construction (fig. 25, p. 110). The nature of their foundations has already been described (p. 6). Only Building XIV, 1 was, comparatively speaking, unrobbed, but even here the walls stood only some 6 in. above floor level. Their surviving surface (pl. IVa; XXXIIa) was flat and level, due to the removal of a tile-course. They were 1 ft. 10 in. to 2 ft. 2 in. wide, except that adjoining Watling Street, which was 1 ft. 5 in. (fig. 27, section B–B¹). The building was not rectangular, the back wall measuring 24 ft. 10 in. and the front 28 ft. 10 in. over all. The resulting trapezoid plan had the effect of throwing out of alignment the façade of XIV, 2 which abutted it. Both buildings were faced with narrow porches or colonnades; the interval between the walls of XIV, 1 at the south-east end was c. 2 ft.; at the north-west end of XIV, 2 it had increased to 4 ft. 3 in.

A porch only 2 ft. wide might be thought so narrow as to be useless; but if the front wall of XIV, 1 carried an open colonnade, the actual area covered by roof would have been 4 ft. 6 in. at its narrowest, sufficient perhaps to shelter customers inspecting merchandise displayed in Room 2. The larger part of the building comprised Room 1 (41 ft. 9 in. by *c.* 22 ft.), which, like Room 2, was floored with pebbles set in brick-earth. The floors in both rooms lay on thick levels of make-up; that in Room 1 was 1 ft.–1 ft. 10 in. above the Antonine fire-debris (fig. 27, section B–B[1]). It is probable that the reason for this was that in the interval the metalling of Watling Street had risen correspondingly, making a new internal level necessary. The upper levels of the street-metalling had been removed here, so that proof was lacking, but a parallel phenomenon can be demonstrated[1] in Buildings XXVII, 2 and XXVIII, 1. The lower layers of make-up had a flat trodden surface; but that it was not an early floor is shown by the absence of a door through wall 1/2 at this level. At a secondary period the south corner of the building had been partitioned off in timber to enclose two small rooms floored in *opus signinum*, in which were set some large flat tiles. The surface was too broken to show whether tiles had originally covered the whole expanse of the concrete: the surviving tiles appeared only around the borders (pl. XXXII*a*). The central slot, 15 in. wide and 6 in. deep, was certainly not a drain (fig. 24, section A–A[1], p. 109).

The debris over the floor in Room 1 produced pieces of painted wall-plaster in green, yellow, red, and blue, and one larger piece had areas of purple and red separated by a narrow white band. Similar plaster fragments were found in the make-up levels below the floor: this latter material was presumably introduced from elsewhere.

Building XIV, 2 had a frontage of almost 45 ft., and chalk foundations unlike the concrete footings of XIV, 1. These, however, went right down to natural soil and imply stout walls (fig. 9, section Y–Z (p. 27)). At the back there was a narrow gap, *c.* 8 in. wide, between the two buildings to take the eaves-drips, but the walls of Rooms 3 and 4 abutted on to those of XIV, 1 and were formally later. The arrangement implies that the rear roofs had parallel ridges at right angles to the street and that those in front were different. There are two possible restorations. If the front of both buildings shared a common ridge parallel with the street its position must lie on the centre line of Room 2 in Building XIV, 1. In Building 2 this could imply a front range of two storeys in Room 3 to allow height for a gently sloping roof over the north-west half of Room 2; its south-east portion would lie below a ridge along the centre line of Room 1 and extending north-east to abut the eaves of Room 3 (see fig. 20).

Alternatively Building 1 had a gable end on the street and Building 2 had a ridge covering Rooms 2 and 3 which either abutted the outside wall of Building 1 at eaves level or else ran over to join its ridge at full height. The second alternative is the more likely since the greater height would probably be required for proper slopes on the rearward roofs. The ridge must have been over wall 2/3 and in either event the south-east end of this wall must have risen above the rear slopes of the roof to carry the front slope at the point of junction with XIV, 1: this may be thought an awkward arrangement. Room 1 of Building 2 is just over 14 ft. wide; its strong foundations do not suggest that it carried a low-level lean-to roof as if it were a mere shed attached to Room 2. If its north-west wall were carried higher to support a simple roof sloping down to the south-east an unnecessary amount of rain-water would fall into the narrow interspace; it can therefore be suggested that its roof was ridged at the same

---

[1] *Antiq. Journ.* xl (1960), 19 for XXVII, 2; ibid. xxxix (1959), 11 for XXVIII, 1.

height as that of Room 2 (see fig. 20). Almost all masonry had been robbed from the footings of XIV, 2, and the floors, deprived of their protection, had disappeared. Above the
debris of the Antonine fire only disturbed layers of dark soil remained.

Between XIV, 2 and XIV, 4 was a space or entry *c*. 14 ft. wide; two bases made of large
flints probably supported a gate. In front of this a gap in the footings, 4 ft. 9 in. wide,
suggested a goods entry into the shop.

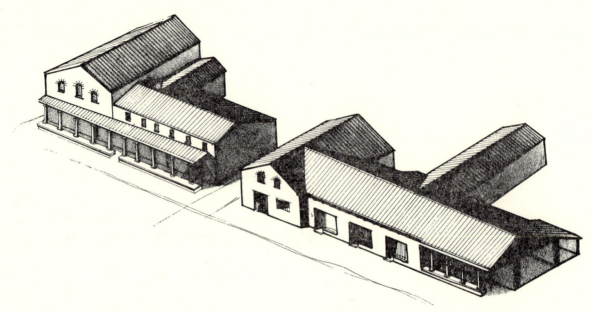

Fig. 20. Reconstruction of the Period III buildings (*drawn by J. C. Randall*).

Building XIV, 4, whose concrete footings resembling those of XIV, 1 had been entirely
robbed away, was of trapezoid shape. Room 2, measuring 26 ft. 3 in. by *c*. 4 ft. 6 in., is best
explained as for a staircase leading to an upper floor. The shop itself, Room 3, measuring
c. 13 ft. by 23 ft., occupied the whole frontage. Little remained inside. Part of a rubble floor
or make-up survived in Room 3, and in Room 1 patches of chalk and rubble may also
represent make-up. No floor surface was to be seen.

Building XIV, 5 had a frontage of *c*. 48 ft. It is described below (p. 102).

Buildings XIV, 6 and XIV, 7 had internal widths of 19 and 20 ft. respectively. Almost all
the walls had been robbed from the chalk footings; a surviving fragment of the rear wall of
XIV, 6 was 1 ft. 9 in. wide. The front walls continued the alignment of those of XIV, 5,
Room 5, but the most northerly wall was reduced in width from 2 ft. to 1 ft. 6 in., presumably
because of the extra wall now introduced immediately behind it. This had the effect of
reproducing the shallow porch in front of Buildings XIV, 1 and 2. Building XIV, 6 had a
series of three pillar-bases measuring 1 ft. 9 in. by 2 ft. 6 in. or 3 ft. on separate chalk footings
(pl. XXXII*b*), whereas in XIV, 7 there was a continuous foundation, the portico being
c. 5 ft. wide.

The front room of XIV, 6 and the back room of XIV, 7 each contained a straight length of independent foundation consisting of trenches 6 ft. 6 in. by 1 ft. 10 in. and 7 ft. by 2 ft. respectively and at least 3 ft. deep, which were filled with layers of flints, chalk, and burnt daub. These might have carried domestic shrines like these already described in the timber-framed buildings of the previous periods (p. 57), but they are somewhat long and narrow for this purpose (the *aediculae* of Period II C were 3 ft. wide); they more probably represent supports for stairs. Room 1 of XIV, 7 also contained a chalk footing parallel to its south-east wall and *c.* 3 ft. 6 in. from it, which appeared never to have been built on; it was covered with a layer of disturbed burnt daub comparable to others in the make-up levels, and was perhaps abandoned as an error in layout, or because of a change of plan. A room like 2 in XIV, 4 would have resulted.

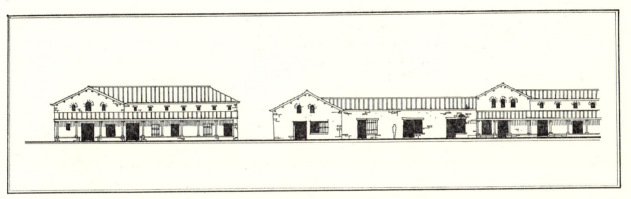

Fig. 21. Elevation of the Period III buildings along Watling Street (*drawn by J. C. Randall*).

Room 3 (XIV, 6) retained traces of a gravel and chalk floor which extended between the pillar bases. In it were two postholes 1 ft. deep and a third, 1 ft. 6 in. deep, up against the wall of Room 2. The latter had cut into the edge of the chalk footings; it had a light-brown filling different from the loose dark soil in the other two which had a packing of tiles and stones round their tops. The purpose of these is obscure, but the single one may have been for scaffolding. Behind both buildings was a gravelled yard in which were some subsidences, filled with black soil, over earlier pits.

Pit 19 was excavated. It was a cylindrical shaft 5 ft. in diameter with a clay lining 1–2 in. thick, dug to a depth of *c.* 14 ft. from the contemporary surface, and was probably intended as a well (fig. 24, section O–O[1]). The top 2 ft. of the side had collapsed, causing a splay into which earlier levels dipped. The filling contained a number of different deposits of varying dates, the reason being that the fillings gradually subsided and had had to be topped up; the black fill at the mouth of this and other pits was seen to be due to late accumulation in the hollow thus caused. The pit must have been dug at a date later than the Antonine fire, since it interrupts the plan of the burnt building, but it seems to have been filled in again before current pottery types had significantly changed. A date of *c.* 160–75 is accordingly assigned to the group from the earliest filling (layer 30 downwards), which included the following samian:

> 30, stamped CIN[NAMI], *c.* A.D. 150–80 (**S 156**)
> 31R, stamped RITOG[ENIM], *c.* A.D. 155–80 (**S 157**)
> 31 (several), 33, and 'cut-glass' jar, Antonine

Layer 29, above this, contained a significant quantity of types not yet in circulation at the time of the fire, including a samian form 79 stamped LVPINI[and moulded-rim dishes such as 1082 and 1086, a late type of poppy-head beaker (undecorated) 1073, and a fragment of indented colour-coated beaker. This is clearly a third-century filling. Layer 28, a plug of gravel with level surface, is therefore recognizable as part of the courtyard floor of Period III, for which layer 29 had been thrown in to make up the level. The gravel produced a fragment of a barbarous radiate coin. Subsidence, however, continued, for covering layer 26 was a floor of flat tiles, clearly sealing a later levelling-up. Layer 26 produced a piece of flanged bowl (cf. 1110) as well as a moulded-rim dish similar to those in layer 29. Sinkage continued and the upper layers are of the late fourth century or later; layer 20 produced a coin of Valentinian I.

Pit 14 was apparently similar, although it was not emptied for more than 3 ft. It was clay-lined and the filling had subsided. It too was probably sealed originally by the floor of the Period III gravel yard. A third pit inside Building XIV, 6 cut through the chalk footings of wall 1/2. It is probably post-Roman and yielded a coin of Helena.

Building XIV, 5

This building, unlike all the others of this period, was partly of masonry, partly of timber; but later subsidence and disturbance prevented recovery of some of the timber walls. The front room, 48 by 13 ft., was bounded by flint-and-mortar walls *c.* 2 ft. wide on chalk footings; the masonry survived only here and there. This front room was divided by the foundation trench for a timber-framed wall which extended south-west as far as Room 3; it was probably a secondary feature contemporary with the cellar, for it ran at a slight angle to the masonry walls and probably superseded a similar wall marked by a line of smaller double postholes close beside it. This earlier line does not cross the front room and is at right angles to its wall. It may be noted that this earlier line, if projected, would form a suitable south-east wall for the tessellation round the mosaic panel at the rear of the site, whereas the oblique wall does not. No wall-trench or postholes, however, were found in this position owing to disturbance.

Both this series of uprights and the larger ones accompanying the oblique trench were driven very deeply by hammering into the underlying deposits, as is vividly illustrated on pl. XXVIIIc, where they can be seen piercing and distorting the *opus signinum* floor of Period II B, Room 30. It seems likely that pile-driving equipment would be required to sink timbers of this size so deeply and with such force. Some posts were over 1 ft. square.

The area marked as Room 3 on the plan (fig. 25) was covered with very ruined patches of tessellation in which were two mosaic panels. It was not possible to tell whether two rooms were involved, and if so whether the lion mosaic in the front room was later than the other and contemporary with the oblique trench. The lion mosaic itself was a small panel *c.* 6 ft. or 6 ft. 6 in. by *c.* 4 ft. 6 in. (pl. XXXIV). It had been much discoloured by fire and distorted by sinkage into a subsidence below. This made its recovery extremely difficult since the edge was standing almost vertical and very loose. The figure of a lion can be seen springing right at a fleeing deer. The motif is extremely rare in Roman Britain; the nearest parallel is also at Verulamium, in the second-century mosaic[1] in Insula XXI Building 2, Room 4. The present panel must date at the earliest from *c.* 275, but more probably belongs to the mid-fourth century, like its neighbour.

Further south-west lay a larger panel forming a rectangle *c.* 5 ft. 6 in. by 6 ft. (pl. XXXIII). Wear and sweeping in Roman times had removed practically the entire pattern save for fragments near the angles and edges, leaving elsewhere a bare expanse of *opus signinum* basis. Such a fate was inclined to overtake fourth-century mosaics at Verulamium, for it can be paralleled in Buildings XIV, 3 and XXVII, 2; it was caused by the thinness of the tesserae used and the poor quality of the fixative.

What survives of the pattern is buds set in rectangular frames at diagonal corners with some perspective boxes adjacent, linked by a short length of guilloche along the side. The pattern is clearly that illustrated on the smaller mosaic in Wheeler, *Verulamium*, pl. XL and XLVI*a* within a wave-border not provided here. That pavement was attributable to the middle of the second century; the present example is just about two centuries later, for a coin of Constantine Caesar (330–5) was found in the make-up beneath it. The pattern is not sufficiently distinctive for us to recognize the 'signature' of a Verulamium school of mosaicists: though one may have existed in the second century,[2] there is at present a dearth of examples in the third century and continuity cannot therefore be proved. The difference in period is responsible for much less careful execution: the angle-bud does not stand diagonally to the panel but lies across the corner. A coin of Victorinus was found on its surface and a barbarous radiate in an interstice left by a missing tessera; these, however, have no evidential value since the mosaic is later than the coins and was completely unsealed: the coins, however, were no doubt circulating in the mid-fourth century. The black-filled hollow over the lion mosaic contained two coins of Constantine and one of Constans Augustus, in addition to five late third-century issues. North-west of Room 3 was a narrow area, 4 ft. wide, with a chalk floor, divided from the gravelled yard by two postholes, and bordered by a foundation trench at its south-west edge. All this area was very disturbed.

The cellar (figs. 22 and 28)

Robbing and disturbance have deprived us of much information concerning these late buildings. All the more important, therefore, is the information yielded by the cellar in XIV, 5. This was a timber-lined construction, in keeping with the character of the whole; but it was evidently an afterthought since the cavity was dug too late to make use of, or affect the construction of, the contiguous masonry walls; it was cut down beside their trench-built foundations and to a greater depth. The cellar, which measured 34 ft. by 14 ft. 3 in., was therefore lined with heavy timber uprights 8–12 in. square and 1½–2 ft. apart, and set in holes at least 1 ft. 6 in. deeper than the floor (pl. XXXV). These would have retained the plank lining of the cavity, no trace of which survived. There was also a boarded floor, resting on joists, the imprint of some of which survived. This, however, must have decayed, for it

---

[1] *Antiq. Journ.* xl (1960), pl. 1.   [2] *Arch. Journ.* cxxiii (1966), 42.

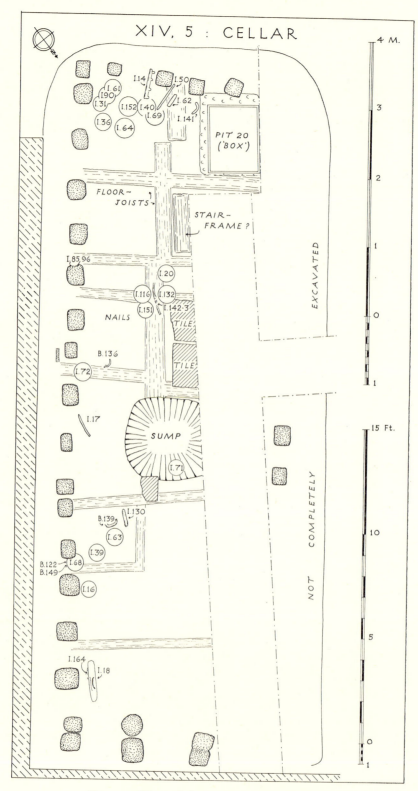

XIV, 5 : CELLAR

I.14
I.50
I.61
I.90
I.31
I.152 I.40
I.62
I.36
I.69
I.141
I.64

PIT 20
('BOX')

FLOOR-
JOISTS

STAIR-
FRAME ?

EXCAVATED

I.85,96

I.20

I.116 I.132
I.151 I.142-3

NAILS

TILE?

B.136
TILE?

I.72

I.17

SUMP

I.71

NOT COMPLETELY

I.130
B.139
I.63
I.39
B.122 I.68
B.149
I.16

I.164
I.18

4 M.

3

2

1

0

1

15 FT.

10

5

0

1

Fig. 22. Plan of the cellar of Period III.

was covered or replaced by an occupation-layer (fig. 28, section K–K¹, layer 55) up to 8 in. thick along the south side, though only *c.* 2 in. thick along the section-face. In the centre of the cellar was a subrectangular pit or sump about 4 ft. square and 2 ft. deep, which seems to have been cut after the wooden floor had been removed since it interrupts a joist-channel; on either side of it were some very large tiles 24–26 in. long and 3 in. thick which sealed two floor-joist channels. Thus it would appear that there were two distinct phases of occupation in the cellar, the first with a wooden floor (which may soon have rotted owing to the percolation of rain water through the packing behind the south-west wall, which seems to have been external): the second when this had been removed and a sump inserted. The sump was filled with layers of yellowish and greyish clay containing few objects: these, however, included the Rhenish motto-beakers fig. 133, 1121–3, the cut-glass beakers fig. 78, 50 and 53, and the disc-brooch fig. 31, 24. Layer 55, the occupation deposit of this secondary phase, contained a great quantity of iron and bronze objects scattered all over the floor (pl. XXXVII). Many of the bronze finds in particular were too decayed to undergo or survive laboratory treatment, and many more were unidentifiable scraps. On fig. 22 the position of those objects is shown which are illustrated in the reports on the bronze and iron finds (pp. 114 ff., 163 ff.). As well as a cut-glass beaker (fig. 78, 51) (one of five in the cellar as a whole), the Rhenish motto-beakers 1114 and 1116, and several other pottery vessels, the cellar contained a great variety of iron tools. These included agricultural implements (17, a bar share; 20, a spade-iron), parts of vehicles (31, a hub-lining; 36, a linch-pin; 39 a pole-tip), carpenter's tools (14, a plane; 16 a small wedge; 85 a joiner's dog), a hipposandal (30), a chopper (40), a plasterer's float (18), a sword (162), as well as a miscellaneous collection of hinges (61, 63–4) and locks (68–9, 71–2). These could hardly be the store or stock of any trader or craftsman except a blacksmith or metal-dealer. The bronze finds were also heterogeneous though in general more decayed and unrecognizable. They included a jug (139), a patera-handle (149), two other handles (122, 136) and also the lid-plate of a wooden box (152).

The cellar was entered by steps at the centre of its south-west side, where two substantial lining-posts had been placed a little forward of their row. The original arrangement was probably a free-standing wooden staircase supported by these posts and by a joist set $3\frac{1}{2}$ in. deep in the subsoil; but belonging to a later phase there were traces of wooden treads set in the partly collapsed packing of the original revetment. The steps had been burnt when the cellar was abandoned (fig. 28, section K–K¹).

Beneath the staircase was a rectangular pit sunk in the floor and lined with wood (Pit 20); the planks were *c.* $\frac{1}{2}$ in. thick, forming a container 3 ft. 4 in. by 2 ft. 6 in., and 3 ft. 3 in. deep below floor level. A chalk packing had been rammed in behind the wood to fill in the cavities. Traces of the planks remained on the floor of the container, and, in places, on the sides right up to the top (pl. XXXVI). Since it was obviously water-tight it might perhaps have been intended as a water-container. Yet a barrel might be thought more suitable for this purpose, and a strong-box is a more probable explanation, confirmed by the well-concealed position in the darkness under the stairs, flush with the floor. Among its contents were:

(*a*) *Glass*. Fig. 78, nos. 48, 49, a pair of cut-glass beakers.
(*b*) *Bronze*. Figs. 35 ff., no. 68, a scoop; 135, a dolphin handle; 140, a Silenus head; 142, a bull's head spout; 143, a jug; 153, a lid-plate; 155, the Verulamium Venus (pls. XLII–XLIVa).

(c) *Iron*. Figs. 63–72, no. 25, a hipposandal; 129, a binding strip; 145, a stand; 155, a bar with double hook; 158, a scraper.

(d) An unidentifiable radiate coin.

Though some of these objects were valuable, they were mixed with others which were not. Moreover, they were not heaped together on the floor of the box as might have been expected if they had been collected for scrap and stored there: they lay separately in different levels of the filling. This consisted of tips of grey sticky occupation earth and yellower cleaner brick-earth. Three whole tiles (1 ft. 4 in. by 11 in. by 1½ in.) lay near the bottom, and there were broken tile fragments higher up. It looks as if the container had been abandoned and filled up with rubbish from the cellar, and the goddess and the other bronzes were discarded and thrown in at the same time. This might perhaps suggest the results of Christian conversion on the owner, though this cannot be pressed: the owner was obviously a scrap merchant.

The secondary occupation, layer 55, which contained so many objects, was sealed by a 3–6-in. layer of debris (54) similar to the chalk and clay packing behind the walls; it may be that at this stage damp had led to a partial collapse of the sides. If so, they were restored, for the new level was covered with more occupation soil. This latest occupation level contained a number of tiles including box flue-tiles, and bones including a pile of beef ribs and the skulls of an ox and horse. There was also a small hoard of four third-century coins (Salonina, Victorinus, Tetricus I or Victorinus, and an unidentifiable *antoninianus*) contained in the remains of what seemed to be a small bronze-bound wooden box. Above this layer was the filling of the cellar after its abandonment, which consisted of uniform tips of rubbly dark earth (layer 9). The main timber uprights of the cellar walls were represented by cavities from about the level of the topmost occupation downwards: above this they had a brown-earth filling different from that of the cellar itself.

The dating evidence for the cellar deposits is as follows. The central sump contained an unidentifiable radiate, and a coin each of Tetricus I and Aurelian. Layer 55, the secondary occupation, produced thirty-six coins:

second-century (10)	Victorinus (3)
denarius of Severus Alexander (1)	the Tetrici (4)
Valerian II (1)	Probus (1)
Gallienus (4)	Carausius (1)
Salonina (1)	uncertain radiates (8)
Postumus (2)	

The latest datable issues are those of Probus (276–82) and Carausius (286–93).

The cellar filling above (layers B I 9 and B II 11) yielded 111 coins:

second-century (1)	the Tetrici (27)
Severus Alexander (1)	Claudius II (10)
Gallienus (9)	Quintillus (1)
Salonina (1)	uncertain radiates (7)
Postumus (3)	barbarous radiates (27)
Victorinus (10)	Carausius (13)
	Constans (341–46) (1)

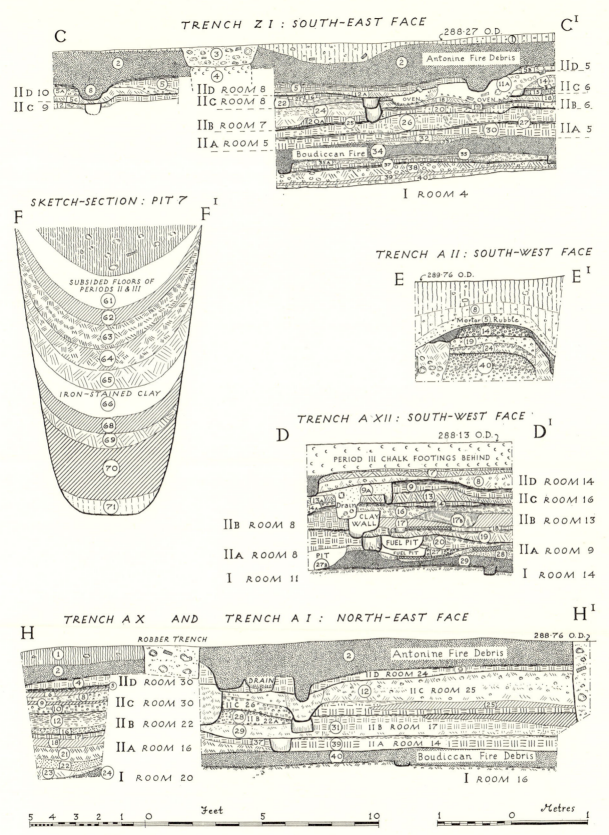

FIG. 23. Sections C–C^I, D–D^I, E–E^I, F–F^I, H–H^I. For positions see fig. 26 (p. 111).

and there was a coin of Gallienus (?) and a barbarous copy of Tetricus II in the burnt debris of the stairs.

It can be accepted as certain that the fourth-century coin, which is quite out of keeping in this assemblage, was introduced in some way from layer 8, a fourth-century levelling-up of the hollow caused by the compaction of the cellar-filling. This layer was very similar in composition and appearance to 9, consisting of earthy rubble; but its coin-list is very different.

Gallienus (2)	Constantius II Aug. (2) (1 barbarous)
Claudius II (1)	Constans or Constantius II (2)
the Tetrici (4)	Constans Aug. (2)
Carausius (6)	barbarous Fel. Temp. Reparatio (10)
Constantine I (4)	minimus (1)
Constantinopolis (1)	Valens (1)
small barbarous	Valentinian I (1)
Gloria Exercitus (1)	Gratian (367–75) (1)
Magnentius (barbarous) (1)	Arcadius (1)

It seems clear that this deposit was laid down c. 360–70 and thereafter one or perhaps four coins were trodden in. We can therefore say that the cellar was filled in sometime after c. 290 (by which date the coins of Carausius may be thought to have become sufficiently plentiful for thirteen of them to be lost in the cellar) and before the time when coins of Constantine I were in common circulation,[1] say 315–20. Later, c. 360–70, the filling was levelled off with more earth and rubble.

When was the cellar constructed? There was no contemporary dating evidence in the cellar itself, for the packing behind the revetment yielded only three irrelevant coins (of Domitian, Trajan, and Hadrian). Its date must depend on that for the buildings as a whole.

Date of Period III

The disturbed condition of the upper levels, where unprotected by walls, meant that only in Building XIV, 1 were sealed and stratified levels relating to Period III preserved intact. As the sections show (figs. 27, 28), considerable layers of make-up had been deposited, owing to the need to raise the floor of the building to contemporary levels. These layers produced the following coins.

T II 5	Pre-third cent. (2)
	Gordian III (1)
T III 6	Tetricus (barbarous) (1)
T III 8	Victorinus (1)
T VI 5	Pre-third cent. (2)
	Claudius II (1)
T VI 6	Pre-third cent. (1)
T VII 5	Pre-third cent. (1)
	Tetricus (1)
T VII 6	Pre-third cent. (2)

[1] Coins of the Tetrarchy and of the first decade of Constantine's reign are rare as site-finds in Britain and need not be expected to appear here in so small a deposit.

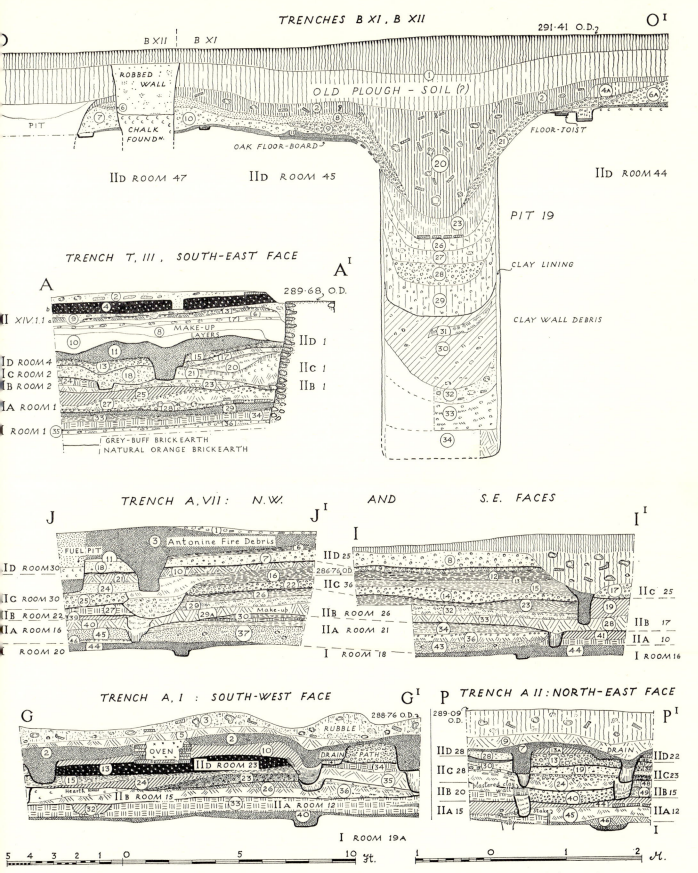

FIG. 24. Sections A–A¹, G–G¹, I–I¹, J–J¹, O–O¹, P–P¹. For positions see fig. 26 (p. 111).

These levels were sealed by the primary floor of Building 1, which accordingly cannot have been laid down before *c.* A.D. 270–5. Since the cellar, as has been explained, was secondary to the masonry walls of Buildings XIV, 4 and 5 (which are assumed to be approximately contemporary with XIV, 1), and since the cellar was abandoned between 290 and 315 after considerable use, it seems probable that a date of *c.* 275 is appropriate to the beginning of Period III. If it had been much later than this a larger number of barbarous radiates might perhaps have been expected in the primary levels. The sequence suggested, accordingly, is:

(i) *c.* 275 construction of masonry buildings

(ii) *c.* 280–90 excavation of cellar

(iii) *c.* 310–15 abandonment of cellar

As for the life of the main buildings, the floors of XIV, 1 had the following coins on their surfaces:

Gallienus (1)	Carausius (2)
Salonina (1)	Allectus (1)
Victorinus (1)	Constantine I (2)
Claudius II	Crispus (1)
(barbarous) (1)	Valentinian I (1)
the Tetrici (6)	Gratian (1)
barbarous	
radiates (6)	

Thus this building survived at least until the third quarter of the fourth century. The evidence from the rest of the site is consistent as far as it goes, but the other buildings had been far more disturbed. The clean red burnt daub of the Antonine fire was almost everywhere covered by a much more earthy layer of burnt daub. Sometimes this deposit was separated from the clean burnt daub by other layers. It was taken to be material disturbed and redeposited at the beginning of Period III as levelling or make-up for floors; some of it may have come from foundation trenches. But few of the floors themselves survived to seal it, and therefore the deposits are open to intrusion. In B I 15, for instance, occurs a coin of Constantius II. There were no coins in B II at these levels. In B IV 3A, disturbed burnt daub, the following coins were found:

Gallienus (1)	Claudius II (1)
the Tetrici (2)	Constans (1)
Victorinus (1)	

This is clearly the pattern of the layers in Building XIV, 1 with the exception of the Constans which is intrusive.

The remaining coins may be listed as follows.

B V 3	Disturbed daub: second cent. (1)	Claudius II (1)	
	Gallienus (1)	Unidentifiable, probably radiates (2)	
B V 5	Disturbed daub: Constans Aug. (1)		
B V 6A	Disturbed daub: Victorinus (1)	Crispus (1)	
	Tetricus I (2)		

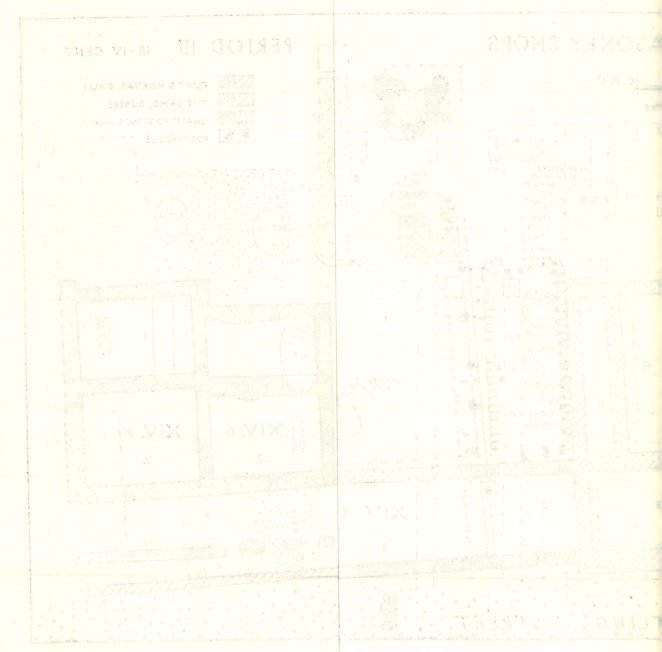

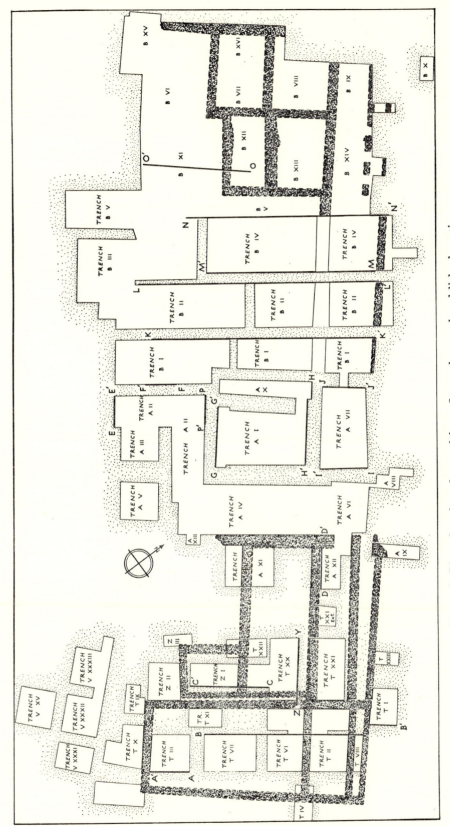

FIG. 26. Plan showing the position of trenches and published sections.

B V 10   Disturbed daub: Victorinus (1)

B VIII 8A Disturbed daub: Claudius II (1)

B XII 3   Uppermost of several make-up layers: Constantine I (1)

                                                House of Constantine (335–41) (1)

B XIV 2   Disturbed daub: barbarous radiate (1)

B XV 9   Disturbed daub: Tetricus I (1)

It will be seen that these layers have a preponderance of late third-century coins, but some fourth-century ones have intruded. Finally, B XI 2, rubble probably from the destruction of Building XIV, 6, yielded a coin (367–75) of Valentinian I. Though the evidence might suggest that this site ceased to be occupied before the end of the fourth century, it would probably be unwise to accept it at its face value. The upper levels have been too thoroughly disturbed for any certainty to be reached about this question, and the deeply dug allotment soil with any later coins it may have contained was removed by mechanical excavation.

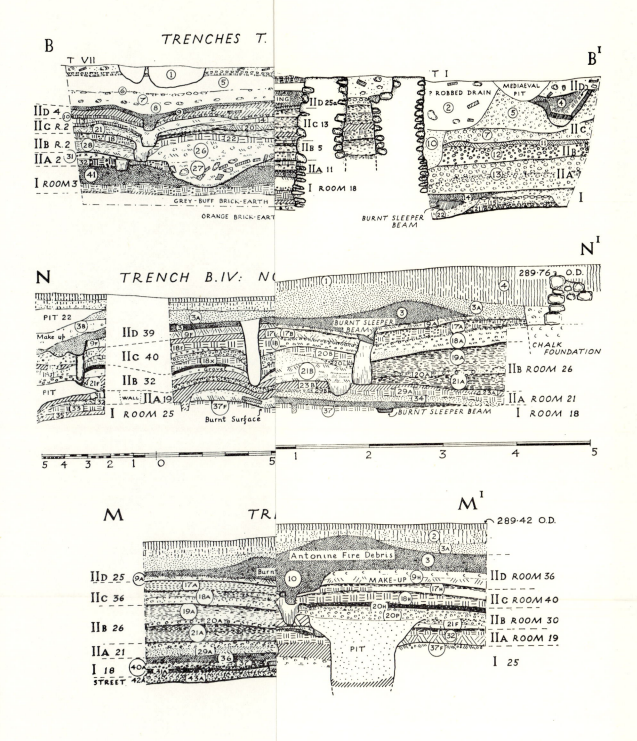

TRENCHES T.

B

T VII

①

⑤

⑥

⑦

⑧

⑨

IID 4 ⑩

IIC R.2 ㉑ ⑱

IIB R.2 ㉘

IIA 2 ㉛ ㉜

I ROOM 3 ㊶

㉖

㉗

GREY-BUFF BRICK-EARTH

ORANGE BRICK-EARTH

ING

IID 25a

IIC 13

IIB 5

IIA 11

I ROOM 18

BURNT SLEEPER
BEAM

B¹

T I

? ROBBED DRAIN

MEDIAEVAL PIT

IID

②

⑤

④

⑦

⑩

⑪

⑫

IIC

IIB

⑬

IIA

④

㉒

I

TRENCH B.IV: NO

N

PIT 22

Make up ③B

⑨F

PIT ㉑F

WALL

③A

⑤

⑨F

⑱F

⑱X

Grove

㉛ ㉜

IIA 19 ㊲F

I ROOM 25 Burnt Surface

IID 39

IIC 40

IIB 32

⑰B

⑰B

⑳B

⑳L

㉑B

㉓B ㉙B

N¹

289.76 O.D.

①

④

③

③A

BURNT SLEEPER
BEAM

⑫A ⑰A

⑱A

⑲A

⑳AP

㉑A

㉙A

㉞

CHALK
FOUNDATION

IIB ROOM 26

IIA ROOM 21

I ROOM 18

㉓A

㊲ BURNT SLEEPER BEAM

5 4 3 2 1 0   5   1   2   3   4   5

M

TR

M¹

289.42 O.D.

②

③A

③

Antonine Fire Debris

⑩

MAKE-UP ⑨H

⑰H

IID 25 ⑨A

IIC 36 ⑰A ⑱A

IIB 26 ⑲A ⑳A

IIA 21 ㉑A ㉙A

I 18 ㊱

STREET ㊵A ㊷A ㊸A

Burnt

⑳H

⑳P

⑱H

㉑F

㉜

㊲F

PIT

IID ROOM 36

IIC ROOM 40

IIB ROOM 30

IIA ROOM 19

I 25

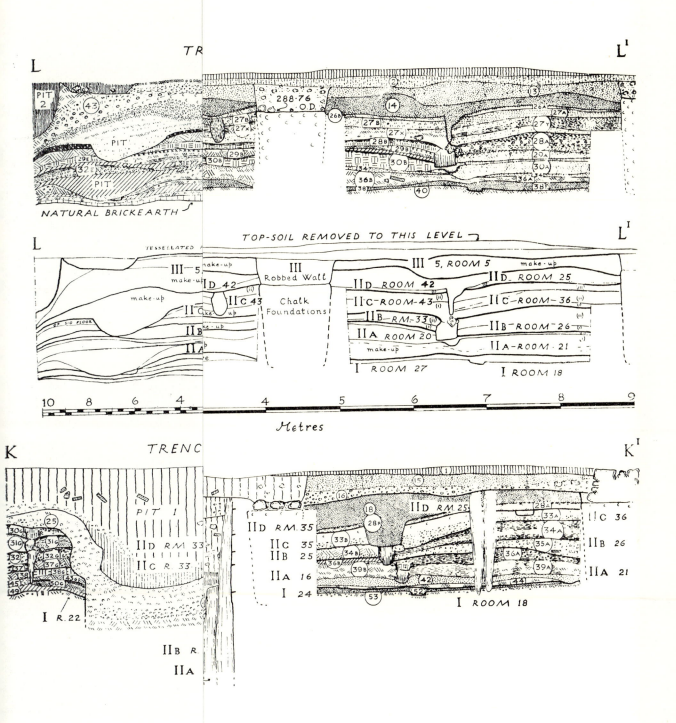

L   TR   **L¹**

PIT 2   (43)

288·76 O.D.

27B   27×

26B

14

(2)

(3)

26A   27A

27Y

28A

28B

27×

29A

29B

30A

30B

30B

32E   31E

29E

30B

34A

36A

38+

36B

38

40

PIT

PIT

NATURAL BRICKEARTH

L   TOP-SOIL REMOVED TO THIS LEVEL   **L¹**

TESSELLATED F

III — 5   make-up

make-up

IID 42 (ii)

IIC 43

IIB

IIA

make-up

OP. S/O FLOOR

III Robbed Wall

Chalk Foundations

III   5, ROOM 5   make-up

IID ROOM 42

IIC-ROOM-43 (ii) (i)

IIB RM-33 (ii) (i)

IIA ROOM 20

make-up

I ROOM 27

IID ROOM 25

IIC-ROOM-36 (ii) (i)

IIB-ROOM-26 (i)

IIA-ROOM 21 (i)

I ROOM 18

```
10      8      6      4        4      5      6      7      8      9
```

Metres

K   TRENC   **K¹**

PIT 1

IID RM 33

IIC R. 33

30B   (25)

31G   31G

32   32C

37   37G

III   38   38G   43G

45   50G

49

I R. 22

IIB R.

IIA

(1)

(15)

(16)

(18)

28B

IID RM 25

28A

33A

34A

IIC 36

IID RM. 35

IIC 35

IIB 25

IIA 16

I 24

33B

34B

36B

39B

35A

36A

39A

IIB 26

IIA 21

(42)

(52)

53

(44)

I ROOM 18

PART II

THE FINDS

MANY PEOPLE have assisted in the preparation of the catalogues below. Dr. W. H. Manning who has made a special study of Romano-British ironwork has kindly reported on the iron objects from Verulamium, and these are accordingly dealt with in a separate section by him. The other objects, of gold, bronze, lead, and bone have been studied by my successive Research Assistants, Miss H. Waugh and Mr. R. Goodburn. Much preliminary work on the brooches, however, was undertaken by Mrs. R. A. Canham, and Mr. M. R. Hull has been generous with his advice. Mr. B. R. Hartley, as well as examining every piece of samian as recorded in the summary Period-lists above, has also contributed a section on the more significant decorated pieces of samian and on the samian potters' stamps (pp. 216–62), and Mrs. K. Hartley has drawn and described the mortarium stamps (pp. 371–81) as well as giving great assistance to our study of the mortaria in general. Much useful work on the classification and drawing of these and the remainder of the pottery was done by Mr. J. A. Ellison; the bulk of the pottery drawings, however, which are published below and the pottery report itself are the work of Miss M. G. Wilson; they form a major contribution to this volume. Finally, Miss D. Charlesworth has contributed an important study of the glass vessels, which is illustrated by drawings by Miss Wilson.

In the catalogues below, the label of the deposit from which the object came (which also enables the layer to be identified on the section-drawings) is given first, followed by the date of that deposit as determined both by its datable finds and by its position in the stratified sequence; then follow the Period number (I, II A, II B, etc., as defined in Part I of this volume) and the Room number on the appropriate Period plan. For the numbering of pits, see p. 263.

I. THE NON-FERROUS OBJECTS

by H. Waugh and R. Goodburn

A. OBJECT OF GOLD

Fig. 32, 25. Pl. XXXVIII*a*. Finger-ring with approximately heptagonal hoop. The outer edge is rounded and somewhat worn. B XI 22, A.D. 300–50. Upper filling of Pit 19.

B. OBJECTS OF BRONZE

(*a*) THE BROOCHES (FIGS. 29–31)

(i) *Derivative forms of the Nauheim type: Camulodunum VII*

1. Plain and rather flattened bow, with a four-turn spring and internal chord. Two turns of the spring and most of the catch-plate are missing. A X 65, A.D. 135–45. II C, Room 28.
2. The undecorated bow, flattened in form and cross-section, tapers to the head and foot from the shoulder. A four-turn spring with internal chord survives broken, but the foot is missing. B I 44, *c.* A.D. 75. II A, Rooms 16, 21, make-up for primary floor.

(ii) *The 'Colchester' type: Camulodunum III*

3. Typical example with an eight-turn spring, small plain side wings and plain bow. The foot is extremely corroded. T III 25, A.D. 85–105. II A, Room 2.
4. Similar to 3, but with six-turn spring. Rather poorly preserved and most of catch-plate gone. A VI 23, A.D. 105–15. II B, Room 5.
5. Small version with bar through its eight-turn spring. Bow has a circular section and surviving side-wing has two transverse shallow flutings on its upper surface. B IV 43 A, *c.* A.D. 49. I, Room 18 or street-metalling below this.

(iii) *Type Camulodunum IV*

6. This has an eight-turn spring which is very corroded and with little of the chord remaining. The perforated catch-plate is thick and is slotted for the pin. A X 25, A.D. 49–60. I, Room 20.
7. A peculiar version of this type. The backward-projecting lug at the head is pierced to take an axial bar for the spring, and head is broken at the hole through which the chord passed. It has small side-wings. Foot is notched rather than knobbed, and the underside of the catch-plate is decorated with two pairs of slight transverse grooves. B VIII 1, A.D. 270–5. Make-up, XIV, 6 Room 2.
8. Similar to 6, but with ten-turn spring. It has solid semi-cylindrical side-wings, each with a groove at the outer end. A X 23, A.D. 60–75. II A, Room 16, make-up.
9. Traces of tinning or silvering remain. There is a small loop at the head to take the chord. Side-wings are semi-cylindrical and have disc-ends pierced for the axial bar. Catch-plate has three pairs of decorative grooves on the pin-holder. Z I 26, A.D. 85–105. II A, Room 5.

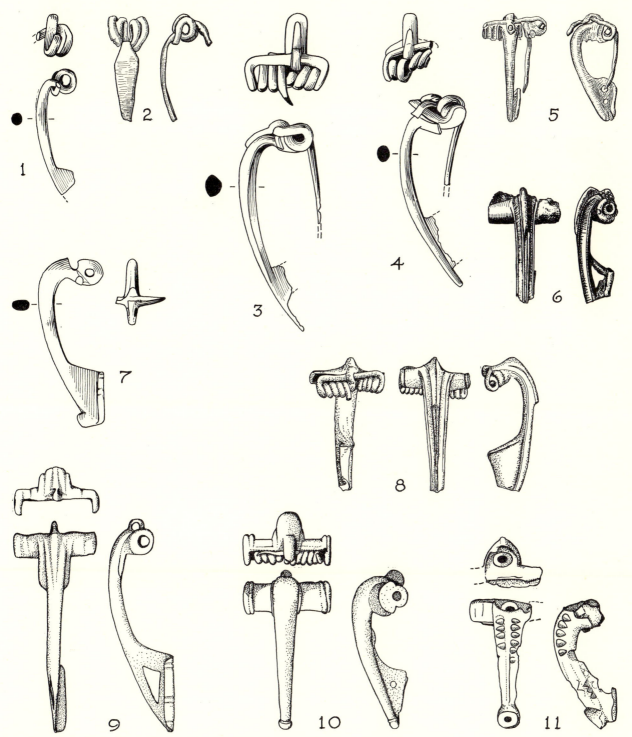

FIG 29. Bronze objects 1–11: brooches ($\frac{1}{1}$).

(iv) *Camulodunum V*

10. 'Dolphin' type, but with the semi-cylindrical side-wings having pierced disc-ends for the axial bar of the twelve-turn spring as in the Polden Hill type. There is no central lug for the bar, and the chord is held by a hook projecting rearwards from the head of the bow. Incised lines run around the margins of the outside of catch-plate and perforation. B I 34A, A.D. 115–30. II B, Room 26.

(v) *The head-stud type*

11. There are circular sockets for studs at the head and on the foot. The bow has slight triangular depressions on either side of a longitudinal rib, but no enamel remains. The surviving wing apparently has transverse flutings, but brooch very corroded. A II 68. Undated pit below II B, Room 14.

(vi) *The sawfish type*

12. Traces of enamel of indeterminate colour remain within lozenges on the bow. Hinged, with devolved crouching-dog form of crest. The lateral teeth are small, and the foot ends in a typical forward-facing knob, although the side-arms are plain except for transverse groove at outer end. A XIII 8, A.D. 105–15. II B, Room 11, primary floor.

(vii) *The Hod Hill type: Camulodunum XVIII, Class A*

13. A variant of this class which has a strongly arched bow and is quite heavily cast. The plain foot tapers to a weakly knobbed terminal. A X 73, A.D. 49–60. I, Room 19, primary floor.

(viii) *The Hod Hill type: Camulodunum XVIII, Class B*

14. A large typical version. Considerably corroded and any silvering has vanished. A I 39, A.D. 75–105. II A, Room 14.

15. A weak version, rather fragmentary, with only vestigial transverse mouldings above and below the panel on the bow. Traces of silvering or tinning remain. B II 32D, A.D. 75–105. II A, Room 19, floor.

16. A typical form, originally tinned or silvered. B IV 42S, A.D. 49–55. I, Room 30, occupation on primary floor.

(ix) *Related hinged brooches*

17. Variant of Hod Hill type, but with slight transverse grooves and ridges on head of bow as in Aucissa type. Upper part only remains, very corroded. B IV 41A, A.D. 49–55. I, Room 18.

18. Has affinities with 'Camulodunum Type XVIII Derivative' described in *Hod Hill*, i (C81–C88, pp. 9–10 and fig. 10). This example, with double groove and punched-dot decoration on bow, is rather corroded and part of catch-plate is missing. T XX 38, *c.* A.D. 49. I, Room 8, occupation below floor (see p. 13).

19. A fine brooch with traces of silvering or tinning and niello inlay leaf-pattern on the bow. Small panel at the head has slightly countersunk seating with central hole, presumably for stud. B IV 3B, third century, make-up, XIV, 5 Room 3.

(x) *Flat strip-bow brooch*

20. Reeded bow resembles Langton Down type, but this has hinged pin. Has some similarity to Hod Hill brooches (*Hod Hill*, i, C30–31, p. 8 and fig. 7) classed as local imitations of Langton Down type. A IV 37, A.D. 105–30. II B, wall-trench 10/11.

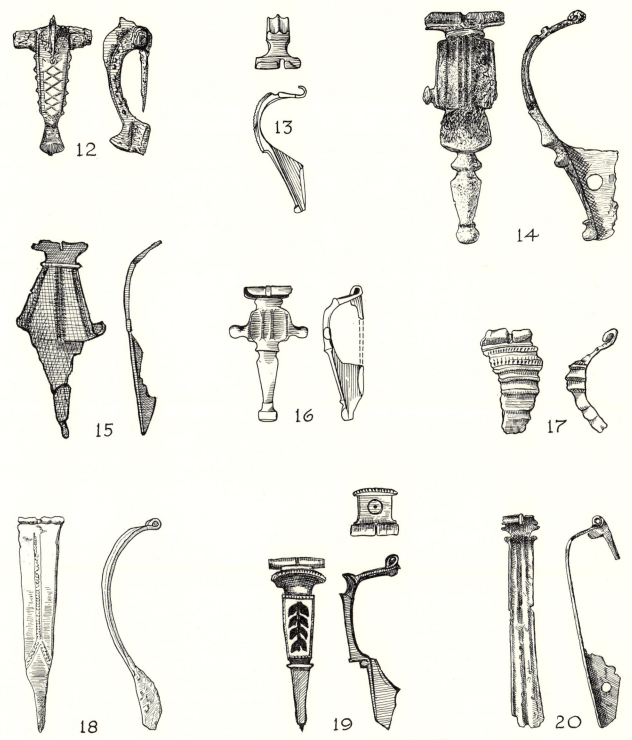

FIG. 30. Bronze objects 12–20: brooches ($\frac{1}{1}$).

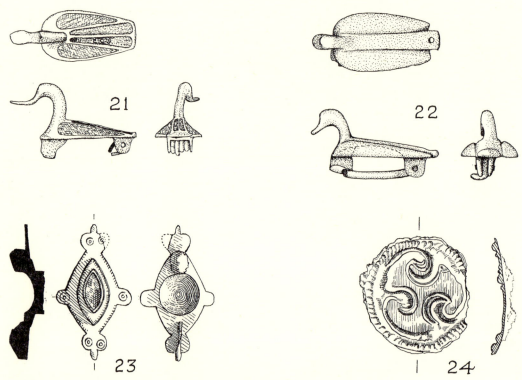

FIG. 31. Bronze objects 21–4: brooches ($\frac{1}{1}$).

(xi) *Plate-brooches*

21. Brooch in the form of a swimming duck, with blue enamel panels for wings and traces of some other colour in panels for the back and tail. Pin is sprung, with axial bar and internal chord. B IV 9F, A.D. 150–155/160. II D, Room 39.

22. A second swimming duck, without enamel but with hinged pin. A I 14, A.D. 150–155/160. II D, silt in drain 23/29.

23. Lozenge-shaped brooch having projections decorated with incised double concentric circles and with incised lines around edges of outer and inner lozenges. Central setting contains decayed enamel. Pin hinged. T III 11, A.D. 155/160. II D, Room 4.

24. Disc with raised beaded border and three curvilinear motifs running into the central field. Heavy corrosion on back probably represents mount of disc-brooch resembling *Richborough IV*, no. 170 (pl. XLV and p. 139) but a relatively weak version of a design in the same native tradition; cf. also M. R. Hull, *Roman Colchester*, 117, fig. 47, 7. B I 59, A.D. 300–15. Sump in cellar floor.

     For another, approximately contemporary example of debased Celtic motifs at Verulamium see the bronze triskele, Wheeler, *Verulamium*, 217, fig. 48.

     See p. 180, no. 57, for an iron penannular brooch.

(b) OTHER OBJECTS OF BRONZE

25. (See Object of Gold, above, p. 114.)

26. Wire finger-ring with rectangular bezel which has crudely engraved, unidentified motif. B I 6A, unstratified.

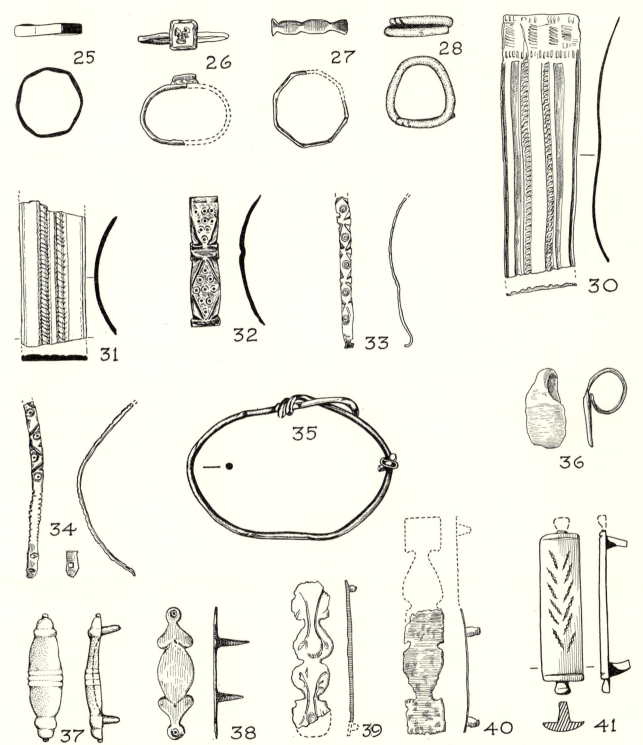

Fig. 32. Gold (25) and bronze objects 26–41 (1/1): for no. 29 see pl. XXXVIII*b*.

27. Octagonal finger-ring with facets narrowing at the angles. No bezel survives and the ring was probably plain. B II 11, A.D. 310–15. III, Building XIV, 5, main cellar-filling.

28. Coiled-wire finger-ring, one terminal with two slight grooves, other seemingly broken off. B II 3, A.D. 370–410+. Rubble over cellar-filling.

29. See pl. XXXVIII*b*. Thin, lozenge-shaped bezel of ring with decorative arrangement of raised dots. B II 37E, A.D. 75–85. II A, accumulation outside Room 19.

30. Part of bracelet with longitudinal grooves and stamped leaf-like motif. Terminal has crudely stamped decoration. B II 36A, A.D. 75–85. II A, Room 21.

31. Fragment of similar bracelet decorated with lines of notches within two pairs of parallel grooves. A IV 33, A.D. 85–105. II A, Room 7.

32. Portion of bracelet with facets and grooves forming lozenge patterns containing punched ring and dot ornament. Motif-units separated by transverse grooves. V XXXIII 1. Unstratified dark soil south-west of XIV, 1.

33. Part of bracelet with incised decoration; part of hook fastening remaining at one end. B I 5, A.D. 370–410+. Rubble over cellar-filling.

34. Similar to no. 32, with an eye for the fastening. B III 7. Late pit in mosaic, XIV, 5 Room 3.

35. Expanding bracelet of wire, with ends wound around hoop; one end broken. B I 8, A.D. 360–70. Secondary make-up of cellar-filling.

36. Ear-ring with loop formed of rod with curved section and expanded flattened end. B IV 23J, A.D. 105–15. II B, Room 29.

37. Mount for leather belt, with acorn terminals and ridges across rather humped back. A I 2, A.D. 155/60. II D, Room 23.

38. Flat mount similar to no. 37, with two spikes for attachment. B II 27X, A.D. 130–40. II C, Room 43.

39. Flat mount, rather damaged but possibly originally silvered, with traces of incised decoration. B VIII 1, A.D. 270–5. III, make-up, XIV, 6 Room 2.

40. Part of belt mount of thin sheet with two of three rivets remaining. B II 41, A.D. 49–75. I, Room 22 (contaminated).

41. Rectangular mount with knob terminals (one missing). Herring-bone pattern of incised lines with feathered edges perhaps once held inlay. A I 38, A.D. 105–15. II B, Room 16.

42. Mount with four transverse ridges, knob terminals, and spikes for attachment. B V 7, A.D. 155/160. II D, Rooms 41–8.

43. Six fittings, each with two long spikes. Five identical, with knobbed ends; sixth has knobbed crescent at a broader end. T VIII 5, A.D. 130–50. II C, Room 13.

44. Pear-shaped fitting with terminal knob and bar-ended rod for attachment at rear. A VII 28, A.D. 105–30. II B, Room 17.

45. Similar fitting to no. 44, but with thin plate at end of mounting-rod. B V 7, A.D. 155/160. II D, Rooms 41–8.

46. Mount in form of stylized phallus with two rivets. Trace of enamel at tip, now yellowish green. B II 27E, A.D. 150–155/160. II D, Room 43.

47. Crudely made phallic amulet with suspension loop. A VI 14, A.D. 130–50. II C, Room 20, south-east wall-trench.

48. Leaf-shaped mount with rivet from which hangs lozenge-shaped pendant with terminals. B V 12, A.D. 140–50. II C, Room 40.

49. Lower part of strap-fitting with circular seating and perforation for a stud. T II 16, A.D. 140–50. II C, Room 4.

50. Part of mount of palmette form decorated with inscribed lines and circles, and with moulded terminal. There is one spike or rivet for attachment. T II 7, A.D. 270–5. III, Make-up, XIV, 1 Room 2.

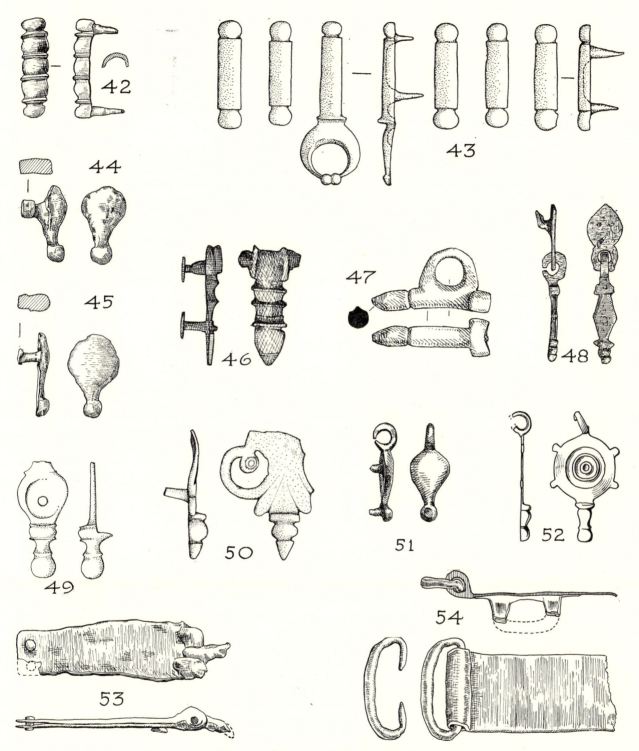

FIG. 33. Bronze objects 42–54 ($\frac{1}{1}$).

51. Leaf-shaped mount with two rivets, having hook for pendant at one end and knob-terminal at other. B IV 3, A.D. 155/160. II D, Rooms 38–42.

52. Pendant, with traces of silvering when found. Circular plate with concentric grooves, four small side-projections and a moulded, knobbed terminal. B II 41, A.D. 49–75. I, Room 22 (contaminated).

53. Corroded belt-plate with hinge and part of pin. Three of four mounting-rivets remain. B I 63, A.D. 60–75. Pit 7, upper filling.

54. Stout plate, broken at one end but retaining hinge-loop and hinge at the other. Mounting prongs at the back, made from one sheet, are broken off. Possibly hasp for lock. A XI 18, A.D. 85–105. II A, Room 7, floor sealing oven.

55. Dress-fastener, with bold dot-and-circle ornament on the discs within the ring forming the head. A variant of J. P. Wild's Class II (*Britannia*, i (1970), 137–55). B IV 38, A.D. 75–85. II A, Room 19.

56. Corroded fastener with section varying from circular to rectangular and broken off at straight end. B XI 11A, A.D. 155/160. II D, wall-trench 45/47.

57. Cruciform tubular object of unknown purpose, rather corroded. B IV 17J, A.D. 145–50. II C, Room 39. Cf. W. J. Wedlake, *Excavations at Camerton, Somerset* (Bath, 1958), fig. 58, no. 10; J. Curle, *Newstead*, pl. LXXVII, 9.

58. Part of pin or *stylus*; small part of head of blade missing. B XIV 4, A.D. 270–5. III, make-up, XIV, 6 Room 3.

59. Pin, broken at tip, with flattened-knob head and groove at top of shank. B IV 21D, A.D. 105–15. II B, Room 34.

60. Similar pin. A I 23, A.D. 130–40. II C, Room 23, primary floor.

61. Pin with mouldings at head, top hollowed to take decorative enamel. B IV 21A, A.D. 105–15. II B, Room 26.

62. (?) Part of belt-buckle, broken off at the ends above the junction with the bar which held the tongue. T XX 31, *c.* A.D. 60. I, Room 8, fuel-pit.

63. Two pieces of bent thin plate with heavy knob terminal at one end and tapering to a damaged foot-like feature at the other. B I 45, A.D. 85–105. II A, accumulation outside (south-west of) Room 17.

64. Hollow handle in form of sleeved arm and hand with fruit held between thumb and forefinger. A I 27, A.D. 105–30. II B, Room 16.

   Hands holding a fruit are found as terminals to pins in bronze (J. P. Bushe-Fox, *Wroxeter*, ii, 13, nos. 10, 11; idem, *Richborough III*, 80, no. 23) or bone (example in Guildhall Museum, London). In view of this association with the toilet the present example, though heavy, should be taken as the terminal of a bone hair-pin suitable to an elaborate coiffure, or perhaps as the handle of a small razor.

65. Seal-box with stud in form of frog on the lid. The innermost moulding is decorated with radial punch-marks. T VI 15, A.D. 140–50. II C, Room 4. Cf. *Richborough V*, p. 101, nos. 183–5, and parallels there cited.

66. Seal-box. Lid has raised mouldings around edge and central perforation to take some form of decoration. Base slightly dished. A I 38, A.D. 105–15. II A, Room 16.

67. Seal-box. Edges of lid decorated with notches, and incised circles at corners; annular area apparently filled with segments of differently coloured enamels including cylindrical depressions with dots of different colour. There is a central dot of azure paste. Projection of lid has disc of enamel and locating pin on underside. There are the usual perforations in base and side. B IX 7, A.D. 130–50. II C, floor below II D, Room 54, found when tracing drain.

68. Large scoop with twisted rod handle. Part remaining is in four fragments. B I, Pit 20: III, box under stairs in cellar, XIV, 5. A.D. 300–15.

69. *Ligula* with flat scoop. Broken off above moulding at constriction of shank. B I 38, A.D. 85–105. II A, accumulation outside (south-west of) Room 17.

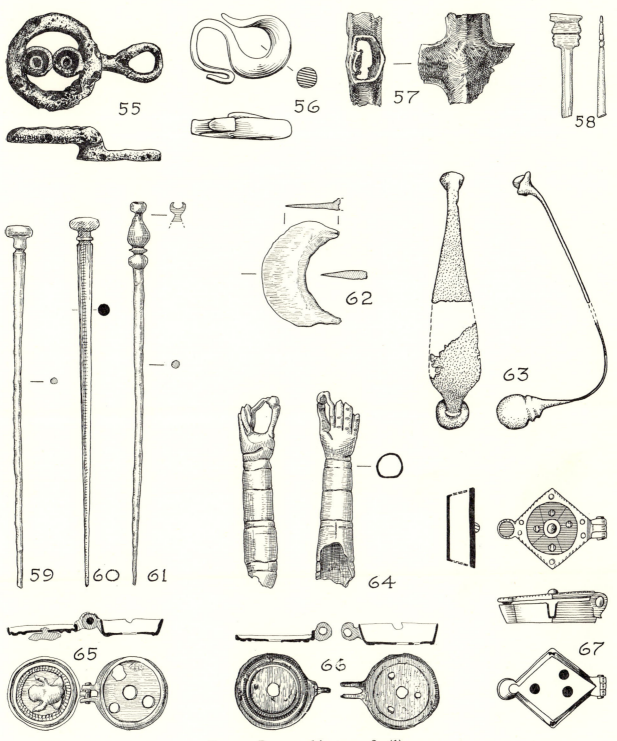

FIG. 34. Bronze objects 55–67 ($\frac{1}{1}$).

70. *Ligula* with cupped scoop, and incised groove on shank. B II 19, A.D. 270–80. Packing of cellar-wall.

71. Instrument with probe at one end and other end broken off on rectangular section beyond mouldings. A II 42, A.D. 75–105. II A, accumulation south-west of Rooms 12–15.

72. Probe with punched-dot decoration above moulding. Other end has smaller probe or is perhaps broken. B III 10, A.D. 270–5. III, make-up, XIV, 5 Room 3.

73. Probe with punched dots spiralling along shank to a series of mouldings. Broken end beyond this perhaps originally formed a *ligula*. A XII 17, A.D. 110–20. II B, Room 13.

74. Spoon, very corroded but with traces of silvering. Bowl pear-shaped and handle-junction plain. B IV 18F, A.D. 135–45. II C, Room 40, secondary floor.

75. Knife-handle, rather corroded, with central decorative opening and terminal suspension loop. Part of the handle is divided to take the blade, which was fixed by three rivets. The central opening holds a small moulded bar and there are perforations for a second. The surfaces are decorated with impressed circles, dotted and incised lines. B IV 23D, A.D. 85–105. II A, Room 23, occupation on primary floor.

76. Stout, curved object with substantial eye for suspension. Possibly toilet implement such as nail-cleaner. V XXXIII 1. Unstratified dark soil south-west of XIV, 1.

77*a*. Length of chain, each link formed of a piece of rectangular-sectioned wire formed into a double loop. Chain attached to crudely made pin by a poorly formed, broken ring.

77*b*. Staple, broken at the ends, found with 77*a*. B II 29C, A.D. 115–30. II B, Room 33.

78. Two links of a chain of same type as 77*a*. T II 24, *c.* A.D. 130. II C, Room 4, make-up.

79. Chain, with links of same type as 77*a*. B XV 11, A.D. 150–155/160. II D, Room 55.

80. Chain attached to a ring by a loop with a terminal knob which holds it in a perforation in a flattened area of the ring. Each link formed of a flat strand, split at each end with the arms folded together. B IV Pit 2. Unnumbered small late pit.

81. Clip or type of split-pin, with ends broken off. B IV 41D, A.D. 49–60. I, Room 26.

82. Chain of three S-shaped links of circular-sectioned wire. B XI 22, A.D. 300–50. Upper filling of Pit 19.

83. Ring of rather pear-shaped section, possibly one of a pair, as a very similar ring came from same layer. B I 9, A.D. 310–15. Cellar-filling.

84. Penannular ring or broken chain-link. B XV 11, A.D. 150–155/160. II D, Room 55.

85. Oval ring of U-shaped section, worn to thin strip at one point. A I 18, A.D. 135–45. II C, Room 24.

86. Crude wire ring with overlapping ends wound around the hoop. B IV 3, A.D. 155/160. II D, Rooms 38–42.

87. Somewhat corroded disc-shaped weight of 4·86 gm. which is 74·95 gr., or approximately $\frac{1}{64}$ of a Celtic pound of 4,770 gr. B XIII 5. III, make-up XIV, 6 Room 2 (Antonine fire, disturbed). For discussion see p. 160.

88. Weight of 53·29 gm. (= 822·37 gr.) with bronze casing around lead core. Two irregular impressions on one flat surface. B II 29B, A.D. 115–30. II B, Room 33. See p. 160.

89. Part of case for weight with traces of lead on inside. B II 29B, as no. 88.

    (Note: a third weight, not illustrated, was found in the same layer. It is a plain circular disc of weight of 2·28 gm. (= 35·19 gr.). See p. 160.)

90. Weight of lead with bronze case. The numeral I is incised on the side. Weight 26·77 gm. (= 413·11 gr.). B IV 17D, A.D. 145–50. II C, Room 45. For discussion see p. 160.

91. Casing, probably for weight, with incised decorative lines on side and base. B IV 34, *c.* A.D. 75. II A, Room 23, make-up.

92. Weight of 277·41 gm. (= 4,280·99 gr.) of lead with part of bronze casing surviving on upper surface and with bronze suspension loop with twist of wire around it. B I 5, A.D. 370–410+. Rubble over cellar-filling. See p. 160.

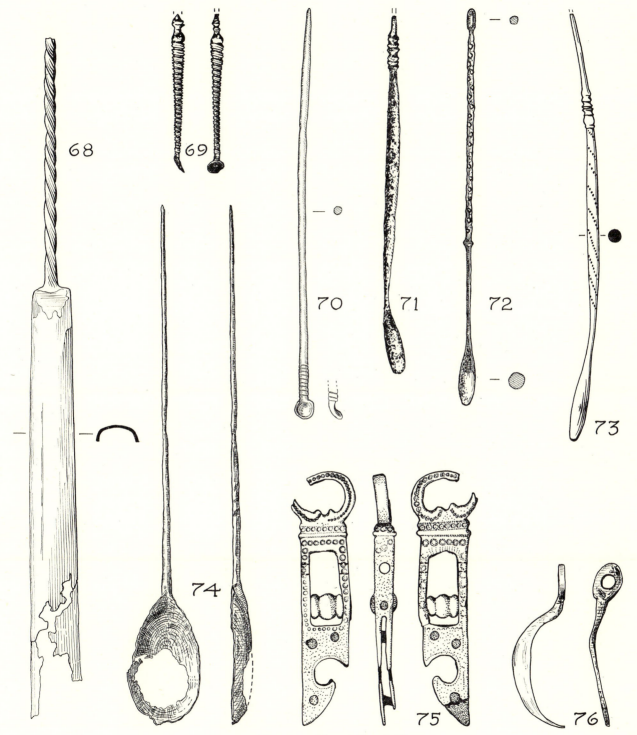

Fig. 35. Bronze objects 68–76 ($\frac{1}{1}$).

93. Rectangular bell with stubs of iron loop to hold clapper inside. B I 9, A.D. 310–15. Cellar-filling.

94. Ribbed hollow cylindrical object. B XIV 10B, A.D. 155/160. II D, Room 25.

95. Cylindrical nozzle-like object with fragment of iron object adhering to the wider end, which has a slot cut in it. Cf. the mounts on the stretcher-bars of a folding stool (Liversidge, *Furniture in Roman Britain*, pls. 40–1). B XV 11, A.D. 150–155/160. II D, Room 55.

96. Decorative stud with notched edge and three concentric zones of enamel, now appearing as varying shades of green; the outer area has five and the adjacent area three segments of darker enamel. B IV 9B, A.D. 150–155/160. II D, Room 42.

97. (Pl. XXXVIII*c*.) Decorative stud, pin broken off, with flat head. Enamels are now azure in central zone and yellow in surrounding zone. Four rings in outer zone are composed of pale yellow glassy substance. T XX 2, A.D. 155/160. II D, Room 10.

98. One of pair of rosette-shaped studs with flat underside and flat-ended shank. Areas of enamel on the surface are now varying shades of green but show that alternate 'petals' were once of different colours. A VII 19, A.D. 115–30. II B, Room 17.

99. Enamelled boss with perforation for pin. At centre, enamel panels outline design of six petals. Around this runs a row of enamel panels of alternating colours, and at edge is border of angular heart-shaped motifs. Original enamel colours, now red and yellow, are uncertain. T XX 9, A.D. 150–155/160. II D, Room 10.

100. Stud with central dot and two concentric grooves. End of pin broken off. A VII 25, A.D. 130–40. II C, Room 30.

101. Decorative stud with shaft-end flattened for attachment. B I 55, A.D. 280–315. Occupation layer in cellar.

102. Thin head of stud with notches around edge. Shank has been wrenched out. B IV Posthole 1, fourth century. XIV, 5, wall 3/6.

103. Double stud with slightly hollowed cone-shaped head. Flat circular foot apparently riveted on. B IV 17B, A.D. 140–50. II C, Room 44.

104. One of pair of handles consisting of loop set on a disc, perforated for attachment, and with a slight offset below the loop. B I 32E, A.D. 105–30. II B, Room 19.

105. Knob-handle which once had rectangular-sectioned shank. B I 9, A.D. 310–15. Cellar-filling.

106. Knob-handle which had square-sectioned iron shank between pair of prongs cast as part of the knob. B I 61, fourth century. Mouth of Pit 7.

107. Knob-handle with groove on the end, defining slight boss with dot in its centre. An irregular rectangular projection for attachment remains at the other end. B I 37G, A.D. 105–15. II B, Room 24.

108. (Pl. XXXVIII*d*.) Hollow mount in form of lion's head; mane and other finer features indicated by slightly curved punch marks. Inside, remains of iron pin for attachment. B I 37D, A.D. 105–15. II B, Room 20.

109. Terminal or handle with concave surface, rather corroded but apparently plain. A VII 32, A.D. 110–20. II B, Room 26.

110. Mount consisting of central knob, with dot at apex, set on circular plate by means of axial rivet and 'washer'. The plate has a large and a small edge-perforation on a diameter: the smaller perforation almost cuts the rim. B II 9, A.D. 270–350. III, gravel floor, XIV, 5 Room 4.

111. Tack with irregular knobbed head and square-sectioned shank. A I 38, A.D. 105–15. II B, Room 16.

112. Small dome-headed tack with pin broken off. T II 24, *c.* A.D. 130. II C, Room 4, make-up.

113. Acorn-shaped terminal, perhaps detached from a drop-handle. B I 9, A.D. 310–15. Cellar filling.

114. Small drop-handle, with terminals flat on one side and moulded on other. A IV 33, A.D. 85–105. II A, Room 7.

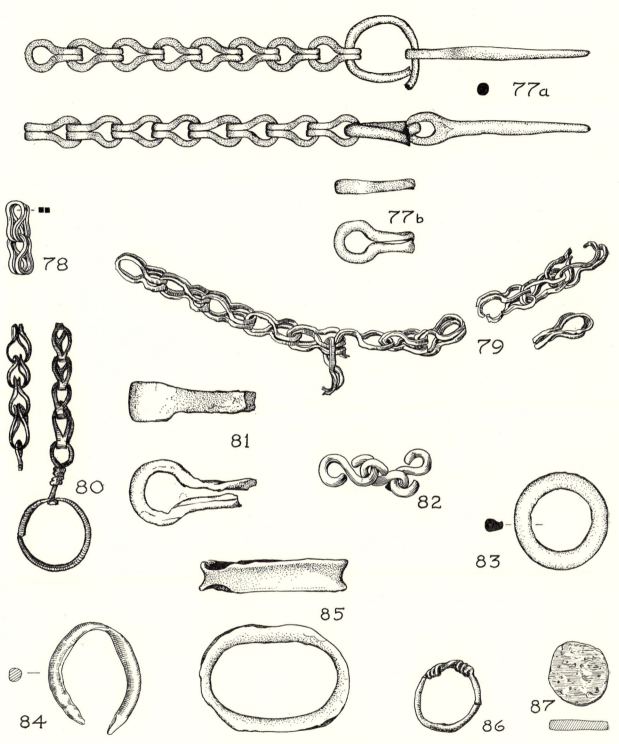

FIG. 36. Bronze objects 77a–87 ($\frac{1}{1}$).

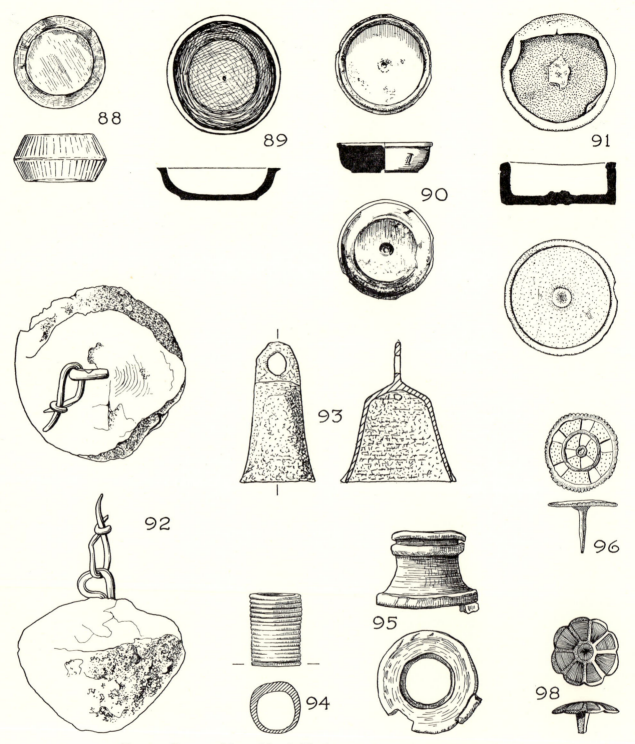

FIG. 37. Bronze objects 88–98 ($\frac{1}{1}$): for no. 97 see pl. XXXVIII*c*.

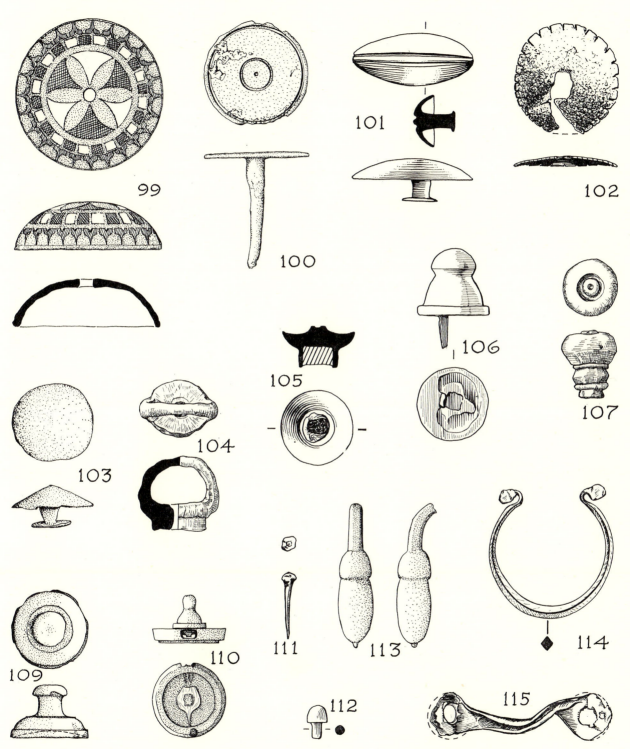

99

100

101

102

103

104

105

106

107

109

110

111

112

113

114

115

Fig. 38. Bronze objects 99–115 ($\frac{1}{1}$): for no. 108 see pl. XXXVIII*d*.

115. Small handle, very distorted, with perforations in flattened-out terminals. B IV 18J, A.D. 130–45. II C, Room 39.

116. Hollow rectangular handle, probably for key. There are traces of solder or lead inside. There is no moulding on the step of the handle adjacent to the loop, merely an incised line. B IV 18E, A.D. 130–45. II C, Room 45.

117. Lock-pin with circular head, notched within the sunken end, possibly for a stud or knob. B II 27B, A.D. 140–50. II C, Room 43. Cf. *O.R.L.* 32, *Zugmantel*, Taf. XIII, no. 71.

118. Smaller lock-pin with circular head. B III 8A, A.D. 150–155/160. II D, Room 43. Cf. *O.R.L.* 32, *Zugmantel*, Taf. XIII, no. 60.

119. Small lock-bolt. T VII 23, *c.* A.D. 130. II B, wall-trench 1/2.

120. Lock-plate with two circular perforations for attachment and rectangular opening for key between them. Z I 20, A.D. 105–15. II B, Room 6.

121. Solid object (? leg) of circular section except for square mouldings above the terminal knob and at the other end which has a circular socket. A IV 33, A.D. 85–105. II A, Room 7.

122. Hollow octagonal object, perhaps a handle, with perforation in one side. Depression in end is fitted with a small iron tube which extends down the inside. B I 55, A.D. 280–315. Occupation layer in cellar.

123. Rectangular plate with groove near one end and short thin tongue at other. Two shallow depressions on back presumably concerned with mounting. A IV 33, A.D. 85–105. II A, Room 7.

124. Harness clip with incised decoration on the hook and circular grooves around holes for studs in the plate. T VII 26, A.D. 105–15. II B, Room 4.
    A military type, published in *Arch. Journ.* cxv (1958), 91 and fig. 7, no. 202; cf. ibid., nos. 153, 180, 247, 262.

125. Harness-fitting, highly ornamented, providing junction for two leather straps, each of which was held in place by two rivets. A VII 33, A.D. 105–15. II B, Room 26.

126. Terret with notched decoration (now scarcely visible) on the rectangular loop. A XII 6, from robber-trench. Cf. *Richborough IV*, 130 and pl. XXXVI, no. 124.

127. Harness ring, broken, with a loop beneath protective masking. A scar on one end of the latter is perhaps only local damage. B V 7, A.D. 155/160. II D, Rooms 41–8.

128. Hook with a loop at one end; two facets towards the point facilitate penetration. Perhaps from a steelyard. T III 32, A.D. 49–60. I, Room 2.

129. Mouth-piece and part of tube of a wind-instrument. Tube has punched decoration in spiral fashion. B III 18, *c.* A.D. 150. II D, Room 31, make-up. Cf. F. Behn, *Musikleben im Altertum und frühen Mittelalter* (Stuttgart, 1954), Taf. 79, Abb. 181, nr. 8.

130. Escutcheon for bowl *c.* 11 cm. in diameter. Suspension-hole somewhat worn by handle. B XIII 5. III, make-up XIV, 6 Room 2 (Antonine fire, disturbed).

131. Small escutcheon. Wear on loop suggests that it was set at a considerable angle to the rim of the vessel. B IV 17B, A.D. 140–50. II C, Room 44.

132. Escutcheon for bucket, with broad triangular attachment plate. B III 19, *c.* A.D. 150. II D, Room 31, make-up. Cf. *O.R.L.* 32, *Zugmantel*, p. 93, fig. 13.

133. Dolphin, probably decoration for the handle of a vessel, attached at the nose and by a groove in the body, which curled around a rod-shaped stem. B I 31D, A.D. 140–50. II C, Room 28. Cf. Wheeler, *Verulamium*, p. 212 and fig. 46, no. 57.

134. Crudely made dolphin, tail broken off, with cylindrical socket behind projecting flange on the snout for attachment to another object. B I 9, A.D. 310–15. III, cellar filling.

135. Dolphin, probably part of handle of vessel, being attached by hollowed snout and body and by flattened underside of tail. Eyes and sides have inlaid blue enamel as indicated by shading, but the rings around the eyes and alternate patches on flanks are now devoid of enamel and show no

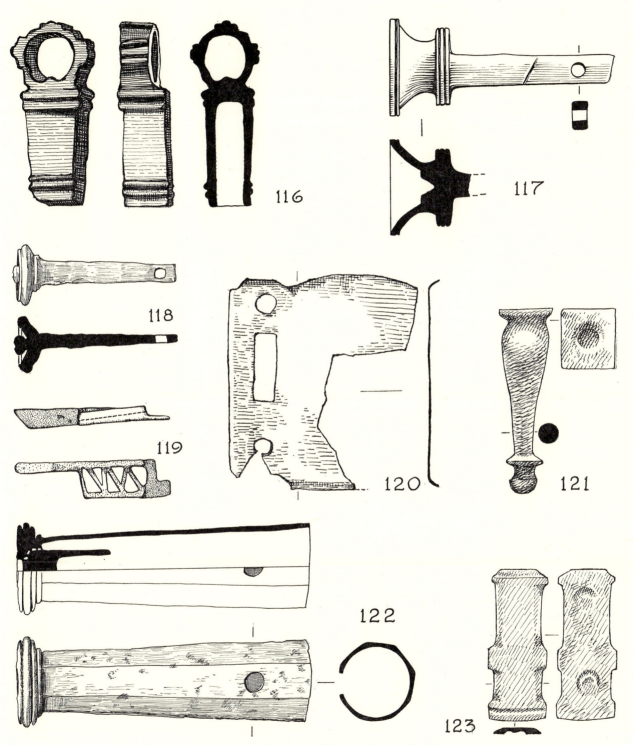

FIG. 39. Bronze objects 116–23 ($\frac{1}{1}$).

trace of having had it. B I Pit 20, A.D. 300–15. Box under cellar stairs. Cf. dolphins on the Amble-teuse vessel in F. Henry, 'Émailleurs d'Occident', *Préhistoire*, ii (1933), fig. 45, no. 1.

136. Handle of jug, circular in section, with flattened plate for attachment to body of vessel on which traces of solder survive. There are remains of another plate at the other end of the handle, which is extremely corroded, for attachment to the rim. B I 55, A.D. 280–315. III, occupation layer in cellar.

137. Handle of jug, probably of type with trefoil mouth, *c.* 16 cm. diameter at the lip, with female head resting on the rim between two projections. Over the head is a leaf-shaped moulding with incised line and circle decoration; a similar leaf, rather damaged, forms the terminal which was attached to the body of the vessel. There are traces of a lightly incised curvilinear design on the back of the handle. A I 20, A.D. 130–40. II C, Room 24. Cf. M. H. P. den Boesterd, *The Bronze Vessels* (Nijmegen 1956), nos. 232–9. Probably South Italian, first or early second century.

138. Fragment of base of *patera*, with raised concentric mouldings. Traces probably of tinning remain on the inner surface. B IV 34, *c.* A.D. 75. II A, Room 23, make-up.

139. Jug, only fragments in extremely corroded state remaining, of turned thin bronze sheet with folding and thickening at the footring and with a slight thickening around the rim. Handle is composed of two sheets, one forming ribbing along the outer surface, the other splayed at the ends inside the vessel to hold the handle in place. B I 55, A.D. 280–315. III, occupation layer in cellar. Cf. M. H. P. den Boesterd, *The Bronze Vessels* (Nijmegen 1956), no. 295, and the parallels there cited, especially *O.R.L.* 15, *Dambach*, Taf. 4, nos. 6 and 8. In the main this seems to be a third-century type.

140. (With pl. XXXVIII*e*.) Mask of an old man with a leafy fillet around his bald head and rather pointed ears, clearly Silenus. Probably once attached as a decorative mount to a vessel since traces of solder remain at the back. B I Pit 20, A.D. 300–15. III, box under cellar stairs.

141. Hollow cylindrical mount with lion's head terminal, cast in one piece. Lion's eyes well modelled, but other features rather crude. Inner end of mount is of irregular form. There is a crude per-foration at this end of the mount, perhaps used for attachment. V XXXII 1. Unstratified dark soil south-west of XIV, 1.

142. (With pl. XXXVIII, *f–i*.) Spout in the form of a fine, naturalistically modelled bull's head with open mouth. The head emerges from a circular mount decorated with an inlaid pattern of ivy leaves in niello (but some of inlay is now returned to silver). The decoration above the head is partly destroyed by a large secondary rectangular notch. B I Pit 20, A.D. 300–15. III, box under cellar stairs.

143. (With pl. XXXIX.) Turned, pear-shaped jug with heavy footring and decorative grooves around neck. The handle, soldered on, is divided at three points and is decorated with stylized leaf motifs. A stylized bovine head, with piercings forming the eyes, forms the attachment to the rim. B I Pit 20, A.D. 300–15. III, box under cellar stairs.

144. Thin cruciform plate with arms which expand irregularly towards the ends. One broken off. B II 17, A.D. 150–155/160. II D, Room 42.

145. Oval plate with central boss, now broken, and four holes for attachment. Presumably decorative, possibly for a box. B I Pit 1. Late Roman. Mouth of Pit 1.

146. Crudely shaped, slightly convex oval plate with carelessly incised lines around border and traces of lines radiating from punch-marks at centre. B II 13. III, make-up, XIV, 5 Room 4 (Antonine fire, disturbed).

147. Decorative mount, with eagle's head modelled in relief at one end of bar which carries four small loops for its attachment and palmette in relief at the other. The rear side of the bar is plain and was fixed to another object, beyond which the eagle's head projected. T XX 31, *c.* A.D. 60. I, Room 8, fuel-pit. (*Note continued on p. 138.*)

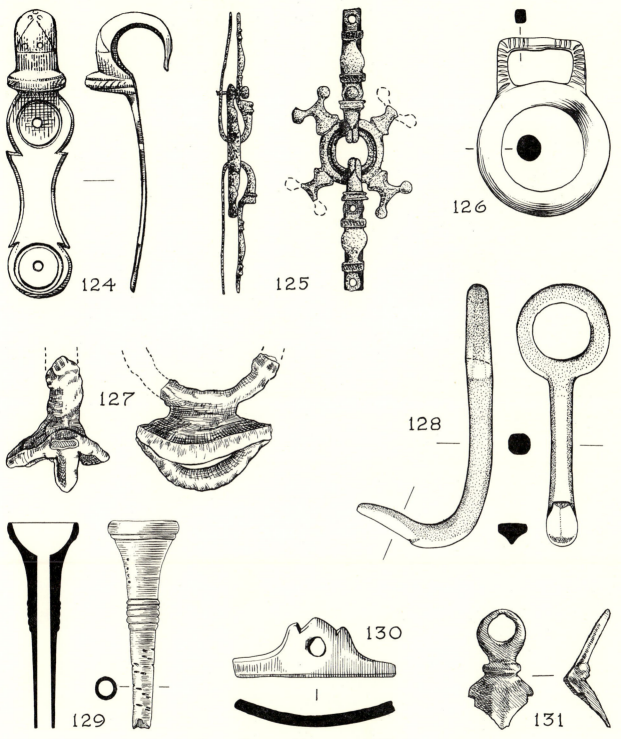

124 125 126 127 128 129 130 131

FIG. 40. Bronze objects 124–31 ($\frac{1}{1}$).

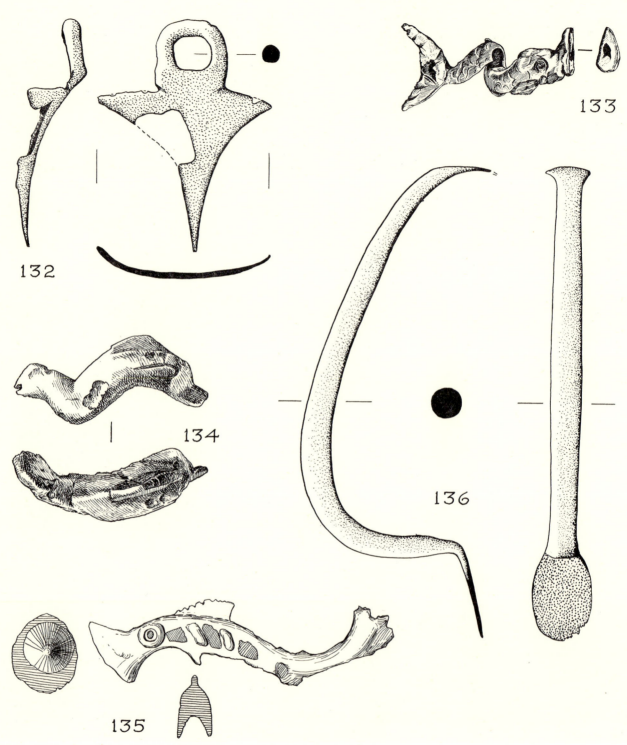

Fig. 41. Bronze objects 132–6 ($\frac{1}{1}$).

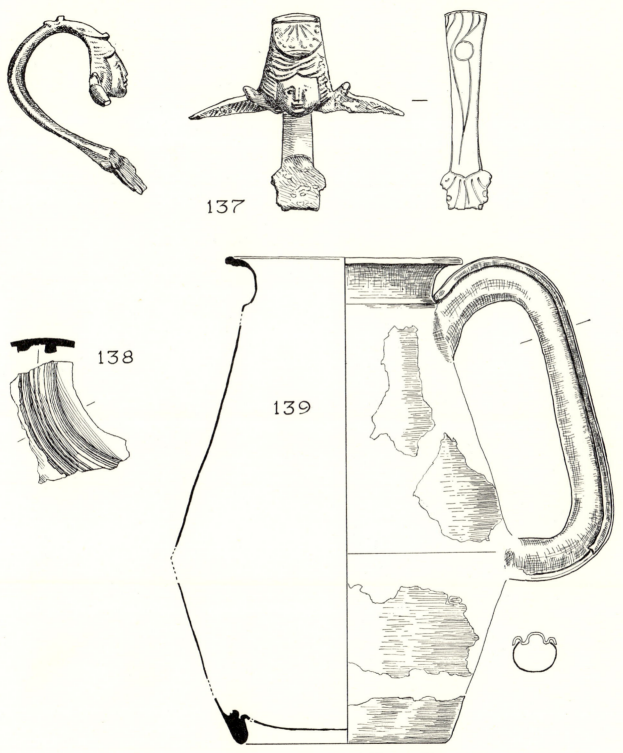

FIG. 42. Bronze objects 137–8 ($\frac{1}{1}$), 139 ($\frac{1}{2}$).

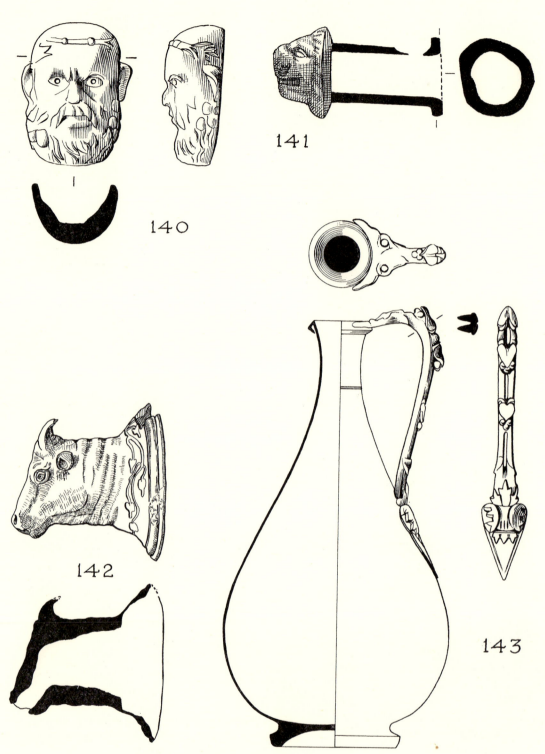

140

141

142

143

FIG. 43. Bronze objects 140–2 ($\frac{1}{1}$), 143 ($\frac{1}{2}$): for nos. 140, 142, and 143 see also pls. XXXVIII, XXXIX.

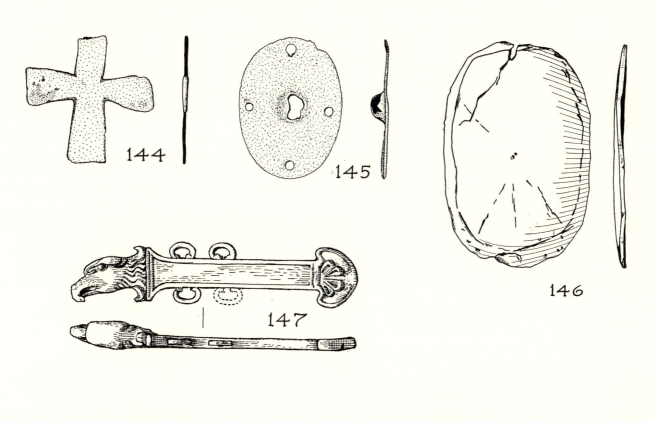

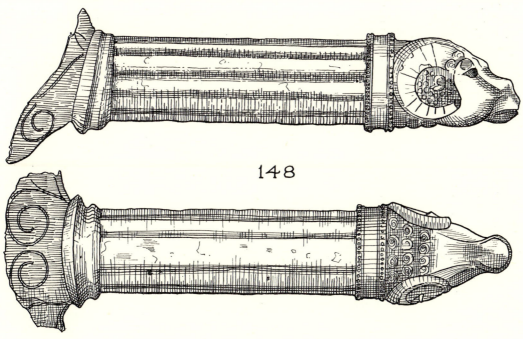

FIG. 44. Bronze objects 144–8 ($\frac{1}{1}$).

We are indebted to Professor H. von Petrikovits for the recognition of this as the model of a *parazonium*. This, as is made clear by Martial xiv, 32:

> *Militiae decus hoc gratique erit omen honoris*
> *arma tribunicium cingere digna latus,*

was a sword of honour worn by tribunes (and more senior officers). Cf. the Prima Porta statue of Augustus (H. Kähler, *Die Augustus-Statue von Primaporta* (Köln, 1959), Taf. 18, and the weapons with eagle-pommels worn by the two porphyry tetrarchs now on St. Mark's, Venice (R. Delbrück, *Antike Porphyrwerke* (Berlin, 1932), Taf. 31; cf. *Berytus*, xiii 1959, pl. XXIII), and for an Etrusco-Roman example with ram's head pommel of the third century B.C. from Chiusi, see Panseri, *La Fabbricazione delle Lame di Acciaio*, Milan, 1957, 37 f. The model here was perhaps made for votive purposes: its early date is noteworthy. On miniature sword-models see K. Raddatz, *Saalburg Jahrbuch*, xii (1953), 60–5, and for parazonia see also R. Egger, 'Aus römischen Grabinschriften', *Sitzungsberichte der Österreichischen Akademie der Wiss.*, ph.-h. Kl. 252, Band 3, 1967, 22 f.

148. *Patera* handle with ram's head terminal. The fluted cylinder is hollow. Found during road-widening work on Bluehouse Hill. Unstratified.

149. (With pl. XL.) Handle of *patera*, filled with some material, with ram's head terminal. Mount for attachment to the vessel has incised curvilinear decoration which is asymmetrical about an axis along the length of the handle. B I 55, A.D. 280–315. Occupation layer in cellar.

    Paterae with handles of this type are of Italian manufacture and first-century date. Cf. M. H. P. den Boesterd, *The Bronze Vessels* (Nijmegen, 1956), no. 68.

150. Heavy plaque with inlaid green enamel leaf-and-crescent motifs separated from blue-enamel background by outlines in upstanding bronze. Central roundel is inlaid with silver-like metal. Notches form edge of design and there is a notch on reverse at approximate mid-point of long side. B I 32F, A.D. 115–30. II B, Room 23.

151. (With pl. XLIV*b*.) Plaque of moulded lead set on bronze backing, in turn supported by iron plate. Design of leaf and feather motifs may have been symmetrical about shorter axis, but the plaque is much corroded. A square plate or other fitting was apparently attached to the centre. The fronds at the side recall the decoration of a Corinthian capital; the central arch perhaps covers an *aedicula*; cf. also the plaque in form of an altar in British Museum (*Guide to the Antiquities of Roman Britain* (1964), p. 56, iv (c) 3 and pl. XXI). Perhaps a *patera* handle. B I 9, A.D. 310–15. III, cellar-filling.

152. Rectangular plate for wooden box lid, with inscribed concentric circles and central perforation to take a stud or boss. Plate was held in place by four pins soldered to the underside, which were flattened out over rectangular washers on the inner surface of the lid. Thickness of wooden lid *c.* 5 mm. B I 55, A.D. 280–315. Occupation layer in cellar.

153*a*. (With pl. XLI.) Approximately square plate for wooden box lid, with openwork border (apparently deliberately cut away on one side), incised concentric circles and a raised annular moulding. The centre is pierced for a stud and there are oblong perforations for mounting towards each corner.

153*b*. Binding for corner of this or a similar box, with openwork decoration along one edge for the front and perforation for attachment.

    Other fragments found with 153*a* and 153*b* include part of another raised annular moulding, perhaps decorating the box in the same way as the end-plate on the casket from Dunapentele in Hungary (*Richborough IV*, pl. XLVIII). B I Pit 20, A.D. 280–315. III, box under cellar stairs.

154. Thin decorative plate with central perforation for fixing. B II 7, fourth century. XIV, 5, wall-trench 2/5.

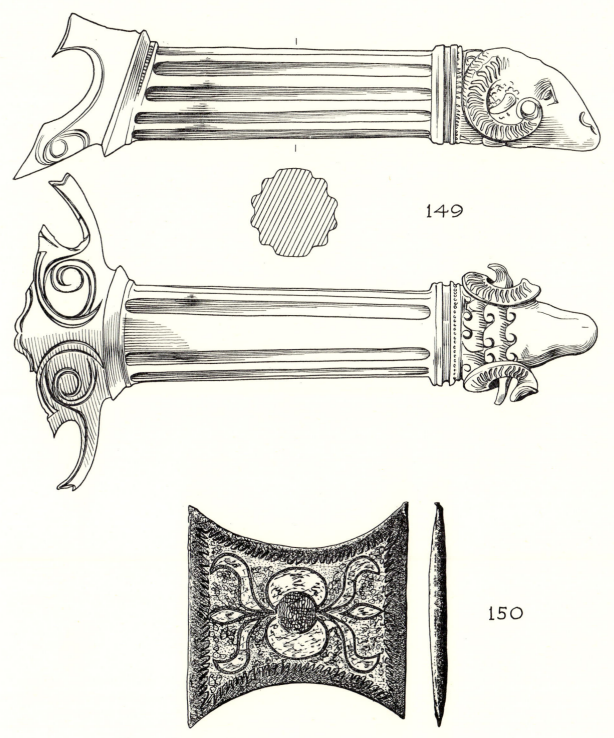

FIG. 45. Bronze objects 149–50 ($\frac{1}{1}$): for no. 149 see also pl. XL.

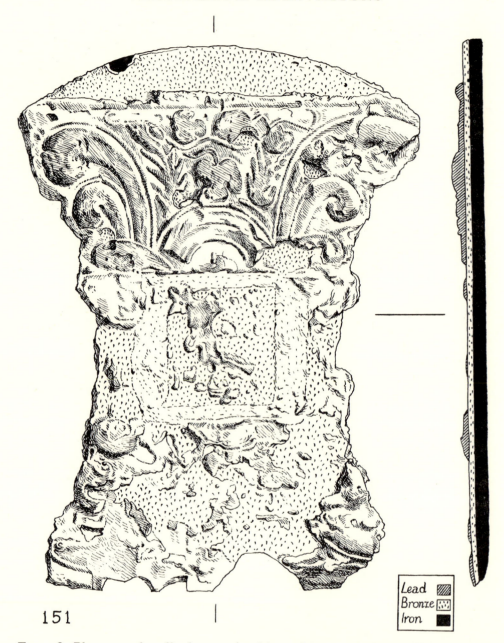

151

Lead
Bronze
Iron

FIG. 46. Plaque or handle (no. 151) of iron, bronze, and lead ($\frac{1}{1}$): see also
pl. XLIV*b*.

155. (Pls. XLII–XLIV*a*.) The Verulamium Venus, *c.* 20 cm. high, with a cloak knotted loosely
about the loins and streaming out behind on either side. In her left hand is an apple or pome-
granate cupped in leaves. Her hair is gathered into two bows on top of the head behind a diadem,
or perhaps more probably is bound by a chaplet of flowers; it is also brought back from the brow
over the ears and is gathered in a roll at the back of the head. A tress falls forward over either

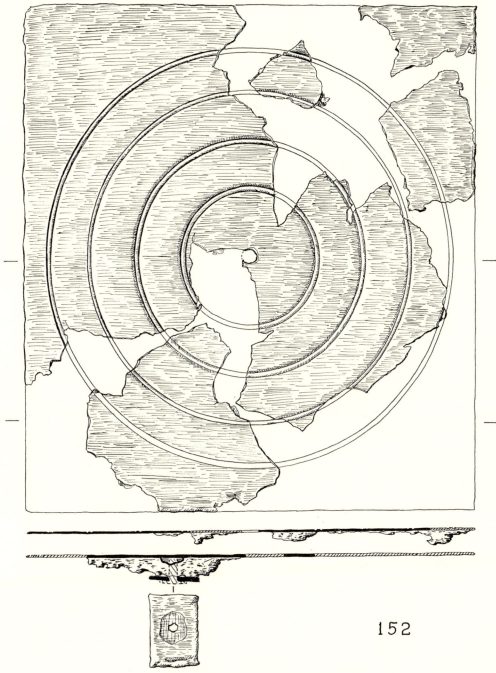

152

FIG. 47. Bronze lid-plate no. 152 ($\frac{1}{1}$).

shoulder. The eyes bear traces of silvering. The thumb of the right hand is restored. For a fuller discussion and references see J. M. C. Toynbee, *Art in Britain under the Romans* (Oxford, 1964), pp. 83–4, pl. XVIII, C, D. The closest parallels to this goddess come from Augst and Trier (see *Ur-Schweiz*, XXV (1961), 21–30, Abb. 13–16, 18). The near resemblance of these, especially the

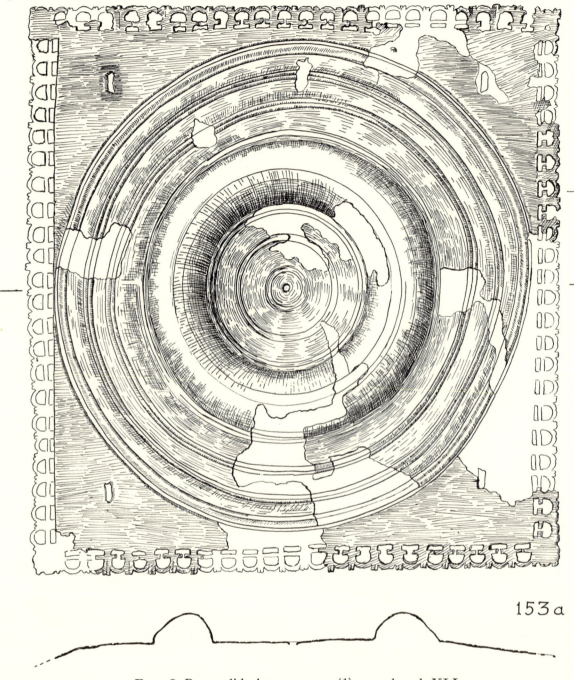

153a

FIG. 48. Bronze lid-plate no. 153a ($\frac{1}{2}$): see also pl. XLI.

Augst figure, indicates that the Venus is a close copy of some lost Hellenistic creation of the second or first century B.C.; cf. A. W. Lawrence, *Classical Sculpture* (London, 1929), pl. 145, and especially M. Bieber, *The Sculpture of the Hellenistic Age* (revised edition, New York, 1961), figs. 609, 610. The copies are likely, in Miss Toynbee's view, to be South Gaulish in origin and of the late first or

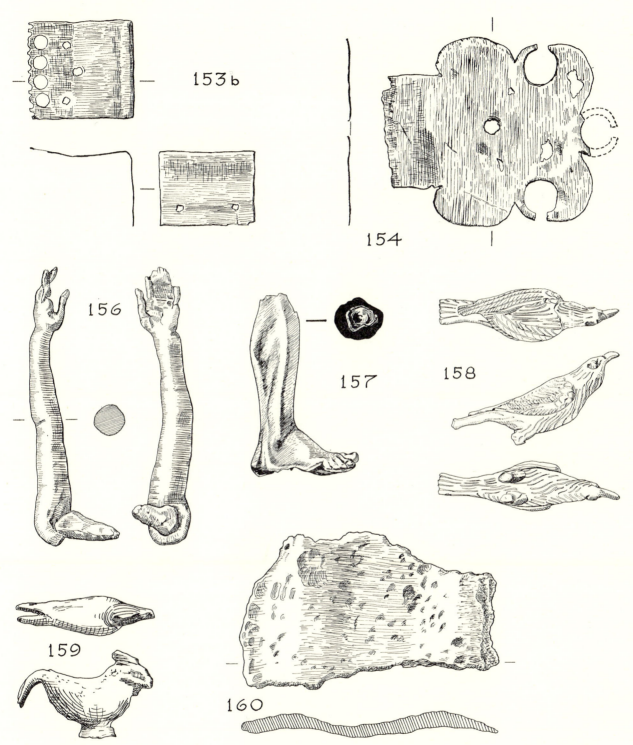

153b

154

156

157

158

159

160

FIG. 49. Bronze objects 153b–160 (all $\frac{1}{1}$ except no. 153b ($\frac{1}{2}$)): for no. 155 see pls. XLII–XLIVa.

second century in date. The presence of the Venus in this early fourth-century context may be due to the intention to reuse the metal. B I Pit 20, A.D. 300–15. III, box under cellar stairs.

156. Model arm and hand with a stout, roughly formed prong for attachment; part of a statuette or perhaps an individual votive object. Since the prong would not effectively retain the arm in position, and as there are slight traces of wear at the junction, this may be part of a moving or adjustable figure. B II 19, A.D. 270–80. III, packing behind cellar wall.

157. Small lower leg and foot, solid except for cavity where it is torn off below knee, perhaps result of faulty casting. Mounting socket in sole. Probably part of statuette rejected by maker. B II 19, A.D. 270–80. III, packing behind cellar wall.

158. Small eagle, well modelled and with plumage indicated by carefully incised lines. Legs and perhaps some of tail broken off. B II 26D, A.D. 150–155/160. II D, Room 36. For parallels see *J.R.S* vii (1917), 103; *Oxoniensia*, xiv (1949), 31.

159. Very crudely formed figure of a cock supported on a small circular stand. B I 22, A.D. 270–80. Make-up south-west of cellar.

160. Fragment of thick casting, perhaps part of drapery of statue broken up for scrap. T VI 28, A.D. 75–85. II A, Room 4. See p. 26.

161. Broken fragment of heavy sheet with relief-moulding at one edge. Possibly fragment of statue. B I 9, A.D. 310–15. Cellar filling. Cf. the fragment of decorated bronze drapery from a statue found outside the south gate, *Hertfordshire Archaeology*, i (1968), 49–50 and pl. 12*b*.

162. Handle with crude mouldings around it at two points of constriction. There are two lateral projections and traces of a third at the top, and a slight groove across the handle near this end. It may have been for a small mirror. A IV, unstratified.

163. Right-angled casting of almost semicircular section, presumably a protective binding-strip. Two attachment-perforations remain at corners and also an indentation for one which was not punched through. B II 19, A.D. 270–80. III, packing behind cellar wall.

164. Thin sheet with two square perforations and part of third. B I 9, A.D. 310–15. Cellar filling.

165*a, b, c.* Thin sheet bronze with perforated punched-dot patterns; (*a*) has a circle with enclosed dots, (*b*) an S-shape, and (*c*) a zigzag. (*b*) also has a line of larger perforations. There is no particular reason to regard this as epigraphic. B I 55, A.D. 280–315. Occupation layer in cellar.

166. Rod with broken-off bifurcation at one end; at other end it is bent over above series of mouldings, ending in knob terminal. Perhaps a medical instrument. A VI 33, A.D. 75–105. II A, Room 10.

167. Tube made of folded sheet, broken at one end. B I 9, A.D. 310–15. Cellar filling.

168. Hook-like object. The rod is flattened to a rectangular section at one end for insertion into another object, and is pierced at its mid-point. Flattened curved end has notch. B I 55, A.D. 280–315. Occupation layer in cellar.

169. Large iron pin or bolt with domed head surfaced with bronze sheet. B I 9, A.D. 310–15. Cellar filling.

170. (Pl. XLV*b*.) Scrap, including several fragments of sheet and a spherical lump, broken chain-link, small stud, three coiled flat strips, end of *ligula*, perforated flat strip. Small piece of slag found with these. B IV 29E, A.D. 75–105. II A, Room 20.

171. (Pl. XLV*c*.) Scrap, including two studs (one with a five-petal motif, perhaps originally enamelled); fragment of decorated strip, perhaps part of bracelet; small curved and tapering mount with two transverse mouldings, concave at back; three fragmentary plates with perforations; possible chain-link; number of small scraps of sheet strip and rod, and three amorphous fragments. Scraps of charcoal and bone were also found. T VI 25, A.D. 105–15. II B, Room 4.

172. (Pl. XLV*a*.) Tightly folded bundle of scrap composed of strips of bronze. On surface is tiny piece of gold sheet, which shows as white triangle on photograph. B XIV 10, A.D. 155/160. II D, wall-trench 25/50.

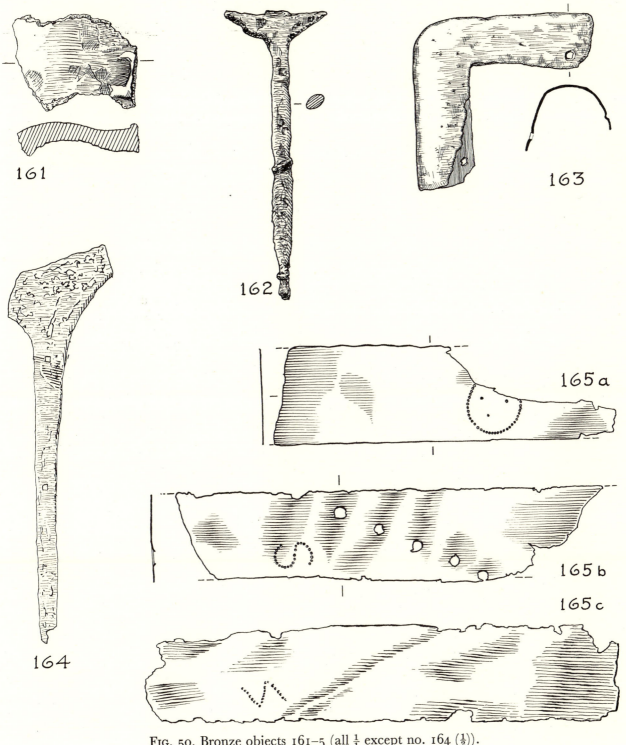

161

162

163

164

165a

165b

165c

FIG. 50. Bronze objects 161–5 (all ½ except no. 164 (⅓)).

C. Object of Speculum

173. Fragment of mirror, diameter *c.* 22 cm., with inscribed concentric lines near edge on both sides. A I 23, A.D. 130–40. II C, Room 23.

D. Objects of Lead

174. Folded bar of lead with pitting, and burring at end, caused by fairly sharp tools, presumably including the one used to fold the bar. B I 31D, A.D. 140–50. II C, Room 28.
175. Fragment of thick sheet, much corroded, with three triangular impressions stamped at one end. A XII 27C, A.D. 75–85. II A, Room 9, in association with a bronze-worker's catchment box (p. 18).
176. Fragment of sheet with three rough square holes along one edge. It has been partly cut and partly torn from some object. B VII 4, A.D. 155/160. II D, Room 52.
177. Ragged fragment of moulding attached to heavy backing plate, which is rectangular and flat at the back although its edges are irregular. B VIII, unstratified.
178. Crude bolt-like object with roughly domed head and flattened, splayed end to the bent shaft. Presumably intended for use in building construction. A II 26, A.D. 130–50. II C, Room 22.
179. Cone-headed pin with shaft which is bent and twisted, the tip broken off. A VII, *c.* A.D. 130. II C, wall-trench 3/10.
180. Broken plate with large oval perforation, decorated by short raised lines at right angles to edges which are defined by continuous raised line parallel to them. Four raised dots within angles. Reverse is plain. B I 9, A.D. 310–15. III, cellar filling.
181. Large flat sheet of hexagonal form, apparently formed in a mould—the underside is rough and the upper smoother where not corroded. At one corner is series of four lines scored parallel to the short side of the sheet. B I Pit 7, A.D. 60–75. Pit 7.
182. Heavy folded sheet, crudely chopped and torn at one end, sawn at the other, and chopped along meeting edges. Perhaps off-cut from preparation of lead pipe. B I 19, A.D. 280–315. Occupation layer in cellar.
183. Much-damaged thin sheet which was formed into a dome shape. Perforation with torn edges at apex probably held mount of harder metal which has been torn out. B I 31D, A.D. 140–50. Ibid.
184. (Pls. XLVI–XLVIIa.) Two fragments of a large, irregular shallow cake of lead, formed by pouring molten metal into shallow depression in ground or base of circular container. Centre of top side is pitted and corroded. Around edges are a large number of random and overlapping impressions made by circular stamp with device having eight radial 'spokes' and a dot at the end of and between each one. Reverse of one part of edge has plain circular depressions, fewer and not corresponding to the obverse impressions. Diameter *c.* 20–25 cm., thickness up to *c.* 1·5 cm. A IV 10, A.D. 155/160. II D, wall-trench 36/37.
185. (Pl. XLVIIb.) Twelve from a series of blank discs, of diameters from 1·5 to 2·1 cm.; about ten broken or damaged, and 100 in good condition. These were examined by Dr. Colin Kraay at the Ashmolean Museum, Oxford. Weights varied between 1·7 and 9·1 gm., although all but eleven discs weighed between 2·9 and 5·9 gm. Breaking these down into 0·5-gm. groups, the following results were obtained:

5·5–6·0 gm.	11 discs
5·0–5·5 gm.	18 discs
4·5–5·0 gm.	18 discs
4·0–4·5 gm.	18 discs
3·5–4·0 gm.	11 discs
3·0–3·5 gm.	8 discs

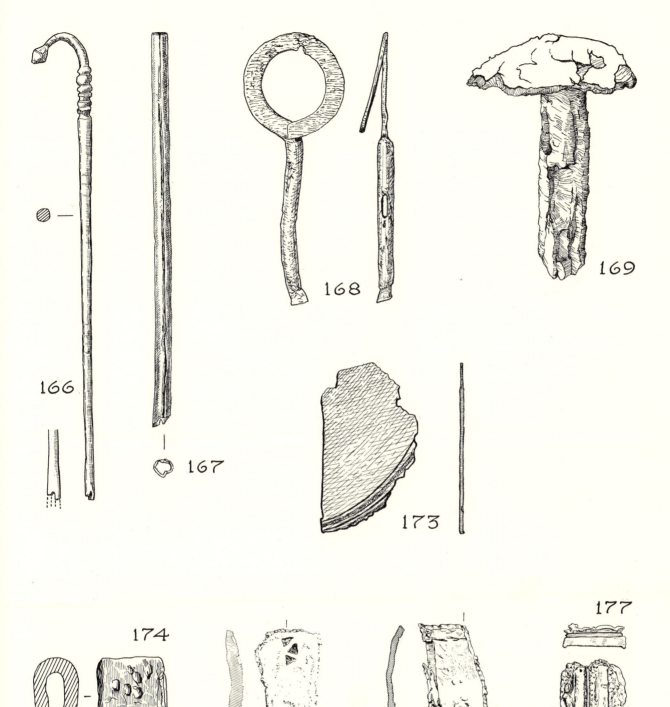

FIG. 51. Objects of bronze (166–9) ($\frac{1}{1}$), speculum (173) ($\frac{1}{2}$), and lead (174–7) ($\frac{1}{2}$): for nos. 170–2 see pl. XLV.

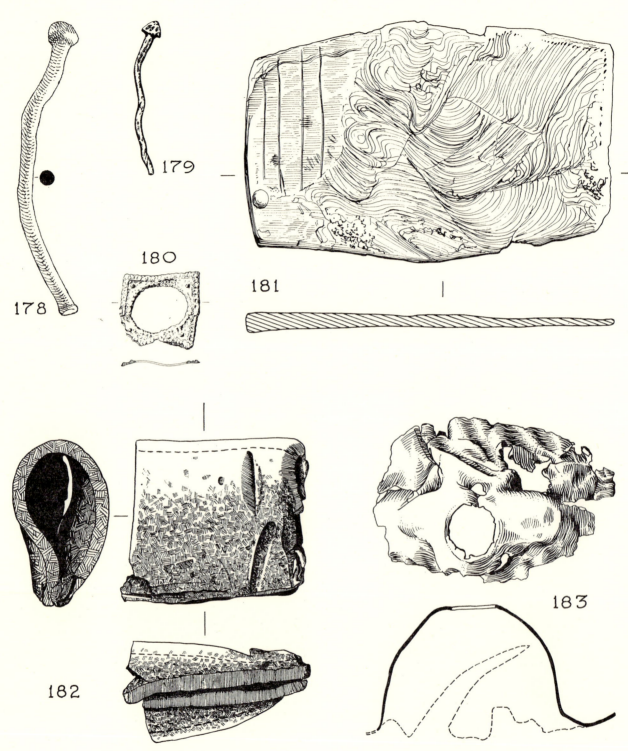

FIG. 52. Lead objects 178–83 (½): for nos. 184–5 see pls. XLVI–XLVIIb.

Dr. Kraay writes: 'I think this is too wide a spread to have much meaning in terms of coinage, so that I suppose these discs had some other purpose.' A V 10, A.D. 155/160. II D, Room 15 (see p. 78).

E. Objects of Bone

Hinges, nos. 186–92.

The purpose of the perforated bone cylinders of the type shown at nos. 186–92 was long in question. They were often suggested to be parts of bone flutes, or, vaguely, 'toggles'. These misconceptions were dispersed by the paper 'Römische Scharnierbänder aus Bein' by Fritz Fremersdorf in *Vjesnika Hravat-skoga Arheološkoga Društva* (Hoffillerov Zbornik), N.S., vols. xviii–xxi (1937–40), pp. 321–37 (Zagreb, 1940). Fremersdorf describes examples found at Vindonissa which still held wooden plugs[1] (Fremers-dorf, p. 326, Abb. 6, 7) and which were identified as hinges by comparison with, for example, the cast of a wooden cupboard with bone hinges at Pompeii, and with wooden examples from Egypt (Fremers-dorf, p. 327, Abb. 8, 9 and p. 332, Abb. 17, 18).

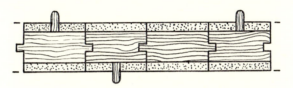

FIG. 53. Diagram to illustrate working of bone hinge (*drawn by R. Goodburn*).

The hinges were made and worked in the following manner (fig. 53), which can be best understood by a study of pl. XLIX, illustrating boxes from the Fayûm, Egypt, now in the Ashmolean Museum, Oxford (1896–1908, E3701). A fairly stout long-bone was turned on a lathe to produce a smooth-surfaced cylinder, which was often decorated with grooves. A cylinder of required length was then sawn from the bone and one, two, or three small holes (depending on the length) were bored through one side of the bone. The centre of the bone was then plugged with a cylinder of wood conforming to the internal cavity of the bone. The ends of this wooden cylinder were trimmed plane with the bone in such a manner as to leave a small projecting spindle or corresponding hollowed well. A number of such units could thus be fitted together to produce cylinders which were able to rotate about the same axis but in different senses (fig. 53). The holes in the cylinder walls were fitted with small wooden pegs; the pegs of alternate cylinders corresponded to holes bored in the edge of the box or cupboard, the rest to holes bored in the lid or door. Thus assembly was carried out by fitting together the cylinders end to end and carefully fixing the pegs of alternate cylinders into the box. The lid could then be fitted on to the remain-ing projecting pegs. Where great strength was not required, a smaller number of pegs could be used; and this explains the existence of spacers, such as no. 192.

An unusual type of cylinder is that represented by no. 191, which is turned from solid bone, only the side pegs being separate parts. This corresponds to the type of hinge employed in small boxes in the Fayûm.

Fremersdorf's paper gives more general information than is necessary or possible to repeat here, describing the use of long decorated pegs in the construction of offset doors and showing examples of

[1] See also Elisabeth Schmid in *Provincialia, Festschrift für Rudolf Laur-Belart* (Basel, 1968), 185 ff., especially Abb. 3.

decorated terminals used to plug the ends of the final bone components of a hinge set. No evidence for these was found at Verulamium.

The photographs of the Fayûm boxes were provided by the Ashmolean Museum. Generous assistance in the production of this note was given by Mr. P. D. C. Brown and Dr. P. R. S. Moorey of the Ashmolean Museum.

186. Hinge turned from a long-bone, with three grooves around either end and two symmetrically placed perforations in the side. B XV 4, A.D. 150–155/160. II D, Room 55, occupation on floor.

187. Fragments of a hinge with two sets of slight grooves which are cut by the perforations; the drill which made these cut into the opposite wall. In one case the scar is deep and oblique, indicating that the bone moved and fragmented during manufacture. It also indicates that the drill being used was high-speed, perhaps worked by a treadle. B XV 3, A.D. 155/160. II D, Room 55, Antonine fire debris.

188. Hinge with one perforation and corresponding slight scar in opposite wall. B XV 4, as no. 186.

189. Hinge with three slight grooves around one end and two perforations, asymmetrically placed. One end is roughly trimmed, and with the splits perhaps indicates reuse. B XII 7, A.D. 270–300+. III, make-up of XIV, 6 Room 1.

190. Hinge with one perforation and with polished surfaces. T XX 12, A.D. 145–50. II C, Room 9.

191. Small hinge turned from wall of thick bone. The hole drilled in the side just perforates the opposite side. Hinge turns upon little spindles, the end of one sawn flat, the other snapped at a turned groove. B IV 29D, A.D. 75–105. II A, Room 22.

192. Turned cylinder with ridged decoration and polished surface One end is sawn flat and preserves working-marks; other is smooth and much abraded. Probably hinge spacer. B I 30C, A.D. 150–155/160. II D, Room 33, floor.

193. Plaque with two rounded and two sawn edges. Decorated with five incised double-ring and dot motifs. B I 28B, A.D. 140–50. II C, Room 35.

194. Triangular plaque with one narrow and one broad groove incised parallel to two sides, and a narrow groove incised parallel to the base. Working marks present on all surfaces. T III 23, A.D. 105–15. II B, Room 1.

195. Part of bobbin-shaped object (no axial hole) with groove around either end. B IV 9B, A.D. 150–155/160. II D, Room 42.

196. Tapering rod with decorative mouldings at head and a flat broader end with traces of iron corrosion upon it. B I 45, A.D. 85–105. II A, accumulation outside Room 17.

197. Needle with plain head, double eye, and broken off above the point. B IV 7, A.D. 150–155/160. II D, Room 40.

198. Needle, with flat head and double eye, broken at both ends. Head decorated with pairs of grooves and notches along the edges. B IV 3, A.D. 155/160. II D, Rooms 38–42, general burnt deposit.

199. Pin with three grooves below rather pointed head. It is slightly curved. Z I 16, A.D. 135–45. II C, Room 8.

200. Pin, broken above point, with series of decorative grooves and oblique notches on head. B IV 17J, A.D. 145–50. II C, Room 39.

201. Pin with plain shaft, tip broken, and head formed of pierced button-like disc fitted on to the shaft. B I 8, A.D. 360–70. III, secondary make-up of cellar filling.

202. Pierced bone disc, possibly pin-head, with three inscribed concentric grooves on upper surface; highly polished. A II 17, A.D. 150–155/160. II D, Room 22, occupation on floor.

203. Triangular plate with three notches in each side, one perforation in the apex and four along the base; perhaps used for tablet-weaving. B XI, plough-soil.

204. Plain triangular plate, of equilateral form with hole near each rounded apex. Used for tablet-weaving of braids. B II 10, A.D. 360–70. III, secondary make-up of cellar filling.

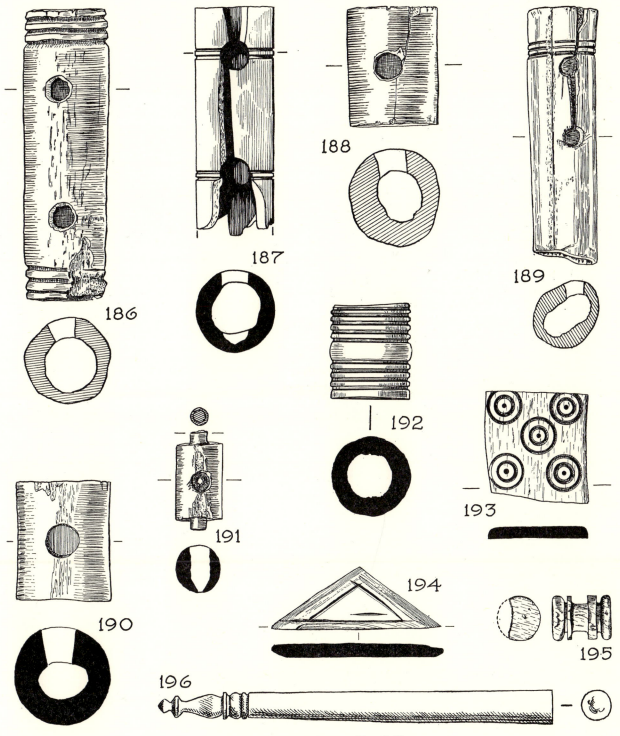

FIG. 54. Bone objects 186–96 ($\frac{1}{1}$).

205. Tooth, the median incisor of small ruminant, probably a small cow,[1] with holes drilled through the root in two places, parallel to the cutting-edge. B IV 17D, A.D. 145–50. II C, Room 45.

206. Spoon. Where the broken handle meets the circular bowl there is a groove forming a V with its apex near base of bowl. B I 12, A.D. 315–60. III, accumulation over south-east wall of cellar.

207. Polished grooved plate for knife-handle which was attached to a similar plate by three bronze rivets. Thickness of plate has been considerably reduced near blade; the rather irregular, less polished finish of this may indicate secondary working. B I 63, A.D. 60–75. Pit 7.

208. Knife-handle formed from two plates with chamfering towards blade and on main edges. End of blade is held in place by iron rivets, with incised circles around each one. T XX 18, A.D. 110–20. II B, Room 7.

209. Knife-handle, polished and simply decorated at the terminal, and sawn to take the iron blade. This is fixed by two iron rivets which also hold in place a decorative bronze mount on either side of the handle. T XXI 21, from robber-trench. Cf. *Richborough IV*, p. 148, no. 224, and pl. LIV, dated to before *c*. A.D. 85.

210. (with pl. XLVIIIa). Finely carved and polished dolphin made from thick wall of a bone. Reverse is fairly flat and there is a drilled oval vertical hole through the body. V XXXIII 3. Late pit south-west of XIV, 2.

211. Die with irregular faces marked with groups of irregularly placed ring-and-dot markings numbering from one to six. Numbers on opposing surfaces add up to seven. B IV 21A, A.D. 105–15. II B, Room 26.

212. Small oval counter with large shallow depression in one side and three pits gouged out of the other. A IV 2, A.D. 155/160. II D, Room 18.

213. Counter similar to 215 but highly polished. Scratches on base seem to include letter M and the numeral VIIII. B I Pit 4, late Roman. Mouth of Pit 4.

214. Small polished counter with incised concentric grooves and central dot in upper surface and faint scratches on base. B I 31D, A.D. 140–50. II C, Room 28.

215. Counter with depression and small central pit in upper surfaces and series of intersecting scratches on base. A IV, unstratified.

F. Objects of Jet

216. Part of bracelet with notches around outer edge of each flat side, producing zigzag effect along edge. B V 2, from robber-trench.

217. Part of bracelet with shallow corresponding notches in each flat side, and below these a band of continuous incised squares. A IV, unstratified.

218. Part of possibly octagonal bracelet with faceted outer edge decorated with a pair of grooves. B I 55, A.D. 280–315. III, occupation layer in cellar.

G. Objects of Shale

219. Part of small bracelet with three grooves bounding two running sets of transverse notches along outer surface. B I 8, A.D. 360–70. III, secondary make-up of cellar filling.

220. Part of rather crudely worked bracelet of varying thickness between two flat sides which have notches along their outer edges. B III 5A, A.D. 350–410+. Dark soil on mosaic, XIV, 5 Room 3.

221. Fragment of fine polished bracelet of ovoid section. B I 9, A.D. 310–15. III, cellar filling.

[1] Kindly identified by Dr. I. W. Cornwall.

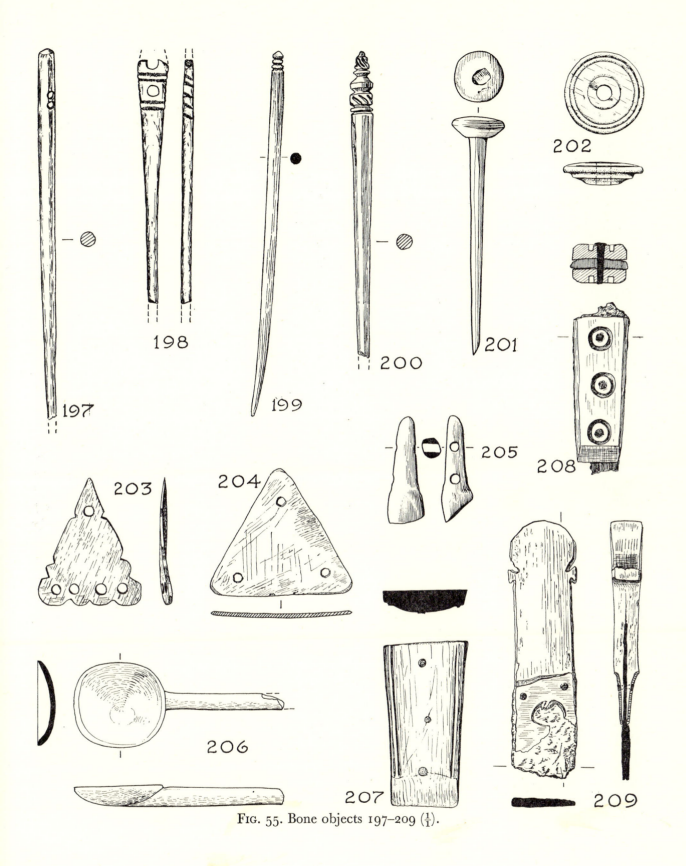

197 198 199 200 201 202 203 204 205 206 207 208 209

FIG. 55. Bone objects 197–209 ($\frac{1}{1}$).

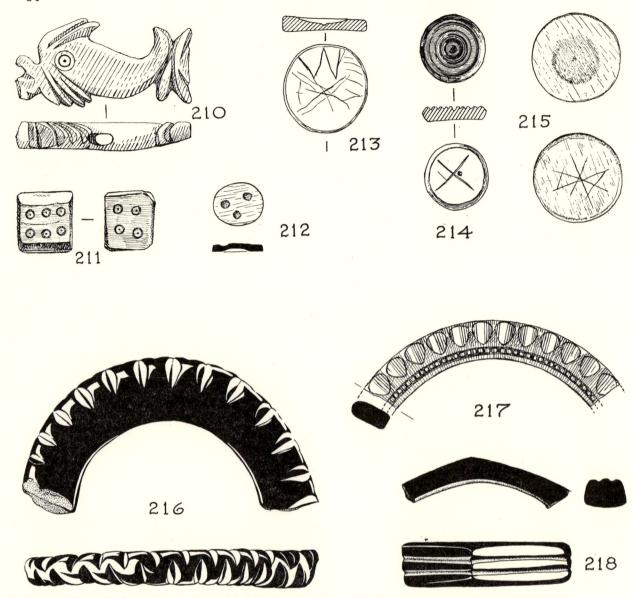

FIG. 56. Bone (210–15) and jet (216–18) objects ($\frac{1}{1}$): for no. 210 see also pl. XLVIIIa.

222. Part of bracelet with two internal facets and rounded exterior. B II 12, A.D. 280–90. III, packing behind cellar wall.

223. Fragment of plain bracelet. B II 10, A.D. 360–70. III, secondary make-up of cellar filling.

224. Fragment of fine bracelet with rounded external section and two internal facets. B I 5, unstratified.

225. Complete bracelet, fractured at one point, with one large and one small internal facet. Outer section rounded. B I Pit 20, A.D. 310–15. III, box under cellar stairs.

226. Discoidal bead with two parallel perforations. Upper surface has shallow groove around raised boss. Tiny central pit in each surface. B II 12, A.D. 280–90. III, packing behind cellar wall.

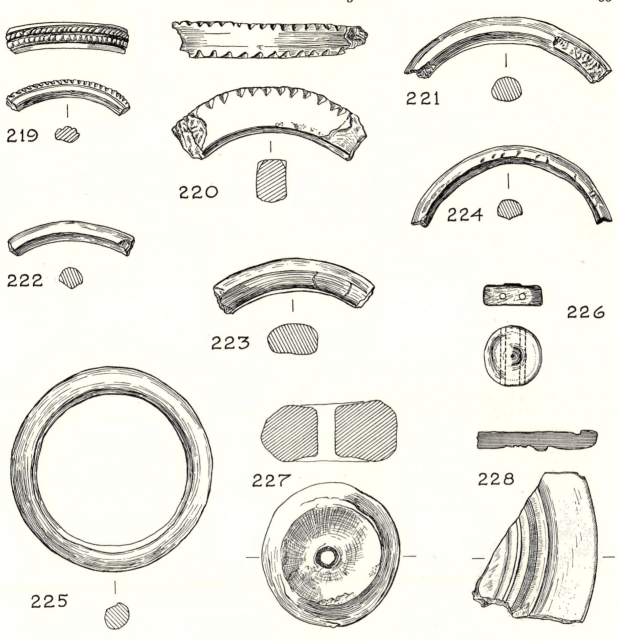

FIG. 57. Shale objects 219–28 ($\frac{1}{1}$).

227. Apparently a spindle-whorl with roughly rounded edges. Thickness varies greatly along one diameter and so the whorl would be unstable in use. Except for the drilled central hole one would see it as a waste-core. B IV 5, from robber-trench.

228. Fragment of turned vessel. Footring defined by two of several concentric grooves on base. Trace of broken-off wall remains. Diameter *c.* 10 cm. B V Pit 2, A.D. 350–410+. Pit 22.

H. Objects of Stone

Grateful acknowledgements are made to Miss H. A. Macdonald and Mr. R. W. Sanderson of the Institute of Geological Sciences, London, for the identifications of most of the stones in this section.

229. Fragments of palette with bevelled edges, composed of a metamorphosed mudstone to which Mr. Sanderson cannot assign a place of origin. B IV 20E, A.D. 115–30. II B, Room 33, secondary floor.

230. (unfigured). Roughly rectangular slab of Purbeck marble, c. 9 by 11 by 1·7 cm. thick. Sides flat, one with very slight groove, but not polished; very slight tooling marks remain. A VI, unstratified.

231. (unfigured). Edge fragment of Purbeck marble slab c. 3·8 to 4·1 cm. thick. One side rough, one polished, and edge smoothed but bearing transverse tooling marks. The angles are rounded. B I 22, A.D. 270–80. III, make-up south-west of cellar.

232. (Pl. XLVIIIb.) One of a number of Purbeck marble slabs of rectangular shape, this one being c. 19·4 by 26·0, by 2·3 to 3·0 cm. thick. The upper surface is smooth and is concave about both major axes. Edges and base are irregular, but the prominences on the base are rather worn. Perhaps the slab was not fixed and was used for mixing or grinding, the to-and-fro motions having produced wear on the base. A IV 12, A.D. 150–155/160. II D, Room 17.

233. (unfigured). Fragment of grey marble similar to Carrara marble. It is 1·8 to 2·1 cm. thick and has two abraded and rounded edges, 8 and 11 cm. long, forming an approximate right angle. One broken edge is fairly straight and the fragment may be mason's waste, perhaps from the Forum. B IV 18B, A.D. 130–40. II C, Room 44, primary floor.

234. (unfigured). Triangular fragment of similar type to above. One edge is abraded and rounded (c. 15 cm.) and two are fairly straight but broken (originally both c. 13 cm.). B II 27B, A.D. 140–50. II C, Room 43.

235. Triangular fragment of Purbeck marble. The broad faces are fairly smooth and regular, one having an upstanding border; thickness is 2·7 cm. generally, and c. 3·3 cm on border. B II Pit 5, late Roman. Mouth of Pit 4.

236. Part of moulding, probably for cornice, of Purbeck marble. There is a hole for the fixing dowel. B V Pit 2A, later fourth century. Pit 22.

237. Large fragment (maximum dimension c. 25 cm.) of oolitic limestone similar to Combe Down type, which is part of torus moulding of column base of diameter c. 84 cm. Above the convex moulding is a roughly flat facet at an angle to the moulding. B I 38, A.D. 85–105. II A, accumulation outside (south-west of) Room 17.

238. (unfigured). Regular rectangular block of slate, 26·1 by 15·1 by c. 3·4 cm. thick, similar to type found in Charnwood Forest area of Leicestershire. One larger face is smooth and slightly concave about a lateral axis and the other is covered by regular sharp tool-marks; the edges appear to be sawn square. It was doubtless a whetstone. A I 9, A.D. 150–155/160. II D, Room 24. See also no. 243.

239. (unfigured). Roughly rectangular block, 20 to 23 cm. long and used as a whetstone, of fine-grained limestone reported to be similar to that found near Upton in Somerset. One broader side (c. 7 cm. thick) and one narrower side (c. 4·5 cm. thick) are smooth although slightly irregular. Other sides, and ends, are rough and irregular. A IV 11, A.D. 155/160. II D, Room 15.

240. (unfigured). Very roughly rectangular block, c. 25 by c. 10 by c. 2·5 cm., with one slightly concave broad surface used as a whetstone. It is a Lower Lias limestone, reported to be similar to that found near Somerton, Somerset. A VI 33, A.D. 75–105. II A, Room 10.

241. (unfigured). Fragment, c. 8 by c. 7 cm., of flat whetstone 1·5 to 1·9 cm. thick. Used on both sides,

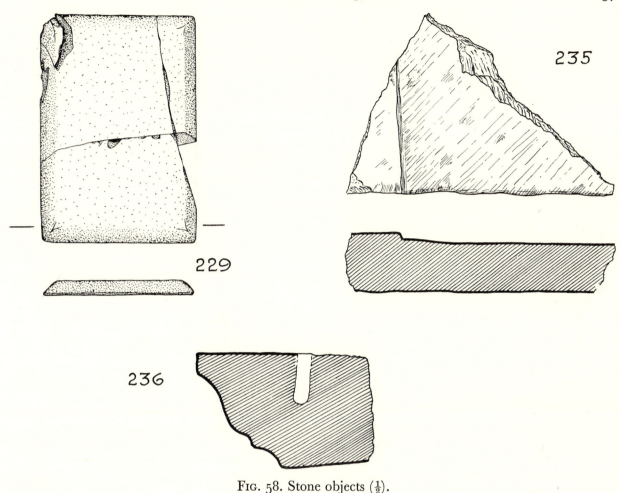

FIG. 58. Stone objects ($\frac{1}{2}$).

which are smooth but slightly irregular. One edge also is slightly worn. The stone is a gritty sandstone similar to the Upper Trenchard Sandstone found near Ellwood, Gloucestershire. A VI 4, A.D. 150–155/160. II D, Room 18.

242. (unfigured). Fragment, *c.* 9 by 5·5 cm., of whetstone *c.* 1 cm. thick, used on one side only. It is of a sandy limestone similar to Collyweston Slate. One edge is worn and convex. B I 6, undated. From robber-trench.

243. (unfigured). Large chunk of red sandstone, 13 to 17 cm. broad and 3·5 to 9 cm. thick, similar to specimen from the Bunter Series at Bromsgrove, Worcestershire; it may be an erratic. It appears to have been used for grinding, as the two larger faces are worn to a saucer shape, and there is a small worn face connecting these two. One larger face has numerous, almost parallel, slight scorings. A I 9, A.D. 150–155/160. II D, Room 24. No. 238 came from same layer.

244. (unfigured). Corner fragment of squarish block of red sandstone similar to that of the Devonian at Viney Hill Quarry in Gloucestershire. One face is very slightly concave, but rotary grinding on the opposite face has produced a deep concavity. Specimen is thus 5 to 6 cm. thick at the

irregularly rectangular edges, but only 1·8 cm. thick at the grinding centre. A+. Unstratified and undated.

245. (unfigured). Smooth tabular hone, measuring *c.* 11·5 by 3 by 0·9 cm., irregular in appearance through long use. It is composed of the rock phyllite and is probably an erratic. B IV 35, A.D. 49–60. I, Room 25.

246. (unfigured). Fragment of little-used hone, 2·3 cm. wide by 1·3 cm. thick, composed of calcareous sandstone similar to a specimen from Wittering, Northamptonshire. A IV 2, A.D. 155/160. II D, Room 18.

The Wroxeter whetstones (D. Atkinson, *Excavations at Wroxeter 1923–27* (Oxford, 1942), 129) were reported (*Arch. Camb.*, lxxxvi (1931), 97) as being of a 'calcareous sandstone containing fragments of lignite, and shells of an *Ostrea* . . . from a narrow, well-defined band in the Great Oolite Series'. The exact locality whence the rock came was suggested to be an area 'where the limestones of the Great Oolite are partly or wholly replaced by so-called estuarine deposits'. It was noted that Watling Street traverses such an area between Stony Stratford and Towcester and that the quarries could have been located there. Thus whetstone no. 246 from Verulamium and those of Wroxeter may derive from a single source.

247. Fragment of Niedermendig lava, *c.* 13 cm. long, perhaps originally part of a quern, but reused since it has two adjacent plane surfaces which lie at an acute angle. Upper surface on section is fairly flat, but others are rough. B IV 3, A.D. 155/160. II D, Room 38–42.

248. Part of upper stone of quern of Niedermendig lava. B I 23, A.D. 155/160. II D, wall-trench 25/35.

249. Very worn fragments of upper stone of Niedermendig lava quern. All faces except the grinding one have groups of parallel tooling marks. B IV 9J, A.D. 150–155/160. II D, Room 43.

250. Fragment of upper stone of Niedermendig lava quern. All faces have groups of parallel tooling lines except for the grinding face where they are radial. B II 36E, A.D. 85–105. II A, accumulation outside Room 19.

251. Part of lower stone of quern of Hertfordshire Puddingstone. A I 29, *c.* A.D. 105. II B, Room 22A, make-up.

252. Lower stone of quern of Hertfordshire Puddingstone, which has suffered burning. A I 9, A.D. 150–155/160. II D, Room 24, occupation on floor.

253. Three fragments of lower quern-stone of Greensand, with roughly worked lower side and evenly worked grinding side. T XXI 23, A.D. 130–50. II C, wall-trench 9/13.

254. Part of lower stone of quern of Niedermendig lava. A II 68, undated pit below II B, Room 14.

255. Several fragments of lower stone of quern of Niedermendig lava. Lower face very irregular. B, unstratified.

256. (unfigured). Fragment of upper quern-stone of Millstone Grit, reported as probably an erratic. There are a number of concentric grooves on the grinding surface; no other surface is complete. A IV 9, A.D. 270–5. III, make-up.

257. (unfigured). Small fragment of upper quern-stone, *c.* 4 cm. thick, of Millstone Grit, probably an erratic. B IV 3, A.D. 155/160. II D, Rooms 38–42.

258. (unfigured). Five *tesserae c.* 1·5 cm. square, some displaying rather worn upper surfaces. They include one of white chalk, and also one of cream limestone and three of creamy-grey limestone which are similar to the White Lias Limestone from the Somerset area. A IV 8, A.D. 155/160. II D, Room 17.

259. (unfigured). Rather coarse *tessera* of upper-surface side 1·4 to 1·6 cm. and of cream White Lias Limestone. A VI 15, A.D. 115–30. II B, Room 26.

No mosaic or tessellated floors were found in the buildings of Period II, and mosaics in general are rare at Verulamium before *c.* A.D. 150. The presence of these mosaic tesserae is therefore worth recording.

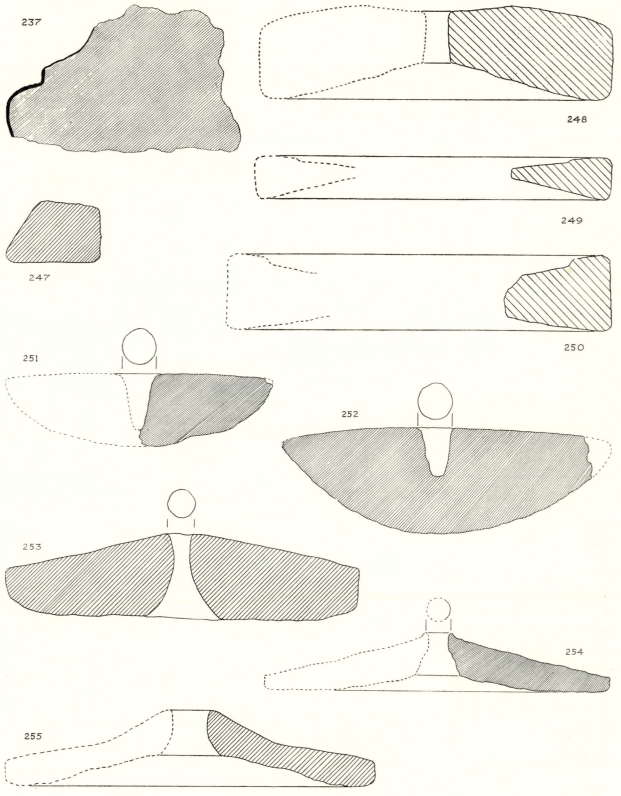

FIG. 59. Stone objects ($\frac{1}{4}$).

Note on the weights (nos. 87–92 above) (S. S. F.)

The Roman pound (*libra*) seems likely to have weighed 5,022 gr.;[1] others give it as 5,050 gr. The Celtic pound, on the other hand, had a weight of 4,770 gr., the difference between them amounting to 16·33 gm., or rather over half a modern ounce. Both were lighter than the present English pound of 7,000 gr. The *libra* was divisible into 12 *unciae*, and it is likely that the Celtic pound was too,[2] though it was also divisible by descending multiples of $\frac{1}{2}$. It is often found that ancient weights discovered in excavations do not reflect exact fractions of either the *libra* or the Celtic pound. Very often they weigh less than the appropriate fraction, a fact which may be explained by loss due to wear and to subsequent corrosion, or by original light weight, or both. Some seem openly fraudulent.[3] The existence of a traditional lighter pound alongside the *libra* in Roman Britain must have been a fruitful source of both confusion and profit.

No. 90 (fig. 37), weighing 413·11 gr., bears the numeral I and may be assumed to represent 1 *uncia*. Twelve *unciae* of this weight would amount to 4,957 gr., considerably more than the Celtic pound but only 65 gr. (4·2 gm.) less than the *libra*, a deficiency of *c.* $\frac{1}{7}$ of a modern ounce. No. 88 with a weight of 822·4 gr. is clearly intended for 2 *unciae*. No. 92 at present weighs 4,281 gr., but much is missing. It can be assumed to represent either a *libra* or a Celtic pound. No. 87, on the other hand, with a weight of 74·95 gr. is no obvious fraction of an *uncia*, but does approximately correspond to $\frac{1}{64}$ of a Celtic pound, being in fact minutely (0·42 gr.) overweight. No. 89 (*b*), not figured, at 35·2 gr., would represent half this again.

BURNT DAUB AND PLASTER
(Plates LIV–LX)

In the following notes the words 'front' or 'obverse' and 'back' or 'reverse' refer to the face of the daub wall and to the back side of the piece of daub which represents the middle of the actual wall where the woodwork was situated. This is because when the daub walls were burnt in the Boudiccan or Antonine fire, the timbers were consumed and the oxidized clay from each half of the wall fell away as separate fragments. When the plate shows both obverse and reverse, the obverse view always lies on the left.

On each piece of burnt daub there are usually two main features to describe. The face of the daub bears some sort of irregularity or pattern designed to roughen the surface to make the plaster, which was applied on top, adhere firmly. These can take the form of slashings with the dauber's trowel or linear grooves made by his finger-tips. Slightly more elaborate are narrow grooves apparently made by a comb. Finally there are stamped patterns of varying complexity. In the examples examined there were no lines of decoration which overlapped. Also, only relatively small pieces of daub were available for study. On the basis of these observations it is equally likely that the patterns were applied with a simple wooden block bearing the design as that they were made with a roller stamp. It would have been much easier to make a flat than a cylindrical stamp. The sides and reverse of each daub fragment usually bear the impressions of the structural woodwork of the wall. These include

---

[1] For discussion of weights see D. F. Allen in S. S. Frere (ed.), *Problems of the Iron Age in Southern Britain* (London, Institute of Archaeology, 1961), Appendix V (p. 302), and R. S. Conway, *Melandra Castle* (Manchester, 1906), 99–110. Cf. also *J.R.S.* lviii (1968), 210, nos. 35, 36; and see *Antiq.*

Journ. xiii (1933), 57, for a *libra*-weight of 5,051 gr.

[2] D. F. Allen, op. cit.

[3] e.g. the Camulodunum 1 and 5 *uncia* weights (Hawkes and Hull, *Camulodunum* (Oxford, 1947), 333).

the parts shown in fig. 4, ground-sill, main uprights, horizontal members, and vertical laths. Instead of laths, wattles—small unworked withies—were sometimes used. In one example there are the impressions of small horizontal woven withies forming hurdling.

1. (Pl. LIV.) Part of wall face bearing parts of two applications of a stamp which has produced ridge and groove pattern of chevron and diamond. There is a 5-cm. gap between the two applications. The reverse of the fragment is abraded and bears no identifiable features. B II 38, A.D. 60. I, Rooms 26–7.

2. Face shows section of stamped pattern apparently comprising linear series of open diamond shapes enclosing slight diamond-shaped boss on flat ground, and with outer area filled with chevrons. Reverse face of fragment shows no recognizable features. B II 38, A.D. 60. I, Rooms 26–7.

3. Face of fragment, 4 cm. thick, shows diamond and chevron stamped pattern. At one point on edge there is a flat upstanding area beyond edge of stamp. Reverse face bears pattern of wood-grain of upright timber. B II 38, A.D. 60. I, Rooms 26–7.

4. Plan view of fragment of daub with one complete hole and parts of four others where the vertical wattles ran through it. Two diameters of the complete hole are 1·6 and 1·8 cm. Site A, Boudiccan fire.

5. (Pl. LV.) Reverse side of fragment with impressions of small horizontal woven withies forming hurdling. A I, A.D. 155/160. II D, north-west wall of Room 23.

6. Unevenly smoothed face of fragment c. 8 cm. thick with enormous trowel-cut pits for keying of plaster, traces of which remain. At the edge is the impression of a vertical timber, 4–5 cm. thick. Parts of the impressions of four vertical woven laths of section c. 4 by 1 cm. remain on reverse; these are contiguous except for the largest longitudinal area seen on the reverse view which is the impression of one of the main vertical timbers. B VII 4, A.D. 155/160. II D, Room 52.

7. (Pl. LVI.) The obverse face of this fragment, which is c. 6 cm. thick, has a cross-hatched keying-pattern apparently made by scoring the surface twice in different directions by means of a comb. The reverse face is now amorphous. B VIII 8, A.D. 155/160. II D, Room 53, wall-trenches.

8. Fragment of c. 4 cm. thickness has smoothed face bearing radiating oblique trowel cuts. An oblique wattle is visible at the bottom of the obverse view. The body of the daub contains flint pebbles, twigs, and grass or straw. One wattle impression is visible on the reverse, at the point where the fragment is labelled. A I, A.D. 155/160. II D, Room 23, north-west wall.

9. Fragment c. 5 cm. thick has included small flints, small pieces of bone, and traces of grass or straw. Smoothed face has oblique trowel cuts forming chevrons and parts of two lines within the chevrons near the edge. On the reverse is the imprint of a lath, 5 cm. wide by c. 1 cm. thick, flanked by two rounded wattles of c. 3 cm. diameter; one is at a slight angle to the lath. Traces of a squared horizontal timber running behind and at right angles to these others remains. On one edge of the fragment (outer edge on plate) is the impression of the wood-grain of a main upright timber which was flush with the surface of the wall. A I, A.D. 155/160. II D, Room 23, north-west wall.

10. (Pl. LVII.) Fragment was originally 4 to 5 cm. thick, presenting a fairly flat face. To facilitate keying of plaster a second coat of daub c. 1 cm. thick was applied and wavy grooves made in this by the dauber's finger-tips. The original face is visible where the second has cracked off (left). The lower edge of the reverse view shows the imprint of what was perhaps a horizontal timber c. 0·8 cm. thick and more than 5 cm. broad. Traces of two laths 0·5 cm. or so thick remain at the extreme side edges of the fragment, passing in front of the horizontal timber and at right angles to it. Two laths, c. 0·6 cm. thick, one passing behind and one in front of the horizontal timber, run at an angle of 75 degrees to it. The centre of the fragment shows a flat area of daub, presumably the impression of a timber which was fitted to the horizontal timber. This complex arrangement of structural members perhaps has some association with the roof construction (see also no. 16 below). B XV 3, A.D. 155/160. II D, Room 55.

11. Massive fragment, almost 8 cm. thick, with irregular scoring on surface. On reverse is the imprint of a vertical timber 4·5 cm. thick at the edge of the fragment. The horizontal member mortised into this does not show, but four vertical woven laths of section 4·5 by 0·5 to 1 cm., two passing either side of it, have left their mark. B XV 3, A.D. 155/160. II D, Room 55.

12. (Pl. LVIII.) Fragment c. 2 to 4 cm. thick which bears zigzag finger-tip marks for keying. This piece apparently fell face downwards, as the original face is well preserved but the thickness is very variable and no trace of timbers remains on the reverse. The latter is smooth but irregular, blackened as though discoloured by superimposed rubbish, and abraded by trampling. B XV 3, A.D. 155/160. II D, Room 55.

13. The irregular surface bears two series of light and approximately parallel vertical scorings. The upper part of the reverse shows part of a horizontal timber c. 1·5 cm. thick, with vertical laths c. 5 by 1 cm., one sloping behind, and one (and part of a second) sloping in front of it. A I, A.D. 155/160. II D, Room 23, north-west wall.

14. (Pl. LIX.) The face bears rather abraded stamping in multiple-chevron form with unstamped fairly flat border. The fragment is up to 9 cm. thick, possibly a combination of two coats 3·5 and 5·5 cm. thick. The reverse view shows four vertical laths sloping alternately to back and front, including widths of 3, 4, and 6 cm. About one-third of the area of the reverse (right) is now amorphous and shows no trace of lath marks, although one edge (outer on plate) has some impression of a vertical timber. B IV 3, A.D. 155/160. II D, Rooms 38–42, general burnt deposit.

15. Crudely finished fragment c. 5 cm. thick, with deep oblique trowel slashes in surface. On reverse are impressions of five contiguous laths, c. 3 cm. wide. One side has the trace of a vertical timber. A I, A.D. 155/160. II D, Room 23, north-west wall.

16. (Pl. LX.) Fragment c. 7 cm. thick has stamped parallel grooves on face with a plain border 2–3 cm. wide, curving up to a void of timbering 3 cm. wide running approximately parallel to the edge of the stamped pattern. The reverse shows five contiguous parallel woven laths, 2·5, 3, 3·5, and (two) 4 cm. wide at an angle of about 50 degrees to the front timber. If the laths were vertical, the timber visible in the wall face would have been an oblique cross-brace, but the difficulties of reconstructing the wall like this suggest that the more likely explanation is that the oblique timber is a roof-beam. If so this gives the approximate pitch of the roof. B VI 8, A.D. 155/160. II D, Room 51, wall-trenches.

17. Two fragments of daub, c. 3·5 cm. thick, bear stamped keying-pattern in form of concentric diamond-shaped grooves on front face. Reverse is abraded and shows no trace of timbers. Also illustrated is fragment of red-painted white plaster, 0·7 cm. thick, which adheres to a layer of daub c. 1·5 cm. thick. This latter bears the concentric diamond pattern on the back, showing that the plaster was not here applied directly to the first coat of daub with keying-marks. T II 8, A.D. 155/160. II D, Room 25A.

18. Fragments of coarse pink-white plaster bearing imprint of herring-bone stamped pattern on the reverse and with thin, fairly smooth greyish layer at face. B VIII 8, A.D. 155/160. II D, Room 53, wall-trenches.

II. THE IRON OBJECTS

by Dr. W. H. Manning, F.S.A.[1]

Fig. 60

1. Bench anvil (?), with a tapering, square-sectioned stem and slightly domed head. Length 14·2 cm. B XV 4, A.D. 150–155/160. II D, Room 55.

   It has the general appearance of a mower's or field anvil but lacks the characteristic supporting loops. The slightly domed head would prevent the edges of the anvil marking the metal being worked on it. In use it was presumably set either in a block of wood or in the bench itself. A smaller but generally similar anvil from Hadrian's Wall Turret 52A is in the Tullie House Museum, Carlisle, while bench anvils with a distinct break between the rectangular head and tang came from Woodcuts (*Cranborne Chase*, i, 86, pl. xxvIII, 12) and London (R. Merrifield, *The Roman City of London*, pl. 125). Room 55 yielded goldsmith's crucibles.

Smiths' sets

The set is a strong chisel used for cutting hot or cold metal and is usually struck with a sledge-hammer.

2. Set, with a stout stem, square and battered at the butt, tapering into a thin edge now badly corroded. Length 14·7 cm. B II 13, A.D. 270–5. III, make-up, XIV, 5 Rooms 2 and 4 (Antonine fire, disturbed).

   Similar tools are known from Loudoun Hill, Ayrshire (Hunterian Museum, Glasgow), London (Guildhall Museum), Chedworth Villa (Site Museum), Silchester (Reading Museum, found with other smith's equipment in the 1900 hoard), etc.

3. Set, with a splayed blade, battered rectangular head and rounded stem. It is much corroded. Length 15·2 cm. A I 9, A.D. 150–155/160. II D, Room 24.

   This is an example of a form of set which continued through the Roman period, other examples coming from Kingsholm, Glos. (presumably first-century A.D., in the British Museum) and Silchester (Reading Museum, from the fourth-century 1900 hoard). The splayed blade suggests that they may have been intended for cutting hot metal.

Smiths' punches

The punch is used on hot metal and may be round, square or any other required shape. It must be long enough to keep the hand clear of the hot metal or be held with a handle. Similar punches are used by carpenters to drive nail-heads below the surface of wood, but these will usually show less sign of battering.

4. Punch, with a battered head tapering to a flattened blade, a feature which may be the effect of corrosion. Length 17·3 cm. A IV 2, A.D. 155/160. II D, Room 17, south-east wall-trench.

   Similar tools come from Silchester (Reading Museum), London (Guildhall Museum), the Eckford, Roxburghs., hoard (*Three Hoards*, fig. 6, E 18), the Blackburn Mill, Berwicks., hoard (*Three Hoards*, 48, fig. 13, B 45–B 47), etc.

[1] To make the record as complete as possible many additional drawings of ironwork were prepared at short notice by Mr. Christopher Saunders, B.A., and Mrs. M. O. Manning, B.A., to whom the writer is most grateful.

5. Punch, with a rectangular cross-section and rounded edges. The head is slightly burred by hammering. Length 11·2 cm. B XV 11, A.D. 150–155/160. II D, Room 55.

The fact that the head is wider than the stem suggests that it was not intended to be driven through the metal and is therefore a punch rather than a small drift.

Fire shovel

Small iron shovels are essentially tools used with a fire, but the fire may vary from the metallurgical furnace to the altar fire. They are characterized by the long, twisted iron handle, usually with a ring at its end. The handle and blade were made separately and welded together.

6. Fire shovel, with a pear-shaped blade and long, twisted handle ending in a plate with a ring at its end to hang it by. Length 87·9 cm. A I 2, A.D. 155/160. II D, Room 23. See pl. XXVII*b*.

Similar shovels come from Newstead, Roxburghs. (*P.S.A.S.* xlvii (1912–13), 388, pl. 2, 5) and the Carrawburgh Mithraeum (*Arch. Ael.* 4th ser., xxix, 84, pl. xv, B).

Axes

The Roman axe is a relatively unspecialized tool and the complete example given below is typical. Many Romano-British axes have lugs on either side of the eye, a characteristic which is particularly common in the first and second centuries A.D.

7. Axe, with an oval eye and an edge which is only slightly wider than the butt. There is no expansion about the eye. It is unusually heavy for its length. Length 19·1 cm. Weight 63 ounces. B I 20, A.D. 155/160. II D, wall-trench 25/35.

Similar axes are known from Silchester in some numbers, with several examples coming from the two fourth-century hoards (1890 and 1900) (Reading Museum), Strageath, Perths. (National Museum, Edinburgh), London (Wheeler, *London in Roman Times*, 78, pl. xxxiv, 8; and examples in Guildhall Museum), etc.

8. Axe blade, broken at the socket; the edge is markedly wider than the socket. One cannot tell if it was originally lugged or not. Length 12·7 cm. B I 69, A.D. 60–75. Pit 7.

9. Axe butt, broken at the socket. It is not lugged, nor is there an expansion around the eye. Length 6·9 cm. B II 5, fourth-century. III, XIV, 5 wall-trench 1/4.

Paring chisels

This form of chisel has a thin, flexible blade which is often splayed to give a very wide edge. It is not struck with a mallet but is used with hand or shoulder pressure to pare the wood. The handle is often made in one piece with the blade.

10. Paring chisel, with narrow blade, splaying slightly at the edge, and a solid handle. The slight ridge between the blade and handle may be intended to represent the stop-ridge of a tanged chisel with a wooden handle. Length 21·1 cm. A IV 8, A.D. 155/160. II D, Room 17.

A similar chisel is known from Caistor-by-Norwich (Norwich Castle Museum), and tanged examples are relatively common, coming from Silchester (Reading Museum), Camulodunum (*Camulodunum*, 343, pl. cv, 6), the Blackburn Mill Hoard (*Three Hoards*, 48, fig. 13, B 44), etc.

Fig. 61

11. Paring chisel, with a massive solid handle which tapers to its junction with the blade, which was originally very wide but of which only a fragment now remains. Length 16·0 cm. B II 13, A.D. 270–5. III, make-up, XIV, 5 Rooms 2 and 4 (Antonine fire, disturbed).

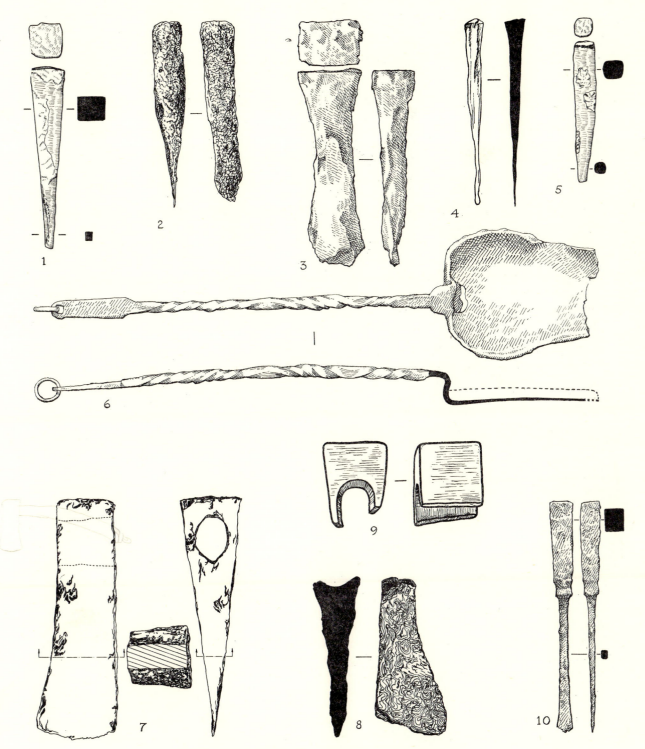

FIG. 60. Iron objects 1–10 (all ⅓ except no. 6 (⅙)).

Such a broad-bladed chisel usually has a stout, solid handle. Other examples come from Caistor-by-Norwich (Norwich Castle Museum), London (Guildhall Museum) and, in some numbers, Silchester (Reading Museum).

Saws

There are two basic forms of Roman saws—hand-saws with a handle at one end of the blade, and bow- or frame-saws where the blade is held at both ends. Complete bow-saw blades are rarely found, but fragments may be recognized with fair certainty by the back and edge being parallel. The teeth of both types often slope markedly in one direction; in a hand-saw this is usually towards the handle so that the blade cuts on the backward pull rather than the forward thrust. The reason for this was to avoid crumpling the thin blade if it stuck in the cut. By analogy it seems likely that the teeth of bow-saws sloped back towards the hand, though the danger of collapsing the blade was obviously less in their case. The teeth may or may not be set, and their number varies with the intended usage of the blade.

12. Hand-saw, with a long, triangular blade and a broad tang, which still retains a rivet, but is broken short. In size and shape it resembles a modern compass-saw. The widening of the blade towards the tang must be to give it strength. The teeth are not set and appear to slope neither backwards nor forwards. There are about eight teeth to the inch which accords with the modern cross-cut saw. Length 41·7 cm. A VI 2, A.D. 155/160. II D, Room 18.

Saws of similar form, but smaller size, come from London (Wheeler, *London in Roman Times*, 79, pl. xxxvi, 5), Caistor-by-Norwich (Norwich Castle Museum), and Chedworth Villa (Site Museum). Another of equal size is known from Great Chesterford, Essex (*Great Chesterford*, 10, pl. 2, fig. 20. It was not part of the hoard of ironwork).

13. Bow-saw blade (fragment), with parallel edges and the teeth sloping in one direction. There are about twelve teeth to the inch which would correspond with the modern panel-saw. The teeth are not set. Length 9·4 cm. A I 26, A.D. 105–30. II B, Room 15. It was found corroded to the hippo-sandal (no. 24 below). Similar fragments come from Hod Hill (Brailsford, *Hod Hill*, i, 14, fig. 13, G 46), Great Chesterford (*Great Chesterford*, 10), Rotherley (*Cranborne Chase*, ii, 132, pl. CIV, 2) and, in some numbers, the Gadebridge Park Villa, Herts. (publication forthcoming).

14. (With pl. L*a*.) Carpenter's plane, consisting of the sole and four rivets. The ends of the sole are turned up slightly, and the mouth is set slightly closer to the toe than the heel. The rivets are still attached to the sole, but the 'iron' is lost. The basic body was of wood. Length 43·9 cm. It is the largest Roman plane known. B I 19, A.D. 280–315. III, occupation layer on cellar floor.

Four planes are known from Roman Britain, one from Silchester (Reading Museum), two from Caerwent (Newport, Mon. Museum), and the Verulamium plane. Others come from Egypt (one), Pompeii (two), and Germany (six).[1] Of these the Egyptian example, which is a small wooden moulding plane, and the two Pompeiian planes, which are smoothing planes, stand apart. The others are all equivalent to the modern jack-plane, and consisted of a wooden body or stock with various iron fittings. Only the 'iron' itself (the cutting blade) *must* be of iron, but some form of iron casing was sometimes added. In our plane and one of the pair from Caerwent the iron work is reduced to the almost minimal form of a sole secured with iron rivets to the wooden stock (which has, of course, vanished).

It is possible that both this plane and the comparable one from Caerwent originally had iron plates on either side of the centre of the stock. Such plates are known on similar planes from Germany (from Saalburg, Feldburg, and Zugmantel) and serve to give added security to a rivet which passes horizontally through the body and supports the plane-iron. Since these plates are not

[1] Details of Roman planes may conveniently be found in W. L. Goodman, *The History of Woodworking Tools* (1964), 43.

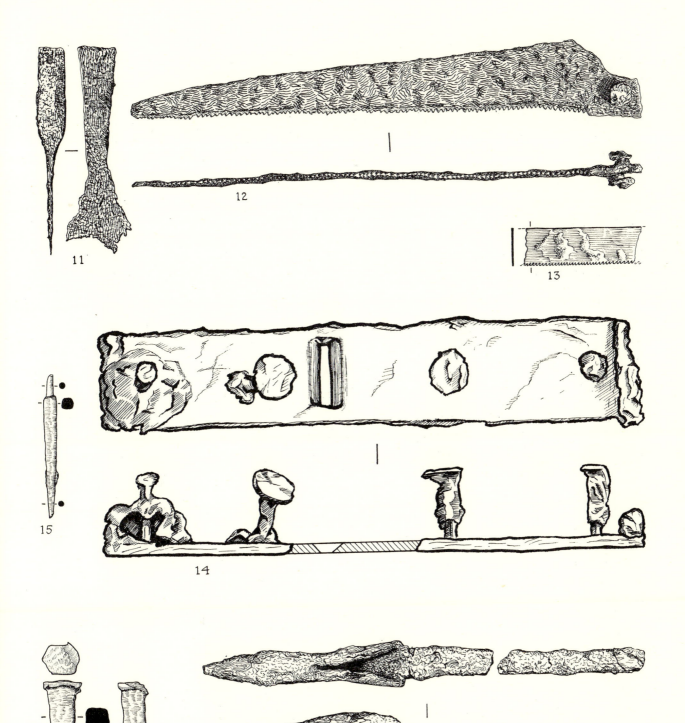

FIG. 61. Iron objects 11–17 ($\frac{1}{3}$).

attached to the sole they could easily become separated from it. The Silchester plane and the second Caerwent plane have sides, at least at the centre of the body, which are welded to the sole but perform a similar function.

Handles were probably carved in the wooden stock between the rivets.

15. Tanged punch (?), with a tapering stem and short tang. The tip of the stem is broken. Length 11·2 cm. B IV 17K, A.D. 140–50. II C, Room 39.

It is most probably a punch although, as the tip of the stem is lost, one cannot be quite certain that it was not, for example, an awl. Such a punch is more likely to have been used by a leather-worker than a smith or even a carpenter.

16. Small wedge or set, with a very battered head. Length 6·1 cm. B I 55, A.D. 280–315. III, occupation layer in cellar.

It could have served either as a cold set, or, perhaps more probably, as a wedge for splitting wood or stone. Similar tools come from Maiden Castle (*Maiden Castle*, 284, fig. 94, 7) and the Jewry Wall, Leicester (*Jewry Wall*, 274, pl. XXIII, *d*, 1 and 2).

17. Winged bar-share, with a flat tang, now broken, running back from a socket formed by the junction of the wings. Length 35·8 cm. B I 55, A.D. 280–315. III, occupation layer in cellar.

The type is best seen in a heavier example from the Box Villa in Wiltshire (*Devizes Museum Catalogue*, ii, 197, pl. LXXX, 1) and in a group from Gettenau in Germany (*Ber. R.G.K.* vii (1912), 157). These latter were found in a hoard with an equal number of coulters suggesting that the type was often used with a coulter, though it would function perfectly well without.

Romano-British plough fittings have been discussed in a paper in *J.R.S.* liv (1964), 54 ff. This form of share is a form of bar-share related to the long plain shares from such sites as Silchester and Great Chesterford (*J.R.S.* liv (1964), 60, fig. 5), and the socketed bar-shares of Iron Age and Roman Britain, e.g. from Glastonbury (*Glastonbury*, ii, 396, fig. 143, z3) and Woodcuts (*Cranborne Chase*, i, 56, pl. XXVIII, 9). The addition of symmetrical 'wings', which run back from what is in effect a socket, serve to increase the cutting edge of the share while retaining the advantages of a pointed tip. In use a wooden share or bar probably fitted into the socket and ran back with the tang to give it additional strength.

Fig. 62

18 (With pl. L*b*.) Plasterer's float, consisting of a long rectangular plate of iron with an arched handle in the centre of its back. It is in a state of advanced corrosion and X-ray photographs merely confirmed that the handle was welded to the plate. Length 55·1 c.m. B I 55, A.D. 280–315. III, occupation on cellar floor.

This is basically a flat board, with a handle on the back, used to smooth the surface of fresh plaster. Normally they were probably made entirely of wood, as they still commonly are; our float is the only one known in iron.

It is possible, but by no means certain, that the plate was strengthened originally with a wooden backing. A relief from Sens shows such a float in use on a newly plastered wall (Espérandieu 2767).

Spade irons

These have been discussed in detail, originally by the late Dr. Philip Corder (*Arch. Journ.* c (1943), 224 f.) and more recently by the present writer in *The Spade in Northern and Atlantic Europe* (ed. Gailey and Fenton (1970), 18). They are a very characteristic Romano-British tool; the edge (or 'mouth') can be either round or straight, and there is a wide variation in the method of attachment to the wooden blade.

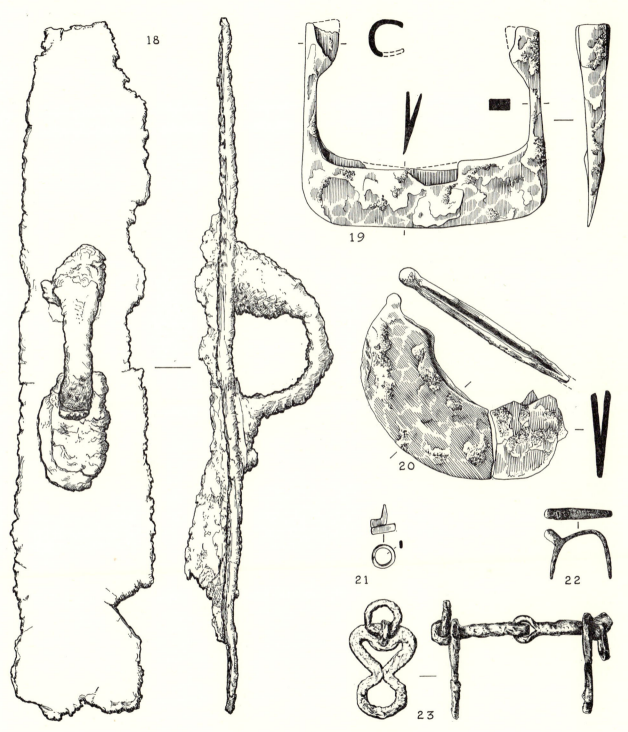

FIG. 62. Iron objects 18–23 (⅓).

19. Spade iron, with a square mouth. The blade has a V-shaped groove in the inner edge to receive the wooden blade. The corners of the mouth are rounded, possibly partly by wear. The arms are straight, without grooves, and end in paired lugs. Corrosion makes it impossible to tell if they were nailed in place. Length 16·5 cm. Width of mouth 20·3 cm. T X 2, unstratified.

It is Type 2B in the writer's classification (*The Spade*, 21 ff.) and is closely paralleled by other examples from Verulamium (Corder, op. cit., 226, fig. 1, 3, and 4, and Wheeler, *Verulamium*, 219, pl. LXV, A, 20); the Chedworth Villa (Corder 230, fig. 4, 26 and another in the Site Museum); Silchester (Corder, 230, fig. 4, 25); and Wilderspool, Lancs. (F. H. Thompson, *Roman Cheshire*, 86, fig. 22, 6).

20. Spade iron (fragment), with a round mouth, now in two pieces. The inner edge is grooved to receive the wooden blade. The arms were probably relatively short continuations of the mouth but are now almost entirely lost. Width 16·3 cm. B I 55, A.D. 280–315. III, occupation layer in cellar.

It is Type 1A in the writer's classification. Better-preserved examples come from Caerwent (Corder, 227, fig. 2, 4); and Combe End (Lysons, *Reliquiae Britannico-Romanae*, ii, pl. i). Other fragments are known and are listed in the writer's paper cited above.

21. Ox-goad, formed by a thin rod coiled into two turns and turned up at the top to form a spike. Length 2·5 cm. A I 2, A.D. 155/160. II D, Room 23.

Similar goads come from many sites including Lydney (*Lydney*, 92, fig. 23, 189), Woodyates (*Cranborne Chase*, iii, 137, pl. CLXXXIII, 17), Rotherley (*Cranborne Chase*, ii, 137, pl. CV, 12), etc. Mounted on the end of a long pole the goad was used by the driver or ploughman to direct the ox.

Spur

Romano-British spurs have been discussed by H. Shortt in a paper in *Antiq. Journ.* xxxix (1959), 62 ff. His classification is dependent on the method of fastening the leather straps to the spur:

1. The hook-spur where the ends of the arms turn back to form hooks. The prick is simple.
2. The loop-spur which has round or rectangular loops at the ends of the arms. The prick is simple.
3. The rivet-spur where the leather is riveted to the ends of the arms. There is usually a hook protruding above the heel-plate and prick.

22. Spur, with a plain but relatively long prick; the ends of the arms are lost. Length 6·9 cm. A XI Pit 1. Post-Roman pit.

The absence of the heel-hook which is characteristic of the rivet-spur suggests that it is either a hook-spur or a loop-spur. Since the hook-spur is a distinct rarity usually found on military sites, one may probably safely accept it as a loop-spur although the other dated examples are earlier. It may, however, be a rubbish survival. Loop-spurs are known from Hod Hill (Brailsford, *Hod Hill*, i, 19, pl. XIII, K 39, K 40, in iron; fig. 2 A 28, A 29, in bronze), London (Wheeler, *London in Roman Times*, 151, fig. 58, in iron coated with bronze), and Longstock (Shortt, op. cit., no. 17, in bronze).

Curb bit

Several forms of curb bit are known from Roman Britain but only one occurs in a civilian context. Basically it consists of a two-link snaffle bit of the normal form with small rings at the ends of the links. Set at right angles to the outer ends of the links, just inside these rings, are figure-of-eight loops with the link itself running through their top edge. In use the small side rings were fastened to the bridle and the reins were attached to the lower part of the loop, which also received a cord passing below the horse's chin. By pulling on the reins this cord was brought against the animal's throat to curb it. The type is notably less severe than the military forms (e.g. *Newstead*, 297, pl. LXXI, 2 and 3) where a sharper reaction was necessary.

23. Curb bit. Length 17·0 cm. B I 9, A.D. 310–15. III, cellar filling.

This is the only complete example of the type known to the writer, although one lacking only one of the side loops comes from Silchester (Reading Museum). The characteristic figure-of-eight side loops are known from Caerwent (Newport Museum), Caistor-by-Norwich (Norwich Castle Museum), etc.

Fig. 63

Hipposandals

The accepted classification is that of Aubert (*Revue des Musées* (Dijon), 1929). He divides them into three groups on form:

1. Those with a long hooked or looped vertical rod at the front, wings at the side and a hooked heel.
2. Those where the wings run forward to meet over the front of the sandal and end with a loop. The heel is hooked.
3. Those where the wings are prolonged forward but do not meet. There is no loop at the front, but the heel is hooked.

It is generally accepted that they are a form of temporary horse-shoe used perhaps when an unshod animal was brought on to metalled roads. If so, the animal's legs would need to be protected against the chafing of the sandals on the adjacent foot. A Gallic origin is usually postulated, but one may note the presence of one from Veii (*Papers of the British School at Rome*, xxiii (1955), 52, fig. 3).

24. Hipposandal, of Aubert Type I with the frontal loop and one wing broken, and the rear hook missing. The corrosion on the undersurface preserved the impression of a fragment of cloth, probably a two-by-one twill (information from Mr. H. W. M. Hodges). A fragment of a saw blade (no. 13 above) was corroded to it, suggesting that both pieces were scrap. Length 12·4 cm. A I 26, A.D. 105–30. II B, Room 15.
25. Hipposandal, probably of Aubert Type I, now in two pieces. The larger fragment consists of the sole and heel, the wings and heel-hook being lost. The smaller piece is the frontal rod and loop. Unfortunately the two were separated before deposition and their highly corroded state prevents absolute certainty that they originally fitted, though there is no reason why they should not come from the same sandal.

Length of sole	15·2 cm.
Length of rod and loop	11·4 cm.

B I Pit 20, A.D. 300–15. III, box below cellar stairs.

26. Hipposandal (fragment), of Aubert Type I. The wings, most of the heel-hook, and all save the base of the frontal rod are lost. Length 17·5 cm. B I 20, A.D. 155/160. II D, wall-trench 25/35.

Complete Class I hipposandals may be cited from London (Wheeler, *London in Roman Times*, 149, fig. 57; and many in the Guildhall Museum), Woodcuts (*Cranborne Chase*, i, 76, pl. XXV, 11), Newstead (National Museum, Edinburgh), etc.

27. Hipposandal, of Aubert Type III. The rear hook is broken and the whole is in a very poor state of preservation. Length 15·0 cm. A VII 3, A.D. 155/160. II D, Room 25.

Other examples of this form are known from Verulamium (Wheeler, *Verulamium*, 221, pl. LXIII, B, 3 and 4, both with a kite-shaped opening in the sole), and from Arlington Bridge, Cambs. (*Proc. Camb. Ant. Soc.* xlv (1952), 61, pl. XII), the Blackburn Mill Hoard (*Three Hoards*, 45, fig. 12, B 21; a kite-shaped opening in the sole and with spikes on the undersurface), Silchester (Reading Museum) and London in some numbers (Guildhall Museum and British Museum).

28. Hipposandal (fragment), of Aubert Type III with the rear hook and one wing missing. Length 17·0 cm. A VI 2, A.D. 155/160. II D, Room 18.

29. Hipposandal heel, with the base of the rear hook. Length 9·1 cm. Found with other scrap. B I 31D, A.D. 140–50. II C, Room 28.

   The bent heel was clearly a source of weakness and dissociated heels are not uncommon finds. Other examples may be mentioned from London (Guildhall Museum), Silchester (Reading Museum), and the Blackburn Mill Hoard (*Three Hoards*, 45, fig. 12, B 20).

30. Hipposandal heel, and rear hook. Length 8·9 cm. B I 55, A.D. 280–315. III, occupation on cellar floor.

Fig. 64

Hub-linings

By lining the outer end of the hub with an iron ring the wear on the axle and hub is much reduced. The normal form of Romano-British hub-lining is a split ring, often with sharp flanges on either side of the junction which were driven into the hub itself to hold the lining firm. All of these rings have a V-shaped cross-section and were used with the wider edge on the outside of the wheel.

31. Hub-lining, formed of a wide split ring with semicircular flanges on either side of the junction. Diameter 10·9 cm. B I 19, A.D. 280–315. III, occupation layer on cellar floor.

   Almost identical linings came from Newstead (*Newstead*, 293, pl. LXX, 9), Loudoun Hill, Ayrs. (Hunterian Museum), the Sandy, Beds., hoard (*Sandy Hoard*, 53, fig. 2, 3), etc.

32. Hub-lining and hub-rim. The hub-rim (or nave band) is a simple band, now incomplete. The hub-lining has the characteristic V-section and originally had flanges on either side of the junction, but only a fragment of one of these remains and their exact form cannot be established. Both the lining and the rim have been distorted into an oval. Diameter of nave-band *c.* 11·9 cm. Diameter of hub-lining *c.* 10·9 cm. A I 26, A.D. 105–30. II B, Room 15.

   The occurrence of the two more or less in their original relative positions is a rarity, hitherto only found on the complete wheels from Newstead (*Newstead*, 292, pl. LXIX, 2) and Bar Hill (*Bar Hill*, 496, fig. 34). Dissociated hub-rims are known from many sites and particularly from hoards of ironwork, including those from the Loudoun Hill hoard (Hunterian Museum), Newstead (National Museum, Edinburgh), etc. Some have a slight 'rim' on their outer edge (e.g. *Newstead*, 293, pl. LXX, 5; *Great Chesterford*, 6; *Sandy Hoard*, 53, fig. 1, 2), but this was not the case with our example.

Linch-pins

Romano-British linch-pins are of two main types:

1. Crescentic-headed, where the head has crescentic arms.
2. Spatulate-headed, where the head is oval.

   Both forms usually have a loop of some form on the head and the lower part of the stem is commonly rebated. They may be subdivided on the details of the loop and other features:

(*a*) Without a loop on the head.
(*b*) With a 'turned-over' loop on the top of the head.
(*c*) With a peg-loop inserted into the head.
(*d*) With a peg-loop and a leaf-shaped step above the head.

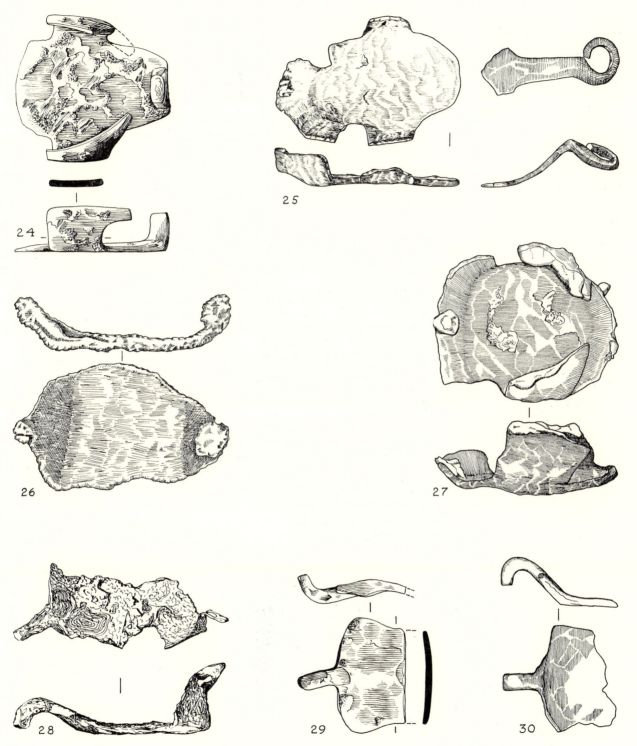

FIG. 63. Iron objects 24–30 ($\frac{1}{3}$).

33. Linch-pin, with spatulate head. The loop is a continuation of the top of the head which is turned over. The lower half of the stem is rebated at the back. Type 2b. Length 17·5 cm. B I 31D, A.D. 140–50. II C, Room 28.

It is a relatively common form occurring at Newstead (*Newstead*, 293, pl. LXX, 1), the Blackburn Mill, Berwicks., hoard (*Three Hoards*, 41, fig. 11, B 4), Caerleon (National Museum of Wales), Caistor-by-Norwich (Norwich Castle Museum), Caerwent (Newport Museum), Silchester (Reading Museum), etc.

34. Linch-pin, with spatulate head. Similar to the preceding. Type 2b. Length 18·3 cm. B I 31D, as no. 33.

35. Linch-pin, with spatulate head. Similar to the two preceding. Type 2b. Length 21·1 cm. B I 31D, as nos. 33, 34, above.

36. Linch-pin, with spatulate head, peg-loop, and a leaf-shaped step above the head. The peg-loop is almost certainly inserted into the head. The stem is not rebated. The 'leaf' is carefully grooved, a detail which serves as a tread and emphasizes the likeness of a leaf. Type 2d. Length 22·9 cm. B I 55, A.D. 280–315. III, occupation layer on cellar floor.

This particular linch-pin is unique in the writer's experience, but similar crescentic-headed pins are known from the Great Chesterford hoard (*Great Chesterford*, 11, pl. 1, fig. 10), the Silchester 1900 hoard (*Archaeologia* lxvii (1901), 247, fig. 4), and the Sandy, Beds., hoard (*Sandy Hoard*, 51, fig. 1, 1). All probably date from the fourth century. The leaf was undoubtedly intended as a step into a vehicle.

Pole-tips

The tip of the draught-pole of a vehicle was often protected with a metal sheath the form of which can vary. One of the simplest forms is a simple cylinder closed at one end where there is a nail hole through it, and possibly cut away to receive the pin to which the yoke was attached. This is seen most clearly in the pole-tip from the Eckford, Roxburgh, hoard (*Three Hoards*, 22, fig. 5, E 3). Of the possible examples from Verulamium two are not sufficiently well preserved to tell if the edge was cut back or not, while a third appears to have had an edge of uniform height. None of the pieces given below must be pole-tips, but this is a probable explanation of their function.

37. Pole-tip (?), consisting of a damaged cylinder with a hole through it at one point, closed at one end by a pierced plate. Diameter 6·1 cm. B I 31D, A.D. 140–50. II C, Room 28.

The hole through the side is probably for a yoke-pin; unfortunately the opposite side is broken away and one cannot tell if there was a corresponding hole there. The hole in the end is almost certainly enlarged by corrosion. It is comparable with the Eckford tip (*Three Hoards*, 22, fig. 5, E 3).

38. Pole-tip (?), consisting of a short cylinder closed at one end. The edge, though damaged, appears to have been of uniform height. There is a large hole in the closed end which is probably enlarged by corrosion. Diameter 6·4 cm. B I 31D, A.D. 140–50. II C, Room 28.

39. Pole-tip (?), consisting of a short cylinder, closed at one end. The edges are badly damaged and there is an enlarged hole in the closed end. Diameter 8·9 cm. B I 55, A.D. 280–315. III, occupation layer in cellar.

Fig. 65

40. Chopper or heavy knife, with a straight back to the blade, which continues the line of the socket, and a curving edge. It is badly damaged. Length 18·3 cm. B I 19, A.D. 280–315. III, occupation layer in cellar.

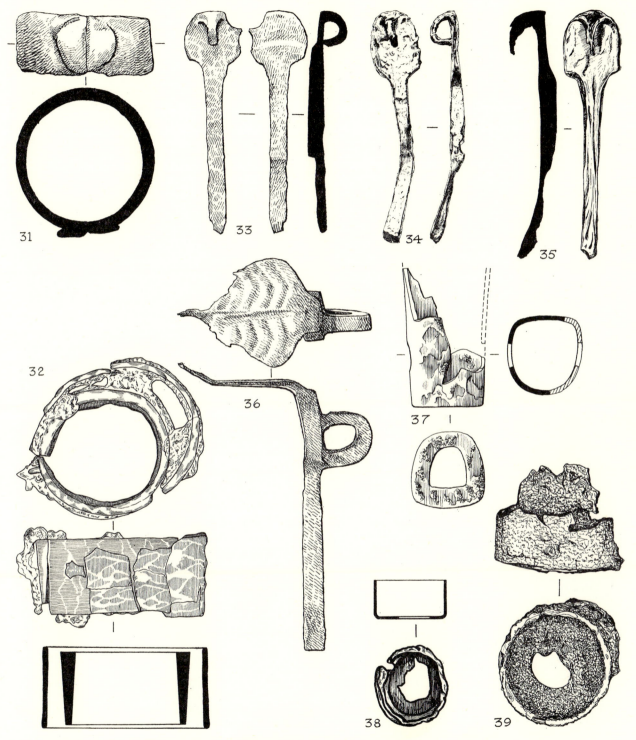

FIG. 64. Iron objects 31–9 ($\frac{1}{3}$).

This is the commonest form of Roman chopper with examples from Kingsholm, Glos. (Lysons, *Reliquiae Britannico-Romanae*, pl. XIII, 1), Caerwent (Newport Museum), the Blackburn Mill Hoard (*Three Hoards*, 47, fig. 12, B 32), Silchester (Reading Museum), Verulamium itself (*Verulamium*, 219, pl. LXIV, B, 14 and 12; the latter tanged not socketed), etc.

41. Knife, with the handle and blade made in one piece. The edge and back of the blade are parallel except at the tip. There is a slight constriction where the blade and handle meet, probably representing a stop-ridge, and the handle ends with a loop. Length 16·5 cm. B II 27Z, A.D. 140–50. II C, Room 41.

Other examples of this type are known from London (Wheeler, *London in Roman Times*, 78, fig. 19. 2—with the maker's stamp: BASILI) and Silchester (Reading Museum).

42. Knife, with a tang, massive stop-ridge, and a blade with a straight edge and back which widens slightly towards the tip where it is broken short. Length 13·2 cm. A IX, unstratified.

An unusual form without any very close parallel known to the writer, although the blade-form occurs on knives from London (British Museum and Guildhall Museum).

43. Knife, with the tips of the 'tang' and blade broken. Length 14·5 cm. A IV 2, A.D. 155/160. II D, Room 18.

The thickness of the tang and its position in line with the back of the blade may indicate that it is part of a thin handle, rather than a true tang. If this is the case the handle probably ended with a loop and it can be compared with knives from Margidunum, Notts. (Nottingham University Museum), Silchester (Reading Museum), Caerwent (Newport Museum), etc. Tanged knives of generally similar shape are in most of the major collections.

44. Shears (fragment), consisting of one blade and almost half the spring with the remains of a loop at its end. Length 12·4 cm. B III 7, A.D. 370–410+. Pit cut into south edge of mosaic, XIV, 5 Room 3.

Roman shears vary considerably in size and function but the general principle is constant. The spring is either a plain U-shape or has the additional 'loop' seen here. Small shears are common finds; an almost complete pair of the same form comes from Richborough (*Richborough II*, 51, pl. XXIV, 67), and fragments from Woodcuts (*Cranborne Chase*, i, 69, pl. XXII, 8), Bokerly Dyke (*Cranborne Chase* iii, 109, pl. CLXXVI, 15), etc.

45. Shears (fragment), consisting of one blade and part of the wide spring. Length 17·8 cm. V XXXII 11, A.D. 130–50. II C, south-west of Room 1.

Similar medium-sized shears with wide springs come from Caerwent (Newport Museum), Silchester (Reading Museum), the Blackburn Mill Hoard (*Three Hoards*, 45, fig. 12, B 29), etc.

46. Spoon, with the knobbed handle and part of the bowl surviving. The bowl would appear to have been oval rather than round. Length 14·5 cm. A IV 8, A.D. 155/160. II D, Room 17.

Small iron spoons are not common; they were usually made in a more noble metal. Small ladles are slightly more common, although it is difficult to draw a distinction between them and large spoons. A smaller spoon is known from Dorchester, Dorset (Dorchester Museum), while a ladle, little longer than a spoon, from Charterhouse, Somerset, is in the Bristol Museum.

47. Bowl, with a simple out-turned rim. The base is largely lost. Diameter 13·2 cm. B XV 10, A.D. 155/160. II D, Room 55.

Iron bowls are very rare, although the thin sheet of which they are made is so easily corroded that they may originally have been more common. They may have been intended for domestic or industrial usage. The slight upward slope of the rim indicates that it is not a shield boss.

48. Vessel wall (fragment), with a rounded rim. Length 4·6 cm. Possibly from a lamp or shallow vessel. B XV 11, A.D. 150–155/160. II D, Room 55.

49. *Stylus.* Both the point and the eraser are damaged and the stem is bent. Length 9·7 cm. A VII, unstratified.

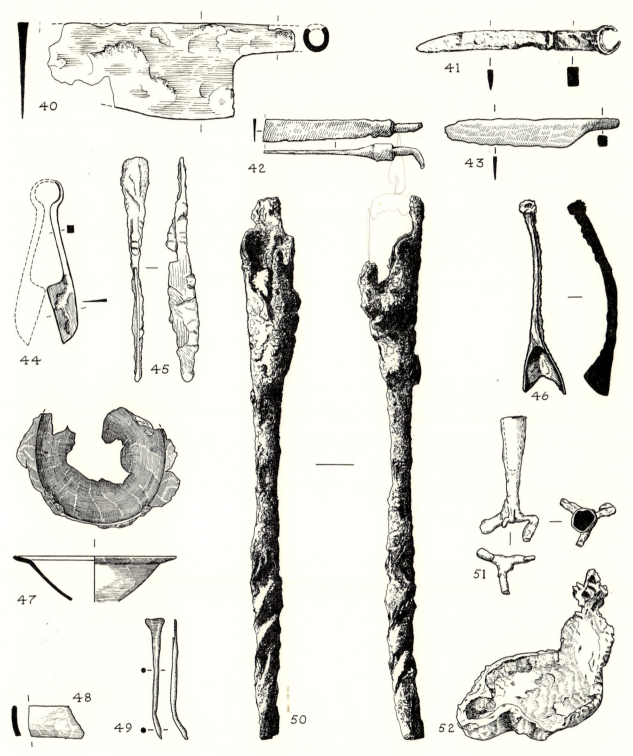

FIG. 65. Iron objects 40–52 ($\frac{1}{3}$).

Such simple *styli* come from many sites including Newstead (*Newstead*, pl. LXXX, 8), Richborough (*Richborough IV*, 153, pl. LIX, 310), Rotherley (*Cranborne Chase*, ii, pl. CV, 3), etc.

50. Candlestick, with a twisted stem and a large socket which was damaged and distorted before deposition. The stem *may* be broken short. Length 36·9 cm. B I 19, A.D. 280–315. III, occupation layer in cellar.

Small socketed candlesticks tapering into a spike at the lower end are found at a number of sites most notably Silchester. Large examples are much rarer and this one, together with a more elaborate example with two sockets pointing in opposite directions from Camerton, Somerset (Wedlake, *Camerton*, fig. 56, no. 20), are the only ones known to the writer. One may note that the Camerton candlestick also has a square-ended stem; both were probably mounted on a wall or in a wooden base.

51. Tripod candlestick, consisting of a conical socket supported by three small, distorted legs, which originally ended in out-turned feet. Length 10·2 cm. B I 9, A.D. 310–15. III, cellar filling.

This is a common form of candlestick and examples come from Silchester (Reading Museum; three examples), Caerwent (Newport Museum), and Lydney, Glos. (*Lydney*, 93, fig. 23, 191, with twisted legs; and 192). The type is seen at its finest in a pair from the Carrawburgh Mithraeum (*Arch. Ael.*, 4th ser. xxix, 84, pl. xv, B) and Bainbridge, Yorks. (*Cumb. and West.* lii (1952), 187, fig. 6) which have spiral ornaments, and drip trays.

52. Open hanging lamp. The top of the stem is broken short. Length 14·0 cm. B XV 11, A.D. 150–155/160. II D, Room 55.

Lamps of this type are relatively common and were suspended by means of a hanger which was linked to a swivel at the top of the stem of the lamp. Complete examples with their hangers come from Newstead (*Newstead*, 307, pl. LXXXIX, 6 and 7), the Bartlow Hills (*Archaeologia*, xxv (1834), 8, pl. II, fig. 10), Guilden Morden, Cambs. (Liversidge, *Britain in the Roman Empire*, fig. 70a), the Gadebridge Park Villa, etc.; and examples which have lost their hangers from the Blackburn Mill hoard (*Three Hoards*, 45, fig. 12, B 26), Bayford, Kent (*Arch. Cant.* xvi (1886), 1–7), etc.

Fig. 66

53. Bucket handle mount (fragment), flattened on one face and rounded on the other. The top is pierced but is now broken. Length 6·6 cm. B I 9, A.D. 310–15. III, cellar filling.

The commonest form of mount is a tapering strip which runs up the side of the bucket and projects beyond the rim, at which point it is thickened and pierced for the handle. A complete example can be seen on the bucket from Newstead (*Newstead*, 310, pl. LXIX, 4) while others occur among the bucket fittings from a well at Woodcuts (*Cranborne Chase*, i, 85, pl. XXVIII, 3–6), in the Brampton hoard (*Brampton Hoard*, 25, 28, and 30), etc.

54. Bucket handle mount, similar to the preceding. Length 12·7 cm. B II 7, fourth century. III, Building XIV, 5 wall-trench 1/4.

55. Bucket handle (fragment), consisting of the hooked end and a fragment of the handle. Length 10·7 cm. B IV 18J, A.D. 130–45. II C, Room 39.

Complete handles come from a number of sites including Bokerly Dyke (*Cranborne Chase*, iii, 106, pl. CLXXVI, 8), Richborough (*Richborough IV*, 155, pl. LXIII, 344), Silchester (Reading Museum, in some numbers), etc.

56. Vessel handle (?) (fragment), consisting of a slightly curving rod, broken at one end, with an oval plate at the other which retains the remains of a rivet. The plate has a concave cross-section. Length 17·3 cm. B XI 29, A.D. 175–275. Pit 19, secondary filling. It is presumably a fixed handle originally riveted to a metal (?) vessel.

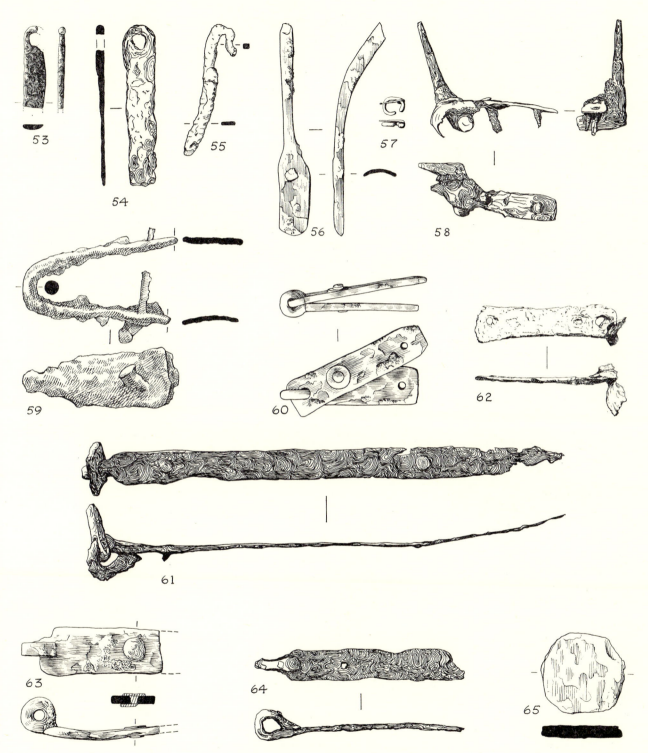

FIG. 66. Iron objects 53–65 ($\frac{1}{3}$).

57. Penannular brooch, formed of a plain hoop, without terminals, with one end of the straight pin twisted around it. Diameter 1·5 cm. B II 3, A.D. 370–410+. Black soil and rubble over XIV, 5.

Such brooches are not common in iron, bronze being a more frequent medium. They have been discussed by Elizabeth Fowler (*P.P.S.* xxvi (1960), 149 f.), our example falling in her Type Aa Another iron example comes from Stubbin Wood, Derbys. (*J. Derbys. Arch. and Nat. Hist. Soc.* lxxvi (1956), 9, fig. 3.2).

Hinges

Three main types of hinges were used in Roman Britain:

1. The drop hinge which is in two parts (*a*) the hinge itself which is usually U-shaped, but can be a single strip thickened and pierced at its end, or even just looped round. (*b*) An L-shaped staple which is driven into the door-jamb. This type is best suited to doors and gates.
2. The loop hinge which again is in two parts, one half usually being a strap which is pierced at one end to form an eye through which the end of the second strap is looped. Alternatively both straps may end in interlinked loops. Such hinges are best used on lids, as they lack the rigidity needed on doors.
3. The strap hinge consisting of two straps with the round plate or plates at the end of one strap fitting between similar plates on the other strap, with a central pivot through them all. The number of plates varies, although three (one and two) is the commonest. These hinges can be used vertically or horizontally.

58. Drop hinge (fragment), and staple. The L-shaped staple, with the characteristic round section of the shorter arm, is complete and has corroded to it about half of the U-shaped (?) hinge with two nails. Length of hinge 10·9 cm.: length of staple 8·9 cm. A I 2, A.D. 155/160. II D, Room 23.

Drop-hinge staples are quite common and examples may be quoted from Silchester (Reading Museum), Woodcuts (*Cranborne Chase*, i, 87, pl. xxviii, 19 and 20), the Carlingwark Loch hoard (*Three Hoards*, 37, fig. 9, c 52), etc.

59. U-shaped drop hinge, with short wide arms which narrow into a round-sectioned bar at the curve of the U. The remains of a nail are set in one arm. Length 13·0 cm. A VII 3, A.D. 155/160. II D, Room 25.

This strengthening of the curve occurs in other drop hinges including examples from Silchester (Reading Museum), and in hinges with more elaborate arms from Lakenheath (British Museum), the Brampton, Cumb., hoard (*Brampton Hoard*, 29, no. 38), etc.

60. Loop hinge, with the loop of one plate passing through a hole in the other. Both straps have two nail-holes but only one nail remains. Length 13·0 cm. B I 31D, A.D. 140–150. II C, Room 28.

This type of hinge is seen at its best in a much larger pair from Newstead (*Newstead*, pl. lxxxiii, 8 and 12), but others come from London (Guildhall Museum) and Bar Hill, Dumbartons. (Hunterian Museum, Glasgow).

61. Loop hinge which is basically similar to the preceding except that one strap is broken short and the other is much longer. There are two nails in the longer arm. Length 34·8 cm. B I 19, A.D. 280–315. III, occupation layer on cellar floor.

62. Loop hinge (?), which has lost the greater part of one strap. There are two nail-holes in the complete strap. Length 11·7 cm. A II 24, A.D. 130–40. II C, Path 26.

63. Drop or loop hinge (fragment), formed of a plate with a well-made loop set at the end of one face. The other end is broken short, but it still retains a nail. The regularity and size of the loop suggests a drop rather than a loop hinge, but one cannot be certain. Length 9·1 cm. B I 55, A.D. 280–315. III, occupation layer in cellar.

64. Loop hinge (fragment), consisting of a narrow, broken plate ending with a turned-over loop. There is a single nail-hole. It is almost certainly one plate from a loop hinge, though it might just possibly have been part of a drop hinge. Length 17·3 cm. B I 19, A.D. 280–315. III, occupation layer in cellar.

65. Disc, possibly the basal lining of the pivot socket of a door. Diameter 6·6 cm. B II 12, A.D. 280–90. III, packing behind cellar wall.

Such discs, often used with iron sheaths for the tenon or socket, are known from a postern gate at Silchester (with a sheath) (*Archaeologia*, lv (1897), 426), and from a gate (with a sheath), from the Basilica, and from House XXIII, Room 7, at Caerwent (Newport Museum).

Fig. 67

Locks and keys

A wide variety of locks and keys were used in the Roman period. The simplest is the *latch-lifter* which was passed through a hole in the door and slid a bolt. The *tumbler lock*, opened with a T-, or L-shaped, *lift key*, is only a little more complex. Here there were two, or occasionally four, tumblers which fell into holes in the bolt to prevent it moving until the key had lifted them; the bolt was probably moved by a string. A slightly more elaborate form of tumbler lock had the tumblers passing through the bolt to be lifted by pushing the key up through the bolt; the key itself then slid the bolt along (*slide keys*). The final form was the *lever lock* which is essentially the same as the modern lock and is opened by turning the key. This is seen at its most complex in a small group of padlocks. The normal padlock was much simpler, the bolt having a set of spring-barbs which spring out when the bolt is pushed into the padlock case, but can be compressed again by the key to allow the bolt to be withdrawn. This is the *barb-spring padlock*.

66. Tumbler lock case (fragment) consisting of a large part of the face with the remains of nails at each of the three surviving corners, a slit for a bolt, and the end of the L-shaped key-hole. On the under-surface the remains of a spring (?) can be seen, probably the spring which held the tumblers in place. The edge of the face is turned down to lap the sides of the case. The whole piece is in an advanced state of corrosion. Length 8·1 cm. A IV 2, A.D. 155/160. II D, wall-trench 16/17.

This type of lock was opened with a slide key. Lock plates in bronze are more common than in iron (e.g. from London: Wheeler, *London in Roman Times*, 73, fig. 17) but an iron example is known from Newstead (*Newstead*, 307, pl. LXXVIII, 12).

67. Lock case (fragments). Two fragments from the top and side of a lock case. The edge of the top is lapped over the upper edge of the side plate, and the smaller fragment retains a nail. In the corner of the larger piece is a small, indeterminate fragment of mechanism. Lengths 6·1 cm.; 3·6 cm. A IV 2, A.D. 155/160. II D, Room 18.

The type of lock is uncertain but it was probably a tumbler or lever lock.

68. Lock (?) (fragment), consisting of two plates, one longer than the other, with a pair of concentric collars set between them. Through the centre of these collars runs a rivet with a massive head, and its tail turned over a square washer. Set slightly in from one edge of the larger upper plate is a rim which at one point appears to take the form of a rectangular tube. Corroded to the outer collar is a strip with a loop end. The fragment is almost certainly part of a mechanism, presumably a lock, but its method of functioning cannot be reconstructed. The collars are not circular wards since the inner one runs from one plate to the other leaving no gap for the key, nor is there a key-hole. Length 8·1 cm. B I 55, A.D. 280–315. III, occupation layer in cellar.

69. Fragment, possibly from a lock. Length 15·2 cm. The function of this object is uncertain, but it probably formed part of a mechanism, and a large and complex lock appears the most probable explanation. B I 19, A.D. 280–315. III, occupation layer in cellar.

70. Fragment, possibly from a lock. Length 18·5 cm. A IV 2, A.D. 155/160. II D, Room 18.

Like the preceding piece this would appear to come from a mechanical device, probably a complex lock.

71. Lever padlock. The case is cylindrical with the edges of one end turned down over the side while the other end was apparently set within the cylinder. The inset end is now badly broken and most of the internal mechanism is lost, but there projects from it a fragment of metal which is probably the remains of the chain which was attached to the lock. The opposite end is more complete, save for a hole at one side, probably an enlargement of the slit which received the free end of the chain, and a pair of holes which may represent the key-hole now blocked by corrosion. Diameter 6·6 cm. B I 55, A.D. 280–315. III, occupation layer in cellar.

This is almost certainly a lever padlock of the type found at the Lullingstone Villa and Caerleon (*Bull. Board of Celtic Studies*, xxii, pt. iv (1968), 410), and in a modified form at the Fishbourne Villa (Site Museum). Unfortunately the mechanism varies from one example to another and when it has been largely lost, as here, it cannot be restored with certainty even with the aid of X-ray photographs.

72. Barb-spring padlock case (fragmentary), consisting of the top of the cylindrical case, parts of the ends, and a large part of the long straight hasp. Length *c.* 45·7 cm. B I 55, as no. 71.

This is an exceptionally large example of a common form. Smaller examples come from Verulamium (*Verulamium*, 219, pl. LXV, A. 15), Silchester (Reading Museum), etc. An example of comparable size and shape comes from Tallington, Lincs. (Lincoln Museum), but the cases of large locks are normally rectangular (e.g. those from *Great Chesterford*, 7, pl. 2, 24, 26, and 27, and Silchester, *Archaeologia*, lvii (1901), 247, fig. 5).

Fig. 68

73. Latch lifter with a flat, damaged handle. Length 22·8 cm. B IV 14, A.D. 270–300+. III, make-up below mosaic, XIV, 5 Room 3. This is a very common type, first appearing in the Iron Age at such sites as Glastonbury (*Glastonbury*, ii, 375, pl. LXII, 156) and occurring at Woodcuts (*Cranborne Chase*, i, 76, pl. XXV, 5), Rotherley (*Cranborne Chase*, ii, 136, pl. CV, 5), Silchester (Reading Museum), and Verulamium itself (*Verulamium*, 219, pl. LXV, B, 21), etc.

74. T-shaped lift key, with an anchor-shaped bit, and a turned-over loop at the end of the shank. Length 10·2 cm. B II 30C, A.D. 75–105. II A, Room 20.

Similar keys are common; examples come from the Brampton, Cumb., Hoard (*Brampton Hoard*, 34, no. 47), London (Wheeler, *London in Roman Times*, 73, pl. XXX, A, 1), Silchester (Reading Museum), etc.

75. Tumbler-lock slide key, of simple form with four massive teeth set at right angles to the bit. The handle is pierced at its top. Length 12·7 cm. B II 13, A.D. 270–5. III, make-up, XIV, 5 Rooms 2 and 4 (Antonine fire, disturbed).

The type is not uncommon and similar examples come from Hod Hill (*Hod Hill*, i, 18, pl. XII, K 10), Verulamium itself (*Verulamium*, 220, pl. LXV, B, 25 and 26), London (Wheeler, *London in Roman Times*, 73, pl. XXX, A, 6–8), etc.

76. Tumbler-lock slide key, basically similar to the preceding. The bit retains only one tooth and is distorted; the shank ends with a small pierced handle. Length 14·5 cm. B IV 36, A.D. 60. I, Rooms 26–31.

77. Tumbler-lock slide key, with a plain bit and pierced handle. Length 7·6 cm. B VI Pit 2, fourth century. Mouth of Pit 14.

This is a common type, both in bronze and iron. Although a similar key from Woodcuts (*Cranborne Chase*, i, 74, pl. XXIV, 4) also lacks teeth on the bit, in both cases this is probably the effect of

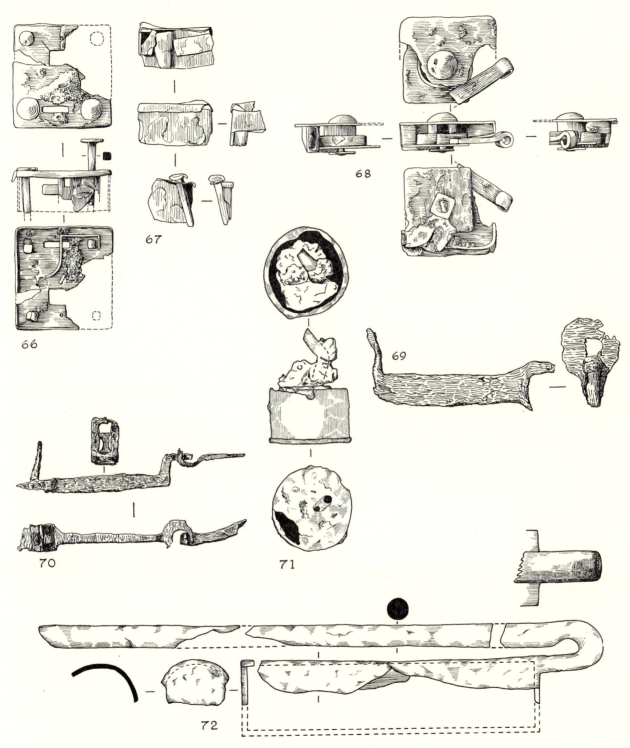

FIG. 67. Iron objects 66–72 ($\frac{1}{3}$).

corrosion. Other examples, with teeth, come from Verulamium (*Verulamium*, 219, pl. LXV, B, 23 and 27), London (Wheeler, *London in Roman Times*, 74, pl. XXX, B, 1, 3, 4, 5), Silchester (Reading Museum), etc.

78. Tumbler-lock slide key, with a pierced handle and slight remains of the teeth on the bit. Length 7·6 cm. B II 27B, A.D. 140–50. II C, Room 43.

79. Lever-lock key, with a rectangular bit with the remains of two slits at the front and three at the bottom, and a round bow. The end of the stem was tubular. Length 5·8 cm. A VI, unstratified.
    Basically similar keys come from many sites including Richborough (*Richborough IV*, 154, pl. LIX, 322), Woodcuts (*Cranborne Chase*, i, 74, pl. XXIV, 7 and 9), London (Wheeler, *London in Roman Times*, 74, pl. XXXI, 1–6, all in bronze), etc.

80. Barb-spring padlock key with a rolled loop at one end of the shank and the remains of the square bit at the other. Length 17·0 cm. B I 9, A.D. 310–15. III, cellar filling.
    Originally the bit will have been rectangular with one or more holes in it. Similar keys come from Rotherley (*Cranborne Chase*, ii, 137, pl. CV, 13), the Great Chesterford hoard (*Great Chesterford*, 7, pl. 2, 25; an unusually large and elaborate key), Silchester (Reading Museum), etc.

81. Barb-spring padlock key similar to the preceding. Length 14·0 cm. B I 27, A.D. 280–90. Packing of cellar steps.

82. T-staple. Length 31·8 cm. B III 17, A.D. 270–300+. III, make-up, XIV, 5 Room 3.
    This is an exceptionally large example of a common type which comes in a wide range of sizes. They could have numerous structural functions, but are known to have held box-flue tiles and other tiles in position. Examples of this size are relatively uncommon but others of some length come from Newstead (*Newstead*, 289, pl. LXVII, 1) and the Brading, I.O.W., Villa (*Brading Ironwork*, 58, fig. 3, g).

83. T-staple with a broken stem. Length 8·4 cm. A I, A.D. 155/160. II D, Room 23, north-west wall-trench.

84. Joiner's dog, with blunted arms. Length of arms 5·8 cm. A VII, c. A.D. 130. II B, wall-trench 22/26.
    A common type which varies greatly in size and was used for joining two pieces of wood. Many are known from Pitt-Rivers's Cranborne Chase sites (e.g. Woodyates, *Cranborne Chase*, iii, 139, pl. CLXXXIV, 7; Woodcuts, *Cranborne Chase*, i, 86, pl. XXVIII, 14; Rotherley, *Cranborne Chase*, ii, 136, pl. CV, 6), Silchester (Reading Museum), etc.

85. Joiner's dog with one arm broken. Length 8·4 cm. B I 55, A.D. 280–315. III, occupation layer in cellar.

86. U-shaped wall hook, with a spike for driving it into wood or a wall. Length 8·4 cm. B II 28C, A.D. 130–40. II C, Room 41.
    It is a common type with many uses and examples may be quoted from Silchester (Reading Museum), Caistor-by-Norwich (Norwich Castle Museum), Caerwent (Newport Museum) and, with a knob at the tip of the hook, from the Brampton Hoard (*Brampton Hoard*, 30, no. 40).

87. U-shaped wall hook with the remains of a spike. Length 9·4 cm. Similar to the preceding. A VI 2, A.D. 155/160. II D, Room 18.

88. U-shaped wall hook which has lost the spike. Length 14·0 cm. Similar to the two preceding. B IV 27X, A.D. 130–40. II C, Room 43.

89. U-shaped wall hook. Length 11·7 cm. A I 13, A.D. 140–50. II C, Room 24.

90. Split-spike loop with the arms bent outwards. Length 11·4 cm. B I 19, A.D. 280–315. III, occupation layer in cellar.
    The outward bend in the arms indicates the thickness of wood through which it was driven. It is a very common type with a multitude of uses; often they hold another split-spike loop to form a simple hinge (e.g. from Woodcuts, *Cranborne Chase*, i, 82, pl. XXVI, 6), or a ring (e.g. *Newstead*, 289, pl. LXVII, 12). Examples of such loops are in all the major site collections such as those from Silchester (Reading Museum), Caerwent (Newport Museum), etc.

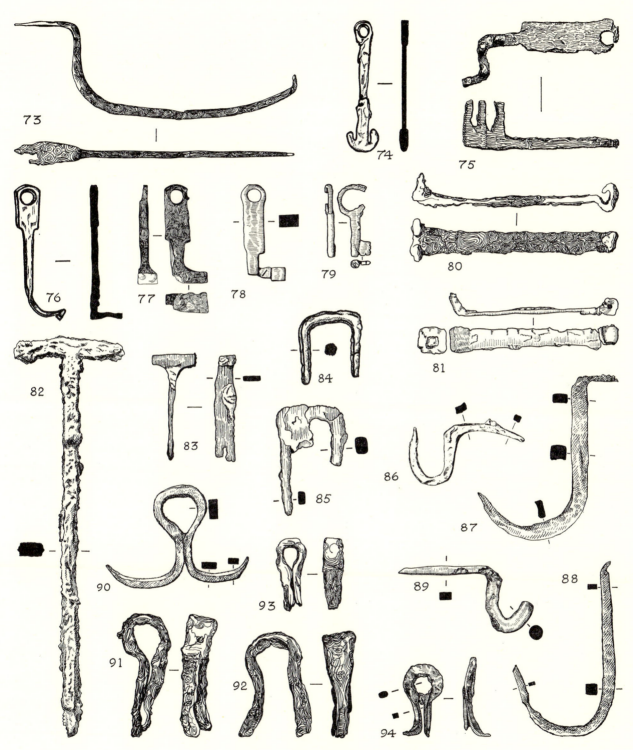

FIG. 68. Iron objects 73–94 ($\frac{1}{3}$).

91. Split-spike loop with straight arms. Length 9·7 cm. B I 9, A.D. 310–15. III, cellar filling.
92. Split-spike loop with the arms forced apart. Length 8·4 cm. B I 9, as no. 91.
93. Split-spike loop. Length 5·8 cm. B I 9, as nos. 90, 91.
94. Split-spike loop. Length 6·4 cm. B XIV 1A, plough-soil.

Fig. 69

95. Ring-headed pin, with a turn-over head. Length 10·7 cm. B IV 23L, A.D. 115–30. II B, Room 34.
    Pins of this type were probably intended to be driven into woodwork. Examples come from
    Newstead (*Newstead*, 289, pl. LXVII, 14), Woodcuts (*Cranborne Chase*, i, 90, pl. XXVII, 3 and pl. XXIX,
    16), Silchester (Reading Museum), etc.
96. Ring-headed pin. Length 10·0 cm. B I 55, A.D. 280–315. III, occupation layer in cellar.
97. Rectangular-headed pin. Length 10·9 cm. Functionally it is no doubt similar to the ring-headed
    pins. B IV 41D, A.D. 49–55. I, Room 26.
98. Ring-headed pin with a short, bent stem. Length 5·3 cm. B I 55, A.D. 280–315. III, occupation
    layer in cellar.

Nails

The great majority of Romano-British nails fall within one of two general types:
    I: with a square sectioned, tapering stem, the larger specimens having a round, conical or pyramidal
      head, often flattened by hammering, the smaller examples having an almost flat head.
    II: with a rectangular sectioned, tapering stem and a triangular head with marked shoulders, but
      of the same thickness as the stem. The top of the head is often rounded by hammering.

Both types have an almost continuous range in length between 2·5 and 3·5 cm., but Type I is far
commoner than Type II.

In publishing the nails from the Brading, I.O.W., Villa, H. F. Cleere produced a detailed classification which included these and other, rarer types (H. Cleere, 'Roman Domestic Ironwork as illustrated by the Brading I.O.W. Villa', *Bull. Inst. Arch.* i, 55 ff.). Later, in publishing the Inchtuthil hoard of nails, he advanced a modified classification (Angus, Brown, and Cleere, 'The Iron Nails from the Roman Legionary Fortress at Inchtuthil, Perths.', *J. Iron and Steel Inst.* cc (1962), 956). Useful as these classifications are, neither group contained all the types found at other sites, the most obvious gap being the complete absence of our Type II nails at Inchtuthil. The subdivisions of the Inchtuthil groups were based on a number of criteria including the thickness of the head, the exact weight, and the section of the stem 0·5 inches below the head, all measurements which the remarkable preservation of part of the hoard made possible but which are less meaningful in the corroded specimens usually found. Sub-divisions, probably based on length, certainly existed, but until more work has been done on large groups it is safer to record the length and not to attempt groupings.

In addition to the nails from the Brading Villa and Inchtuthil, quite large groups are published from Woodcuts (*Cranborne Chase*, i, 94, pl. XXX), Bokerly Dyke (*Cranborne Chase*, iii, 126, pl. CLXXXI), and Newstead (*Newstead*, 289, pl. LXVII).

  99. Nail, Type I. Length 14·7 cm. B I 11, A.D. 310–15. III, cellar filling.
100. Nail, Type I. Length 12·2 cm. V XXXII 3, A.D. 270–300. Metalling south-west of XIV, 1.
101. Nail, Type I. Length 10·9 cm. B I 9, A.D. 310–15. III, cellar filling.
102. Nail, Type I. Length 10·2 cm. A IV 8, A.D. 155/160. II D, Room 17.
103. Nail, Type I. Length 9·7 cm. A V 10, A.D. 155/160. II D, Room 15.
104. Nail, Type I. Length 9·7 cm. B V 5, Antonine fire, disturbed. II D, Rooms 41–8.
105. Nail, Type I. Length 9·7 cm. A IV 2, A.D. 155/160. II D, Room 18.

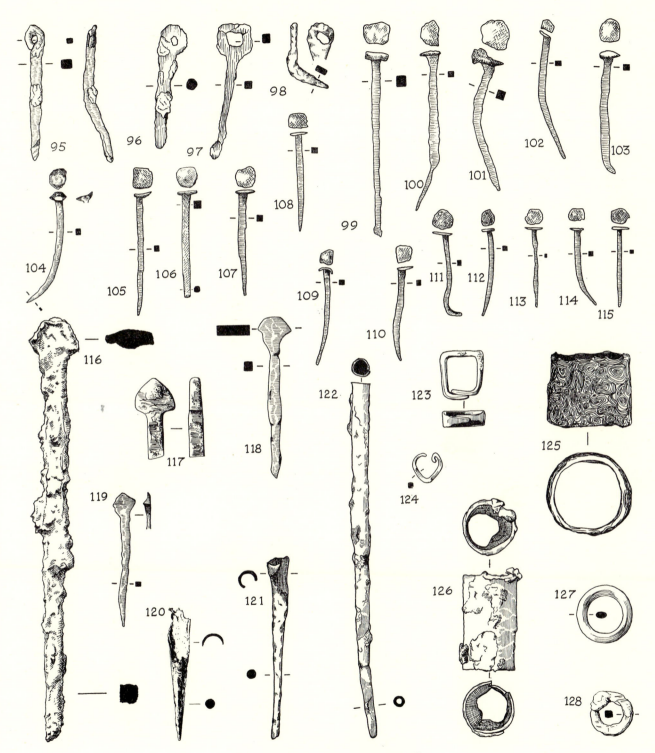

FIG. 69. Iron objects 95–128 (⅓).

106. Nail, Type I. Tip broken. Length 8·4 cm. B I 18, A.D. 155/160. II D, Rooms 25, 35.
107. Nail, Type I. Length 8·4 cm. B I 18, as no. 106.
108. Nail, Type I. Length 7·9 cm. B V 7, A.D. 155/160. II D, Rooms 41–8.
109. Nail, Type I. Length 7·9 cm. B V 7, as no. 108.
110. Nail, Type I. Length 7·4 cm. A IV 2, as no. 105.
111. Nail, Type I. Length 7·1 cm. A IV 8, as no. 102.
112. Nail, Type I. Length 6·9 cm. B VII 4, A.D. 155/160. II D, Room 52.
113. Nail, Type I. Length 6·4 cm. A XI 3, Antonine fire, disturbed. II D, Room 13.
114. Nail, Type I. Length 6·1 cm. A IV 8, as no. 102.
115. Nail, Type I. Length 6·4 cm. T II 8, A.D. 155/160. II D, Room 25A.
116. Nail, Type II. Length 33·8 cm. B I 55, A.D. 280–315. III, occupation layer in cellar.
117. Nail, Type II. Head and top of stem. Length 6·4 cm. B I 55, as no. 116.
118. Nail, Type II. Length 13·0 cm. B I 9, A.D. 310–15. III, cellar filling.
119. Nail, Type II. Length 10·7 cm. B V 22, A.D. 155/160. II D, Interspace north-west of Room 43.
120. Ferrule, with a broken socket. Length 10·7 cm. A II 16, A.D. 150–155/160. II D, Room 19.
      Simple conical ferrules are common finds which could have a number of functions. The most probable is that they shod the ends of sticks or spears, but it should be remembered that similar objects were used until recently to sheath the tips of wooden pitchforks.
      Similar ferrules come from Rotherley (*Cranborne Chase*, ii, 138, pl. cvi, 10), Woodcuts (*Cranborne Chase*, i, 90, pl. xxix, 19), Newstead (*Newstead*, 280, pl. lviii, 6), Silchester (Reading Museum), etc.
121. Ferrule, with a damaged socket. Length 15·0 cm. B I 11, A.D. 310–15. III, cellar filling.
122. Long ferrule (?), tapering evenly from a narrow socket into a solid tip. Length 28·0 cm. B XV 11, A.D. 150–155/160. II D, Room 55.
      Although it is presumably a ferrule it cannot have been intended for rough usage. I know of no other example of comparable length.
123. Ferrule-binding (?), formed by bending a small piece of iron rod into a rectangle. Length 3·8 cm. A I 2, A.D. 155/160. II D, Room 23.
      This is the type of binding which would serve to prevent the end of a wooden stick from splitting. Almost identical pieces are published from Woodcuts (*Cranborne Chase*, i, 90, pl. xxix, 20) and Rotherley (*Cranborne Chase*, ii, pl. cv, 9), whilst a small square collar from Newstead (*Newstead*, 288, pl. lxvi, 5) may have served a similar function.
124. Ferrule-binding (?), similar to the preceding, but forced open. Length 2·5 cm. A X 23, A.D. 75–80. II A, Room 16, make-up.
125. Collar. Diameter 6·9 cm. B I P.H. 5, A.D. 155/160. II D, posthole in wall-trench 25/30.
      Such collars could have a multitude of functions. They are rarely published, but there are many in the Silchester and other collections.
126. Collar or binding. Diameter 4·3 cm. B XV 11, A.D. 150–155/160. II D, Room 55.
127. Ring, with an oval cross-section. Diameter 4·6 cm. B I 31D, A.D. 140–50. II C, Room 28.
      Such rings are very common and could have many uses. Examples are published from Woodcuts (*Cranborne Chase*, i, 83, pl. xxvii, 1), the Brampton hoard (*Brampton Hoard*, 36, no. 51), etc. and there are many examples in all the major collections.
128. Ring, with a square cross-section. Diameter 3·6 cm. A VI 19, A.D. 130–50. II C, Room 19.

Fig. 70

Bindings

A great deal of Roman woodwork was strengthened and protected by iron plates and bindings. In many cases these are nothing more than strips of iron which were nailed to the wood, but occasionally

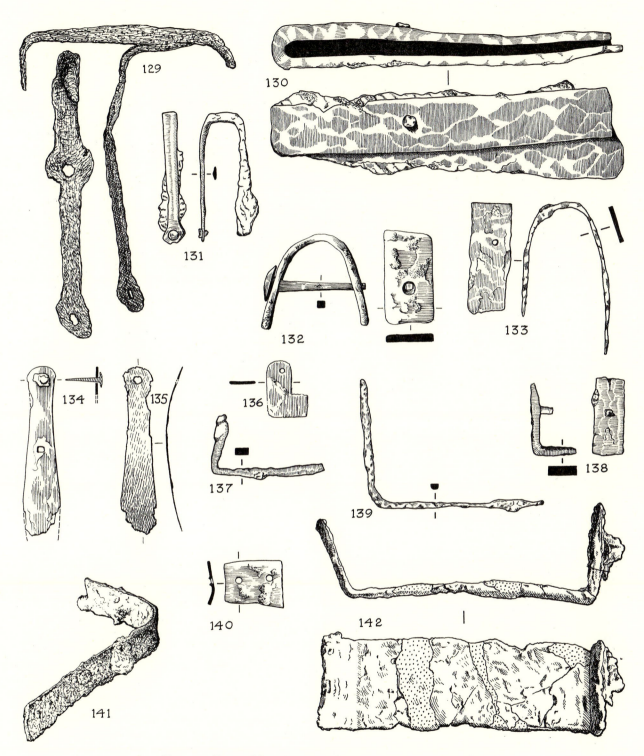

FIG. 70. Iron objects 129–42 (all ⅓ except no. 141 (⅙)).

they achieve some degree of elaboration. The majority of the more elaborate pieces were made for a specific purpose and without the woodwork their exact use is not clear; nor, of course, can we reasonably expect to find parallels for such pieces.

129. Binding, consisting of a strip, expanded around nail-holes at its tip and near the top; at the top it is welded at right angles to a bar which tapers into down-turned spikes at its ends. Length 22·9 cm. B I Pit 20, A.D. 300–15. III, box below cellar stairs.

Its exact purpose is not obvious; the strip was nailed to wood, and the spikes driven into, or turned over, more wood, but it was obviously made with a specific function in mind.

130. Binding (?) formed of a long bar bent double with the remains of a nail on one side. Length 28·8 cm. B I 55, A.D. 280–315. III, occupation layer in cellar.

131. U-shaped binding, with a rivet through the expanded end of one arm. The other arm is set in an immovable mass of corrosion, but was probably similar. Length 10·4 cm. B V 19, A.D. 155/160. II D, Room 43, wall-trench. It is probably from a chest or something similar.

132. U-shaped binding (fragment) with a nail between the two limbs; the arms were originally longer. Length 7·4 cm. B I 55, as no. 130.

U-shaped bindings are quite common, and were often used to strengthen doors. Published examples come from the West Gate and a postern at Silchester (*Archaeologia*, lii (1891), 756, pl. XXXIII, fig. 5; ibid. lv (1897), 427), the Great Chesterford hoard (*Great Chesterford*, 7, pl. I, fig. 16), the Brampton hoard (*Brampton Hoard*, 34, no. 51), etc.

133. U-shaped binding with a single nail-hole. Length 12·2 cm. B XI 28, A.D. 270–300+. Yard floor sunk in Pit 19.

134. End of binding or hinge, with two nail-holes, one retaining a nail. Length 13·5 cm. A IV 2, A.D. 155/160. II D, Room 18.

135. End of binding with a terminal nail-hole. Length 13·0 cm.

The thinness and curve of the metal suggest that it may have bound a vessel or possibly a chest lid. A IV 2, as no. 134.

136. L-shaped plate, with a nail-hole in one arm; the other arm probably broken short. Probably a reinforcement for the corner of a wooden object. Length 4·6 cm. B IV 23B, A.D. 90–105. II A, Room 23.

137. L-shaped strip, probably a fragment of binding. Length 9·4 cm. B I 66, A.D. 60–75. Pit 7.

138. L-shaped binding (fragment), still retaining a nail. Length 6·1 cm. A I 2, A.D. 155/160. II D, Room 23.

139. L-shaped strip, probably a fragment of binding. Length 15·2 cm. B I 9, A.D. 310–15. III, cellar filling.

140. Plate, pierced by two nail-holes. Length 4·6 cm. A I 2, as no. 138.

141. Binding, bent through a right angle and now broken at its ends. There are the remains of a nail-hole at the end of the shorter arm. Length 28·0 cm. B I 55, A.D. 280–315. III, occupation layer in cellar.

142. Binding, turned down at the ends. No nail-holes are visible but it is in a very poorly preserved state. Length 20·3 cm. B I 55, as no. 141.

Fig. 71

143. Binding (fragment), turned over at one end and broken. It is very corroded but what appears to be the remains of a nail can be seen near the end. Length 28·0 cm. B I 55, with no. 142.

144. Binding (?), slightly constricted at its centre with turned-up ends. Length 17·8 cm. A IV 8, A.D. 155/160. II D, Room 17.

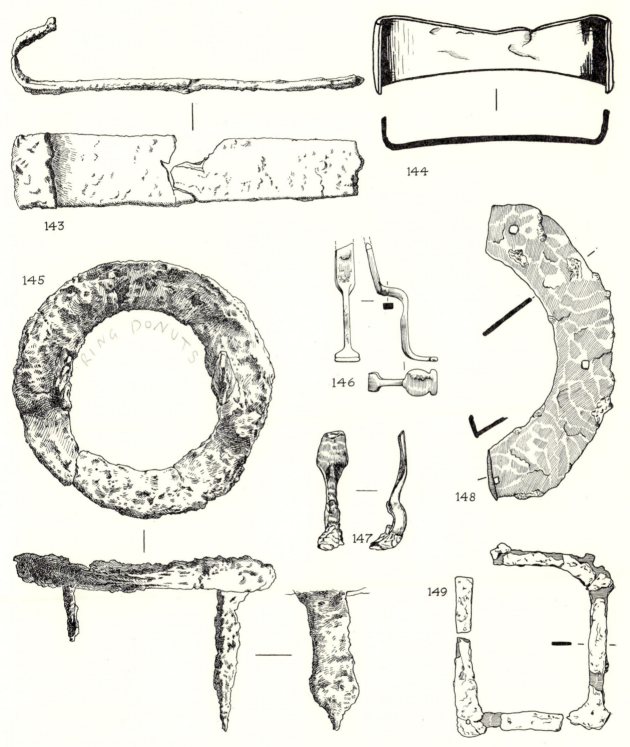

FIG. 71. Iron objects 143–9 ($\frac{1}{3}$).

145. Stand (?), formed of a flat ring with a pair of legs set opposite each other. Both of the legs are broken short. Diameter 20·3 cm. B I Pit 20, A.D. 300–15. III, box below cellar stairs.

Although some form of stand appears to be the most probable explanation it is by no means certain.

146. Leg and foot (?), possibly from a box or tripod. Length 9·4 cm. B I 37G, A.D. 105–15. II B, Room 24.

The 'foot' is clearly complete but the top of the leg is broken. The present angle of the top of the leg may be the result of its being bent when it was broken.

147. Leg and foot, probably from a box or vessel. Length 9·7 cm. B I 55, A.D. 280–315. III, occupation layer in cellar.

148. Flat ring (fragment). Somewhat under half the ring with three nail-holes survives. It is turned up at one end, probably when it was broken. Length 23·4 cm. A VII 3, A.D. 155/160. II D, Room 25.

Similar rings come from the Carlingwark Loch hoard (*Three Hoards*, 37, fig. 9, C 38), Silchester (Reading Museum), and Caistor-by-Norwich (Norwich Castle Museum). When publishing the Carlingwark Loch example Professor Piggott suggested that it might be the rim of a circular shield-boss; but this suggestion must be rejected, since it is clearly one of a group none of which shows any signs of the central boss. More probably they strengthened the centre of a circular wooden structure formed of separate segments.

149. Square frame with circular, pierced expansions at the corners. One corner is lost. Length 14·0 cm. B I 55, as no. 147.

It is presumably a reinforcing binding, but its exact purpose is not obvious.

Fig. 72

150. Stud on a fragment of sheet, probably a fragment from an iron-bound box or casket. Length 4·1 cm. B XIII 9, A.D. 155/160. II D, south-east wall-trench of Room 48.

Iron-cased caskets with similar studs and other mounts have been found at a number of sites including Radnage, Bucks. (*Antiq. Journ.* iii (1923), 152) and Boxmoor, Herts. (British Museum). Very large iron strong boxes are known from Pompeii with almost identical studs (Museo Nazionale, Naples).

151. Plate (fragment) bent and broken at one end. Length 10·9 cm. B I 55, A.D. 280–315. III, occupation layer in cellar.

152. Socket with a strengthening bar which will have run back along a wooden handle. There is a nail-hole at the end of the bar. Length 22·4 cm. It could come from a variety of tools. B I 19, A.D. 280–315. III, occupation layer in cellar.

153. Terminal ending in a loop (fragment). Length 6·9 cm. A I 2, A.D. 155/160. II D, Room 23.

154. Terminal ending in a loop (fragment). Length 7·9 cm. B III 10A, A.D. 270–300+. III, make-up, XIV, 5 Room 3.

155. Bar with a double hook through it at one end. Length 28·4 cm. B I Pit 20, A.D. 300–15. III, box below cellar stairs. The bar is broken and incomplete.

156. Round collar and rectangular plate, with a nail through them. Whether the collar is welded to the plate is uncertain, but the position of the nail suggests that it is not. Length 4·3 cm. B I 9, A.D. 310–15. III, cellar filling.

157. Bolt (?). An L-shaped bar ending with a disc head. Length 25·4 cm. B I 9, as no. 156.

It *may* have been a bolt moving in iron loops with the disc head serving as a stop to prevent it pulling out, while the shorter arm formed the handle. Other uses are, however, equally probable.

158. Scraper (?), with a tang, down-turned blade and slightly curving edge. The whole is distorted but apparently complete. Length 10·7 cm. B I Pit 20, as no. 155.

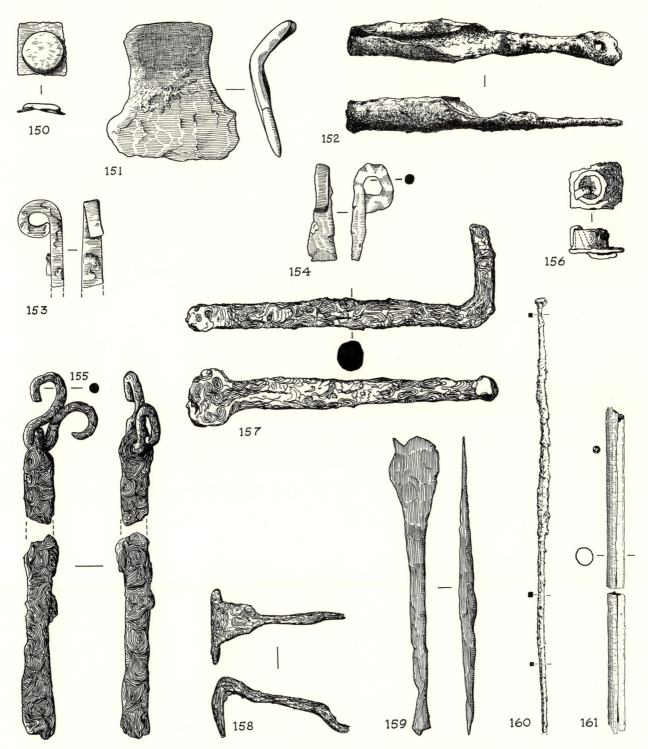

150

151

152

153

154

155

156

157

158

159

160

161

FIG. 72. Iron objects 150–61 (all ⅓ except no. 160 (⅙)).

Tanged 'scrapers' of this general type come from Housesteads (Museum of Antiquities, Newcastle), Silchester (Reading Museum), Caistor-by-Norwich (Norwich Castle Museum), and Chalton, Hants (*Antiq. Journ.* xxxvii (1957), 218, fig. 2 B).

159. Modelling tool (?), consisting of a central stem with a flat blade at one end, and what appears to be the remains of a second blade at the other end. Length 23·8 cm. B II 26G, A.D. 150–155/160. II D, Room 32.

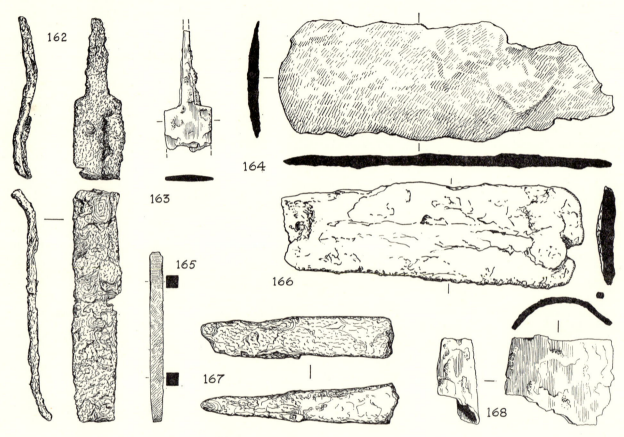

FIG. 73. Iron objects 162–8 (⅓).

Double-bladed modelling tools or spatulas are not uncommon though they are usually smaller than this. Many come from London (Guildhall Museum), Silchester (Reading Museum), etc.

160. Rod, with a square cross-section, and a flat, bulbous end; the other end is probably broken. Length 68·6 cm. B XV 3, A.D. 155/160. II D, Room 55.

It could have had many functions, but is probably a part of some larger and more complex object.

161. Tube, formed by rolling a sheet of iron. The junction is open and it is broken at both ends and in the middle. Length 51·1 cm. B I 18, A.D. 155/160. II D, Rooms 25, 35, Antonine fire debris.

No comparable length of tubing is known to the writer. It could have had many functions; if the join was originally sealed in some way it might have been used as a pipe, but there is, in fact, little sign that this was so. It is perhaps more likely that it encased a wooden rod.

Fig. 73

162. Sword, which has been violently broken. The tip is missing and it is in a very poor state of preservation. Length 31·8 cm. B I 55, A.D. 280–315. III, occupation layer in cellar.

   X-ray photographs (taken by Mr. H. W. M. Hodges) reveal that it is not pattern-welded.
Although swords are more commonly found on military sites a number are known from civilian
sites including London (Guildhall Museum), where it may have had a military origin, and Silchester
(1890 hoard; *Archaeologia*, liv (1894), 140, fig. 1). The sword is too damaged for a meaningful
discussion of the type.

163. Sword (fragment), part of the tang and blade. Length 9·4 cm. Z I 12, A.D. 130–50. II C, Room 7.

164. Bar of irregular shape. Length 27·2 cm. Probably scrap. B I 55, as no. 162.

165. Bar of rectangular section, probably broken at the ends. Length 13·2 cm. It may originally have
been a punch. B IV 17D, A.D. 145–50. II C, Room 45.

166. Bar of irregular shape. Length 24·4 cm. Probably scrap. B I 16, A.D. 270–5. III, make-up, XIV, 5.

167. Bar of irregular shape. Length 15·7 cm. Probably scrap. B III, in mouth of late pit.

168. Semicircular plate of irregular shape. Length 8·7 cm. Probably a piece of scrap binding. B I 31D,
A.D. 140–50. II C, Room 28.

III. THE GLASS

by Dorothy Charlesworth, F.S.A.

The glass which is discussed is only a part of the total amount found in the excavations. Many of the pieces could not be identified. This applies particularly to the fragments of bottle glass, undecorated, convex blown glass which might come from one of a number of different shapes made at any time in the first three centuries A.D. There are also some base and rim fragments which could not be assigned to a type or to an exact date and were left out. Only a few unidentified pieces have been included, each for a particular reason, the technique, the metal or the decoration singling it out. With so much material unidentifiable on the one hand and other types immediately recognizable from even the smallest fragment, no accurate conclusions on the use of glass in this part of Verulamium can be drawn. It is, however, worth noting the quantity of good-quality cut-glass of third-century date on the one hand, and the absence (with two exceptions) of the fine wares of the early to middle part of the first century on the other.

(i) *Moulded dish*

Fig. 74, 1. B IV 18J, A.D. 130–45. II C, Room 39. The glass of the early to middle first century A.D. is hardly represented at Verulamium, but there is one fragment of thick emerald-green glass dish formed in a mould and polished. The inner surface is smooth. The rim has been accented on the outer surface by a groove and a rib below it in false relief. The fragment is too small to give the shape of the vessel but the metal and technique indicate that it was made in the first half of the first century A.D. or earlier. The use of the rich emerald-green and the production of plain moulded shapes died out by the middle of the century, and in Britain examples are found only on a few sites, mainly in the south-east, such as London and Camulodunum.

(ii) *Mould-blown bowls and beakers*

The following list shows the pieces present with their stratigraphy and its dating.

1. Fig. 74, 2. B I 70, A.D. 60–75. Pit 7.
2. Fig. 74, 3. B I 70, A.D. 60–75. Pit 7.
3. A I 38, A.D. 105–15. II B, Room 16.
4. B IV 21A, A.D. 105–15. II B, Room 26.
5. T II 1. Unstratified. XIV, 1.
6. Z I 1, A.D. 270–5. III, make-up for XIV, 2.

Mould-blown, decorated vessels are most common in the first century A.D. They are made in a two- or three-part mould, the junctions of which are visible on the finished vessel. In contrast with all other forms of decoration the glass is of uniform thickness throughout; where there is a boss or rib on the outside there is a hollow inside. Fragments of only four vessels in this technique were found.

Two are from ribbed bowls, one in deep-blue glass (no. 3), the other natural-green (no. 1, fig. 74, 2), a type made in both Syria–Palestine and Italy in the mid first century A.D. and found occasionally on sites in the south-east England, for example at London (Wheeler, *London in Roman Times*, 122, fig. 42, 5). Those at Camulodunum (p. 299, no. 548–9), although not identical, belong to the same general class.

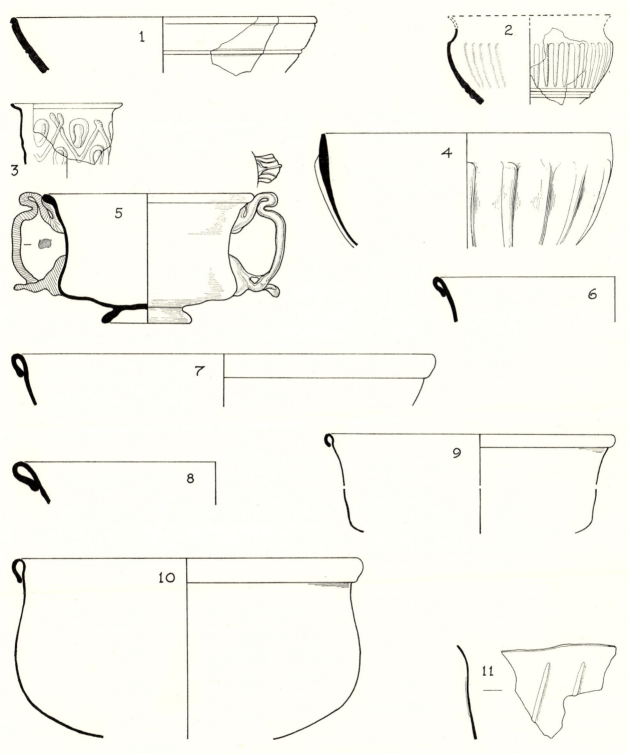

FIG. 74. Glass vessels 1–11 ($\frac{1}{2}$).

The other three pieces come from two beakers, both in yellowish glass decorated with lotus-bud in a diamond grid. Three pieces found in different seasons (nos. 4, 5, 6) belong to the same beaker and the rim fragment (no. 2, fig. 74, 3) may also be from this beaker. It is the same colour but clearer. This may only be differential weathering. The outsplayed rim is unusual: normally it is upright and either left rough or rounded in the flame. Some beakers have a dot alternating with the lotus-bud and no grid (Isings form 31).

The origin of the beakers is probably various, Syria–Palestine, Egypt, and Italy. They have a wide distribution. A typical example is illustrated in *Masterpieces of Glass* (British Museum, 1969), no. 62. They are not well dated. The fragment in amber colour found at Corbridge and the York beaker (R.C.H.M. *Eburacum*, fig. 88, HG 273) cannot be earlier than Flavian. Others are known from Bath and London. Several examples have been found at Pompeii, one at Nijmegen *c.* A.D. 30–70 and one in the pre-Hadrianic rubbish pit at Vindonissa (Isings, pp. 45–6). The Newport Pagnell beaker of this type, with dots alternating with the buds, is probably not from a Saxon grave but is a first-century vessel like the rest (D. B. Harden in *Dark Age Britain* (1956), 135–6). The lotus bud in a diamond grid is also used for a drinking horn (*Masterpieces*, no. 66).

(iii) *Pillar-moulded bowls*

The following list shows the pieces present with their stratigraphy and its dating.

1. Fig. 74, 4. A VII 32, A.D. 110–20. II B, Room 26.
2. T II 5, A.D. 270–5. III, make-up XIV, 1.
3. T II 19, A.D. 130–40. II C, Room 13.
4–7. A VI 23 (four examples), A.D. 105–15. II B, Room 26.
8. B I 38, A.D. 85–105. II A, accumulation outside Room 17.
9. B II 32G, A.D. 85–105. II A, accumulation outside Room 17.
10. B II 11, A.D. 310–15. III, cellar filling.
11. B I 68, A.D. 60–75. Pit 7.
12. B I 70, A.D. 60–75. Pit 7.
13. B I Pit 20, A.D. 280–315. Box below cellar stairs.
14. B I Pit 21, A.D. 49–60 (?). Pit cut by north-west corner of cellar.
15. B III 10B, A.D. 270–5. III, make-up, XIV, 5.
16. B V 21B, A.D. 270–5. III, make-up, XIV, 5.
17. T XX 23, A.D. 105–15. II B, Room 7.

These broad-ribbed bowls, made in a mould and polished inside and on the rim, are one of the most common first-century types of vessel, partly because the thick glass is durable and partly because even small fragments are recognizable. Pieces of seventeen bowls were found, all except one in natural-green glass. The exception (no. 17) is in a deep amber colour, popular in the first century A.D.

No individual descriptions are given as there is no complete bowl-section available. One typical fragment is illustrated (fig. 74, 4). All the vessels belong to the normal first-century B.C./A.D. type with broad, long ribs continuing under the base of the vessel and with two wheel-cut grooves on the base inside. These bowls (Isings form 3a) cannot be closely dated. This form is the most common of the three main subdivisions of the type, all of which are found in both the eastern and western provinces of the empire. The other two are short-ribbed bowls, the ribbing ending on the side of the vessel (Isings form 3c). One, with thick widely spaced ribs and (generally) two wheel-cut lines below the rim on the inside, was probably not made after the end of the first century B.C. There is one example in a grave, probably Augustan, at Samothrace (*J. Glass Studies*, ix (1967), 39). The only known example in Britain is from a pre-Roman grave at Hertford Heath (*Archaeologia*, ci (1967), 52). Its absence from Verulamium and even Camulodunum is worth noting. The other short-ribbed bowl, with closely set ribs, is found at Camulodunum (pp. 301 f., no. 61) but not at Verulamium. Numerous examples of first-century A.D. long, broad-ribbed bowls can be cited. The variations in proportion of depth to rim-diameter seem to have no significance. There are many at Camulodunum and at Richborough, Caerleon, London, etc. One example from Colchester is of particular interest for it was found in the First Pottery Shop, Insula 19, which also contained a bowl of the same shape in pottery. The shop was burned in A.D. 60 (M. R. Hull, *Roman Colchester*, 156–8). Two of the latest dated examples, in contexts where they cannot be survival material, are those from Pfünz, first occupied *c.* A.D. 90–100 and Benwell, on Hadrian's Wall, first occupied *c.* A.D. 122 (*AA*[4], iv (1927), 175). See also the mould-blown ribbed bowls mentioned above, section (ii).

(iv) *Handled bowl* (B II Pit 9, *c.* A.D. 105. Pit 9. Fig. 74, 5)

This incomplete bowl in poor quality blue-green glass, with a slightly everted rim rounded in the flame, straight side and pad base, is the cheap version of the cut-glass bowl, in imitation of silver work, made in the first centuries B.C. and A.D. The blown vessel is probably not earlier than the middle of the first century A.D. An example was found in the potter's shop, Colchester (*Roman Colchester*, 157–8), thought to have been burnt down in Boudicca's revolt. Similar bowls have been found at Pompeii and in the pre-Hadrianic rubbish pit at Vindonissa. Isings form 39.

(v) *Bowls with hollow tubular rims*

The following list shows the pieces present with their stratigraphy and its dating.
1. Fig. 74, 6. T XX 10, A.D. 155/160. II D, north-west wall-trench of Room 10.
2. Fig. 74, 7. T II 19, A.D. 130–40. II C, Room 13.
3. Fig. 74, 8. A VII 32, A.D. 110–20. II B, Room 26.
4. Fig. 74, 9. B XV 4, A.D. 150–155/160. II D, Room 55.
5. Fig. 74, 10. A XIII 8, A.D. 105–15. II B, Room 11.
6. Fig. 74, 11. T II 19, as no. 2 above.
7. B I 40A, A.D. 75–105. II A, wall-trench, Room 17.
8. A VI 15, A.D. 130–40. II C, Room 13.
9. B IV 23D, A.D. 90–105. II A, Room 23.
10. A IV 28, A.D. 105–30. II B, Room 11.
11. A VII 32, as no. 3 above.
12. A X 19, A.D. 85–105. II A, Room 16.
13. B II 27D, A.D. 140–50. II C, Room 40.
14. B IV 3A, A.D. 155/160. II D, Antonine fire (disturbed).
15. A X 70, A.D. 75–90. II A, Room 16.
16. B III 7 and B III 9, A.D. 350–410+. XIV, 5.
17. B XI 29, A.D. 175–275. Pit 19, later filling.
18. B XIV 8, A.D. 270–5. III, make-up, XIV, 6.

These are one of the most persistent types of glass vessel. They appear on wall-paintings at Pompeii and the Boscoreale villa (before A.D. 79), and one was found in a Saxon grave at Highdown. Except in graves they are seldom found intact. The rim and/or base is found but the thin sides are smashed. This is the case here, where rims of seventeen bowls have been found (and one body sherd, no. 6). One of these rims, no. 1 (fig. 74, 6) is in deep-blue glass, a metal which suggests a first-century date. Five are in yellowish-green; three of these are from large bowls, no. 3 (fig. 74, 8), no. 7, and a third (no. 2, fig. 74, 7) represented by joining pieces found in different seasons; the remaining two, nos. 8, 9, are from smaller bowls, one of which has unusually heavy flaking iridescent weathering. The remainder, e.g. fig. 74, 9 and 10, are all in natural-green glass. Both plain and ribbed bowls are known: a fragment of one ribbed bowl, no. 6 (fig. 74, 11) in yellowish-green glass, is illustrated. A complete example of this latter type is shown in *Antiquities of Roman Britain* (British Museum), pl. xii, 6.

(vi) *Bottles*

The following list shows the pieces present with their stratigraphy and its dating.

1. Fig. 75, 12. A XI 14, A.D. 105–30. II B, Room 12.
2. Fig. 75, 13. B XI 20, late fourth century. Mouth of Pit 19.
3. Fig. 75, 14. A IV 2, A.D. 155/160. II D, Room 18.
4. Fig. 75, 15. B II 19, A.D. 280–90. III, packing behind cellar wall.
5. Fig. 75, 16. T VII 5, A.D. 270–5. III, make-up, XIV, 1.
6. Fig. 75, 17. T II 8, A.D. 155/160. II D, Room 25A. Distorted by fire.
7. Fig. 75, 18. T VII 9, A.D. 155/160. II D, Rooms 6, 7. See below.
8. Fig. 75, 19. B I 30C, A.D. 150–155/160. II D, Room 33.
9. T VII 26, A.D. 105–15. II B, Room 4, make-up.
10. T XX 2, A.D. 155/160. II D, Room 10.
11. A II 7, A.D. 155/160. II D, Rooms 20–2.
12. A VI 9, A.D. 130–40. II C, Room 19.
13. A VII 29, A.D. 120–30. II B, Room 29.
14. B I 31D, A.D. 140–50. II C, Room 28.
15. B I 30A, A.D. 150–155/160. II D, Room 26.
16. B I Pit 7, A.D. 60–75. Pit 7.
17. B II Pit 6, A.D. 150–155/160. II D, Room 33, fuel-pit.
18. B II 28E, A.D. 135–45. II C, Room 37.
19. B IV Pit 7, A.D. 145–50. II C, small pit in Room 37.
20. B IV 3, A.D. 155/160. II D, Rooms 38–42.
21. B IV 13, A.D. 130–50. II C, Room 37.
22. A XI 13, A.D. 115–30. II B, Room 12.
23. B III 1. Unstratified. Plough-soil over XIV, 5 Room 3.
24, 25. B III 10C, A.D. 270–300+ (two examples). III, make-up, XIV, 5 Room 3.
26. B III 11, A.D. 155/160. II D, Room 31.
27. B III 6, A.D. 270–300+. III, make-up below mosaic, XIV, 5 Room 3.
28. B III Pit 1, A.D. 370–410+. Late pit cutting south edge of mosaic XIV, 5 Room 3.
29. B XI 11, A.D. 155/160. II D, Room 45.
30, 31. B XIII 4, fourth century (two examples). III, disturbed burnt daub in XIV, 6 Room 2.
32. B XIII 6, A.D. 270–5. III, make-up, XIV, 6 Room 2.

Pieces of thirty-two bottles were identified and there are fragments of natural-green glass which could also be from bottles but are not distinctive. Most of the identified pieces were from square bottles but the rim, neck, and handle is similar whether the body be square, rectangular, octagonal, hexagonal, or triangular in section, or cylindrical. Fig. 75, 12, 13, and 15 show the typical rim and handle. Two fragments (nos. 30, 32) are definitely part of cylindrical bottles.

The most interesting fragments are the marked bases. Some have only a circle (fig. 75, 16) or concentric circles (fig. 75, 14, and 17, the latter distorted by fire; also nos. 22, 26, and 30 (unfigured)). One (fig. 75, 18) has part of an inscription ..]ERC[.. retrograde (*JRS* xlviii (1958), 153, no. 15). Mr. R. P. Wright quotes a circular stamp **MERCO F** (*CIL* xii, 5696, 11) as a possible clue to its completion. Another fragment has part of a square with a circle (fig. 75, 19).

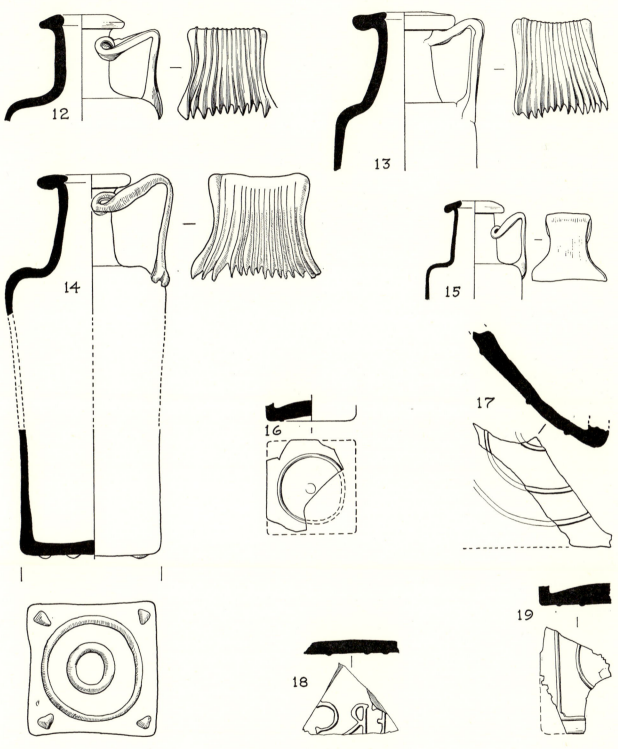

FIG. 75. Glass vessels 12–19 ($\frac{1}{2}$).

The period during which these bottles were most common was A.D. 70–120, but they first appear about ten years earlier and probably continued to be made until *c.* A.D. 140 (*J. Glass Studies*, viii (1966), 26 f., for square bottles; *Studies in Glass History* (ed. R. J. Charleston, Wendy Evans, A. E. Werner, 1970) for cylindrical). Most are mould-blown although some of the angular-bodied bottles are free-blown and flattened. From fragments it is difficult to decide on the technique. All are green or blue-green in colour from the impurities, mainly iron, in the sand or silica which is the basic material of all glass. None is deliberately coloured.

(vii) *Flagons*

The following list shows the pieces present with their stratigraphy and its dating.

1. Fig. 76, 20. B VI 10, A.D. 155/160. II D, Drain 51/56.
2. Fig. 76, 21. B I 70, A.D. 60–75. Pit 7.
3. T VI 28, A.D. 75–80. II A, Room 4, make-up.
4. T VI 7, A.D. 270–5. III, make-up, XIV, 1.
5. T VII 23, *c.* A.D. 130. II B, wall-trench 2/4.
6. A I 23, A.D. 130–40. II C, Room 23, concrete floor.
7. A I 27, A.D. 115–30. II B, Room 16.
8. A II 42, A.D. 75–105. II A, accumulation outside Rooms 12, 15.
9. B IV 23J, A.D. 105–15. II B, Room 29.
10. B I 70, as no. 2 above.
11. B VII 4, A.D. 155/160. II D, Room 52.
12. B XIII 7, A.D. 155/160. II D, Room 49.
13. { T XX 31, A.D. 60. I, Room 8, fuel-pit.
     { W VIII 10. Beneath Insula XXVIII, 1 Room 2.
     { V XV 13. Insula XIV, south-west of 1, Room 2.
14. A II 30, A.D. 130–40. II C, Room 28.
15. B I 51, A.D. 49–60. I, interspace 21/22.
16. B I 63, A.D. 60–75. Pit 7.
17. B XI 12, A.D. 150–155/160. II D, Room 46, floor.
18. A I 23, as no. 6 above.
19. A II 44, A.D. 105–15. II B, path 18.
20. B XV 11, A.D. 150–155/160. II D, Room 55.
21. T II 19, A.D. 130–40. II C, Room 13.

These are represented in most cases by handles. There are twenty-one vessels. Thirteen of these are in natural-green glass (nos. 1 (fig. 76, 20), 3–12, 17, 22). Five are in deep blue (nos. 2 (fig. 76, 21), 13, represented by three pieces of the same vessel from widely separated spots, and 14–16). Two are in amber colour (18, 19) and one in wine colour (20). This last is not a common colour for these flagons. The rich blue is generally associated with first-century glass. It is not always possible from the handle to tell whether the flagon is of the early to mid-first-century type or of the later group of *c.* A.D. 70–150, made in the Seine/Middle Rhine area. Only fragments of the neck and body would determine this, for the earlier flagons have a shortish, wide neck expanding gradually into a globular or conical unribbed, but not necessarily undecorated, body, while the later ones have a tall, narrow neck constricted at the base, and frequently a ribbed or else plain body. There is also more variety of body-shape in the later group. The flat strap-handle or handle with a single central rib is usually associated with conical-bodied flagons, the rib being carried down as a long 'tail' at the lower sticking part. Three or four ribbed handles come from globular or bulbous vessels, the ribs forming a 'claw' to grip on to the shoulder. Typical shapes are illustrated in *Arch. Ael.* xxxvii, 51, fig. 8.

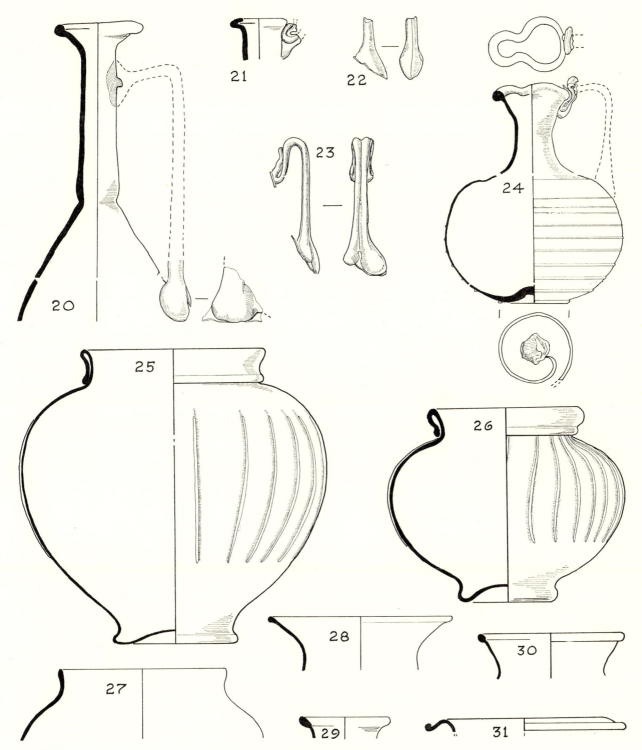

Fig. 76. Glass vessels 20–31 ($\frac{1}{2}$).

Fragments from globular ribbed bodies could be taken as further examples of these flagons but it is equally possible for them to be from jars (see below). Without the rim it is impossible to tell, as the same coloured metals are used, and the shape up to the shoulder is the same. Both globular ribbed jars and flagons are contemporary and from the same factories. Seven of these ribbed body-fragments are in natural-green (nos. 1–7 below); three are in light amber colour (nos. 8–10), one in deep blue (no. 11), and the rest in olive-green (nos. 12–14).

Body fragments.

1. A I 23, A.D. 130–40. II C, Room 23.
2. A II 26, A.D. 130–50. II C, Room 22.
3. A II 42, A.D. 75–105. II A, accumulation outside Rooms 12, 15.
4. A IV 33, A.D. 85–105. II A, Room 7.
5. B IV 10, A.D. 155/160. II D, wall-trench 36/37.
6. A XI 18, A.D. 150–155/160. II D, Room 45, floor.
7. B I 67. Unstratified. Collapsed upper filling, Pit 7.
8. B IV 10, A.D. 155/160. II D, wall-trench 36/37.
9. A I 23, A.D. 130–40. II C, Room 23.
10. A VII 32, A.D. 110–20. II B, Room 26.
11. B I 38C, A.D. 120–30. II B, Room 24.
12. A VII 32, as no. 10 above.
13. B IV 20E, A.D. 115–30. II B, Room 33.
14. B I 70, A.D. 60–75. Pit 7.

(viii) *Jugs*

The following list shows the pieces present with their stratigraphy and its dating.

1. Fig. 76, 22. A II 2 unstratified.
2. Fig. 76, 23. A IV 41, A.D. 60. I, Room 14.
3. Fig. 76, 24. {B XI 27, A.D. 275–300+. Pit 19.
            {B XI 29, A.D. 175–275. Pit 19.

Spouted vessels seem common only in the period from the later first to the third century. They are smaller than the flagons, and therefore two blue-green handle fragments (nos. 1 and 2) are assigned to this class. A third (Isings form 56a) is represented by rim to shoulder, base and some wall fragments (no. 3, fig. 76, 24) of a blue-green jug decorated with a spiral trail covering the entire body and ending at the base where it is cut off by the scar of the pontil. The trail must have been added while the vessel was still on the blow-pipe, before being held on the pontil for the rim to be finished. A second-century ribbed version of this jug and undecorated jugs have been found in Cologne (Fremersdorf, *Das natur-farbene sogenannte blaugrüne Glas in Köln*, T. 15 and 62). Vessels of similar shape and size, but with a round lip instead of a spout, are also known.

(ix) *Globular ribbed jars*

The following list shows the pieces present with their stratigraphy and its dating.

1. Fig. 76, 25. B I 64, 65, 67; A.D. 60–75. Pit 7.
2. Fig. 76, 26. B II Pit 9, *c.* A.D. 105. Pit 9.
3. T II 19, A.D. 130–40. II C, Room 13.
4. T VI 28, A.D. 75–80. II A, Room 4, make-up.

5. B I 36A, A.D. 85–105. II A, Room 21.
6. B II Pit 9, as no. 2 above.
7. A XI 16, A.D. 85–105. II A, Room 7.

Some fragments which could be from vessels of this type are listed with the flagons, from which they cannot be distinguished. Only where there is a rim is the vessel certainly a jar. One nearly complete jar in blue-greenish glass is no. 2 (fig. 76, 26). It shows the characteristic hollow tubular collar-rim and the open pushed-in base ring. The ribbing is formed by a slight inflation of the paraison (the gathering of glass) in a ribbed mould. It is then withdrawn and fully inflated. Six other vessels of this type have been recognized (nos. 1 (fig. 76, 25), and 3–7). The first is in deep blue glass, the others all in natural green.

(x) *Jars*

The following list shows the pieces present with their stratigraphy and its dating.

1. Fig. 76, 27. B II 7, fourth century. Wall-trench north of cellar.
2. Fig. 76, 28. B I 55, A.D. 280–315. III, occupation layer in cellar.
3. Fig. 76, 29. B II 32E, A.D. 90–105. II A, accumulation outside Room 19.
4. Fig. 76, 30. T XXII 2, A.D. 155/160. II D, Room 10.
5. Fig. 76, 31. B XV 4, A.D. 150–155/160. II D, Room 55.

There is no complete jar, only rim-fragments of five, all in natural-green glass. There are two rim types. Two examples, no. 1 in blue-green glass and no. 2 in green glass, have rounded rims. Both are probably first or second century in date. The other three have infolded rims. No. 3 is from a small jar in thin greenish glass, of first- or second-century type. No. 4 in poor yellowish-green glass might be late Roman but it is not distinctively a late metal, and poor-quality glass was put on the market occasionally in earlier periods. This is confirmed by the context.

The remaining rim, no. 5, also infolded at the edge, is outsplayed so that a lid can rest on it. This is a first- and second-century type of bulbous, almost globular jar, sometimes called a cinerary urn because a number have been found containing burials, for example at West Mersea (*Antiq. Journ.* iv, 268) and York (*Eburacum*, fig. 89, 1948, 3. 1).

(xi) *Flasks*

The following list shows the pieces present with their stratigraphy and its dating.

1. Fig. 77, 32. B IV 3, A.D. 155/160. II D, Rooms 38–42.
2. Fig. 77, 33. B III 10A, A.D. 270–5. III, make-up, XIV, 5.
3. Fig. 77, 34. B I 39B, A.D. 75–105. II A, Room 16.
4. Fig. 77, 35. B I 48, A.D. 85–105. II A, accumulation outside Room 17.
5. Fig. 77, 36. B II 42, A.D. 49–75. I, Room 22 (contaminated).
6. Fig. 77, 37. T III 9, early fourth century. III, make-up for secondary *opus signinum* floor, XIV, 1 Room 2.
7. Fig. 77, 38. B I 36A, A.D. 85–105. II A, Room 21.
8. Fig. 77, 39. B V 29, A.D. 270–5. III, make-up, XIV, 5 Room 4.
9. T XX 21, A.D. 105–15. II B, Room 7.
10. A VI 33, A.D. 75–105. II A, Room 10.
11. B III Pit I, late fourth century. Mouth of Pit 2.
12. B XV 11, A.D. 150–155/160. II D, Room 55.

Most of these are utilitarian vessels, for holding oils and unguents, made in natural-green glass. Two pieces (nos. 1 and 2, fig. 77, 32, 33) are of better-quality colourless glass with a trail round the neck. Such flasks, often with quite elaborate decoration, were common in the second and third centuries.

There is a considerable variety of size. The three smallest were probably for perfumes (nos. 3 (fig. 77, 34), 9 and 10). The drop-shaped body is typical of the first and second centuries. Three are slightly larger with a more or less conical body and of the same date (nos. 4 (fig. 77, 35), 11, 12). The neck to shoulder fragment (no. 5, fig. 77, 36) is also contemporary but from a larger, bulbous-bodied flask; and there are two rim and neck fragments probably from similar, but still larger, flasks (no. 6 (fig. 77, 37) and no. 7 (fig. 77, 38)). The base of a later type of perfume flask, with a very much flattened body, was also found (no. 8, fig. 77, 39).

(xii) *Double-handled flask*

Fig. 77, 40. A IV 33, A.D. 85–105. II A, Room 7.

One complete handle and a fragment of another in greenish glass are all that remain of the vessel. It was probably a miniature amphora. This shape is found in glass (Isings form 60) in the first century and at the same time also a two-handled flask with a base ring (Isings form 15). The amphorisk appears again in the fourth century, but the metal and context of these handles indicate a first- to second-century date.

(xiii) *Beakers and bowls with cut decoration*

The following list shows the pieces present with their stratigraphy and its dating.

1. Fig. 77, 41. B XV 4, A.D. 150–155/160. II D, Room 55.
2. Fig. 77, 42. B XV 4, as no. 1.
3. Fig. 77, 43. B XV 4, as no. 1.
4. Fig. 77, 44. B II 26A, A.D. 150–155/160. II D, Room 25.
5. Fig. 77, 45. A VI 15, A.D. 115–30. II B, Room 26.
6. Fig. 77, 46. { Z I 5, A.D. 150–155/160. II D, Room 8.
 B V 29, A.D. 270–5. III, make-up, XIV, 5 Room 4.
7. Fig. 77, 47. A IV 4, A.D. 270–5. III, make-up, XIV, 2 Room 2.
8. Fig. 78, 48. B I Pit 20. A.D. 300–15. III, box under cellar stairs.
9. Fig. 78, 49. B I Pit 20, as no. 8.
10. Fig. 78, 50. B I 59, A.D. 300–15. III, sump in cellar floor.
11. Fig. 78, 51. B I 55, A.D. 280–315. III, occupation layer in cellar.
12. Fig. 78, 52. B I 9, A.D. 310–15. III, cellar filling.
13. Fig. 78, 53. B I 59, as no. 10.
14. Fig. 78, 54. { B XV 11, A.D. 150–155/160. II D, Room 55.
 B XV 4, A.D. 150–155/160. II D, Room 55.
    both in occupation material in different parts of the room among and below the Antonine fire debris.
15. Fig. 78, 55. A V+. Unstratified.
16. Fig. 78, 56. B IV 18F, A.D. 135–45. II C, Room 40.

All these vessels are in good colourless glass of second- to fourth-century date. Many are in small fragments. In some cases fragments of an identical pair have been found together, e.g. the two facet-cut beakers nos. 1 and 2 or the large beakers nos. 8 and 9 found in the box in the cellar; and no. 12 pairs with no. 13. In all these cases the cutting is a characteristic feature of the vessel. Other beakers of late fourth-century date, including those decorated with cut lines, are treated in another section (p. 210) with the plain examples of the same type, because in their case the decoration is merely a variation, not an essential characteristic.

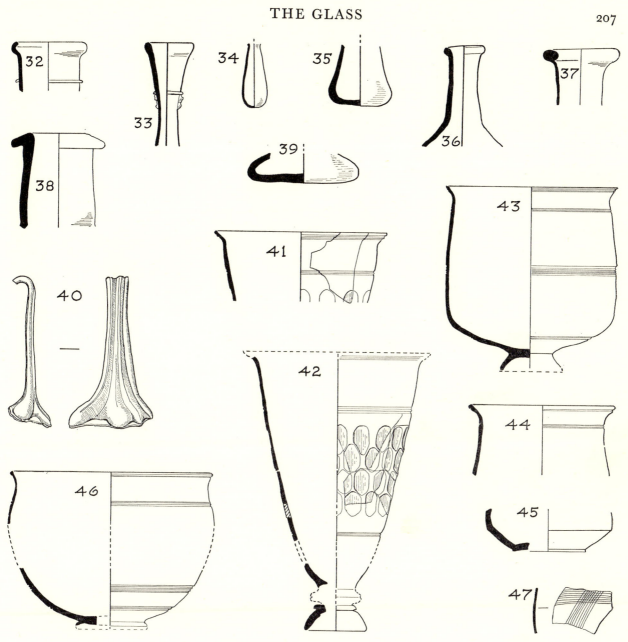

FIG. 77. Glass vessels 32–47 ($\frac{1}{2}$).

1. Facet-cut beakers. Nos. 1, 2 (fig. 77, 41, 42)

Two beakers found together in II D, Room 55, in the occupation material engulfed by the Antonine fire, were in a shattered condition and incomplete, and may have been subjected to a sudden change of temperature. Another vessel from this room shows positive traces of fire. Although there is no sign, such as partial melting, that they have been affected by the fire, it is difficult otherwise to account for the state of this relatively thick metal. Had the fault been too rapid annealing they would probably have shattered when the closed diaper of facets, which covered the greater part of the side, was cut. The type is a well-known one of Flavian–Trajanic date. A complete one (probably Alexandrian but they were also made in Italy) from Barnwell is in the British Museum (*Antiquities of Roman Britain* (1958), pl. xi *d*); cf. also one from Euenheim bei Euskirchen in the Köln Museum (O. Doppelfeld, *Römisches und fränkisches Glas in Köln*, 1966, Taf. 40) on which the restoration of fig. 77, 42 is based. Dated examples are published from the Caerleon amphitheatre with a coin of Domitian and late first- to second-century pottery (*Archaeologia*, lxxviii, 170) and from Chester with Flavian pottery (*Liverpool Annals*, xxiii, 36). It should be noted that there are similar beakers with coarser cutting in the later Roman period, and the closed diaper is also used to decorate bowls as late as the fourth century.

2. Carinated beakers

Three examples have been identified. One is nearly complete, but with part of its rim distorted, melted in the Antonine fire (no. 3, fig. 77, 43). This beaker has a ground rim decorated with two cut lines, two more below the rim and a broader band round the girth. Below the carination are two further lines where the side slopes steeply to a small pad base formed into a footring. A similar rim fragment, but with a different spacing of the cut lines was found (no. 4, fig. 77, 44) and a base (no. 5, fig. 77, 45) with no footring, only ground flat.

This is a second-century type of vessel. The Hardknott example must date *c.* A.D. 125–70 (*C. & W.* 59, 38, fig. 3, 3), and the stratification here conforms.

3. Two pieces, a rim and a base found in different seasons (no. 6, fig. 77, 46) seem to be parts of the same vessel. Both have firmly cut lines and the colourless metal with cloudy weathering looks identical. The outsplayed rim is ground smooth and has two lines below it. The base fragment has a set of two lines with a set of three further up the side. The base itself is a pad of glass added to the blown vessel; probably it was originally shaped into a footring but now it is flat, and the rough edges suggest that the foot was damaged in antiquity and the ring cut away to make the vessel stable. The type was almost certainly made in the Rhineland in the second or third century. A similar beaker from Cologne is illustrated by Fremersdorf, *Die römische Gläser mit Schliff, Bemalung und Goldauflagen* (1967), pl. 15.

4. Another fragment of Rhenish glass, also of second- or third-century date, is decorated with evenly cut and spaced groups of lines forming a diamond grid or a cross-hatching. The shape cannot be restored (no. 7, fig. 77, 47). Fremersdorf (op. cit., p. 111) illustrates a flask with this decoration from Cologne and there are fragments in the Saalburg Museum.

5. Beakers with zoned decoration

In 1959 a large number of similar vessels decorated with zoned patterns made up of oval or circular facets and broad cut lines were found in the cellar of Building XIV, 5 (nos. 8–13, fig. 78, 48–53). In all, seven vessels were identified, none complete, and some obviously part of the same matching set, purchased together.

The decoration is not identical on each vessel but has many elements in common, and the shape is similar. All have a slightly outsplayed rim, knocked off and lightly ground to smooth it, and a bulbous body curving in to a small flat base consisting of a circular facet cut to give stability. The metal thickens gradually from rim to base and the decoration seems to be unpolished, but as all the pieces are abraded and dulled this is not certain. Other beakers of the same type also appear to have unpolished cutting. The fragments immediately divide into two groups, those from vessels with cross-hatched diamonds as a major element in the design, and those with circular facets in which the centre is left proud. An element which appears on both is the 'ear of wheat' which is in the upper zone of the design in one case (fig. 78, 53) and in the lower zone of the Pit 20 beakers linked by a festoon.

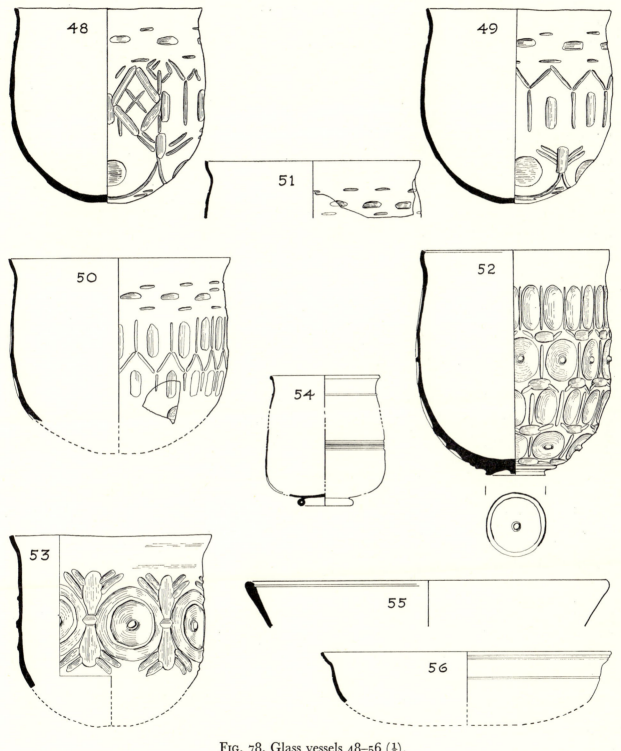

FIG. 78. Glass vessels 48–56 (½).

There are many minor variations, but this shape and the decoration associated either with these bag-shaped beakers or with straight-sided beakers, as at York (*Eburacum*, fig. 88), are a common find in the Cologne area, where they were made (Fremersdorf, op. cit., pl. 55, 57, 60–2, 66–70) and also in Britain, for example in London (Wheeler, *London in Roman Times*, fig. 42, 1, 2), Wroxeter (i, pl. XII, 4), Richborough (*II*, 52), Silchester, and Lullingstone. Beakers with circular facets with the raised centre are known from Piercebridge, the Stanton Chair villa and Caistor-by-Norwich. In spite of the wealth of material the dating is uncertain. They belong to the third century but such a distinctive type of decoration is not likely to have been produced over a long period of time. The close dating of the present examples is significant.

6. Fragments of a small beaker in very thin glass were found in 1960 (no. 14, fig. 78, 54), in a deposit sealed by the Antonine fire. The rim is lightly ground and has a fine trail below it. A band of cut lines decorate the side. It is extraordinary that such fine glass could be cut without breaking. The shape is not altogether certain from the surviving pieces which appear partly to overlap but do not join.

7. Pieces of rims of shallow bowls or dishes were found. No. 15 (fig. 78, 55), is of good colourless glass, thickening rapidly towards the rim, which has a cut line on the underside. The shape of the vessel is uncertain.

The second (no. 16, fig. 78, 56) has an S-shaped curve of rim and side reminiscent of a group of round-based shallow bowls of mid-fourth-century date. These are variously decorated. There is no decoration on what little survives of this bowl and it may, as the stratification suggests, be of much earlier date. It is of colourless glass, polished with cut lines below the rim and another accenting the 'shoulder'. The complete shape seems to be the same as that of a bowl from grave 99 at Ospringe, decorated in that case with a closed diaper of facets (Whiting, Hawley, and May, *Excavations of the Roman Cemetery at Ospringe, Kent*, 35, pl. 32).

(xiv) *Beaker with moulded (?) decoration.* Fig. 79, 57. B I 55, A.D. 280–315. III, occupation layer in cellar.

This fragmentary beaker in thick colourless glass, now clouded, is of the same shape as the beakers with cut decoration (see fig. 78, nos. 48–50). The rim is slightly outsplayed and ground, the glass thicker towards the base. The decoration is four rows of raised rings. These are not cut: the outline is not sharp enough. They may be trailed, but it seems more likely that the beaker was formed in a mould. As with the pillar-moulded bowl (see p. 198) the inside of the vessel is smooth. This beaker is contemporary with the cut beakers of the same shape.

(xv) *Late Roman beakers*

The following list shows the pieces present with their stratigraphy and its dating.

1. Fig. 79, 58. B I 59, A.D. 300–15. III, sump in cellar floor.
2. Fig. 79, 59. B I 55, A.D. 280–315. III, occupation layer in cellar.
3. Fig. 79, 60. B V Pit 2A, late fourth century. Pit 22.
4. Fig. 79, 61. { B I 55, as no. 2 above.
                { B I 59, as no. 1 above.
5. Fig. 79, 62. B VII 3C, A.D. 270–5. Chalk foundation of XIV, 7.
6. B I 9, A.D. 310–15. III, cellar filling.
7. B I 9, as no. 6 above.

Fragments of seven late Roman beakers were found, six in colourless glass with iridescent or clouded weathering, and one in thicker greenish metal (no. 4, fig. 79, 61).

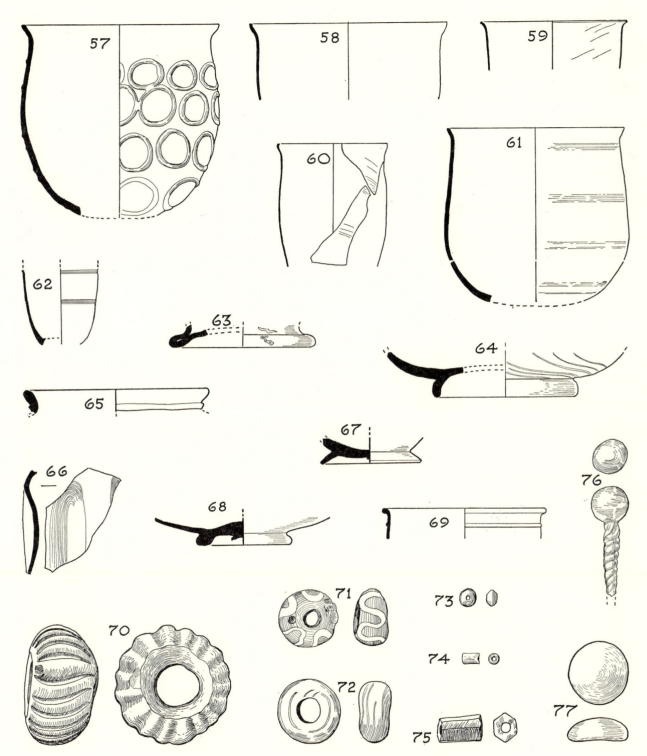

FIG. 79. Glass vessels 57–69 ($\frac{1}{2}$) and glass objects 70–7 ($\frac{1}{1}$).

The rim fragments (nos. 1, 2, 3 (fig. 79, 58–60) and no. 6) in thin colourless glass of poor quality knocked off and unworked, with the result that the edge is rough, are from beakers of the type found at Winthill (*JRS* xlvii (1957), 232). Two are of the same shape but decorated with wheel-cut lines. On the rim- and side-fragments (no. 7) there is only a faintly cut line below the rim; but on the base fragment, which is in better-quality glass (no. 5, fig. 79, 62), are two sets of two firmly cut lines.

The five fragments composing no. 4 (fig. 79, 61) do not give a complete section of a beaker. The rim is now badly chipped but seems to have been left rough as in the case of the colourless beakers. Below it are faintly cut lines, and the body fragments show that there were four sets of two lines round it. The metal has pin-head bubbles in it but has not weathered. There is no apparent difference in date between the decorated and undecorated beakers. They occur commonly in late Roman graves in the middle Rhineland (see Isings form 106), and in Britain on many sites such as Silchester (forum excavation 1869), Wroxeter, Corbridge, and Traprain Law. A very similar vessel but with a rounded, thickened rim is also found, but starting at a slightly later date and continuing into the post-Roman period; this is the immediate forerunner of the Saxon cone-beaker.

These vessels are generally termed beakers but it is possible that they were lamps. The rough rim would make them inconvenient for drinking, and in the Near East this is a well-known lamp-form of the Byzantine period (Crowfoot and Harden in *J. Egyptian Archaeology* (1931)).

(xvi) *Millefiori*
1. Fig. 79, 63, B II 19, A.D. 280–90. III, packing behind cellar wall.
2. Fig. 79, 64. A XII 10, A.D. 150–155/160. II D, Room 25B.

One of the two pieces of millefiori glass (no. 1) is an unusual one, part of the open base-ring of a blown vessel, a jar, or flagon. The metal is emerald-green with short rods of opaque yellow and patches of opaque red. The blowing of a vessel inevitably distorts any pre-arranged floral or formal pattern, and for blown glass only these 'marbled' or 'dappled' effects were used. Most millefiori is made in a mould. Examples date from the second century B.C. to the middle of the first century A.D. by which time it seems to have gone out of use. Blown millefiori (i.e. metals with the contrasting colours embedded in the ground colour as opposed to those where the polychrome is on the outer surface only) is rare in the first century A.D., the only examples being small flasks, generally of a dark colour streaked with white. One is known, in metal similar to this Verulamium fragment, a small flask in the Ray Smith collection (*Glass from the Ancient World*, Corning, 1957, no. 141), dated there rather on the late side to the first or second century A.D.

Examples of third-century blown millefiori have also been found, and the Verulamium fragment belongs to this group. One is a small flagon from grave 235 in Jakobstrasse, Köln, with coins of Trajan, Victorinus, Postumus, and Constantius Chlorus, a late third-century grave. Another, a bowl, comes from a grave at Sackrau of *c*. A.D. 300 (Fremersdorf, *Römisches Buntglas in Köln, die Denkmäler des römischen Köln*, iii, p. 51).

No. 2 (fig. 79, 64). Base of bowl in green glass with rods of opaque yellow, and added base ring. The vessel is made in a mould in the normal manner of first-century B.C./A.D. millefiori. The base ring is not common on vessels in millefiori metal. It is heavily weathered.

(xvii) *Miscellaneous fragments*
Some fragments seem worth recording although the type of vessel to which they belong has not been determined.

1. Fig. 79, 65. Deep-blue glass, hollow tubular rim from a beaker or small jar. First century. T VI 24, A.D. 105–15. II B, Room 3.

2. Colourless glass fragment with a thin, marvered blue trail running horizontally. Probably Rhenish, later second or third century. B XIV 8, A.D. 270–5. III, make-up, XIV, 6 Room 3.

3. Fig. 79, 66. Thick colourless glass fragment from the side of an indented beaker. The thickness of 2 mm. is unusual for this type of vessel. First or second century. B II 2. II D, Rooms 32–42, Antonine fire, disturbed.

4. Fig. 79, 67. Base ring in good colourless glass, dulled and clouded, formed by cutting from a moulded blank shape. The inner surface is concave, the outer flat with the centre left proud. The technique is most common in the first century in the Alexandrian and Italian factories. B XVI 3, A.D. 155/160. II D, Room 57.

5. Fig. 79, 68. Base of a blown vessel in colourless glass with milky weathering with a trailed-on footring and a pontil-mark at the centre. The irregularity of the ring and its rounded contour contrast with the sharper outline of the previous piece. Second to third century. B I 9, A.D. 310–15. III, cellar filling.

6. Fig. 79, 69. Colourless glass rim fragment. The tip of the rim is rounded in the flame and outsplayed; below is a trail of the same metal. This is probably from a straight-sided bowl of a type known from the Baldock cemetery (*Arch. Journ.* xcix, 276). Probably second century. A II 2. Unstratified.

(xviii) *Window-glass*

1. T III 6, A.D. 270–5. III, make-up, XIV, 1 Room 1.
2. T III 10, A.D. 270–5. III, make-up, XIV, 1 Room 1.
3. T III 11, A.D. 155/160. II D, Room 4.
4. T III 12, A.D. 155/160. II D, wall-trench 1/4.
5. T II 8, A.D. 155/160. II D, Room 25A.
6. B VII 4, A.D. 155/160. II D, Room 52.
7. B XV 11, A.D. 150–155/160. II D, Room 55.
8. V XXXIV 6, A.D. 155/160. II D, Room 1.
9. T III 8, A.D. 270–5. III, make-up, XIV, 1 Room 1.
10. T II 19, A.D. 130–40. II C, Room 13.
11. T II 26, A.D. 95–105. II A, Room 11.
12. T II 3, A.D. 350–410+. Rubble over XIV, 1 Room 2.
13. B XI 2. Unstratified rubble, yard south-west of XIV, 6.
14. B I 68, A.D. 60–75. Pit 7.

A quantity of window-glass, all blue-green or green, the same quality as the bottle glass, was found. Many pieces evidently came from burned buildings (nos. 1–8). All the pieces are rough on one side and smooth on the other, c. 3–5 mm. thick. the typical window-glass of the first or second century A.D. In no case was it possible to reconstruct a complete pane.

The technique of manufacture is uncertain. The glass might be blown in a cylindrical shape and cut to open out flat or, as seems more probable, formed by pouring into a mould. The possibilities are discussed by D. B. Harden in *Glastechnische Berichte*, viii (1959), 8–16, and in E. M. Jope (ed.), *Studies in Building History*, and by G. C. Boon in *J. of Glass Studies*, viii (1966), 41–7.

(xix) *Beads*

The following list shows the pieces present with their stratigraphy and its dating.

1. Fig. 79, 70. A II 26, A.D. 130–50. II C, Room 22.
2. Fig. 79, 71. B XV 7, A.D. 155/160. II D, Room 55.
3. Fig. 79, 72. T XX 23, A.D. 105–15. II B, Room 7.

4. Fig. 79, 73. B I 15, A.D. 270–5. III, Antonine fire (disturbed): make-up, XIV, 5.

5. Fig. 79, 74. B I 9, A.D. 310–15. Cellar filling.

6. Fig. 79, 75. B I 8, A.D. 360–70. III, secondary make-up of cellar filling.

7. A II 44, A.D. 105–15. II B, path 18.

8. B I 27, A.D. 280–90. III, packing of cellar wall.

9. B IV 7, A.D. 150–155/160. II D, Room 40.

10. A XII 6, robber-trench.

11. B IV 15, A.D. 270–300+. III, make-up below mosaic, XIV, 5 Room 3.

12. T II 36, A.D. 60. I, Rooms 6, 18.

13. T VII 28, A.D. 105–30. II B, Room 2.

14. T XX 18, A.D. 110–20. II B, Room 7.

15. V XXXI 4. Unstratified.

16. B IV 20E, A.D. 115–30. II B, Room 33.

17. B VI 1, A.D. 350–410+. Rubble over XIV, 7.

18. B II 3, A.D. 370–410+. Rubble over XIV, 5.

19. B VI 1, A.D. 370–410+. Rubble over XIV, 7.

20. A II 48, A.D. 105–30. II B, Room 15.

21. A XII 9, A.D. 140–50. II C, Room 16.

22. A XII 8, c. A.D. 150. II D, Room 14 make-up.

23. A VI 21, A.D. 130–50. II C, Room 13.

24. B IV 19A, A.D. 120–30. II B, Room 26.

25. B XI 1. Plough-soil.

The twenty-five beads are all of well-known but undatable types. The melon-shaped beads both of turquoise frit and deep-blue glass (nos. 1 (deep blue), 7–15) are found on most Roman sites. The dark annular bead no. 2 (fig. 79, 71) in blue with a white trail, the annular green bead no. 3 (fig. 79, 72) accidentally streaked with purple, one in deep-blue glass (no. 25), and one in natural-green (no. 16), are equally frequent finds. There are beads of these types from Newstead (Curle, *Newstead*, 336, pl. 91) and Richborough (*Richborough IV*, p. 149, pl. LV), for example.

The small beads are often found spaced out on bronze chain-bracelets or necklaces. Three small blue beads (nos. 4 (fig. 79, 73), 17, 18) and seven green (nos. 5 (fig. 79, 74), 6, 20–4), one of them (no. 6, fig. 79, 75) a well-made hexagonal bead, may have been used in this way.

(xx) *Objects*

1. Gaming counters

1. Fig. 79, 77. B I 54, A.D. 300–15. III, tertiary floor of cellar.

2. T II 4, A.D. 275–300+. III, Floor XIV, 1 Room 2.

3. A VI 33, A.D. 75–105. II A, Room 10.

4. B IV 18H, A.D. 130–40. II C, Room 40.

5. A VI 33, as no. 3 above.

6. B IV 40D, A.D. 49–60. I, Room 26.

Monochrome counters c. 1–2 cm. in diameter are a common find on Roman sites. All have rather rough flat bases and smooth, rounded tops. They are all made as counters and are not merely reused fragments. The colours vary so that the different players can distinguish their pieces, although here there is no suggestion that the six counters are part of a single set, such as was found in a grave at Lullingstone (*J.R.S.* xliv, 133). Four are green (nos. 1–4), one blue (no. 5), and one of dark iridescent glass (no. 6).

2. Stirring rod. Z I 22, A.D. 130–40. II C, Room 8.

The piece of twisted, green glass rod was used for stirring cosmetics or unguents imported in small flasks. When complete the rod sometimes has an ornamental head or terminates in a flat stud or a ring. They are found throughout the Roman period.

3. Pin. Fig. 79, 76. A III, unstratified.

Glass pins may have been used as hair ornaments or possibly in clothing, but they are rather thick for pushing through any fabric. This pin in green glass has a globular head and is drawn out spirally.

IV. THE SAMIAN WARE

by B. R. Hartley, F.S.A.

All the fragments of plain and decorated samian ware, as well as the potters' stamps, have been examined and are listed in the tables (pp. 14–102). It is neither practicable, nor indeed desirable, to discuss and illustrate it all, since a surprisingly high proportion was residual in the contexts in which it was found and was not, therefore, useful for dating. The general principle adopted has been to illustrate all the available decorated ware from Period I (D1–14), from Pit 7 (D15–50) which gave a particularly large and interesting group of importance for dating the redevelopment of the site, and from the Antonine fire (D113–42). Apart from the large collection of more or less complete Flavian vessels found in deposits of Periods II A and II B (D64–81, see p. 28), only a selection of the decorated ware from other periods is presented. In general this is pottery important for dating, or pottery of particular intrinsic interest. No attempt has been made, for instance, to illustrate the readily identifiable standard bowls of Drusus I (X–3) or Igocatus, since they do not add to their known repertoires. All the potters' stamps are discussed and illustrated. The die numbers used in the Leeds catalogue are noted for each stamp to facilitate comparison, particularly in discussing stamped decorated ware. For these, the roman numeral defines the reading, the lower-case letter gives the precise stamp. Forms are noted in the traditional Dragendorff–Déchelette–Knorr–Walters series with slight modifications. Form 27g is form 27 with foot-stand groove; form 33a is form 33 with internal fluting at the junction of base and wall, usually with external grooves at the top and bottom of the wall.

Apart from a few problem pieces (such as D85), the Lezoux and East Gaulish decorated sherds are not difficult to assign to their sources, and usually to a particular potter or group of potters. For South Gaulish bowls, and to some extent for the sherds from Les Martres-de-Veyre, the situation is much more difficult, since stamps and signatures in the moulds rarely appear for form 29, which was normally stamped after moulding with a stamp which does not necessarily have a direct connection with the mould-maker. Secondly, forms 30 and 37 rarely have stamps at all. The result is that it is often impossible to assign South Gaulish sherds to the men responsible for the moulds, except of a few potters who used mould-stamps (such as Crucuro, Germanus, or Mercato) or who seem to have used their own moulds for form 29 and consistently stamped their bowls (e.g. Bassus–Coelus or Germanus). Nevertheless, it is worth attempting to trace stamped parallels for South Gaulish decorated sherds, since ultimately the complicated cross-links will have their own stories to tell, and dating-evidence often accrues from the process.

A brief note on the sources of the Verulamium samian is desirable. In the first century virtually all of it came from the factories at La Graufesenque, near Millau. The only exception is the presence of a little ware from the early Lezoux firms which exported to southern Britain under Nero and Vespasian (fig. 80), and possibly one sherd from Montans (S36). The second-century situation is more complicated. Under Trajan, in common with the rest of Britain, Verulamium drew partly on La Graufesenque, largely on Les Martres-de-Veyre and conceivably on Montans, though the few sherds from the latter are more likely to be Hadrianic. In the first half of Hadrian's principate Lezoux became the chief source, as usually in Britain. East Gaulish ware scarcely appears at all in the groups considered, though the exceptions, D132, from Chémery-Faulquemont, and D126, from Blickweiler, are particularly useful in providing much-needed evidence for dating products of these early East Gaulish centres. Later in the second century, and in the third century, Verulamium received much samian ware from Rheinzabern, though there is none in the groups discussed below.

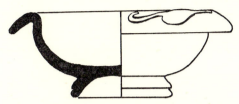

FIG. 80. First-century Lezoux ware, form 35 ($\frac{1}{2}$). From T VI 35 (II B, Room 4, make-up, c. A.D. 105 (p. 44)). Reddish-buff micaceous paste; orange-red gloss all worn away internally below rim and to a large extent also externally: foot-stand worn, but has a definite groove around it as not infrequently with first-century Lezoux examples.

Parallels for figure-types are quoted, wherever possible, from Hermet's and Déchelette's series, since Oswald's corresponding ones are usually not so readily identifiable.

The following abbreviations, other than self-evident ones, are used in the text:

Atkinson 1942: D. Atkinson, *Report on Excavations at Wroxeter, 1923–1927*.
BM: British Museum.
D.: Figure-type in J. Déchelette, *Vases ornés de la Gaule romaine*, tome ii (1904).
Baillie Reynolds 1938: P. K. Baillie Reynolds, *Excavations on the site of the Roman fort of Kanovium*.
GH: Guildhall Museum.
van Giffen 1940–44: Valkenburg report in *Jaarverslag van de Vereeniging voor Terpenonderzoek*, 25/28.
van Giffen 1948–53; ibid. 33/37.
Hermet 1934: F. Hermet, *La Graufesenque (Condatomago)*, tome ii.
H.: Figure-type in *Hermet 1934*.
Karnitsch 1959: P. Karnitsch, *Die Reliefsigillata von Ovilava*.
Knorr, *Aislingen*: R. Knorr, *Die Terra-Sigillata-Gefässe von Aislingen* (Jahrb. des Hist. Vereins Dillingen xxv, 1912).
Knorr 1919: R. Knorr, *Töpfer und Fabriken verzierter Terra-Sigillata des ersten Jahrhunderts*.
Knorr 1952: R. Knorr, *Terra-Sigillata-Gefässe des ersten Jahrhunderts mit Töpfernamen*.
Krämer 1957: W. Krämer, *Cambodunum Forschungen*, i (1953).
LM: London Museum.
Mary 1967: G. T. Mary, *Novaesium I (Die südgallische Terra Sigillata aus Neuss)*, Limesforschungen Band 6.
NMA: National Museum of Antiquities, Edinburgh.
O.: Figure-type in F. Oswald, *Index of Figure-Types on Terra Sigillata* (1936–7).

Oswald, *Stamps*: F. Oswald, *Index of Potters' Stamps on Terra Sigillata* (1931).

Stanfield 1929: J. A. Stanfield, 'Unusual forms of Terra Sigillata' (*Arch. Journ.* 86 (1929), 113 ff.).

S. & S.: J. A. Stanfield and Grace Simpson, *Central Gaulish Potters* (1958).

Terrisse 1969: J.-R. Terrisse, *Les céramiques sigillées gallo-romaines des Martres-de-Veyre* (Gallia Supplement XIX).

Ulbert 1959: G. Ulbert, *Die römischen Donau-Kastelle Aislingen und Burghöfe*, Limesforschungen Band 1.

Ulbert 1969: G. Ulbert, *Das frührömische Kastell Rheingönheim*, Limesforschungen Band 9.

Walke 1965: N. Walke, *Das römische Donaukastell Straubing-Sorviodurum*, Limesforschungen Band 3.

PERIOD I

Potters' stamps

S1. B I 51 (p. 22; fig. 81). Crestio of La Graufesenque (*Hermet 1934*, pl. 110, 43). Form 29, without decoration, stamped OF·CRE[STIO] (Ia). Crestio reserved this stamp for use on form 29 and dishes, usually the larger varieties with rouletted bases. Another example from Verulamium is on an unusual dish best described as form 15/18R, having the external profile of form 18 but with an internal quarter-round moulding (this dish was from a Boudiccan level). It is evident that the die had a long life, since stamps from it appear at the Nijmegen fortress (3), Chester (2), York? (Yorkshire Museum without definite provenance) and, most surprisingly, at Castledykes (A. S. Robertson, *The Roman Fort at Castledykes*, fig. 34, 4). The latter must be a survival, but on the other evidence it is doubtful if the stamp could have been used before about A.D. 55. *c.* A.D. 55–70.

S2. A IX 5 (p. 20; fig. 81). Meddillus of La Graufesenque (*Hermet 1934*, pl. 111, 100). Form 29 stamped ME⊕ILLVS (IVa). This stamp is almost invariably on form 29 (seventy-two examples), but it is recorded thrice on form 27 too. Some of the typologically early bowls stamped by Meddillus have links with Bassus-Coelus, Crestio, Primus, and other primarily Neronian potters (cf. *Knorr 1919*, Taf. 55, B, G, J, and K), and the decoration of this piece is similarly early. On the other hand, the stamp is very common at sites first occupied under the Flavians (e.g. Caerleon, Cardiff, Chester—far removed from any possible site for the putative early fort—and York (3); he also produced form 37). A.D. 60 would, therefore, be about the earliest date possible. *c.* A.D. 60–85.

S3. T III 35 (p. 20; fig. 81). Murranus of La Graufesenque (*Hermet 1934*, pl. 112, 110). Form 18 stamped OF.MVRRAN (IVd). Murranus began work under Claudius, but was basically a Neronian potter. This stamp is always on dishes, and there is no evidence for its precise date, unless two examples on burnt dishes at Colchester are accepted as involved in the Boudiccan destruction. *c.* A.D. 50–70.

S4. A IX 5 (p. 20; fig. 81). Primus of La Graufesenque (*Hermet 1934*, pl. 112, 132). Form 27g stamped OFPRIM (XIIIa). This stamp was found in both of the pottery shops destroyed in A.D. 60–1 at Colchester (Hull, *Roman Colchester*, fig. 79, 13; the other unpublished). It is almost invariably on cups (forms 24/25, 27, 33, or Ritterling 8). Only two examples come from probably Flavian contexts (Chester and Nijmegen fortresses). *c.* A.D. 55–70.

S5. T VI 34 (p. 21; fig. 81). Same potter as no. 4. Form 18 stamped OF PRIM (XIIIe). An uncommon stamp of Primus. Another example from Nijmegen is on a heavily burnt cup of form 27, perhaps involved in the Batavian revolt. *c.* A.D. 55–75.

Decorated ware

D 1–8. All A IX 5 (p. 20), and South Gaulish ware from La Graufesenque.

D 1. (Fig. 83). Form 29, part of the lower zone with large winding scroll. It is not possible to assign this to a particular potter, since the elements of the decoration were all used by many. The larger of

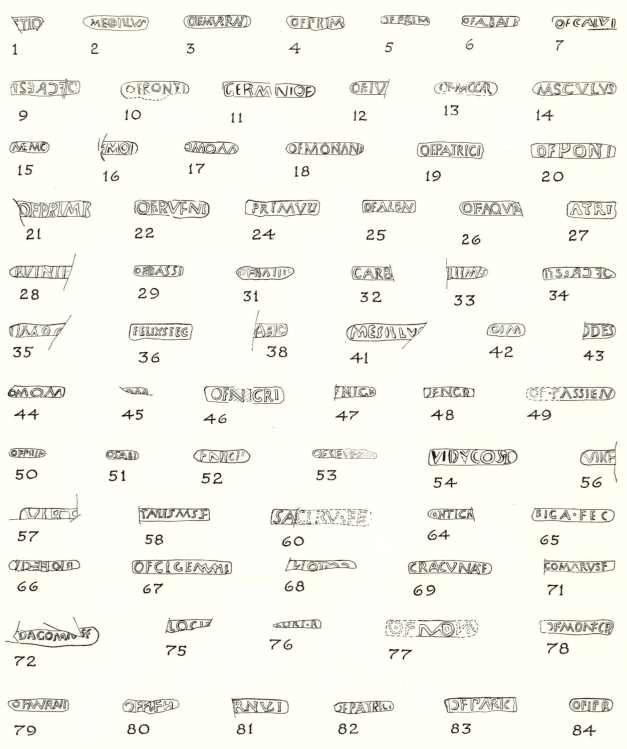

Fig. 81. Samian potters' stamps, S1–84 ($\frac{1}{1}$).

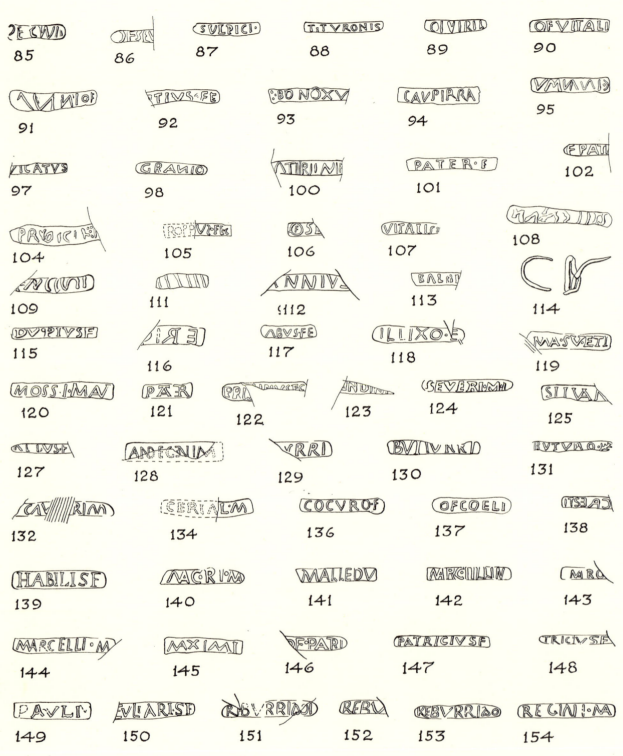

FIG. 82. Samian potters' stamps, S 85–155 ($\frac{1}{1}$). (Note: 154 should read 155.)

MEⓉILLVS

FIG. 83. Decorated samian 1–14 ($\frac{1}{2}$).

the two leaves occurs on bowls from moulds signed by Modestus (one also stamped by Felix), Masclus, Marinus, and Matugenus. The smaller leaf was used by Senicio and probably also by Celadus and Crestio. The scroll-binding is common to Crestio, Gallicanus, Masclus, and Senicio. For a sherd probably from the same mould at Rheingönheim see *Ulbert 1969*, Taf. 5, 12. The connections suggest a date *c*. A.D. 50–65.

D2. (Fig. 83.) Form 30 with alternating panels containing saltires and arcades. All the details occur frequently on bowls from moulds signed in the decoration by Masclus (*Germania*, xxxviii (1960), p. 60, 9 and 10 and p. 61, 16) and attribution to him seems certain, though the ovolo does not seem to be known on signed pieces (cf. *Hermet 1934*, pl. 77, 3). Masclus was basically a Neronian potter.

D3. (Fig. 83.) Form 30, similar to the last (cf. *Germania*, loc. cit.) and probably also by Masclus.

D4. (Fig. 83.) Form 30. The style is not unlike that of the last two bowls, but this time it should be assigned almost certainly to Martialis. A bowl from Usk (*Monmouthshire Antiquary*, i (1962), 2), stamped in the mould **MARTIALIS**, has all the same details and a closely similar arrangement (cf. also *Antiq. Journ.* x, 123, fig. 5*x*). *c*. A.D. 50–65.

D5. (Fig. 83.) Form 30, probably assignable to Martialis, since it has the same ovolo as the Usk bowl noted under no. 4, as well as the same trilobed plant in a similar saltire. *c*. A.D. 50–65.

D6. (Fig. 83.) Form 30. The general style recalls Masclus, who used the same ovolo and leaf-tips (*Germania*, xxxviii, 59, 6). The eagle is very uncommon (only Hawkes and Hull, *Camulodunum*, pl. xxxiii, 19 has been noted otherwise), but it is a reversed match of one used by Masclus and Ingenuus (BM, M 444 and *van Giffen 1941–4*, Afb. 59, 2; *Knorr 1919*, Taf. 41, 47). Probably the two eagles were modelled at the same time but the die for this one was soon broken.

D7. (Fig. 83.) Form 29, stamped internally by Meddillus (see S2). The style of decoration is not one normally associated with Meddillus and the mould was no doubt bought from another potter. A bowl from Kempten (*Krämer 1957*, Taf. 24, 16) is probably from the same mould. A similar scroll, but with an extra leaf, is on a form 29 at Neuss stamped **VAPVSV** (XIIIb) (*Mary 1967*, Taf. 6, 2, and 17) and also on a bowl from Strasbourg stamped **OF.RVFINI** (IIb) (Château des Rohans 3970) but with a bird replacing one of the bunches of grapes in the lower part. Typologically, the decoration would be dated *c*. A.D. 50–65, so it is quite consistent with presence in Period I.

D8. (Fig. 83.) Form 29. The elements of the upper scroll, acorn, spiral, and stirrup-leaf, all appear on form 29 at Hofheim, stamped internally **OFBAS[SI COEI]** (IIIa) (*Knorr 1919*, Taf. 12D, wrongly assigned to Bassus). An unstamped piece from London is from the same mould as the Hofheim bowl (*Knorr 1952*, Taf. 7C). No close parallel has been noted for the lower zone. *c*. A.D. 50–65.

D9–14. All South Gaulish, probably all from La Graufesenque.

D9. A XI 26 (p. 21; fig. 83). Form 29. A small fragment of the upper zone with a continuous scroll. Both the fabric and the large, well-separated beads suggest Claudian manufacture. Cf. Hawkes and Hull, *Camulodunum*, pl. xxx, 19 and *Hermet 1934*, Taf. 36, 43.

D10. A IV 41 (p. 21; fig. 83). Form 29, burnt. Despite the survival of the full scheme of decoration, no potter can be suggested for this piece. The scroll of the upper zone is reminiscent of a bowl stamped by Carillus from Strasbourg (reproduced in Knorr, *Aislingen*, Taf. VIII, 3) and also of some work by Frontinus (Bushe-Fox, *Richborough III*, pl. xxvi, 3). The untidy wreath of the lower zone has only been noted on a bowl from Period III at Cambodunum (*Krämer 1957*, Taf. 26, 2). Similar festoons with beaded yokes and containing the same birds are on a bowl from La Graufesenque stamped **OF.LVCCEI** (Rodez Mus.), but the pendants are different and I know no parallel for the ones on this piece. Such links as there are, are therefore with both Claudio-Neronian and Neronian-Vespasianic potters. Neronian manufacture with use in A.D. 60–1 seems reasonable.

D11. B IV 37D (p. 22; fig. 83). A small fragment of form 29, with brilliant glaze, from the lower zone of a bowl with large scroll. No useful comment is possible on the decoration, but the fabric suggests Neronian date.

D12. B IV 41L (p. 23; fig. 83). A small fragment of form 29 with parts of both zones. The lower one has a continuous chevron-wreath and tendrils parallel to it, in a style used by Bilicatus, Felix, and Modestus. The leaf was also used by Bilicatus (*Knorr 1919*, Taf. 15F and K). Claudio-Neronian rather than Neronian. *c.* A.D. 45–60.

D13. B IV 41S (p. 23; fig. 83). A poorly moulded form 29 with blurred wreath and festoons. The general style is close to work stamped by Aquitanus (*Knorr 1919*, Taf. 9L) and the rosette is precisely matched on an Aquitanus bowl from Leicester but also, with the same festoons, on an unpublished bowl from Rheingönheim (Speyer Mus.) stamped in the base [OF•CR]ESTIO (Ia). *c.* A.D. 50–65.

D14. B II 40 (p. 22; fig. 83). A small fragment of form 30, interesting primarily for the ovolo with vertically split tongue (cf. *Hermet 1934*, pl. 35 *bis*, 4). This ovolo was presumably used at La Graufesenque in view of Hermet's record, but it was copied much later at Montans by such potters as Chresimus and Malcio (*Bull. Soc. arch. hist. lit. et scient. du Gers*, lxv (1964), 296, AA7); cf. D 91.

PERIOD II

PIT 7

Potters' stamps

S6. (p. 25; fig. 81.) Albanus of La Graufesenque (*Hermet 1934*, pl. 110, 2). Form 27g stamped OFALBANI (Ib). All fifty-eight records of this stamp are on form 27, usually with grooved footrings. There are eight stamps from Flavian foundations, but none from a definitely pre-Flavian context. There are, however, two records of a similar stamp (Ia) on form 24/25, so Albanus probably began work under Nero. It may be noted that Dr. Oswald (*Stamps*, p. 9) includes under the same heading the work of an earlier Albanus making, *inter alia*, Ritterling 5. *c.* A.D. 65–80.

S7. (p. 25; fig. 81.) Calvus of La Graufesenque (*Hermet 1934*, pl. 110, 22). Form 27 stamped OFCALVI (IIIp). This stamp is comparatively uncommon and only once occurs at a Flavian foundation. Calvus probably began work under Nero, *c.* A.D. 65. Of the four hundred or so stamps reading OFCALVI only twenty are from late Vespasianic or Domitianic foundations, but many are from sites abandoned by about A.D. 80, so it is doubtful if Calvus was at work after A.D. 85. *c.* A.D. 65–85.

S8. (p. 24.) Crestio or La Graufesenque (*Hermet 1934*, pl. 110, 43). Form 29 stamped [OF]CREST[IO] (Ic). With only two exceptions, this stamp is always on form 29 (twenty noted). No Flavian sites are involved and one record in Valkenburg Period III (*van Giffen 1940–44*, 226, no. 40) must be earlier than A.D. 70. *c.* A.D. 55–70. See D15 (fig. 84).

S9. (p. 24; fig. 81.) Crestus or Crestio of La Graufesenque (*Hermet 1934*, pl. 110, 43). Probably form 29, stamped OFCREƧT[I] retro. (IVa). Whether this and similar stamps belong to the same potter as the last is uncertain. It is, however, definitely later than S8, since records from Flavian foundations are not uncommon (Nijmegen fortress and the site of Ulpia Noviomagus (5), Caerleon, Chester, Carlisle, and York are all included). There is, however, one record on form 24/25 from Strasbourg (a burnt cup, perhaps lost in A.D. 69–70). *c.* A.D. 65–80.

S10. (p. 24; fig. 81). Frontinus of La Graufesenque (*Hermet 1934*, pl. 111, 56). Form 18 stamped OFRONTI (XVIIa). There is little specific evidence for the date of this stamp, which is usually on form 18, occasionally on form 15/17. However, nothing suggests pre-Flavian activity for Frontinus, and his work, though not this stamp, is common at Agricolan sites in Britain. *c.* A.D. 70–90.

S11. (p. 25; fig. 81.) Germanus of La Graufesenque (*Hermet 1934*, pl. 111, 64). Form 29 stamped GER‑MANIOF (XIIa). The stamp is almost invariably on form 29, with only two records on form 18. Only four examples out of a total of thirty-four are from Flavian foundations. *c.* A.D. 60–75. See D16.

S12. (p. 25; fig. 81.) Iucundus of La Graufesenque (*Hermet 1934*, pl. 111, 68). Form 18 stamped OF.IV [CVN] (IIIf). All examples of the stamp are on dishes, with no certain instance of form 15/17. One comes from Period IV at Valkenburg (A.D. 70 or later). Many other stamps of Iucundus come from Flavian sites, including Agricolan ones in Britain, but he was at work by A.D. 60 at the latest judging by his decorated ware. His early stamps are in the genitive without *of(ficina)*. In view of the lack of records at Agricolan sites, this particular stamp may be dated *c.* A.D. 65–80.

S13. (p. 24; fig. 81.) Maccarus of La Graufesenque (*Hermet 1934*, pl. 111, 80). Form 27g stamped OF.MACCAR (VIIIe). Maccarus worked primarily under Claudius and this piece must be residual. *c.* A.D. 40–55.

S14. (p. 24; fig. 81.) Masc(u)lus of La Graufesenque (*Hermet 1934*, pl. 111, 98). Form 18 stamped MASCVLVS (XVIIb). An uncommon stamp, only otherwise known on form 15/17 Alésia, 15/17 or 18 London and 18 Silchester. However, XVIIa is identical in lettering, though slightly smaller, and the die may have been moulded from an impression of XVIIb. The smaller version appears four times at Flavian sites, the larger is probably to be dated *c.* A.D. 55–70.

S15. (p. 25; fig. 81.) Memor of La Graufesenque (*Hermet 1934*, pl. 114, 20). Form 27g stamped MEMO (XIIIa). A rather uncommon stamp, always used on form 27, with Nijmegen (Ulpia) and Chester as the only dated sites. Other stamps are recorded on form 24/25, once certainly, one probably, and his common MEMORISM (IIIa) stamp occurs occasionally at Agricolan foundations. Memor specialized in making form 27, but he also produced moulds, bowls from which occur in the Pompeii hoard of A.D. 79 (*J.R.S.* iv, pl. XIV). *c.* A.D. 65–85.

S16. (p. 25; fig. 81.) Modestus of La Graufesenque (*Hermet 1934*, pl. 112, 195). Form 27g stamped [O]FMOI (probably VIIa' rather than VIIa). The die originally gave stamps reading OFMOD, but it was later broken and the ends filed off diagonally, giving stamps /OFMOI/ (VIIa'). The first version was used occasionally on Ritterling 8 and form 24/25 before the Boudiccan rebellion (Hull, *Roman Colchester*, fig. 99, 23), but the later one has been noted twenty times from Flavian foundations. The dates implied are: VIIa *c.* A.D. 55–65; VIIa' *c.* A.D. 65–75. The latter occurs, presumably as a survival, at Broomholm.

S17. (p. 24; fig. 81.) Mommo of La Graufesenque (*Hermet 1934*, pl. 112, 106). Form 27g stamped OMOM (XIa). All seventy-two examples of this stamp are on form 27; six come from Flavian foundations, so it should be one of his later dies, *c.* A.D. 65–80.

S18. (p. 24; fig. 81.) Montanus of La Graufesenque (*Hermet 1934*, pl. 112, 118). Form 18 stamped OFMONTANI (Ib). All records are on form 15/17 or 18 or 18R, and include York and the Nijmegen and Strasbourg fortresses. A closely similar stamp (Ia) occurs at Caerleon and Carmarthen. Montanus must have begun work by A.D. 60 (Hull, *Roman Colchester*, fig. 99, 13 for one of his early stamps). Dr. Oswald's records (*Stamps*, 210) include much of the work of Montanus of La Madeleine under this potter. *c.* A.D. 65–80.

S19. (p. 24; fig. 81.) Patricius of La Graufesenque (*Hermet 1934*, pl. 112, 119). Form 18 stamped OF.PATRICI (Ig). An uncommon stamp of Patricius, only noted five times before, and not at closely dated sites. However, none of Patricius' stamps has been recorded on pre-Flavian forms or in definitely pre-Flavian contexts, while many come from Flavian foundations. *c.* A.D. 70–90.

S20. (p. 24; fig. 81.) Pontus of La Graufesenque (Oswald, *Stamps*, 243). Form 18 stamped OFPONTI (VIIIe). This stamp is usually on form 18 or 29 and has only been seen otherwise once on form 27. There are no dated sites, though his other stamps are all common on Flavian sites. *c.* A.D. 65–90. See D67, below.

S21. (p. 24; fig. 81.) Primus of La Graufesenque (*Hermet 1934*, pl. 112, 132). Form 18R stamped OFPRIMI, a dot in the first half of the M (IXb). A definitely pre-Flavian stamp confined to forms 29, 15/17R and 18R. *c.* A.D. 50–65.

S22. (p. 24; fig. 81.) Rufinus of La Graufesenque (*Hermet 1934*, pl. 112, 141). Form 15/17 stamped OF.RVFNI (IVa). This stamp is almost invariably used on forms 15/17 or 18, generally the latter. A record from Valkenburg Period III demonstrates pre-Flavian use (*van Giffen 1948–53*, p. 144, 309), but six stamps are from Flavian foundations, none Agricolan. *c.* A.D. 65–80.

S23. (p. 24.) CV[or CΛ[retro. on form 27, South Gaulish and Flavian. The stamp has not been identified.

It can scarcely be coincidence that while almost all these stamps are known from Flavian sites only one (S16) is recorded at a site founded under Agricola. Only four, S8, 13, 14 and 21 are definitely pre-Flavian. The weight thus falls *c.* A.D. 65–80 and, with the lack of Agricolan parallels, a date rather before A.D. 80 seems certain for the filling of the pit.

Decorated ware from Pit 7 (D15–50)

All South Gaulish and probably all from La Graufesenque.

D15. (p. 24; fig. 84.) Form 29, stamped internally [OF]CREST[IO] (Ic). The rather stiff arrangement is paralleled on a bowl with the same stamp at Utrecht which also has the same chevron and festoon pendants. Similar festoons also appear in the Pompeii Hoard (*J.R.S.* iv, 29: OFVITA). The gadroons and chevron-wreath were also used in this way by Iucundus (*Knorr 1919*, Taf. 43F), Meddillus (*Knorr 1919*, Taf. 55B; *Knorr 1952*, Taf. 40D), Pontus (OF.PONTI VIIIa. Wiggonholt, Worthing Mus.), and Vitalis (*Knorr 1919*, 83D), though rather similar schemes could be used by earlier potters, such as Ardacus (*Knorr 1952*, Taf. 2C). This is probably late work of Crestio of *c.* A.D. 60–70. See S8.

D16. (p. 24; fig. 84.) Form 29, stamped internally GERMAN̂IOF. This is the early work of Germanus, made, if indeed he did make the mould, before he had developed his highly individual style. The lower zone is very close to one on a bowl from Vechten with the same stamp (Rijksmus. van Oudheiden, Leiden VF 1387) and is matched at La Graufesenque (*Hermet 1934*, pl. 102, 50). The use of the bifid bud attached to the scroll of the upper zone is characteristic of Germanus (cf. *Hermet 1934*, pl. 42, 1). *c.* A.D. 60–75. See S11.

D17. (p. 24; fig. 84.) Form 29, The upper zone of festoons with birds (O. 2298 and 2249) is close to one on a bowl stamped OFVITΛL at Ovilava (*Karnitsch 1959*, Taf. 9, 1) and Vitalis used the festoon pendant of this piece (*Knorr 1919*, Taf. 83, 15), as did Germanus on another Verulamium bowl to be published later. The leaves of the lower zone are also on the other Verulamium bowl and on one from Vechten stamped by Vitalis (*Knorr 1919*, Taf. 84J). *c.* A.D. 65–80.

D18. (p. 24; fig. 84.) Form 29. The upper zone has a rather flat continuous scroll with a leaf used by Licinus in a generally similar one (*Knorr 1919*, Taf. 47F). The leaves in the scroll of the lower zone were used by several potters, including Frontinus, Montanus, Passenus, and Secundus, the closest parallel noted being a bowl in the London Museum stamped OF.PASSIEN (IIIb). *c.* A.D. 50–65.

D19. (p. 24; fig. 84.) Form 29. The upper zone has panels of animals (including *Hermet 1934*, pl. 26, 63) alternating with panels of small leaves. The divisions between them are unusual in consisting of double wavy lines on each side of rosettes top and bottom, an arrangement only otherwise noted on form 29 at Leicester, stamped OFMONT̂I.CR and on a bowl from Heerlen with the same wreath in the lower zone (*L'Antiquité Classique*, xvii (1948), 246, no. 1). For the leaves cf. Coelus (*Knorr 1919*, Taf. 23A). In the lower zone the wreath of poorly impressed overlapping leaves is matched on bowls stamped by Rufinus at Chester and Virtus at York. The festoons are most closely, though not precisely, matched in another Verulamium bowl stamped GERMA͡NIF (B I 45), but the pendants cannot be paralleled. c. A.D. 65–80.

D20. (p. 24; fig. 84.) Form 29. Panels with dog (*Hermet 1934*, pl. 26, 40 = O. 2015) in the upper zone. The lower zone has a similar series of festoons to a bowl from Neuss stamped OFPRIMI (IXb), but the pendants have only been noted on a bowl of S. Iulius Iucundus from Vechten. The general style is much closer to the work of Flavian than earlier potters. c. A.D. 70–85.

D21. (p. 24; fig. 85.) Form 29. The rather unusual scroll in the upper zone is virtually identical to one on a bowl from York stamped PRIMVꝤFE. Perhaps even closer, since the piece also has the reversed S-gadroons of the Verulamium sherd, is a Vechten bowl stamped OFCOELI (*Knorr 1919*, Taf. 24C). At the bottom of the lower zone is a wreath using the same leaf as the scroll, but the top wreath of the zone seems to be unparalleled on stamped pieces. This bowl was presumably closely connected with Coelus, c. A.D. 65–80.

D22. (p. 24; fig. 85.) Form 29. In style the upper zone is close to D19 above. The leaves in the panel with diagonal wavy lines are not very common and have only been noted on bowls stamped by Rufinus and Vanderio. The animals are lion (D.747/8) and dog (D.916 approximately). Flavian rather than earlier. c. A.D. 70–85.

D23. (p. 24; fig. 85.) Form 29. Part of the upper zone with a continuous scroll reminiscent of D21. The use of a bird perched on the end of a tendril is paralleled on a bowl stamped OF.VITALI at Wroxeter (*Atkinson 1942*, pl. 68, 52R) and the same bird used in this way is on a bowl in the Pompeii Hoard (*J.R.S.* iv, pl. IX, 49). c. A.D. 65–80.

D24. (p. 24; fig. 85.) Form 29, a small fragment from the upper zone, probably assignable to Meddillus, as it is identical to a bowl stamped by him (*Knorr 1952*, Taf. 39C). This is unlikely to be his earliest work, however. c. A.D. 65–80.

D25. (p. 24; fig. 85.) Form 29. The festoons, birds, and pendants all appear on the Leicester bowl referred to under D19. Free, plain rings are not common in South Gaulish work, but were certainly used by Meddillus and Passenus. c. A.D. 60–75.

D26. (p. 24; fig. 85.) Form 29. A small part of the lower zone with one of the large plants more commonly seen partly impressed as a 'filler'. On form 29 it is noted completely impressed on bowls of Flavius Germanus at Alésia and Vitalis at Nijmegen. c. A.D. 70–85.

D27–30. (p. 24; fig. 85.) Small fragments of form 29, all from different bowls, not assignable to makers. D27 is interesting for the unusual pendant. All could be either Neronian or early Flavian.

D31. (p. 24; fig. 85.) Form 30, complete, but unstamped. Two main panels, four times repeated, separated by narrow panels using the small bifid bud characteristic of Germanus. This may be his work, since a similar panel containing only four tendrils is on a bowl of his from La Graufesenque (*Hermet 1934*, pl. 100, 17) and the ovolo may be one on a bowl from Ostia stamped GERMA͡NI in the decoration (*Knorr 1952*, Taf. 28F). c. A.D. 65–80.

D32. (p. 24; fig. 85.) Form 30, complete, with two panels repeated four times. The gladiators (O. 1007, 1008) occur together frequently on bowls of Crucuro, who also used the ovolo tongue with four prongs. If, as seems likely, this is his work, then it is probably one of his earliest pieces. c. A.D. 70–80.

D33. (p. 24; fig. 85.) Form 30. The ovolo and general style are reminiscent of work attributed to Masculus (*Knorr 1952*, Taf. 36A). What seem to be the same leaves (and birds?) are on a form 29 from Rheingönheim stamped OF LABIONIS (*Knorr 1919*, Textbild 43), and there is a rather similar piece from Risstissen (*Ulbert 1959*, Taf. 54, 9). c. A.D. 55–75.

D34. (p. 24; fig. 86.) Form 30 with one of the common ovolos of the Pompeii Hoard (*J.R.S.* iv, pl. XIII, 65), used by Mommo and possibly Memor (ibid. pl. XIV). Both potters regularly used corner tassels, but neither the leafy (olive?) festoon nor the cogged medallion seems to be known on stamped bowls. For the festoon on form 29, see Kenyon, *Jewry Wall Report*, 61, no. 10, assigned

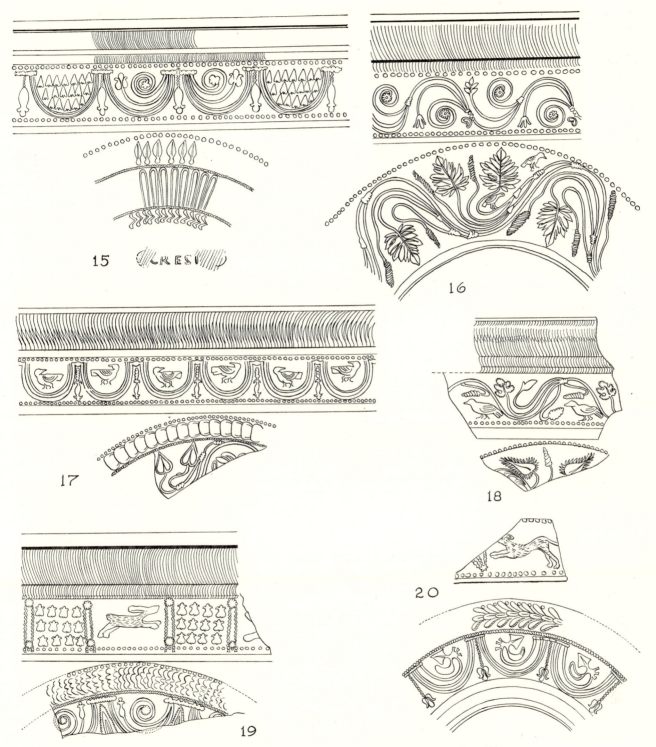

15 ⟨CRESI⟩

16

17

18

20

19

FIG 84. Decorated samian 15–20 ($\frac{1}{2}$), with stamp S 8 ($\frac{1}{1}$).

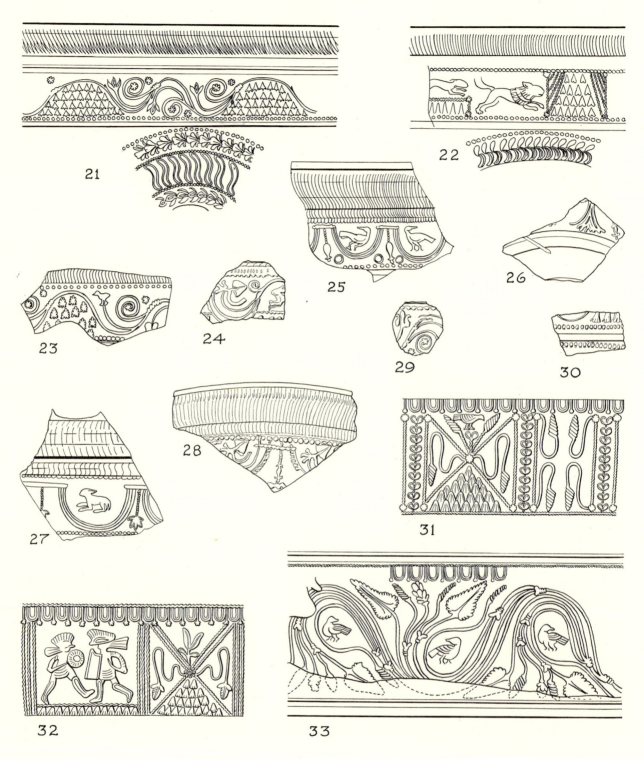

FIG. 85. Decorated samian 21–33 ($\frac{1}{2}$).

by Oswald to Mommo, and for its use on rather later pieces cf. *Ann. of Arch. and Anth.* xi, 68. *c.* A.D. 70–85.

D35. (p. 24; fig. 86.) Form 30. This and the next piece have early versions of the ovolo tongue with trident end which became so characteristic, in coarser versions, of the mid- and late Flavian South Gaulish bowls.

D36. (p. 24; fig. 86.) Form 30, with strap handle and, presumably, spout (cf. *Stanfield 1929*, 122 for the similar form 37). The figure is a variant of H. 19, 84. There is nothing to indicate the potter. *c.* A.D. 70–90.

D37. (p. 24; fig. 86.) Form 30. Panels, including a boar (H. 27, 34). Flavian.

D38. (p. 24; fig. 86.) Form 30. Panels with a Jupiter (H. 18, 1) and lion (H. 25, 12). For a similar arrangement of the lion and the leaf on a tassel cf. D68 (Severus IIIa), but the style is common. Flavian.

D39. (p. 24; fig. 86.) Form 30. Panels with one of the common combinations of leaf-tips and wavy-lines normal on form 30 for Flavian potters (e.g. Mommo, *Knorr 1952*, Taf. 77D).

D40. (p. 24; fig. 86.) Form 37 in the style of Germanus. For the large and small dolphins see *Knorr 1919*, Taf. 35, details 42 and 51; for the bird ibid. 44. The festoon made up from separate impressions of a bud (ibid. 61) is unusual. *c.* A.D. 70–85.

D41. (p. 24; fig. 86.) Form 37. The ovolo and beaded borders are both uncommon. Several fragments of a bowl by the same potter have been found at Margidunum (Oswald, *The Terra Sigillata of Margidunum*, pl. xiv, 2: there assigned to Albinus, but on insufficient evidence). The piece is presumably Vespasianic.

D42. (p. 24; fig. 86.) Form 37 in the style of Frontinus. For the stumpy gadroons cf. Curle, *Newstead*, p. 209, 1 and 4 (same bowl). The leaf in the scroll is *Knorr 1919*, Taf. 33, 2. *c.* A.D. 70–90.

D43. (p. 24; fig. 86.) A small fragment of form 37 with the ovolo with large rosette on the tongue used commonly by Frontinus, and no doubt by other contemporary potters. This occurs frequently at Inchtuthil and Camelon as well as in the Pompeii Hoard (*J.R.S.* iv, *passim*). *c.* A.D. 70–90.

D44. (p. 24; fig. 86.) Form 37 with the four-pronged tongue to the ovolo used by M. Crestio and Crucuro (*Knorr 1919*, Textbild 5), but perhaps here by another potter, though the medallions and panels with leaf-tips and wavy-lines are on form 37 with stamps of M. Crestio at Nijmegen (Mus. Kam M1020) and Strasbourg (Château des Rohans 5475). D72 has several points in common, and C. I(ulius) Sa(binus) used similar saltires and panels with the medallion (*Hermet 1934*, pl. 82, 7). Generally similar bowls are not uncommon among the unpublished Newstead material and at Caerhun (*Baillie Reynolds 1938*, S142). The figure-types are: dog (H. 26, 63), hare (H. 26, 56), Cupid (D. 280), and sheep (O. 1858). *c.* A.D. 75–90.

D45. (p. 24; fig. 86.) Form 37, possibly by Memor, who used the gadroons and saltire on a bowl from Richborough with his mould-signature (unpublished: Site Museum v, 153). Cf. also *J.R.S.* iv, pl. xiv and *Fundberichte aus Schwaben*, xvii (1909), Taf. iv, 1 with a signature interpreted by Knorr as Sasmonos, but surely also Memor's. *c.* A.D. 70–90.

D46. (p. 24; fig. 87.) Form 37 with wavy-lines and a chevron wreath below. Typologically this looks later than most of the pit material and one wonders whether it might not be intrusive.

D47. (p. 24; fig. 87.) Form 37 fragment with part of a zone of festoons. Flavian.

D48. (p. 24; fig. 87.) Form 37 fragment with a large trident tongue to the ovolo. Such pieces had begun to appear by A.D. 79 at latest on the evidence of the Pompeii hoard (*J.R.S.* iv, *passim*).

D49. (p. 24; fig. 87.) Form 37 fragment, having an ovolo with large rosette to the tongue. Flavian.

D50. (p. 24; fig. 87.) Form 37, a small fragment with a boar (H. 27, 34). Flavian.

Only one of the decorated pieces in the pit is necessarily pre-Flavian (D18). On the other hand, the high proportion of forms 29 and 30 is striking. There are a few links in the decorated ware

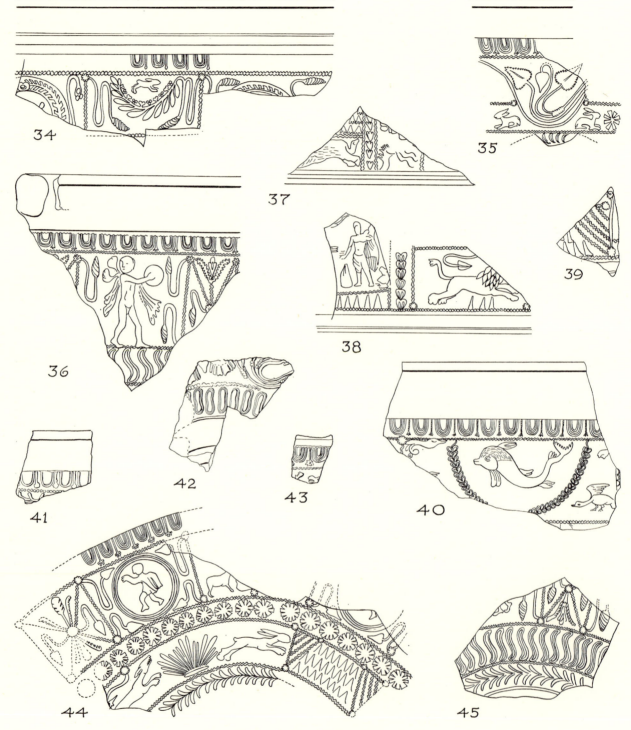

FIG. 86. Decorated samian 34–45 ($\frac{1}{2}$).

with the Pompeii hoard of A.D. 79 and with Agricolan Scotland, where the decorated bowls of Frontinus, for instance, are common. Nevertheless, there seems to be nothing in the pit, with the possible exception of D46—a small fragment—which is necessarily later than A.D. 75. Taken with the evidence of the potters' stamps, it seems clear that the pit must have been filled by A.D. 75 or very soon after.

PIT 10

Potter's stamp

S24. B IV Pit 10 (p. 25; fig. 81). Primulus of La Graufesenque (*Hermet 1934*, pl. 112, 131). Form 15/17 stamped PRIMVLI (Vd). The stamp was used only on plates, rather more often on form 18 than form 15/17. It occurs at Usk, Corbridge, and at Nijmegen (fortress and Ulpia Noviomagus). Primulus was at work under Nero, since he made, if rarely, both Ritterling 8 and form 24/25. This die, however, is more likely to be Flavian in view of the sites noted above. *c.* A.D. 70–85.

PERIOD IIA

Potters' stamps

S25. A VI 31 (p. 32; fig. 81). Albanus of La Graufesenque (S6, above). Form 27g OF.ALBAN (IIa). Always on form 27, this stamp has only once been recorded outside Britain (at Groesbeek, Holland). Chester provides the only instance of a Flavian site. Probably *c.* A.D. 65–85.

S26. A VI 31 (p. 32; fig. 81). Aquitanus of La Graufesenque (*Hermet 1934*, pl. 110, 11). Form 15/17 or 18 stamped OFAQVITAN (IIb). This stamp is on a burnt dish from one of the shops destroyed in A.D. 60–1 at Colchester (Hull, *Roman Colchester*, fig. 99, 19). *c.* A.D. 50–65.

S27. B I 38 (p. 35; fig. 81). Ater(?) of South Gaul. Form 27 stamped ΛTRI. This stamp is usually attributed to a somewhat nebulous Ater of South Gaul (Oswald, *Stamps*, 25), but is in fact almost certainly from a broken die of Patricius. The character of the letters is close to many Patricius stamps and there are good parallels for continuing use of badly broken dies (e.g. all stamps reading T+.OFFIC are stamped with a die originally giving RVTTI.OFFIC). However that may be, the stamp is certainly Flavian and occurs at Caerleon, Chester, and York. *c.* A.D. 70–90.

S28. B IV 33 (p. 37; fig. 81). Avinius of South Gaul, probably La Graufesenque. Form 18 stamped ΛVINII (Ia). This is an excessively rare stamp only noted in Britain elsewhere on form 18 London (LM A22860), where it is broken in the same place. Fortunately the stamp appears complete at Bavai on form 18 (*Pro Nervia*, III, iii, 48, no. 132) and it is evident that no letters are lost on the Verulamium stamp. Both form and fabric are consistent with Flavian date.

S29. B I 38 (p. 35; fig. 81). Bassus of La Graufesenque (*Hermet 1934*, pl. 110, 16). Form 18 stamped OF.BASSI (IIIe). *c.* A.D. 45–65.

S30. B I 38 (p. 35). Same potter. Form 18, stamped [OFB]ASSI (IIIp). An uncommon stamp of Bassus, only otherwise recorded at La Graufesenque, Ubbergen (Oppidum Batavorum) and London. Pre-Flavian. *c.* A.D. 50–70.

S31. A II 42 (p. 33; fig. 81). Bassus and Coelus (*Hermet 1934*, pl. 110, 17). Form 27g stamped OFBΛSSIC. The only other example is from La Graufesenque (Millau Mus.), but the partnership was certainly Neronian to early Flavian.

S32. B I 38 (p. 35; fig. 81). Carbo of La Graufesenque (*Hermet 1934*, pl. 110, 25). Form 18 stamped CARB[ONISM] (VIa). Flavian activity is implied by records at Corbridge, Wilderspool, the Nijmegen fortress (3), and the Ulpia Noviomagus cemetery. The first two have stamps reading ARBONISΛ, as often with this die—hence records under Arro (Oswald, *Stamps*, 23). The others have the full version. Normally the stamp is on form 18 or 18R, but it was used twice on cups by impressing only the beginning and end of the stamp, resulting in CAIISM on form 27 at Exeter (Mus. 368) and CAISM at Strasbourg on form 24/25 (Château des Rohans 21717f). The latter suggests the possibility of pre-Flavian beginning, strengthened by the use of another die on form 24/25 at Autun. *c.* A.D. 65–85.

S33. B II 30C (p. 38; fig. 81). Catullinus of Central Gaul. Form 27, stamped [CAT]VLLINVS (IIb), slightly burnt. This stamp is uncommon and has only been seen otherwise on form 27 at Wroxeter, and on form 18/31 at London (4), Heerlen and Utrecht. The fabrics suggest manufacture at Les Martres-de-Veyre rather than Lezoux. Though obviously not datable from independent evidence, the forms and fabrics would be consistent with Trajanic or early Hadrianic date. Probably *c.* A.D. 100–25.

S34. A VI 31 (p. 32; fig. 81). Crestus or Crestio of La Graufesenque (*Hermet 1934*, pl. 110, 43). Form 27 stamped OFCREȘTI retro. (IVa). See S9 and S96. *c.* A.D. 65–80.

S35. B I 38 (p. 35; fig. 81). Domitus of Les Martres-de-Veyre (*Terrisse 1969*, pl. LII). Form 33a stamped DOMII retro. (VIIIa). This stamp is very common in Britain, but is probably one of the potter's earliest ones, since it (unlike one of the others) is absent from the groups associated with the London Second Fire. It also appears in the Nijmegen fortress. *c.* A.D. 100–20.

S36. A II 59 (p. 33; fig. 81). Felix of South Gaul. Form 18 stamped FELIXS.FEC (XXXa). This stamp is not recorded either from Montans or La Graufesenque, but typologically the dish looks Claudian and could well be from Montans.

S37. B I 45 (p. 35). Germanus of La Graufesenque (see D16). Form 29 stamped GERMANIF (XXIIIb), inside the base. No decoration survives. The stamp is normally on form 29, but has also been noted on form 15/17. *c.* A.D. 65–85.

S38. A II 59 (p. 33; fig. 81). Labio of La Graufesenque (*Hermet 1934*, pl. 111, 72). Form 18 stamped [OF.L]ABIO (IVg). Labio probably had a lengthy career. The stamps in OF.LABIO are usually early, though this one occurs in the Chester fortress. *c.* A.D. 50–70.

S39. T VI 22A. Form 37 with the stamp MC[retro. in the decoration. Although noted on preliminary examination, the sherd and drawing seem to have been mislaid and the piece will have to be discussed in a future report.

S40. T III 27 (p. 28). Form 29, base only, stamped ME⊕I]LLVS (IIIa). See S2 for the same stamp.

S41. T VII 36 (p. 29; fig. 81). Meddillus (?) of La Graufesenque. Form 18R stamped MESILLVS[FI. The equation with Meddillus is highly likely, since the Gaulish barred d or dd is frequently replaced by s or ss (D. Ellis Evans, *Gaulish Personal Names*, 367: J. Whatmough, *The Dialects of Ancient Gaul*, Grammar part i, 105.) This stamp is only known elsewhere at London and Périgueux on form 33(a?). *c.* A.D. 60–80.

S42. A IV 42 (p. 31; fig. 81). MIO retro. on form 27g (Ia). This stamp is unique. It may be an illiterate cypher, though Dr. Oswald assigned the stamp MIO to a somewhat hypothetical Miccio of South Gaul. This stamp is likely to be Flavian, judging by the form and fabric of the Verulamium cup.

S43. B II 37E (p. 36; fig. 81). Modestus of La Graufesenque (*Hermet 1934*, pl. 112, 105). Form 15/17 or 18 stamped [OFM]ODES (IVa). There is no evidence allowing this stamp to be dated closely. Probably *c.* A.D. 50–70.

S44. A VII 42 (p. 38; fig. 81). See S 45.

S45. B II 36E (p. 36; fig. 81). Mommo of La Graufesenque. Both the same stamp as S17, above. *c.* A.D. 65–80.

S46. A I 39 (p. 33; fig. 81). Niger of La Graufesenque (*Hermet 1934*, pl. 112, 113). Form 29 base stamped OF[NI]GRI (IIa). This bowl is partly unglazed inside the footring. This is the only stamp of Niger commonly used on form 29 (thirty-eight examples, with another sixteen on dishes). It has only been noted twice from Flavian foundations, presumably as a survival. *c.* A.D. 50–70. (A fragment of the lower zone survives, but shows only straight gadroons, not illustrated.)

S47. A IV 40 (p. 31; fig. 81). Niger (as last, S46). Form 15/17 or 18 stamped [O]FNIGR (IVa). At Valkenburg this stamp occurs in Period II (*van Giffen 1940–44*, p. 232, no. 89), and it also appears in the ditch of the Cirencester fort in a group of *c.* A.D. 55–65 (*Antiq. Journ.* xlii, 3 f.). A probable example comes from the fortress baths at Caerleon, presumably a survival. *c.* A.D. 45–65.

S48. A II 42 (p. 33; fig. 81). Niger (as last two). Form 27g stamped OFNGR (Va). An uncommon stamp, usually on form 27. No close dating. Probably Neronian.

S49. B I 38 (p. 35; fig. 81.) Passienus of La Graufesenque (*Hermet 1934*, pl. 112, 117). Form 29, without decoration, stamped [OF.P]ASSIEN (IIIb). This stamp is always on form 29 (some forty examples). No Flavian sites are involved. *c.* A.D. 45–65.

S50. B II 30C (p. 38; fig. 81). Primus of La Graufesenque (*Hermet 1934*, pl. 112, 132). Ritterling 8 stamped OFPRIM (XIIIc). An uncommon stamp, but also on Ritterling 8 at Alésia and so probably one of Primus's early ones. *c.* A.D. 45–60.

S51. A X 21 (p. 33; fig. 81). Sabinus of La Graufesenque (*Hermet 1934*, pl. 112, 145). Form 27g stamped OSABI (XXIIa). Stamps with this reading are uncommon, but seem to be largely Neronian or early Flavian. This one appears at Ubbergen (Oppidum Batavorum). *c.* A.D. 55–75.

S52. A VII 42 (p. 38; fig. 81). Senicio of La Graufesenque (*Hermet 1934*, pl. 112, 156). Form 24/25 stamped ENICI (VIIa'). This is from a worn or mutilated die of Senicio. The original version appears on Ritterling 8 and 9 in Claudio-Neronian contexts; the reduced one is recorded several times on forms 24/25 and 27. *c.* A.D. 55–65.

S53. A IV 38 (p. 30, fig. 81). Severus of La Graufesenque (*Hermet 1934*, pl. 112, 160). From 27g stamped OFSEVERI (VIIIa). A Neronian to early Flavian stamp, usually on form 27, known from York, the Nijmegen fortress and Ulpia (3), and twice, burnt, in the Burghöfe Geschirrdepot (*Ulbert 1959*, 42, 77; Munich: Prähistorisches Staatssammlung, 1955, 129). *c.* A.D. 65–80.

S54. Pit 9 (in B II 32G) (p. 34; fig. 81). Viducos of Les Martres-de-Veyre (*Terrisse 1969*, pl. LIV). Form 33a stamped VIDVCOSF (VIIIa). As often with early products of Les Martres, more than 85 per cent of the examples of this stamp are in Britain. Only one burnt sherd with it is published as from the burnt deposit of the London Second Fire at Regis House (*Antiq. Journ.* xxv, 70), but in fact another was found there (GH 1932.193). In addition, six more burnt vessels with the stamp have now been noted from London (all on form 33a). This should mean that the stamp was in use at least as late as A.D. 120. However, it is absent from Hadrian's Wall and so is unlikely to have been used much later. The initial date can only be guessed. It is clear that Les Martres was exporting to Britain before the Trajanic evacuation of Scotland, and this stamp could theoretically be as early as A.D. 100. It must, therefore, fall in the range A.D. 100–25, and probability favours a date *c.* A.D. 105–20.

S55. B II 32E (p. 37) The same stamp as S54.

S56. B I 38 (p. 35; fig. 81). Virthus of La Graufesenque (*Hermet 1934*, pl. 113, 180). Form 18R, burnt, stamped VIRTH[VSFECIT] (Ia). Virthus certainly began work under Claudius, but this stamp is probably not his earliest, though it does not appear at any Flavian sites. *c.* A.D. 50–65.

S57. B II 32F (p. 34; fig. 81.) Same potter as the last. Form 15/17 or 18 stamped VIRT[HV] (VIIIa). This stamp has been noted in the Yorkshire Museum (unprovenanced, but probably from York). It is probably one of the latest used by Virthus. *c.* A.D. 55–70.

S58. B II 32D (p. 36; fig. 81). Vitalis of Les Martres-de-Veyre (*Terrisse 1969*, pl. LIV). Form 18/31 stamped [V]ITALISMSF (XLVIa). This stamp is normally on early varieties of form 18/31, more rarely on form 27 or form 15/17. Two examples from the London Second Fire (*Antiq. Journ.* xxv, 76) and two burnt ones from London. *c.* A.D. 100–25.

It will be observed that almost all the potters' stamps are residual in Period IIa contexts. If it were not for the four stamps of Central Gaulish potters from Les Martres-de-Veyre

(S35, 56, 57, and 58), it would be possible to think of a relatively early Flavian date for the end of this period. As it is, the comparative rarity of second-century pieces must be given full weight and it seems clear that the end of period IIA must have come in the decade A.D. 100–10.

Decorated ware

D51–63. All South Gaulish.

D51. A VII 42 (p. 38; fig. 87). Form 37, probably the same bowl as D73, q.v.

D52. B I 38 (p. 35; fig. 87). Form 30. A small fragment which could be either Neronian or early Flavian.

D53. B I 38 (p. 35; fig. 87). Form 29, probably a Neronian piece. The hare is H. 26, 38.

D54. B II 32E (p. 36; fig. 87). Form 29. Too little of the decoration is left for useful discussion. Probably Flavian.

D55. B II 32E (p. 36; fig. 87). Form 29. The badly blurred scroll recalls ones used by such potters as Patricius (*Knorr 1952*, Taf. 50). *c.* A.D. 70–85.

D56. B II 32E (p. 36; fig. 87). Form 37, probably by Frontinus, cf. *Knorr 1952*, Taf. 25. *c.* A.D. 70–90.

D57. B II 32E (p. 36; fig. 87). Form 37, ovolo, with large rosette to the tongue, used by Frontinus and his contemporaries. *c.* A.D. 70–90.

D58–61. All B II 32E (p. 36; fig. 87). At least three different bowls of form 37, all in the style of Frontinus, *c.* A.D. 70–90.

D62. B II 37E (p. 36; fig. 87). Form 37. There are resemblances with Memor's work, especially in the alternation of gadroons and figures (cf. *Fundberichte aus Schwaben*, xvii (1909), Taf. iv, 1 and the note under D45). Several of the motifs were also used by Frontinus, however (cf. *Knorr 1952*, Taf. 25). *c.* A.D. 70–85.

D63. B IV 29A (p. 38; fig. 87). Form 29/37, with normal profile for form 29, but with the rim and plain band of form 37, as *Stanfield 1929*, 10. The upper zone is identical to one on a bowl from Nijmegen stamped OFPRIMI (*Hermet 1934*, pl. 119, 4 and *Knorr 1919*, Taf. 67K). The lower zone is close to some work of Vitalis (*J.R.S.* iv, pl. v, 29 and *Knorr 1919*, Taf. 83D). *c.* A.D. 65–80.

PERIOD IIA/IIB

Under this heading is recorded the scattered group of complete vessels, mostly decorated, referred to above (p. 28).

Potters' stamps

S59. A VII 19, 28, 32, 33, 41, and 42. Pontus of La Graufesenque (*Hermet 1934*, pl. 112, 125). Form 29 stamped in the base OF PONTI (VIIIe). The stamp is discussed under no. S20 above. Here *c.* A.D. 65–80, in view of the decoration (D. 67 below). See fig. 88.

S60. A VII 27 (fig. 81). Sacirus of Central (?) Gaul. Form 18/31 stamped •SA[CIRV•FE] (VIa). A rare stamp only known at Alésia, Cirencester, York, and Vichy. The fabrics have a peculiar range, sometimes matching South Gaulish standards, sometimes Les Martres-de-Veyre. Probability favours the latter on three counts: the forms are close to normal Central Gaulish versions of forms 18/31 and 18/31R; names in Sacir- are typical of Central Gaul and, finally, the character of the lettering looks like Central Gaulish work. If this is correct, then an early potter of Les Martres-de-Veyre working under Trajan.

S61. A VII 33. Severus of La Graufesenque (*Hermet 1934*, pl. 112, 160). Form 29 stamped in the base (F)ISEV[ERI] retro. (IIIa). The beginning of the stamp is usually badly impressed, and it has been recorded (Oswald, *Stamps*, 44) as BISENESI. Most of the records are in the Rhineland, but the

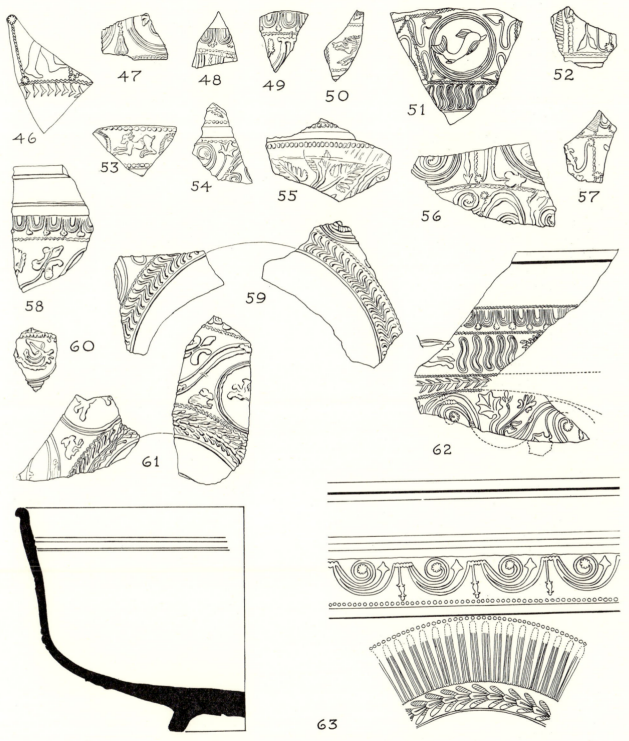

FIG. 87. Decorated samian 46–63 ($\frac{1}{2}$).

stamp is twice on form 27 at Corbridge. The decoration (D. 68, below) is in accord with a date *c*. A.D. 70–85 and nothing in the record for the stamp conflicts. See fig. 89.

S62. A VII 24, 28, and 29. A fragmentary cursive signature. The bowl is discussed under D. 76, below.

S63. A VII 19, 28, 32, 33, 41, and 42. Traces of a cursive signature, for which see D. 75, below.

Decorated ware (D64–81)

All South Gaulish and from La Graufesenque. See p. 28 for the circumstances of discovery.

D64. A VII 26 and 29 (fig. 88). Form 29. The scroll of the upper zone, but reversed, is on form 29 from Vindonissa stamped OFPRIM (*Knorr 1952*, Taf. 51B). A close parallel to the medallion of the lower zone is known from La Graufesenque on bowls stamped internally OFNIGRI and OFNIGRI.AND (*Hermet 1934*, pl. 106, 14). Certainly pre-Flavian, *c*. A.D. 50–65.

D65. A VII 28 (fig. 88). Form 29 with a common type of scroll in the upper zone. Perhaps more likely to be pre-Flavian, though more or less close early Flavian parallels are to be found (e.g. *Knorr 1912*, Taf. VIII, 2). *c*. A.D. 55–75.

D66. A VII 28, 32, 33, 41, and 42 (fig. 88). Form 29 with complete scheme. The scroll of the upper zone is repeated at Newstead (Curle, *Newstead*, p. 211, 5) and there are very similar ones at Rottweil (*Knorr 1912*, Taf. III, 2; Taf. X, 1). A bowl stamped OFSABIN internally, from Mainz, offers the same arrangement for part of the upper zone and also has the same festoons and stirrup-leaves (*Knorr 1919*, Taf. 69B). For the festoons there is also a parallel from Wroxeter stamped OFCOTOI, retro. (Bushe-Fox, *Wroxeter 1913* pl. XIII, 1). *c*. A.D. 65–80.

D67. A VII 19, 28, 32, 33, 41, and 42 (fig. 88). Form 29, complete, stamped internally OFPONTI (VIIIe: see S59). For the medallions with large and small hares cf. *Knorr 1919*, Taf. 64F (OF PASSIENI). The medallions and small hares are on a bowl involved in the Boudiccan destruction at Colchester, Hull, *Roman Colchester*, fig. 101, 4 stamped OFFEICIS. The figure-types of the upper zone are, left to right, dogs (H. 26, 18), hares (H. 26, 63 and 26, 54), hare to left (H. 26, 28), does (H. 27, 33), draped man (H. 18, 53), hare (H. 26, 55), and man (H. 21, 182 variant). The lower zone adds birds (H. 28, 39, and 40) and a small bird (H. 28, 67) used as a 'filler'. A scroll close in character is known from Rottweil (*Knorr 1912*, Taf. IV, 3). *c*. A.D. 65–80.

D68. A VII 33 (fig. 89). Form 29 stamped internally OFISEV[ERI] retro. (IIIa, see S61). The same general style appears on bowls stamped by Severus from Caerleon (VIa) and Rottweil (*Knorr 1952*, Taf. 83A). There are also links, for the lower zone, with Carillus (Ia, Strasbourg published in Knorr, *Aislingen*, Taf. VIII, 3) and Meddillus (IVa, form 29, York). The figures in the upper zone are: dog (H. 26, 22), man with torch (H. 19, 98), hare (H. 26, 66), and lion (D. 771). The lower zone adds what is probably the bear H. 26, 3. *c*. A.D. 70–85.

D69. A VII 19, 32, and 33 (fig. 89). Form 29. The hunting scene above has links with Crucuro (BM M1362) and the same conventional bush and grass-blades appear on form 37 at Inchtuthil. No close parallel has been noted for the lower zone, though the wreath of overlapping leaves is common enough in Flavian contexts (e.g. *Knorr 1912*, Taf. V, 11). *c*. A.D. 75–85.

D70–1. A VII 28 and 32 (fig. 89). Small fragments of form 37, close to D72 in character and possibly from the same bowl.

D72. A VII 33 (fig. 90). Form 37. This and the last two fragments have an ovolo with four-pronged tongue used by M. Crestio and Crucuro (*Knorr 1919*, Textbild 5). There are close connections with D44 above. The general style may be matched at Caerhun (*Baillie Reynolds 1938*, S142). For the large rosettes and unusual festoon of the lower zone see *Walke 1965*, Taf. 6, 31 (Straubing) and *Knorr 1912*, Taf. XXIII, 1 and 3 (Rottweil). The figures are: lion (D. 770) and Pan (H. 19, 94). *c*. A.D. 75–95.

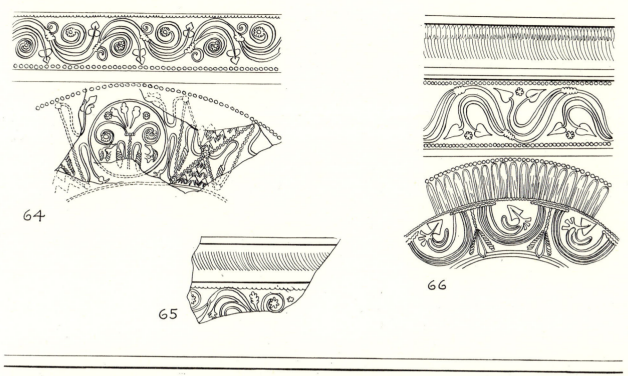

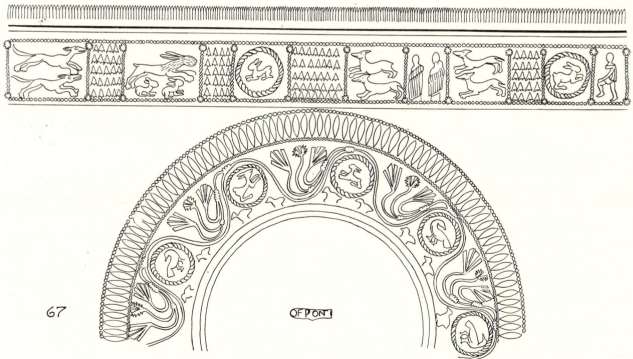

FIG. 88. Decorated samian 64–7 and stamp S 59 ($\frac{1}{2}$).

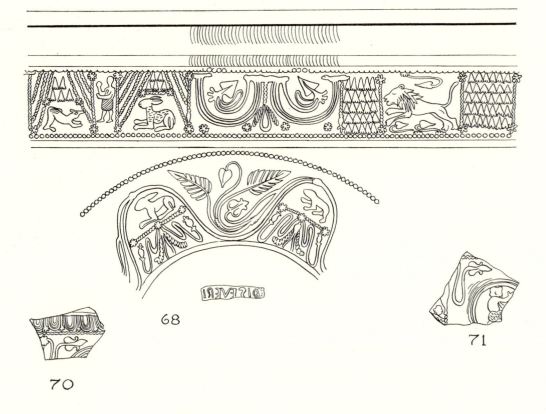

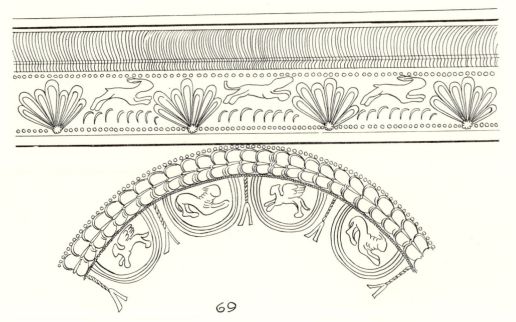

FIG. 89. Decorated samian 68–71 (½), with stamp S 61 (¼).

FIG. 90. Decorated samian 72–4 ($\frac{1}{2}$).

D73. A VII (fig. 90). Form 37. This bowl, probably the same as D51, also has the ovolo with four-pronged tongue, though the style is very different from the last. The ovolo suggests Crucuro or M. Crestio, and the upper zone recalls *Knorr 1912*, Taf. III, 2 and X, 1, both from Rottweil. For the general style cf. also *J.R.S.* iv, pl. XVI, 78 and a Camelon bowl (NMA, FX128). The dolphin is D. 2389. *c.* A.D. 75–95.

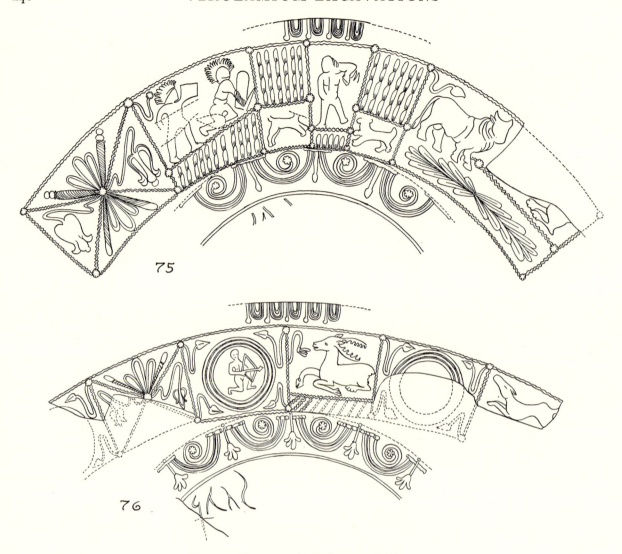

FIG. 91. Decorated samian 75–6 ($\frac{1}{2}$).

D74. A VII 33 (fig. 90). Form 37, again with the same ovolo. This is close to stamped bowls of M. Crestio. One from London (BM, M554) has the same gadroons and sphinx (H. 25, 5) in a festoon. Others at London (BM, 1928. 7. 13) and Utrecht have the bear (H. 26, 1) in a medallion and saltires with the same details in all but the upper quadrant. *c.* A.D. 75–95.

D75. A VII 19, 28, 32, 33, 41, and 42 (fig. 91). Form 37. This bowl has several unusual features for which no exact parallels seem to be available, including the peculiar saltire and the curious arrangement of the panel with a bull. However, it does seem to be closely related to D76, which has the same ovolo and a somewhat similar saltire. The identified figures are: gladiators (H. 21, 172 and 173) and bull (H. 23, 256). See also D76.

D76. A VII 24, 28, and 29 (fig. 91). Form 37, connected with the last but also having links with stamped bowls of two potters. Both the leaves and also the medallion with archer (H. 23, 263) occur on bowls, stamped in the mould, by C. Valerius Albanus. The medallion with archer was used similarly by Crispus on form 29 from Vechten, Nijmegen, and Wroxeter. It is not impossible that the incomplete mould-signature is one of Albanus. The stag is H. 27, 4 variant, and the dog H. 26, 39. *c.* A.D. 75–90.

D77. A VII 32 and 33 (fig. 92). Form 37 with the same ovolo as the last two bowls. There are links with bowls stamped by Meddillus (IVa). The large leaves are on one of his bowls from Vechten and a similar lower zone occurs on another at York. The figures are: dog (H. 26, 29), boar (H. 27, 44), stag (H. 27, 10) and, in the lower zone, dog (H. 26, 28) and hare (H. 26, 72 but larger). The scroll is also close to one on a bowl from Southwark stamped QVINTIO (Va) (Chelmsford Museum B18517). The next bowl is clearly from the same workshop. *c.* A.D. 75–95.

FIG. 92. Decorated samian 77 ($\frac{1}{2}$).

D78. A VII 38 (fig. 93). Form 37, very close in details to the last and presumably also connected with Meddillus or Quintus or contemporaries. All the figures are also on D77. *c.* A.D. 75–95.

D79. No ref. (fig. 93). Form 37, perhaps by M. Crestio (cf. *Knorr 1952*, Taf. 19A, which includes the *bestiarius*, H. 24, 283, lion, H. 25, 11, and corner tassels). The ovolo, however, seems to be the one on the probable Memor bowl from Rottweil (*Fundberichte aus Schwaben*, xvii, Taf. IV, 1) and the vertical element in the saltire is also attested for Memor (*J.R.S.* iv, pl. XIV, 1) and Crispus (on form 29 from Wroxeter). The pan is H. 19, 93. *c.* A.D. 75–90.

D80. A VII 32 (fig. 94). Form 37 with some links with the last, but not necessarily by the same potter. For the large leaf in a similar scroll cf. *Archaeologia*, lxiv, 306, 64 (Camelon). The figures are: boar (H. 27, 50 variant), lion (close to D. 748) and gladiator (H. 21, 140). *c.* A.D. 75–100.

D81. A VII 32 and 33 (fig. 94). Form 37 with connections with M. Crestio and Crucuro. The horizontal element in the saltire is on stamped examples of form 37 by the former at Utrecht and Gloucester.

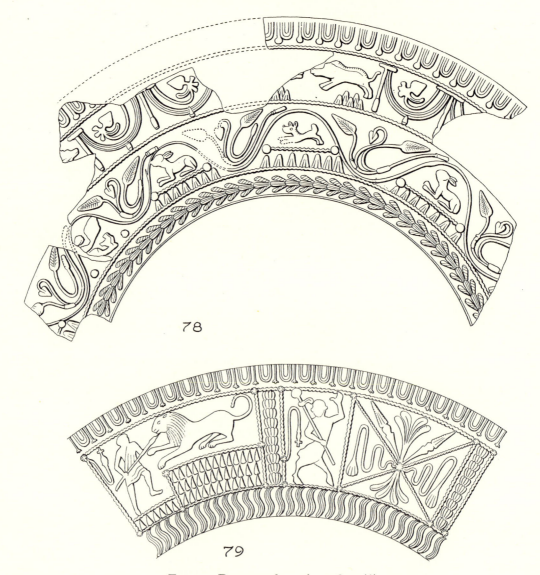

FIG. 93. Decorated samian 78–9 ($\frac{1}{2}$).

For the wreath and general composition see *Knorr 1919*, Taf. 28, also by M. Crestio. But *Knorr 1954*, Taf. 20A offers points of comparison with Crucuro. The figures are: maenad (H. 20, 112), dog (H. 26, 18), Venus (H. 18, 21) and gladiators (H. 21, 154, and 150). *c.* A.D. 75–95.

PERIOD IIB

Potters' stamps

S64. B IV 21A (p. 50; fig. 81). Antigrus of Lezoux (?). Form 29 stamped in the base ΛΝΤΙGR[V] (Ia). Only part of a leaf survives of the decoration. The coarse yellowish-brown, micaceous fabric with matt-orange glaze is one used by many first-century potters of Lezoux, and this bowl was almost certainly made there. The stamp is only known otherwise from Poitiers on forms 18 and 24/25. As with many early Lezoux stamps, the lettering is poor and the serifs are made by jabbing a stylus into the clay of the die, thus appearing as projecting blobs on the stamp. First-century Lezoux ware is always rare in Britain and seems to have been imported only under Nero and in the early Flavian period. It occurs in Wales, but not on the northern military sites. *c.* A.D. 55–75.

S65. B I 32X (p. 48; fig. 81). Biga of Central Gaul, probably Lezoux. Form 18/31, stamped BIGA·FEC (Ia). Only one stamp of Biga is known Lezoux (from a different die), but the fabrics are typical Lezoux ones. There are two examples of this stamp in Chesters Museum (presumably from Hadrian's Wall), and one from Wroxeter seems certainly to be earlier than the forum (*Atkinson 1942*, p. 265 with p. 119). Other stamps are certainly from Hadrian's Wall and the Saalburg Erdkastell (before A.D. 139). *c.* A.D. 120–35.

S66. B IV 23J (p. 51; fig. 81). Bio of La Graufesenque (*Hermet 1934*, pl. 110, 19). Form 27g stamped BIOFECIT retro. (IIc). Bio's activity was entirely pre-Flavian, though this particular stamp has not been noted from dated contexts (and is only known otherwise at Vechten and Alésia). *c.* A.D. 45–65.

S67. Z I 18 (p. 45; fig. 81). Cl(audius?) Gemma of La Graufesenque (*Hermet 1934*, pl. 110, 35). Form 18 stamped OFCLGEMME (IIa). A difficult stamp to interpret certainly, but *nomen* and *cognomen* seems probable rather than an association of two potters Cl(arus?) and Gemma. Dating evidence is meagre, but the stamp is on form 18R at Catterick and a stamp with *cognomen* alone comes from Period IV at Valkenburg (*van Giffen 1948–53*, pp. 138, 223). Probably Flavian.

S68. T VII 26 (p. 43; fig. 81). Cotto of La Graufesenque (*Hermet 1934*, pl. 110, 38). Form 18 stamped COTTON retro. (VIIa). There is no independent dating for this stamp, but other ones of Cotto are common in Flavian and Flavian-Trajanic contexts. *c.* A.D. 75–110.

S69. T I 12 (pp. 53, 54; fig. 81). Cracuna of Lezoux, where the stamp has been recorded twice. Form 27 stamped CRACVNA·F (IIa). This stamp occurs seven times in Scotland and is, therefore, at least partly Antonine, though not late in the period, since it is often on form 27 and reaches Lower Germany (where Lezoux stamps later than *c.* A.D. 150 are excessively uncommon). Oswald (*Stamps*, 93) confuses the issue by equating him with a later East Gaulish potter of the same name, as well as with a late Antonine Cracina of Lezoux. It would not be impossible for Cracuna to have begun work as early as A.D. 130 (cf. p. 54), though positive evidence is lacking.

S70. B I 47 (p. 49). Crestio of La Graufesenque (*Hermet 1934*, pl. 110, 43). Form 24/25 stamped CRESTIO (XVIa). *c.* A.D. 45–60.

S71. B I 32X (p. 48; fig. 81). Dagomarus of Les Martres-de-Veyre (*Terrisse 1969*, pl. LII). Form 33 stamped [DΛ]GOMARVSF (IIIb). Nine examples of this stamp come from the London Second Fire (*Antiq. Journ.* xxv, 75), but none is known from the Hadrian's Wall system. *c.* A.D. 110–25.

S72. B II 30G (p. 49; fig. 81). The same potter, but possibly from Lezoux rather than Les Martres. Form 18/31 stamped DAGOMARVS·F (VIIa). Dagomarus certainly migrated to Lezoux, where he used the stamp DAGOMΛ: it is possible that the die for VIIa travelled with him, since it sometimes is on vessels in what looks like one of the common Lezoux fabrics. This stamp does not occur in the London Second Fire, but is known from Hadrian's Wall (Chesters Museum). *c.* A.D. 115–30.

S73. A XI 13 (p. 46). GIIM[on form 27. Probably Central Gaulish, though the potter has not been identified and the last surviving letter might be a sloping B.

S74. T XX 18 (p. 45). Germanus of La Graufesenque. Form 37 with the mould-stamp [GERMA]NI in the decoration. *c.* A.D. 70–85.

S75. B I 32X (p. 48; fig. 81). Logirnus of La Graufesenque (*Hermet 1934*, pl. 111, 81). Form 18R stamped LOGI[RN] (XId). One of the less common stamps of Logirnus. Flavian, as records from Inchtuthil and Camelon show.

S76. T XX 23 (p. 45; fig. 81). Lorius of South Gaul, probably La Graufesenque. Form 18 stamped LORI.R (Ia). Eight examples of this stamp are known, all on form 15/17 or 18, but none from closely dated sites. The significance of the final R is obscure. Probably pre-Flavian.

S77. A II 52 (p. 46; fig. 81). Mona—? of South Gaul, probably La Graufesenque. Form 15/17 or 18 stamped [OF]MO[ИΛ] (Ia). The stamp is common at Flavian foundations, including the Saalburg Erdkastell, but it has also been found at Burghöfe (*Ulbert 1959*, Taf. 41, 38); it should therefore be dated *c*. A.D. 70–100.

S78. B IV 23J (p. 51; fig. 81). Monticus and Cres— or Mont— Cres— of La Graufesenque (*Hermet 1934*, pl. 112, 109). Form 29, without decoration, stamped [O]FMONTI.CR (IIIa). It is doubtful if Oswald's Monticus of La Graufesenque (*Stamps*, p. 211) has a separate existence, since the stamps in OFMONTICI, etc., all prove to be the same as the Verulamium one, and OFMONTC could belong to the same man or men, especially as the lettering is almost identical. Interpretation as a man with *nomen* and *cognomen* is probably to be preferred to an association of two potters. The stamp is usually on plain forms, but has been seen on form 29 at Alésia, Nijmegen, and Utrecht Museum. Records in Flavian contexts are known, but a Neronian beginning is probable, especially as one of the Burghöfe stamps (*Ulbert 1959*, Taf. 41, 39) is on a burnt cup. *c*. A.D. 65–80.

S79. T XX 18 (p. 45; fig. 81). Murranus of La Graufesenque (*Hermet 1934*, pl. 112, 110). Form 27 stamped OFMVRANI (VIa). Almost certainly this is a late stamp of Murranus in view of records at Chester, Valkenburg Periods III/IV (*van Giffen 1948–53*, pp. 142, 281–2) and the Nijmegen fortress (4). *c*. A.D. 60–75.

S80. B II 28A (p. 50; fig. 81). Niger? of La Graufesenque. Form 27 stamped OFNI (XIIIa), twice. This is likely to be a stamp of Niger, and not a late one, since it is on Ritterling 9 at Sels and Vechten. *c*. A.D. 40–65.

S81. A VI 23 (p. 44; fig. 81). Paternulus of Central Gaul, probably Lezoux. Form 27 stamped [PAT]ERNVLI (Ia) with the only known die for this potter. Oswald (*Stamps*, 231) tentatively suggested origin at Lezoux and Flavian date. The claim of Lezoux is increased slightly by the recent discovery of the stamp there, but the date is another matter. Not a late potter, since the stamp is usually on form 27. Flavian date is, however, ruled out by the fabrics, which seem to be standard ones of the Lezoux export period (not before A.D. 120–5). The probable solution is that Paternulus worked for a short time in the 120s, but note the primary position in Period II B.

S82. A VI 23 (p. 44; fig. 81). Patricius of La Graufesenque (*Hermet 1934*, pl. 112, 119). Form 18 stamped OFPATRICI (Ie). Many examples from Flavian sites. *c*. A.D. 70–90.

S83. A II 52 (p. 46; fig. 81). Same potter as last. Form 27g stamped OFPATRIC. This stamp is unique. *c*. A.D. 70–100.

S84. B IV 23J (p. 51; fig. 81). Presumably Primus of La Graufesenque. Form 27g stamped OI'IPR (VIIIa). This stamp has only been noted elsewhere at Colchester, twice, once on a burnt cup of form 24/25. *c*. A.D. 50–70.

S85. B IV 20E (p. 52; fig. 82). Secundus of La Graufesenque. Form 27 stamped SECVND retro. (probably XXXIj, but the stamp has not been relocated). This stamp occurred twelve times on burnt vessels in the Burghöfe Geschirrdepot (*Ulbert 1959*, Taf. 41, 76). It is only otherwise known from the Nijmegen fortress. *c*. A.D. 60–75.

S86. B IV 21L (p. 53; fig. 82). Severus and Pudens, presumably of La Graufesenque, since Severus and Pudens are both attested there (*Hermet 1934*, pl. 112, 135, and 160). Form 18 stamped OF·SEV[ER+] (IIIa'). This is a reduced version of an original OF.SEVERP (IIIa), well known from Flavian sites (Caerleon, Corbridge, and Nijmegen fortress and Ulpia). The interpretation of the final P is secured by the existence of the stamp FSEVERPVD (Ia). *c*. A.D. 70–90.

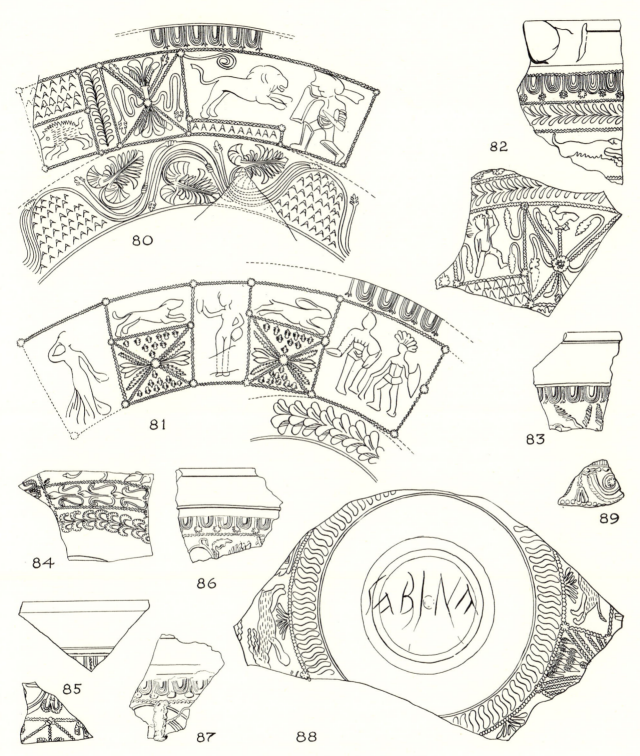

FIG. 94. Decorated samian 80–9 ($\frac{1}{2}$).

S87. A II 39 (p. 46; fig. 82). Sulpicius of La Graufesenque. Form 27 stamped SVLPICI· (XIIa). The stamp has been noted seven times from Flavian foundations. Probably *c.* A.D. 80–110.

S88. B I 38E (intrusive, cf. p. 48; fig. 82). Tituro of Lezoux. Form 33 stamped TITVRONIS with the tops of the first six letters missing (VIc). This is a late Antonine stamp, used frequently on forms 79 and 80. *c.* A.D. 160–200.

S89. A VI 23 (p. 44; fig. 82). Virilis of La Graufesenque (*Hermet 1934*, pl. 113, 178). Form 18, stamped OIVIRIꞮ (VIIIa). There is no satisfactory evidence for dating this stamp, though others of Virilis are common in Flavian contexts. *c.* A.D. 65–90?

S90. B I 32X (p. 48; fig. 82). Vitalis of La Graufesenque (*Hermet 1934*, pl. 113, 179). Form 18R stamped OFVITALI (IVb). This stamp is used only on dishes, usually the rouletted varieties, but there is no specific evidence for its date. However, there does not seem to be any reason to accept it as a pre-Flavian stamp and the period A.D. 70–100 is likely for its use.

Decorated ware

D82. A XII 23A (p. 44; fig. 94). Form 37 with strap-handle, and presumably spout (cf. *Stanfield 1929* fig. 3, 7, and 8). The saltire is close to work of Memor (*J.R.S.* iv, pl. xiv, 73 and 74). The ovolo with large rosette (used by Frontinus) is common at Inchtuthil and Camelon. The Cupid is H. 18, 37. Cf. D45. *c.* A.D. 75–95.

D83. T XX 18 (p. 45; fig. 94). Form 37 in the characteristic style of Germanus of La Graufesenque (*Hermet 1934*, pls. 99–102). *c.* A.D. 70–85. See S 74.

D84. A XIII 8 (p. 46; fig. 94). Form 37 by X-2 of Les Martres-de-Veyre. Cf. *S. & S.*, pl. 4, 44. *c.* A.D. 100–20.

D85. A XIII 8 (p. 46; fig. 94). Form 37, Central Gaulish. The style is unusual and neither the ovolo nor the very fine beads above it can be matched on stamped bowls. The piece is no doubt Trajanic or early Hadrianic, but it is not clear whether it is from Les Martres-de-Veyre or Lezoux.

D86. A XIII 6 (p. 46; fig. 94). Form 30, South Gaulish. Ovolo with a large rosetted tongue, perhaps by Frontinus or a contemporary, *c.* A.D. 70–90.

D87. A II 51 (p. 46; fig. 94). Form 37, South Gaulish, in the style of Frontinus (cf. D58–61, above). *c.* A.D. 70–90.

D88. B IV 21E (p. 52; fig. 94). Form 37, South Gaulish, with S-shaped gadroons below a hunting scene with deer (H. 27, 18) and grass-tufts. There are also panels of wavy-lines and leaf tips. The borders are rather coarse and suggest the period A.D. 85–105. For a graffito *post cocturam* see p. 364.

D89. B IV 21D (p. 52; fig. 94). Form 29, South Gaulish. Clearly residual and probably pre-Flavian rather than Flavian.

PERIOD IIC

Potters' stamps

S91. B I 31D (p. 66; fig. 82). Annius of Lezoux. Form 18/31 stamped ΛИИІoF (XIIa). There were two Central Gaulish Annii, or else a potter of this name migrated from Les Martres-de-Veyre (*Terrisse 1969*, pl. LII) to Lezoux, where the Verulamium stamp occurs in the Collection Rambert. Other stamps of the Lezoux potter are from Hadrian's Wall, in a late Hadrianic context (*Trans. Cumb. and West. Arch. Soc.* xxx, 186, no. 6. Die XIa), and Falkirk (NMA, Edinburgh FR 188. Die XVIa). *c.* A.D. 130–50.

S92. B IV 18J (p. 69; fig. 82). Attius of Central Gaul, probably the Lezoux potter rather than Attius of Les Martres (*Terrisse 1969*, pl. LII). Form 18/31R stamped [AT]TIVS.FE (Xa). The best-dated example of the stamp comes from the Saalburg Erdkastell (*Saalburg Jahrbuch*, xxvii (1970), 29), so it was certainly in use by A.D. 139 at the latest. *c.* A.D. 125–55.

S93. A II 24 (p. 65; fig. 82). Bonoxus of Central Gaul, probably of Les Martres to judge by the fabrics, though his work has not been recorded there. Form 27 stamped ∴BONOXV[S.Ł∴] (Ia). Other stamps of Bonoxus occur on Hadrian's Wall, but none is known from Scotland. This stamp is known from Forden Gaer (evacuated *c.* A.D. 125?) and at Corbridge. *c.* A.D. 115–35.

S94. B IV 17J (p. 69; fig. 82). Caupirra of Lezoux. Form 33 stamped CAVPIRRA (IVa). This piece is probably intrusive in Period IIC (cf. p. 73) since, although his work is not very common, Caupirra's associations are mid- to late Antonine. This stamp is on form 33 in a late Antonine group at Astwick (*VCH Bedfordshire*, 2, p. 4) with stamps of Aucella (2), Calvinus, Doeccus (2), Macrinus, Maternus, and Sacrillus. *c.* A.D. 155–85.

S95. A II 29 (p. 66; fig. 82). Cinnamus of Lezoux. Form 33 or 33a stamped C•INNMV retro. with a dot in the first half of the second N (= $\widehat{\text{NA}}$?) (VIIa). Like most plainware stamps of Cinnamus, this is not common, and it is arguable that it, and many of the others, belong to his early phase before he began specializing in producing moulds. However that may be, it occurs on form 27 and on form 33 with mouldings as on the early 33a variant. At Lezoux plain samian of forms 27 and 33a stamped by Cinnamus with another die was found in a pit dated *c.* A.D. 130–45, where it was associated with much work of Sacer, Attianus, Drusus, Granio, and other primarily Hadrianic potters, as well as with wasters of form 37 in what looks like a 'proto-Cinnamus' style. While the Verulamium stamp is not necessarily quite as early as the Lezoux one, it certainly need not be as late as A.D. 150. Provisionally, it may be placed *c.* A.D. 140–55.

S96. T II 19 (p. 62). Crestio or Crestus of La Graufesenque. Form 18 stamped [OFC]REꙄTI retro. (IVa). The same stamp as S9 and S34 above (pp. 223, 232). Clearly residual.

S97. B IV 17K (p. 70; fig. 82). Divicatus of Lezoux, where this stamp is known. Form 33 stamped [DI]VICATVS (IIIa). Divicatus used several closely similar stamps, most of which are found both on form 27 and form 80, some appearing in Scotland. That he was entirely Antonine in date is likely, the most probable range being *c.* A.D. 140–70.

S98. B V 12 (p. 70; fig. 82). Granio of Lezoux. Form 33 stamped GRANIO (IIIa). This stamp occurs at Lezoux in the pit of *c.* A.D. 130–45 noted under S95. It is there on ten wasters of form 27 and one of form 18/31. At Clermont-Ferrand (Coll. Souchon), it has been found on the prototype of form 80 paralleled by a comparable form 79 also present in the Lezoux pit. *c.* A.D. 130–50.

S99. B IV 18F (p. 70). Lupinus or Lupus of Lezoux. Form 38 stamped LVPIN[. The stamp has not been identified, but is presumably Antonine, though evidence at Lezoux suggests that form 38 was made occasionally there late in Hadrian's reign.

S100. A II 23 (p. 63; fig. 82). Materenus or -ius of Central Gaul, probably Lezoux. Form 33, with very thin base, stamped [M]ATIIRIINIF. This is the only stamp known to have been used by the potter. It occurs on form 27 at York and on form 18/31 at Caerleon (2) and Cannstatt. This piece, and the potter, must be dated from the context at Verulamium.

S101. T XXI 16 (p. 62; fig. 82). Pater of Lezoux. Form 18/31 stamped PATER.F (XIXa). This stamp occurred at Lezoux in the pit (of *c.* A.D. 130–45) noted under S95 and S98, above, on form 33a. It also comes from one of the wells of the Saalburg Erdkastell (before A.D. 139, *Saalburg Jahrbuch*, xxvii (1970), 30) and twice at Newstead (NMA, FRA 1548, 1550). It should be remarked that the same stamp recorded on form 45 at Leicester (Kenyon, *Jewry Wall Site*, 50, no. 10) is really on form 81, as at Wroxeter and Wilderspool. *c.* A.D. 130–50.

S102. B II 27B (p. 68; fig. 82). Patillus of Central Gaul. Form 18/31R stamped F PATI[LLVS] (Ia). Only one other example of this stamp is known, on form 27 from Canvey Island. Both that and the Verulamium dish look like Hadrianic-Antonine work. The initial letter is mysterious. It could perhaps be F(ecit) with the usual order inverted or possibly an abbreviated *nomen*, as with F. Albinus, where the F probably stands for Florius or the like.

S103. A I 13 (p. 65). Patricius of La Graufesenque, rather than Pater of South Gaul, since the style of lettering is identical to that of many Patricius stamps. Form 15/17 or 18 stamped PA[TRI] (XXVb). Flavian.

S104. B IV 18J (p. 69; fig. 82). An obscure stamp on form 18/31R which may be rendered PRYD.IC.L.I. Oswald (*Stamps*, 245) records under Pridiclus. The origin is uncertain, since the Verulamium piece looks Central Gaulish, as does one from Southwark (Verulamium Mus. assigned wrongly to St. Albans by Oswald). But dishes from Caerleon and Strasbourg have been noted as 'probably East Gaulish' by Miss B. M. Dickinson. The forms are 18/31 or 31 and 18/31R, with Hadrianic-Antonine appearances.

S105. T III 16 (p. 60; fig. 82). Roppus of La Graufesenque (*Hermet 1934*, pl. 112, 140). Form 15/17 or 18 stamped [ROPP]V&.FEC (IIIa). Valkenburg Period III has an example on form 15/17 or 18 (*van Giffen 1948–53*, pp. 144, 308), but it also appears at Nijmegen Ulpia twice, and in the Strasbourg fortress. *c.* A.D. 60–80.

S106. A I 18 (p. 64; fig. 82). Severus of La Graufesenque (*Hermet 1934*, pl. 112, 160). Form 18R stamped Ⓕ SE[VERI] (VIe). *c.* A.D. 65–85.

S107. T III 18 (p. 60; fig. 82). Vitalis of La Graufesenque (*Hermet 1934*, pl. 113, 179). Form 27(?) stamped VITALIS[F] (LIIIa). *c.* A.D. 70–90.

S108. A VI 22 (p. 63; fig. 82). Form 18/31, Central Gaulish. An illiterate stamp not known elsewhere. The form suggests Hadrianic or early Antonine date.

S109. B II 28E (p. 68; fig. 82). Form 18/31, Central Gaulish. A similar illiterate stamp to the last and of the same date.

S110. A II 19 (p. 65). Form 27, South Gaulish. An illiterate stamp of the kind common on form 27 in the Flavian period particularly.

S111. A I 31 (p. 47; fig. 82). Form 27g, South Gaulish. A potter's mark with diagonal strokes only. The form suggests Neronian or early Flavian date (*recte* under Period II B).

Decorated ware

D90. B II 28E (p. 68; fig. 95). Form 37, South Gaulish. There are parallels for both the ovolo and the chevron-wreath from the Pompeii hoard (e.g. *J.R.S.* iv, pl. xv, 71). *c.* A.D. 75–90.

D91. B II 17J (p. 69; fig. 95). Form 37, South Gaulish, with a very deep plain band and multiple grooves above the ovolo, which has a split tongue. The distinctive ovolo was used frequently by Chresimus and Malcio of Montans. The figure is H. 20, 133. As stamps and decorated ware of Chresimus and the closely related potter Felicio, also of Montans, appear in Scotland on sites with no Flavian occupation, production of this ware must have continued down to A.D. 140 at least. On the other hand, similar pieces occur in the Second Fire at London (*Antiq. Journ.* xxv, p. 66, 4), before about A.D. 125. The activity of these late potters at Montans therefore probably falls *c.* A.D. 115–45, and the Verulamium bowl will be in its true context. See also D109.

D92. B I 18, V 12, and XI 17 (pp. 70, 88, 92; fig. 95). Form 37 in the distinctive style of Acaunissa of Central Gaul and with the only ovolo certainly used by him. For the tendrils and leaves cf. *Trans. Cumb. and West Arch. Soc.*, N.S., xxx, 184, from the Birdoswald Alley. The figures are: Pan (D. 421, there slightly misdrawn) and Venus (D. 188). An unpublished bowl from Heronbridge is probably from the same mould (W. J. Williams collection). Three bowls of Acaunissa are known from Scotland and he may be dated *c.* A.D. 125–45.

D93. B IV 18B (p. 71; fig. 95). Form 37 in the style of Igocatus (X-4) of Les Martres-de-Veyre. For the figure and tier of baskets in his work see *S. & S.*, pl. 17, 222. *c.* A.D. 100–20.

D94. B IV 17E and IV 9J (IID) (pp. 72, 87; fig. 95). Form 37 by an anonymous Hadrianic-Antonine potter, presumably of Lezoux. The ovolo was used, though rarely, on bowls in standard Cinnamus

FIG. 95. Decorated samian 90–104 ($\frac{1}{2}$).

style, though no stamped examples have been noted. The figures are: Minerva (D. 77), Osiris (O. 711A), and warrior (O. 177A). There are several links, particularly the use of the chevron-leaves, with another anonymous potter, whose work is known at Lezoux, who used a distinctive ovolo with a tongue ending in an X in a blob (cf. *Derbyshire Arch. Journ.* lxxxi (1961), p. 96, 20). The potter with the X-ovolo has several bowls in Scotland (e.g. *Proc. Soc. Ant. Scot.* lxxxiv, p. 27, no. 6 from an Antonine I group and mistakenly assigned to the Small S potter). In view of this, and the Cinnamus link, a date *c.* A.D. 130–60 seems certain.

PERIOD IID

A. FLOORS AND OCCUPATION

Potters' stamps

S112. Z I 5 (p. 82; fig. 82). Annius of Lezoux (cf. S91 above). Form 31 stamped ΛNNIV[SF] (XIVa). This stamp is not common, but like S91 it occurs at Birdoswald. *c.* A.D. 130–50.

S113. A II 13 (p. 84; fig. 82). Balbinus of Les Martres-de-Veyre (*Terrisse 1959*, pl. LII). Form 18/31 stamped BΛLBI[NVS.I:] (IIa). This stamp has often been recorded under F.ΛLBINVSF, as the B was partly made by jabbing a stylus into the die and light impressions give an initial I:. Similarly, the stamp usually recorded as IIΛIBINI.M belongs to this man. The latter is common in the Second Fire groups at London (*Antiq. Journ.* xxv, 75 and *Richborough V*, 133), but the Verulamium stamp is not, and may be slightly later, perhaps *c.* A.D. 125–40.

S114. V XXXIII 5 (p. 82; figs. 82 and 95). Criciro of Lezoux. Form 37 with the familiar CR signature below the decoration, from the mould. Criciro is not an easy potter to date closely. On the one hand, his decorated ware is closely related to that of Sacer and Attianus, on the other, to that of Divixtus. His work is common in Scotland, but also occurs on Hadrian's Wall, where it is not clear whether it belongs to Period Ia or Ib, or both. Broad dating within the range A.D. 135–75 is needed to cover all the possibilities.

S115. B V 23A (p. 88; fig. 82). Duppius of Lezoux. Form 80 stamped DVPPIVSF (Ib). This stamp, and the similar Ic, is found on form 27, on form 33, and on form 80. Antonine date is confirmed by several examples from Corbridge, and by its presence in an Alcester pit of *c.* A.D. 150, twice on form 27. Early versions of form 80 were current by A.D. 140 at the latest, but this cup is nearer to the standard version and could scarcely be earlier than A.D. 150. The stamp is to be dated *c.* A.D. 145–70, and this piece probably to A.D. 150–70.

S116. A I 10 (p. 84; fig. 82). Ericus of Lezoux(?). Form 18/31 stamped ERIC[VM] retro. (IIIa). Some of Ericus' fabrics are unusual, others match standard ones from Lezoux. This stamp is rare, and only otherwise recorded from London, Nijmegen, Friedberg, and Mainz. Other stamps occur at Camelon on forms 18/31 and 27 (NMA, FX 250, 272). The distribution in Germany is so considerable (fourteen examples) that much of his work must be earlier than A.D. 150. A general date *c.* A.D. 135–65 is likely.

S117. Z I 5 (p. 82; fig. 82). Iabus of South Gaul, presumably La Graufesenque. Form 18 stamped ΛBVSFE (IIIa′). A reduced version of an original IΛBVSFE. The original is certainly Claudio-Neronian (Valkenburg Period I), but the reduced versions cannot be seriously later, since it appears on Ritterling forms 8 and 9 at Nijmegen. *c.* A.D. 50–65.

S118. B II 27E (p. 87; fig. 82). Illixo of Lezoux, where this stamp appears on forms 18/31 and 33 (Collection Mathonnière-Plicque). Like most stamps of Illixo, this is known on form 27 (Habert, *La Poterie antique parlante*, 642), but no dated sites are involved. Other stamps are known from Old Kilpatrick (2) and Newstead. Probably *c.* A.D. 145–75.

S119. B XV 11A (p. 88; fig. 82). Mansuetus of Lezoux. Form 33 stamped MA.SV.ETI (VIIIb). One of the earlier stamps of Mansuetus, who was primarily late Antonine, as his record for other stamps shows (many examples come from Hadrian's Wall, where the context must be the Period Ib occupation). This stamp appears on form 27 at York and on form 18/31R at London and must have been in use by A.D. 160 at the very latest. c. A.D. 150–70.

S120. V XXXIII 6 (p. 82; fig. 82). Mossius of Lezoux, where the stamp occurs on forms 33 and 38. Form 33 stamped MOSSI.MAN (IIIa). Like Mansuetus, Mossius worked mainly in the late Antonine period, though he occasionally made form 27 and so must have begun work by A.D. 160 at the latest. This stamp could not be earlier than A.D. 150 and is probably rather later than that. c. A.D. 155–75 is the probable range.

S121. Z II 9 (p. 82; fig. 82). Pater of Lezoux (cf. S101). Form 31 stamped PATER (XVa). This stamp is probably slightly later than XIXa, but was used on form 27 at Godmanchester (St. Ives Museum) and Paris (Musée Carnavalet). c. A.D. 135–55.

S122. B I 27X (p. 85; fig. 82). Priscinus of Lezoux. Form 27 stamped PRI[SC]INVSFC (IIIa). At Lezoux the stamp appears in a Hadrianic to early Antonine group at the Ligonne workshops, where he made form 27 and form 33a. c. A.D. 125–50.

S123. A I 14 (p. 84; fig. 82). Secundinus of Central Gaul. Form 18/31 stamped [SEC]VNDINI (Vk). It is not clear whether this belongs to Secundinus of Les Martres-de-Veyre or to one of the many Secundini of Lezoux. Its use on form 27, 18/31 and 18/31R, together with the frequent records in the Rhineland, suggests Hadrianic or early Antonine date at the latest.

S124. A IV 19 (p. 83; fig. 82). Severus of Central Gaul, probably Lezoux, though origin at Les Martres-de-Veyre is not impossible. Form 33 stamped SEVERI.M.I. This stamp is nothing to do with the well-attested late Antonine potter, since it is used on form 27 at Orleans (Museum 15551) and form 33a at Wilderspool (Warrington Museum 1130). Another example from Chester is on a typologically Hadrianic or early Antonine form 18/31R (*Journ. Chester and N. Wales Arch. Soc.* n.s. xxxiii, pl. xx, 55). c. A.D. 125–50.

S125. A VII 11 (p. 86; fig. 82). Silvanus of Central Gaul. Form 27 stamped SILVAN[I] (XVIIIj). This stamp is usually on form 27, sometimes form 18/31. The forms are typically Hadrianic-Antonine, but whether this is Silvanus of Les Martres-de-Veyre or Silvanus of Lezoux is not clear. The former is slightly more likely, though the stamp is known at Carnuntum (*Carn. Jahrb.* 1959, 52, no. 9), where Les Martres products of this date are unusual. Probably c. A.D. 130–50.

S126. B XV 11 (p. 88). Illiterate stamp IAXXVXI[on form 18/31R. Hadrianic or early Antonine.

Decorated ware

D95. V XXXI 10 (p. 81; fig. 95). A small fragment of form 37, presumably from a freestyle bowl, with the small conventional plant (*S. & S.*, fig. 22, 16) used at Les Martres-de-Veyre and at Lezoux by Sacer and his associates. This appears to be Lezoux fabric. c. A.D. 125–45.

D96. V XXXIII 11 (p. 82; fig. 95). Form 37 with a neat wavy line below an ovolo with prominent rosette-tongue. This ovolo appears on bowls in the style of Paterclus at Bedford Museum and Wilderspool. The figure is perhaps D. 527, which was used commonly by members of the Quintilianus Group at Lezoux, including Paterclus (*S. & S.*, pl. 72, 35, poorly impressed). c. A.D. 125–50.

D97. V XXXIII 5 (p. 82; fig. 95). Form 37 with large winding scroll, close to examples from moulds signed by Attianus of Lezoux (*S. & S.*, pl. 87, 21). The ovolo is similar to the one on D110, below, also used by the Sacer-Attianus Group. c. A.D. 125–50.

D98. V XXXIII 5 (p. 82; fig. 95). Form 37, from a mould signed CR by Criciro of Lezoux. This has Criciro's large ovolo (*S. & S.*, fig. 33, bottom, 1). The figure-types are: D. 793, D. 799, D. 867, and D. 960 *bis*, all already known on Criciro's bowls. For the date see S114.

D99. V XXXII 12 (fig. 95). Form 37, South Gaulish. Ovolo with a three-pronged tongue above panels bordered by coarse wavy lines. The lion (D. 762) is derived from the Germanus repertoire, but bowls of this class are rarely stamped, and the potter cannot be named. The absence of such pieces from Inchtuthil and Camelon is striking and this should mean that they were not reaching Britain before A.D. 90. *c.* A.D. 90–110.

D100. A IV 8 (p. 91; fig. 95). Form 37. Both the ovolo and the small tree were used by Bassus at Lezoux, where they appear together on a signed mould. The mask athwart the panel junction (D. 713) also occurs at Lezoux with the same ovolo, on bowls belonging to one of the Quintilianus Group, conceivably Bassus. *c.* A.D. 125–45.

D101. A IV 12 (p. 83; fig. 95). Form 37 in the characteristically untidy style belonging to the earlier work of Docilis of Lezoux (cf. *S. & S.*, pls. 91 ff.). *c.* A.D. 130–55.

D102. A I 12 (p. 84; fig. 95). A small fragment of form 37, apparently Central Gaulish, with a sharp wavy-line border and an unusual, though blurred, ovolo. The bird (D. 1009) was used by Banuus, Divixtus, Paternus, and Solinus, but this fragment does not match any of their work and is presumably by an obscure potter. Late Hadrianic or Antonine.

D103. A I 9 (p. 85; fig. 95). A small fragment of form 37, probably by one of the Sacer Group. The ovolo was used initially by Sacer, later by Criciro and Cinnamus. The festoon appears on bowls in the style of Attianus (*S. & S.*, pl. 87, nos. 23 and 24) or Martialis/Martinus (whichever is the correct reading of the difficult cursive signature), some of whose work is indistinguishable from the Attianus parallels quoted. *c.* A.D. 130–50.

D104. A I 9 (p. 85; fig. 95). Form 37 in the style of a potter of the Cerialis–Cinnamus Group whose moulds were probably bought by Aventinus, since his plain ware stamps frequently appear on them (*S. & S.*, pl. 156, with no. 6 particularly closely related to the Verulamium bowl). The connections of the decoration suggest the period A.D. 145–70 for these bowls, and the site-evidence for the associated AVENTINI.M stamp (Ia) is in accordance. The figure-types on the Verulamium bowl are: warrior (D. 103), bust (*S. & S.*, fig. 46, 4, perhaps a mutilated partial impression of some such types as D. 523) and hare (D. 950a) *c.* A.D. 145–70.

D105. B IV 9A (p. 85; fig. 96). Form 37, three fragments in the style of X-6 of Lezoux (cf. *S. & S.*, pls. 75–6 and fig. 18, 3 for the ovolo). The lion seems to be the one of the Hercules and lion (O. 996) impressed separately. *c.* A.D. 125–50.

D106. B IV 7 (p. 87; fig. 96). A small fragment of form 37 with close-set medallions having plain double borders. The general arrangement is reminiscent of the work of Sissus II (not the Sissus connected with the Quintilianus Group, *S. & S.*, pl. 77, bottom 2 and 3, who may be termed Sissus I, but the man who signed moulds in cursive script, ibid., no. 1). The leaf and medallions are both on an unpublished bowl from Wroxeter with part of his mould-signature. The bird appears to be D. 1001. Some bowls of Sissus II have connections with X-5, X-6, the Cassia–Tittius firm and, marginally, with Docilis. His bowls are relatively common in Antonine Scotland, where Camelon, for instance, has several. In view of all this evidence a date *c.* A.D. 135–65 is likely for Sissus II.

D107. B IV 7 (p. 87; fig. 96). A small fragment with the Cerialis–Cinnamus ovolo (*Proc. Soc. Ant. Scot.* xciv, 103 with *Gallia*, xxvii, 3 ff.). The acanthus occurs on bowls in the style of the potters using this ovolo not infrequently and has been noted on pieces with the bowl-makers' stamps of Aventinus and Sennius (*S. & S.*, pl. 156, 4 and 9; pl. 166, 4). The figure-types are the rear of a stag or doe (D. 852 or, more probably D. 878) and dog (D. 919). *c.* A.D. 145–75.

D108. B II 27E (p. 87; fig. 96). Form 37, late South Gaulish ware. This is from a badly moulded bowl with panels, including a lion (*Hermet 1934*, pl. 25, 17). *c.* A.D. 90–110.

D109. B II 27E (p. 87). Probably part of the same bowl as D91, q.v. (p. 248).

D110. B V 26 (p. 88; fig. 96). Form 37. A small fragment with the same ovolo as D97, but not from the same bowl. Presumably by one of the Sacer Group. *c.* A.D. 130–50.

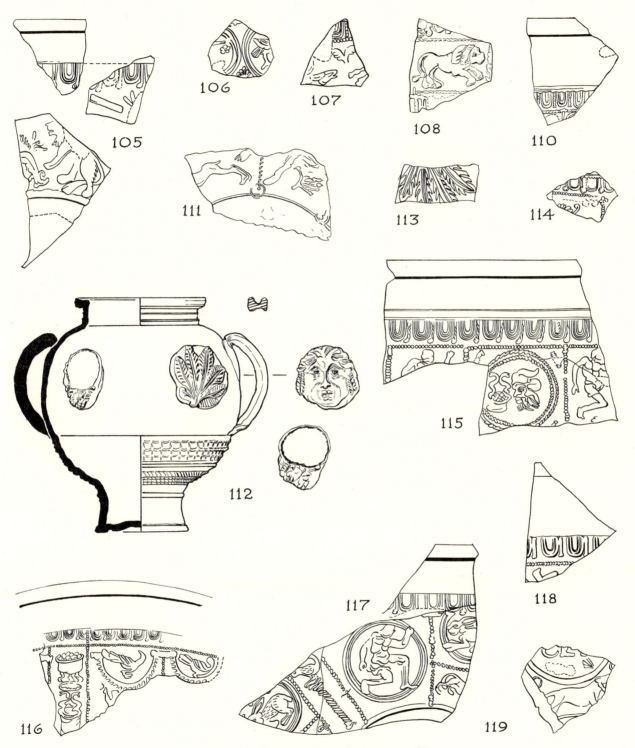

FIG. 96. Decorated samian 105–19 ($\frac{1}{2}$).

D111. B V 26 (p. 88; fig. 96). Form 37, Central Gaulish. The panels have borders of widely spaced, irregular beads ending below in large rings. No potter can be suggested for this piece. Stylistically, it could equally be late Hadrianic or Antonine.

D112. B XV 4 (p. 88; fig. 96). Complete jar, Déchelette form 74 variant (Déchelette, *Vases ornés de la Gaule romaine*, ii, pl. 1, 3), in the so-called 'black samian' fabric. The appliqué decoration has the mask D. 116, part of another mask, and a leaf (not in D. as an appliqué type, but probably a reduced copy of the moulded type D. 1168). For similar jars from Britain see *Antiq. Journ.* xxxvii, 34 ff. Evidence of date is largely lacking, and the Verulamium piece is most useful, since it demonstrates that these appliqué jars were in use by about the middle of the second century. They must overlap in date with the comparable moulded jars and cups with 'black' coat, since the latter were made by a Paternus (whether the potter using the small PATERNIM stamp, who made them, is to be distinguished from the well-known Paternus of Lezoux or not, he cannot have been at work before about A.D. 145). See pl. LI.

The somewhat artificial nature of modern classification is well shown by this and similar pieces, since, without moulded or appliqué decoration, they would normally be described as colour-coated ware. At Lezoux the samian potters, from the early second century onwards at least, regularly made beakers and jars in colour-coated fabrics alongside samian ware. Recent excavations at Lezoux have shown that colour-coated forms and 'black samian' were fired together in the same kiln under reducing conditions. The same slip was evidently used for both.

PERIOD IID

B. Fire Deposits

Potters' stamps

S127. A I 2 (p. 92; fig. 82). Slightly burnt. Albus of La Graufesenque (*Hermet 1934*, pl. 110, 4). Form 27g stamped ΛLIVS.F[I] (VIIa'). Many impressions of this stamp were made after the die, originally giving ALBVS.FE, had become partly filled with clay. Probably *c.* A.D. 55–75.

S128. A VI + (fig. 82). Heavily burnt and so presumably derived from the fire. Andegenus of Lezoux. Form 31 stamped ANDEGENIM (Ia). This stamp is in a large pit-group of early Antonine samian at Alcester. It also appears on form 18/31R, typologically late Hadrianic or early Antonine, at Great Chesterford and Richborough. *c.* A.D. 130–60.

S129–30. A II 7 and B IV 2 (pp. 91, 94; fig. 82). One burnt. Butturrus of Les Martres-de-Veyre (*Terrisse 1969*, pl. LII). Both form 33, stamped BVTTVRRI. The stamp occurs at Les Martres on a form intermediate between Ritterling 8 and Dragendorff 40, on form 27 Carlisle, form 27g London, form 38 Corbridge and Wroxeter and on form 79 Vichy? (Moulins Museum VM47), but form 33 is normal. Dated sites include Camelon (NMA FX 266) and Newstead (Hunterian Museum). Les Martres was scarcely exporting to Britain after A.D. 160, and the occurrence of form 27 with this stamp shows it to be used earlier than that. *c.* A.D. 140–65.

S131. T III 11 (p. 89; fig. 82). Burnt. Buturo of Central Gaul, probably Les Martres-de-Veyre judging by the fabrics, though his work has not been found there. Form 33 stamped .BVTVRO.✷ (IIa). This is from the only die of Buturo so far attested. Apart from Corbridge (P34) there are no independently dated sites, though the dishes are of forms (18/31 and 18/31R rather than 31 and 31R, and ought not to be late in the Antonine period. A date *c.* A.D. 135–65 would be consistent with the meagre evidence.

S132. T III 11 (p. 89; fig. 82). Burnt. Caupirra of Lezoux (cf. no. S94). Form 44 stamped CΛV[.PI]RI.ΛM (VIa). This stamp is on mid- to late Antonine forms (31 and 31R) and also occurs at Benwell

(*Arch. Ael.* 4th ser. v. 60, no. 4) and Birrens (information from Dr. A. S. Robertson and Mrs. J. P. Wild), where it should belong to the Period Ib occupation and its equivalent, respectively. It would be difficult to begin it before A.D. 155, and A.D. 155–85 is the likely range within which it falls.

S134. B XIV 8 (fig. 82). Burnt. Cerialis of Lezoux. Form 33 stamped [CERI.A]L.M (VIa), found in a third-century deposit, but clearly derived from the fire. This stamp was used by Cerialis mainly on form 33, but it has also been noted on form 27 twice, so it was in use before A.D. 160. This is presumably the potter associated with Cinnamus in his early days (*S. & S.*, pl. 164, bottom, 3; *Richborough V*, 130). He must have been at work by A.D. 140 or so. *c.* A.D. 140–60.

S135. B I 15, B IV 3, B IV 3A (pp. 93, 94). Burnt. Cintusmus of Lezoux. Form 37 with Cinnamus Ovolo 2, stamped on the rim CINT[VS]MVSF (VIIIa). This stamp is frequently on the rims of bowls of form 37. The association are with Cinnamus (ovolos 1 and 2 and both the large CIN-NAMI stamp and the small plain ware CINNAMIM stamp impressed in the moulds), Albucius (*S. & S.*, fig. 51, 3) and, possibly, Attianus or Criciro (Juhász, *Die Sigillaten von Brigetio*, iii, 2). On plain ware the stamp is known from Castlecary (NMA, FZ56), Newstead (Mason collection) and Greatchesters. *c.* A.D. 150–80. See D122.

S136. B I, 18 (p. 93; fig. 82). Burnt. Cocuro of Central Gaul, possibly Les Martres-de-Veyre. Form 33 stamped COCVRO.F (Ia). The recorded sites do not help greatly with dating, only Corbridge and Maryport being significant. The forms involved suggest late Hadrianic or early Antonine date, *c.* A.D. 130–55.

S137. B I 18 (p. 93; fig. 82). Burnt. Coelus of La Graufesenque, where this has been found (Millau Mus.). Form 18 stamped OFCOELI (Ib). Clearly residual. *c.* A.D. 65–85.

S138. Z II 5 (p. 89; fig. 82). Crestio or Crestus of La Graufesenque. Form 18 stamped OF CREƧTI retro. (IVa). See S9.

S139. A I 2 (p. 92; fig. 82). Burnt. Habilis of Lezoux. Form 33 stamped HABILISF (Ib). Habilis was a fully Antonine potter, whose work occurs on Hadrian's Wall (presumably Period Ib) with this stamp on form 38 at Chesters Museum (3661/2343). It also appears once on form 80 at Wroxeter. Probably *c.* A.D. 150–80.

S140. B IV 3 (p. 94; fig. 82). Unburnt. Macer of La Graufesenque, where the stamp is known on form 29 (Rodez Museum). Form 18 stamped M͡AC•RI•M͡A (IVa). Often on form 29, and occurring at Camelon (NMA, FX296), this should belong to *c.* A.D. 70–90.

S141. B II 14A (p. 93; fig. 82). Unburnt. Malledo of Lezoux. Form 31 stamped MALLEDV (VIIa). This stamp is not well dated; it only occurs on forms 31 and 33. For what it is worth, the excellent velvety glaze of this piece suggests early rather than late Antonine date, though Malledo certainly worked down to A.D. 175 or so. Probably *c.* A.D. 150–70.

S142. B II 14A (p. 93; fig. 82). Burnt. Marcellinus of Les Martres-de-Veyre (*Terrisse 1969*, pl. LIII). Form 42 stamped MARC•IILINI̩ (Vd or Vd′). This stamp is usually on forms 27, 27g, or 42. One example (unburnt) came from the London Second Fire at Regis House, but five others from London are burnt. It must, therefore, have been in use by A.D. 125 at the latest. A broken version, with the final I missing, occurs on form 33. The Verulamium stamp could be either. *c.* A.D. 115–35, in view of total absence from Antonine foundations.

S143. A IV 11 (p. 91; fig. 82). Burnt. Marcellinus of Central Gaul, probably Les Martres-de-Veyre, and possibly a stamp figured from there (*Terrisse 1969*, pl. LIII). Form 18/31R stamped M͡ARC [ELLINI] (Va). The only other known example is also from Verulamium on form 18/31R (in private hands). If Les Martres, then almost certainly Hadrianic.

S144. B I 18 (p. 93; fig. 82). Burnt. Marcellus of Lezoux. Form 18/31R stamped MARCEL.LI.M (IXb). This is probably a stamp of the Marcellus who worked at the Ligonne site at Lezoux, making forms 18/31, 18/31R, and 27. The contexts at Lezoux demand a date *c.* A.D. 130–55, though this stamp is not known there or at any independently dated site.

S145. B XI 11 (p. 95; fig. 82). Heavily burnt. Maximus of Lezoux. Form 33 stamped MAXIMI• (XVIIIa). With only two exceptions, on forms 27 and 31, all thirty-seven examples of the stamp known are on form 33, all in Britain. Apart from Corbridge, there are no dated contexts. Probably *c.* A.D. 150–80.

S146. B XIV 9 (p. 96; fig. 82). Unburnt. Patricius of La Graufesenque. Form 27 stamped OF.PATRI (Vc). Flavian.

S147. A I 2 (p. 91; fig. 82). Burnt. Patricius of Lezoux. Form 33 stamped PATRICIVSF(XXa). The stamp is known from Newstead (NMA, FRA 1549) and Corbridge (K126), but not otherwise from dated sites. Patricius tended to specialize in making form 18/31R. Some of his stamps are on form 27 occasionally. He probably worked *c.* A.D. 145–75.

S148. T III 11 (p. 89; fig. 82). Burnt. A partial impression of the same stamp as the last.

S149. B IV 3 (p. 94; fig. 82). Burnt. Paullus of Lezoux. The stamp is on form 27 and is very indistinct. It probably reads PAVLL.M and, whether it belongs to the potter who made decorated bowls or not, it is surely to be equated with the man who stamped PAVLVSM (*sic*) retro. on form 27 and whose work occurs in the Birdoswald Alley (*Trans. Cumb. and West. Arch. Soc.*, N.S. xxx, 187). *c.* A.D. 135–60.

S150. B I 18 (p. 93; fig. 82). Burnt. Peculiaris of Lezoux. Form 33 stamped [PE]CVLIARISF (VIa). This stamp occurs on a considerable variety of forms, including 27, 33, 31, 79, and 80, with six records in Antonine Scotland. It was no doubt in use for a long time and two examples in Chesters Museum are probably from Hadrian's Wall (3734/2397 and 3308/2153), and presumably Period Ib, rather than Ia. Probably *c.* A.D. 140–70.

S151–4. T III 10, burnt; B II 14, burnt; B IV 3A and B VII 4, burnt (pp. 93–6; fig. 82). Other burnt examples unstratified. Reburrus of Lezoux. All form 33 with more or less complete versions of the stamp REBVRRIωOI (Va). Reburrus evidently had a long and complicated career. Many stamps, including this, occurred at Lezoux in a large group of *c.* A.D. 150–60. It is known on forms 18/31, 18/31R, 31, 33, 38, 79, and 27, the latter demonstrating that the die was in use before A.D. 160. He bought moulds of Casurius, whose earliest decorated ware is *c.* A.D. 160 (*Antiq. Journ.* xlvi, 103). Stamps from another die occur on burnt vessels at Gauting (*Ber. R.G.K.* 46/47 (1965–6), 77 ff.), where it is difficult to avoid the conclusion that the large quantity of burnt Antonine samian is connected with the invasion of A.D. 162 or (less probably) the Marcomannic incursion of A.D. 167. *c.* A.D. 150–80.

S155. T I 4 (p. 92). Unburnt. Reginus of Central Gaul, possibly the potter of Les Martres-de-Veyre. Form 33 stamped REGINI.MA (IVa). This is not a particularly common stamp, but it has been noted on forms 18/31, 27, 33, and 38. Probably early Antonine.

Of the twenty-seven stamps noted from the Antonine fire levels, or derived from them, four are South Gaulish and clearly residual (S127, 137, 138, and 140). Trajanic stamps are absent and purely Hadrianic ones rare. For the first time Antonine potters are in the majority, many of the stamps being found also in Scotland. With few exceptions the potters in question made form 27, however, and that may be taken to indicate that they were at work before A.D. 160 at the latest, since the form is virtually absent from Period Ib contexts on Hadrian's Wall and in the Antonine levels of forts in the hinterland reoccupied in the mid-Antonine period. The latest potter in the Fire Groups seems to be Caupirra (S132), though Habilis (S139) and Malledo (S141) cannot have been at work much before A.D. 160. Taking their evidence as a whole, the stamps clearly imply a date after A.D. 150, but almost certainly before A.D. 160. The most probable period is *c.* A.D. 155–60.

It is of interest to note that plain ware certainly, or probably, from the kilns at Les Martres-de-Veyre was still in use at the time of the destruction, another parallel with Antonine Scotland, but a difference from Hadrian's Wall and the reoccupied forts in its hinterland.

The plain samian is not here studied in detail, but the salient points may be noted. Neglecting the obviously residual pieces, the order of frequency of forms, with approximate figures based on a rim-count, is: form 33 (70), 31 (60), 18/31 (21), 18/31R or 31R (17), 27 (14), 38 (8), 36 (7), Curle 11 (7), 46 (6), Curle 15 (4), 44 (3), jars with 'cut-glass' facets (3), 35/36 (2), 42 (2). Forms 15/31, 79/80, Curle 21 (?), Curle 23, Ludowici Tg and the samian inkwell are all represented by single fragments. There is no conflict here with the evidence of the stamps, especially as the dishes classed as form 31 tend to be the shallower, earlier variety rather than the deep version of Pudding Pan Rock times. The vessels noted as 18/31R or 31R do not seem to include the fully developed late Antonine form either.

Decorated ware

D113. T X 5 (p. 89; fig. 96). Burnt. Form 37, a small fragment from a bowl with large winding scroll. This could be Hadrianic-Antonine or Antonine (cf. D120 below for a possible early date).

D114. V XXXII 7 (p. 89; fig. 96). Unburnt. Form 37, probably from Les Martres-de-Veyre, where the ovolo and the use of a bead-row above it may be paralleled (*Terrisse 1969*, pl. XLIII, 260). Probably late Trajanic or Hadrianic.

D115. T III 11 (p. 89; fig. 96). Burnt. Form 30 in the standard style of Cinnamus of Lezoux with his ovolo 2 (*S. & S.*, fig. 47, 2). The decoration consists of alternating panels with an athlete (D. 394) in one and the double chevron-medallion with Pan-mask (D. 675) and dolphin-stand (D. 1069A) in the other. *c.* A.D. 150–75.

D116. T III 11 (p. 89; fig. 96). Burnt. Form 37 in the more regular panelled style of Docilis of Lezoux, but with a small ovolo not apparently recorded on a stamped or signed bowl. The tier of baskets, etc., is normal for him, as are the festoons and the small warrior (O. 210A) (cf. *S. & S.*, pls. 91–3). The bird (O. 2251) is probably the matching piece to the reversed one on *S. & S.*, pl. 92, 12.

Recent finds in Britain and at Lezoux support the Hadrianic-Antonine dating proposed by Miss Simpson (*S. & S.*, 178), though they may call for extension of activity to *c.* A.D. 160. The Mumrills bowl (*Proc. Soc. Ant. Scot.* xciv, 101, no. 3) is now firmly assignable to Docilis, since a sherd of it with his intra-decorative cursive signature was found in later excavations. Its close connections with Casurius suggest contact between the two potters. Casurius was almost certainly making plain ware in the 150s, but his earliest decorated ware is unlikely to be much earlier than A.D. 160. For Docilis a date of *c.* A.D. 130–60 is now required, with the bowls in the style with large, neat panels, as at Mumrills, coming towards the end of the range. The discovery of many sherds in this style at Lezoux in a context requiring a date *c.* A.D. 150–60 confirm this. The Verulamium bowl should fall *c.* A.D. 130–55.

D117. T III 12 (p. 89; fig. 96). Burnt. Form 37 by one of the potters normally using a straight line below the ovolo. (Here the ovolo is superimposed on the line.) This device was used by many potters, but notably by Secundus of Lezoux (cf. *Proc. Soc. Ant. Scot.* xciv, 103; *Gallia*, xxvii, p. 6, 4). Although this ovolo is not attested on a Secundus bowl, he did use the rest of the decorative motifs on bowls with his more usual ovolo approximating to ovolo 3 of Cinnamus. For the hare (D. 950 variant) bowls from Chester and Manchester; for the column a bowl from Caernarvon (*Arch. Camb.* 1962 p. 121, no. 24); for the athlete (D. 394) a bowl from Saltney (*Ann. Arch. and Anthr.* xxii, pl. III) and for the panther (D. 799) a bowl from South Shields (Museum BA 32). There is little doubt that the piece is to be assigned to Secundus, whose styles show some affinities with Cinnamus and his firm. A date of introduction before A.D. 150 is unlikely, since bowls in

Secundus style are relatively common in Scotland but also appear on Hadrian's Wall and in the reoccupied hinterland forts. In view of this, a general date of c. A.D. 150–80 seems likely. The bowl from the Corbridge 'destruction of A.D. 197' (*S. & S.*, 260) must be set aside as dating evidence, in view of the present uncertainties about the nature and date of that deposit.

D118. A I 2 (p. 91; fig. 96). Burnt. A small fragment of form 37 with the ovolo with beaded tongue used by Cerialis, Cinnamus, Anunus, Paullus, and others (cf. *Gallia*, xxvii, 3 ff.). This ovolo is usually on unsigned and unstamped bowls. It almost certainly came into use in the 140s on the available evidence from Lezoux. The proportions of bowls from Scotland, Hadrian's Wall, and Hinterland forts are again of interest. c. A.D. 145–70. (See D119).

D119. A I 2 (p. 91; fig. 96). Burnt. Possibly from the same bowl as the last, this is assignable to Cerialis or Cinnamus on the strength of the leafy frond in the field (*Gallia*, xxvii, p. 6). The thick single-bordered festoon, the sphinx (D. 496) and panther (D. 798) are regular elements in the Cerialis–Cinnamus style. c. A.D. 145–70.

D120. A I 2 (p. 91; fig. 97). Burnt. Large fragments of a bowl in the style of Attianus of Lezoux. All the elements of decoration, including the stag (D. 867) and birds (D. 1019 and O. 2298) are known on stamped bowls (*S. & S.*, pls. 85 ff.). The association of Attianus at Lezoux and the paucity of his bowls in Scotland suggest a date c. A.D. 130–50.

D121. T II 8 (p. 92; fig. 97). Slightly burnt. Form 37 probably assignable to Sacer of Lezoux. The simple panels, with Hercules (D. 464) and a caryatid (D. 655 or 657) alternating, have neat rosettes at the corners, as on bowls from the Saalburg and Cannstatt (*S. & S.*, pl. 84, 14 and 15). The ovolo, not known on stamped bowls, is better seen on D124 below. Its punch may well have been transmitted from Les Martres-de-Veyre to Lezoux, as with many used by Sacer and Attianus, since the ovolo appears on bowls in what seems to be Les Martres fabric. c. A.D. 125–50.

D122. B I 15, B IV 3, B IV 3A (pp. 93–4; fig. 97). Burnt. Several sherds of a small form 37 in the style of Cinnamus and with his ovolo 2 (*S. & S.*, fig. 47, 2), stamped on the rim by Cintusmus (see S135). The simple panelled style is standard work of Cinnamus, the panels having: (i) a candelabrum (D. 1113A), (ii) Vulcan (D. 39, without tongs), and (iii) stag (D. 852), partly impressed and springing from an acanthus leaf, as often in the work of Cinnamus. c. A.D. 150–80.

D123. B I 21 (p. 93; fig. 97). Unburnt. Form 37 in the style of Silvio (*S. & S.*, pl. 33). This style is common to Les Martres-de-Veyre and Lezoux, though whether because the potter has migrated from the one to the other or whether because he sold moulds to Lezoux is not clear. Bowls in this style at Lezoux appear in context of A.D. 125–45, so the production at Les Martres is unlikely to be early Trajanic. c. A.D. 115–35.

D124. B I 21 (p. 93; fig. 97). Burnt. Form 37 with the same ovolo as D121. c. A.D. 145–70.

D125. A X 2 (p. 93; fig. 97). Burnt. A fragment of form 37 from a bowl with large scroll decoration, also having across the main tendril partial impressions of the small vine scroll used by Drusus and his contemporaries. There is an exact parallel from the Lezoux pit of A.D. 130–45 referred to under S95 above. In the pit were other fragments by the same potter, many having the distinctive ovolo of D127 below. c. A.D. 130–50.

D126. B III 11 (p. 93; fig. 97). Burnt. A complete form 37 from the East Gaulish kilns at Blickweiler. For the ovolo see Knorr and Sprater, *Die westpfälzischen Sigillata-Töpfereien von Blickweiler und Eschweiler Hof* (1927), Taf. 82, 32; the tritons ibid., Taf. 71, 14 and 15; the birds, Taf. 80, 7 and 8; the ship Taf. 71, 12 without the sail or sailor (as on Taf. 57, 7); the vine is not exactly paralleled there, but cf. Taf. 81, 22; the bifid plant Taf. 81, 51. For a rather similar composition with the ovolo of Austrus cf. ibid., Taf. 33, 2. This piece, like most decorated bowls from Blickweiler or La Madeleine, was not stamped and the potter's name cannot be guessed. Blickweiler ware was current before the Antonine period on the evidence of the potters' stamps from the Saalburg Earth Fort, including those of Austrus, who must have left Lezoux for Blickweiler by A.D. 135

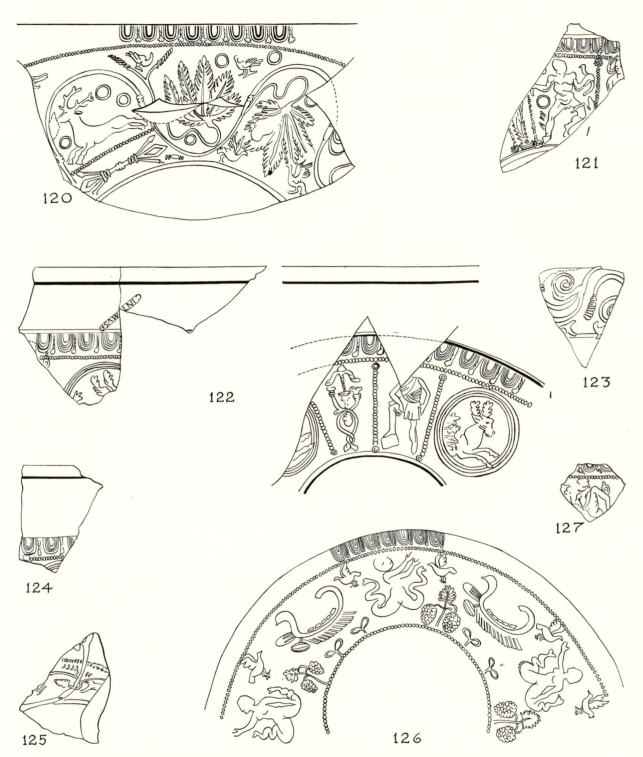

FIG. 97. Decorated samian 120–7 and stamp S135 (½).

or so. The context of this piece provides useful evidence for the date of one of the slightly later Blickweiler styles.

D127. B II 13 (p. 93; fig. 97). Burnt. Form 37 with the ovolo referred to under D125 above. The Vulcan (D. 39, with tongs) also occurs on bowls in the same pit. c. A.D. 130–50.

D128. B IV 3, 3a; B V 21 (pp. 94–5; fig. 98). Burnt. Form 37 in an unusual style. There are two points of contact with the style of the potter of *S. & S.*, pl. 77, 4, whose name is not known though contemporaneity with Priscinus is evident in the basal wreath and the use of rings at the bottom of the vertical borders. This is scarcely enough to establish identity in view of the differences, however. The Pan (D. 424) is only attested for Aventinus I (*S. & S.*, pl. 156, 2), and neither the dolphin nor the gladiator have precise parallels. On general grounds of style one would expect this interesting piece to be Hadrianic or early Antonine.

D129. B IV 3 (p. 94; fig. 98). Burnt. Form 37. A simple large scroll in the manner of Sacer (*S. & S.*, pl. 83, 8) or Cinnamus (Juhász, *Brigetio*, tab. IV, 7) in his early work; probably the latter, since the striated ring occurs on bowls in the Cerialis–Cinnamus style. c. A.D. 140–70.

D130. B IV 3 (p. 94; fig. 98). Burnt. A small fragment of form 37 with Amazon (D. 153) and acanthus leaf. Perhaps by one of the Sacer–Attianus Group, since they regularly used both motifs. The ovolo is not well enough preserved for a decision. Hadrianic-Antonine.

D131. B IV 3 (p. 94; fig. 98). Burnt. Form 37, thin. The ovolo is the one used on D97 above, but scarcely here by Sacer, who did not have borders of wavy lines. Hadrianic-Antonine.

D132. B IV 3A (p. 94; fig. 98). Unburnt. Form 37, ovolo only. This almost certainly belongs to the same bowl as a piece from Period II D (B IV 9G), also figured here, in the style of Satto or Saturninus of Chémery-Faulquemont. The fragment fits precisely against rubbings of their commonest ovolo. Evidently residual and from II D, though certainly late Hadrianic or Antonine.

D133. B IV 3A (p. 94; fig. 98). Burnt. Form 37. A fragment in the style of Docilis with the same tier of baskets and a trace of the candelabrum of the Mumrills bowl referred to under D116, above. c. A.D. 130–60.

D134. B V 9 (p. 95; fig. 98). Form 37 rim with graffito *post cocturam*]NI. The ovolo only survives. It might be one used by Bassus of Lezoux. Hadrianic or early Antonine.

D135. B V 7 (p. 95; fig. 98). Burnt. A fragment from a freestyle bowl of form 37 with parts of a lion (D. 799), stag (D. 867) and the serpent on rock (D. 960 *bis*), together with the tail of another lion (D. 766). All the types were used by Sacer, Attianus, and Criciro. The composition is most reminiscent of the latter (*S. & S.*, pl. 118), c. A.D. 140–70.

D136. B V 7 (p. 95; fig. 98). Burnt. Form 37 with ovolo 3 of Cinnamus (*S. & S.*, fig. 47, 3) and a simple scheme of three panels repeated with (i) Cupid (D. 236); (ii) festoon containing hare (D. 950a); (iii) medallion containing bird (D. 1038) over another motif not preserved. Typical work of Cinnamus. c. A.D. 150–75.

D137. B VI 10 (p. 96; fig. 98). Unburnt. Form 37. A fragment from a bowl with similar arrangement to D120 above, and presumably also by Attianus.

D138. B XIV 16 (p. 96; fig. 98). Unburnt. Form 37. Presumably residual, since it is in the unmistakable style of Igocatus of Les Martres-de-Veyre (*Terrisse 1969*, pls. XIV–XV), with the draped man (D. 523), lioness (D. 793 partly impressed), and the legs of the Perseus (D. 146) which form a major part of his repertoire of types. c. A.D. 100–20.

D139. B VIII 5 (fig. 98). Heavily burnt. Form 37. This piece seems to disclose connections with Docilis, who used both the ram's horn and the lozenge, as well as astragali horizontally at the bottoms of bead-rows. The figure appears to be a slightly larger version of a Hercules (D. 751). The ram's horn is used similarly on a burnt bowl from Gauting (*B. Röm. Germ. Komm.* 46–7 (1965–6), Taf. 49, 15), there mistakenly assigned to Casurius, and perhaps to be assigned to the Hadrianic fire at Gauting rather than the Antonine one. c. A.D. 130–60.

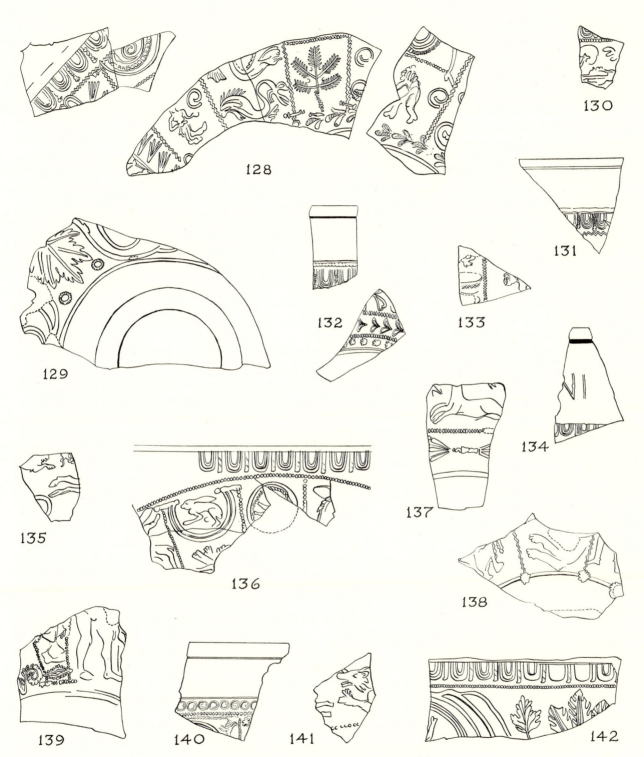

FIG. 98. Decorated samian 128–42 (½).

D140. A IV 1 (fig. 98). Burnt, from disturbed daub layer. Form 37, with rings replacing the ovolo and with borders of medium-sized and fine beads below. Part of a medallion, or more probably a small vine-scroll, since it is combined with a tendril and trilobed leaf as on the Heronbridge bowl of Drusus II and a bowl in the same style from Holt (*S. & S.*, pl. 89, 12; *Y Cymmrodor*, xli, fig. 49, 150). Perhaps by Drusus II, then. *c.* A.D. 125–50.

D141. B XI 20 (fig. 98). Burnt, and so presumably derived from fire. Form 37, freestyle, with border of large beads below the decoration. This device is so unusual as to suggest the work of Austrus or one of his associates, such as Secundinus. The bear (O. 1620) was used by both. *c.* A.D. 125–45, or *c.* A.D. 125–35, if Austrus (cf. note under D126).

D142. B III 5 (fig. 98). Burnt, from disturbed daub. Form 37, with ovolo 3 of Cinnamus and scroll in his normal style. (*S. & S.*, pl. 162, 60). *c.* A.D. 150–80.

Leaving aside seven sherds which are either residual or unassignable, and the Blickweiler bowl (D126), which has to be dated from its context here, the potters best represented are the Sacer–Attianus–Drusus Group (nine sherds), Docilis (three), Criciro (one), Cerialis–Cinnamus (three), Cinnamus (five), and Secundus (one). All these potters except the last began work before A.D. 150, often well before, but their bowls were, sometimes at least, still in use at the time of the fire. The Cinnamus pieces all belong to his main period of production, when he was using ovolos 2 and 3, but probably before ovolo 1 had been introduced, and there is no reason to doubt that they were only used after A.D. 150 (cf. *S. & S.*, p. 271). There are, therefore, at least six bowls in the group which must be later than A.D. 150, but work of late Antonine potters, characteristic of Period Ib on Hadrian's Wall or the Hinterland forts reoccupied at about the same time, is entirely absent. This agrees remarkably well with the date suggested (p. 256) from the potters' stamps. It is clear that the fire fell in the decade A.D. 150–60 and, allowing time for the introduction and use of the standard Cinnamus style and the work of Secundus, a date in the middle of the decade or in its second half seems most likely. Comparison with the decorated bowls from the Wroxeter Gutter (*Atkinson 1942*, 132 ff.) is instructive. The latter group must be later than A.D. 160, but probably not much later (cf. Wacher (ed.), *The Civitas Capitals of Roman Britain*, 58, note 13). There is almost no point of contact with the Verulamium material. On the other hand, the bowls from the general debris of the destruction at Wroxeter, which include a high proportion of residual pieces, not all necessarily in use at the time of the destruction, have many links with the Verulamium group, though some bowls are clearly later. At Verulamium one misses entirely the work of Paternus and his associates, Advocisus and Casurius, to name only a few of the commoner potters who must have been at work by A.D. 160 or very soon after.

LATER SECOND-CENTURY DEPOSITS

S156. Pit 19 (p. 102). Cinnamus of Lezoux. Form 30, stamped CIN[NAMI] (IVb). This is the normal large Cinnamus stamp. *c.* A.D. 150–80.

S157. Pit 19 (p. 102). Ritogenus of Lezoux. Form 31R, stamped RIIOG[ENIM] (IIb). This stamp is known from Hadrian's Wall but, unlike his others, does not appear in Scotland. Ritogenus seems to have been largely a mid-Antonine potter. *c.* A.D. 155–80.

V. THE OTHER POTTERY

In general the pottery is catalogued in chronological groups by period, according to its context in the sequence of buildings (e.g. Periods I, II A, etc.). But *Amphorae* and *First-century imported fine wares* have been abstracted and are described separately at the beginning of the catalogue. Both are of non-British origin and both have a high survival rate in residual contexts which do not give a true picture of their date of manufacture. Also abstracted are vessels in *Belgic-type coarse ware from later levels*. These are residual in their contexts but give a conspectus of the types present.

In the remainder of the catalogue the pottery of each period is classified under subheadings by shape with the exception of the first group comprising *Fine Wares*, which are mainly colour-coated vessels of various types. The date given is that of the deposit, and where not specifically stated is that given in the period-heading. Where the presence of secondary floors or occupation levels enables a period to be subdivided, a narrower date-range within the over-all limits of the period itself has been assigned. This is naturally to some extent arbitrary but takes account of the associated samian and coin evidence.

The *mortaria* have been examined by Mrs. K. F. Hartley, and we are much indebted to her for assigning them where possible to their place or region of manufacture. She has also provided an approximate date-range derived from her own wide studies. Except where mortaria occur in sufficient number to be grouped according to their origin this general date-range is given before the place of manufacture, which is followed by the number and date of the layer in which the individual vessel under discussion occurred (e.g. 'pre-Flavian, south-east Britain or import; T VI 35, A.D. 49–60'); in the former case it precedes the deposit number and its date e.g. 'A.D. 100–40; B IV 3C, A.D. 155/160'.

A description of the layer is given only where this does not appear in the tables on pp. 20–5, 28–39, 43–53, 60–72, and 81–97. To save confusion on the plans some pits have been renumbered thereon, thus avoiding duplication of the same figure or the necessity to add the trench number. In these lists the pottery label is given first and the number as shown on the plans second, e.g. 'B IV Pit 10. Pit 10' or 'B XI Pit 1. Pit 19'.

The samian tables illustrate in an unarguable form the high survival-rate of sherds as residual material. This has posed a serious problem in the classification of the coarse pottery which in itself is not controlled by the exact criteria applicable to samian ware. What was to be included, and what rejected as out of context? The solution adopted here is unavoidably to some extent subjective, though the large bulk of the sample has facilitated the identification of the life-span of most types. Considerations taken into account include the amount of wear or abrasion and the size of sherds, and the extent to which the appearance of types in successive levels is coherent and continuous. Where reasonable doubt survives about whether a type is in context or residual it has been included, but information (without a drawing) is also provided about appearances in later contexts when consideration of numbers, continuity, or typology suggest that the vessel is residual therein. Vessels clearly out of context have been omitted except for exceptional pieces deserving publication in their own right.

Further working lists and drawings of the types, and of the groups in which they occur, exist in card-index form bound in Moore's Modern Method binders, and these will be placed in the Verulamium Museum with the finds themselves when publication is complete.

Lengthy discussion of types and citation of parallels has been avoided, since it would have added very considerably to the length of the report, which rests on its own internal validity. Some short comments may, however, be offered.

(i) Black-burnished ware, category A, has been identified where possible; category B, however, in the south of Britain is much less easy to isolate, and this has not been attempted consistently. For this ware see *P.S.A.S.* xciv (1960–1), 126–31.

(ii) No. 35, a Belgic beaker with hollow cordons, is a native type not found in the southern half of the Catuvellaunian area; it appears to be local to the Northamptonshire–north Buckinghamshire region (*Arch. Journ.* cxxiv (1967), 82 and figs. 10, 35; 12, 53).

(iii) The fine mica-coated beakers (nos. 125–9), bowls (nos. 215–17), and tripod bowl (no. 231) from Pit 7 are almost certainly imports from the Continent to judge by their skilled technique and early date (A.D. 60–75). Cf. Camulodunum form 95. They were very soon copied, however, for nos. 312–14 are clearly in local shapes and come from deposits of Flavian age. No. 216 is perhaps the ancestor of Gillam's type 192 which appears on Hadrian's Wall in the period A.D. 120–40.

(iv) The well-documented appearance of colour-coated wares is worthy of attention. Apart from imported 'varnish wares' of the pre-Flavian period (nos. 27, 29) only roughcast beakers are found in the first century. But vessels like no. 397 make their appearance *c.* A.D. 110 though in small quantity; the source is probably continental: vessels of this type were made at Lezoux. True hunt cups of apparently Nene Valley type are first found *c.* A.D. 135–40 (nos. 555–7) and so is a 'Castor box' (no. 558); the latter is earlier both in type and date than the standard Castor-ware 'boxes', and its source is unknown. By A.D. 150 the beakers have become well established (nos. 791–6). Tall beakers, on the other hand, do not appear until well after the Antonine fire, and probably *c.* A.D. 200 or a little later (nos. 1056 ff.).

(v) The so-called 'unguent jars' (nos. 476–80, 636–41, 882–5, 1099, and fig. 141, nos. 15, 16) first appear in the period A.D. 105–30. They were found in some numbers by Wheeler in the Triangular Temple (*Verulamium*, 191, fig. 32, 45, and pl. LIX), where they undoubtedly were employed for a ritual purpose. On the present site, however, they just as clearly had an industrial purpose. Two were certainly used as crucibles (p. 366). The others contained no evidence of use, but their restricted distribution—in Period II B to Rooms 12, 13, and 14 and the colonnade nearby, in II C to Rooms 15, 16, 27, and 39, and only slightly wider in Period II D—clearly points to a specialist purpose, which was probably concerned with metal-working. It might be interesting to work out the distribution of other types too.

(vi) The hollow raised bosses on nos. 906 and 947 are of interest as perhaps suggesting that the hollow boss is not necessarily an indication of Romano-Saxon cultural fusion (e.g. no. 1203B) but on the contrary a long-lived if uncommon tradition of Romano-British potcraft. Note also no. 128, a probable import (section (iii), above).

(vii) The great bulk of the coarse pottery was certainly locally manufactured at kilns at Verulamium itself (*Antiq. Journ.* xxi (1941), 271 ff.; *Hertfordshire Archaeology*, i (1968), 22 ff.), or in the neighbourhood of Radlett and Brockley Hill. Trade in pottery over longer distances is perhaps best documented by a study of the mortaria; this will be a feature of a subsequent volume. Mortaria from the Oxford region first appear in the present sequence soon after A.D. 130, only two decades at the most after the potters of the Oxford region began their manufacture. It is possible, however, that other types of ware from the Oxford region reached Verulamium slightly earlier. No. 524, a buff-ware vessel with orange-painted decoration, is dated A.D. 105–15, and is therefore broadly contemporary with very similar painted vessels from Dorchester on Thames (*Arch. Journ.* cxix (1962), 136–7, nos. 71–4). Like them it is likely to have been made at a pottery in the Oxford region. From the second decade of the fourth century there is evidence that red colour-coated vessels were arriving from the same source (no. 1149, 1196, etc.). We are indebted to Mr. C. J. Young for making the identifications.

Nos. 694 and 696 are probably to be ascribed to kilns in London; for a discussion of the type represented by no. 696 see P. Corder in *Antiq. Journ.* xxi (1941), 296–8. Finally it is possible to suggest that no. 1243 may have been made in one of the kilns of the Farnham region. (See Surrey Archaeological Society, *A Survey of the Prehistory of the Farnham District* (1939), 231–5, R. 3, R. 12, R. 24.)

CATALOGUE OF THE POTTERY
by M. G. Wilson, F.S.A.

AMPHORAE
(For Amphora-stamps see p. 370)

Fig. 99
1. Smooth hard orange-buff ware, cream slip, Z I 39, pre A.D. 49. I, below Room 4.
2. Hard yellow-buff granulated ware, grey core, Z I 39, pre A.D. 49. I, below Room 4.
3. Orange-buff ware, B IV 35, A.D. 49–60. I, Room 25.
4. Hard granulated buff ware, A I 40, A.D. 60. I, Rooms 15–16, burnt debris. Another from B IV 18B, A.D. 130–40. II C, Room 44.
5. Hard finely granulated buff ware. Stamp on handle SAENIN.B. B I 68, A.D. 60–75. Pit 7. Others of this type, not with stamps, come from B IV 21M, A IV 21, A.D. 145–50 (II C, Room 37); T I 5, A.D. 140–50 (II C street-metal); A VI 3, A.D. 150–155/160 (II D, Room 18 occupation on floor); A I 2, A.D. 155/160 (II D, Room 23); B XIV 7 (III, disturbed burnt-daub make-up (XIV, 6)); and from T VI 8, A.D. 270–5 (III, make-up (XIV, 1)). Cf. no. 10.
6. Pinkish-buff micaceous ware with small white and grey grits. B I 38, A.D. 85–105. II A, outside Room 17.
7. Hard buff rather finely granulated ware, A IV 42, A.D. 75–105. II A, outside Room 7.
8. Hard buff slightly micaceous ware with some small white grits, A VII 34, A.D. 85–105. II A, Room 8. Another from T III 27, A.D. 85–105 (II A, Room 1).
9. Similar ware to 8 but with smoothed surface, A II 42, A.D. 75–105. II A, outside Room 12. Spanish, Dressel form 20.
10. Cf. no. 5. A I 31, A.D. 105–30. II B, Room 17.
11. Orange-buff ware, cream slip, A VI 23, A.D. 105–15. II B, Room 26, early floor. Another from A XII 12, A.D. 115–30 (II B, Room 26, latest floor). Dressel form 38, (?) Italian.

12. Smooth deep buff micaceous ware, T XXI 19, A.D. 110–20. II B, Room 5, intermediate floor. Another from Z I 22, A.D. 130–40 (II C, Room 8).
13. Hard granulated orange-pink ware, B IV 20J, A.D. 115–30. II B, Room 29, make-up for *opus signinum* floor.
14. Rather smooth cream ware, pink core, T VII 21, A.D. 130–40. II C, Room 2.
15. Hard finely granulated pinkish-buff slightly micaceous ware, B IV 17K, A.D. 140–50. II C, Room 39.
16. Similar ware to 15. B I 31E, A.D. 140–50. II C, Room 27. Another from T XX 18, A.D. 110–20 (II B, Room 7).
17. Pinkish-buff ware, cream slip, T VII 17, A.D. 130–50. II C, Room 3. Spanish, Dressel form 20.
18. Hard buff rather finely granulated ware, pink core, V XXXIV 10, A.D. 150–155/160. II D, Room 1. Dressel form 38. Another with two dipinti on neck . . .]GΛ (vertical), . . .] .INI CELL (horizontal, below) (pl. LIII, c) from V XXXIV 2, A.D. 375–410+. (*J.R.S.* l (1960), 242, no. 40). Similar rim from T XX 18, A.D. 110–20 (II B, Room 7).

Fig. 100

19. Hard creamy-buff finely granulated ware, B XI 13, A.D. 270–5. III make-up, yard behind XIV, 6, probably residual. Another from A XI 16, A.D. 85–105 (II A, Room 7). Spanish, Dressel form 20.
20. Hard pinkish-buff finely granulated ware, slightly micaceous, A I 5, A.D. 270–5. III make-up (XIV, 4) perhaps residual.
21. Finely granulated buff ware, micaceous light reddish-buff slip, B I 9, A.D. 310–15. III cellar filling.
22. Hard micaceous light reddish-buff ware; shoulder and lower part of handles added from a similar amphora, B I 9, A.D. 310–15 (two). III, cellar filling.

First-century Imported Fine Wares

23. Bowl perhaps derived from samian form 24/25 (cf. Camulodunum form 58A), in fine hard smoothly burnished cream ware, residual in B II Pit 9, *c.* A.D. 105. II A, Pit 9.
24. Plate in terra nigra, B II 38, A.D. 60. I, Rooms 26–7.
25. Plate in terra nigra, T II 43, pre A.D. 49. Below I, Rooms 6 and 18.
26. Plate in terra nigra, T VII 53, pre A.D. 49. Old plough-soil.
27. Plate in fine buff micaceous ware, good orange-red coating inside and on rim, dull reddish-buff matt coating elsewhere; residual in T VIII 5, A.D. 130–50. II C, Room 13.
28. Roughcast bowl in fine yellow paste, with yellow-brown slightly 'metallic' coating, A X 72, A.D. 49–60. I, Room 19A.
29. Bowl with applied scale and edge of 'raspberry' roundel (cf. Camulodunum form 62B) outside, roughcast inside, in fine cream paste with slightly 'metallic' yellow-brown coating, darker outside, T VII 49, A.D. 49–60. I, Room 1.
30. Roughcast beaker in fine white paste with yellow-brown slightly 'metallic' coat, B IV 37, A.D. 49–60. I, Room 25 floor. Others from B I 42A, A.D. 60–75 (II A, Rooms 16–21, burnt daub make-up); and, residually, from T XX 18, A.D. 110–20 (II B, Room 7). Cf. 232; also 52, 101, 233, 396, 555, 780–89, 1070.
31. Similar to 30. T XX 38, *c.* A.D. 49, I, Room 8.
32. St. Rémy beaker in very fine hard white paste, covered in thin yellow glaze over applied cable-pattern strips, B IV Pit 10, A.D. 60–75. Pit 10. Reconstructed with a base in identical ware from B I Pit 7, A.D. 60–75 (Pit 7). A similar decorated sherd from B IV Pit 8, A.D. 75–105 (Pit 2); a handle from B IV 29B, A.D. 75–85 (II A, Room 23); and a base with glossy bright greenish-yellow glaze from B IV 29E, A.D. 75–105 (II A, Room 20) are all residual.

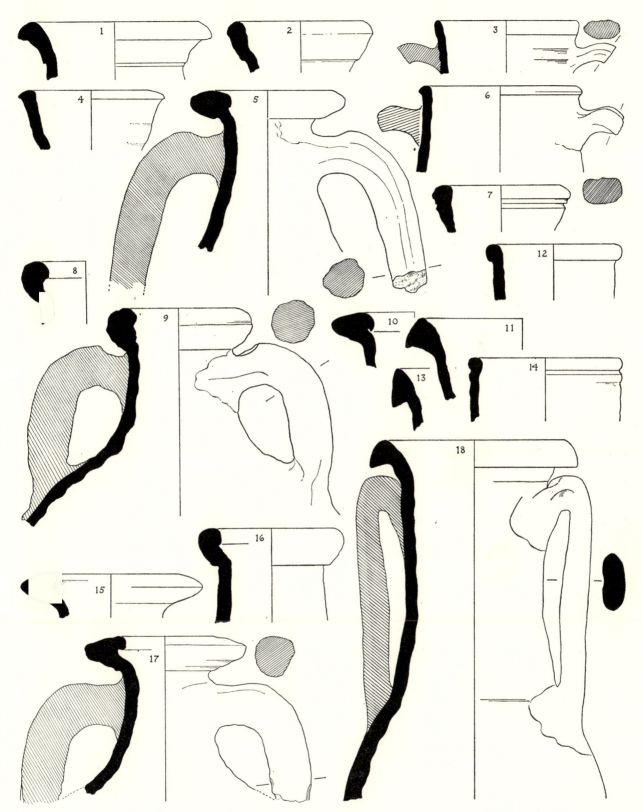

FIG. 99. Pottery vessels: amphorae nos. 1–18 ($\frac{1}{4}$).

33. St. Rémy beaker-sherd with applied decoration, in very fine hard white paste, covered outside only in yellow to green glaze; residual in B IV 23J, A.D. 105–15. II B, Room 29.

34. St. Rémy beaker with a pattern of barbotine dots, in very fine hard white paste, covered with brownish-yellow glaze, B II 40, A.D. 55–60. I, Room 22. The lower part has been reconstructed from a decorated sherd in B II 37E, A.D. 75–85 (accumulation outside II A, Room 19); a plain sherd in B I 48, A.D. 85–105 (outside II A, Room 17); and a base with glossy yellow-green glaze in A XI 20, A.D. 85–105, II A, Room 7. All three are residual.

Belgic Coarse Pottery in Later Layers

35. Beaker with hollow cordons and pattern of diagonal combing, in rather coarse dark grey ware with burnished dark grey-brown surface; residual in B I 38, A.D. 85–105. II A, outside Room 17. Another piece of the same beaker in B I 63, A.D. 60–75. Pit 7. Others were found, also residually, in T VII 39, A.D. 75–85 (II A, Room 3); B I 37F, A.D. 105–15, and B I 32F, A.D. 115–30, both II B, Room 23.

36. Jar with shoulder cordons in coarse granulated dark grey to buff ware; residual in B XI 22, A.D. 300–50. Upper filling of Pit 19.

37, 38. Jars with neck cordons, in finely granulated black to buff burnished ware; residual in A X 22, A.D. 60–75. II A, Room 16, burnt daub make-up.

39. Jar with burnished diagonal lines on shoulder, in coarse granulated unevenly burnished grey-brown ware; residual in B XI 22, A.D. 300–50. Upper filling of Pit 19.

40. Jar with roughly rilled body, in coarse granulated grey-brown ware, with burnished rim; residual in A X 19, A.D. 85–105. II A, Room 16.

41. Pedestal base in hard finely granulated pinkish-buff ware; residual in A I 29, c. A.D. 105. II B, Room 22A.

42. Pedestal base in smooth burnished grey-black ware, repaired with a plug of lead inside and a thin lead plate beneath, perhaps to fill up a hole deliberately bored in the base; residual in B I 38, A.D. 85–105. Outside 11 A, Room 17.

Period I: Pottery from Layers Dated Before A.D. 49

43. Flagon with a fragment of a three-ribbed handle, in hard finely granulated light reddish ware with cream slip, T I 15, street-metalling.

44. Bowl with horizontal and vertical furrowing, in rather coarse red-brown ware with white grits, blackened surface, burnished on rim and shoulder, B IV 44. Old plough-soil.

45. Imitation Arretine cup, cf. Loeschcke 8, 8A; Ritterling 5, though without rouletting on the rim, in fine hard burnished grey ware, T VI 40. Below I, Room 6.

46. Dish in rather granulated grey burnished ware, roughly finished, Z I 39. Below I, Room 4.

Period I: Pottery from Layers Dated c. A.D. 49

47. Jar in coarse rather finely granulated grey-black ware, unevenly burnished, T II 40. I, Room 6.

48. Jar with internally grooved rim, in coarse finely granulated red-brown ware with black surface, B IV 43A. I, Room 18 or street-metalling below this. Cf. 81–2, 197–9, 390, 481–5, 656–66, 897–909, 1050, 1062, 1080.

49, 50. Jars with rilling on shoulder: 49 in coarse granulated grey ware, partly red surface, burnished on rim and near base, T XX 38. I, Room 8, occupation below floor. No. 50 in rather coarse grey-brown ware, T VII 51. I, Room 3, occupation below floor.

51. Mortarium in smooth hard white ware, burnt; Claudian, south-east Britain or import; T II 40. I, Room 6.

FIG. 100. Pottery vessels: amphorae nos. 19–22; first-century imported wares nos. 23–34; Belgic coarse
pottery in later layers nos. 35–42; Pottery of Period I, nos. 43–51 (¼).

PERIOD I: POTTERY FROM LAYERS DATED A.D. 49–60

Fig. 101

52. Roughcast beaker in fine hard buff paste with brown coating, B II 41, A.D. 49–75. I, Room 22 (contaminated). Cf. 30–1, 101, 232–3, 396, 555, 780–9, 1070.

Flagons

53. Finely granulated white ware, Z I 37. I, Room 4.
54. Hard rather finely granulated buff ware, T VII 46. I, Room 3.
55. Ware as 54. B I 52, A.D. 60. I, Rooms 18–24.
56. Light reddish granulated ware, B IV 40D. I, Room 26.
57. Hard, rather finely granulated buff ware, T VII 46. I, Room 3.
58. Hard, rather finely granulated white ware, Z I 35. I, Room 4.

Ring-necked flagons

59. Rather finely granulated pink ware, B II 40, A.D. 55–60. I, Room 22.
60. Hard, rather finely granulated white ware, A X 71. I, Room 19A, secondary oven.

Beakers

61. Carinated beaker or jar in rather coarse burnished dark grey ware, B IV 36, A.D. 60. I, Rooms 26–31.
62. Butt beaker with burnished lattice decoration, in light reddish rather granulated ware, grey core, smoothly burnished rim and shoulder, B IV 40B. I, Room 27.
63. Rusticated beaker in fine hard deep pink slightly burnished ware, B II 40, A.D. 55–60. I, Room 22.
64. Poppyhead beaker or jar in finely granulated grey ware, burnished blue-grey slip on upper two-thirds of body, A IV 41, A.D. 60. I, Room 15.

Jars

65. Burnished diagonal lines on shoulder; finely granulated dark grey ware, partly burnished surface, T XX 30, A.D. 60. I, Room 6, tub. Cf. 149–56, 269, 383–5, 431–42, 607–12, 843.
66. Hard grey-buff burnished ware, B IV 41S. I, Room 30.
67. Rather coarse grey-brown burnished ware, B I 51. Interspace 21/22.
68. Light grey-brown burnished ware, B I 51. Interspace 21/22.
69. Grey granulated ware, B II 41, A.D. 49–75. I, Room 22 (contaminated).
70. Unevenly burnished orange-red ware, grey core, B IV 36, A.D. 60. I, Rooms 26–31. Cf. 162, 167, 183, 266–8, 443–6, 605.
71. Unevenly burnished coarse dark grey ware, T II 39. I, Room 6.
72. Ware as 71. B IV 41A. I, Room 18.
73. Grey-brown burnished ware, B I 51. Interspace 21/22.
74. Partly burnished rather coarse light grey ware, B I 51. Interspace 21/22.
75. Coarse granulated brownish-buff ware, B I 51. Interspace 21/22.
76. Rather granulated light grey burnished ware, A XI 25. I, Room 12, floor. Another in grey-brown ware, A XI 26, A.D. 60. I, wall-trench 9/10. Cf. 172.
77. Rather finely granulated light grey ware, slightly burnished, B IV 35. I, Room 25.
78. Ware as 77. B I 51. Interspace 21/22.
79. Hard dark grey granulated ware, A IV 41, A.D. 60. I, Room 15. Another, in dark blue-grey ware with lighter core, B I 63, A.D. 60–75. Pit 7.
80. Grey granulated ware, B II 42, A.D. 49–75. I, Room 22 (contaminated).

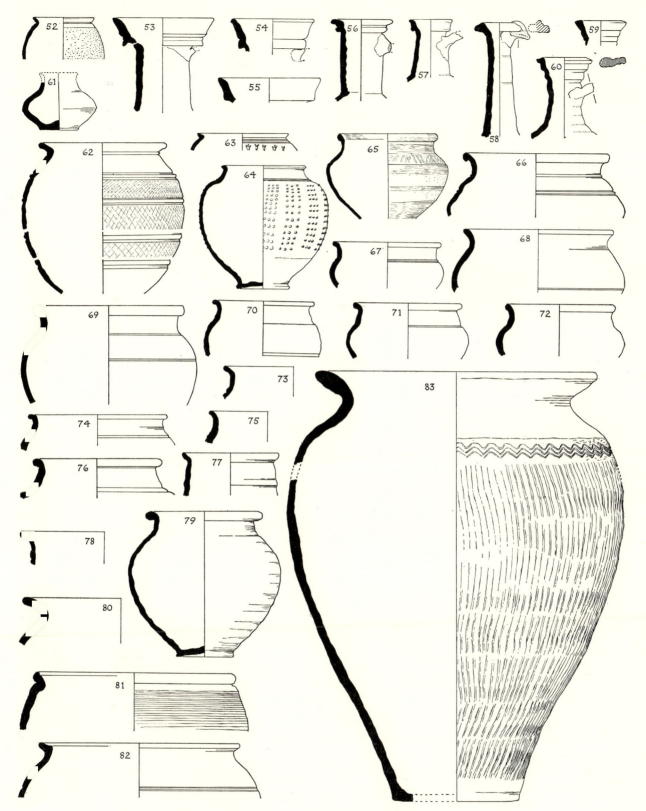

FIG. 101. Pottery vessels nos. 52–83 from deposits down to A.D. 60 ($\frac{1}{4}$).

Jars with internally grooved rims. Cf. 48, 197–9, 390, 481–5, 656–66, 897–909, 1062, 1080.

81. Coarse calcite-gritted ware, burnt red, T XX 37. I, Room 8, floor, Cf. 482, 1050.
82. Dark-grey burnished ware, B II 42, A.D. 49–75. I, Room 22 (contaminated).

Storage jars. Cf. 200–4, 487, 667–8, 912–21, 1243

83. Grooved wavy lines on shoulder, vertical furrowing below; coarse granulated reddish to dark-grey ware, light grey core, B II 40, A.D. 55–60. I, Room 22.

Fig. 102

84. Rather coarse burnished grey-buff ware, T VII 48. I, Room 3.
85. Very coarse granulated grey ware, burnished lines on neck and shoulder, furrowed body, T XX 38, *c.* A.D. 49. I, Room 8, occupation below floor.
86. Very coarse granulated grey-brown ware, unevenly burnished, B IV 41S. I, Room 30.

Bowls

87. Hard rather granulated red-brown ware, grey core, roughly finished, Z I 37. I, Room 4.
88. Rather coarse orange-buff ware, grey core, trace of mica on surfaces, B IV 41S. I, Room 30.
89. Rather coarse grey-brown ware, dark burnished rim, incised wavy line on shoulder, B II 40, A.D. 55–60. I, Room 22. Another in B II 37E, A.D. 75–85 (outside II A, Room 19). Cf. 327.
90. Dark grey rather granulated ware, partly burnished, T XX 31, A.D. 60. I, Room 8, fuel-pit.

Imitation Gallo-Belgic plates

91. Coarse dark grey-brown granulated ware, unevenly burnished inside, and on lower half outside, T VII 46. I. Room 3.
92. Rather coarse dark grey-brown ware, smooth surfaces, burnished on rim, B I 41, A.D. 60–75. II A, Rooms 16–21, burnt daub make-up.

Mortaria (see p. 263 for note on the dates given).

93. Hard cream ware, pink core, grey and red grits; pre-Flavian, south-east Britain or import; T VI 35. I, Room 6, secondary floor.
94. Rim profile too close to spout for accuracy; hard cream ware, grey and white grits; probably Colchester; B IV 36, A.D. 60. I, Rooms 26–31.
95. Hard buff rather finely granulated ware, dark grey and translucent light grits; *c.* A.D. 55–90, Verulamium region; A I 40, A.D. 60. I, Rooms 15–16.
96. Hard rather finely granulated ware burnt pink, dark grey and translucent light grits; Verulamium region; A I 40, A.D. 60. I, Rooms 15–16.
97. Hard yellow-buff ware, light grey core, white, grey, and buff grits; pre-Flavian, source unknown; A I 41. I, Room 15.

Pottery of the general date of Period I, from later layers

98. Mortarium in smooth hard burnt ware, small white and grey grits; pre-Flavian, Kent or Colchester; T III 11, A.D. 155/160. II D, Room 4.
99. Mortarium in finely granulated buff ware, worn; Claudian-Neronian, source unknown; B II 27D, A.D. 140–50. II C, Room 40.
100. Jar with rilled shoulder in rather coarse light grey-brown ware, B I 47, A.D. 105–15. II B, Room 24. Other examples of this type came from T VI 29, A.D. 60 (I, Room 6); A VII 43, *c.* A.D. 60–75 (II A, Room 21, burnt-daub make-up); A II 61, A.D. 75–85 (outside II A, Rooms 12 and 15); A II 58, A.D. 75–105 (outside II A, Rooms 12 and 15); and B I 45, A.D. 75–90 (outside II A, Room 17). Cf. 272, 275.

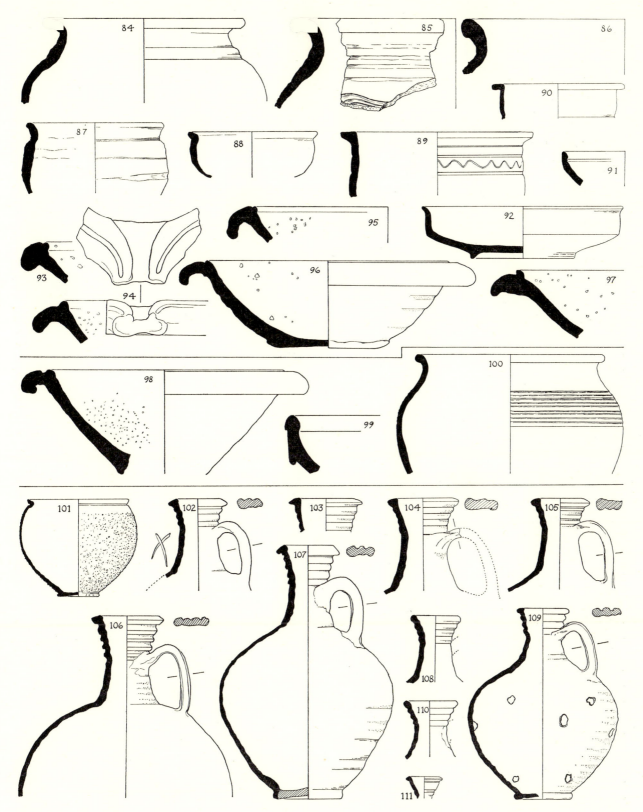

Fig. 102. Pottery vessels from deposits dated A.D. 49–60 (nos. 84–100) and A.D. 60–75 (nos. 101–9) (¼).

II A: POTTERY DATED A.D. 60–75

Fine ware

101. Roughcast beaker in fine hard light reddish paste, dark grey metallic coating, B I 70. Pit 7. Cf. 30–1, 52, 232–3, 396, 555, 780–9, 1070.

Ring-necked flagons. Cf. 238–41, 375–8, 403–10, 559–73, 798–811, 1071–2, 1107.

102. Hard finely granulated buff ware, with graffito on neck opposite the handle, B I 63–70. Pit 7. Another, without graffito, from T VII 36, A.D. 75–85. II A, Room 3.
103. Finely granulated light grey ware, B I 63. Pit 7. Cf. 238.
104. Hard granulated buff ware, B I 70. Pit 7.
105. Hard finely granulated orange-buff ware, B I 70. Pit 7. Another rim from T VII 39, A.D. 75–85, II A, Room 3; and others, residually, from B II 17, A.D. 150–155/160 (II D, Room 42, occupation) and B I 22, A.D. 270–80 (III, make-up (XIV, 5)).
106. Hard rather finely granulated light buff ware, B I 69. Pit 7.
107. Hard granulated yellow-buff ware, B I 63–70. Pit 7.
108. Ware as 107, pinkish-buff, B IV Pit 10. Pit 10.
109. Hard rather finely granulated orange-buff ware, perforated after firing by unevenly spaced rows of holes, one in base, B I 66. Pit 7.
110. Ware as 109. B I 63–70. Pit 7.
111. Fine hard buff ware, perhaps mica-coated, B I 66. Pit 7.

Fig. 103

Other flagons

112. Finely granulated white ware, A VII 43, *c.* A.D. 60–75. II A, Room 21, burnt daub make-up. Cf. 235.
113. Orange-buff granulated ware, B I 70. Pit 7.
114. Hard yellow-buff granulated ware, B I 63–70. Pit 7.

Two-handled flagons

115. Hard finely granulated pinkish-buff ware, B I 70. Pit 7.
116. Hard yellow-buff granulated ware, pink core, B I 63–70. Pit 7.
117. Hard finely granulated pinkish-buff ware, perhaps two-handled, B I 63–70. Pit 7.

Narrow-necked jars. Cf. 245–50, 412–18, 822–35, 1074, 1152–4, 1231–4.

118. Rather coarse orange-brown ware, burnt grey, B I 70. Pit 7.
119. Rather granulated grey-brown burnished ware, resembling Belgic, A X 22. II A, Room 16, burnt daub make-up.
120. Fine light grey burnished ware, B I 63. Pit 7.
121. Grey burnished ware, B I 63. Pit 7.
122. Finely granulated deep buff ware. B I 66. Pit 7.
123. Ware as 122, buff, B I 68. Pit 7.
124. Rather coarse light grey burnished ware, brown on rim, B I 69. Pit 7.

Mica-coated beakers

125. Finely granulated brownish-buff paste, B I 63–70. Pit 7.
126. Very fine pinkish-buff paste, with pattern of barbotine dots, B I 63 and 64. Pit 7.

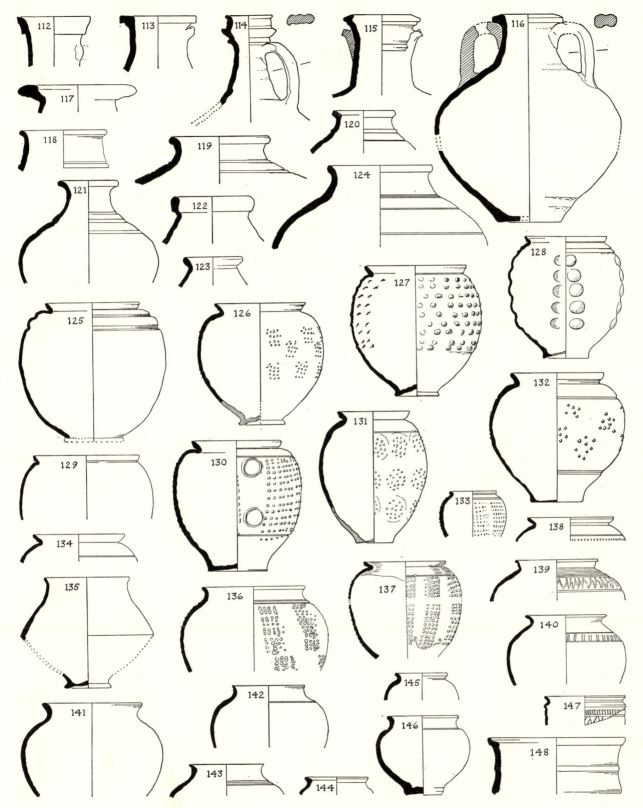

FIG. 103. Pottery vessels nos. 112–48 from deposits dated A.D. 60–75 ($\frac{1}{4}$).

127. Finely granulated brownish-buff paste, with raised bosses in horizontal rows, B I 63–70 (four), Pit 7. Others from A II 56, A.D. 60–75 (Pit 8); A I 33, A.D. 75–105 (II A, Room 12); and, residually, from A II 39, A.D. 105–115 (II B, Room 10). Cf. 947.

128. Fine buff paste, with large raised bosses in vertical rows, B I 64. Pit 7. Sherds of this type from A XI 23, A.D. 75–85 (II A, Room 7); Z I 25, A.D. 85–105 (II A, Room 5); T VII 29, A.D. 85–105 (II A, Room 3) and, residually, from T XX 15, A.D. 105–30 (two) (II B, Room 7); Z I 22, A.D. 130–40 (II C, Room 8); T XX 13, A.D. 140–50 (II C, Room 9); and T XXI 14, A.D. 140–50 (II C, Room 13).

129. Fine hard buff paste B I Pit 7. Pit 7. Cf. 380, 583, 1046, and 836 (indented).

Other beakers

130. Fine burnished cream ware, with panels of barbotine dots alternating with circles, B I 68. Pit 7. Others from B I 66 (Pit 7) and B IV Pit 10 (Pit 10), of the same date.

131. Fine hard burnished light grey ware, with barbotine dots arranged in rows of circles. Pit 7. Others from B I 63 (two), 65, 66 (two), 63–70 all of the same date and pit; from B I 36A, A.D. 85–105, II A, Room 21; and in yellowish-buff ware from A II 55, A.D. 75–150, confused levels collapsing towards a pit in trench B III.

132. Ware as 131. B I 66. Pit 7.

133. Fine hard grey ware, light grey burnished slip, with panels of barbotine dots, B I 65. Pit 7. Cf. 136–7, 255, 424–8, 598–604, 837–9, 1047–9, 1073.

134. Fine hard burnished grey ware. Pit 7.

135. Carinated beaker in fine hard burnished grey ware from B I 66, 67. Pit 7. Others residual in A I 38, A.D. 105–15 (II A, Room 16); B IV 17H, A.D. 130–50 (II C, Room 40). Sherds with a sharper angle in this ware came from T I 19, A.D. 60 (I, Room 18, burnt daub) and, residually, from A I 25, A.D. 130–50 (II C, Room 25). Cf. 419, 581.

136. Light grey finely granulated ware, darker burnished surface or slip, with panels of barbotine dots, B I 63 (two). Pit 7. Another from B I 70, ibid. For comparisons see under 133.

137. Fine hard grey ware, light grey burnished slip on upper part of body, with panels of barbotine dots, B I 64. Pit 7.

138. Fine hard burnished brown-grey ware, rouletted band on shoulder, B I 65. Pit 7.

139. Fine hard burnished grey ware, rouletted pattern on shoulder, B I 66. Pit 7.

140. Ware as 139, incised vertical lines on shoulder, A VI 38. Pit 12.

141. Beaker or jar in hard rather finely granulated light grey ware, darker burnished slip, B I 64. Pit 7. Cf. 164.

142. Beaker or jar in hard finely granulated blue-grey ware, lighter core, burnished slip, B I 70. Pit 7. Another from B IV 31, A.D. 85–105. II A, Room 19.

143. Ware as 142, with lighter slip, B I 63–70. Pit 7.

144. Hard light grey ware, B I 63. Pit 7.

145. Fine hard burnished grey ware, B I 63–70 (two). Pit 7.

146. Hard finely granulated light buff ware, traces of burnished red slip, A VI 38. Pit 12.

147. Slightly micaceous fine hard pinkish-buff ware, rouletted band on shoulder and incised lattice below, B I 49. Occupation and make-up below II A, Room 17. Another from A II 42, A.D. 75–105. Outside II A, Rooms 12–15.

148. Rather coarse burnished grey-black ware, B I 64. Pit 7.

Fig. 104

Jars with burnished or incised shoulder decoration. Cf. 65, 269, 383–5, 431–42, 607–12, 843.

149. Hard roughly burnished dark grey ware, incised diagonal decoration, B IV Pit 10. Pit 10.

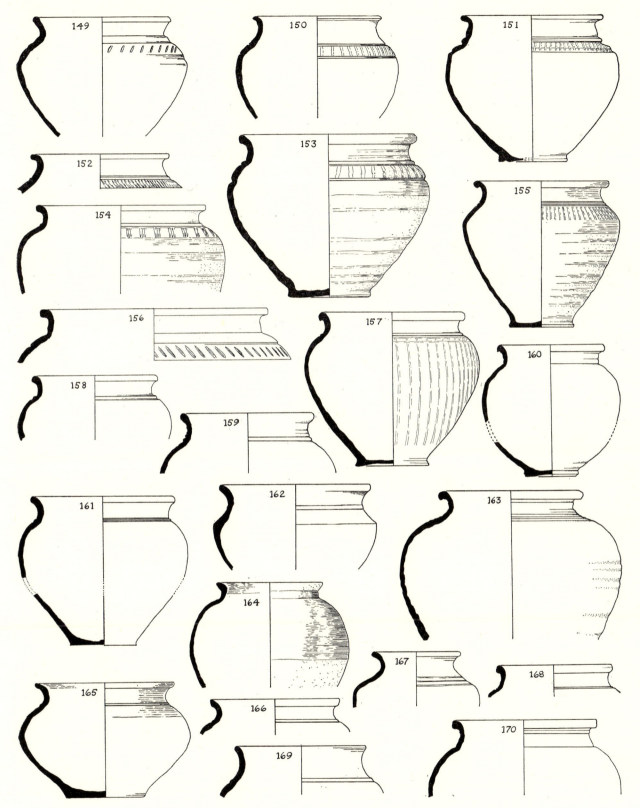

FIG. 104. Pottery vessels nos. 149–70 from deposits dated A.D. 60–75 ($\frac{1}{4}$).

150. Rather coarse dark grey-brown ware, unevenly burnished surface, burnished vertical decoration, B I 70. Pit 7. Another from B I 63, ibid.
151. Ware as 150. B I 66. Pit 7.
152. Ware as 150, with diagonal burnished decoration, B I 63. Pit 7.
153. Hard rather finely granulated grey ware, partly burnished surface, with burnished diagonal decoration, B I 63–70. Pit 7.
154. Light grey ware, orange-brown where the surface is burnished, with vertical burnished decoration, B I 64. Pit 7.
155. Light grey finely granulated ware, partly burnished surface, burnished vertical decoration, B IV Pit 10. Pit 10.
156. Rather finely granulated light grey-brown ware, incised diagonal decoration, B I 70. Pit 7.

Jars

157. Finely granulated dark grey-brown micaceous ware, with smooth surface, burnished on rim, neck, and base, and burnished vertical decoration on body, B I 70. Pit 7. A smaller jar, diameter 10 cm., from B I 64, ibid.
158. Light blue-grey granulated ware, lighter core, B I 62. Pit 7.
159. Hard rather finely granulated grey ware, lighter core and slip. Pit 7.
160. Hard dark grey granulated ware, lighter core, B I 64. Pit 7.
161. Light blue-grey granulated ware, light-grey core, B I 64. Pit 7.
162. Hard rather light grey granulated ware, lighter core, partly burnished surface, B I 63. Pit 7. Another residual in A VI 9, A.D. 130–40 (II C, Room 19). Cf. 70, 167, 183, 266–8, 443–6, 605.
163. Hard light grey rather finely granulated ware, B IV Pit 10. Pit 10. Another from B I 64. Pit 7.
164. Rather finely granulated grey ware, darker burnished slip, B I 64. Pit 7. Cf. 141.
165. Light grey-brown ware, with dark, partly burnished surface, B I 63 (two). Pit 7.
166. Smooth hard burnished grey ware, A VII 43, c. A.D. 60–75. II A, burnt-daub make-up of Room 21.
167. Light grey burnished ware, B I 68. Pit 7. For comparisons see under 162.
168. Hard finely granulated grey ware. Pit 7.
169. Rather coarse grey-brown ware, darker burnished surface, B II Pit 11. Pit 11.
170. Hard rather finely granulated buff ware, B I 63–70. Pit 7. Cf. 458–62, 469, 634–5, 645–55, 871–81, 1061, 1077–8, 1109.

Fig. 105
171. Orange-buff finely granulated ware, partly burnished, B I 67. Pit 7.
172. Pinkish-buff rather finely granulated ware, burnt grey, B I 69, 70, 71. Pit 7. Cf. No. 76.
173. Ware as 172. B I 63. Pit 7.
174. Grey granulated ware, B I 65. Pit 7. Another residual in B II 28G, A.D. 130–50. (II C, Room 32).
175, 176, 177. Hard finely granulated grey ware. Pit 7.
178. Grey ware, B I 63. Pit 7. Cf. 292.
179. Light grey granulated ware, burnished, B IV Pit 10. Pit 10. Others from B I 63, A.D. 60–75 (Pit 7), B I 38, A.D. 85–105 (II A, outside Room 17), and residual in A II 39, A.D. 105–15 (II B, Room 10), and B I 14A, fourth century.
180. Rather coarse light grey ware, darker surface, B I 66. Pit 7.
181. Finely granulated pinkish-buff ware, dark blue-grey surface, B I 64. Pit 7.
182. Hard light grey ware, B I 68. Pit 7.

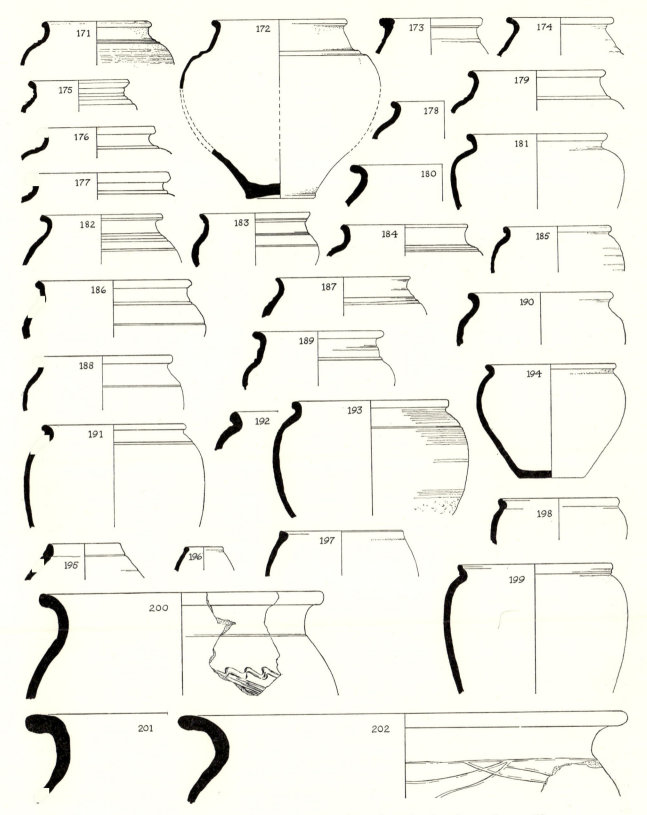

FIG. 105. Pottery vessels nos. 171–202 from deposits dated A.D. 60–75 (¼).

183. Rather finely granulated dark grey ware, smooth surface, B I 69. Pit 7. Cf. 70, 162, 167, 266–8, 443–6, 605.
184. Light grey rather finely granulated ware, B I 65. Pit 7. Others from B I 62, B I 64 (Pit 7 (two)); A IV 42, A.D. 75–105 (accumulation outside II A, Rooms 7–12); T VII 29, A.D. 85–105 (II A, Room 3); and residual in A VII 28, A.D. 105–30 (II B, Room 17).
185. Coarse granulated dark grey ware B I 64. Pit 7.
186. Rather coarse but finely granulated dark grey-brown ware, unevenly burnished, similar to Belgic fabric and probably residual, B I 68. Pit 7.
187. Grey-brown unevenly burnished ware, B I 63. Pit 7. Perhaps residual.
188. Ware as 187 but darker, B I 70 (two). Pit 7. Cf. 303.
189. Rather coarse light brownish-grey ware, darker burnished surface, B I 70. Pit 7.
190. Coarse dark grey-brown unevenly burnished ware, B I 70 (two). Pit 7.
191. Coarse dark grey granulated ware, burnished rim, B I 70. Pit 7.
192. Grey-buff granulated ware, one burnt or fired red; diameter 20 cm., A IV 39 (two). II A, Room 7, burnt daub make-up.
193. Coarse dark grey to reddish ware, slight rilling on body, burnished rim, B I 65. Pit 7.
194. Rather coarse granulated light grey to reddish ware, B I 63. Pit 7.
195. Finely granulated burnished buff ware, B I 64 and 69. Pit 7.
196. Ware as 195. B I 63. Pit 7.

Jars with internally grooved rims. Cf. 48, 81–2, 390, 481–5, 656–66, 897–909, 1062, 1080.
197. Rather finely granulated light buff ware, B I 66. Pit 7.
198. Rather coarse brownish-buff ware, B I 63. Pit 7. Another from T I 14, A.D. 60 (I, Room 18).
199. Buff calcite-gritted ware, B I 68. Pit 7. For calcite-gritted parallels, cf. 81, 482, 666, 1050.

Storage jars. Cf. 83–6, 487, 667–8, 912–21, 1243.
200. Very coarse granulated grey-brown ware, unevenly burnished, with diagonal furrowing below scored wavy lines, B I 51C. II A, Room 17, make-up.
201. Ware as 200; diameter 57 cm., B I 71. Pit 7.
202. Ware as 200, with burnished shoulder-decoration, B IV Pit 10. Pit 10.

Fig. 106
203. Ware as 200. B I 71. Pit 7.
204. Rather coarse grey-buff ware, darker surface, unevenly burnished rim and shoulder, scored decoration below, B I 66. Pit 7.

Bowls with plain wide rims. Cf. 326–31, 488–502, 691–3.
205. Hard dark blue-grey granulated ware, lighter core, B I 65. Pit 7. This is the same type as 331.
206. Hard light-grey ware, B I 69. Pit 7.

Other bowls
207. Slightly granulated burnished dark grey ware, B I 71. Pit 7.
208. Rather soft and finely granulated buff ware, B I 63–70. Pit 7.
209. Pinkish-buff ware, cream surface, B I 63–70. Pit 7.
210. Fine cream ware, with rouletting on body, B I 63–70. Pit 7.

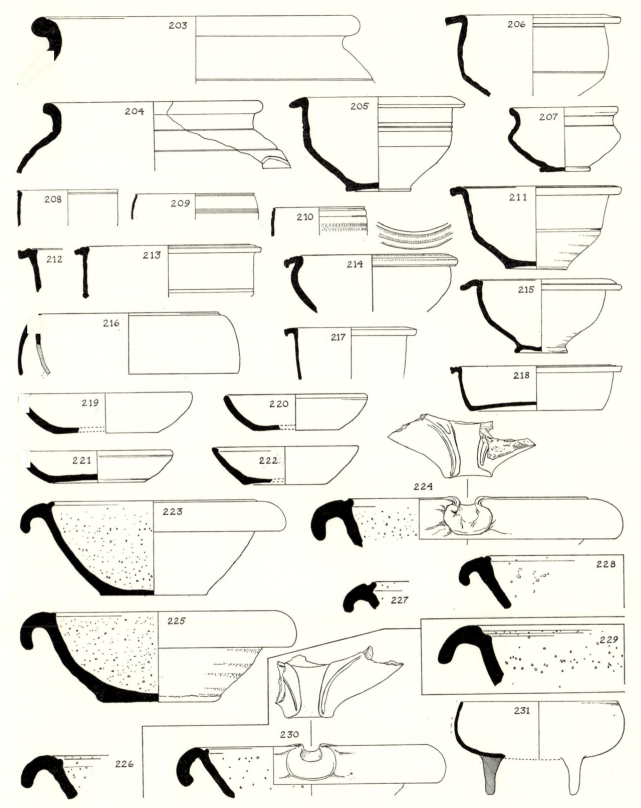

FIG. 106. Pottery vessels nos. 203–31 from deposits dated A.D. 60–75 (¼).

Reeded-rim bowls. Cf. 332–42, 393–5, 503–13, 669–89, 926–40.

211. Hard grey granulated ware, B I 70. Pit 7.
212. Hard finely granulated grey ware; diameter 24 cm., B I 63. Pit 7.
213. Hard finely granulated buff ware, B I 71. Pit 7.
214. Rather coarse dark grey-brown burnished ware, with rouletted rim. Pit 7.

Mica-coated bowls. Cf. 231, 312–4, 516, 693, 947–50.

215. Fine hard light grey-buff paste, burnished surface, probably with mica worn off, B I 63. Pit 7. Two others, with mica, from B I 67, ibid.
216. Fine hard pinkish-buff paste, grey core, B I 63–70. Pit 7.
217. Ware as 216. B I 64. Pit 7.

Dishes with plain rims. Cf. 346–9, 526–30, 736–41, 992–8, 1066, 1093, 1112, 1129, 1178–81, 1198, 1219–21, 1265–74

218. Mica-coated grey ware. Pit 7. Others from B I 63–70 of the same date, ibid.; B II 37E, A.D. 75–85 (outside II A, Room 19), and residually from A II 12 and B I 27X, both A.D. 150–155/160 (II D, Rooms 20 and 26).
219. Hard rather finely granulated blue-grey ware, B I 63. Pit 7.
220. Ware as 219, with lighter core, B I 63. Pit 7.
221. Grey granulated ware, burnished inside and on rim, B I 64. Pit 7.
222. Coarse, unevenly burnished, granulated dark grey-brown ware, A VI 38. Pit 12.

Mortaria made in the Verulamium region (see p. 263 for note on the dates given).

223. Hard finely granulated buff ware, smoothed surface, white and grey grits; Flavian; B I 63. Pit 7.
224. Hard rather finely granulated pinkish-buff ware, with white, grey, and reddish grits; Flavian; B I 63 and 70. Pit 7.
225. Hard orange-buff granulated ware, with white, black, and grey grits; Flavian; B I 63. Another from B I 66. Pit 7.
226. Hard rather finely granulated buff ware, white and dark grey grits; Flavian; A X 22. II A, Room 16, burnt daub make-up.
227. Ware as 226; Flavian; Pit 7.
228. Ware as 226; Flavian; A X 22. II A, Room 16, burnt daub make-up.
229. Ware as 226; A.D. 70–90; B II 41, A.D. 49–75. I, Room 22 (contaminated).

Pots from B I 67, mixed levels at the top of Pit 7 following a collapse of the section (i.e. not all certainly deriving from its original filling).

230. Mortarium with rim in the style of Devalus; hard buff granulated ware, white and grey grits; Flavian, Verulamium region; B I 67.
231. Tripod bowl in mica-coated fine pinkish-buff ware, B I 67.

PERIOD II A: POTTERY FROM LAYERS DATED A.D. 75–105

Fig. 107

Fine ware

232. Roughcast beaker in fine hard white paste, yellow-brown slightly metallic coating, A VI 35, A.D. 75–85. II A, Room 11. Another from T XX 18, A.D. 110–20 (II B, Room 7). Cf. 30, 31, 52, 101, 396, 555, 780–9, 1070.

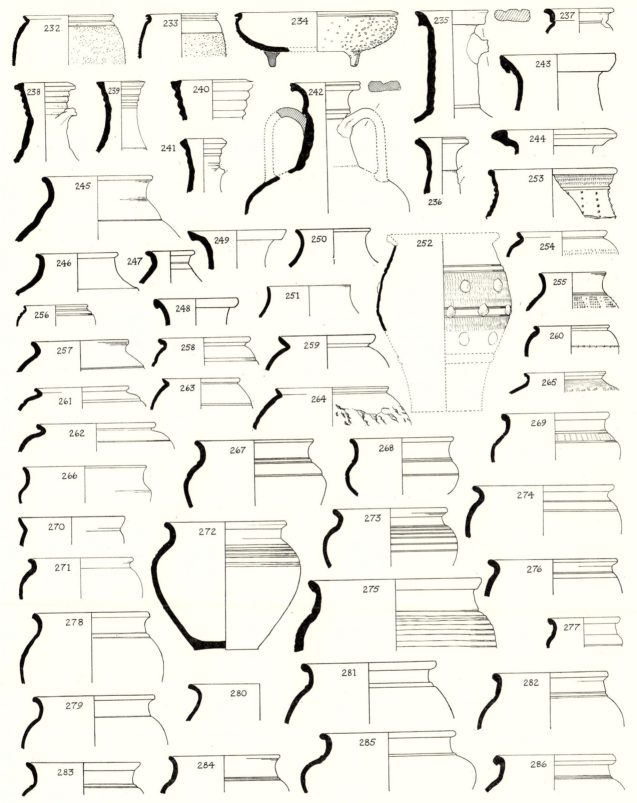

FIG. 107. Pottery vessels nos. 232–86 from deposits dated A.D. 75–105 (¼).

233. Roughcast beaker in fine hard buff paste, black coating, B II 32 E, A.D. 90–105. Outside II A, Room 19. A similar beaker with orange paste, dark grey coating, residual in A II 7, fourth century (III, timber wall-trench (XIV, 5)).
234. Roughcast tripod bowl in fine hard pinkish-buff paste, orange to brown coating, slightly metallic inside, A II 61, A.D. 75–85. Outside II A, Rooms 12–15.

Flagons

235. Hard rather finely granulated buff ware, A I 37, A.D. 85–105. II A, Room 16. Another from A IV 42, A.D. 75–105 (outside II A, Room 7). Cf. 112.
236. Hard orange-buff granulated ware, A II 42, A.D. 75–105. Outside II A, Room 12.
237. Hard finely granulated buff ware, T III 26, A.D. 75–85. II A, Room 2.

Ring-necked flagons. Cf. 102–11, 375–8, 403–10, 559–73, 798–811, 1071–2, 1107.

238. Hard pinkish-buff finely granulated ware, B I 36A, A.D. 85–105. II A, Room 21.
239. Hard yellow-buff rather finely granulated ware, B I 45, A.D. 75–90. Outside II A, Room 17.
240. Ware as 239. Z I 29, A.D. 75–85. II A, Room 5.
241. Ware as 239. B I 36A, A.D. 85–105. II A, Room 21.

Two-handled flagons

242. Hard pinkish-buff granulated ware, B II 37E, A.D. 75–85. Outside II A, Room 19.
243. Hard finely granulated burnished buff ware, perhaps a two-handled type, T III 25, A.D. 85–105. II A, Room 2.
244. Hard rather finely granulated buff ware, perhaps a two-handled type, B I 38, A.D. 85–105. Outside II A, Room 17. Another residual in T II 8, A.D. 155/160 (II D, Room 25A).

Narrow-necked jars. Cf. 118–24, 412–18, 822–35, 1074, 1152–4, 1231–4.

245. Rather coarse light grey-brown ware, unevenly burnished, B I 36A, A.D. 85–105. II A, Room 21.
246. Finely granulated grey-brown burnished ware, A VI 35, A.D. 75–85. II A, Room 11.
247. Grey ware. B II 32E, A.D. 90–105. Outside II A, Room 19.
248. Dark grey granulated ware with traces of lighter slip, B II 31E, A.D. 90–105. Outside II A, Room 19.
249. Fine hard light grey ware, slightly burnished black surface, B I 38, A.D. 85–105. Outside II A, Room 17.
250. Fine hard light grey ware, B II 37E, A.D. 75–85. Outside II A, Room 19. Another from B I 35A, A.D. 105–15 (II B, Room 26).

Beakers and small jars

251. Carinated beaker in fine burnished grey-brown micaceous ware, T XXI 24, A.D. 85–105. II A, Room 11, secondary occupation.
252. Buff beaker in rather soft orange-buff ware, grey core, with rouletted body and rows of applied bosses, T III 27, A.D. 85–105. II A, Room 1.
253. Carinated beaker in fine hard burnished light grey ware, with rouletted neck, and vertical rows of applied dots on body, B I 38, A.D. 85–105. Outside II A, Room 17.
254. Beaker in fine hard grey ware, burnished rim and shoulder, with light rouletting on body, A X 19, A.D. 85–105. II A, Room 16. Cf. 422–3.

255. Poppyhead beaker in fine hard light grey burnished ware, B II 32G, A.D. 85–105. Outside II A, Room 17. Cf. 133, 136–7, 424–8, 598–604, 837–9, 1047–9, 1073.
256. Beaker or jar in fine hard burnished light grey ware, B IV 32, A.D. 75–90. II A, Room 19.
257. As 256. A II 42, A.D. 75–105. Outside II A, Rooms 12–15.
258. As 256. B IV 31, A.D. 85–105, II A, Room 19.
259. As 256. B II 36A, A.D. 75–85. II A, Room 21.
260. Fine hard brownish-buff ware, with applied dots set in a shallow groove, B II 32E, A.D. 90–105. Outside II A, Room 19.
261. Fine hard burnished pinkish-buff ware, B I 45, A.D. 75–90. Outside II A, Room 17.
262. Hard rather finely granulated blue-grey ware, partly burnished, T VII 29, A.D. 85–105. II A, room 3.
263. Slightly burnished black ware, B I 38, A.D. 85–105. Outside II A, Room 17.
264. Rusticated beaker in dark grey granulated ware, A II 42, A.D. 75–105. Outside II A, Rooms 12–15.

Jars

265. Fine dark grey burnished ware, with finely rilled shoulder and scored decoration below, T III 27, A.D. 85–105. II A, Room 1. Cf. 694.
266. Fine hard light grey ware, darker burnished slip, B I 38, A.D. 85–105. Outside II A, Room 17. Cf. 70, 162, 167, 183, 443–6, 605.
267. Coarse dark grey burnished ware, B II 37E, A.D. 75–85. Outside II A, Room 19.
268. As 267 but finer. B IV 29A, A.D. 75–90. II A, Room 21. For comparisons see under 266.
269. Hard finely granulated grey-black burnished ware, reddish core, with burnished lines on shoulder, B IV 33, A.D. 49–75 (?) Outside II A, Room 19: see note on no. 363. Cf. 65, 149–56, 383–5, 431–42, 607–12, 843.
270. Grey burnished ware, B II 32E, A.D. 90–105. Outside II A, Room 19.
271. Rather finely granulated dark grey ware, reddish-buff core, A VI 31, A.D. 85–105. II A, Room 10.
272. Coarse granulated dark grey-brown ware, B II 37E, A.D. 75–85. Outside II A, Room 19. Cf. 100.
273. Light grey ware with darker surface, A II 62, A.D. 75–85. Outside II A, Rooms 12–15. Another from T XX 13, A.D. 140–50 (II C, Room 9), perhaps residual.
274. Rather finely granulated light grey ware, B I 36A, A.D. 85–105. II A, Room 21.
275. Coarse granulated grey-brown ware, burnished rim and neck, A VI 35, A.D. 75–85. II A, Room 11. Cf. 100.
276. Finely granulated dark grey ware, B II 32E, A.D. 90–105. Outside II A, Room 19.
277. Fine hard burnished light grey ware, B IV Pit 8, A.D. 75–105. Pit 2.
278. Dark blue-grey granulated ware, lighter core, B I 38X, A.D. 85–105. Outside II A, Room 17.
279. Hard burnished grey ware, B II 37E, A.D. 75–85. Outside II A, Room 19.
280. Ware as 279. A VI 31, A.D. 85–105. II A, Room 10.
281. Finely granulated dark grey ware, B II 32E, A.D. 90–105. Outside II A, Room 19.
282. Buff granulated ware, B II 32E, A.D. 90–105, ibid.
283. Light grey burnished ware, B II 32E, A.D. 90–105, ibid.
284. Dark grey burnished ware, B II 37E, A.D. 75–85, ibid.
285. Rather coarse burnished grey ware, B IV 29D, A.D. 75–105. II A, Room 22. Others from B I 51, A.D. 49–60 (I, Interspace 21/22); B I 70, A.D. 60–75 (Pit 7); A II 42, A.D. 75–105 (outside II A, Rooms 12–15); T XX 18, A.D. 110–20 (II B, Room 7); B IV 21B, A.D. 105–15 (II B, Room 34); and residual in T VI 21, A.D. 130–40 (II C, Room 4); B II 17, A.D. 150–155/160 (II D, Room 42).
286. Light grey granulated ware, B I 36A, A.D. 85–105. II A, Room 21.

Fig. 108

287. Hard rather finely granulated buff ware, T III 27, A.D. 85–105. II A, Room 1.

288. Ware as 287. A I 37, A.D. 85–105. II A, Room 16.

289. Grey granulated ware, B II 37E, A.D. 75–85. Outside II A, Room 19. Others from B IV Pit 10 (Pit 10); B I 70 (Pit 7); both A.D. 60–75.

290. As 289. A XI 23B, A.D. 75–85. II A, Room 7.

291. Hard rather finely granulated light grey ware, T III 26, A.D. 76–85. II A, Room 2.

292. Coarse granulated dark grey ware, A VI 31, A.D. 85–105. II A, Room 10. Cf. 178.

293. Coarse grey ware, B II 37E, A.D. 75–85. Outside II A, Room 19.

294. Rather coarse burnished grey ware, A IV 42, A.D. 75–105. Outside II A, Room 7.

295. Coarse, unevenly burnished grey-brown granulated ware, A IV 38, A.D. 75–85. II A, Room 7.

296. Coarse granulated dark grey ware, with graffito SAX (p. 364) B II 37E, A.D. 75–85. Outside II A, Room 19.

297. Ware as 296, grey-brown, B I 38, A.D. 85–105. Outside II A, Room 17.

298. Finely granulated buff ware, B I 38A, A.D. 75–105. II A, Room 21.

299. Hard granulated buff ware, A IV 34, A.D. 85–105. II A, Room 7.

300. Ware as 299. B II 36A, A.D. 85–105. II A, Room 21.

301. Coarse granulated grey-brown ware, B IV 29A, A.D. 75–90. II A, Room 21, perhaps residual. Others from B IV 37S, A.D. 49–60 (I, Room 30); A II 56, A.D. 60–75 (Pit 8); B I 36A, A.D. 85–105 (II A, Room 21); and residual in B II 28A, A.D. 115–30 (II B, Room 26), and A II 19, A.D. 140–50 (II C, Path 26).

302. Rather coarse grey-brown ware, burnished rim and shoulder, B I 48, A.D. 85–105. Outside II A, Room 17.

303. As 302. A I 37, A.D. 85–105. II A, Room 16. A similar jar in thinner ware from A I 27, A.D. 105–30 (II B, Room 16). Cf. 188.

304. Coarse granulated dark grey-brown ware, burnished rim and shoulder, A X 19, A.D. 85–105. II A, Room 16. Perhaps, like 301, residual.

305. Hard dark grey ware, B I 48, A.D. 85–105. Outside II A, Room 17.

306. Buff granulated ware, B II 32F, A.D. 75–105. II A, Room 17.

307. Coarse grey ware with reeded rim, B II 37E, A.D. 75–85. Outside II A, Room 19.

Storage jar

308. Very coarse granulated grey-brown ware, unevenly burnished rim and neck, with multiple scored wavy lines between horizontal and vertical furrowing, B IV 32, A.D. 75–90. II A, Room 19.

Tazze. Cf. 705, 922–5.

309. Hard rather finely granulated buff ware, smoked grey inside, A IV 40, A.D. 75–105. Outside II A, Room 7.

310. Ware as 309. B II 30B, A.D. 75–105. II A, Room 20.

311. Ware as 309. B IV 30C, A.D. 75–105. II A, Room 20.

Mica-coated bowls. Cf. 215–18, 516, 693, 947–50.

312. Orange-buff paste, grey core, A XI 20, A.D. 85–105. II A, Room 7.

313. As 312. B II 30C, A.D. 75–105. II A, Room 20.

314. Fine reddish-buff paste, A I 37, A.D. 85–105. II A, Room 16.

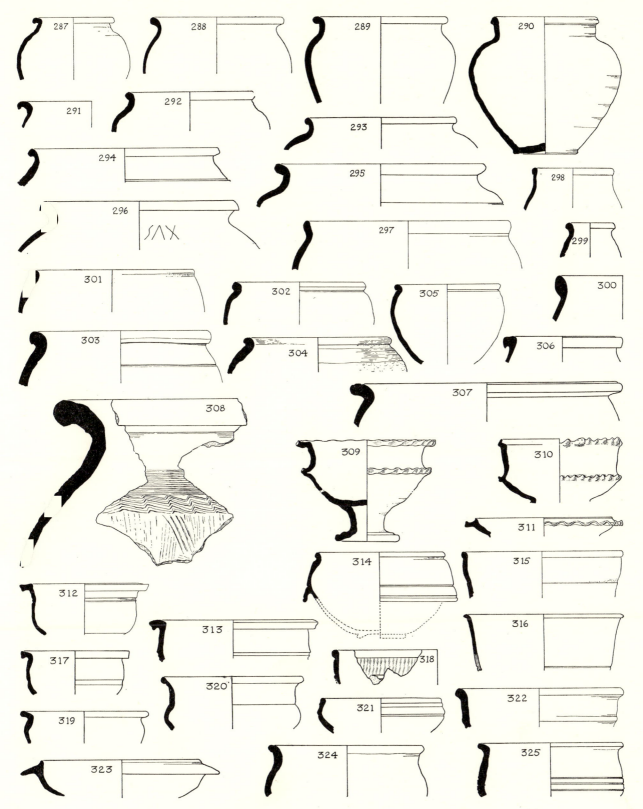

Fig. 108. Pottery vessels nos. 287–325 from deposits dated A.D. 75–105 (¼).

Bowls

315. Finely granulated pinkish-buff ware, B I 38, A.D. 85–105. Outside II A, Room 17.
316. Hard finely granulated buff ware, burnished orange slip, B II 32E, A.D. 90–105. Outside II A, Room 19. Cf. 517.
317. Hard rather finely granulated blue-grey ware, lighter core, A XI 19, A.D. 85–105. II A, Room 7.
318. Bowl imitating samian form 37, in fine burnished dark grey ware, reddish core, with rouletted neck, T III 25, A.D. 85–105. II A, Room 2. Cf. 523, 694, and 265 (jar).
319. Dark grey burnished ware, T III 25, A.D. 85–105. II A, Room 2.
320. Dark grey-brown burnished ware, A XII 27, A.D. 75–85. II A, Room 9.
321. Hard grey burnished ware, A II 42, A.D. 75–105. Outside II A, Rooms 12–15.
322. Buff ware, B II Pit 10, A.D. 75–105. Unnumbered pit outside II A, Room 17.
323. Fine hard light grey ware, burnished inside and on rim and flange, A IV 33, A.D. 85–105. II A, Room 7.
324. Rather coarse grey-brown burnished ware, A IV 42, A.D. 75–105. Outside II A, Room 7.
325. Coarse granulated grey-brown ware, burnished lip, A IV 42, A.D. 75–105. Outside II A, Room 7.

Fig. 109

Bowls with plain wide rims. Cf. 205–6, 488–502, 691–3.

326. Rather coarse burnished dark grey-brown ware, B I 48, A.D. 85–105. Outside II A, Room 17.
327. Orange-grey burnished ware, B II 37E, A.D. 75–85. Outside II A, Room 19. Cf. 89.
328. Hard light grey burnished ware, B I 38, A.D. 85–105. Outside II A, Room 17. Others from B II 32G of the same date (outside II A, Room 17), and residual in B I 28C, A.D. 150–155/160 (II D, Room 33).
329. Ware as 328. A I 37, A.D. 85–105. II A, Room 16.
330. Hard dark blue-grey finely granulated ware, lighter core, partly burnished, A IV 33, A.D. 85–105. II A, Room 7. Others from Z I 26, A.D. 85–105 (two), and Z I 27, A.D. 75–105, all II A, Room 5.
331. Hard dark blue-grey granulated ware, lighter core, B II 37E (three), A.D. 75–85. Outside II A, Room 19. Others from B IV 32, A.D. 75–90 (II A, Room 19); B II 36E, A.D. 85–105 (outside II A, Room 19); A XI 14, A.D. 105–30 (II B, Room 12); and residual in B IV 7, A.D. 150–155/160 (II D, Room 40). This is the same type as 205.

Reeded-rim bowls. Cf. 211–13, 393–5, 503–13, 669–89, 926–40.

332. Hard finely granulated grey ware, lighter core, B IV 31, A.D. 85–105. II A, Room 19.
333. Ware as 332, blue-grey. A XI 20, A.D. 85–105. II A, Room 7.
334. Ware as 333. B IV 31, A.D. 85–105. II A, Room 19.
335. Ware as 332. B IV 31, A.D. 85–105. II A, Room 19.
336. Light grey granulated ware, B II 32G, A.D. 85–105. Outside II A, Room 17.
337. Dark grey granulated ware, B IV 29A, A.D. 75–90. II A, Room 21.
338. Ware as 337, burnished below carination, B I 36A, A.D. 85–105. II A, Room 21.
339. Grey-brown rather finely granulated ware, A VI 31, A.D. 85–105. II A, Room 10.
340. Orange-buff granulated ware, B I 38, A.D. 85–105. Outside II A, Room 17.
341. Hard buff granulated ware, B II 32E, A.D. 90–105. Outside II A, Room 19.
342. Ware as 341. A IV 26, A.D. 85–105. II A, Room 7.
343. Bowl or dish with slightly beaded and flanged rim in hard grey-buff rather granulated ware, T VII 35, A.D. 85–105. II A, Room 3. Cf. 515, 728, 965, 1084, 1260, 1287.

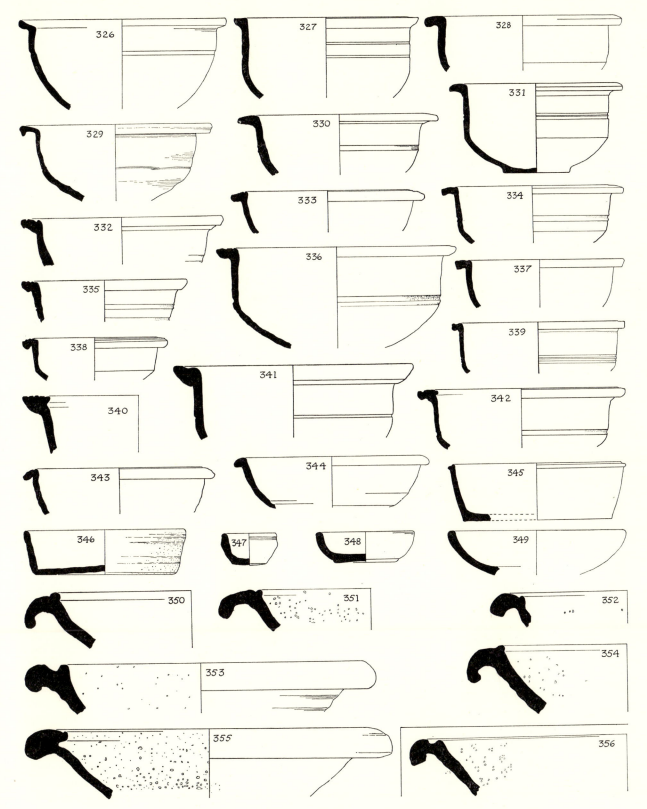

FIG. 109. Pottery vessels nos. 326–56 from deposits dated A.D. 75–105 ($\frac{1}{4}$).

Dishes

344. Buff granulated ware, smooth burnished surfaces, B II 32E, A.D. 90–105. Outside II A, Room 19. Cf. 724–7, 952–4, 1063–5, 1082–6, 1177, 1215, 1262–4.

345. Dark grey granulated ware, lighter core, B I 38X, A.D. 85–105. Outside II A, Room 17. Another from B I 63, A.D. 60–75. Pit 7.

Dishes with plain rims. Cf. 219–22, 526–30, 736–41, 992–8, 1066, 1093, 1112, 1129, 1178–81, 1198, 1219–21, 1265–74.

346. Hard rather finely granulated yellow-buff ware, with lines of burnishing, B II 32B, A.D. 75–105. II A, Room 20.

347. Coarse granulated grey-brown ware, roughly made, cf. crucibles, A IV 33, A.D. 85–105. II A, Room 7.

348. Blue-grey granulated ware, lighter core, B IV 29A, A.D. 75–90. II A, Room 21. A smaller dish in this ware, diameter 7·2 cm., from B IV 21A, A.D. 105–15. II B, Room 26.

349. Dark grey burnished ware, B I 38, A.D. 85–105. Outside II A, Room 17.

Mortaria (see p. 263 for note on the dates given)

350. Smooth hard buff ware, cream slip; Flavian, Colchester or Kent; A VI 33, A.D. 75–105. II A, Room 10.

351. Hard cream ware, grey and white grits; Flavian, Colchester or Kent; A X 19, A.D. 85–105. II A, Room 16.

352. Smooth buff ware, grey grits; late first, or second century; south-east Britain, possibly Kent; A II 42, A.D. 75–105. Outside II A, Rooms 12–15.

353. Smooth hard pinkish-buff ware, white grits; c. A.D. 70–110, Bushe-Fox 26–30, south-east Britain; B I 38, A.D. 85–105. Outside II A, Room 17. Cf. 533, 743.

354. Smooth hard orange-buff ware, grey and white grits; Flavian, south-east Britain or import; A VI 36, A.D. 75–105. IIA, Room 10.

355. Hard buff ware, grey and a few reddish grits; late first to early second century, probably south-east Britain; B II 32G, A.D. 85–105. Outside II A, Room 17.

356. Smooth hard buff ware, grey and white grits; A.D. 70–120, almost certainly Kent; not from this group but residual in Z I 2, Antonine fire. II D, Room 8.

Fig. 110

Mortaria made in the Verulamium region

357. Hard rather finely granulated buff ware, grey and white grits; pre- or early Flavian; T II 26, A.D. 95–105. II A, Room 11, occupation on layer 27.

358. Hard yellow-buff granulated ware, grey and white grits; A.D. 70–110; Z I 26, A.D. 85–105. II A, Room 5.

359. Ware as 358; stamp VIANVACAE (counterstamp of ALBINVS), A.D. 65–95, probably second half of this period; A VI 31, A.D. 85–105. II A, Room 10. Cf. 365, 545–6. See p. 371.

360. Ware as 358; Flavian; A VI 31, A.D. 85–105. II A, Room 10.

361. Ware as 358; diameter 14·5 cm., pre-Flavian; A VI 35, A.D. 75–85. II A, Room 11. Another, also residual in B I 9, A.D. 310–15.

362. Hard rather finely granulated buff ware, grey, brown, and white grits; Flavian; T III 25, A.D. 85–105. II A, Room 2.

363. Ware as 362; A.D. 70–90; B IV 33, A.D. 49–75(?). Outside II A, Room 19; layer 33 appeared to be of Period I (see fig. 27) but not sealed by burnt debris; the vessel was presumably trodden in.

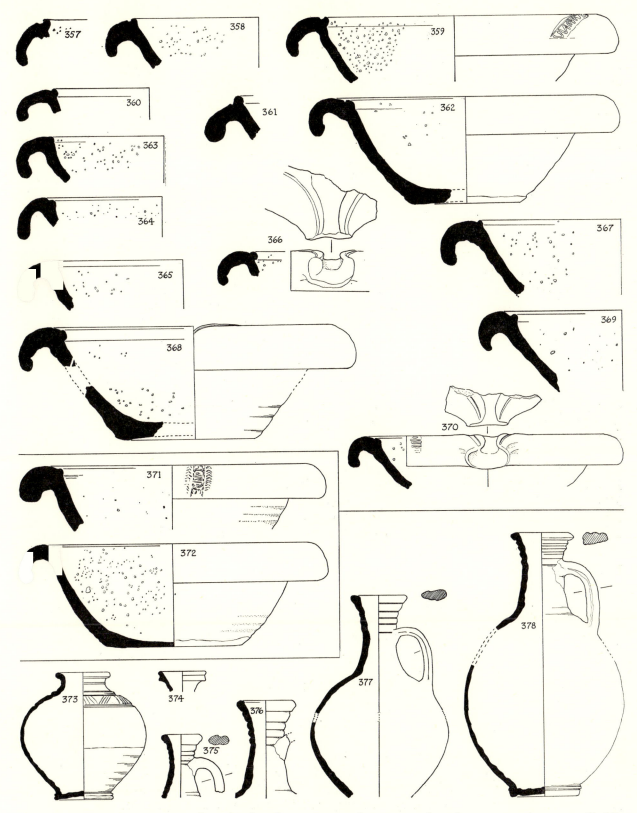

FIG. 110. Pottery vessels from deposits dated A.D. 75–105 (nos. 357–72) and *c*. A.D. 105 (nos. 373–8) ($\frac{1}{4}$).

364. Ware as 362; A.D. 70–95; A II 42, A.D. 75–105. Outside II A, Rooms 12–15.
365. Ware as 362; stamp F.LVGVDV (counterstamp of ALBINVS), A.D. 65–95; T VII 36, A.D. 75–85. II A, Room 3. Cf. 359, 545–6. See p. 371.
366. Hard yellow-buff granulated ware, brown, grey, and white grits; Flavian; A VI 31, A.D. 85–105. II A, Room 10.
367. Hard rather finely granulated buff ware, smoothed surface, white and grey grits; A.D. 70–95; B I 38, A.D. 85–105. Outside II A, Room 17.
368. Hard granulated buff ware, white, grey, and brown grits; A.D. 70–100; B I 45, A.D. 85–105. Outside II A, Room 17.
369. As 368; A.D. 70–110; A VI 30, A.D. 75–105. II A, Room 10.
370. Hard buff finely granulated ware, grey and white grits; illiterate stamp, A.D. 95–135; Z I 26, A.D. 85–105. II A, Room 5.

Mortaria residual in later layers

371. Hard rather finely granulated orange-buff ware, grey grits; stamp SECVNDVS, A.D. 65–95, Verulamium region; A II 26, A.D. 130–50. II C, Room 22. See pp. 378–9.
372. Hard rather finely granulated buff ware, grey, white, and reddish grits (burnt); A.D. 65–95, Verulamium region; V XXXII 11, c. A.D. 150. II D, Room 2, make-up.

POTTERY FROM LAYERS DATED c. A.D. 105

373. Narrow-necked jar in hard dark grey ware, buff core, lighter burnished slip on upper part, with burnished diagonal lines on shoulder, B II Pit 9. Pit 9.
374. Flagon, in hard burnished dark grey ware, A II 47. II B, Room 14, make-up.

Ring-necked flagons. Cf. 102–11, 238–41, 403–10, 559–73, 798–811, 1071–2, 1107.

375. Hard buff rather finely granulated ware, B II Pit 9. Pit 9.
376. Hard buff granulated ware, B II Pit 9. Pit 9.
377. Ware as 376, smoothed near base, B II Pit 9. Pit 9.
378. Hard rather finely granulated orange-buff ware, smoothed near base, B II Pit 9. Pit 9.

Fig. 111
Beakers

379. Poppyhead beaker in hard burnished grey ware, lighter slip to bottom of decoration, B II Pit 9. Pit 9.
380. Mica-coated beaker in fine reddish-buff paste, A I 29. II B, make-up for Room 22A. Another from A X 17, A.D. 85–105 (II A, Room 16). Cf. 129, 583, 1046, and 836 (indented).

Jars with burnished lattice decoration. Cf. 429, 430, 613–22, 624, 845–56, 1125, 1155, 1187.

381. Hard grey-brown burnished ware, with light grey slip to bottom of lattice, B II Pit 9. Pit 9.
382. As 381. B II Pit 9. Pit 9.

Jars with burnished shoulder-decoration. Cf. 65, 149–56, 269, 383–5, 431–42, 607–12, 843.

383. Hard finely granulated grey ware, burnished lighter slip on upper half, B II Pit 9. Pit 9.
384. Ware as 383. B II Pit 9. Pit 9. Two more from T III 24, A.D. 115–30 (II B, Room 2).
385. Hard finely granulated dark grey ware, upper half burnished, B II Pit 9. Pit 9.

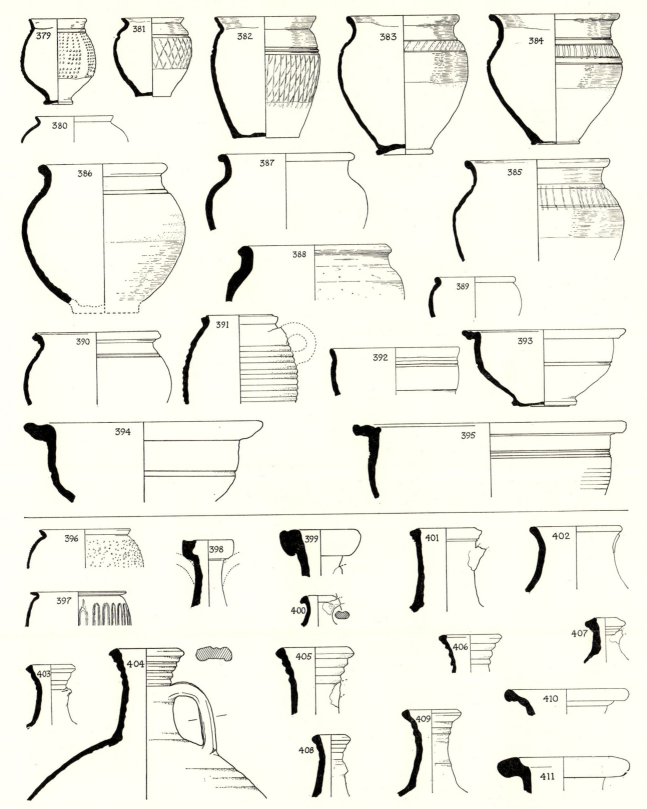

FIG. III. Pottery vessels from deposits dated *c.* A.D. 105 (nos. 379–95) and A.D. 105–30 (nos. 396–411) (¼).

Jars

386. Hard buff granulated ware, lower half burnished, B II Pit 9. Pit 9.
387. Coarse granulated dark grey-brown ware, A II 47. II B, Room 14, make-up.
388. Coarse granulated dark grey-brown ware, unevenly burnished, A I 29. II B, make-up for Room 22A; perhaps residual.
389. Rather granulated grey-brown ware, lighter core, T VII 33. II A, wall-trench 1/3.

Jars with internally grooved rims. Cf. 48, 81–2, 197–9, 481–5, 656–66, 897–909, 1050, 1062, 1080.

390. Finely granulated light grey ware, partly burnished, A I 29. II B, make-up for Room 22A.
391. Rather finely granulated reddish-buff ware, perhaps two-handled, A II 47. II B, Room 14, make-up.

Bowl

392. Finely granulated reddish burnished ware, A II 47. II B, Room 14, make-up.

Reeded-rim bowls. Cf. 211–13, 332–42, 503–13, 669–89, 926–40.

393. Smooth hard grey-brown burnished ware, B II Pit 9. Pit 9.
394. Hard granulated buff ware, B II Pit 9. Pit 9.
395. Hard rather finely granulated buff ware, smoothed surface B II Pit 9. Pit 9.

PERIOD II B: POTTERY DATED A.D. 105–30

Fine ware

396. Roughcast beaker in fine hard white paste, 'metallic' dark grey-brown coating, B IV 21Y, A.D. 105–15. II B, Room 33. Cf. 30–1, 52, 101, 232–3, 555, 780–9, 1070.
397. Colour-coated beaker in fine hard white paste, grey-brown 'metallic' coating, with barbotine loops, B IV 23L, A.D. 115–30. II B, Room 34. A sherd from B III 24, c. A.D. 130 (II C, Room 31 make-up); another beaker, with orange paste, from A VI 23, A.D. 105–15 (II B, Room 26). See p. 264.

Flagons

398. Hard granulated buff ware, B IV 21L, A.D. 115–30. II B, Room 34.
399. Smooth hard cream ware, A VII 32, A.D. 110–20. II B, Room 26.
400. Orange-buff ware, A I 27, A.D. 105–30. II B, Room 16.
401. Hard rather finely granulated white ware, T VII 28, A.D. 105–30. II B, Room 2.
402. As 401, cream, B IV 20P, A.D. 115–30. II B, Room 30.

Ring-necked flagons, Cf. 102–11, 238–41, 375–8, 559–73, 798–811, 1071–2, 1107.

403. Pale buff granulated ware, B IV 21G, A.D. 105–30. II B, Room 28.
404. Hard rather finely granulated buff ware, A I 27, A.D. 105–30. II B, Room 16. Another from B I 70, A.D. 60–75 (Pit 7).
405. Ware as 404. A VI 23, A.D. 105–115. II B, Room 26.
406. Ware as 404. A XI 13A, A.D. 105–30. II B, Room 8.
407. Ware as 404. T XX 18, A.D. 110–20. II B, Room 7.
408. Ware as 404. B I 32F, A.D. 115–30. II B, Room 23.
409. Ware as 404. B I 32F, A.D. 115–30. II B, Room 23.

Flagons, perhaps two-handled

410. Fine hard cream ware, grey core, B IV 21A, A.D. 105–15. II B, Room 26.
411. Ware as 404. A VII 32, A.D. 110–20. II B, Room 26.

Fig. 112

Narrow-necked jars. Cf. 118–24, 245–50, 822–35, 1074, 1152–4, 1231–4.

412. Rather finely granulated burnished grey-brown ware, A I 26A, *c.* A.D. 130. II B, wall-trench 15/16.
413. Finely granulated burnished light grey ware, A II 48, A.D. 105–30. II B, Room 15.
414. Light grey burnished ware, B IV 23J, A.D. 105–15. II B, Room 29.
415. Hard grey ware, lighter burnished surface, B IV 19A, A.D. 115–30. II B, Room 26.
416. Fine hard dark grey burnished ware, A I 26, A.D. 105–30. II B, Room 15.
417. Hard finely granulated buff ware, B I 31C, A.D. 115–30. II B, Room 24.
418. Ware as 417. A VI 23, A.D. 105–15. II B, Room 26.

Beakers and small jars

419. Carinated beaker in fine hard light grey mica-coated ware, A I 38, A.D. 105–15. II B, Room 16. perhaps residual. Cf. 135, 581.
420. Beaker or jar in rather finely granulated grey-white ware, B II 28A, A.D. 115–30. II B, Room 26.
421. Beaker or jar in fine burnished dark grey ware, A VII 32, A.D. 110–20. II B, Room 26.
422. Rouletted beaker in hard burnished light grey ware, B IV 23Z, A.D. 105–15. II B, Room 27. Cf. 254.
423. Rouletted beaker in finely granulated burnished orange-buff ware, A VII 39. This layer, it is now thought, is more likely to belong to II A, Room 16 (A.D. 85–105) than to be make-up below II B, Room 22, *c.* A.D. 105 (see fig. 24). Cf. 254.

Poppyhead and similar beakers. Cf. 133, 136–7, 255, 598–604, 837–9, 1047–9, 1073.

424. Fine hard burnished grey ware, B II 29A, A.D. 105–15. II B, Room 26.
425. Ware as 424. B II 30G, A.D. 105–15. II B, Room 23. Another from B I 36A, A.D. 85–105 (II A, Room 21).
426. Fine hard grey-brown ware, burnished slip, with circular barbotine decoration, A XI 11A, A.D. 105–30. II B, wall-trench 8/12.
427. Fine hard burnished grey ware, with diamond-shaped barbotine decoration, A IV 32, A.D. 105–30. II B, Room 12.
428. Fine hard grey ware, lighter burnished slip, with diamond-shaped barbotine decoration, A IV 35, A.D. 105–30. II B, Room 11.

Jars with burnished lattice decoration. Cf. 381–2, 613–22, 624, 845–56, 1125, 1155, 1187.

429. Fine hard grey ware, burnished slip on rim and shoulder, A X 12, A.D. 105–30. II B, Room 22.
430. Fine hard burnished light grey ware, B II 29A, A.D. 105–15. II B, Room 26.

Jars with burnished shoulder-decoration. Cf. 65, 149–56, 269, 383–5, 607–12, 843.

431. Rather coarse burnished dark grey ware, B I 37G, A.D. 105–15. II B, Room 24.
432. Fine hard grey ware, partly burnished, T VII 28, A.D. 105–30. II B, Room 2.
433. Hard rather dark grey burnished ware, A VII 32, A.D. 110–20. II B, Room 26.
434. Dark grey-brown ware, unevenly burnished, A VII 33, A.D. 105–15. II B, Room 26.

435. Hard grey-brown ware, light grey burnished slip, A I 26, A.D. 105–30. II B, Room 15.
436. Light grey burnished ware, B IV 23J, A.D. 105–15. II B, Room 29.
437. Rather dark grey-brown burnished ware, T XX 18, A.D. 110–20. II B, Room 7.
438. Fine hard grey ware, lighter burnished slip, A VII 29, A.D. 120–30. II B, Room 29.
439. Light brown ware, dark grey burnished surface, B I 32G, A.D. 115–30. II B, Room 24.
440. Hard burnished light grey ware, A II 40, A.D. 115–30. II B, Path 18. Another from B II 27A, A.D. 140–50 (II C, Room 36).
441. Dark grey ware, partly burnished, T VII 23, c. A.D. 130. II B, wall-trench 1/2.
442. Ware as 441. A I 31, A.D. 105–30. II B, Room 17.

Plain jars with carinated shoulders. Cf. 70, 162, 167, 183, 266–8, 605.
443. White granulated burnished ware, B II 29C, A.D. 115–30. II B, Room 33.
444. Rather coarse dark grey ware, unevenly burnished, T VII 28, A.D. 105–30. II B, Room 2.
445. Grey burnished ware, A VII 29, A.D. 120–30. II B, Room 29. Two others from A VII 32, A.D. 110–20. II B, Room 26.
446. Hard light grey ware, darker burnished slip, A II 39, A.D. 105–15. II B, Room 10.

Other plain jars
447. Fine hard light grey ware, B IV 20E, A.D. 115–30. II B, Room 33.
448. Rather finely granulated buff ware, T III 23, A.D. 105–15. II B, Room 1.
449. Hard burnished light grey ware, A X 15, A.D. 115–30. II B, Room 22.
450. Ware as 448, partly burnished, T XX 18, A.D. 110–20. II B, Room 7.
451. Hard grey ware, T XX 18, A.D. 110–20. II B, Room 7.
452. Hard rather finely granulated grey ware, A VII 28, A.D. 105–30. II B, Room 17.
453. Hard burnished grey ware, A VI 23, A.D. 105–15. II B, Room 26.
454. Rather coarse grey-brown ware, smoothly burnished, A IV 32, A.D. 105–30. II B, Room 12. Another, less coarse, from A VI 4, A.D. 150–155/160 (II D, Room 18).
455. Rather coarse light grey ware, darker burnished surface, B IV 23L, A.D. 115–30. II B, Room 34.

Jars mainly in buff ware. Cf. 170, 634–7, 645–55, 871–81, 1061, 1077–8, 1109.
456. Hard buff granulated ware, B IV 19Z, A.D. 115–30. II B, Room 26. Another from B IV 3, A.D. 155/160. (II D, Rooms 38–42).
457. Hard rather finely granulated orange-buff ware, B IV 23J, A.D. 105–15. II B, Room 29.
458. Hard orange-buff ware, B I 38E, A.D. 105–15. II B, Room 19.
459. Ware as 458. B I 32G, A.D. 115–30. II B, Room 24.
460. Hard granulated buff ware, B IV 23J, A.D. 105–15. II B, Room 29. Another from B IV 23L, A.D. 115–30. II B, Room 34.
461. Ware as 460. B IV 23L, A.D. 115–30. II B, Room 34.
462. Ware as 460. B II 29G, A.D. 115–30. II B, Room 23.
463. Hard light grey ware, B II 29C, A.D. 115–30. II B, Room 33.
464. Hard buff granulated ware, B IV 23J, A.D. 105–15. II B, Room 29.

Fig. 113
Jars mainly in grey ware
465. Hard light grey granulated ware, A VII 29, A.D. 120–30. II B, Room 29.
466. Ware as 465. B II 30E, A.D. 105–30. II B, Room 27. Another from B IV 23J, A.D. 105–15 (II B, Room 29).

FIG. 112. Pottery vessels nos. 412–64 from deposits dated A.D. 105–30 ($\frac{1}{4}$).

467. Ware as 465. B IV 21D, A.D. 105–15. II B, Room 34.
468. Rather dark grey burnished ware, T XX 18, A.D. 110–20. II B, Room 7.
469. Dark grey-brown granulated ware, B II Pit 8, A.D. 115–30. Unnumbered pit in II B, Room 33.
470. Hard smoothly burnished dark grey ware, B II 30G, A.D. 105–15. II B, Room 23.
471. Fine hard buff ware, B II 28A, A.D. 115–30. II B, Room 26.
472. Rather granulated dark grey burnished ware, T XX 23, A.D. 105–15. II B, Room 7.
473. Coarse grey-brown ware, unevenly burnished rim and shoulder, B II 28A, A.D. 115–30. II B, Room 26, probably residual. Others from Z I 37, A.D. 49–60 (I, Room 4); A XI 22, A.D. 75–85 (II A, Room 7); A VII 32, A.D. 110–20 (II B, Room 26); and residually in T III 21, A.D. 130–40 (II C, Room 1).
474. Hard light grey ware, A II 40, A.D. 115–30. II B, Path 18, perhaps residual.
475. Hard rather finely granulated buff ware, T XX 18, A.D. 110–20. II B, Room 7.

Unguent jars, Cf. 636–41, 882–5, 1099 and fig. 141, 15, 16 (used as crucibles).
476. Hard buff ware, A II 57, A.D. 105–30. II B, Room 14.
477. Ware as 476. A II 57, A.D. 105–30. II B, Room 14.
478. Hard rather finely granulated buff ware, A XII 17, A.D. 110–20. II B, Room 13.
479. Ware as 478. A XI 11, A.D. 115–30. II B, Room 12.
480. Ware as 478. A VI 23, A.D. 105–15. II B, Room 26.

Jars with internally grooved rims, Cf. 48, 81–2, 197–9, 390, 656–66, 897–909, 1050, 1062, 1080.
481. Grey ware, B IV 21E, A.D. 105–15. II B, Room 33.
482. Orange-buff calcite-gritted ware, B II 20, A.D. 115–30. II B, Room 33. For calcite-gritted parallels cf. 81, 199, 666, 1050.
483. Hard finely granulated buff ware, A IV 37, A.D. 105–30. II B, wall-trench 10/11.
484. Hard buff granulated ware, B IV 20J, A.D. 115–30. II B, Room 29.
485. Jar with reeded rim and scored wavy lines on body; ware as 484, B I 32Y, A.D. 115–30. II B, Room 20.
486. Jar with reeded rim and scored vertical lines on neck, in hard grey ware, B I 37G, A.D. 105–15. II B, Room 24.

Storage jar. Cf. 83–6, 200–4, 667–8, 912–21, 1243.
487. Hard rather finely granulated light grey ware, T XX 23, A.D. 105–15. II B, Room 7.

Bowls with plain wide rims. Cf. 205–6, 326–31, 691–3.
488. Hard dark grey ware, smoothed near base, A VII 32, A.D. 110–20. II B, Room 26.
489. Hard light grey ware, B IV 20E, A.D. 115–30. II B, Room 33.
490. Coarse granulated grey burnished ware, with diagonal burnished lines on shoulder, Z I 20A, A.D. 105–15. II B, Room 7.
491. Hard dark grey ware, lighter core, A VII 33, A.D. 105–15. II B, Room 26.
492. Hard light grey ware, A VI 23, A.D. 105–15. II B, Room 26.
493. Smooth hard grey ware, T XX 18, A.D. 110–20. II B, Room 7.
494. Light grey granulated ware, with burnished vertical lines on body, B II 29C, A.D. 115–30. II B, Room 33.
495. Smooth hard dark grey burnished ware, A I 31, A.D. 105–30. II B, Room 17.
496. Finely granulated grey ware, A I 27, A.D. 105–30. II B, Room 16.

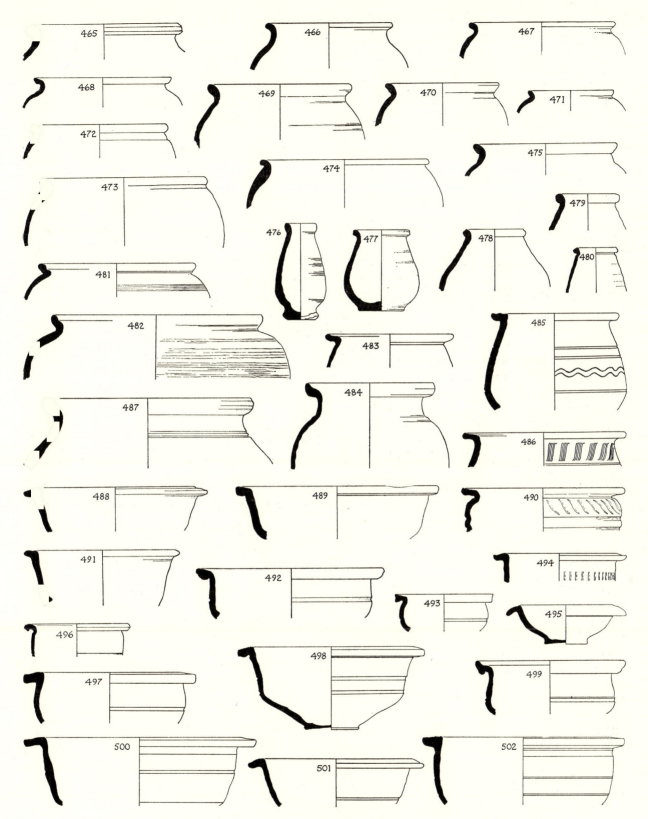

FIG. 113. Pottery vessels nos. 465–502 from deposits dated A.D. 105–30 ($\frac{1}{4}$).

497. Rather finely granulated grey ware, lighter core, B IV 21L, A.D. 115–30. II B, Room 34. Another from A VI 23, A.D. 105–15 (II B, Room 26).

498. Ware as 497, dark blue-grey, A I 27, A.D. 105–30. II B, Room 16. Cf. 334.

499. Smooth grey ware, pink core, B IV 20J, A.D. 115–30. II B, Room 29, make-up for *opus signinum* floor.

500. Finely granulated light grey ware, B I 32G, A.D. 115–30. II B, Room 24.

501. Hard buff granulated ware, B IV 23J, A.D. 105–15. II B, Room 29. A similar rim from A I 27, A.D. 105–30. II B, Room 16.

502. Ware as 501. A II 50, A.D. 105–15. II B, Room 15.

Fig. 114

Bowls and dishes with reeded rims. Cf. 211–13, 332–42, 393–5, 669–89, 926–40

503. Hard grey granulated ware, A VII 32, A.D. 110–20. II B, Room 26.

504. Ware as 503. B IV 23L, A.D. 115–30. II B, Room 34.

505. Ware as 503, smoothed near base, A VI 23, A.D. 105–15. II B, Room 26.

506. Ware as 503. B I 38E, A.D. 105–15. II B, Room 19.

507. Smooth light grey ware, B IV 21A, A.D. 105–15. II B, Room 26.

508. Hard buff granulated ware, Z I 20, A.D. 105–15. II B, Room 6.

509. Hard finely granulated orange-buff ware, B II 28B, A.D. 115–30. II B, Room 33.

510. Hard buff granulated ware, A IV 37, A.D. 105–30. II B, wall-trench 10/11.

511. Ware as 510. B I 47, A.D. 105–15. II B, Room 24.

512. Ware as 510. B IV 23J, A.D. 105–15. II B, Room 29.

513. Ware as 510, with burnished surface, A VII 29, A.D. 120–30. II B, Room 29.

514. Dish with slightly reeded rim, in hard burnished light grey ware, A VI 23, A.D. 105–15. II B, Room 26.

515. Dish with beaded rim and short flange, in hard grey-buff rather finely granulated ware, burnished on rim and flange, T VII 26, A.D. 105–15. II B, Room 4. Cf. 343, 728, 965, 1084, 1260, 1287.

Bowls

516. Mica-coated reddish ware, B IV 19Z, A.D. 115–30. II B, Room 26. Cf. 215–18, 231, 312–14, 693, 947–50.

517. Orange-buff granulated ware with burnished lines, B IV 19A, A.D. 115–30. II B. Room 26. Cf. 316.

518. Hard pinkish-buff ware, A I 27, A.D. 105–30. II B, Room 16. Cf. 700.

519. Brownish-buff burnished ware, B II 28A, A.D. 115–30. II B, Room 26.

520. Pinkish-buff granulated ware, B II 30E, A.D. 105–30. II B, Room 27.

521. Hard grey-brown unevenly burnished ware, B II 29B, A.D. 115–30. II B. Room 33.

522. Smooth hard burnished light grey ware, A II 49, A.D. 105–15. II B, Room 15.

523. Bowl imitating samian form 37, with rouletted neck as 318, in the same fine dark grey burnished ware, T XX 23, A.D. 105–15. II B, Room 7. Cf. 318, 694, and 265 (jar).

524. Bowl with orange-painted vertical lines, in hard rather finely granulated light buff ware, T VII 26, A.D. 105–15. II B, Room 4. Cf. 1245.

Mica-coated plate and dishes, Cf. 739–41, 998, 1086.

525. Plate in hard rather finely granulated light grey paste, B IV 23J, A.D. 105–15. II B, Room 29. This resembles Gallo-Belgic forms, e.g. no. 25, and is likely to be first century.

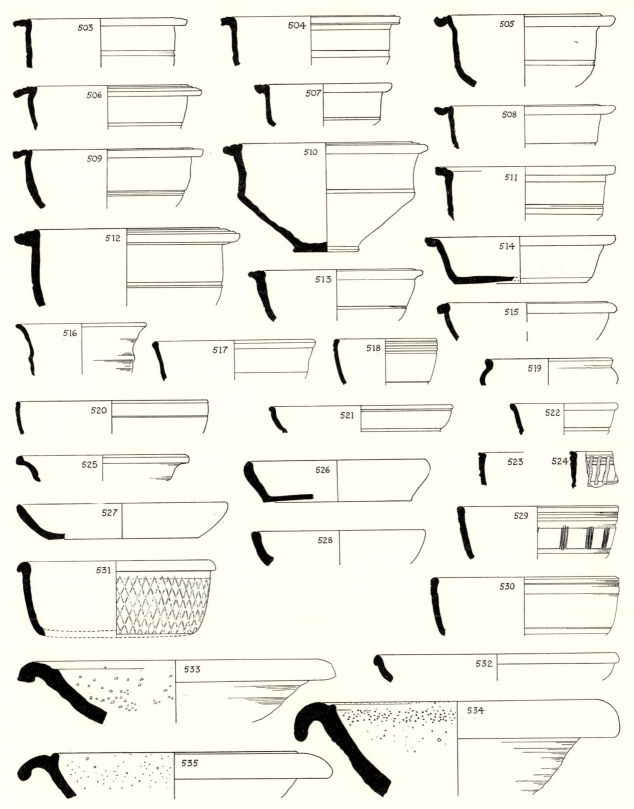

FIG. 114. Pottery vessels nos. 503–35 from deposits dated A.D. 105–30 ($\frac{1}{4}$).

526. Dish in orange-buff paste, A II 48, A.D. 105–30. II B, Room 15.
527. Ware as 526. A X 15, A.D. 115–30. II B, Room 22. Others from B II 30H, A.D. 105–30 (II B, Room 23); B II 28B, A.D. 115–30 (II B, Room 33); A II 26 (II C, Room 22), B IV 17E (II C, Room 45), and B II 37G (II C, Room 32), all A.D. 130–50; B IV Pit 5, A.D. 140–50 (II C, Pit 16); B IV 9A (II D, Room 25), and B II 26F (II D, Room 33), both A.D. 150–155/160; T I 4 A.D. 155/160 (II D, Room 25A, wall-trench); and residual in B XI 5, fourth century (XIV, 6, yard).

Dishes with plain or slightly beaded rims. Cf. 219–22, 346–9, 736–41, 992–8, 1066, 1093, 1112, 1129, 1178–81, 1198, 1219–21, 1265–74.
528. Rather finely granulated burnished ware, burnt grey, A XII 16, A.D. 115–30. II B, Room 13.
529. Finely granulated light reddish ware, cream slip, with scored vertical lines, B IV 21G, A.D. 105–30. II B, Room 31.
530. Hard light reddish finely granulated ware, B I 37D, A.D. 105–15. II B, Room 20.

Dishes with moulded rims
531. Grey buff burnished ware, with burnished lattice, A I 38, A.D. 105–15. II B, Room 16. Another from A I 25, A.D. 130–50 (II C, Room 25). Cf. 706–23, 966–91, 1087–90, 1111, 1176, 1216–17, 1261, 1286.
532. Rather finely granulated pinkish-buff ware, B II 30G, A.D. 105–15. II B, Room 23.

Mortaria (see p. 263 for note on the dates given).
533. Smooth hard buff ware with white, black, grey, and a few red grits; perhaps a late variant of Bushe-Fox 26–30, *c.* A.D. 90–120, south-east Britain or continent; A II 53, A.D. 105–30. II B, Room 14. Cf. 353, 743.
534. Smooth hard buff ware, grey grits; A.D. 60–90, south-east Britain, possibly Kent; A II 39, A.D. 105–15. II B, Room 10.
535. Smooth hard cream ware, white and grey grits; probably early second century, south-east Britain, possibly Kent; B IV 23J, A.D. 105–15. II B, Room 29.

Fig. 115
Mortaria made in the Verulamium region
536. Hard rather finely granulated yellow-buff ware, with grey, white, and a few red grits; A.D. 60–90; A XII 16, A.D. 115–30. II B, Room 13.
537. Hard granulated buff ware with white and red grits; Flavian; A VII 23, A.D. 115–30. II B, Room 26.
538. Hard rather finely granulated buff ware, with white and grey grits; A.D. 70–90; B IV 21Y, A.D. 105–15. II B, Room 33.
539. Ware as 538. Flavian; B IV 23J, A.D. 105–15. II B, Room 29.
540. Ware as 538, with grey and brown grits; Flavian; A VI 23, A.D. 105–15. II B, Room 26.
541. Ware as 538, with grey, white, and red grits; Flavian; T VI 22, A.D. 105–30. II B, Room 4.
542. Ware as 538. A.D. 70–95; B II 28A, A.D. 115–30. II B, Room 26.
543. Ware as 538, with grey and brown grits; A.D. 70–90; A VI 23, A.D. 105–15. II B, Room 26.
544. Hard yellow-buff rather finely granulated ware, with white, grey and brown grits; like vessels of Albinus, A.D. 65–95; T XX 23, A.D. 105–15. II B, Room 7.
545. Hard rather finely granulated buff ware, with grey grits; stamp ALBINVS, A.D. 65–95; A VI 23, A.D. 105–15. II B, Room 26. Cf. 359, 365. See p. 371.

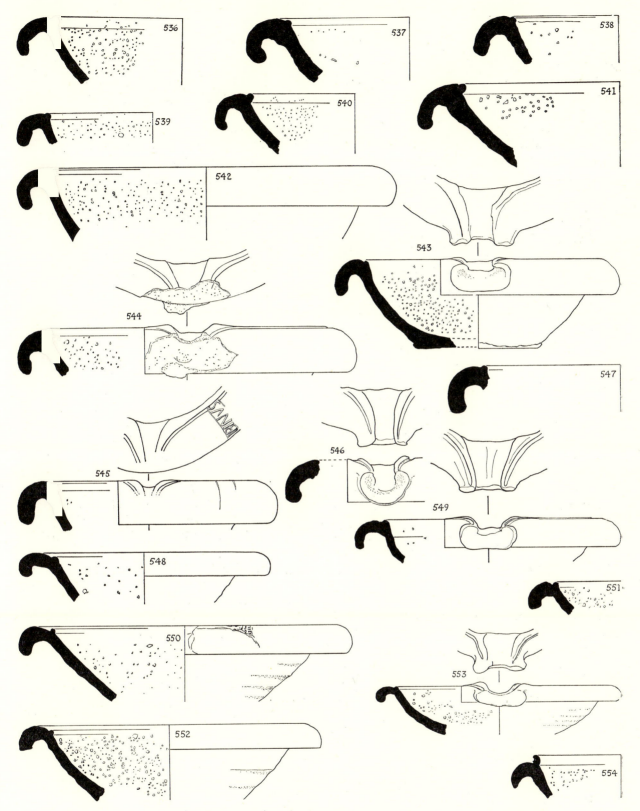

Fig. 115. Pottery vessels nos. 536–54 from deposits dated A.D. 105–30 ($\frac{1}{4}$).

546. Ware as 545; stamp ALBINVS, A.D. 65–95; T VII 26, A.D. 105–15. II B, Room 4, Cf. 359, 365.

547. Hard buff granulated ware; A.D. 70–100; B I 38E, A.D. 105–15. II B, Room 19.

548. Hard rather finely granulated buff ware, with white grits; c. A.D. 90–135; B I 37G, A.D. 105–15. II B, Room 24.

549. Hard white granulated ware, with grey grits; A.D. 80–110; A IV 35, A.D. 105–30. II B, Room 11.

550. Hard yellow-buff rather finely granulated ware, with grey, white, and red grits; stamp CA (retro), A.D. 110–45; A II 37, A.D. 105–30. II B, Room 10. See p. 380.

551. Ware as 550; part of leaf stamp [stamp of TMH], A.D. 110–45; A XI 13, A.D. 115–30. II B, Room 12. See p. 379.

552. Ware as 550; A.D. 110–50; A XI 11, A.D. 115–30. II B, Room 12.

553. Ware as 550, brownish-buff; A.D. 110–50; A II 40, A.D. 115–30. II B, Path 18.

554. Ware as 550, pinkish-buff; A.D. 120–60; T XX 18, A.D. 110–20. II B, Room 7.

Pottery from Layers Dated A.D. 130–50

Fig. 116

Fine ware, colour-coated

555. Indented beaker in fine hard orange-buff paste, grey-brown coating, with traces of roughcast inside, B II 28G, A.D. 130–50. II C, Room 32. Cf. 787–9, 1070; also (plain) 30–1, 52, 101, 232–3, 396, 780–6.

556. Beaker with barbotine decoration in fine hard white paste, dark grey-brown coating, B IV 21X, A.D. 130–45. II C, Room 37. Cf. hunt cups 791–5, 1045, 1144.

557. As 556, with part of barbotine animal, B IV 17F, A.D. 140–50. II C, Room 40.

558. 'Castor box' in hard reddish paste, grey core, grey-brown coating, rouletted, B IV 17J, A.D. 145–50. II C, Room 39. Another from B V 12, A.D. 140–50 (II C, Room 40). See p. 264.

Ring-necked flagons. Cf. 102–11, 238–41, 375–8, 403–10, 798–811, 1071–2, 1107.

559. Hard reddish paste, white slip, B IV 17K, A.D. 140–50. II C, Room 39. Others from B IV 17E, A.D. 145–50 (II C, Room 45) and B II 27G, A.D. 130–50 (II C, Room 33). This type was almost certainly made at the pottery outside the London Gate of the town (Stadium site Kiln I, *Hertfordshire Archaeology*, i (1968), 22 ff.).

560. Ware as 559. B IV 21X, A.D. 130–45. II C, Room 37. Another from Z II 7, A.D. 155/160 (II D, wall-trench 3A/5).

561. Ware as 559. T I 10, A.D. 130–50. II C, Room 13, front wall-trench.

562. Ware as 559. B II 27X, A.D. 130–40. II C, Room 43.

563. Hard rather finely granulated whitish-buff ware, B IV Pit 7, A.D. 145–50. Small pit in II C, Room 37.

564. Ware as 563. T II 19, A.D. 130–40. II C, Room 13.

565. Hard orange-buff granulated ware, A IV 20, A.D. 130–40. II C, Path 21.

566. Ware as 565. A II 22, A.D. 130–50. II C, Room 23.

567. Hard rather finely granulated buff ware, B IV 19D, A.D. 130–40. II C, Room 45. Others from B V 32, A.D. 150–155/160 (II D, Room 42A) and Z I 2, A.D. 155/160 (II D, Room 8).

568. Hard rather finely granulated pinkish-buff ware, A IV 20, A.D. 130–40. II C, Path 21.

569. Ware as 568. B IV 17B, A.D. 140–50. II C, Room 44.

570. Ware as 568. B I 31E, A.D. 140–50. II C, Room 27.

571. Hard orange-buff granulated ware, B II 27G, A.D. 130–50. II C, Room 33.

572. Ware as 571, yellow-buff, B IV 17K, A.D. 140–50. II C, Room 39.

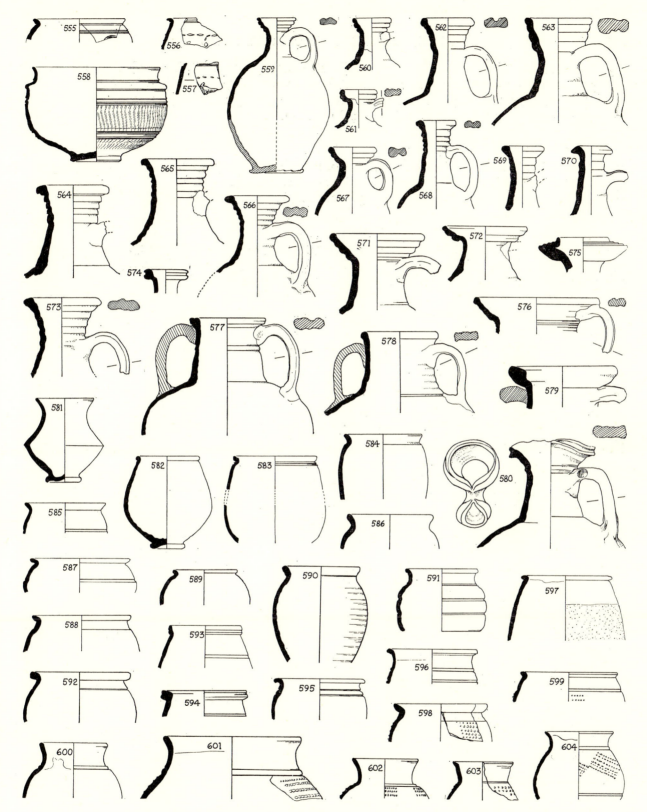

FIG. 116. Pottery vessels nos. 555–604 from deposits dated A.D. 130–50 (except 583, q.v.) ($\frac{1}{4}$).

573. Hard rather finely granulated buff ware, B IV 18D, A.D. 135–45. II C, Room 46. Others from A II 39, A.D. 105–15 (II B, Room 10); B II 28C, A.D. 130–40 (II C, Room 41); B IV 18J, A.D. 130–45 (II C, Room 39); A II 36, c. A.D. 150 (II C, Room 22, Pit 5); A II 19, A.D. 140–50 (II C, Path 26); and A II 16, A.D. 150–155/160 (II D, Room 19).

Other flagons

574. Smooth hard orange-buff ware, B I 31E, A.D. 140–50. II C, Room 27.
575. Hard rather finely granulated orange-buff ware, A II 24, A.D. 130–40. II C, Path 26.
576. Smooth cream ware, T XXI 16, A.D. 130–40. II C, Room 13.

Two-handled flagons

577. Hard rather finely granulated buff ware, A I 23, A.D. 130–40. II C, Room 23.
578. Hard finely granulated orange-buff ware, B IV 21X, A.D. 130–45. II C, Room 37.
579. Hard granulated cream ware, B IV 17K, A.D. 140–50. II C, Room 39.

Pinched-mouth flagon. Cf. 821.

580. Hard orange-buff granulated ware, B IV Pit 5, A.D. 140–50 (two), II C (Room 45) Pit 16. Similar spouts from A IV 20, A.D. 130–40 (two) (II C, Path 21).

Beakers and small jars

581. Carinated beaker in fine hard grey ware, with burnished slip, B III 20, A.D. 140–50. II C, Room 31, votive deposit (p. 57). Cf. 135, 419.
582. Beaker in fine hard burnished cream ware, B IV 17K, A.D. 140–50. II C, Room 39. Cf. 841.
583. Mica-coated beaker in fine buff paste, A X 7, A.D. 150–155/160 II D, Room 29. Another from A X 3, A.D. 150–155/160 (II D, Room 29). Cf. 129, 380, 1046 and 836 (indented). Note: this vessel is misplaced here: the drawings had already been mounted before a dating mistake was realized. The vessel's correct position, in Period II D, should be after no. 836.
584. Beaker or jar in unevenly burnished grey granulated ware, B IV 17K, A.D. 140–50. II C, Room 39. A similar one in burnished dark grey ware from B IV 18J, A.D. 130–45 (II C, Room 39) and, in light grey ware, from B IV 3, A.D. 155/160; another, burnt red, from B IV 3A, Antonine fire, disturbed (both II D, Rooms 38–42).
585. Fine hard burnished light grey ware, B II 27F, A.D. 130–40. II C, Room 33.
586. Hard light grey ware, T VI 19, A.D. 130–40. II C, Room 4.
587. Fine burnished grey ware, T VI 20, A.D. 130–40. II C, Room 3.
588. Fine hard burnished light grey ware, B IV 17J, A.D. 145–50. II C, Room 39.
589. Rather dark grey granulated ware, buff core, A IV 20, A.D. 130–40. II C, Path 21.
590. Hard orange-red ware, smoothly burnished, but with pronounced wheelmarks, B IV 18B, A.D. 130–40. II C, Room 44.
591. Hard rather finely granulated pinkish-buff ware, Z I 17, A.D. 135–45. II C, Room 8.
592. Hard finely granulated buff ware, B IV 17K, A.D. 140–50. II C, Room 39.
593. Ware as 592. A II 19, A.D. 140–50. II C, Path 26.
594. Cream granulated ware, B II 27Y, A.D. 130–40. II C, Room 36.
595. Hard grey ware, T XXI 23, A.D. 130–50. II C, wall-trench 9/13.
596. Fine hard grey ware, lighter burnished slip, B IV 18A, A.D. 135–45. II C, Room 36.
597. Beaker imitating fine-ware roughcast, in finely granulated light grey-buff ware, with burnished light grey slip on rim and shoulder, B IV 17J, A.D. 145–50. II C, Room 39. Another in dark grey ware from this layer.

Poppyhead and similar beakers. Cf. 133, 136–7, 255, 424–8, 837–9, 1047–9, 1073.

598. Beaker or jar with barbotine panels, in fine hard grey ware, with lighter burnished slip, A II 26, A.D. 130–50. II C, Room 22. Another from B XI 7A, A.D. 155/160 (II D, Room 46).

599. Ware as 598, B IV 17B, A.D. 140–50. II C, Room 44.

600. Beaker with plain body in fine hard grey-brown ware, burnished light grey slip, B IV 17F, A.D. 140–50. II C, Room 40.

601. Beaker with barbotine panels in hard grey ware, burnished lighter slip, B IV 17C, A.D. 140–50. II C, Room 46.

602. As 601, B II 28E, A.D. 135–45. II C, Room 37. Others from A IV 18, A.D. 130–40 (II C, Interspace 14/17); B IV 3, A.D. 155/160, (II D, Rooms 38–42); and A IV 1, Antonine fire, disturbed (II D, Rooms 17, 18).

603. Fine hard burnished light grey ware, A II 24, A.D. 130–40. II C, Path 26.

604. Fine hard grey ware, lighter burnished slip, A II 22, A.D. 130–50. II C, Room 23. Others from A II 44, A.D. 105–15 (II B, Path 18); and A IV 20, A.D. 130–40 (II C, Path 21).

Fig. 117

Jars with carinated shoulders, plain. Cf. 70, 162, 167, 183, 266–8, 443–6.

605. Hard rather finely granulated dark grey ware, burnished especially on rim and shoulder, A II 36, c. A.D. 150. II C, Room 22, Pit 5, demolition pit.

606. Fine hard grey-brown ware, burnished grey slip, B V 12, A.D. 140–50. II C, Room 40.

Jars with carinated shoulders and burnished decoration. Cf. 65, 149–56, 269, 383–5, 431–42, 843.

607. Fine hard grey ware, lighter burnished slip, Z I 22, A.D. 130–40. II C, Room 8.

608. Ware as 607. B II 27G, A.D. 130–50. II C, Room 33. Others from B I 36A, A.D. 85–105 (II A, Room 21); and B I 18, A.D. 155/160 (II D, Rooms 25, 35).

609. Hard burnished grey ware, B IV 17K, A.D. 140–50. II C, Room 39.

610. Hard finely granulated light grey ware, burnished slip on upper part, T III 20, A.D. 135–50. II C, Room 1.

611. Hard grey-brown ware, burnished grey-black slip, A I 25, A.D. 130–50. II C, Room 25. Another from B II 27X, A.D. 130–40 (II C, Room 43).

612. Hard dark grey rather finely granulated ware, burnished on neck, B II 28F, A.D. 130–40. II C, Room 33.

Jars with burnished lattice decoration. Cf. 381–2, 429, 430, 624, 845–56, 1125, 1155, 1187.

613. Hard grey granulated ware, burnished rim and shoulder, B IV 17J, A.D. 145–50. II C, Room 39. Another from B IV 9B, A.D. 150–155/160 (II D, Room 42).

614. Hard finely granulated grey ware, burnished slip, B IV 27X, A.D. 130–40. II C, Room 43. Others from T VII 23, c. A.D. 130 (II B wall-trench 1/2); and B IV 18J, A.D. 130–45 (II C, Room 39).

615. Ware as 614. B IV 17K, A.D. 140–50. II C, Room 39. Another from B IV 19J, A.D. 130–40 (II C, Room 39); and a rim each from B II 28B, A.D. 115–30 (II B, Room 33) and A II 27, A.D. 130–50 (II C, Room 22).

616. Ware as 614. A XI 10, A.D. 130–50. II C, Room 16.

617. Ware as 614. B IV Pit 7, A.D. 145–50. Small pit in II C, Room 37.

618. Black-burnished ware, category A, B IV 19D, A.D. 130–40. II C, Room 45.

619. Hard finely granulated grey-black burnished ware, B IV 17J, A.D. 145–50. II C, Room 39.

620. Hard grey granulated burnished ware, B IV Pit 5, A.D. 140–50. II C (Room 45), Pit 16. Another from A IV 12, A.D. 150–155/160 (II D, Room 17).
621. Hard light grey granulated ware, B IV 17K, A.D. 140–50. II C, Room 39.

Other jars in grey or brown ware.

622. Hard light grey granulated burnished ware, probably with burnished lattice, B IV, Pit 7, A.D. 145–50. Small pit in II C, Room 37.
623. Orange-brown unevenly burnished ware, B II 27D, A.D. 140–50. II C, Room 40.
624. Hard burnished grey-brown granulated ware, probably with lattice, B IV 17K, A.D. 140–50. II C, Room 39. Others from B IV 19D, A.D. 130–40 (II C, Room 45); and B I 18, A.D. 155/160 (II D, Rooms 25, 35).
625. Hard light grey granulated ware, B II 27A, A.D. 140–50. II C, Room 36.
626. Ware as 625. B II 27B, A.D. 140–50. II C, Room 43.
627. Hard dark grey finely granulated ware, B II 27D, A.D. 140–50. II C, Room 40. Cf. 654.
628. Hard light grey rather finely granulated ware, A II 23, A.D. 130–40. II C, Path 21. Another, with thinner rim, from A I 25, A.D. 130–50 (II C, Room 25); and a smaller jar (diameter 14 cm.) from A I 12, A.D. 150–155/160 (II D, Room 24). Cf. 868.
629. Hard light grey burnished ware, B II 27B, A.D. 140–50. II C, Room 43. Cf. 858.
630. Hard rather finely granulated grey ware, B I 31X, A.D. 140–50. II C, Room 27.
631. Hard finely granulated grey ware, B IV 17J, A.D. 145–50. II C, Room 39.
632. Ware as 631, light grey, A I 15, A.D. 145–50. II C, Room 24.
633. Ware as 631, Z I 22, A.D. 130–40. II C, Room 8.

Jars in buff ware. Cf. 170, 458–62, 464, 645–55, 871–81, 1061, 1077–8, 1109.

634. Hard buff granulated ware, B II 27D, A.D. 140–50. II C, Room 40.
635. Ware as 634, finely granulated, B IV 22, A.D. 130–50. II C, wall-trench 44/36. Another from B II 28B, A.D. 115–30 (II B, Room 33).

Unguent jars. Cf. 476–80, 882–5, 1099 and fig. 141, 15, 16 (used as crucibles).

636. Hard finely granulated light grey ware, B I 31E, A.D. 140–50. II C, Room 27.
637. Hard finely granulated buff ware, A XII 13A, A.D. 130–50. Interspace 12/16. Others from A XII 12, A.D. 115–30 (II B, Room 26), A XII 9A (II C, Interspace 12/16), A XII 13 (II C, Room 16) and A XI 12 (II C, Room 15), all A.D. 130–40; A XI 10 (two), A.D. 130–50 (II C, Room 16); and B IV 17K, A.D. 140–50 (II C, Room 39).
638. Ware as 637. A X 63, A.D. 145–50. II C, Room 28.
639. Ware as 637, perhaps used as a crucible, A XI 12, A.D. 130–40. II C, Room 15.
640. Ware as 637, A I 16, A.D. 130–50. II C, Room 24.
641. Ware as 637. A XI 10, A.D. 130–50. II C, Room 16.

Jars with frilled rims

642. Hard buff granulated ware, with one or perhaps two handles 3·8 cm. wide, B IV 17K, A.D. 140–50. II C, Room 39.
643. Ware as 642, more finely granulated, B II 27X, A.D. 130–40. II C, Room 43.

Painted jar

644. Smooth white ware, with red painted band on shoulder, B IV 18J, A.D. 130–45. II C, Room 39.

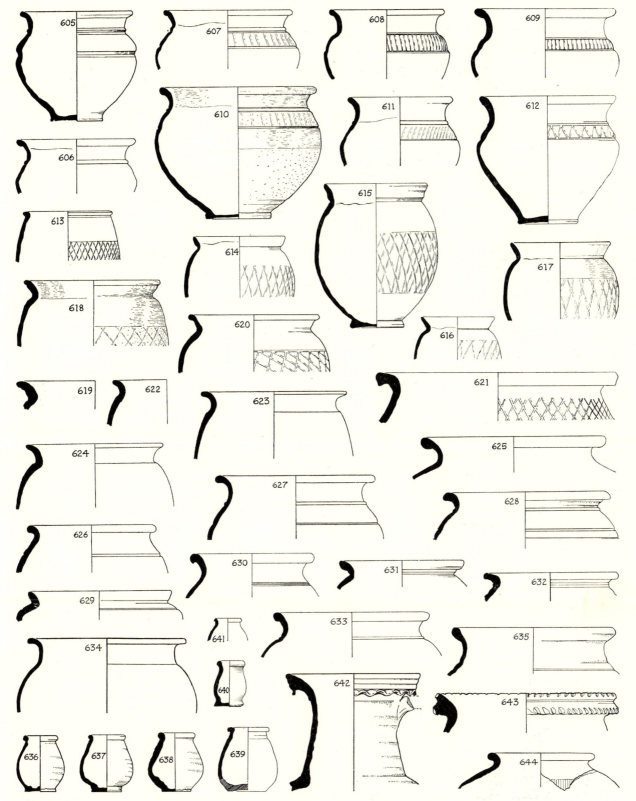

FIG. 117. Pottery vessels nos. 605–44 from deposits dated A.D. 130–50 ($\frac{1}{4}$).

Fig. 118

Jars mainly in buff ware. Cf. 170, 458–62, 634–5, 871–81, 1061, 1077–8, 1109.

645. Smooth hard orange-buff ware, B IV 17K, A.D. 140–50. II C, Room 39.

646. Hard rather finely granulated grey-buff ware, B II 27H, A.D. 130–50. II C, Room 31.

647. Rather finely granulated grey ware, B IV 18J, A.D. 130–45. II C, Room 39. Another from B IV 17K, A.D. 140–50 (II C, Room 39).

648. Hard finely granulated buff ware, B I 31X, A.D. 140–50. II C, Room 27.

649. Hard granulated buff ware, B II 28F, A.D. 130–40. II C, Room 33. Others from A X 65, A.D. 135–45 (II C, Room 28); A IV 20, A.D. 130–40 (II C, Path 21); A VII 5 (II D, Room 24) and B I 27D (II D, Room 28), both A.D. 150–155/160.

650. Ware as 649. A IV 20, A.D. 130–40. II C, Path 21.

651. Hard finely granulated dark grey ware, B IV 21X, A.D. 130–45. II C, Room 37.

652. Hard finely granulated buff ware, B IV 17J, A.D. 145–50. II C, Room 39. Others from A IV 18, A.D. 130–40 (II C, Interspace 14/17); B IV Pit 7, A.D. 145–50 (small pit in II C, Room 36); and T XX 2, A.D. 155/160 (II D, Room 10). Cf. 879.

653. Ware as 652. B IV 18F, A.D. 135–45. II C, Room 40, secondary floor. Three others from B IV 17F, A.D. 140–50 (II C, Room 40, occupation on 18F).

654. Ware as 652. B IV 17K, A.D. 140–50. II C, Room 39. Others from A II 36, *c.* A.D. 150 (II C, Room 22, Pit 5, demolition pit); and A VI 8, A.D. 130–40 (II C, Room 13). Cf. 627.

655. Ware as 652. B IV, Pit 5, A.D. 140–50. II C, (Room 45), Pit 16. Others from T III 20, A.D. 135–50 (II C, Room 1); B IV 17K, A.D. 140–50 (II C, Room 39); A I 12 (II D, Room 24), A I 14 (II D, Drain 23/29), and B IV 9B (II D, Room 42), all A.D. 150–155/160; Z II 7, A.D. 155/160 (II D, wall-trench 3A/5).

Jars with grooved or reeded rims. Cf. 48, 81–2, 197–9, 390, 481–5, 897–909, 1050, 1062, 1080.

656. Hard buff granulated ware, B II 27F, A.D. 130–40. II C, Room 33.

657. Ware as 656. B IV 17J, A.D. 145–50. II C, Room 39.

658. Ware as 656. T XX 13, A.D. 140–50. II C. Room 9.

659. Ware as 656, orange-buff, B IV 19D, A.D. 130–40. II C, Room 45. Others from B I 31E, A.D. 140–50 (II C, Room 27); and B II 28B, A.D. 115–30 (II B, Room 33).

660. Ware as 656. A IV 20, A.D. 130–40. II C, Path 21.

661. Ware as 656, orange-buff, B IV 18A, A.D. 135–45. II C, Room 26.

662. Ware as 656, more finely granulated, B IV 17A, A.D. 140–50. II C, Room 36. Similar rims from A IV 21, A.D. 130–50 (II C, Room 17); and A VII 19, A.D. 115–30 (II B, Room 17).

663. Hard rather finely granulated light grey ware, B IV 19D, A.D. 130–40. II C, Room 45.

664. Hard buff granulated ware, A IV 20, A.D. 130–40. II C, Path 21. Cf. 901.

665. Ware as 664, more finely granulated, A II 22, A.D. 130–50. II C, Room 23. Others from B II, Pit 8, A.D. 115–30 (shallow scoop in II B, Room 33); B II 27C, and B II 27Z (both II C, Room 41, A.D. 140–50); and similar rims from A VII 9, A.D. 145–50 (II C, Room 36) and B V 26, *c.* A.D. 150 (make-up, II D, Room 42A).

666. Coarse buff calcite-gritted ware, B IV 17K (four), A.D. 140–50. II C, Room 39. Others from B II 28F, A.D. 130–40 (II B, Room 33); A II 23, A.D. 130–40 (II C, Path 21); T I 5, A.D. 140–50 (street-metalling); A I 13, A.D. 140–50 (II B, Room 24); T I 8, A.D. 140–50 (street-metalling); B IV 17J, A.D. 145–50 (II C, Room 39); B V 23A, *c.* A.D. 150 (II D, Room 43, make-up); B V 23, A.D. 150–155/160 (II D, interspace north-west of Room 43); A I 2 (II D, Room 23); A X 2 (II D, Room 29); B VII 8 (II D, Room 51, wall-trench); B IX 4 (II D, Room 54); and B XIII 9 (II D, Room 48, south-east wall-trench), all A.D. 155/160. Cf. 81, 199, 482, 1050.

FIG. 118. Pottery vessels nos. 645–82 from deposits dated A.D. 130–50 (¼).

Storage jars. Cf. 83–6, 200–4, 487, 912–21, 1243.

667. Coarse light grey-brown calcite-gritted ware, B IV 17J, A.D. 145–50. II C, Room 39. Cf. 915–19.

668. Very coarse granulated dark grey ware, unevenly burnished, B IV 18J, A.D. 130–45. II C, Room 39. Another from A VII 19, A.D.115–30 (II C, Room 17).

Reeded-rim bowls. Cf. 211–13, 332–42, 393–5, 503–13, 926–40.

669. Hard rather finely granulated buff ware, A II 23, A.D. 130–40. II C, Path 21. Another from T I 9, *c.* A.D. 150 (II D, north-east wall-trench, Room 25A); and similar rims from B IV 18J, A.D. 130–45 (II C, Room 39), and B IV 3, A.D. 155/160 (II D, Rooms 38–42).

670. Ware as 669. A IV 13, A.D. 130–50. II C, Room 37. Another from B IV 17R, A.D. 145–50 (II C, Room 39).

671. Hard granulated buff ware, B IV 17K, A.D. 140–50. II C, Room 39.

672. Ware as 671. B II 28F, A.D. 130–40. II C, Room 33. Another from B II 27B, A.D. 140–50 (II C, Room 43) and a rim from B II 26D, A.D. 150–155/160 (II D, Room 36).

673. Ware as 671. T VII 11, A.D. 140–50. II C, Room 4.

674. Hard finely granulated grey-buff ware, B IV 17F, A.D. 140–50. II C, Room 40.

675. Hard buff granulated ware, B IV 18F, A.D. 135–45. II C. Room 40.

676. Ware as 675. B IV 17K, A.D. 140–50 (two). II C, Room 39.

677. Ware as 675. A II 30, A.D. 130–40. II C, Room 28.

678. Hard buff rather finely granulated ware, A XI 12, A.D. 130–40. II C, Room 15.

679. Hard buff granulated ware, B IV 17K, A.D. 140–50. II C, Room 39. Another from B IV 17J, A.D. 145–50 (II C, Room 39).

680. Hard buff rather finely granulated ware, B I 31D, A.D. 140–50. II C, Room 28. Another from B V 7A, A.D. 155/160 (II D, Room 45).

681. Hard orange-buff granulated ware, B II 27F, A.D. 130–40. II C, Room 33. Others from B II 28F, A.D. 130–40 (II C, Room 33), and B II 27A, A.D. 140–50 (II C, Room 36).

682. Ware as 681, buff, A IV 20, A.D. 130–40. II C, Path 21, make-up.

Fig. 119

683. Hard buff granulated ware, B IV 17K, A.D. 140–50. II C, Room 39. Others from B IV 18B, A.D. 130–40 (II C, Room 44); A I 12, A.D. 150–155/160 (three) (II D, Room 24); B IV 3A, Antonine fire, disturbed (II D, Rooms 38–42).

684. Ware as 683. B IV 18A, A.D. 135–45. II C, Room 36. Others from A II 19, A.D. 140–50 (II C, Path 26), and B I 27B, A.D. 150–155/160 (II D, Room 27).

685. Hard rather finely granulated buff ware, A II 24, A.D. 130–40. II C, Path 26.

686. Ware as 685. B IV 18M, A.D. 140–50. II C, Room 37.

687. Ware as 685. B IV 17K, A.D. 140–50. II C, Room 39.

688. Ware as 685. B IV 17K, A.D. 140–50. II C, Room 39.

689. Hard grey ware, partly burnished, A VI 9, A.D. 130–40. II C, Room 19.

690. Hard grey ware, evenly rilled, B IV 17J, A.D. 145–50. II C, Room 39.

Bowls with plain wide rims. Cf. 205–6, 326–31, 488–502.

691. Hard, finely granulated light grey ware, A II 24, A.D. 130–40. II C, Path 26.

692. Dark grey burnished ware, reddish core, B I 32A, A.D. 140–50. II C, Room 27.

693. Mica-coated fine buff ware, T XX 13, A.D. 140–50. II C, Room 9. Cf. 215–18, 231, 312–14, 516, 947–50.

FIG. 119. Pottery vessels nos. 683–723 from deposits dated A.D. 130–50 ($\frac{1}{4}$).

Other bowls

694. Bowl imitating samian form 37, in finely micaceous smooth dark grey burnished ware with grooved decoration (the base added from another bowl of this type), T III 18, A.D. 130–50. II C, Room 2. Others from A I 27, A.D. 105–30 (II B, Room 16); Z I 21, A.D. 135–45 (II C, Room 8); and sherds from T III 23, A.D. 105–15 (II B, Room 1); Z I 20, A.D. 105–15 (II B, Room 6); A XI 17, A.D. 105–30 (II B, Room 13); T III 15, A.D. 150–155/160 (II D, Room 1). Cf. 318, 523, and 265 (jar).

695. Bowl apparently imitating type 694, but in rather finely granulated dark grey burnished ware, with burnished lattice decoration, T II 19, A.D. 130–40. II C, Room 13.

696. Bowl imitating samian form 30, in hard dark grey burnished ware, decorated with stamped concentric circles, Z I 22, A.D. 130–40. II C, Room 8. Cf. 947.

697. Bowl imitating samian form 30, in fine hard grey burnished ware, with rouletted diamond-shaped decoration, A II 55, A.D. 75–150. Layers collapsed into pit in II C, Room 22.

698. Bowl in hard grey burnished ware, B IV 18A, A.D. 135–45. II C, Room 36.

699. Bowl imitating samian form 29, in rather finely granulated buff ware, A II 30, A.D. 130–40. II C, Room 28.

700. Bowl in hard finely granulated orange-buff ware, with burnished cream slip outside, A I 25, A.D. 130–50. II C, Room 25.

701. Fine hard reddish-buff burnished ware, T III 14, A.D. 140–50. II C, Room 2, secondary floor.

702. Smooth orange-buff ware, B II 29E, A.D. 130–40. II C, Room 37.

703. Hard cream ware, B II 27B, A.D. 140–50. II C, Room 43.

704. Smooth hard burnished grey ware, lighter core, B IV 17F, A.D. 140–50. II C, Room 40.

Tazza. Cf. 309–11, 922–5.

705. Hard granulated light grey-buff ware, B IV 17K, A.D. 140–50. II C, Room 39. Cf. 922.

Dishes with moulded rims and burnished decoration. Cf. 531, 966–91, 1087–90, 1111, 1176, 1216–17, 1261, 1286.

706. Dish or bowl in hard grey granulated burnished ware, B IV 17K, A.D. 140–50 (two). II C, Room 39. Another from B IV 3C, A.D. 155/160 (II D, Room 43), and a similar dish from B IV 17J, A.D. 145–50 (II C, Room 39).

707. Dish in hard grey granulated ware, lighter core, B IV 17K, A.D. 140–50. II C, Room 39. Similar deep dishes from B IV 18A, A.D. 135–45 (II C, Room 36); A VI 14, A.D. 130–50 (II C, Room 20, south-east wall-trench); B II 28E, A.D. 135–45 (II C, Room 37).

708. Hard dark grey granulated burnished ware, A II 36, *c.* A.D. 150. Pit 5. Cf. 1111.

709. Ware as 708. B IV 17J, A.D. 145–50. II C, Room 39. Others from B IV 9A, A.D. 150–155/160 (II D, Room 25); A XI 4A (II D, north-west wall-trench of Room 13), B I 18 (II D, Rooms 25, 35) and B XV 12 (II D, drain outside Room 55), all A.D. 155/160. A similar dish, in black-burnished A ware, residual in T X 4, A.D. 270–5 (III, make-up outside XIV, 1).

710. Dish with internally grooved rim, in hard rather finely granulated grey burnished ware, B IV 17J, A.D. 145–50. II C, Room 39.

711. Dish in finely granulated, rather coarse grey to buff burnished ware, A IV 21, A.D. 130–50. II C, Room 17.

712. Dish or bowl in ware similar to 711, A VI 20, A.D. 130–40. II C, Path 21, make-up.

713. Dish in hard dark grey burnished ware, A II 24, A.D. 130–40. II C, Path 26. Another from A IV 2, A.D. 155/160 (II D, Room 18).

714. Ware as 713. A XI 10A, A.D. 130–50. II C, wall-trench 15/16.

715. Hard grey-buff burnished ware, B IV 17K, A.D. 140–50. II C, Room 39. Others, the colour ranging from dark to light grey, from B IV 17E, A.D. 145–50 (II C, Room 45); B IV 17K (II C, Room 39), and B IV, Pit 5 (four) (Pit 16), both A.D. 140–50; and residual in B XIII 6 (III, make-up, XIV, 6, Room 2); B V 8 (III, make-up, XIV, 5, Room 4) both A.D. 270–5; and B II 15, A.D. 270–80 (III, make-up XIV, 5, south-west of cellar).

716. Hard grey burnished ware, B II 27B, A.D. 140–50. II C, Room 43. Others from B IV Pit 5, A.D. 140–50 (two) (Pit 16); B II 26A, A.D. 150–155/160 (II D, Room 25); A I 2 (II D, Room 24); B VI 8 (II D, Room 51, wall-trenches); and T X 5 (II D, Room 1), all A.D. 155/160; B IV 3A, Antonine fire, disturbed (II D, Rooms 38–42).

717. Hard dark grey burnished ware, with lattice similar to 716, B II 27B, A.D. 140–50. II C, Room 43.

718. Ware as 717. B III 26, A.D. 140–50. II C, filled-in wall-trench beneath Aedicula B. Others from B IV 19B, A.D. 115–30 (II B, Room 33); B II 26F, A.D. 150–155/160 (II D, Room 33); Z I 2, A.D. 155/160 (II D, Rooms 5, 8, 10).

719. Dish with flanged rim, in rather coarse but finely granulated buff burnished ware (burnt), similar to black-burnished ware, A VI 6, A.D. 140–50. II C, Room 13. Others from A VII 19, A.D. 115–30 (II B, Room 17) and A VII 9, A.D. 145–50 (II C, Room 36), perhaps the same dish, in black ware.

720. Hard grey burnished ware, A IV 20, A.D. 130–40. II C, Path 21 make-up.

721. Hard light grey burnished ware, B IV 17J, A.D. 145–50. II C, Room 39. Another from B XI 30, A.D. 160–75 (Pit 19); and a smaller dish from B IX 4, A.D. 155/160 (II D, Room 54).

722. Hard dark grey burnished ware, brown core, A IV 20, A.D. 130–40. II C, Path 21 make-up.

723. Hard grey burnished ware, B IV 17R, A.D. 145–50. II C, Room 39.

Fig. 120

Plain dishes with moulded rims. Cf. 344, 952–64, 1063–5, 1082–6, 1177, 1215, 1262–4.

724. Hard grey ware, burnished inside, B II 27G, A.D. 130–50. II C, Room 33. Another from B XV 11, A.D. 150–155/160 (II D, Room 55).

725. Hard grey ware, burnished rim, B II 27F, A.D. 130–40. II C, Room 33.

726. Hard dark grey granulated ware, lighter core, B IV 17K, A.D. 140–50. II C, Room 39.

727. Hard light grey ware with burnished bands, A II 23, A.D. 130–40. II C, Path 21.

Dishes with flanged or grooved rims

728. Dish with beaded and flanged rim, in hard grey-buff rather finely granulated ware, B IV 19M, A.D. 140–50. II C, Room 37. Cf. 343, 515, 965, 1084, 1260, 1287.

729. Dish with slightly grooved rim and finely rilled sides, in coarse light grey-buff calcite-gritted ware, T I 7, A.D. 130–45, street-metalling. Cf. 1259.

Dishes with slightly beaded or plain rims, and burnished decoration. Cf. 999–1007, 1051, 1091–2, 1120, 1128, 1175, 1218.

730. Rather coarse grey-black ware, unevenly burnished, A II 24, A.D. 130–40. II C, Path 26. Another from B V 23, A.D. 150–155/160 (II D, interspace north-west of Room 43).

731. Handled dish in rather finely granulated grey-black ware, unevenly burnished inside, smoothed outside, B IV 17K, A.D. 140–50. II C, Room 39. Others from A I 2, A.D. 155/160 (II D, Room 23) and, in black-burnished ware, residual in B I 5, A.D. 350–410+ (III, over cellar (XIV, 5)). Cf. 1044.

732. Ware as 731. B IV 17K, A.D. 140–50. II C, Room 39. Another from T XX 2, A.D. 155/160 (II D, Room 10).

733. Dark grey burnished ware, B IV 17J, A.D. 145–50. II C, Room 39.

734. Ware as 733. A II 36, *c.* A.D. 150. Pit 5. Another, in light grey ware, from A I 12, A.D. 150–155/160 (II D, Room 24).
735. Hard grey burnished ware, B IV 17K, A.D. 140–50. II C, Room 39.

Dishes with plain rims, undecorated. Cf. 219–22, 346–9, 526–30, 992–8, 1066, 1093, 1112, 1129, 1178–81, 1198, 1219–21, 1265–74.

736. Hard grey burnished ware, B IV 17J, A.D. 145–50. II C, Room 39. Another from B IV 17K, A.D. 140–50 (II C, Room 39).
737. Hard light grey burnished ware, B IV 18F, A.D. 135–45. II C, Room 40.
738. Hard buff ware, B I 31E, A.D. 140–50. II C, Room 27. Another from T XX 2, A.D. 155/160 (II D, Room 10)

Mica-coated dishes Cf. 525–7, 998, 1086.

739. Dish or bowl in smooth buff paste, grey core, B III 19, *c.* A.D. 150. II D, Room 31, make-up.
740. Dish in hard buff paste, A I 24, A.D. 140–50. II C, Room 23. Others from A VI 19, A.D. 130–50 (II C, Room 19); T I 5, A.D. 140–50 (street-metalling); T XXI 12A, A.D. 150–155/160 (II D, cupboard floor in Room 10).
741. Hard red-buff paste, grey core, A X 63, A.D. 145–50. II C, Room 28.

Mortaria made in south-east Britain. (See page 263 for note on the dates given.)

742. Smooth hard deep buff ware, pink core, white and translucent grits; Trajanic-Hadrianic, perhaps from Kent; B IV 17B, A.D. 140–50. II C, Room 44.
743. Smooth hard deep buff ware, grey and white grits; cf. Bushe-Fox 26–30, A.D. 70–120; B II 28F, A.D. 130–40. II C, Room 33. Cf. 353, 533.
744. Hard yellow-buff ware, white and red-brown grits; A.D. 110–40, Colchester or Kent; T I 5, A.D. 140–50. Street-metalling.
745. Ware as 744; probably *c.* A.D. 130–80, Colchester or Kent; B V 12, A.D. 140–50. II C, Room 40.
746. Smooth hard buff ware, deep pink core, white grits; *c.* A.D. 100–50, perhaps Kent or Colchester; B IV 18B, A.D. 130–40. II C, Room 44.
747. Smooth buff ware, white grits; A.D 130–80, Colchester; A II 24, A.D. 130–40. II C, Path 26.

Mortaria made in the Oxford region

748. Hard buff ware, pink and white translucent grits; A.D. 110–40; B IV 18B, A.D. 130–40. II C, Room 44.
749. Hard cream ware; A.D. 110–40, possibly Oxford region; A I 25, A.D. 130–50. II C, Room 25.

Mortaria made in the Verulamium region

750. Hard rather finely granulated orange-buff ware, grey, white, and red grits; Flavian-Trajanic; A II 27, A.D. 130–50. II C, Room 22.
751. Ware as 750, buff; Flavian-Trajanic; B IV 17K, A.D. 140–50. II C, Room 39.
752. Hard buff granulated ware, dark and light grey grits; style of Lallans, Flavian-Trajanic; B IV 17J, A.D. 145–50. II C, Room 39. Another from B IV 18B, A.D. 130–40 (II C, Room 44).
753. Hard buff granulated ware, pink core, white, grey, and red grits; A.D. 80–120; B IV 18H, A.D. 130–40. II C, Room 40.
754. Ware as 753; A.D. 80–120; T II 19, A.D. 130–40. II C, Room 13. Possibly residual.

Fig. 121

755. Hard buff rather finely granulated ware, white grits, diameter 16·5 cm.; A.D. 90–130; B IV pit 5, A.D. 140–50. Pit 16.

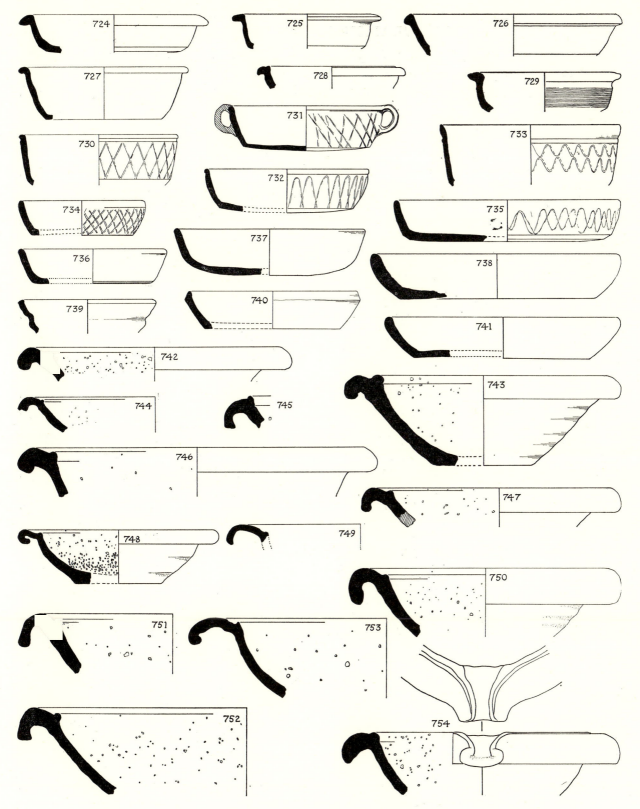

FIG. 120. Pottery vessels nos. 724–54 from deposits dated A.D. 130–50 ($\frac{1}{4}$).

756. Ware as 755, white and grey grits; A.D. 90–120; B II 28E, A.D. 135–45. II C, Room 37.

757. Ware as 755, white and grey grits; A.D. 90–130; B IV 22, A.D. 130–50. II C, wall-trench 36/44.

758. Ware as 755, grey grits; second century, probably first half; B IV 19D, A.D. 130–40. II C, Room 45.

759. Ware as 755, grey and red grits; A.D. 100–40; A IV 20, A.D. 130–40. II C, Path 21.

760. Hard orange-buff rather finely granulated ware, white and grey grits; A.D. 100–40; B IV 18A, A.D. 135–45. II C, Room 36.

761. Hard whitish-buff granulated ware, brown grits; A.D. 100–40; B III 20, A.D. 140–50. II C, Room 31.

762. Hard buff rather finely granulated ware; A.D. 110–40; A I 25, A.D. 130–50. II C, Room 25.

763. Hard buff granulated ware, white and grey grits; A.D. 110–40; B I 31E, A.D. 140–50. II C, Room 27. Another from B XV 11, A.D. 150–155/160 (II D, Room 55).

764. Ware as 763; first half of second century, probably pre-A.D. 140; B IV 17J, A.D. 145–50. II C, Room 39.

765. Ware as 763; A.D. 110–40; A IV 19, c. A.D. 150. Make-up, II D, Room 15.

766. Hard buff rather finely granulated ware; A.D. 110–40; A II 27, A.D. 130–50. II C, Room 22.

767. Hard yellow-buff rather finely granulated ware, grey grits; A.D. 110–40; B II 27X, A.D. 130–40. II C, Room 43.

768. Ware as 767, grey and white grits; A.D. 110–50; A XI 8, A.D. 140–50. II C, Room 15.

769. Hard buff rather finely granulated ware, grey grits, part of stamp border (stamp of Driccius) A.D. 110–50; T XXI 16A, A.D. 130–40. II C, Room 9. See p. 381.

770. Ware as 769, grey, white, and red-brown grits; A.D. 100–50; A XI 8, A.D. 140–50. II C, Room 15.

771. Hard yellow-buff rather finely granulated ware, white and grey grits; A.D. 130–60; B IV 17F, A.D. 140–50. II C, Room 40.

772. Ware as 771, buff; A.D. 120–50; B IV, Pit 5, A.D. 140–50. Pit 16.

773. Ware as 771; A.D. 130–70; B IV 17A, A.D. 140–50. II C, Room 36.

774. Hard buff rather finely granulated ware, grey core, grey and white grits; A.D. 130–70; B IV 21M, A.D. 145–50. II C, Room 37.

775. Hard rather granulated buff ware, white, grey, and red-brown grits; A.D. 130–90; B V 12, A.D. 140–50. II C, Room 40.

776. Hard rather finely granulated buff ware, white and grey grits; A.D. 140–80+; B IV Pit 7, A.D. 140–50. Small pit in II C, Room 37.

777. Hard buff granulated ware; A.D. 140–200; B IV 21X, A.D. 130–45. II C, Room 37.

778. Ware as 777, white, grey, and red-brown grits; A.D. 140–200. A VI 8, A.D. 130–40. II C, Room 13.

779. Hard rather finely granulated orange-buff ware, white and grey grits; A.D. 110–40; residual in B III 25, A.D. 270–300+. III, (?) make-up against north side of Aedicula A.

POTTERY FROM LAYERS DATED A.D. 150–155/160

(An asterisk denotes a pot almost certainly from the Antonine fire, but found in a disturbed layer.)

Fig. 122

Fine wares: (a) roughcast beakers. Cf. 30–1, 52, 101, 232–3, 555, 1070.

780. Fine hard white paste, dark grey-brown coating, B IV 3, A.D. 155/160. II D, Rooms 38–42. Others from A IV 20, A.D. 130–40 (II C, Path 21, make-up); T I 10, A.D. 130–50 (II C, Room

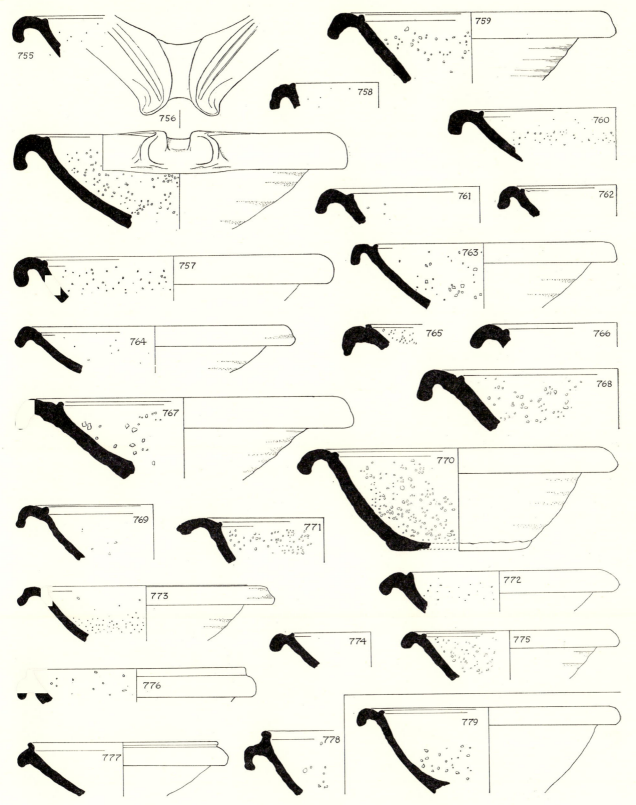

FIG. 121. Pottery vessels nos. 755–79 from deposits dated A.D. 130–50 ($\frac{1}{4}$).

13, wall-trench); B II 27C, A.D. 140–50 (II C, Room 41); A VI 4 (two), A.D. 150–155/160 (II D, Room 18); B IV 7, A.D. 150–155/160 (II D, Room 40); A VI 2 (II D, Room 18), T III 11 (II D, Room 4), B XV 3 (II D, Room 55), Z II 7 (II D, wall-trench 3A/5), all A.D. 155/160; B IV 3A, Antonine fire (disturbed) (II D, Rooms 38–42); residually in B V 21A, B V 28, B V 29 (all III, make-up, XIV, 5 Room 4), and V XXXII 4 (III, make-up south-west of XIV, 1), all A.D. 270–5.

781. Fine hard white paste, slightly 'metallic' dark brown to orange coating, T XX 10, A.D. 155/160. II D, north-west wall-trench of Room 10.

782. Ware as 781, dark grey-brown coating, B XV 3, A.D. 155/160. II D, Room 55.

783. Fine hard orange paste, dark grey-brown slightly 'metallic' coating, B IV 3A, Antonine fire (disturbed). II D, Rooms 38–42. Others from A I 13, A.D. 140–50 (II C, Room 24); A I 18, A.D. 135–45 (II C, Room 24); B VI 17B, A.D. 140–50 (II C, Room 44).

*784. Fine hard orange-buff paste, 'metallic' grey coating, B IV 3A, Antonine fire (disturbed). II D, Rooms 38–42.

785. Fine hard white paste, 'metallic' grey-brown coating, A I 2, A.D. 155/160. II D, Room 23.

786. Ware uncertain, V XXXIII 6, A.D. 150–155/160. II D, Room 2A.

*787. Roughcast beaker with indented sides, in fine orange-buff paste, grey-brown slightly 'metallic' coating (worn), B IV 3A, Antonine fire (disturbed). II D, Rooms 38–42. Indented sherds from B V 23, A.D. 150–155/160 (II D, interspace north-west of Room 43) and B XI 7A, A.D. 155/160 (II D, Room 46). Cf. 555, 1070.

788. As 787, in fine hard cream paste, dark grey 'metallic' coating, B I 18, A.D. 155/160. II D, Rooms 25, 35.

789. As 787 in fine hard buff paste, dark grey coating, B II 14, A.D. 155/160. II D, Rooms 32/42.

Fine wares: (b) colour-coated beakers

790. Beaker with indented sides, in fine hard white (burnt) paste, grey-brown coating, T III 11, A.D. 155/160. II D, Room 4. Cf. 1059, 1060, 1105–6, 1130–2.

*791. Beaker with barbotine hound, in fine hard white paste, dark grey-brown 'metallic' coating, A XI 3, Antonine fire (disturbed). II D, Room 13. Cf. 556–7, 1045, 1144, 1205.

*792. Similar to 791, with red-brown coating, darker inside, A IV 1, Antonine fire (disturbed). II D, Rooms 17, 18. Others from A IV 2, A.D. 155/160 (II D, Room 18); A V 11, A.D. 200–225/250 (Pit 21).

793. Similar to 791, with barbotine hare, B IV 7, A.D. 150–155/160. II D, Room 40.

*794. Beaker with barbotine leaf, in fine hard cream paste, dark grey-brown 'metallic' coating, B VII 9, Antonine fire (disturbed). II D, Room 52.

795. Beaker with barbotine decoration, in fine hard reddish-grey paste, dark grey 'metallic' coating, T XXI 10, A.D. 150–155/160. II D, Room 25b, floor.

796. Fine hard white paste, 'metallic' red-brown coating, B XV 3, A.D. 155/160. II D, Room 55.

797. Bowl imitating samian form 40, in fine hard orange paste, glossy 'metallic' black coating. Probably made at Lezoux. B III 9C, (?) A.D. 150–155/160. Posthole perhaps associated with Aedicula.

Ring-necked flagons. Cf. 102–11, 238–41, 375–8, 403–10, 559–73, 1071–2, 1107.

798. Hard granulated buff ware, A VII 3, A.D. 155/160. II D, Room 25.

799. Flagon similar to 800 (upper part only figured), T XX 2, A.D. 155/160. II D, Room 10.

800. Hard finely granulated buff ware, smoothed especially on lower half of body, A I 2 (two), A.D. 155/160. II D, Room 23.

801. Ware as 800, from the same layer.

802. Ware as 800. B XV 11, A.D. 150–155/160. II D, Room 55.

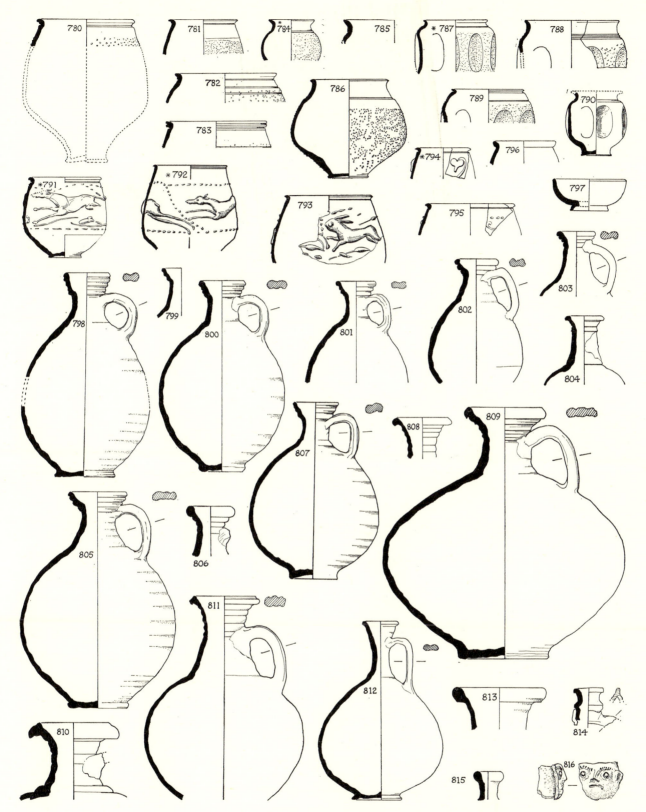

FIG. 122. Pottery vessels nos. 780–816 from deposits dated A.D. 150–155/160 (¼).

803. Smooth hard cream ware, B V 22, A.D. 155/160. II D, interspace north-west of Room 43.
804. Ware as 803. B XIV 10, A.D. 155/160. II D, wall-trench 25/50.
805. Hard finely granulated buff ware, smooth surface, A VII 3 (two), A.D. 155/160. II D, Room 25. Another from B IV 17K, A.D. 140–150 (II C, Room 39), and a similar rim from B II 17, A.D. 150–155/160 (II D, Room 42).
806. Ware as 805. B V 7, A.D. 155/160. II D, Rooms 41–8.
807. Hard reddish ware, white slip, A IV 2, A.D. 155/160. II D, Room 18. Others from B IV 17K, A.D. 140–50 (II C, Room 39); B XV 3, A.D. 155/160 (II D, Room 55).
808. Rather finely granulated orange-buff ware, A X 7, A.D. 150–155/160. II D, Room 29.
809. Hard finely granulated buff ware, smoothed surface, B XV 4, A.D. 150–155/160. II D, Room 55.
810. Ware as 809. T III 11, A.D. 155/160. II D, Room 4.
811. Ware as 809, smoothed near base, B XIII 9, A.D. 155/160. II D, south-east wall-trench of Room 48.

Other flagons

812. Smooth hard reddish-grey paste, cream slip, B XIII 9, A.D. 155/160. II D, south-east wall-trench of Room 48.
813. Hard granulated buff ware, B IV 3, A.D. 155/160. II D, Rooms 38–42.
814. Rather finely granulated white ware, with the end of the handle wrapped round the neck, T XX 8, A.D. 150–155/160. II D, Room 10.
815. Mica-coated buff ware, red core, A VII 5, A.D. 150–155/160. II D, Room 24.
816. Face mask in relief, probably the top of a flagon, in hard granulated buff ware, red core, T XXIII 3, A.D. 155/160. II D, front wall-trench, Room 25A.

Fig. 123

Two-handled flagons

817. Flagon likely to have had two handles, in hard rather finely granulated buff ware, A I 12, A.D. 150–155/160. II D, Room 24.
818. Flagon likely to have had two handles, ware as 817, B VI 8, A.D. 155/160. II D, wall-trenches of Room 51. Similar rims from A I 10, A.D. 150–155/160 (II D, Room 23); A VII 5, A.D. 150–155/160 (II D, Room 24).
819. Hard granulated buff ware, B IV 3, A.D. 155/160. II D, Rooms 38–42.
820. Hard rather finely granulated buff ware, B XV 11, A.D. 150–155/160. II D, Room 55.

Pinched-mouth flagon. Cf. 580.

821. Ware as 820. A IV 2, A.D. 155/160. II D, Room 18. A similar spout from A I 12, A.D. 150–155/160 (II D, Room 24).

Narrow-necked jars. Cf. 118–24, 245–50, 412–18, 1074, 1152–4, 1231–4.

822. Fine hard orange-buff ware, cream slip, with combed decoration, B XIV 10, A.D. 155/160. II D, wall-trench 25/50. Another, without the lower zone of decoration, from Z I 2, A.D. 155/160 (II D, Room 8). Sherd from A XI 4, A.D. 155/160 (II D, Room 13).
823. Ware as 822. A VII 5, A.D. 150–155/160. II D, Room 24.
824. Hard rather finely granulated orange-buff ware, B IV 9A, A.D. 150–155/160. II D, Room 25.
825. Ware as 824, buff, T III 11, A.D. 155/160. II D, Room 4.

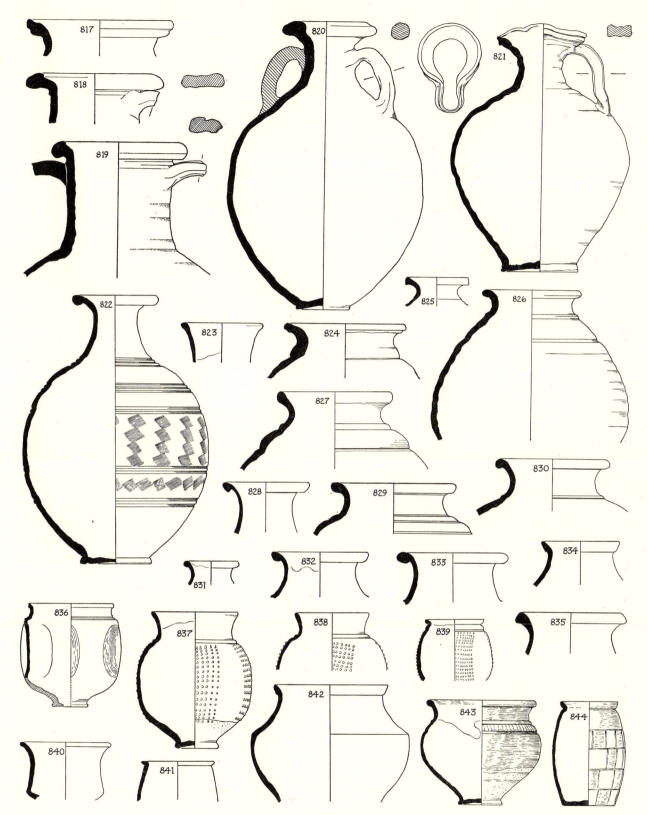

Fig. 123. Pottery vessels nos. 817–44 from deposits dated A.D. 150–155/160 ($\frac{1}{4}$).

826. Hard rather finely granulated grey-brown ware, burnished horizontal lines from rim to shoulder, A I 14, A.D. 150–155/160. Silt in II D, Drain 23/29. Another, in grey ware, from A VII 8, of the same date (II D, Room 25 floor).

827. Hard light grey burnished ware, A I 12, A.D. 150–155/160. II D, Room 24.

828. Ware as 827. A I 14, A.D. 150–155/160. Silt in II D, Drain 23/29.

829. Ware as 827. B II 14, A.D. 155/160. II D, Rooms 32–42. Similar rim from B I 27C, A.D. 150–155/160 (II D, Room 33).

830. Hard light grey granulated ware, A I 14, A.D. 150–155/160. Silt in II D, Drain 23/29.

831. Hard grey ware, lighter burnished slip, A I 2, A.D. 155/160. II D, Room 23. Others from A I 12, A.D. 150–155/160. (II D, Room 24) and A XI 4C, A.D. 155/160 (II D, north-west wall-trench of Room 13).

832. Ware as 831. B V 22, A.D. 155/160. II D, interspace north-west of Room 43.

833. Hard burnished light grey ware, B I 18, A.D. 155/160. II D, Rooms 25, 35.

834. Hard light grey ware, dark burnished slip, A II 13, A.D. 150–155/160. Gravel path, II D, 20/27.

835. Hard grey burnished ware, A II 14, A.D. 150–155/160. II D, Path 20/27.

Mica-coated beakers

836. Mica-coated beaker with indented sides. B VIII 8, A.D. 155/160. II D, wall-trenches of Room 53. Base reconstructed from one found residually in B III 10D, A.D. 270–5 (III, make-up in Pit 4). An indented sherd in this ware from Pit 7, A.D. 60–75.
Beaker no. 583 above properly belongs here.

Poppyhead and similar beakers. Cf. 133, 136–7, 255, 424–8, 598–604, 1047–9, 1073.

837. Fine hard grey ware, lighter burnished slip from rim to bottom of panels, B III 11, A.D. 155/160. II D, Room 31. Others from T VII 17, A.D. 130–50 (II C, Room 3); T I 5, A.D. 140–50 (street-metalling); A XII 10 (II D, Room 25B), B II 26A (II D, Room 25), both A.D. 150–155/160; A IV 11, A V 6 (both II D, Room 15), B XIV 10 (II D, wall-trench 25/50), B V 22 (II D, interspace north-west of Room 43), T XX 2 (II D, Room 10), Z I 2 (three) (II D, Room 8), all A.D. 155/160; B IV 3A (II D, Rooms 38–42), A IV 1 (II D, Rooms 17, 18) both Antonine fire (disturbed); A V 11 (two), A.D. 200–225/250 (Pit 21); B XIV 12, A.D. 270–5 (III, make-up of XIV, 6 Room 3).

838. Ware as 837, grey slip, T XX 2 (two), A.D. 155/160. II D, Room 10. Another from B VI 4, A.D. 155/160 (II D, Room 56).

839. Beaker or jar in ware as 837, B V 7, A.D. 155/160. II D, Rooms 41–8. Others from B II 2, Antonine fire (disturbed) (II D, Rooms 32–42) and residually in B XI 10 (yard metalling south-west of XIV, 6) and B XI 10A (III, wall-trench) both A.D. 270–300+.

Other beakers

840. Carinated beaker in smooth hard burnished grey-buff (burnt) ware, Z I 2, A.D. 155/160. II D, Room 8.

841. Beaker in smooth hard burnished buff ware, A IV 2, A.D. 155/160. II D, Room 18. Another, in light red ware, cream slip, from A X 7, A.D. 150–155/160 (II D, Room 29). Cf. 582.

Jars

842. Fine hard ware (burnt red), smoothly burnished slip, A I 2, A.D. 155/160. II D, Room 23.

843. Hard light grey ware, burnished slip, with burnished shoulder-decoration, B XV 3 (three),

A.D. 155/160. II D, Room 55. Others from A I 31 (rim to cordon), A.D. 105–30 (II B, Room 17); T III 19, *c.* A.D. 130 (II B, wall-trench 1/2); B IV 18B (II C, Room 44), A II 30 (II C, Room 28), both A.D. 130–40; A I 18 (II C, Room 24), B IV 18A (II C, Room 36), B IV 18D (II C, Room 46), all A.D. 135–45; T I 10, A.D. 130–50 (II C, Room 13, wall-trench); A XI 8 (II C, Room 15), B IV 17B (two) (II C, Room 44), all A.D. 140–50; A I 15, A.D. 145–50 (II C, Room 24); A IV 19, *c.* A.D. 150 (II D, make-up of Room 15); A I 30 (II D, in clay of north-west wall, Room 23), B IV 9B (II D, Room 42), B V 23 (II D, interspace north-west of Room 43), B XV 4 (two) (II D, Room 55), T XXI 10 (II D, Room 25B, floor), all A.D. 150–155/160; A I 2 (II D, Room 23), A VII 3 (two) (II D, Room 25), B IV 10 (II D, wall-trench 36/37), B XV 7A (II D, Room 55), T II 8 (II D, Room 25A), T XXI 5 (II D, Rooms 10, 25B), all A.D. 155/160; B XIV 5 (II D, Room 50), B XVI 6 (in oblong trench, XIV, 7, Room 1), both Antonine fire (disturbed); and residual in A V 8, A IV 9, B XIV 8, all A.D. 270–5 (III, make-up). Cf. 65, 149–56, 269, 383–5, 431–42, 607–12.

844. Orange-brown ware, decorated with grooved lines, the surface burnished except in alternate squares, A I 2, A.D. 150–155/160. II D, Room 23.

Fig. 124

Jars with burnished lattice on body. Cf. 381–2, 429, 430, 613–22, 624, 1125, 1155, 1187.

845. Handled jar in fine hard ware (burnt red), burnished cream slip, T XX 2, A.D. 155/160. II D, Room 10. A similar jar, though found without the handle, in grey ware with slip, from Z I 2, A.D. 155/160 (II D, Room 8).

846. As 845. B XVI 7, Antonine fire (disturbed), III, filling of oblong trench, XIV, 7, Room 1.

*847. Hard dark grey ware, burnished above and below lattice, Z II 2. III, Pit outside XIV, 2. Smaller jar (diameter 10·8 cm.) from B I 31G, A.D. 130–50 (II C, Room 32).

848. Hard finely granulated buff ware, burnished above lattice, A VII 3, A.D. 155/160. II D, Room 25. Similar jars in grey ware from B II 27Y, A.D. 130–40 (II C, Room 36) and Z I 12, A.D. 130–50 (II C, Room 7).

849. Hard rather finely granulated light grey ware, burnished above lattice, A II 13, A.D. 150–155/160. II D, Path 20/27.

850. Fine hard grey ware, burnished above and below lattice, B IV 3, A.D. 155/160. II D, Rooms 38–42.

851. Hard finely granulated grey-brown ware, burnished above and below lattice, A IV 11, A.D. 155/160. II D, Room 15.

852. Rather coarse but finely granulated grey-brown ware, unevenly burnished, likely to have burnished lattice, A IV 12, A.D. 150–155/160. II D, Room 17. Another, in grey-black ware, from A X 3, of the same date (II D, Room 29).

853. Fine hard grey burnished ware, with lighter slip to bottom of lattice, A VII 3, A.D. 155/160. II D, Room 25. Another from A X 2, A.D. 155/160 (II D, Room 29).

854. Fine hard grey-brown burnished ware, grey slip on rim and shoulder, B V 23, A.D. 150–155/160. II D, interspace north-west of Room 43.

855. Ware as 854, light grey, T I 9, *c.* A.D. 150. II D, make-up below beam of front wall, Room 25A.

856. Hard dark grey burnished ware, B I 30E, A.D. 150–155/160. II D, Room 26, floor.

857. Ware as 856, grey, perhaps plain, B IV 7, A.D. 150–155/160. II D, Room 40.

Other jars

858. Hard light grey burnished ware, B II 14, A.D. 155/160. II D, Rooms 32–42. Others from B II 27B, A.D. 140–50 (II C, Room 43); B IV 3B (III, make-up, XIV, 5, Room 3). Cf. 629.

859. Ware as 858. A I 12, A.D. 150–155/160. II D, Room 24.

860. Hard light grey granulated burnished ware, B IV 3, A.D. 155/160. II D, Rooms 38–42.

861. Fine hard burnished cream ware, B VII 8, A.D. 155/160. II D, Room 51.

862. Hard buff rather finely granulated ware, B V 7, A.D. 155/160. II D, Rooms 41–8.

863. Ware as 862, with cream slip, Z II 7, A.D. 155/160. II D, wall-trench 3A/5.

864. Fine grey-brown ware, burnished light grey slip on rim and shoulder, A IV 8, A.D. 155/160. II D, Room 17.

865. Fine hard grey ware, burnished slip, B XVI 3, A.D. 155/160. II D, Room 57.

866. Hard light grey burnished ware, with burnished decoration above neck cordon, B XIII 7, A.D. 155/160. II D, Room 49.

867. Dark grey granulated ware, B II 27E, A.D. 150–155/160. II D, Room 43, make-up.

868. Hard rather finely granulated grey ware, A II 14, A.D. 150–155/160. II D, Path 20/27. Cf. 628.

869. Ware as 868. B XIII 9, A.D. 155/160. II D, south-east wall-trench of Room 48.

870. Hard grey burnished ware, A VIII 8, A.D. 150–155/160. II D, Room 25 floor.

Jars in hard buff ware. Cf. 170, 458–62, 464, 634–5, 645–55, 1061, 1077–8, 1109.

871. Finely granulated, T XX 2, A.D. 155/160. II D, Room 10.

872. Rather finely granulated light grey-buff, A IV 2, A.D. 155/160. II D, Room 18. Another from A IV 8, A.D. 155/160 (II D, Room 17).

873. Rather finely granulated, A I 10, A.D. 150–155/160. II D, Room 23.

874. Ware as 873, with neck cordon, A I 2, A.D. 155/160. II D, Room 23. Another from Z I 2, A.D. 150/155 (II D, Room 8).

875. Ware as 873. A I 2, A.D. 155/160. II D, Room 23.

876. Ware as 873. A VI 3, A.D. 150–155/160. II D, Room 18. Others from B V 23 (II D, interspace north-west of Room 43) and B V 32 (II D, Room 43), both of the same date.

877. Ware as 873, orange-buff, A IV 8, A.D. 155/160. II D, Room 17.

878. Ware as 873, A IV 8, A.D. 155/160. II D, Room 17. Others from B IV 18J, A.D. 130–45 (II C, Room 39); A IV 20, A.D. 130–40 (II C, Path 21); B V 23A, c. A.D. 150 (II D, make-up for Room 43); A II 14, A.D. 150–155/160 (II D, Path 20/27); B V 21 (II D, Rooms 38–42), A IV 2(II D, Room 18), and T XX 2 (II D, Room 10), all A.D. 155/160.

879. Finely granulated, A IV 2 (two), A.D. 155/160. II D, Room 18. Others from T XX 14A, A.D. 130–50 (II C, Room 12); A VI 4, A.D. 150–155/160 (II D, Room 18). Cf. 652.

880. Granulated, B III 11, A.D. 155/160. II D, Room 31.

881. Rather finely granulated light grey-buff; used as container for purple-red pigment, A IV 2, A.D. 155/160. II D, Room 18. Others, without the pigment, from B IV 23A, A.D. 85–105 (II A, Room 2); A I 12, A.D. 150–155/160 (II D, Room 24); B V 7 (II D, Rooms 41–8) and B XV 3 (II D, Room 55) both A.D. 155/160; and residually in B XI 14 (III, yard-metalling south-west of XIV, 6) and T III 10 (III, make-up for XIV, 1 Room 1), both A.D. 270–5.

Fig. 125

Unguent jars. Cf. 476–80, 636–41, 1099 and fig 141, 15, 16 (used as crucibles).

882. Hard finely granulated buff ware, partly smoothed surface, B V 23, A.D. 150–155/160. II D, interspace north-west of Room 43. Others from B XIII 9, A.D. 150–155/160 (II D, south-east wall-trench, Room 48); B XIII 7, A.D. 155/160 (II D, Room 49).

883. Ware as 882. A I 12, A.D. 150–155/160. II D, Room 24.

884. Light grey-brown ware, A I 2, A.D. 155/160. II D, Room 23. Another, in burnt granulated ware, from T XXI 7, A.D. 155/160 (II D, wall-trench 10/25B).

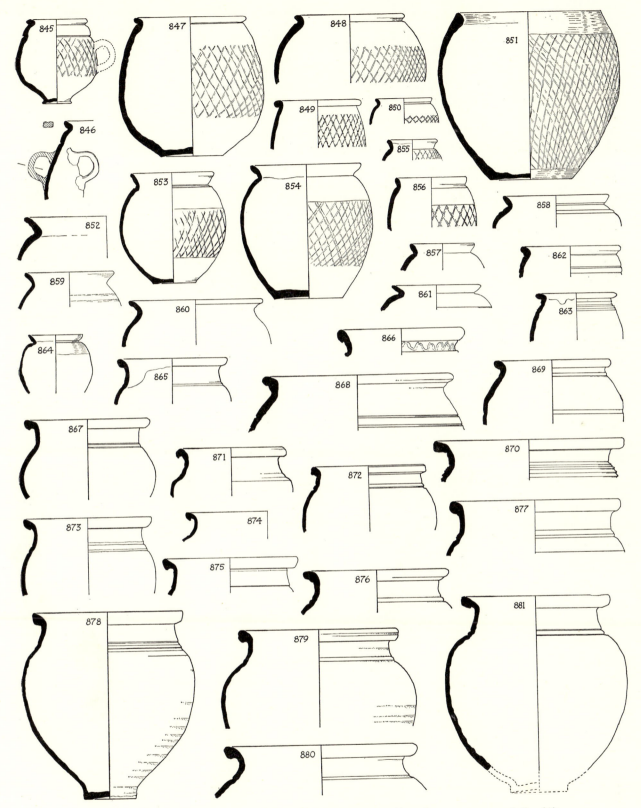

FIG. 124. Pottery vessels nos. 845–81 from deposits dated A.D. 150–155/160 ($\frac{1}{4}$).

885. Hard finely granulated buff ware, T XX 2, A.D. 155/160. II D, Room 10. Others in this shape, but lacking a rim, from B II 30E, A.D. 105–30 (II B, Room 27); B IV 17B, A.D. 140–50 (II C, Room 44); B IV 17F, A.D. 140–50 (II C, Room 40); A VII 3, A.D. 150–155/160 (II D, Room 25).

Triple vases. Cf. fig. 143, 13 in pipeclay.

886. Joined in the centre; slightly granulated buff ware, smoothed surfaces, A IV 8, A.D. 155/160. II D, Room 17.
887. Joined at the basal ring; burnt granulated ware, B XV 11, A.D. 150–155/160. II D, Room 55.

Other jars

*888. Handled jar in rather coarse, finely granulated buff ware, smoothed surfaces, B IV 13, A.D. 270–300. III, make-up, XIV, 5 Room 3. Another from A I 2, A.D. 155/160 (II D, Room 23).
889. Rather soft buff ware, B IV 3, A.D. 155/160. II D, Rooms 38–42.
890. Rather coarse buff ware (burnt) with very large grits, A IV 2, A.D. 155/160. II D, Room 18.
*891. Fine hard grey ware, lighter burnished slip (burnt), B V 5, Antonine fire (disturbed). II D, Rooms 41–8.
892. Ware as 891. B IV 9A, A.D. 150–155/160. II D, Room 25.
893. Ware as 891. T XXI 5, A.D. 155/160. II D, Rooms 10, 25B.
894. Hard grey granulated ware, burnished rim and shoulder, B V 22, A.D. 155/160. II D, interspace north-west of Room 43.

Calcite-gritted jars. Cf. 1100, 1159–60, 1209–10, 1242, 1283.
895. Coarse buff ware, B VII 4, A.D. 155/160. II D, Room 52.
896. Ware as 895. B IV 9F, A.D. 150–155/160. II D, Room 39, floor.

Jars with internally grooved rims. Cf. 48, 81–2, 197–9, 390, 481–5, 656–66, 1050, 1062, 1080.
897. Hard rather finely granulated buff ware, A IV 2, A.D. 155/160. II D. Room 18. A similar, smaller jar from B V 9, the same date (II D, south-east wall-trench of Room 45).
898. Ware as 897, perhaps originally grey (burnt), B VII 4, A.D. 155/160. II D, Room 52.
899. Ware as 897. A I 12, A.D. 150–155/160. II D, Room 24.
900. Ware as 897. A V 6, A.D. 155/160. II D, Room 15. Larger jars in this shape (diameter 14·8 cm.) from B IV 9D, A.D. 150–155/160 (II D, Room 40, floor); B IV 3, A.D. 155/160 (II D, Rooms 38–42); and a rim from B IV 18J, A.D. 130–45 (II C, Room 39).
901. Ware as 897, smoothed near base, T I 6, A.D. 155/160. II D, front wall-trench, Room 25A. Cf. 664.
902. Coarse granulated cream ware, A VII 3, A.D. 155/160. II D, Room 25.
903. Hard rather finely granulated buff ware, B XV 12, A.D. 155/160. II D, Drain outside Room 55. Another from T XI 11, A.D. 150–155/160 (II D, Room 4, floor).
904. Ware as 903. T XX 2, A.D. 155/160. II D, Room 10. Another from B IV 17C, A.D. 140–50 (II C, Room 46).
905. Ware as 903. A I 2, A.D. 155/160. II D, Room 23. Another from B II 14, A.D. 155/160 (II D, Rooms 32–42). Similar rim from A I 13, A.D. 140–50 (II C, Room 24).
906. Jar decorated with raised bosses, unevenly spaced, with diagonal burnished lines between, and burnished loops below, in hard grey-brown rather finely granulated ware, red-brown inside, burnished on rim, shoulder, and cordons, A I 14, A.D. 150–155/160. II D, silt in Drain 23/29.
907. Hard rather finely granulated ware (burnt), B IV 3, A.D. 155/160. II D, Rooms 38–42.
908. Smooth hard orange ware, B II 26D, A.D. 150–155/160. II D, Room 36.

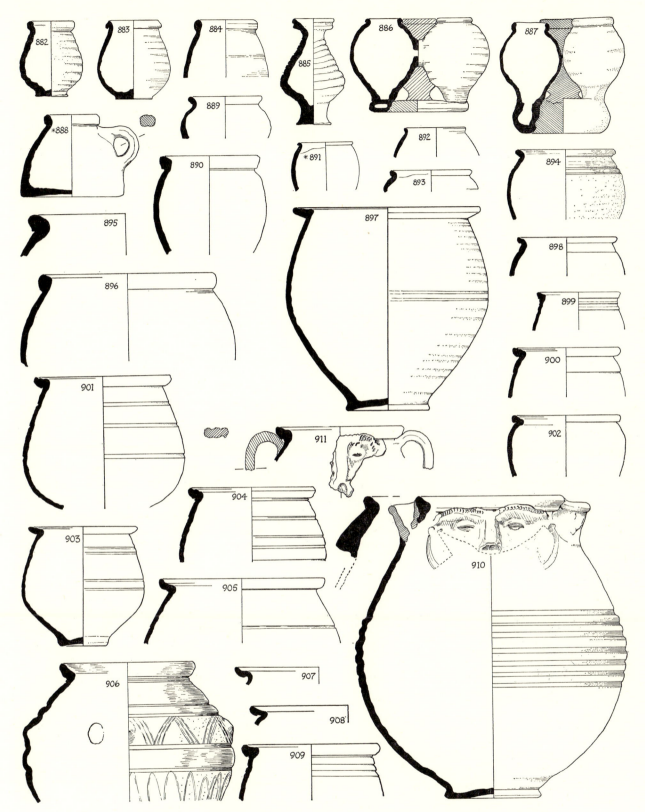

FIG. 125. Pottery vessels nos. 882–911 from deposits dated A.D. 150–155/160 ($\frac{1}{4}$).

909. Hard light grey-buff rather finely granulated ware, T XX 2, A.D. 155/160. II D, Room 10. Another from B IV 17C, A.D. 140–50 (II C, Room 46).

910. Jar with part of human face in relief, the ears formed into tubular spouts or handles, in hard buff rather finely granulated ware, B V 23, A.D. 150–155/160. II D, interspace north-west of Room 43. Others from B IV 17J, A.D. 145–50 (II C, Room 39); B IX 9, A.D. 270–300+ (residual) (III, yard-metalling south-west of XIV, 6); and a sherd from T XX 2, A.D. 155/160 (II D, Room 10). Cf. 1079.

911. Jar similar to 910, but with loop handles, Z I 2, A.D. 155/160. II D, Room 8.

Fig. 126

Storage jars. Cf. 83–6, 200–4, 487, 667 (calcite), 668, 1243.

912. Coarse granulated buff ware, A IV 2, A.D. 155/160. II D, Room 18.

913. Rather coarse granulated grey ware, B II 26A, A.D. 150–155/160. II D, Room 25.

914. Hard granulated ware (burnt red), with burnished lattice on shoulder, surface burnished on upper part, and near base, B XV 3, A.D. 155/160. II D, Room 55.

915. Coarse buff ware with rather fine calcite grit, smoothed surface, A IV 2, A.D. 155/160. II D, Room 18.

916. Coarse light grey-buff calcite-gritted ware, B VII 4, A.D. 155/160. II D, Room 52.

917. Very coarse light grey-buff ware with large calcite grits, lightly rilled shoulder and furrowed body, A IV 2, A.D. 155/160. II D, Room 18. Another from A IV 8, A.D. 155/160 (II D, Room 17).

918. Coarse buff calcite-gritted ware, B XIV 10, A.D. 155/160. II D, wall-trench 25/50. Similar rims from B XIII 5, Antonine fire (disturbed) (II D, Room 48); and residually from B XI 9 (III, yard-metalling south-west of XIV, 6), B XII 7 (III, make-up of XIV, 6 Room 1), both A.D. 270–300+; B XIV 12, A.D. 270–5 (III, make-up of XIV, 6 Room 3).

919. Very coarse buff calcite-gritted ware, with rilled shoulder and furrowed body, B XI 17, A.D. 150–155/160. II D, Room 44.

920. Very coarse granulated grey-brown ware, rilled shoulder, burnished rim and neck, A IV 12, A.D. 150–155/160. II D, Room 17. Similar rim from A I 11, the same date (II D, Room 23).

921. Jar with two countersunk handles, plugged into body, and shallow incised wavy line decoration, in hard rather finely granulated reddish-buff ware, A I 2, A.D. 155/160. II D, Room 23. Another from B II 2 (burnt), Antonine fire (disturbed) (II D, Rooms 32–42).

Fig. 127

Tazze. Cf. 309–11, 705.

922. Hard grey-buff granulated ware, B II 27E, A.D. 150–155/160. II D, Room 43. Another from B II, undated. Cf. 705.

923. Hard buff finely granulated ware, smoked grey inside, A V 3 and 6, A.D. 155/160. II D, Room 15.

*924. Ware as 923, burnt, A IV 5, A.D. 350–410+ (residual) (III, outside (south-west of) XIV, 4): part of the same tazza was found in A IV 2, A.D. 155/160 (II D, Room 18). Similar tazza from T III 23, A.D. 105–15 (II B, Room 1).

925. Hard slightly granulated buff ware, smoked grey, B VIII 5, A.D. 155/160. II D, Room 48.

Bowls with reeded rims. Cf. 211–13, 332–42, 393–5, 503–13, 669–89.

926. Hard finely granulated buff ware, partly burnished, B VII 8A, A.D. 155/160. II D, wall-trench 47/48.

927. Hard grey ware, partly burnished, Z I 2, A.D. 155/160. II D, Room 8.

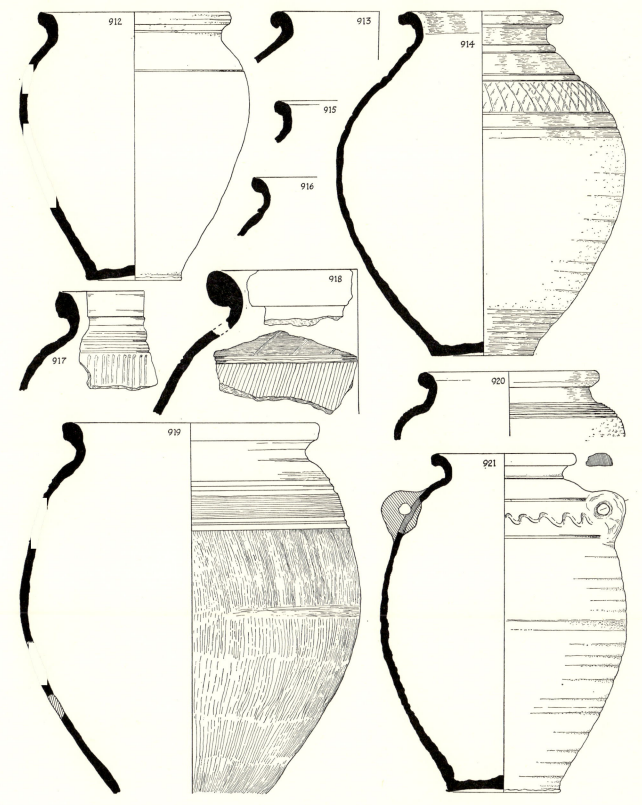

FIG. 126. Pottery vessels nos. 912–21 from deposits dated A.D. 150–155/160 (¼).

928. Hard buff granulated ware, used to contain red pigment, B V 23, A.D. 150–155/160. II D, interspace north-west of Room 43. See p. 382.

929. Ware as 928. A IV 8 (three), A.D. 155/160. II D, Room 17. Others from A II 27, A.D. 130–50 (II C, Room 22); A II 36 c. A.D. 150 (Pit 5); B XIII 9, A.D. 155/160 (II D, Room 48, south-east wall-trench); B IV 3A, Antonine fire (disturbed) (II D, Rooms 38–42).

930. Hard rather finely granulated buff ware, A VII 3, A.D. 155/160. II D, Room 25.

931. Ware as 930. B II 14, A.D. 155/160. II D, Rooms 32–42. Others from B IV 18G, A.D. 130–40 (II C, Room 38); A IV 12, A.D. 150–155/160 (II D, Room 17); A II 20 (II D, Room 20), B II 26B (II D, Room 42) both A.D. 150–155/160; Z I 2, A.D. 155/160 (II D, Room 8).

932. Ware as 930. A IV 2 (two), A.D. 155/160. II D, Room 18.

933. Hard buff granulated ware, B V 23, A.D. 150–155/160. II D, interspace north-west of Room 43.

934. Ware as 933. B II 14 (three), A.D. 155/160. II D, Rooms 32–42. Others from B II 27X, A.D. 130–40 (II C, Room 43); A II 19, A.D. 140–50 (II C, Path 26); T I 9, c. A.D. 150 (II D, north-east wall-trench, Room 25A); A II 13 (II D, Path 20/27), B I 27B (II D, Room 27), B II 26B (II D, Room 42), all A.D. 150–155/160; Z I 2, A.D. 155/160 (II D, Room 8).

935. Ware as 933. A I 12, A.D. 150–155/160. II D, Room 24. Another from A I 2, A.D. 155/160 (II D, Room 23).

936. Hard rather finely granulated buff ware, T I 9, c. A.D. 150. II D, north-east wall-trench, Room 25A.

937. Hard grey-buff ware, A VII 5, A.D. 150–155/160. II D, Room 24.

938. Hard orange-buff granulated ware, B II 27E, A.D. 150–155/160. II D, Room 43. Similar rim from A I 21, A.D. 130–40 (II C, Room 24).

939. Smooth hard orange-buff ware, B I 30X, A.D. 150–155/160. II D, Room 27.

940. Ware as 939, buff, B V 7, A.D. 155/160. II D, Rooms 41–8.

941. Hard burnished grey ware, lighter slip on rim, B III 12, A.D. 150–155/160. II D, Room 31. Similar bowls, with unreeded rim, from B I 27B (II D, Room 27), and B II 26A (II D, Room 25) of the same date.

Other bowls

942. Similar to 941, but with plain flange, B II 27E, A.D. 150–155/160. II D, Room 43.

943. Hard rather finely granulated buff ware, B VII 4, A.D. 155/160. II D, Room 52.

944. Hard yellow-buff granulated ware, B VII 4. Ibid.

945. Fine burnished ware (burnt red), burnished line decoration, A X 3, A.D. 150–155/160. II D, Room 29.

946. Dark grey burnished ware, burnished line decoration, A I 12, A.D. 150–155/160. II D, Room 24.

Mica-coated bowls. Cf. 215–18, 231, 312–14, 516, 693.

947. Bowl imitating samian form 30 in mica-coated fine red-buff ware (worn), with raised bosses arranged in vertical lines, Z I 5, A.D. 150–155/160. II D, Room 8. Cf. 127–8, 696.

948. Smooth hard orange-buff ware, perhaps mica-coated, A II 14, A.D. 150–155/160. II D, Path 20/27.

949. Mica-coated hard buff ware, A II 7, A.D. 155/160. II D, Rooms 20–22.

950. Mica-coated smooth red-buff ware, Z III 4, A.D. 155/160. II D, wall-trench 5/11.

Plain dishes with moulded rims. Cf. 344, 724–7, 1063–5, 1082–6, 1177, 1215, 1262–4.

951. Smooth hard burnished red-buff ware B II 26F, A.D. 150–155/160. II D, Room 33.

952. Orange-buff granulated ware, B II 27E, A.D. 150–155/160. II D, Room 43.

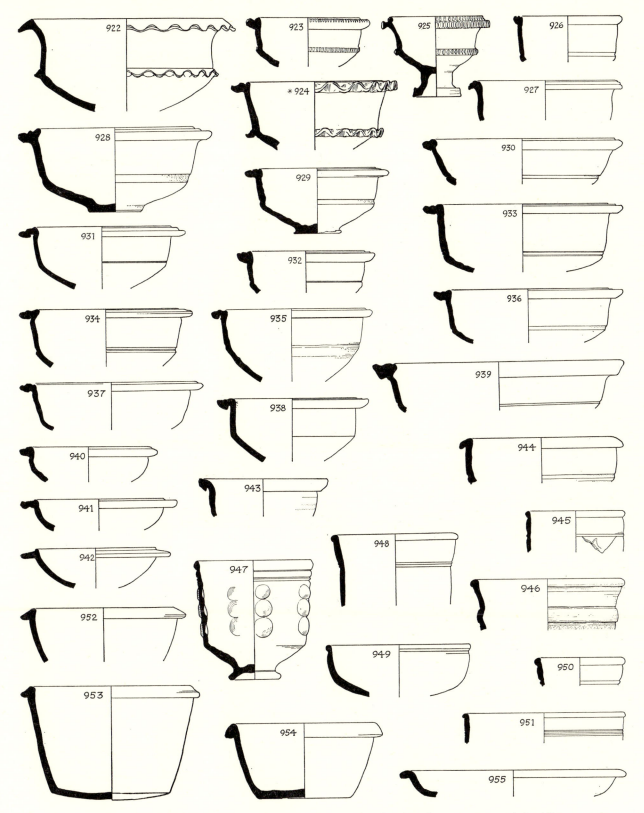

FIG. 127. Pottery vessels nos. 922–55 from deposits dated A.D. 150–155/160 ($\frac{1}{4}$).

953. Dish or bowl in burnished red-brown ware, A I 2, A.D. 155/160. II D, Room 23.
954. Smooth hard burnished orange-buff ware, B IV 3, A.D. 155/160. II D, Rooms 38–42.
955. Ware as 954, light reddish, A X 3, A.D. 150–155/160. II D, Room 29. Another, with grey core, from A II 14, the same date (II D, Path 20/27).

Fig. 128.

956. Ware as 954. B IV 3, A.D. 155/160. II D, Rooms 38–42.
957. Hard grey burnished ware, A I 2, A.D. 155/160. II D, Room 23. Others from A IV 12, A.D. 150–155/160 (II D, Room 17); B XI 30, A.D. 160–75 (Pit 19).
958. Dark grey-brown burnished ware, A XI 4C, A.D. 150–155/160. II D, north-west wall-trench, Room 13. Another from A IV 12, the same date (II D, Room 17).
959. Hard grey burnished ware (burnt) B I 18, A.D. 155/160. II D, Rooms 25, 35.
960. Hard grey burnished ware, B IV 9J, A.D. 150–155/160. II D, Room 43, floor
961. Hard dark grey burnished ware, B V 23, A.D. 150–155/160. II D, interspace north-west of Room 43.
962. Hard light grey rather finely granulated ware, burnished, A I 9, A.D. 150–155/160. II D, Room 24.
963. Hard burnished grey ware, B XV 12, A.D. 155/160. II D, drain outside Room 55.
964. Ware as 963. A X 2, A.D. 155/160. II D, Room 29.
965. Dish with bead and flanged rim, ware as 964 (burnt), B II 27E, A.D. 150–155/160. II D, Room 43. Cf. 343, 515, 728, 1084, 1260, 1287.

Dishes with moulded rims and burnished decoration. Cf. 531, 706–23, 1087–90, 1111, 1176, 1216–17, 1261, 1286.

966. Hard grey ware, burnished inside and on rim, T I 9, *c.* A.D. 150. II D, north-east wall-trench, Room 25A.
967. Hard light grey burnished ware, A II 18, A.D. 150–155/160. II D, Room 22, floor. Others from B II 26D, A.D. 150–155/160 (in grey-black ware) (II D, Room 36); B IV 3, A.D. 155/160 (burnt red) (II D, Rooms 38–42).
968. Hard dark grey rather finely granulated ware, burnished, A IV 12, A.D. 150–155/160. II D Room 17. Another from T XXII 2, A.D. 155/160 (II D, Room 10).
969. Hard grey ware, burnished mottled surfaces, B VII 4, A.D. 155/160. II D, Room 52.
970. Hard burnished grey ware, Z I 2, A.D. 155/160. II D, Room 8.
971. Hard burnished dark grey ware, B IV 9A, A.D. 150–155/160. II D, Room 25.
972. Hard burnished grey ware (burnt), graffito BO, A X 2, A.D. 155/160. II D, Room 29. Another, without graffito, from Z III 4, the same date (II D, wall-trench 5/11).
973. Ware as 972. A IV 8, A.D. 155/160. II D, Room 17. Others from T XXI 5, A.D. 155/160 (II D, Rooms 10, 25B); B XV 11 (diameter 12 cm.), A.D. 150–155/160 (II D, Room 55); and residual in B XI 13A, A.D. 270–5 (III, make-up, yard south-west of XIV, 6).
974. Hard grey ware, burnished mottled surfaces, B VII 4, A.D. 155/160. II D Room 52. Others from B IV 18J, A.D. 130–45 (II C, Room 39); B V 12, A.D. 140–50 (II C, Room 40); B I 18 (II D, Rooms 25, 35), B II 14 (two) (II D, Rooms 32–42), B IV 10 (II D, wall-trench 36/37), B V 7 (II D, Rooms 41–8), T III 11 (II D, Room 4), all A.D. 155/160; A V 11, A.D. 200–225/250 (Pit 21); and residually from B XIII 6 (III, make-up, XIV, 6 Room 2), B V 23B (III, make-up, XIV, 5 Room 4) both A.D. 270–5; B IV 14A, A.D. 270–300 (III, make-up XIV, 5 Room 3) B XI 10, A.D. 270–300+ (III, yard-metalling south-west of XIV, 6).
975. Hard burnished light grey ware, A I 12, A.D. 150–155/160. II D, Room 24.
976. Ware burnt red, lighter burnished slip, A VII 3, A.D. 155/160. II D, Room 25.

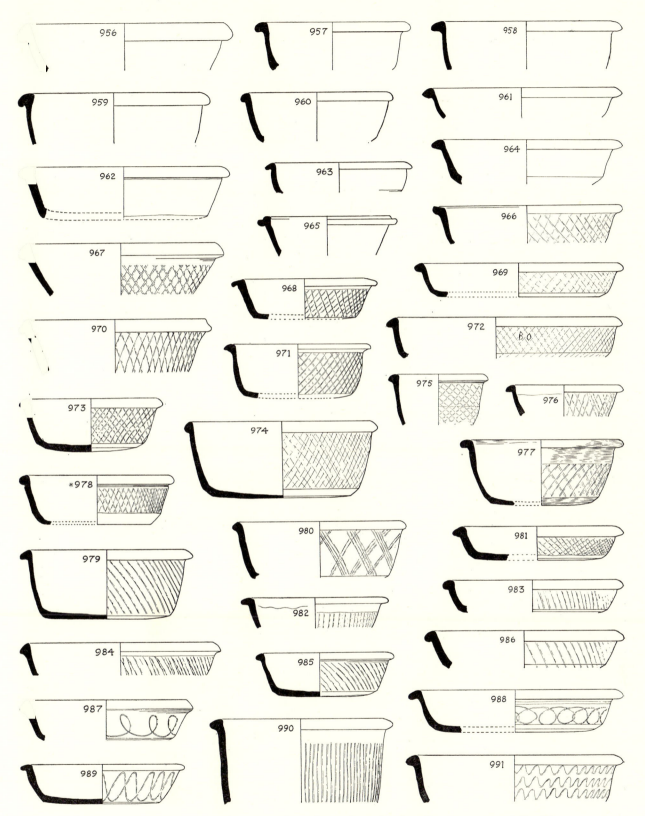

FIG. 128. Pottery vessels nos. 956–91 from deposits dated A.D. 150–155/160 ($\frac{1}{4}$).

977. Ware as 976, with slip to top of lattice, A I 2, A.D. 155/160. II D, Room 23. Others from A VII 3 (II D, Room 25), B VI 8 (grey) (II D, wall-trench of Room 51), both of the same date.

*978. Hard burnished light grey ware, A IV 1, Antonine fire (disturbed) II D, Rooms 17, 18. Another, dark grey, from B V 23, A.D. 150–155/160 (II D, interspace north-west of Room 43).

979. Hard mottled light grey-buff burnished ware, A VII 3, A.D. 155/160. II D Room 25. Another from B V 32, A.D. 150–155/160 (II D, Room 42A).

980. Hard burnished grey ware, Z I 2, A.D. 155/160. II D, Room 8. Another from T XXI 5, the same date (II D, Rooms 10, 25B).

981. Hard grey-brown burnished ware, lighter slip inside and to bottom of lattice, A VII 5, A.D. 150–155/160. II D, Room 24.

982. Ware as 981 (burnt), slip on upper part only, B V 7, A.D. 155/160. II D, Rooms 41–8. Another, also burnt, from B IV 3A, Antonine fire (disturbed) (II D, Rooms 38–42).

983. Hard mottled grey-buff burnished ware, A VI 2, A.D. 155/160. II D, Room 18.

984. Hard grey-black ware, burnished inside and on rim, B IV 3C, A.D. 155/160. II D, Room 43. Another from B V 7, the same date (II D, Rooms 41–8).

985. Hard burnished mottled grey-brown ware, T XX 2, A.D. 155/160. II D, Room 10. Others from B IV 3 (II D, Rooms 38–42), A IV 2 (II D, Room 18), both A.D. 155/160.

986. Ware as 985. B V 7, A.D. 155/160. II D, Rooms 41–8.

987. Hard grey burnished ware, A I 10, A.D. 150–155/160. II D, Room 23. Another from A IV 2, A.D. 155/160 (II D, Room 18). Similar larger dish (diameter 24 cm.) From B II 14, A.D. 155/160 (II D, Rooms 32–42).

988. Hard burnished grey-black ware, A I 14, A.D. 150–155/160. II D, Drain 23/29. Another from B II 27Z, A.D. 140–50 (II C, Room 41); and residual in A V 8 (grey), A.D. 270–5 (III, make-up south-west of XIV, 4); B I 22 (light grey), A.D. 270–80 (III, make-up south-west of cellar).

989. Ware as 988 (burnt), Z I 2, A.D. 155/160. II D, Room 8.

990. Burnished ware, burnt red, T III 11, A.D. 155/160. II D, Room 4.

991. Hard burnished light grey ware, A IV 14, A.D. 150–155/160. II D, Room 16, floor.

Fig. 129

Dishes with slightly beaded or plain rims, undecorated. Cf. 219–22, 346–9, 526–30, 736–41, 1066, 1093, 1112, 1129, 1178–81, 1198, 1219–21, 1265–74.

992. Hard light grey rather finely granulated ware, burnished, A IV 2, A.D. 155/160. II D, Room 18.

993. Hard burnished grey ware, darker outside, T III 11, A.D. 155/160. II D, Room 4. Another from B V 12, A.D. 140–50 (II C, Room 40).

994. Hard burnished light grey ware, B IV 9J, A.D. 150–155/160. II D, Room 43, floor.

995. Ware as 994, grey, T I 4, A.D. 150–155/160. II D, clay of north-east wall, Room 25A. Another from T III 6, A.D. 270–5 (III, make-up, XIV, 1 Room 1).

996. Ware as 994. A II 16, A.D. 150–155/160. II D, Room 19. Another from A X 2, A.D. 155/160 (II D, Room 29).

997. Hard light grey-brown ware, unevenly burnished, B IV 7, A.D. 150–155/160. II D, Room 40. Cf. 1091, 1112, 1272.

*998. Mica-coated ware (burnt red), B IV 3A, Antonine fire (disturbed) (II D, Rooms 38–42). Another from A IV 2, A.D. 155/160 (II D, Room 18). Cf. 525–7, 739–41, 1086.

Dishes with slightly beaded or plain rims, and burnished decoration. Cf. 730–5, 1051, 1091–2, 1120, 1128, 1175, 1218.

999. Rather coarse, unevenly burnished dark grey-brown ware, B IV 9F, A.D. 150–155/160. II D, Room 39, floor. Another, in grey-black ware, from A I 15, A.D. 145–50 (II C, Room 24).

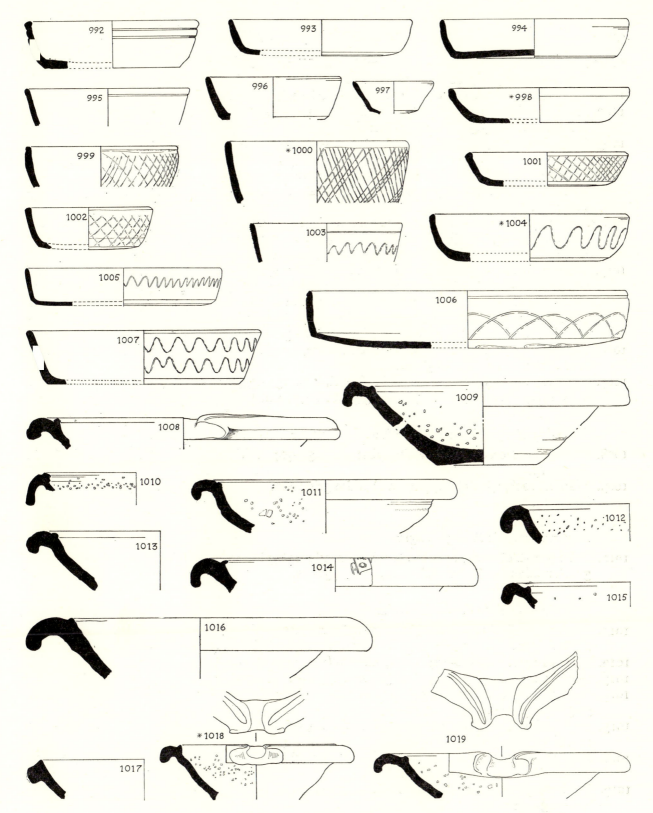

FIG. 129. Pottery vessels nos. 992–1019 from deposits dated A.D. 150–155/160 ($\frac{1}{4}$).

*1000. Hard mottled light grey ware, burnished inside and on rim, A II 5, A.D. 270–5. III, make-up south-west of XIV, 4. Another from Z II 7, A.D. 155/160 (II D, wall-trench 3A/5).

1001. Hard dark grey ware, grey-buff burnished surface, T I 9, c. A.D. 150. II D, street-metalling.

1002. Hard burnished light grey ware, A I 12, A.D. 150–155/160. II D, Room 24. Another from B I 19, A.D. 280–315 (III, cellar floor, XIV, 5).

1003. Hard burnished grey ware, A I 10, A.D. 150–155/160. II D, Room 23. Others in light and dark grey, from B IV 17J, A.D. 145–50 (II C, Room 39), B IV 3 (II D, Rooms 38–42), B XIV 10 (II D, wall-trench 25/50), T III 11 (II D, Room 4), T III 8 (II D, Room 25A), all A.D. 155/160; and residually in T VII 5, A.D. 270–5 (III, make-up, XIV, 1 Room 1); B IV 4, A.D. 350–410+ (XIV, 5).

*1004. Hard burnished mottled light grey ware, III, make-up, XIV, 5 Room 4. Others from A II 16, A.D. 150–155/160 (II D, Room 19); B XIII 4, Antonine fire, disturbed (II D, Room 48); and residually in B II Pit 5, late fourth century (mouth of Pit 4).

1005. Ware as 1004. A I 10, A.D. 150–155/160. II D, Room 23. Others, in light or dark grey, from B IV 9J, A.D. 150–155/160 (II D, Room 43, floor); T III 11 (II D, Room 4), T X 5 (II D, Room 1), T XXI 5 (II D, Rooms 10, 25B), all A.D. 155/160; B XVI 7 (burnt) Antonine fire (disturbed) (III, oblong trench in XIV, 7 Room 1); and residually in T III 6, A.D. 270–75 (III, make-up, XIV, 1 Room 1) and B XI 4B (burnt), 270–300+(yard south-west of XIV, 6).

1006. Hard dark grey rather finely granulated ware, burnished inside, smoothed outside, B IV 3, A.D. 155/160. II D, Room 38–42.

1007. Hard dark grey burnished ware, B II 27E, A.D. 150–155/160. II D, Room 43. Others from B IV 17K, A.D. 140–50 (II C, Room 39); B IV 9F, A.D. 150–155/160 (II D, Room 39, floor).

Mortaria probably made at Colchester (see page 263 for note on the dates given).

1008. Smooth hard cream ware, white grits; A.D. 130–70; A IV 19, c. A.D. 150. II D, make-up in Room 15.

1009. Ware as 1008, with black, grey, and white grits; A.D. 130–70; A X 7, A.D. 150–155/160. II D, Room 29.

Mortarium made in the Oxford region

1010. Hard grey-buff ware, brown and white translucent grits; early or mid-second century; B IV 3A, Antonine fire (disturbed). II D, Rooms 38–42.

Mortaria made in the Verulamium region

1011. Hard rather finely granulated yellow-buff ware, grey and white grits; probably A.D. 90–130+; B VI 11, A.D. 150–155/160. II D, in clay of standing timber-framed clay wall 55/56.

1012. Ware as 1011. A.D. 100–40; B I 18, A.D. 155/160. II D, Rooms 25, 35.

1013. Ware as 1011. A.D. 100–40; B IV 3C, A.D. 155/160. II D, Room 43.

1014. Hard granulated buff ware, stamp ROA; A.D. 110–50; B IV 10, A.D. 155/160. II D, wall-trench 36/37. See p. 378.

1015. Hard rather finely granulated orange-buff ware, grey grits; A.D. 110–40; B IV 9, A.D. 150–155/160. II D, Room 24.

1016. Hard rather finely granulated ware, burnt grey, with white and grey grits; A.D. 100–40; A II 7, A.D. 155/160. II D, Rooms 20–2.

1017. Hard finely granulated buff ware: second century, post-Hadrianic; B II 14, A.D. 155/160. II D, Rooms 32–42.

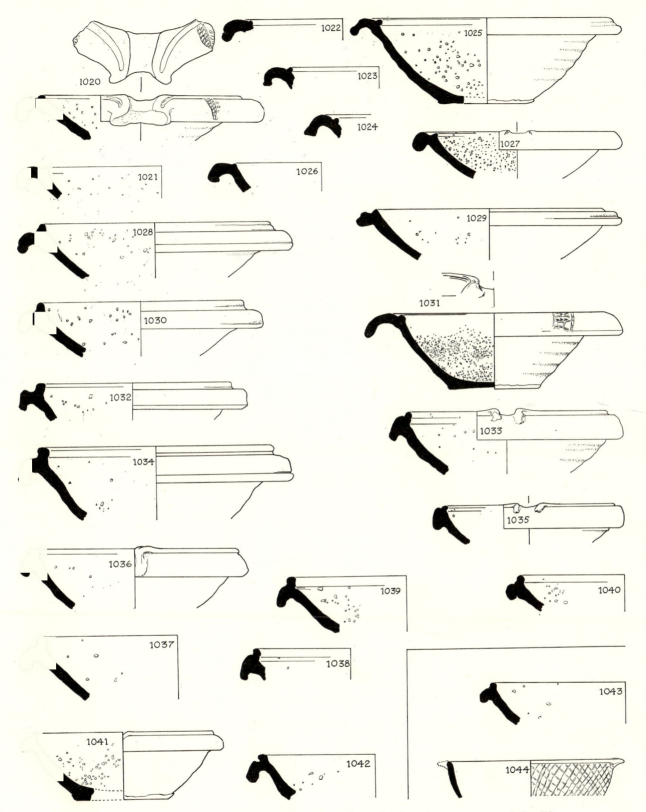

FIG. 130. Pottery vessels nos. 1020–44 from deposits dated A.D. 150–155/160 ($\frac{1}{4}$).

*1018. Hard buff granulated ware (burnt), white and grey grits; A.D. 110–50; B IV 3A, Antonine fire (disturbed). II D, Rooms 38–42.

1019. Hard rather finely granulated buff ware, white and grey grits; A.D. 120–45, style of Lallans and Saturninus; B IV 3, A.D. 155/160. II D, Rooms 38–42.

Fig. 130

1020. Ware as 1019, grey and red-brown grits; part of two stamps [of **MELVS**] A.D. 110–35; A XI 7, c. A.D. 150. II D, Room 13, make-up. See p. 376.

1021. Hard orange-buff finely granulated ware, white and dark grey grits; A.D. 110–40; A I 14, A.D. 150–155/160. II D, silt in Drain 23/29.

1022. Hard rather finely granulated buff ware; A.D. 110–50; A XII 10, A.D. 150–155/160. II D, Room 25B.

1023. Hard buff granulated ware; A.D. 110–50; Z I 2, A.D. 155/160. II D, Room 8.

1024. Ware as 1023, with fragment of unidentifiable stamp border; A.D. 110–50; Z I 6, A.D. 150–155/160. II D, oven in Room 8.

1025. Hard finely granulated buff ware, white and grey grits; A.D. 120–50; B XIV 14, A.D. 150–155/160. II D, Room 50.

1026. Hard granulated ware (burnt); A.D. 120–60; A I 2, A.D. 155/160. II D, Room 23.

1027. Hard orange-buff granulated ware, grey, white, and translucent grits; A.D. 130–70; B II 14, A.D. 155/160. II D, Rooms 32–42.

1028. Hard rather finely granulated buff ware, grey and red grits; A.D. 130–80; B V 7A, A.D. 155/160. II D, Room 45.

1029. Hard buff granulated ware, white and grey grits; A.D. 130–70; B II 14, A.D. 155/160. II D, Rooms 32–42.

1030. Hard buff rather finely granulated ware, white and brown grits; A.D. 140–80; B IV 3, A.D. 155/160. II D, Rooms 38–42.

1031. Ware as 1030, brown grits; part of stamp S]ARRI[VS, A.D. 135–75; A IV 8, A.D. 155/160. II D, Room 17. See p. 378.

1032. Hard finely granulated grey-buff ware, white and grey grits; A.D. 140–200; A II 7, A.D. 155/160. II D, Rooms 20–2.

1033. Hard orange-buff granulated ware, white and grey grits; A.D. 140–200; B IV 7, A.D. 150–155/160. II D, Room 40. With part of the same in B IV 18C, A.D. 135–45 (II C, Room 45).

1034. Ware as 1033, white and grey grits; A.D. 140–200; A IV 2, A.D. 155/160. II D, Room 18. Others from A VI 8, A.D. 130–40 (II C, Room 13); B IV 3A (burnt), Antonine fire (disturbed) (II D, Rooms 38–42), with a sherd of the same in B IV 3, A.D. 155/160 (ibid.).

1035. Hard buff granulated ware, white grits; A.D. 140–20; A IV 11, A.D. 155/160. II D, Room 15.

1036. Hard rather finely granulated buff ware, grey grits; A.D. 140–200; T XX 2, A.D. 155/160. II D, Room 10.

1037. Ware as 1036, white and brown grits; c. A.D. 150–200; A X 2, A.D. 155/160. II D, Room 29.

1038. Hard finely granulated yellow-buff ware, grey and white grits; c. A.D. 150–200; B IV 9D, A.D. 150–155/160. II D, Room 40.

1039. Ware as 1038, buff; A.D. 150–200; T XXI 7, A.D. 155/160. II D, wall-trench 10/25B.

1040. Hard rather finely granulated buff ware, grey core, with white, grey, and brown grits; A.D. 150–200; B V 9, A.D. 155/160. II D, south-east wall-trench, Room 45.

1041. Hard finely granulated buff ware, with grey, red-brown and white grits, the spout formed by pressing out the bead; A.D. 150–200+; B V 32, A.D. 150–155/160. II D, Room 42A.

1042. Hard rather finely granulated buff ware, with grey and white grits; A.D. 150–200; Z I 2, A.D. 155/160. II D, Room 8.

POTTERY OF THE GENERAL DATE OF PERIOD II D FROM LATER LAYERS

1043. Mortarium in hard finely granulated light grey-buff ware, with white and grey grits; A.D. 140–200, Verulamium region; T VII 6, A.D. 270–5. III, make-up, XIV, 1 Room 1.

1044. Dish with lobe handle(s) and burnished lattice, in hard dark grey rather finely granulated ware, unevenly burnished on rim, handle, and interior, B XIII 10, A.D. 270–5. III, make-up, XIV, 6 Room 2. Cf. 731.

POTTERY FROM LAYERS DATED A.D. 160–75

Fig. 131

Fine ware

1045. Beaker with barbotine decoration in fine hard light reddish ware, dark grey-brown coating (worn), B XI 30. Pit 19. Cf. 556–7, 791–5, 1144.

Beakers

1046. Mica-coated fine light reddish paste, B XI 30. Pit 19. Cf. 129, 380, 583.

1047. Poppyhead beaker in fine hard grey ware, burnished slip. B XI 30. Pit 19. Another from B VII 4, A.D. 155/160 (II D, Room 52). Cf. 133, 136–7, 255, 424–8, 598–604, 837–9, 1073.

1048. As 1047. B XI 30. Pit 19.

1049. As 1047, light grey ware and slip, B XI 30. Pit 19.

Jar with internally grooved rim. Cf. 48, 81–2, 197–9, 481–5, 656–66, 897–909, 1050, 1062, 1080.

1050. Coarse buff calcite-gritted ware, finely rilled, B XI 30. Pit. 19. For calcite-gritted parallels cf. 81, 199, 482, 666.

Dish with plain rim and burnished lattice. Cf. 730–5, 999–1007, 1091–2, 1120, 1128, 1175, 1218.

1051. Hard rather granulated dark grey ware, burnished especially inside and on rim, B XI 30. Pit 19.

Mortarium made at Colchester (see page 263 for note on the dates given).

1052. Hard finely granulated cream ware, with grey-white grits; probably A.D. 130–80; B XI 30. Pit 19.

Mortaria made in the Verulamium region

1053. Hard finely granulated yellow-buff ware, with grey and brown grits; A.D. 140–20; B XI 30. Pit 19.

1054. Ware as 1053; A.D. 140–200; B XI 30. Pit 19.

Mortarium of the same general date from a later layer

1055. Hard yellow-buff granulated ware, grey core, with grey and white grits; A.D. 140–200, Verulamium region; B VII 3B. III, make-up, XIV, 6 Room 1.

POTTERY FROM LAYERS DATED A.D. 200–225/250 AND (*) 200–75

Fine wares

1056. Rhenish-ware beaker with barbotine decoration, in smooth hard orange paste, dark grey-brown 'metallic' coating, A V 11. Pit 21. Cf. 1118.

1057. Beaker with barbotine hound, in fine hard orange-buff paste, dark grey-brown 'metallic' coating, lighter inside, A V 11. Pit 21.

1058. Beaker with barbotine scale-pattern, in fine hard grey paste, buff core, black coating, A V 11. Pit 21. Reconstructed from a base with scale-pattern, in white paste with grey coating, from T II 8, A.D. 155/160. II D, Room 25A. Cf. 1141–3.

1059. Beaker with barbotine scale-pattern between indentations, in hard white paste, with dark-brown coating, A V 11. Pit 21. Another, lacking the rim, from B XI 21, A.D. 270–300+ (III, Yard metalling south-west of XIV, 6). Sherds from A IV 2, A.D. 155/160 (II D, Room 18); A IV 4 (III, make-up, XIV, 2 Room 2), A II 5 (III, make-up south-west of XIV, 4), both A.D. 270–5; B I 11 (in orange-buff paste), A.D. 310–15 (III, cellar filling, XIV, 5).

*1060. Beaker with indented sides, in fine hard white paste, dark grey-brown 'metallic' coating, A V 1, A.D. 200–75 (disturbed top of Pit 21). Similar base from B II 3, A.D. 370–410+ (rubble over cellar filling, XIV, 5). Cf. 790, 1105–6, 1130–2.

Jars

1061. Hard finely granulated buff ware, A V 11. Pit 21. Cf. 170, 458–62, 464, 634–5, 645–55, 871–81, 1077–8, 1109.

1062. Jar with internally grooved rim, in hard grey ware, A V 11. Pit 21. Cf. 48, 81–2, 197–9, 390, 481–5, 656–66, 897–909, 1050, 1080.

Plain dishes with moulded rims. Cf. 344, 724–7, 952–64, 1082–6, 1177, 1215, 1262–4.

1063. Hard grey ware, lighter burnished slip, A V 11. Pit 21.

1064. Hard mottled grey-black burnished ware, A V 11. Pit 21.

1065. Ware as 1064, grey, A V 11. Pit 21.

Dish with plain rim. Cf. 219–22, 346–9, 526–30, 736–41, 992–8, 1093, 1112, 1129, 1178–81, 1198, 1219–21, 1265–74.

1066. Hard burnished grey-black ware, A V 11. Pit 21.

Mortaria made at Colchester, of the same general date but from later layers (see page 263 for note on the dates given).

1067. Hard pinkish-buff ware, with white grits; late second, or third century; B II 2, Antonine fire (disturbed). III, make-up, XIV 5.

1068. Smooth hard cream ware; *c.* A.D. 200–300; B I 5, A.D. 370–410+. Rubble over cellar filling, XIV, 5.

1069. Ware as 1068, with grey grits; probably A.D. 200–50; B I 5, A.D. 370–410+.

POTTERY FROM LAYERS DATED A.D. 270–5 AND 175–275

Fig. 132

Fine ware

1070. Roughcast beaker in fine hard white paste, dark grey-brown 'metallic' coating, B VII 3B. III, make-up, XIV, 6 Room 1. Cf. 555, 787–9, also (plain) 30–1, 52, 101, 232–3, 396, 780–6.

Ring-necked flagons. Cf. 102–11, 238–41, 375–8, 403–10, 559–73, 798–811, 1107.

1071. Hard rather finely granulated buff ware, T III 8. III, make-up, XIV, 1 Room 1.

1072. Ware as 1071. A II 11. Make-up south-west of XIV, 4. Others from A IV 11, A.D. 155/160 (II D, Room 15); B II 15, A.D. 270–80 (III, make-up of XIV, 5, south-west of cellar); AII 34 (unnumbered pit south-west of XIV, 4). Similar rim from B IV 18J, A.D. 130–45 (II C, Room 39).

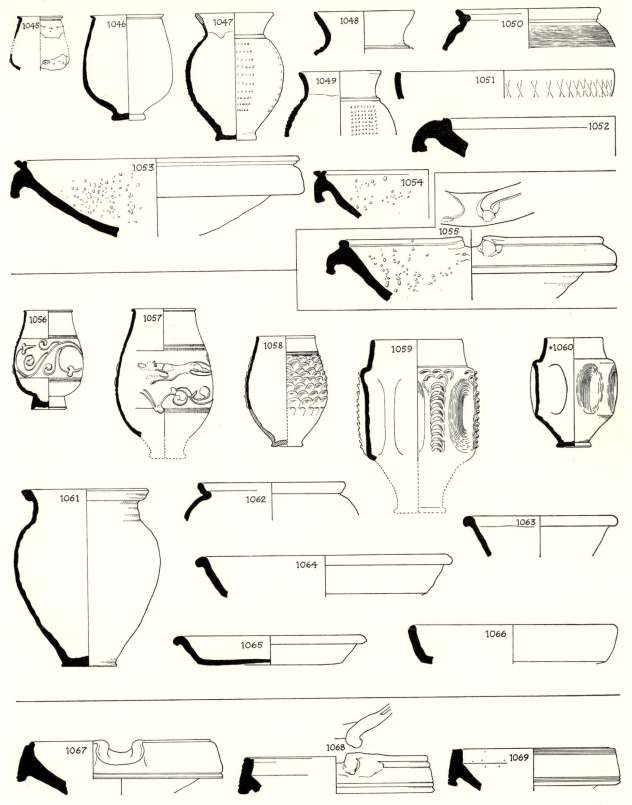

FIG. 131. Pottery vessels from deposits dated A.D. 160–75 (nos. 1045–55) and A.D. 200–75 (nos. 1056–69) (¼).

Poppyhead beaker. Cf. 133, 136–7, 255, 424–8, 598–604, 837–9, 1047–9.

1073. Hard rather finely granulated burnished dark grey ware, slip on upper part, B XI 29, A.D. 175–275. Pit 19, upper filling.

Narrow-necked jar. Cf. 118–24, 245–50, 412–18, 822–35, 1152–4, 1231–4.

1074. Rather coarse, hard granulated light grey burnished ware, A VII 2. III, make-up, XIV, 4 Room 3.

Jars

1075. Hard rather granulated grey ware, sharply rilled shoulder, B V 29. III, make-up, XIV, 5 Room 4.
1076. Smooth reddish-buff micaceous ware, cream slip, A I 5. III, make-up, XIV, 4 Room 1.

Jars in buff ware. Cf. 170, 458–62, 464, 634–5, 645–55, 1061, 1109.

1077. Hard buff ware, A I 5. III, make-up, XIV, 4 Room 1.
1078. Hard rather finely granulated yellow-buff ware, B XI 29, A.D. 175–275. Pit 19.
1079. Face-mask fragment in relief, in hard buff ware, probably from a jar as 910, 911. T VI 6. III, make-up, XIV, 1 Room 1.

Jar with internally grooved rim. Cf. 48, 81–2, 197–9, 390, 481–5, 656–66, 909, 1050, 1062.

1080. Hard light grey granulated ware, B V 31. III, make-up, XIV, 5 Room 3.

Bowl

1081. Hard rather granulated grey ware, burnished rim and neck, rilled shoulder, B V 28. III, make-up, XIV, 5 Room 4. Another from T XX 2, A.D. 155/160 (II D, Room 10).

Plain dishes with moulded rims. Cf. 344, 724–7, 952–64, 1063–5, 1177.

1082. Hard grey ware, mottled grey-buff burnished surfaces, B XI 29, A.D. 175–275. Pit 19.
1083. Ware as 1082, light grey, B XI 29, A.D. 175–275. Pit 19.
1084. Dish with groove on rim, forming a small bead, in hard finely granulated dark grey ware, burnished rim, B V 29. III, make-up, XIV, 5 Room 4. Cf. 343, 515, 728, 968, 1260, 1287.
1085. Hard dark grey ware, burnished mottled surfaces, B XI 29, A.D. 175–275, Pit 19.
1086. Mica-coated dish with buff paste, grey core, B XI 29, A.D. 175–275. Pit 19. Probably residual, cf. 525–7, 739–741, 998.

Dishes with moulded rims and burnished decoration. Cf. 531, 706–23, 966–91, 1111, 1176, 1216–17, 1261, 1286.

1087. Hard light grey ware, partly burnished slip, B XI 29, A.D. 175–275. Pit 19.
1088. Hard dark grey ware, surfaces burnished except in decorated zone, T III 8. III, make-up, XIV, 1 Room 1. Another from T XI 5 (III, make-up, XIV, 1 Room 1).
1089. Smooth hard dark grey burnished ware, B III 4. III, make-up, XIV, 5 Room 3. Cf. 977, 1004.
1090. Hard rather dark grey ware, burnished inside and on rim, T VI 7. III, make-up, XIV, 1 Room 1.

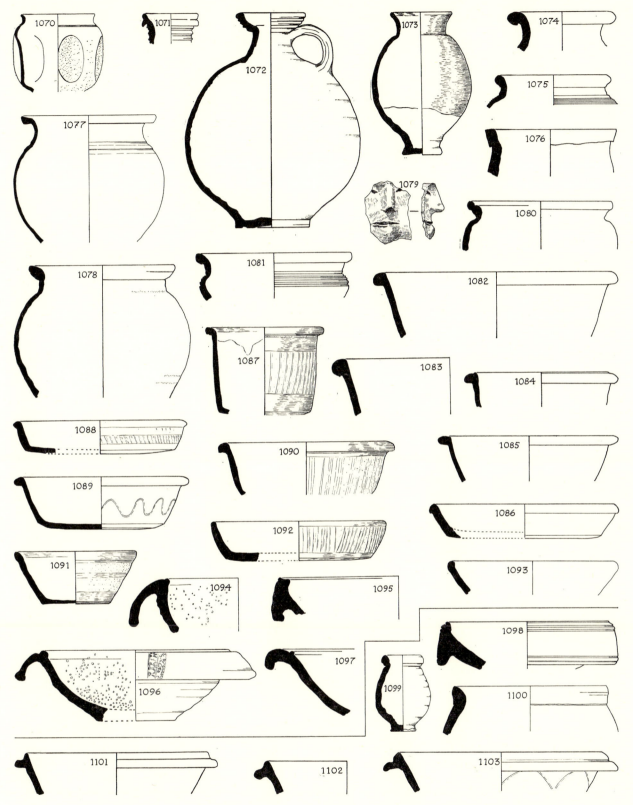

FIG. 132. Pottery vessels from deposits dated A.D. 270–5 (nos. 1070–97) and A.D. 270–90 (nos. 1098–1103) ($\frac{1}{4}$).

Dishes with plain rims and burnished decoration. Cf. 730–5, 999–1007, 1051, 1120, 1128, 1175, 1218.

1091. Hard finely granulated dark grey ware, partly burnished, B XI 29, A.D. 175–275. Pit 19. Cf. 997, 1112, 1272.

1092. Hard dark grey ware, unevenly burnished surfaces, except in decorated zone, T VI 7. III, make-up, XIV, 1 Room 1.

Dish with plain rim, undecorated. Cf. 219–22, 346–9, 526–30, 736–41, 992–8, 1066, 1112, 1129, 1178–81, 1198, 1219–21, 1265–74.

1093. Smooth hard burnished dark grey ware, T III 10. III, make-up, XIV, 1 Room 1.

Mortaria (see p. 263 for note on the dates given).

1094. Hard deep buff finely micaceous ware, with grey grits; probably by Gaius Atisius Sabinus (or G. Atisius Gratus) who probably worked in Gallia Narbonensis; primarily Flavian; T VI 8. III, make-up, XIV, 1 Room 1.

1095. Hard buff granulated ware, with grey and white grits; probably third century, Verulamium region; A I 3. III, make-up, XIV, 4 Room 1.

1096. Smooth hard cream ware, translucent pink and grey grits; illiterate stamp, *c.* A.D. 140–80, Oxford region; T XI 5. III, make-up, XIV, 1 Room 1. See p. 381.

1097. Hard yellow-buff rather finely granulated ware; stamp ΛRIINTX (? retro), A.D. 110–40, Verulamium region; T XI 5. Ibid. See p. 379.

POTTERY FROM LAYERS DATED A.D. 270–90

1098. Mortarium in smooth hard deep buff ware; third century, Colchester; B I 25, A.D. 270–80. III, make-up, XIV, 5 south-west of cellar.

1099. Unguent jar in finely granulated orange-buff ware, B II 18, A.D. 280–90. III, chalk packing behind cellar wall. Cf. 476–80, 636–41, 882–5 and fig. 141, 15, 16 (used as crucibles).

1100. Jar in coarse buff calcite-gritted ware, B II 12, A.D. 280–90. III, packing behind cellar wall. Cf. 895–6, 1159–60, 1242, 1283.

Bowls with flanged rims, undecorated. Cf. 1110, 1127, 1162–9, 1211–13, 1248–54, 1292.

1101. Hard grey-black burnished ware, B II 15, A.D. 270–80. III, make-up, XIV, 5, south-west of cellar.

1102. Ware as 1101, burnished inside and on rim, B I 25, A.D. 270–80. III, make-up, XIV, 5, south-west of cellar.

Bowl with flanged rim and burnished decoration. Cf. 1126, 1170–4, 1193, 1255–7, 1285, 1293.

1103. Rather coarse grey-black ware, unevenly burnished inside, and on rim and flange, B I 25, A.D. 270–80. III, Make-up, XIV, 5, south-west of cellar. Cf. 1170.

POTTERY FROM LAYERS DATED A.D. 270–300+

Fig. 133

Fine ware

1104. Rhenish-ware beaker in very fine hard orange paste, glossy 'metallic' black coating, the base broken and subsequently trimmed, B III 15. III, make-up below mosaic, XIV, 5 Room 3.

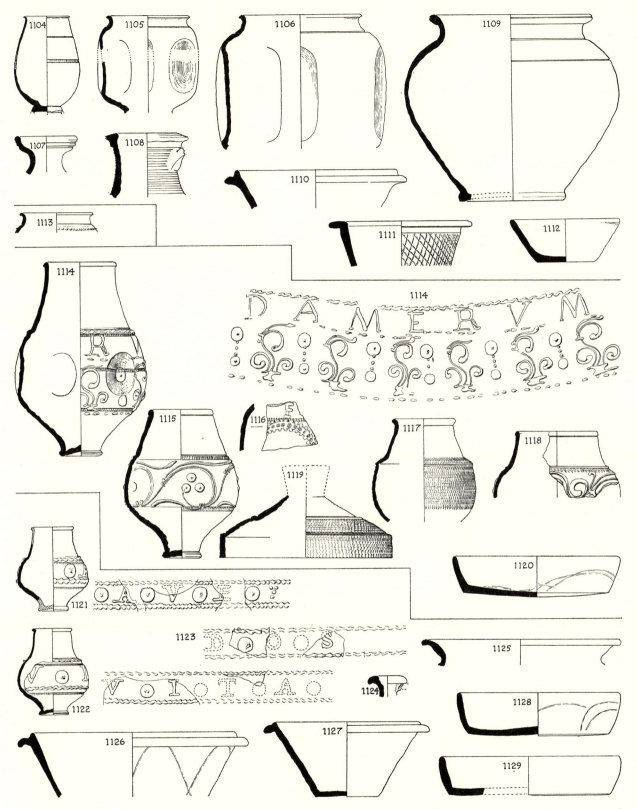

FIG. 133. Pottery vessels from deposits dated A.D. 270–300+ (nos. 1104–12); A.D. 280–315 (nos. 1113–20) and A.D. 300–15 (nos. 1121–9) (¼).

1105. Beaker with indented sides, in hard buff paste, 'metallic' grey-brown coating, B III 15. Ibid. Cf. 790, 1059, 1060, 1130–2.
1106. As 1105. B IV 14. III, make-up below mosaic. XIV, 5 Room 3.

Flagons

1107. Ring-necked flagon in hard buff ware, B IV 15A. III, make-up below mosaic, XIV, 5 Room 3. Cf. 102–111, 238–41, 375–8, 403–10, 559–73, 798–811, 1071–2.
1108. Hard finely granulated ware (burnt red), B XII 7. III, make-up, XIV, 6 Room 1.

Jar

1109. Hard rather finely granulated light grey-buff ware, partly smoothed surface, B V 17. III, yard south-west of XIV, 6. It is possible that this layer has a terminal date later than 300+. Cf. 170, 458–62, 464, 634–5, 645–55, 871–81, 1061, 1077–8.

Plain bowl with flanged rim. Cf. 1101–2, 1127, 1162–9, 1211–13, 1248–54, 1292.

1110. Hard light grey burnished ware, B IV 14. III, make-up below mosaic, XIV, 5 Room 3. Similar rim from B XI 26, A.D. 300–50 (Pit 19).

Dishes

1111. Grey-black burnished ware, with burnished lattice, B II 19, A.D. 280–90. III, packing behind cellar wall. Probably residual, cf. 708.
1112. Hard finely granulated light grey-buff ware, B III 15. III, make-up below mosaic, XIV, 5 Room 3. Another, in smooth hard red-brown ware, grey-brown surface, from the same layer. Cf. 997, 1091, 1272.

POTTERY FROM LAYERS DATED A.D. 280–315

Fine ware: (a) beakers with white decoration. Cf. 1121–3, 1133–9, 1143.

1113. Beaker in fine hard reddish paste, highly 'metallic' grey coating, with white barbotine dots, T X 3, A.D. 280–90. III, make-up outside (south-west of) XIV, 1.
1114. Rhenish-ware beaker in fine hard orange paste, dark grey-brown 'metallic' coating, the sides having six circular indentations, with white-painted inscription **DA MERVM**, and white barbotine decoration, B I 55. III, cellar, occupation layer. See pl. LIc. Similar sherds from B I 9, A.D. 310–15. (III, cellar-filling); B II 2, Antonine fire (disturbed) (II D, Rooms 32–42).
1115. Beaker in fine hard buff (or white) paste, dark grey-brown coating, with white barbotine decoration, B I 55. III, cellar, occupation layer. Similar sherds, with orange coating inside, from B I 8, A.D. 360–70 (III, secondary make-up of cellar filling).
1116. Sherd of beaker in hard yellow-buff paste, grey core, highly 'metallic' dark-grey coating, with white-painted **E**, above wreath in white and brown paint, B I 19A. III, cellar, occupation layer.

Fine ware: (b) other beakers

1117. Rouletted beaker in hard orange-buff paste, dark brown coating, B I 55. III, cellar, occupation layer. Shoulder sherd from B XIV 15A, Antonine fire (disturbed) (II D, Room 50).
1118. Beaker with barbotine decoration, in hard finely granulated buff ware, dark grey-brown coating, B I 55. III, cellar, occupation layer. Another from B I 9, A.D. 310–15 (III, cellar-filling). Cf. 1056.

1119. 'Castor Box' lid in hard orange paste, dark grey coating outside, grey-brown inside, B I 55. III, cellar occupation layer. Similar rim, in buff paste, from B XI 22, A.D. 300–50. Pit 19, cf. layer 23.

Dish with plain rim and burnished decoration. Cf. 730–5, 999–1007, 1051, 1091–2, 1120, 1128, 1175, 1218.

1120. Hard rather granulated dark grey ware, more burnished inside, with burnished arcading, B I 55. III, cellar, occupation layer. Another from B I 9, A.D. 310–15 (III, cellar filling).

POTTERY FROM LAYERS DATED A.D. 300–15

Fine ware. Cf. 1113–16, 1133–9, 1143.

1121. Rhenish-ware beaker in fine hard grey paste, reddish core, grey-black 'metallic' coating, with white barbotine inscription AVE (incomplete) and decoration, cf. *CIL* xiii, 10018, 31e¹ (AVE). B I 59. III, sump in cellar floor. Similar sherds from T III 6, A.D. 270–5 (III, make-up, XIV, 1 Room 1); B I 55, A.D. 280–315 (III, cellar, occupation layer); B I 12 (two), A.D. 315–60 (III, accumulation over south-east wall of cellar).

1122. As 1121, with inscription VI[; cf. *CIL* xiii, 10018, 191 (VITA). B I 59. III, sump in cellar floor.

1123. Inscription fragment from beaker similar to 1121–2, showing separate letters OS (incomplete); cf. *CIL* xiii, 10018, 69 (DOS). B I 59. III, sump in cellar floor.

Flagon

1124. Hard rather finely granulated light reddish ware (worn), B I 58B. III, secondary occupation level in cellar.

Jar

1125. Black-burnished A ware, B I 59, III, sump in cellar floor. Cf. 381–2, 429, 430, 613–22, 624, 845–56, 1155, 1187.

Bowls with flanged rims

1126. Rather finely granulated grey ware, burnished especially inside, with burnished arcading, B I 59. III, sump in cellar floor. Cf. 1103, 1193, 1255–7, 1285, 1293.

1127. Hard grey ware, grey-buff core, burnished inside, and partly outside, B I Pit 20. III, 'Box' in cellar floor. Cf. 1101–2, 1110, 1211–13, 1248–54, 1292.

Dishes with plain rims

1128. Black-burnished A ware, with burnished arcading, B I 59. III, sump in cellar floor. Cf. 730–5, 999–1007, 1051, 1091–2, 1120, 1128, 1175, 1218.

1129. Smooth hard burnished grey-black ware, B I 59. III, sump in cellar floor. Another in light grey ware from the same layer; two others in grey-black ware from B I 9, A.D. 310–15 (III, cellar filling). Cf. 219–22, 346–9, 526–30, 736–41, 992–8, 1066, 1093, 1112, 1178–81, 1198, 1219–21, 1265–74.

POTTERY FROM MAIN FILLING OF CELLAR (B I 9) DATED A.D. 310–15

Fig. 134

Fine ware: (a) Beakers with indented sides. Cf. 790, 1059, 1060, 1105–6.

1130. Rhenish-ware beaker in fine hard orange paste, grey core, glossy 'metallic' dark grey coating, orange-brown inside.

1131. Beaker with white-painted circle and central dot, set in shallow circular indentations, alternating with narrow vertical indentations, in rather coarse hard orange-buff paste, and coating.

1132. Hard white paste, 'metallic' black coating.

Fine ware: (b) beakers with white decoration. Cf. 1113–16, 1121–3, 1143.

1133. Hard buff paste, 'metallic' dark grey coating, orange-brown at base, with white barbotine decoration.

1134. Rather coarse hard reddish-buff paste, 'metallic' black coating, with white barbotine decoration, reconstructed with rim and sherd of a second beaker. Cf. 1137.

1135. Fine hard white paste, dark grey 'metallic' coating, white barbotine decoration.

1136. Hard buff paste, 'metallic' grey-brown coating, white barbotine decoration.

1137. Hard buff paste, 'metallic' black coating, dark brown inside, with white barbotine decoration. Cf. 1134.

1138. Hard orange-buff paste, 'metallic' dark grey to brown coating, with white barbotine decoration.

1139. Hard, rather coarse buff paste, 'metallic' brown coating, matt orange inside, with white barbotine decoration.

Fine ware: (c) rouletted beaker

1140. Hard orange-buff paste, highly 'metallic' dark grey coating, orange-brown inside.

Fine ware: (d) beakers with barbotine scale-pattern. Cf. 1058–9.

1141. Hard buff paste, dark grey to brown 'metallic' coating. Oxford region.

1142. Hard white paste, 'metallic' grey to orange-brown coating, purple inside.

1143. Hard buff paste, dark grey to brown 'metallic' coating outside, matt orange inside, with white-painted dots. Cf. 1113–16, 1121–3, 1133–9.

Fine ware: (e) beaker with colour-coated barbotine decoration. Cf. 556–7, 791–5, 1045, 1205.

1144. Fine hard white paste, dark-grey to brown 'metallic' coating.

Fine ware: (f) plain beaker

1145. Hard red to grey paste, grey-brown coating, Cf. 1224.

Fine ware: (g) flagon

1146. Handle joined to rim by projecting knob on either side of two vertically projecting spurs, with a narrower vertical projection broken off. This suggests a metal prototype with hinged lid. Hard orange-buff paste, slightly 'metallic' dark to orange-brown coating. Two were found.

Fine ware: (h) bowls

1147. Rouletted bowl in hard white paste, 'metallic' red-brown coating, brown inside.

1148. Hard light reddish-buff paste, dark grey-brown coating, with traces of white-painted decoration on rim.

Fine ware: (i) red colour-coated bowls. Cf. 1196–7, 1200–04, 1228–30, 1280–1, 1290.

1149. Hard reddish paste, micaceous red coating. Oxford region.

1150. Bowl with burnished wavy-line decoration between narrow concentric circles, in hard reddish paste, grey core, with micaceous brownish-buff coating. Not from Oxford region.

1151. Rouletted bowl in hard orange-buff paste, and coating.

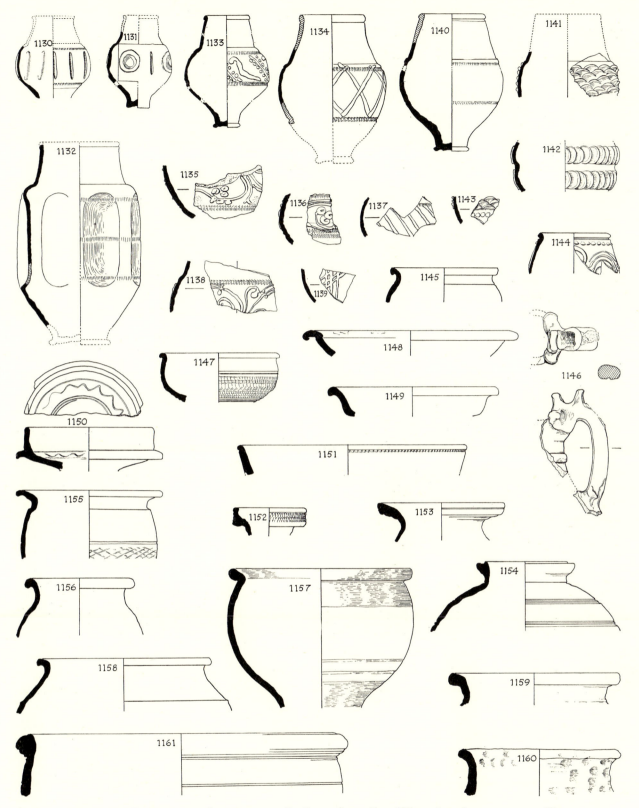

FIG. 134. Pottery vessels nos. 1130–61 from the cellar filling dated A.D. 310–15 (¼).

Narrow-necked jars. Cf. 118–24, 245–50, 412–18, 822–35, 1074, 1231–4.

1152. Rouletted jar in hard rather granulated cream ware. Cf. 1232.
1153. Smooth hard light grey burnished ware.
1154. Hard grey ware, lighter core, partly burnished.

Jars

1155. Black-burnished A ware. Cf. 381–2, 429, 430, 613–22, 624, 845–56, 1125, 1187.
1156. Hard granulated grey ware, partly burnished.
1157. Hard finely granulated grey ware, partly burnished.
1158. Hard grey granulated ware.

Calcite-gritted jars. Cf. 895–6, 1100, 1209–10, 1242, 1283.

1159. Coarse buff calcite-gritted ware, grey core.
1160. Very coarse buff calcite-gritted ware, grey core, roughly finished, showing finger-impressions.

Bowl

1161. Hard finely granulated cream ware, unevenly burnished.

Fig. 135

Plain bowls with flanged rims. Cf. 1101–2, 1110, 1127, 1211–13, 1248–54, 1292.

1162. Black-burnished A ware (three).
1163. Rather granulated grey-black burnished ware, lighter core.
1164. Black rather finely granulated ware, partly burnished outside.
1165. Smooth hard burnished grey-black ware.
1166. Smooth hard burnished light grey ware.
1167. Hard light grey ware, burnished inside, and partly outside.
1168. Rather finely granulated grey-black ware, smoothly burnished.
1169. Hard rather granulated grey ware, burnished inside and on flange.

Bowls with flanged rims and burnished decoration. Cf. 1103, 1126, 1193, 1255–7, 1285, 1293.

1170. Black-burnished A ware (burnt grey outside). Cf. 1103.
1171. Black-burnished A ware.
1172. Dark grey granulated ware, black surface, burnished flange.
1173. Rather finely granulated grey ware, burnished especially inside and on flange.
1174. Light grey granulated ware, partly burnished. Cf. 1256–7.

Dishes

1175. Dish with plain rim and burnished decoration, in black-burnished A ware. Another in the same ware, slightly thicker, from this layer; and from B I 8 (two), A.D. 360–70. Cf. 730–5, 999–1007, 1051, 1091–2, 1120, 1128, 1218.
1176. Dish with moulded rim and burnished decoration, in rather granulated grey-black ware, burnished especially inside and on rim. Cf. 531, 706–23, 966–91, 1087–90, 1216–17, 1261, 1286.
1177. Plain dish with moulded rim, in hard rather finely granulated black ware, burnished inside, partly burnished and roughly finished outside. Cf. 344, 724–7, 952–64, 1063–5, 1082–6, 1215, 1262–4.

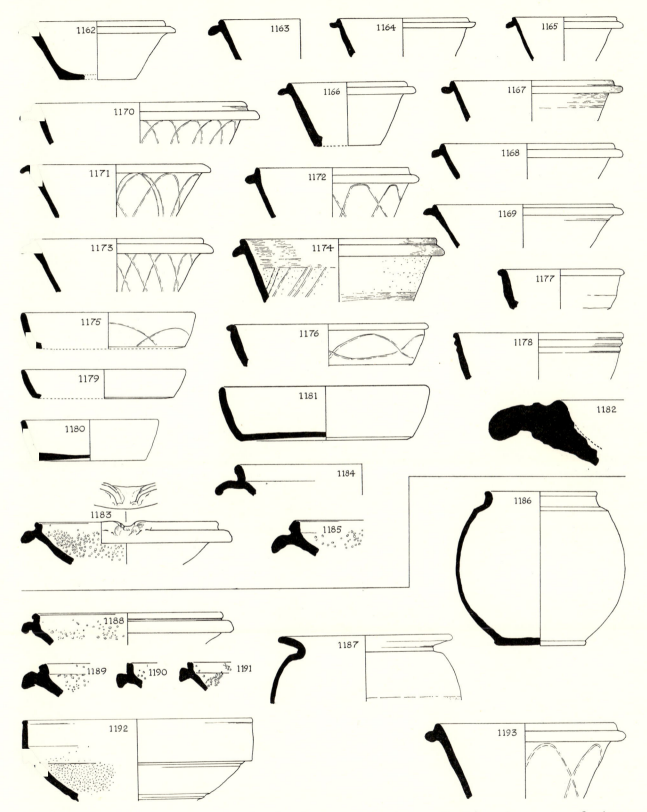

FIG. 135. Pottery vessels from deposits dated A.D. 310–15 (nos. 1162–85) and A.D. 275–360 (nos. 1186–93) (¼).

Dishes with plain, or slightly beaded rims, undecorated. Cf. 219–22, 346–9, 526–30, 736–41, 992–8, 1066, 1093, 1112, 1129, 1198, 1219–21, 1265–74.

1178. Rather finely granulated grey-black ware, burnished inside, and partly outside.
1179. Black-burnished A ware, burnished inside.
1180. Hard rather granulated grey burnished ware.
1181. Hard rather granulated dark grey burnished ware.

Mortarium (see p. 263 for note on the dates given).

1182. Hard buff granulated ware, smooth yellow surface (worn) diameter 84 cm.; late second, or early third century, perhaps from the Silchester area.

Mortaria made in the Oxford region

1183. Hard finely granulated yellow-buff ware, with translucent red-brown and grey grits; probably third century.
1184. Smooth hard white ware, with translucent light brown grits; late third or fourth century.
1185. Hard finely granulated cream ware, with translucent red-brown and grey grits; date as 1183.

POTTERY FROM VARIOUS LAYERS DATED BETWEEN A.D. 275 AND 360

Jars

1186. Hard grey burnished ware, B XI 26, A.D. 300–50. Pit 19.
1187. Hard finely granulated dark grey ware, burnished rim and shoulder, B I 12, A.D. 315–60. III, accumulation over south-east wall of cellar. Cf. 381–2, 429, 430, 613–22, 624, 845–56, 1125, 1155.

Mortaria made in the Oxford region

1188. Hard finely granulated buff ware, reddish core, with translucent pink grits; third century, or possibly later; B I 61, A.D. 280–350. III, floors subsiding into mouth of Pit 7.
1189. Ware as 1188, with translucent white and grey-brown grits; third century or later; B II Pit 3, fourth century. Small unnumbered pit in XIV, 5 Room 2.
1190. Hard finely granulated cream ware, with translucent grey and white grits; fourth century; B XIV 3, A.D. 275–350+. Floor, XIV, 6 Room 3.
1191. Smoth hard pinkish-cream ware, translucent grey and pink grits; fourth century; B XIV 3, A.D. 275–350+. Floor, XIV, 6 Room 3.
1192. Smooth hard orange-red paste, glossy orange-red coating, with translucent grey and white grits; fourth, or very late third century; B I 12, A.D. 315–60. III, accumulation over south-east wall of cellar. Cf. 1222, 1278–9, 1288.

Bowl with flanged rim and burnished decoration. Cf. 1103, 1126, 1170–4, 1285, 1293.

1193. Black-burnished A ware, B I 12, A.D. 315–60. III, accumulation over south-east wall of cellar.

POTTERY FROM FOURTH-CENTURY LAYERS

Fig. 136

Fine ware: (a) colour-coated

1194. Flanged bowl in hard white paste, dark grey coating, B II 5. III, wall-trench 1/4, XIV, 5. Cf. 1206, 1225–6.
1195. Dish in hard white paste, 'metallic' brown coating, V XXXII 1. Dark soil south-west of XIV, 1, unstratified.

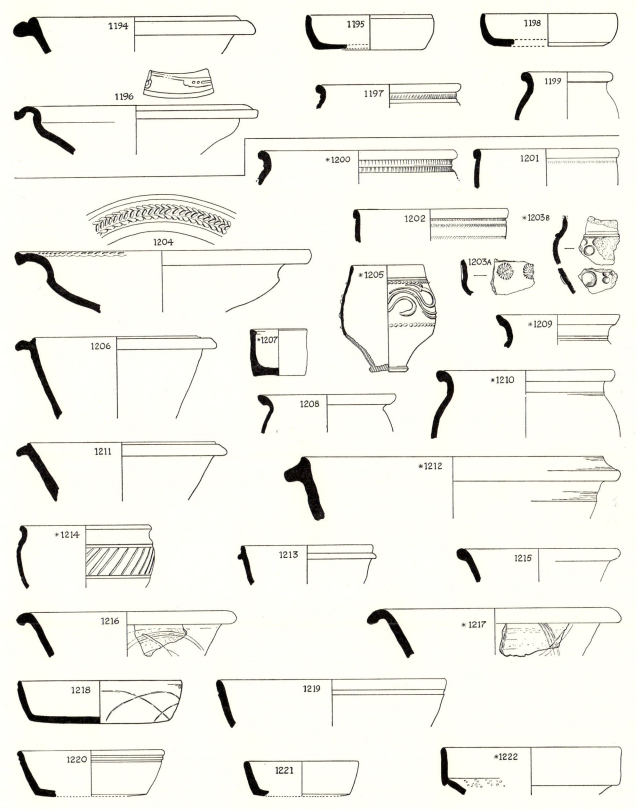

FIG. 136. Pottery vessels from deposits dated to the fourth century (nos. 1194–9) and A.D. 360–70 (nos. 1200–22) (¼).

Fine ware: (b) red colour-coated bowls. Cf. 1149–51, 1200–4, 1228–30, 1280–1, 1290.

1196. Bowl with white-painted design on rim, in hard orange-red micaceous paste, grey core, with red coating, B XIII 3. Floor, XIV, 6 Room 2. Oxford region.

1197. Rouletted bowl in fine hard orange-red paste and micaceous coating, B VIII 2A. Disturbed make-up, XIV, 6. Oxford region.

Coarse ware

1198. Dish with plain rim, in burnt ware (reddish-grey) rather unevenly burnished, B XIII 4. Antonine fire (disturbed). XIV, 6 Room 2. This might be Antonine as it is burnt. Cf. 219–22, 346–9, 526–30, 736–41, 992–8, 1066, 1093, 1112, 1129, 1178–81, 1219–21, 1265–74.

1199. Jar in hard light grey ware, B IV 6. Dark soil over mosaic, XIV, 5 Room 3.

Pottery from Layers Dated Late Fourth Century (*), and a.d. 360–70

Fine ware: (a) red colour-coated bowls. Cf. 1149–51, 1196–7, 1228–30, 1280–1, 1290.

*1200. Rouletted bowl in hard reddish-buff paste, micaceous orange-red coating, B I Pit 4, late fourth century. Pit 4. Oxford region.

1201. As 1200. B I 8, a.d. 360–70. III, secondary make-up of cellar filling. Another from B I 9, a.d. 310–15 (III, cellar filling). Oxford region.

1202. As 1200. B I 8, a.d. 360–70. III, secondary make-up of cellar filling. Oxford region.

1203A. Hard orange-red paste and coating, with stamped rosettes, B I 8. Ibid. Oxford region.

*1203B. Upper sherd with parts of four stamped circles, lower sherd with boss surrounded by shallow groove, and three stamped circular hollows, in reddish-buff micaceous paste, grey core (worn), orange-red coating outside, with horizontal brown streaks: the sherds are burnt, but the coating is inferior to the normal. B I Pit 4, late fourth century. Pit 4.

1204. Bowl with stamped decoration on rim, in hard orange-red paste and burnished surface, grey core, B I 8, a.d. 360–70. III, secondary make-up of cellar filling. Not from the Oxford region.

Fine ware: (b) colour-coated

*1205. Beaker with barbotine decoration, in fine hard white paste, orange-brown to grey 'metallic' coating, B I Pit 1, late fourth century. Pit 1. Base reconstructed from one of two others in B I 5, a.d. 370–410+ (rubble over cellar filling); another from B I Pit 4, late fourth century (Pit 4). Cf. beakers with cornice rims, 556–7, 791–5, 1045, 1144.

1206. Flanged bowl in hard white paste, 'metallic' grey coating, B I 8, a.d. 360–70. III, secondary make-up of cellar filling. Cf. 1194, 1225–6.

Jars

*1207. Hard buff ware, B I Pit 4, late fourth century. Pit 4.

1208. Hard finely granulated yellow-buff ware, B I 8, a.d. 360–70. III, secondary make-up of cellar filling. This ware is common in the second and third centuries, cf. 462.

Calcite-gritted jars. Cf. 895–6, 1100, 1159–60, 1242, 1283.

*1209. Grey calcite-gritted ware, B I Pit 4, late fourth century. Pit 4.

1210. Grey-brown calcite-gritted ware, B II Pit 5, late fourth century. Pit 4.

Plain bowls with flanged rims. Cf. 1101–2, 1110, 1127, 1162–9, 1248–54, 1292.

1211. Smooth hard grey ware, dark burnished surfaces, B I 8, A.D. 360–70. III, secondary make-up of cellar filling.

*1212. Coarse grey-buff calcite-gritted ware, B I Pit 4, late fourth century. Pit 4. Cf. 1258.

1213. Bowl or dish in hard grey ware, reddish core, partly burnished, B I 8, A.D. 360–70. III, secondary make-up of cellar filling.

Bowl with grooved decoration

*1214. Hard grey ware, darker burnished surface and rim, B I Pit 4, late fourth century. Pit 4.

Plain dish with moulded rim. Cf. 344, 724–7, 952–64, 1063–5, 1082–6, 1177, 1215, 1262–4.

1215. Rather finely granulated grey-black burnished ware, red core, B I 8, A.D. 360–70. III, secondary make-up of cellar filling.

Dishes with moulded rims and burnished decoration. Cf. 531, 706–23, 966–91, 1087–90, 1111, 1176, 1216–17, 1261, 1286.

1216. Hard rather finely granulated grey ware, burnished inside and on rim, B I 8, A.D. 360–70. III, secondary make-up of cellar filling.

*1217. Ware as 1216, grey-brown, partly burnished outside as well, B I Pit 1, late fourth century. Pit 1.

Dish with plain rim and burnished decoration. Cf. 730–5, 999–1007, 1051, 1091–2, 1120, 1128, 1175.

1218. Hard rather finely granulated dark grey ware, burnished inside and on rim, smoothed outside, B I 8, A.D. 360–70. III, secondary make-up of cellar filling.

Dishes with plain, or slightly beaded rims, undecorated. Cf. 219–22, 346–9, 526–30, 736–41, 992–8, 1066, 1093, 1112, 1129, 1178–81, 1198, 1265–74.

1219. Smooth hard burnished grey ware, lighter core, B I 8, A.D. 360–70. III, secondary make-up of cellar filling.

1220. Hard light grey burnished ware, B I 8, A.D. 360–70. Ibid.

*1221. Black-burnished A ware, B I 8, A.D. 360–70. Ibid.

Mortarium made in the Oxford region (see p. 263 for note on the dates given).

*1222. Hard light reddish paste, orange-red coating, with translucent pink and grey grits; fourth, or very late third century; B I Pit 4, late fourth century. Pit 4. Others from B I 15, Antonine fire (disturbed) (III, make-up, XIV, 5 Room 2); B I Pit 1 (Pit 1), B I Pit 4 (Pit 4), both late fourth century; B I 5 (rubble over cellar filling), B III 5 (disturbed debris over mosaic, XIV, 5 Room 3), B III 5B (ibid.); B IV Pit 1 (Pit 2), all A.D. 350–410+. Cf. 1192, 1278, 1288.

POTTERY FROM LAYERS DATED A.D. 350–410+

Fig. 137

Fine ware: (a) colour-coated

1223. Beaker in smooth light red dishpaste and red colour coating, B IV 1. Plough-soil. Another from B II 2 (earthy burnt daub, XIV, 5 Room 4).

1224. Beaker in fine hard white paste, grey-brown coating (worn), orange-brown inside, B I 5, A.D. 370–410+. Rubble over cellar filling. Cf. 1145.

1225. Flanged bowl in hard white paste, 'metallic' orange-brown coating, B I 5, A.D. 370–410+. Ibid. Cf. 1194, 1206.
1226. As 1225. B III 5B. Disturbed debris over mosaic, XIV, 5 Room 3.
1227. Dish in hard white paste, 'metallic' dark grey to brown coating, B I 5, A.D. 370–410+. Rubble over cellar filling. Others from B III 5 (two), A.D. 350–410+ (disturbed debris over mosaic, XIV, 5 Room 3); B I 9, A.D. 310–15 (III, cellar filling).

Fine ware: (b) red colour-coated bowls. Cf. 1149–51, 1196–7, 1200–4, 1280–1, 1290.

1228. Fine hard orange-red paste and burnished surface, B I 5, A.D. 370–410+. Rubble over cellar filling. Not from the Oxford region.
1229. Ware as 1228, with pattern of stamped whole and half rosettes, B IV Pit 1. Pit 2. Oxford region.
1230. Ware as 1228, with white-painted decoration, B I 5, A.D. 370–410+. Rubble over cellar filling. Oxford region. Nos. 1229–30 are more obviously colour-coated than 1228.

Narrow-necked jars. Cf. 118–24, 245–50, 412–18, 822–35, 1074, 1152–4.

1231. Jar with frilled rim, and traces of dark grey paint on rim and neck, in hard light reddish-buff ware, B III 5B. Disturbed debris over mosaic, XIV 5, Room 3.
1232. Sherd with scored wavy line between double rouletted bands, in hard rather finely granulated yellow-buff ware, B I 5, as 1230.
1233A. Sherd, probably from narrow-necked jar, with stamped shoulder decoration, in hard finely granulated grey ware, burnished, B I 5, A.D. 370–410+. Rubble over cellar filling.
1233B. As 1233A, in hard grey ware, grey-black burnished slip, B I 5. Ibid.

Jars

1234. Sherd with finger-impressed applied shoulder band, in hard rather finely granulated grey ware, brown core, B I 5. Ibid. Cf. 1282.
1235. Rather coarse orange-buff burnished ware, grey core, B I 5, A.D. 370–410+. Ibid.
1236. Hard granulated buff ware, grey core, B III 5. Disturbed debris over mosaic, XIV, 5 Room 3.
1237. Hard light reddish ware, grey core, cream slip, with red-painted decoration on rim, B III 5. Ibid.
1238. Hard grey burnished ware, evenly rilled shoulder, B VI Pit 2. Mouth of Pit 14.
1239. Hard finely granulated grey ware, rilled shoulder, B I 5, A.D. 370–410+. Rubble over cellar filling.
1240. Ware as 1239. B I 5. Ibid. Another, in light grey burnished ware, from B I Pit 7, late fourth century. Mouth of Pit 7.
1241. Ware as 1239. B I Pit 4. Pit 4.
1242. Coarse grey calcite-gritted ware, B I 5, A.D. 370–410+. Rubble over cellar filling. Cf. 895–6, 1100, 1159–60, 1209–10, 1242, 1283.

Storage jar. Cf. 83–6, 200–4, 487, 667–8, 912–21.

1243. Hard finely granulated burnished blue-grey ware, cf. products of Farnham kilns (p. 265). B III 5. Disturbed debris over mosaic, XIV, 5 Room 3.

Bowls

1244. Smooth orange-buff burnished ware, B III 5B. Disturbed debris over mosaic, XIV, 5 Room 3.
1245. Hard light reddish ware, white slip, with red-painted stripe, B I 5, A.D. 370–410+. Rubble over cellar filling. Others from B II 4, A.D. 275–300+ (make-up below mosaic XIV, 5 Room 3); B I 8, A.D. 360–70 (III, secondary make-up of cellar filling). Cf. 524.

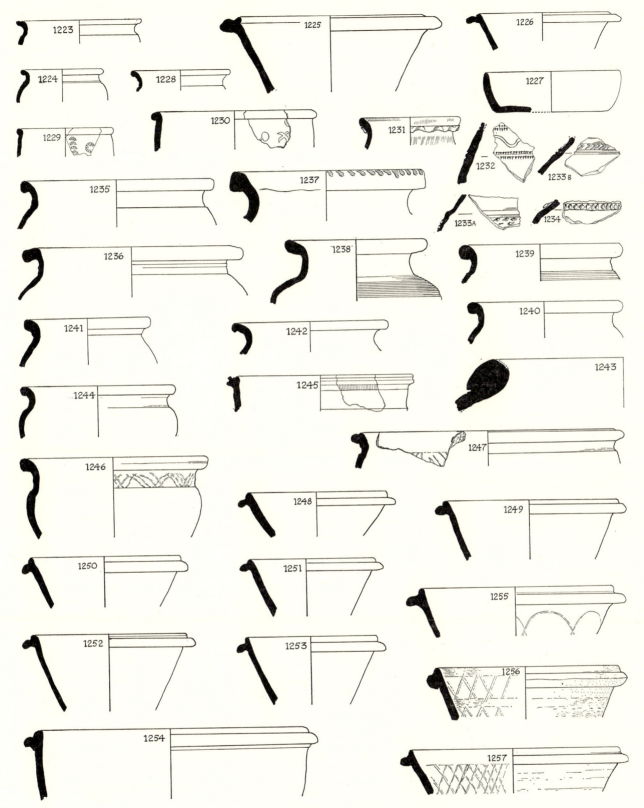

FIG. 137. Pottery vessels nos. 1223–57 from deposits dated A.D. 350–410+ ($\frac{1}{4}$).

1246. Hard rather granulated grey ware, partly burnished surface, with burnished decoration on neck, B I 5, A.D. 370–410+. Rubble over cellar filling.
1247. Hard finely granulated blue-grey ware, burnished surfaces, with burnished decoration inside, B III 5A. Dark soil on mosaic, XIV, 5 Room 3.

Plain bowls with flanged rims. Cf. 110–12, 1110, 1127, 1162–9, 1211–13, 1292.

1248. Black-burnished A ware, B I 5, A.D. 370–410+. Rubble over cellar filling.
1249. Ware as 1248. B I 5. Ibid. Another from B I 9, A.D. 310–15 (III, cellar filling).
1250. Ware as 1248. B I 5. Ibid.
1251. Hard light grey burnished ware, B I 5. Ibid.
1252. Smooth hard dark grey burnished ware, B V Pit 2. Mouth of Pit 22.
1253. Ware as 1252. B III 5B. Disturbed debris over mosaic, XIV, 5 Room 3.
1254. Hard rather granulated grey ware, partly burnished, B I 5, A.D. 370–410+. Rubble over cellar filling.

Bowls with flanged rims and burnished decoration. Cf. 1103, 1126, 1170–4, 1193, 1285, 1293.

1255. Black-burnished A ware, B I 5, A.D. 370–410+. Ibid.
1256. Hard finely granulated light grey ware, partly burnished lighter slip inside to top of flange, partly burnished outside, B III 5B. Disturbed debris over mosaic, XIV, 5 Room 3. Cf. 1174, 1293 and 1286 (dish).
1257. Rather granulated light grey ware, partly burnished, B I 5, A.D. 370–410+. Rubble over cellar filling. Cf. 1174, 1293 and 1286 (dish).

Fig. 138

Bowls in calcite-gritted ware

1258. Bowl with flanged rim, in coarse grey-buff rilled ware, B I 5, A.D. 370–410+. Ibid. Cf. 1212.
1259. Ware as 1258. B VI Pit 2. Mouth of Pit 14. Cf. 729.

Dish with flanged rim. Cf. 343, 515, 728, 965, 1084, 1287.

1260. Hard grey ware, more burnished inside, B I 5, A.D. 370–410+. Rubble over cellar filling.

Dish with moulded rim and burnished decoration. Cf. 531, 706–23, 966–91, 1087–90, 1111, 1176, and especially 1216, 1217.

1261. Hard grey-brown rather finely granulated ware, burnished inside and on rim, partly outside, B I 5, A.D. 370–410+. Ibid.

Plain dishes with moulded rims. Cf. 344, 724–7, 952–64, 1063–5, 1082–6, 1177, 1215.

1262. Hard finely granulated grey ware, black surfaces, partly burnished outside and on rim, B I 5, A.D. 370–410+. Ibid.
1263. Smooth hard grey-brown burnished ware, B V Pit 2. Mouth of Pit 22.
1264. Hard burnished dark grey ware, B VI Pit 2. Mouth of Pit 14.

Dishes with slightly beaded, or plain rims, undecorated. Cf. 219–22, 346–9, 526–30, 736–41, 992–8, 1066, 1093, 1112, 1129, 1178–81, 1198, 1219–21.

1265. Hard rather granulated light grey ware, partly burnished, B III 5A. Dark soil on mosaic, XIV, 5 Room 3. Cf. 995.

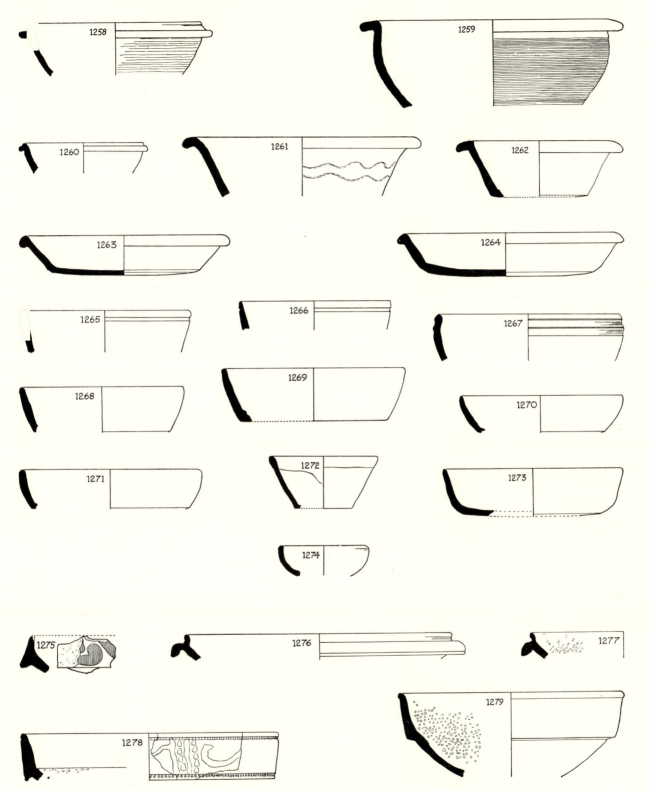

FIG. 138. Pottery vessels nos. 1258–79 from deposits dated A.D. 350–410+ (¼).

1266. Hard grey ware, burnished inside and on rim, B III 5A. Ibid.

1267. Hard light grey finely granulated ware, burnished inside, B IV Pit 1. Pit 2.

1268. Black-burnished A ware, B I 5, A.D. 370–410+. Rubble over cellar filling.

1269. Ware as 1268. B I 5. Ibid. Two others from B I 8, A.D. 360–70 (III, secondary make-up of cellar filling).

1270. Ware as 1268. B I 5. Ibid.

1271. Ware as 1268. B I 5 (two), A.D. 370–410+. Ibid. Others from B I 9, A.D. 310–15 (III, cellar filling); B I 8, A.D. 360–70 (III, secondary make-up of cellar filling).

1272. Hard rather granulated grey ware, rim dipped in grey slip, inside of dish burnished, B I 5, A.D. 370–410+. Ibid. Cf. 997, 1091, 1112.

1273. Hard grey rather granulated ware, unevenly burnished, B III Pit 1A. Pit 2.

1274. Hard light grey rather finely granulated ware, B IV Pit 3. Mouth of Pit 3. Cf. fig. 141, 19 (crucible).

Mortarium made at Hartshill, Mancetter (see p. 263 for note on the dates given).

1275. Rather smooth white ware, yellow-brown painted decoration on flange, with dark brown grits; A.D. 240–340; B V Pit 2. Mouth of Pit 22.

Mortaria made in the Oxford region

1276. Smooth hard reddish ware, grey core, white slip, with translucent pink grits: this ware usually has a red colour-coat; after A.D. 250; B I 5, A.D. 370–410+. Rubble over cellar filling.

1277. Smooth hard burnt ware, with translucent pink and grey grits; fourth century(?); B I 5. Ibid.

1278. Hard orange-red paste and coating, white-painted decoration between rouletted bands, with grey, white, and brown translucent grits; fourth century; B I 5. Ibid. Cf. 1192, 1222, 1288.

1279. Smooth hard orange-red paste and coating, with red, grey, and white translucent grits; almost certainly fourth century, though the ware did start in the late third; B V Pit 2. Mouth of Pit 22. Cf. 1192, 1222, 1288.

POTTERY FROM LAYERS DATED A.D. 375–410+

Fig. 139

Fine ware: red colour-coated bowls. Cf. 1149–51, 1196–7, 1200–4, 1228–30, 1290.

1280. Hard light red paste, orange-red coating, T I 2. Robbed drain. Not from Oxford region; perhaps Nene Valley.

1281. Hard red paste and coating, T XI 2. Building debris over floor of XIV, 1 Room 1. Probably from Oxford region.

Jars

1282. Hard grey finely granulated burnished ware, red core, with finger-nail impressions on shoulder cordon, T I 2. Robbed drain. Cf. 1234.

1283. Coarse grey-brown calcite-gritted ware, T I 2. Ibid. Cf. 895–6, 1100, 1159–60, 1209–10, 1242.

Bowl

1284. Fine hard burnished grey ware. T I 2. Ibid.

Bowl with flanged rim, and burnished decoration. Cf. 1103, 1126, 1170–4, 1193, 1255–7, 1293.

1285. Hard light grey burnished ware, A I 4. Chalk patch in XIV, 4 Room 1.

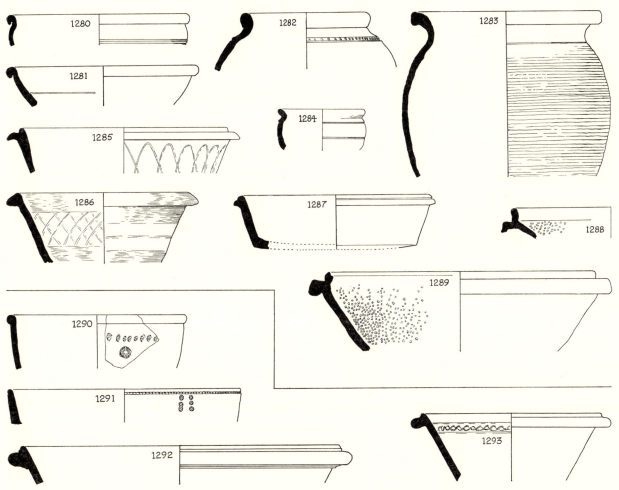

FIG. 139. Pottery vessels from deposits dated A.D. 375–410+ (nos. 1280–9) and A.D. 370–410+ (nos. 1290–3) (¼).

Dish with moulded rim, and burnished decoration. Cf. 531, 706–23, 966–91, 1087–90, 1111, 1176, 1216–17.

1286. Hard grey ware, partly burnished, T I 2. Robbed drain. Another, in light grey ware, from B I 5, A.D. 350–410+ (rubble over cellar filling).

Dish with flanged rim. Cf. 343, 515, 728, 965, 1084, 1260.

1287. Hard dark grey burnished ware, T I 2. Ibid.

Mortaria made in the Oxford region (see p. 263 for note on the dates given).

1288. Hard orange-red ware and coating, with translucent grey and red grits; fourth century; T I 2. Ibid. Cf. 1192, 1222, 1278–9.

1289. Smooth hard cream ware, with translucent grey and pink grits; fourth century; T I 2. Ibid. Others from B II 2 (earthy burnt daub, XIV, 5 Room 4); B I 8, A.D. 360–70 (III, secondary make-up of cellar filling); B III 5B, A.D. 350–410+ (disturbed debris over mosaic, XIV, 5 Room 3); T II 3, A.D. 375–410+ (building debris over floor of XIV 1 Room 2).

POTTERY FROM B II 3, A LATE RUBBLE LAYER OVER CELLAR,
A.D. 370–410+

Fine ware: (a) red colour-coated bowl. Cf. 1149–51, 1196–7, 1200–4, 1228–30, 1280–1.

1290. Hard light red ware and coating, grey core, with stamped whole and half rosettes. Oxford region. A sherd, with row of half rosettes, from B I Pit 4, late fourth century (Pit 4).

Fine ware: (b) colour-coated dish

1291. Hard light red ware, red-brown coating, with rouletted rim and white-painted decoration.

Bowls with flanged rims

1292. Hard burnished grey ware. Cf. 1101–2, 1110, 1127, 1162–9, 1211–13, 1248–54.
1293. Hard light grey ware, partly burnished outside, with burnished decoration inside. Cf. 1103, 1126, 1170–4, 1193, 1255–7, 1285, especially 1256–7.

GRAFFITI ON POTTERY

Fig. 140

1.]HIIRMOGANAX[*J.R.S.* xlviii (1958), p. 154, no. 36. Presumably a name, Hermoganax. Cut, before firing, on an amphora sherd in pinkish-buff paste with cream slip, V XXXII 3A, A.D. 270–5. III, make-up for metalled surface outside (south-west of) XIV, 1.

2.]LIASMVLTASOLIINDAVIDIIS *J.R.S.* xlviii (1958), pp. 154 f., no. 40.]LIAS multa sol(v)enda vides. 'It would seem that the intended phrase was metrical. . . .' Unsuitably cut on the reeded rim of a carinated bowl in buff ware, V XXXIII 7, A.D. 150–155/160. II D, Room 2A.

3.]PIIO[*J.R.S.* li (1961), p. 197, no. 43. On the inside of a plate in terra rubra 1, residual in B IV 21A, A.D. 105–15. II B, Room 26.

4. SΛX (complete). *J.R.S.* xlix (1959), p. 139, no. 31. On the shoulder of a jar, fig. 108, 296, B II 37E, A.D. 75–85. II A, accumulation outside Room 19.

5.]TΛCITΛ[probably incomplete. *J.R.S.* xlviii (1958), p. 154, no. 35. On a sherd of Antonine samian form 33, Z II 3. Late pit outside (south-west of) XIV, 2.

6. (With pl. LIII, A) BONI (complete). On a sherd of samian form 36, probably Antonine, B II 14, A.D. 155/160. II D, Rooms 32–42.

7. CIILIIR *J.R.S.* xlviii (1958), p. 154, no. 39. On a sherd, showing part of a charioteer's arm, from a beaker in orange-red paste with dark brown colour-coating, T IX 1. Late pit outside (south-west of) XIV, 1.
   Celer is presumably a name auspiciously attributed to the charioteer.

8. MM on plain band above the ovolo of a samian form 37, East Gaulish, late second or early third century, B I 9, A.D. 310–15. III, cellar filling.

9. (Pl. LIII, B.) Base of samian form 18R with thunderbolt (left) and (?) bow and arrow. B II 32G, A.D. 85–105. II A, outside Room 17.

10. SABINA on samian form 37, A.D. 80–100. See pp. 52, 246 and fig. 94, 88. B IV 21E, A.D. 105–15. II B, Room 33.

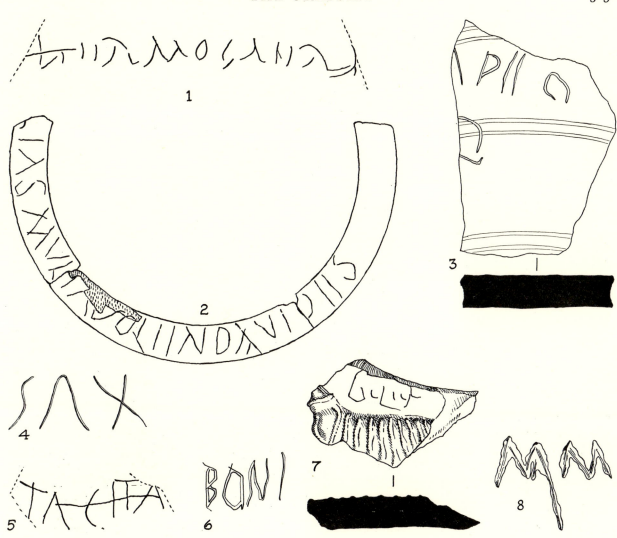

FIG. 140. Graffiti on pottery nos. 1, 2 ($\frac{1}{2}$), nos. 3–8 ($\frac{1}{1}$). See also pp. 261, no. D 134 and 335, no. 972.

CRUCIBLES

Fig. 141

1. Oval crucible, hand made in clay burnt grey, encrusted with green- to copper-coloured glassy deposit, B I 65, A.D. 60–75. Pit 7. Similar sherd with base 1·25 cm. thick, B I 67, undated collapsed section in Pit 7, and another with a smear of gold inside, B I 63, A.D. 60–75. Pl. LII B.
2. As no. 1, but with grey, less glazed deposit, and a single circular perforation, B I 67, undated collapsed section in Pit 7.
3. As no. 1, but with grey, less glazed deposit, B I 66, A.D. 60–75, Pit 7.
4. As no. 1, in gritty clay, with grey, less glazed deposit, B I 66, A.D. 60–75. Pit 7.

5. As no. 1, in gritty clay, with dark green glazed deposit, B I 63, A.D. 60–75. Pit 7. Similar sherds from A XI 25, A.D. 49–60 (I, Room 12); A XII 12, A.D. 115–30 (II B, Room 26) with a speck of copper inside.

6. Clay prop for keeping crucibles such as 1–5 upright in the furnace, roughly made in similar clay, burnt grey, with glazed deposit, B I 67, undated collapsed section in Pit 7.

7. Crucible in hard buff granulated ware, with glazed deposit outside, and metallic traces inside, B II 35, A.D. 60–75. II A, Room 20, burnt daub make-up.

8. Fragment of lower part of small jar or flagon used as crucible, in hard granulated ware, burnt grey, with a thick glazed deposit, grey to purple outside, green inside, B I 67, undated collapsed section in Pit 7. Another vessel used in this way, base diameter 6 cm., from B IV 23B, A.D. 90–105 (II A, Room 23) and two, one with base diameter 3½ cm., from B IV 3, A.D. 155/160 (II D, Rooms 38–42, Antonine fire debris).

9. Crucible in the shape of a small dish, in hard buff granulated ware, burnt grey, with trace of glazed deposit inside, A XI 11A, A.D. 105–30. II B, wall-trench 8–12.

10. As 9. Z I 12, A.D. 130–50. II C, Room 7.

11. As 9, burnt red, but with no adhering deposit, T I 10, A.D. 130–50. II C, Room 13, wall-trench.

12. Hand-made crucible in smoothed grey-brown clay, with glazed deposit inside, subsequently buried with infant inhumation, B IV 17C, A.D. 140–50. II C, Room 46.

13, 14. Granulated clay burnt grey, with glazed deposit inside, B XV 11, A.D. 150–155/160. II D, Room 55. There were twenty-one small crucibles similar to nos. 13, 14, in this room, some with traces of gold inside. Pl. LIIa.

15, 16. Unguent jars used as crucibles, in hard granulated ware burnt grey, B XV 11, A.D. 150–155/160. II D, Room 55. Found with two more of the same type. Pl. LIIa. Cf. fig. 125, 882–4, etc.

17. Lower half of small jar or flagon, used as a crucible, in hard granulated clay, burnt grey, with coarser clay roughly moulded round it, filled with fine sand when found, in the same group of crucibles as 13–16, B XV 11, A.D. 150–155/160. II D, Room 55.

18. Small dish in hard buff rather finely granulated ware, perhaps intended for a crucible, B V 9, A.D. 155/160. II D, Room 45, south-east wall-trench.

19. As 18, in hard granulated ware, burnt grey, with traces of metal on both surfaces, B VIII 1, A.D. 270–5. III, make-up, XIV, 7 Room 2.

20. As 18, in hard cream ware, smooth surface, with some red-buff clay adhering to lower part and base, but with no signs of use, B XI 30, A.D. 160–75. Pit 19.

21. As 18, in rather finely granulated ware, burnt grey, with traces of metal adhering, B IV Pit 3, A.D. 350–410+. Mouth of Pit 3. Cf. fig. 143, 10 (lamp).

LAMPS

Fig. 142

1. Fine white paste, orange-brown coating, B XIV 9A, A.D. 270–5. III, make-up, XIV, 6 Room 3. Cf. Wheeler, *London in Roman Times*, fig. 15, Type III a.

Open lamps and fillers in coarse ware

2. Lamp with lug handle, in buff granulated ware, smoked, B IV 17K, A.D. 140–50. II C, Room 39.

3. Lamp with nozzle pinched out, in hard finely granulated buff ware, smoked inside, T XX 13, A.D. 140–50 (two). II C, Room 9. Cf. Wheeler, *London in Roman Times*, fig. 14, 1.

4. Small lamp-filler, similar to 3, unused, Z I 18, A.D. 115–30. II B, Room 6.

5. Lamp or filler, unused, as 3, A XI 7, A.D. 150–155/160. II D, Room 13, make-up. Similar fragment from A XI 10, A.D. 130–50 (II C, Room 16).

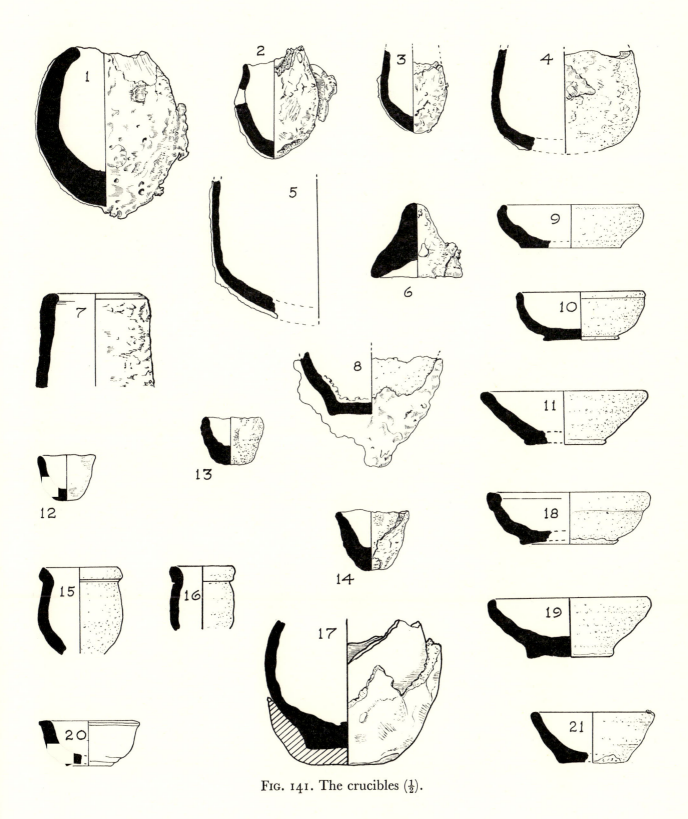

Fig. 141. The crucibles ($\frac{1}{2}$).

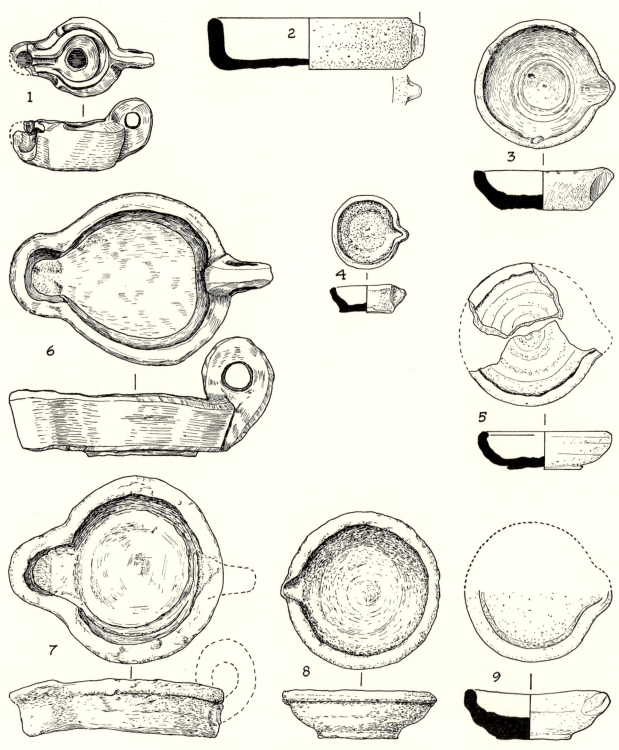

FIG. 142. Lamps, nos. 1–9 (½).

6. Lamp with nozzle and handle, in finely granulated buff ware, surface smoothly but unevenly burnished, smoke-blackened inside, B XV 4, A.D. 150–155/160. II D, Room 55. Cf. Wheeler, *London in Roman Times*, pl. XXIX, 7.

7. Similar to 6, but with flat base, handle broken off, burnt red outside, probably in Antonine fire, B XV 4. As no. 6.

8. Lamp similar to 3 but with footring, smoked inside, B XV 4. As no. 6.

9. As 3, smoked, A V 11, A.D. 200–225/250. Pit 21.

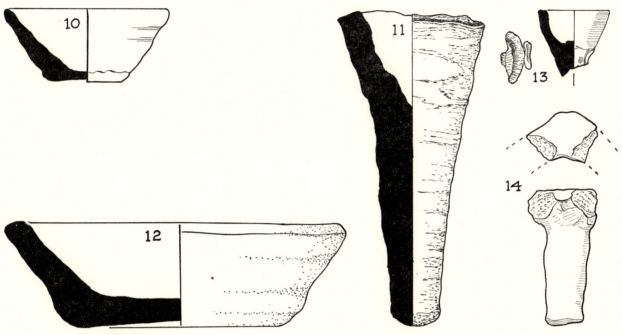

FIG. 143. Lamps, nos. 10–12 and clay objects, nos. 13–14 ($\frac{1}{2}$).

Fig. 143

10. Small dish, similar to a crucible, in hard light reddish ware, smoke-blackened inside as if used for a lamp, B VI Pit 2, A.D. 350–410+. Pit 14. Cf. fig. 141, 21 (crucible).

Pottery bases used as lamps

11. Amphora base in hard buff granulated ware, smoke-blackened, A XI 25, A.D. 49–60. I, Room 12.

12. Mortarium base with broken edge unevenly rounded off, in hard buff granulated local ware, smoked inside, A VII 42, A.D. 75–85. II A, Room 14.

OBJECTS OF CLAY

13. Vase, one of a set of three attached to a basal ring, in white pipeclay, B XI 29, A.D. 175–275. Pit 19. Cf. fig. 125, nos. 886–7 in coarse ware.

14. Fragment of a stand, consisting of a vertical support attached to the corner of two horizontal bars in smooth pinkish-buff clay, showing no signs of use, A VI 23, A.D. 105–15. II B, Room 26.

THE AMPHORA STAMPS (fig. 144)

The name Callender followed by a number refers to the numbered index of stamps in Callender, *Roman Amphorae* (London, 1965). This reference is followed by his dating of the stamp, where available, and then by details of the find-spot, and its date. Gratitude is due to Dr. Callender for examining these stamps and reporting on them; his full report is abbreviated here since full details have since been provided in his book.

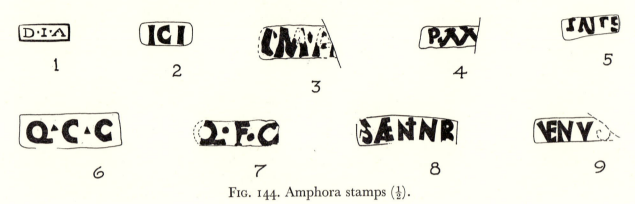

FIG. 144. Amphora stamps (½).

1. **D.I.A.** See Callender no. 535, dated (?) A.D. 90–140 (probably South Spanish). T VI 14, A.D. 140–50. II C, Room 4.
2. **L(?)CI** or **L(?)C** and triangular stop. The upper part of I stands proud, having filled the die, and may represent a stop. See Callender no. 826, no date given (South Spanish). T VII 17, A.D. 130–50. II C, Room 3.
3. **L.M.A.** See Callender no. 887, no date given (almost certainly South Spanish). A III, unstratified.
4. **P.M**. . . See Callender nos. 1344 (b) to 1356. B II 37E, A.D. 75–85. II A, accumulation outside Room 19.
5. **PNSI** or **PNS** and leaf stop. See Callender no. 1361, dated second century (?), T, unstratified.
6. **Q.C.C** (with triangular stops). See Callender no. 1428, dated A.D. 80–130 (?). B I 9, A.D. 310–15. III, cellar filling.
7. **Q.F.C.** See Callender no. 1449, dated *c.* A.D. 120–60 (South Spanish). Z III 5, *c.* A.D. 150. II D, Room 3B.
8. **. . .SAENIN.B**? See Callender no. 1559 (b), dated *c.* A.D. 80/90–130/140 (South Spanish). B I 68, A.D. 60–75. Pit 7.
9. Read as **SAENE** by Dr. Callender (Callender no. 1559 (p)), but more likely to be **VENVS.** . (**VENVSTI**). See Callender no. 1776 (b), (possibly Italian). B IV 9J, A.D. 150–155/160. II D, Room 43.

VI. THE MORTARIUM STAMPS

by K. F. Hartley

In the following catalogue the stamps are treated as far as possible alphabetically. The numbers refer to the stamps drawn on figs. 145 and 146. Then is given the layer-number of the deposit in which the figured stamp occurred and its date, followed by those of other (unfigured) examples of the same die. However, when the vessel bearing the stamp has been figured in the Pottery Report above, only the number of the vessel in that report is given with its date (e.g. 'No. 359') without further details, which can be obtained by cross-reference.

1. B XIII 4, Antonine fire (disturbed). Over II D, Room 48. The two slightly burnt fragments from one mortarium each carry a fragmentary potter's stamp impressed along the rim. Together they allow]VTOR to be read. This stamp is unknown elsewhere but it can be attributed with virtual certainty to Adiutor, a potter who worked in Gallia Belgica, perhaps in the vicinity of Bavai where eight of his mortaria have been noted (*Pro Nervia*, tome i, fasc. i, 59). Two other stamps of his are known from Britain, both from Colchester, one in a pit dated to c. A.D. 100 and perhaps indicating activity in the late first or early second century (M. R. Hull, *Roman Colchester*, 126, no. 24).

2–11 Albinus.

2. B I 45, A.D. 85–105. II A, outside Room 17.
3. B II 31E, A.D. 90–105. II A, outside Room 19.
4. No. 359. A.D. 85–105.
5. T VII 29, A.D. 85–105. II A, Room 3. Others from Z I 26, A.D. 85–105 (II A, Room 5); B+, unstratified.
6. B I 38, A.D. 85–105. II A, outside Room 7. Others no. 365, A.D. 75–85, and from B I 38 (another); A VI 29, A.D. 75–105 (II A, Room 11); T VI 8 (III, residual); B I 64, A.D. 60–75 (Pit 7). Probably also from A II 42, A.D. 75–105 (II A, outside Rooms 12, 15); T VII 19, A.D. 140–50 (II C, Room 4); B I 65, A.D. 60–75 (Pit 7).
7. B I 45, A.D. 85–105. II A, outside Room 17. Others no. 545, A.D. 105–15, and from A VII 33, A.D. 105–15 (II B, Room 26) (with F. LVGVDV stamp 8).
8. B I Pit 7, A.D. 60–75. Pit 7. Another example cited under 7.
9. B I 32G, A.D. 115–30. II B, Room 24. Others from B I 63 (two), A.D. 60–75 (Pit 7); B I 45, A.D. 85–105 (II A, outside Room 17); B I 38, A.D. 85–105 (II A, outside Room 17).
10. A VII 32, A.D. 110–20. II B, Room 26. Others from B IV 23B, A.D. 85–105 (II A, Room 23); T XX 15, A.D. 105–30 (II B, Room 7); B I 45 (three), A.D. 85–105 (II A, outside Room 17); B I 63, A.D. 60–75 (Pit 7).
11. B IV 21A, A.D. 105–15. II B, Room 26. No. 546 (A.D. 105–15) is probably from the same die.

Stamps 2, 3, 5, 7, 9, and 11 are from six different name dies of Albinus. Stamp 4 was invariably used in conjunction with stamp 3, the name on one side of the spout, the counterstamp in a corresponding position on the other side; it appears to read VIΛNVΛCΛE retrograde. Stamps 6, 8, and 10 are counterstamps presenting a more or less complete version of F. LVGVDV, and were used respectively with stamps from the same dies as 5, 7, and 9. Stamp 11 had a similar counterstamp, but no counterstamp was used with stamp 2.

All of the stamps drawn on figs. 145–6 are from different vessels, and other stamps from the same dies are recorded alongside. One piece only, from A VII 33, is sufficiently complete to have both name and counterstamp (7 and 8); all of the other stamps or counterstamps of Albinus listed are probably from different vessels, though some pieces are too fragmentary for certainty.

Albinus was by far the most prolific mortarium-maker in Britain. More than 250 mortaria of his are now recorded, including eleven from Scotland; the two individual sites with most stamps are London (86) and Verulamium (48). Few are from dated sites or deposits; these include one from Inchtuthil, c. A.D. 83–7, three from the Neronian-Flavian fort at Baginton, Wars., and two from pits at Wroxeter, containing only pre-Flavian and Flavian material (D. Atkinson, *Report on Excavations at Wroxeter, 1923–7* (1942), 278, nos. M1, and E46); two stamps from Newstead must be earlier than A.D. 105 (J. Curle, *Newstead*, 265). The rims used are entirely appropriate and his generally Flavian date is beyond question, though slightly earlier activity is possible. A date of c. A.D. 65–95 is indicated.

Although one stamp of his has been found at Radlett and one at Brockley Hill (see below), no certain kiln has yet been found for Albinus. However, he and a few other mortarium makers (see Oastrius (?), no. 32, and Ripanus, no. 33), regularly used counterstamps such as **F. LVGVDV** (presumably *f(actum) Lugudu(ni)*, **FEC LVGD** and **LVGD.F.** These undoubtedly establish manufacture at a place called Lugdunum. It has been usual to assume that these potters, and others clearly allied but not using these counterstamps (e.g. Matugenus; Doinus, nos. 19–20; Marinus, no. 31; Sollus, no. 38, etc.), worked either at Lyons, Lugdunum Batavorum, or Lugdunum Convenarum. It is now certain that they all worked in Britain for the following reasons:

(a) Although the stamps of many of the potters concerned are common in Britain, not one is recorded from the whole of Gaul, nor are there any mortaria of similar forms and fabrics there.

(b) Matugenus, Melus (and probably Doinus and Ripanus among others) are known to have worked at Brockley Hill, where kilns and waste pottery, and a clay name-die of Matugenus, have been found (*Trans. London and Middlesex A.S.* n.s. X, i, 1; X, iii, 201; XI, ii, 173; XI, iii, 259; XVII, i, 60 (name-die); XIX, 65). Potters were also making mortaria at kilns at Radlett (see Castus, no. 15) and at Verulamium (see Roa, no. 34). All used fabric and grit indistinguishable from that of Albinus.

(c) A few stamps of Matugenus record him as the son of an Albinus, and the similarity of his mortaria to those of Albinus leaves no doubt that his father was indeed the mortarium-manufacturer.

(d) The very heavy distribution of Albinus' work at Verulamium (48) and London (86) is paralleled by the distribution for Matugenus, Sollus, and others. It suggests that these two towns were their main home market.

The makers of mortaria in these potteries south of Verulamium, headed by Albinus, may be described with no exaggeration as controlling at least half of the market for mortaria in Britain in Flavian and early Trajanic times. Only one group of potters, working in Kent or less probably in Gallia Belgica, provided serious competition (*Richborough V*, 179, footnote). It is therefore to be expected that a very large number of kilns existed between Verulamium and London, and in the vicinity of Watling Street for easy transport. Lugdunum is surely to be sought in this area. The counterstamp **VIANVACAE** remains unexplained but on balance is likely to be a place-name also, since no potters in this region give names of associates, workmen, or slaves, and the practice is, indeed, very rare anywhere in Britain. Growing evidence supports the possibility that potters of any substance had kilns in more than one place, perhaps separated by only a few miles.

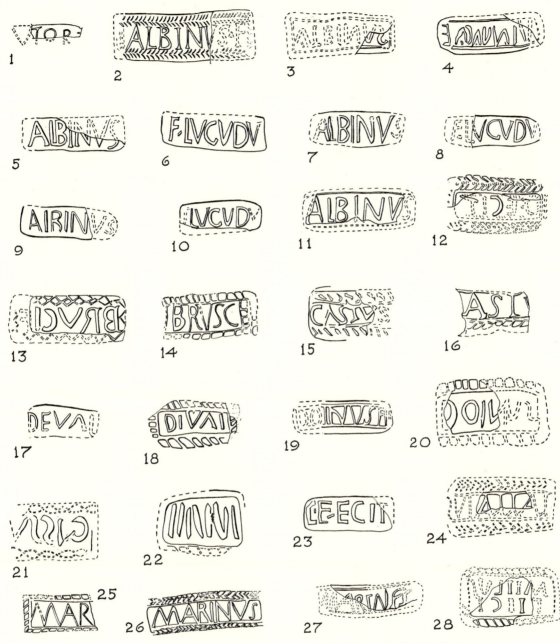

FIG. 145. Mortarium stamps nos. 1–28 (½) (*drawn by K. F. Hartley*).

12. Z I 12, A.D. 130–50. II C, Room 7. A fragment from the upper border of a counterstamp of G. Attius Marinus, giving FECIT retrograde when complete.

    G. Attius Marinus is of particular interest because he used three different fabrics, each with its own distribution pattern. This leaves little doubt that he migrated twice during his working life (*Bulletin of the Institute of Archaeology*, London, v (1965), 33–6). The rim-forms associated, and the dating evidence, show that his activity began in the vicinity of Colchester, perhaps about A.D. 90.

Mortaria in this fabric have been found at: Caerleon, Colchester (3), London, Monmouth, and Leicester. This is a wide distribution for a first-century potter working in this area. Perhaps attracted by the success of the potters of the Verulamium region he moved to Radlett, where his mortaria were found at kilns used also by Castus (*V.C.H. Hertfordshire*, part 5, 161–2; *Proc. Soc. Ant. London*, 2nd series, xvii (1899), 266, two examples of FECIT stamps, and four described as undecipherable but clearly stamps of G. Attius Marinus, drawn upside down). These mortaria are in fabric typical for potters working in the Verulamium region (*Antiq. Journ.* xxi (1941), 272, for an excellent description of the fabric). His Radlett mortaria are relatively few and reached only a small market: Brockley Hill, Godmanchester, London, and Verulamium (3 including this).

His remaining stamped mortaria were made in the midlands in a totally differing fabric, their distribution being: Ashley, Northants; Baginton (2); Barton-on-Humber; Brough-on-Noe; Elslack; Grainsby, Lincs.; High Cross; Holditch, Staffs.; Littlechester; Lincoln (2); Leicester (11); Melandra Castle (2); Rocester; Slack; Templeborough (4); Tripontium; Wall (2); Wilderspool (5); and York. The white pipeclay fabric and a waster found at Hartshill in Warwickshire, indicate that it was in the potteries there and at Mancetter two miles away that his major production took place. The date of his work there is within the period A.D. 100–30. There is no site evidence to date his Radlett production but the rims suggest that it fell, as might be expected, between the Colchester and midland period; and the proportion indicates a limited activity. A date of A.D. 95–105 should more than cover the period of his Radlett production.

13. A IV 12 (A.D. 150–155/160, II D, Room 17) and A IV 2 (A.D. 155/160, II D, Room 18), joining.

The retrograde stamps on this mortarium are of Brucius, or Bruccius as another die gives the name. Thirty-three mortaria of this potter have been noted from sites in England and Wales; ten of these (reading Bruccius) are from the kiln-area at Brockley Hill and it may be assumed that he worked there, at least while using that die.

There is no site evidence to date his work; his rim-profiles are basically mid- to late Flavian in type and there is enough change to suggest that the die giving Bruccius may be the earlier one. A date *c.* A.D. 80–110 ought to cover his activity.

14. A IV 11, A.D. 155/160. II D, Room 15.

This stamp is from one of the seven dies of Bruscius; on all but one of these the name was abbreviated to BRVSC or BRVSCI. A kiln where he worked with another mortarium-maker, Junius, was excavated recently at Hartshill, and it is likely that he also had kilns at Mancetter, two miles away. Seventeen of his mortaria are now known from other sites in England and seven from Antonine deposits in Scotland (e.g. Mumrills, *P.S.A.S.* xciv (1960–1), 110–11). The stamps from the Antonine occupation of Scotland, and the association with Junius, together point to a date *c.* A.D. 140–70 for his work. Midland mortaria were rarely distributed as far south as Verulamium (cf., however, no. 35, below).

15. B IV 17K, A.D. 140–50. II C, Room 39.

A stamp from one of the five dies noted so far for Castus. More than twenty-two of his stamps, though none from this die, were found at two kilns at Radlett (*Proc. Soc. Ant. London*, 2nd series, xvii, 266) and twenty-two other stamps have been noted from other sites, mostly in the Verulamium–London region, but ranging as far north as Slack, Yorks.

There is no site evidence for his date but the presence at the Radlett kilns of mortaria of G. Attius Marinus, identical in form and fabric to those of Castus at Radlett, suggest contemporary production there. G. Attius Marinus' activity there is dated within the period A.D. 95–105 (see no. 12). Castus' mortaria from Radlett, however, clearly antedate most of his known work.

The range of rims used by Castus throughout his activity is unusually large, and some would hardly be out of place in the mid-second century. Stamps from the die represented here occur only on distinctly late rims; a date within the period A.D. 110–40 would certainly cover the use of this die.

16. B II 28B, A.D. 115–30. II B, Room 33.

An incomplete stamp reading]ASTV[. No other stamp from this die is known but the characteristics of both stamp and mortarium would fit Castus. A.D. 100–40 should cover the possible period of production.

17. B II 36E, A.D. 85–105. II A, outside Room 19.

A stamp from one of the six dies known for Devalus, complete impressions giving DEVAI. Twenty-six stamps of Devalus are known from sites in the midlands and south, and one comes from the fort at Castledykes. Fabrics, rims, and distribution leave no doubt that Devalus worked in the potteries near Verulamium. His forms are basically Flavian, and the Castledykes stamp must have reached the site during the last two decades of the century and probably *c.* A.D. 81–7.

18. B I 65, A.D. 60–75. Pit 7.

This stamp reading DIVAI is unique and is probably complete. It is from another die of Devalus, using I instead of E. Flavian but not closely datable, apart from the evidence here.

19. T III 23, A.D. 105–15. II B, Room 1.

A broken stamp reading]INVSF from one of the four dies of Doinus. More than a hundred stamps of Doinus have been found at sites throughout England, Wales, and Scotland, a typical distribution for the foremost potters working in the Verulamium area in the Flavian period. Ten of these stamps come from the Brockley Hill pottery, strongly suggesting activity there. The stamps from Flavian forts in Scotland at Loudon Hill, Newstead (2), and Dalswinton II (*Trans. Dumfries and Galloway N.H. and A.S.* xxiv, 21), and the rims used, all attest a date of A.D. 70–110 to cover the whole of his work. The Dalswinton mortarium is from the same die as no. 20 (below) and, judging by its findspot, must have been in use in the last stages of the occupation. Changes in his rims and stamps tend to suggest that no. 20 is from his last die and no. 19 from an earlier one to be dated A.D. 70–100.

20. B II 28G, A.D. 130–50. II C, Room 32.

A fragmentary stamp from what is probably the latest of Doinus' four dies, and certainly to be dated within the period A.D. 85–110 (see no. 19).

21. B V 31, residual in III, make-up, XIV, 5 Room 3.

A poor impression of a retrograde stamp of Gissus, probably a variant of the well-attested name Cissus (Holder, *Alt-celtischer Sprachschatz*, s.v.). No good impressions of his name-stamp have been found, but many show traces of surprisingly fine cable borders. Five of his stamps have been found recently at Brockley Hill, strongly suggesting that he worked there especially in view of the rarity of his work: his only other stamps are from Brentford, London, and Verulamium (2). A date in the period A.D. 100–40 would cover the rims used.

22. B II 28E, A.D. 135–45. II C, Room 37.

A virtually complete retrograde stamp, possibly to be interpreted as the genitive of Junius. This potter is not to be confused with the Antonine one of the same name working in the potteries at Hartshill and Mancetter, Wars. The fabric and forms point to production in the Verulamium region, and a stamp of his has been found in the kiln area at Radlett and another at Brockley Hill. The only other stamps known are the present example and one from London. He was presumably making mortaria on only a small scale, and his rims point to activity within the period A.D. 100–40.

23. A VI 23, A.D. 105–15. II B, Room 26. Another from A VII 27, A.D. 105–30 (II B, Room 22).

Both stamps read L. FECIT; the F having a bottom stroke like an E. The L could be the initial letter of the potter's name but it might conceivably be expanded as Lugduni. The fabric and rims clearly point to the Verulamium region potteries. Only nine of these stamps are known, but the market extended into the west midlands to Wroxeter and Chester. The rim-profiles are basically Flavian, and a date *c.* A.D. 70–100 is indicated.

24. B II 32E, A.D. 90–105. II A, outside Room 19.

A fragmentary retrograde stamp of Lallans. Thirty-eight stamps, all from one die, are known, from England as far north as Aldborough, and in Wales. His work is entirely in accordance with manufacture in the Verulamium region, and five stamps at Brockley Hill suggest that he may have worked there. A stamp from Heronbridge is dated to the early second century, and his rim-types suggest a date within the period A.D. 90–130. He has some affinities with Saturninus (no. 36 below).

25. A VI+, unstratified.

There are two impressions, close together, of a stamp reading MAR[, or possibly MAVR[. This is the most complete example of this stamp found, but as Mar- is so common a first syllable no conjecture may usefully be made on the complete name. Only further stamps will settle the matter, but it is either the work of an unknown potter or from a new die of Maurus. Only three other stamps from the same die are known, from Wroxeter (2) and from a kiln primarily used by Maurus and Sennius at Mancetter (*Trans. Birmingham A.S.* lxxvii (1959), 11–12). The creamy white fabric is typical of Mancetter and Hartshill, and the rim-forms so closely match those of Sennius and Maurus that the potter may be ascribed to Mancetter with confidence, whether equated with Maurus or not. The association with these potters points to a date c. A.D. 160–90.

26. T XX 23, A.D. 105–15. II B, Room 7.

A stamp from one of the six dies of Marinus. There is no connection between this potter and G. Attius Marinus. Sixty-nine stamps come from sites throughout England, with five from Newstead. Eight of the stamps are from the kiln-site at Brockley Hill and it is probable that he worked there for a time at least. The Newstead examples are earlier than A.D. 105 (J. Curle, *Newstead*, 265) and a FECIT counterstamp of his was found in a pit filled c. A.D. 90 at Richborough (J. P. Bushe-Fox, *Richborough IV*, 251, 17 (B) i). His rims are comparable in range with those of Doinus and a similar date, c. A.D. 70–110, is likely.

27. A VI 23, A.D. 105–15. II B, Room 26.

This fragmentary stamp is from a die which gives MARTN (T with only half a bar at the top), followed inexplicably by FS, and is presumably to be assigned to Martinus or Marinus. In view of the doubt it must be treated separately. Nine stamps are known from the same die, all from the south except for one from Castleshaw, Yorks. The mortaria are typical of products of the Verulamium area, and the profiles point to a date within the period A.D. 70–110.

28. A VI 16, A.D. 130–45. II C, Room 20. Another on no. 1020, c. A.D. 150.

Fragmentary stamps of Melus I. When complete the stamp reads MIILVS/FIICI (the F lacks the lower bar), retrograde. Three other dies are known. Melus worked at Brockley Hill, where twenty-five of his stamped mortaria have been found (*Trans. London and Middlesex A.S.* XI, iii, 259–76). Nineteen stamps have been noted from sites in the south and midlands. The range of his forms is closely similar to that of Castus and a similar date c. A.D. 95–135 is likely. The example figured is certainly later than A.D. 110, and no. 1020 is likely to be.

29. T VIII 5, A.D. 130–50. II C, Room 13. Another from Z I 2, A.D. 155/160 (II D, Room 8).

This stamp reading FECIT was used with a name-stamp of Moricamulus. The fabrics and rims are typical of the potteries near Verulamium. Thirty-six stamps of Moricamulus are known from England and Wales, as far north as Corbridge. A stamp at Richborough was found in a pit whose filling is dated A.D. 80–90 by the excavator (J. P. Bushe-Fox, *Richborough IV*, 249, 26A). The rims are comparable to those of Doinus and a date A.D. 70–110 is fairly certain.

30. A XII 6. Robber-trench.

A fragment from a name stamp of Moricamulus. This die was used alone, being impressed on each side of the spout. See no. 29.

31. B II, unstratified.

An almost complete retrograde stamp from one of the four dies of Mossius. A clay die used by

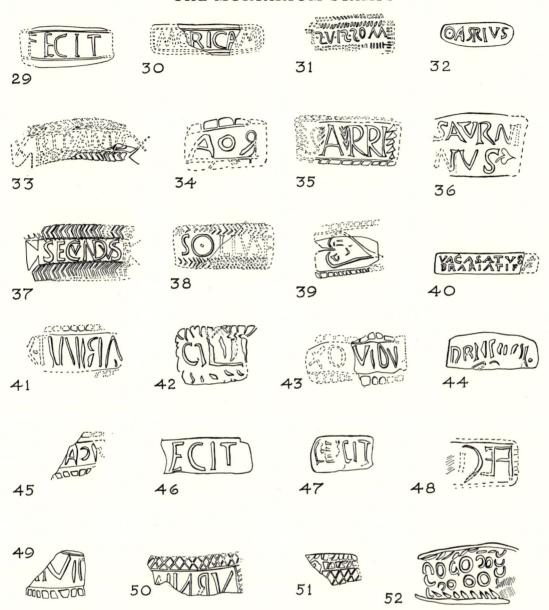

FIG. 146. Mortarium stamps nos. 29–52 ($\frac{1}{2}$) (*drawn by K. F. Hartley*).

him (but not for this stamp) was found at Hartshill in 1960 (*J.R.S.* li (1961), 195, 15), where he undoubtedly worked, though a stamp from the kilns at Mancetter may indicate that he worked there also. Excluding finds from these sites, sixteen stamps are known, all from sites in the midlands and north except for this Verulamium example. A stamp from Rough Castle is clearly Antonine, as his rim-forms suggest. A date *c.* A.D. 135–75 seems likely.

32. B I 6. Robber-trench.

Oastrius (**S**, **T**, and **R** ligatured) seems to be the most likely reading of this stamp. Darrius might have been suggested, but the first letter is clearly an **O**. Neither name is recorded, though compare

Darra (F. Oswald, *Index of Potters' Stamps on Terra Sigillata*, 103). This potter used a counterstamp, not preserved on this vessel, reading LVGD.F, the G in the form of a reversed D (see nos. 2–11, Albinus, for comments on the use of these counterstamps). His work is similar to that of Albinus, Sollus, and Secundus, all working in the potteries near Verulamium. Twelve stamps from this die and its mate are known, all from the south and midlands. His rims indicate activity in the period A.D. 65–95.

33. B I 64, A.D. 60–75. Pit 7.

A fragment from a stamp reading RIPANVS. A counterstamp reading FECIT was often used with it, but occasionally he used a stamp reading LVGV[with this name die. Taking into consideration the identical fabric and rim-forms used, as well as the LVGV... counterstamp, it seems reasonably certain that this Ripanus should be identified with Q. Rutilius Ripanus, who used a counterstamp reading LVGVDV | FACTVS. The stamps giving only RIPANVS, like this example, may well belong to the later part of his career.

Two of his name-stamps, three of his FECIT stamps, and one LVGV[stamp were found at the kilns at Brockley Hill. There is thus little doubt that he worked there at some time. Fourteen stamps have been noted elsewhere, from sites in the south and midlands. A stamp from the early fort at Baginton supports the early date of A.D. 65–95 suggested by his rims.

34. No. 1014, A.D. 155/160.

This stamp reading ROA, retrograde, may be intended as a trademark rather than a name. His stamps have never been found outside Verulamium where eleven have been noted. Seven of these were found in Pit 6 in Insula V, a pit whose filling included waste pottery from a kiln; and though the kiln was not found it cannot have been far away (*Antiq. Journ.* xxi (1941), 271–98). Dr. Corder dated the material in the pit to A.D. 120–60. The illustrated mortaria I–M could certainly not be earlier than A.D. 140 and would fit A.D. 160 well enough, but none of the mortaria of Roa and the illiterate potter mentioned need be as late as this. It would be difficult to see them as contemporaries of the others. A date of A.D. 110–50 would fit their products better.

35. No. 1031, A.D. 155/160.

An almost complete stamp from the most commonly used of the seven dies of Sarrius, whose kilns have been found at Mancetter, and who may also have worked at Hartshill. He is known to have worked also at Rossington Bridge, near Doncaster, but this example is from his midland workshop. Excluding stamps from the kilns, seventy-one examples are known from sites in England, and fourteen from Scotland, making him the most prolific second-century mortarium potter in Britain. In England, as with most of the midland potters, his markets were mostly in the midlands and north, and Verulamium is outside the main marketing area for his work (as it is, indeed, also for Bruscius (no. 14), Mossius (no. 31), and Mar . . . (no. 25)).

The commonness of his work in Antonine deposits in Scotland suggests the basic date (*P.S.A.S.* xciv (1960–1), 111–12); but a stamp recorded from Birdoswald in Period I A (*C. & W.*, 2nd ser. xxx, 187, 2 'with illegible stamp') might suggest he was at work before A.D. 140. On the other hand, he was almost certainly using the same kiln as the late Antonine potter Junius at Mancetter. A date of A.D. 135–75 is likely to cover his activity.

36. B IX 2 (Antonine fire, disturbed, over II D, Room 54). Another from B II 28C, A.D. 130–40 (II C, Room 41).

An almost complete stamp of Saturninus I. Twenty-seven of his stamps are recorded from sites throughout England, including seven from Brockley Hill where he probably worked. A stamp from Milecastle 50 T.W. may be dated to within a few years of A.D. 125 (*C. & W.*, 2nd ser. lii, 34, fig. 7, no. 38). The rims used by Saturninus I suggest activity *c.* A.D. 100–30.

37. No. 371, A.D. 130–50.

An almost complete stamp from the only die used by Secundus. The treatment of the stamp is very reminiscent of two of Ripanus' stamp-types (including no. 33), and at least four mortaria of Secundus have been found at the Brockley Hill kilns (*Trans. London and Middlesex A.S.*, N.S. x, ii, 7), where detached spouts are mentioned in connection with his vessels; this probably means they are wasters, since the addition of clay to make the spout leads to weakness, and they often detach themselves during firing. Twenty-three stamps have now been found in other sites throughout England, and one in Scotland, at Camelon. The first-century date of Secundus' rim-forms is beyond doubt, and the Camelon example must clearly belong to the Flavian occupation. The rims point to a date *c.* A.D. 65–95.

38. A II 47, *c.* A.D. 105. II B, Room 14, make-up.

This stamp is from the most commonly used of the three dies of Sollus. Seventy stamps are known from sites throughout England, including thirty-two from London, one from the kilns at Brockley Hill and three from Flavian forts in Scotland. His fabric, forms, and distribution are all typical of major potters in the potteries near Verulamium in the Flavian period. His rims are consistent with a date of A.D. 70–100.

39. No. 551, A.D. 115–30. Another from site A, unstratified.

This unusual leaf-stamp was used as a counterstamp by a potter whose stamp reads **TMH**. There are marks inside the leaf which could represent letters but cannot be read with any confidence. **TMH** presumably represents *tria nomina*. Nine stamps are known from vessels made by this potter, all in the south-east. A stamp from Colchester was in a deposit containing Flavian and very early second-century material (*Trans. Essex A.S.*, 3rd ser. I, i, 16, no. 7). A date of *c.* A.D. 110–45 would agree well with the rims used.

TMH is one of the few potters for whom there is evidence for migration, in this instance from the vicinity of Colchester to that of Verulamium. The fabrics produced in these two areas differ notably in texture, and the apparent visual difference has been checked by spectrographic analysis (*Bulletin of the Institute of Archaeology*, London, v (1965), 41, no. 223 and 42, no. 222). No. 551 was certainly made in the Verulamium region, but the other is likely to be from Colchester.

40. T III 11, A.D. 155/160. II D, Room 4.

Two fragments from different sides of the same vessel, each with a stamp reading **VACASATVS/ BRARIATIF**, placed along the rim. The sensible habit of stamping along the rim, instead of across it, was common among Gaulish potters (see Adiutor, no. 1). Vacasatus is of more than usual interest because he was the son of Brariatus, the most prolific mortarium-manufacturer in Gallia Belgica, who probably worked at Bavai (*Pro Nervia*, tome i, fasc ii (1923), 114–27). Vacasatus' mortaria and their distribution point to his working in Gallia Belgica also.[1] One other mortarium of Vacasatus is known in Britain, from Gloucester (*Trans. Bristol and Glouc. A.S.* lxvii, 377, and fig. 2, 4). His work is datable to the second century, since it occurs at Arentsburg (Holwerda, 130, no. 27) which only has the very latest of the regular South Gaulish samian ware.

41. B IV 3A (Antonine fire, disturbed, over II D, Room 38–42). Another from T XI 5 (no. 1097), A.D. 270–5 (III, make-up, XIV, 1 Room 1).

This retrograde stamp is hardly ever completely impressed. The **A** is almost certainly the first letter, and the reading **ARIINT**, probably followed by an **X** as space filler, is likely. The names Arentius, Arenus, and Arenticus are all recorded (Holder, *Alt-celtischer Sprachschatz*). There is no doubt that he was a local potter, for of the twenty-three stamps known, thirteen are from Verulamium, five are from London, and the rest from other sites in south-eastern England. One stamp comes from Brockley Hill. His rims indicate activity in the first half of the second century, perhaps within the period A.D. 110–40.

[1] Professor J. E. Bogaers informs us that the stamp of Vacasatus listed under *dolia* in *CIL* xiii, 10005, 25 is in fact on a mortarium. There is therefore no longer any evidence to show that this potter made amphorae as has been suggested e.g. by M. H. Callender, *Roman Amphorae*, under no. 1753.

This potter's stamps like those of Junius I (no. 22), and nos. 42–4 are barely literate, a sad fall from the usually clear stamps of Albinus, Matugenus, Sollus, and their contemporaries. It is not a matter of some potters being more literate than others, for the late stamps of Matugenus, Doinus, and Sollus, and even two of Albinus, show unmistakable tendencies in this direction. The change to semi-literate stamps accelerated in the early second century, and by A.D. 150 or 160 there is no sign that potters in the Verulamium area were stamping mortaria at all. These changes coincided largely with the loss of their Province-wide markets, for during the Trajanic-Hadrianic period the potters at Mancetter and Hartshill, headed by the migrant G. Attius Marinus, were gradually taking over the northern military market, as well as supplying the midlands. Indeed comparison of the Flavian with the second-century mortaria of the Verulamium region shows the mortaria themselves deteriorating in quality. Whether this was the cause or the result of losing the market it is difficult to say, but it is notable that the midland mortaria were gaining in quality at this time. Whatever the precise reason for the deterioration, the fact that potters like Sollus could use both good stamps like no. 38 and a semi-literate one may well indicate that the fine early stamps were the work of professional die-makers, the later ones being made by the potters themselves.

42. A XI 8, A.D. 140–50. II C, Room 15.

A less literate stamp than no. 41, perhaps reading CILV[; Cillus is recorded as a name (Holder, *Alt-celtischer Sprachschatz*). All four stamps known are from Verulamium, and the potter probably worked *c.* A.D. 95–135 to judge from his rims.

43. B IV 18J, A.D. 130–45. II C, Room 39.

The two incomplete stamps on this mortarium, when conflated, give the possible reading OVIDV[with an initial X as a space-filler. Only one other mortarium of his is known, also from Verulamium. They were clearly made locally and the rims suggest a date of A.D. 110–50.

44. T VI 20, A.D. 130–40. II C, Room 3. Another from Z I 26, A.D. 85–105 (II A, Room 5).

Another semi-literate stamp by a potter using local fabric. It is possible to read DRICCIVS, and there was a potter of this name working at Radlett (see no. 54). While the possibility may be held in mind, the extreme difference in rims makes it less likely that they are the same. A date of *c.* A.D. 95–135 is indicated by his rims.

45. No. 550, A.D. 105–30.

A fragmentary retrograde stamp]CA[of an otherwise unknown potter. The name may well begin with C, but this is not absolutely certain. The fabric is a local one and the form points to a date of A.D. 110–45.

46. A VI 23, A.D. 105–15. II B, Room 26. Another from B II 32F, A.D. 75–105 (II A, Room 17).

This incomplete stamp reading]ECIT appears on both sides of the mortaria of this potter. A recent find from Brockley Hill makes it possible to equate this stamp with a counterstamp reading EECIT, used (only rarely) by Doinus (see nos. 19 and 20) with an early name-stamp which is not among those illustrated here. *c.* A.D. 70–100.

47. A VI 31, A.D. 85–105. II A, Room 10.

A badly smeared stamp which was clearly intended to read FECIT. Unfortunately no other example is recorded from the same die and the name of the potter remains unknown. The fabric is local, and the form suggests a date within the period A.D. 80–120.

The practice of using a separate stamp reading FECIT was a common one in the potteries near Verulamium; elsewhere its use is reserved to G. Attius Marinus and certain potters working at or near Colchester in the late first or early second centuries. Otherwise with few exceptions F(ecit) was included in the name die after the name, or the nominative or genitive form of the name was used alone.

48. B II 26A, A.D. 150–155/160. II D, Room 25.

A fragmentary retrograde FECIT stamp, otherwise unrecorded. This belonged to a local potter, probably of the period A.D. 110–40.

49. V XXXIII 10, A.D. 130–50. II C, Room 5.

A fragmentary stamp reminiscent of Ovidus (no. 43), but not from the same die, and quite possibly by another potter. A date within the period A.D. 110–50 is likely.

50. A II 39, A.D. 105–15. II B, Room 10.

An incomplete retrograde stamp otherwise unrecorded, with a neat criss-cross border. Only the discovery of more complete examples will allow the potter to be identified; but this mortarium is a local product, probably of the period A.D. 90–140.

51. T XI 6, A.D. 270–5. III, make-up, XIV, 1 Room 1. Another from T XI 5 (same date and context).

These two stamps are certainly from the same vessel. No other stamp from the same die is known, but the fabric and particularly the crystalline pink and brownish grit allow the mortarium to be identified as a product of one of the kilns near Oxford, such as that at Cowley (*Oxoniensia*, vi (1941), 9–22) where very similar mortaria were stamped with meaningless trademarks. A date of A.D. 140–80 would fit the rim used. See no. 1096.

52. B IV 22, A.D. 130–50. II C, wall-trench 36/44.

This trademark was not made with a die but is a graffito *ante cocturam*. A slightly different version, now incomplete, was made on the other side of the spout. The fabric is local, and this is the only known example of the use of a graffito in place of a stamp by a potter of the Verulamium region. In fact the practice is rare everywhere. A date *c.* A.D. 100–35 seems likely for the rim used.

53. A II 39 (not drawn), A.D. 105–15. II B, Room 10.

A fragmentary stamp, too indistinct to draw. The fabric is local and the rim probably belongs to the period A.D. 110–40.

54. No. 769, A.D. 130–40 (not drawn.)

This fragment preserves part of the border of a stamp, almost certainly the lower border of one used by Driccius, but unfortunately none of his known stamps are complete enough for direct comparison to be made. He worked at Radlett, *c.* A.D. 110–50, a date which accords with this mortarium.

VII. REPORT ON SAMPLES OF DEPOSITS
by Dr. I. W. Cornwall

1. Site B. *Bronze working slab* (pp. 18, 19).

   The sample contains considerable copper and a small amount of tin-salts, in approximately the correct proportions to represent 10 per cent tin-bronze.

   The coarser acid-insolubles, after treatment with concentrated hydrochloric acid consisted of quartz- and flint-sand with much wood-charcoal (mainly birch), small clay-aggregates fired red and a mass, some 1 cm.³, of sintered quartz and clay, which had evidently been subjected to a high temperature.

   These constituents confirm the association of the material with a hearth or furnace and bronze-working and suggest that the place was perhaps a foundry-floor.

2. B IV 21A, *Trampled earth with* (?) *iron slag.* II B, Room 26 (pp. 42–3).

   The washed sample showed a good deal of charcoal and burnt earth and clay, mostly in smallish crumbs, but this was only evidence of the presence of hearth-material, possibly only dumped ashes.

   A small fraction (perhaps 5 per cent) was separated from this using a small permanent magnet, which proved, on visual examination under the binocular, to consist of flakes of magnetite ('blacksmith's scales') and globules of glassy slag with blowholes and heat-polished surfaces. These prove that iron-smelting and working took place at no great distance, though perhaps not at the exact spot from which the sample was taken.

3. *Red deposit* in bowl no. 928 from B V 23, Interspace north-west of Room 43 (p. 332).

   Sandy intensely ferruginous clay (not natural, I think), fired at red heat for some time with dehydration of iron oxides (limonite-yellow) to haematite, Fe_2O_3. Impure red ochre, artificially, perhaps fortuitously, formed.

INDEX

PLATE I

Trench A IV: General view of the excavations, looking N., showing the two fires

PLATE II

a. Trench B IV looking E. Period II B Rooms 30–2 in foreground; stone wall of Period III in background

b. Trench B IV at Period I level (p. 9)

PLATE III

a. General view of XIV, Buildings 6 and 7, looking S.W.

(photo: J. H. Brown)

b. Burnt remains of Excavation hut, showing floor-joists (p. 75)

PLATE IV

a. Trench T XX looking E, showing section of Periods I–II D and of the chalk foundations of XIV, 2; Building XIV, 1 in background (p. 6)

b. Chalk foundations of XIV, 6 and wall-trenches of II D Rooms 48–50 in foreground: permanent display of Period I plan in background (pp. 6, 80)

PLATE V

a. S.E. section of Trench B IV with walls of Period I exposed: N.E. portion

b. S.E. section of Trench B IV with walls of Period I exposed: S.E. portion

PLATE VI

a. Trench Z I, S.E. face. Compare fig. 23, Section C–C^{I} (p. 107)

b. Trench T XX, N.E. face. Compare fig. 9, Section Y–Z (p. 27)

PLATE VII

a. Trench Z I, S. corner, showing stratification

b. Trench T VII, E. corner, showing stratification: compare fig. 27, Section B–B¹ for left-hand face

PLATE VIII

b. The same after further excavation: Wall-trench 7/25A of
Period II D

a. Trench T II, S. face showing continued use of same line for
wall-trenches of successive Periods (p. 9). Compare fig. 27,
Section B–B¹

PLATE IX

a. Trench T XX, N.W. face showing chunky daub of Boudiccan fire between 1 and 2 ft., and Antonine fire in top 2 ft.; compare fig. 7 (p. 17)

b. Trench T III, N.E. face, showing Period I wall above the lowest label and Period II A Wall 1/2 slightly higher, left. The prominent gravel floor half way up is layer 18, floor of II C Room 2, fig. 24, Section A–A¹ (p. 109)

PLATE X

a. Trenches A IV–VI looking S.W.: Period I, Rooms 13–16 exposed

b. Trench B IV: Period I buildings exposed: foreground, right, Fuel-pit of II A Room 23 (p. 27)

PLATE XI

a. Trench T XX: Period I Wall-trench 6/8 cut by Pit 13; left, the Tub (p. 15 and fig. 6)

b. Trench A I: foreground, the Bin in I Room 15; background, I, Rooms 16 and 20 (p. 18)

PLATE XII

a. Trench A II: wattle sockets of I, Room 21 (p. 9)

b. Trench B I: wattle sockets of I, Room 19A, looking N.E. (p. 9)

PLATE XIII

a. Trench B II, Period I Rooms 18 (foreground) and 27 with bronze-working boxes: left, similar box in II A Room 20 (p. 18)

b. Trench B II looking N.: Period II A, Wall 17/19 showing surviving beam (pp. 9, 28)

PLATE XIV

a. Trench B II, looking S.W.: II B, Room 30 back left, 32 right; chalk floor of II C Room 41 in section, centre

b. Trench T VII looking E.: II B, Room 2 right; Room 3 top; Room 4 left

PLATE XV

a. Trench B IV: hoard of *denarii* in II B, Room 34, beside
Wall-trench (p. 43)

b. Trench B IV: skeleton of dog in II C, Room 40 (p. 57)

PLATE XVI

a. Trench T VI looking E.: Period II C Wall-trench 3/4 at level of layer 15
(pp. 9, 54) (cf. fig. 27, Section B–B¹)

b. Trench B I: oven in II C, Room 27 (p. 56)

PLATE XVII

a. Trench B III: *aediculae* from the S.E., showing the step added in Period II D (pp. 57 ff.)

b. The *aediculae* with the step of Period II D removed

c. The *aediculae* from the N.W., showing the packing of Period II D. The back wall has been removed

PLATE XVIII

a. Aedicula A from the N.E. showing votive pot (p. 57)

b. Aedicula A from the S.W.

PLATE XIX

a. Aedicula A from the S.E., with step of Period II D

b. The *aediculae* from the E. (p. 57)

PLATE XX

a. Trench B IV, looking E.: Period II D, Rooms 36–9 in foreground (p. 74)

b. Trench B IV, looking S.W.: Period II D, Room 25 (foreground) with Rooms 42–36 behind (p. 80)

PLATE XXI

a. Trench B IV, looking E.: Period II D, Wall-trench 25/42 and rough chalk packing of hollow
(p. 80)

b. Trench A VII, looking W.: Wall-trenches 25/30, drain (left) and fuel-pit in Room 30 (p. 79)

PLATE XXII

a. Trench A XI, looking S.: chalk foundation of XIV 2, and chalk floor of Period II D, Room 13 beyond: Wall-trench 13/14 left foreground

b. Trench T II, looking W.: II D, Wall-trench 7/25A, with walls of XIV, 1 Room 2 (p. 9)

PLATE XXIII

a. Keying for wall-plaster: II D, Room 23, Wall 23/24

b. The main frame: II D, N.W. wall of Room 23, looking N.W.

c. Hurdle-frame, II D, Wall 23/24, looking N.E.

d. II D, Wall 17/23, looking S.E.

The dissection of timber-framed walls: Trench I, Period II D (pp. 6 ff.)

PLATE XXIV

a. Trench A I: II D, N. Corner of Room 23 (pp. 6, 81)

b. Trench A I: II D, Room 24, looking S.W. (p. 79)

c. Trench A X: II D, S.W. Wall of Room 30 (p. 81)

PLATE XXV

b. Trench T XI, looking S.W.: II D, Room 4, hearth (p. 76)

a. Trench A I, looking S.E.: II D, Wall 23/24 (pp. 6, 78)

PLATE XXVI

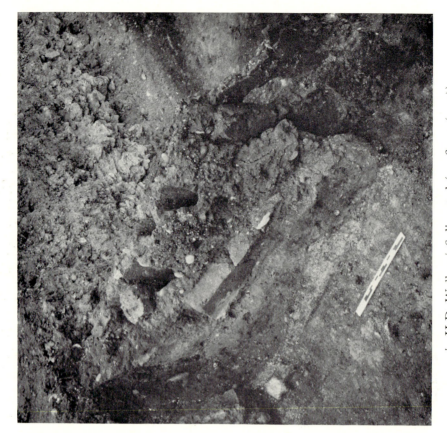

b. II D, Wall 55/56 dissected (see fig. 4 (p. 7))

a. Trench B XV, looking N.: II D, Wall 55/56 (pp. 7 f.)

PLATE XXVII

a. Chalk foundations of Building XIV 7, looking N.E., with II D plank-lined drain (centre) and Wall 55/56 (left foreground) (pp. 9, 76)

b. Trench A I, looking N.W.: iron shovel (Fig. 60, 6) beside N.W. wall of II D, Room 23 (pp. 78, 81)

PLATE XXVIII

a. Trench T XXI, looking S.W.: section of tub in II D, Room 10 (p. 76)

b. Trench A IV, looking S.W.: hearth and vessels in II D, Room 17 (p. 78)

c. Trench B II, looking S.W.: *opus signinum* floor of II B, Room 30 pierced by post-holes of Period III partition (pp. 41, 102)

PLATE XXIX

a. Trench B XI: floor-joists and planks of II D, Room 46 (p. 74)

b. Trench B XIII, looking S.E.: floor-planks in II D, Room 49 and sleeper
beam of Wall 48/49 (p. 75)

PLATE XXX

a. Trench B XI, looking N.: II D, Room 46, showing masonry packing in Wall-trench 46/52 (p. 80)

b. Trench T I looking N.E.: external Wall-trench of Room 25A with stamped daub (p. 77)

PLATE XXXI

b. Trench B XV, looking S.E.: fallen pottery in II D, Room 55, beside S.W. Wall (p. 80)

a. Trench B XV, looking N.E.: fallen pottery in II D, Room 55 (p. 80)

PLATE XXXII

a. Trench T III, looking S.: XIV, 1 Room 1, late subdivision (p. 99)

b. Trench B XIV, looking N.W.: pillars of XIV, 6 Room 3 (p. 100)

PLATE XXXIII

a. Mosaic floor in XIV, 5 Room 3, looking S.E. to the *aedicula* of Period II C (p. 103)

b. The mosaic looking S.W.

PLATE XXXIV

a. The Lion and Stag mosaic of XIV, 5 Room 3, looking S.W. (pp. 102 f.)

b. The same, remounted

PLATE XXXV

b. The cellar, looking N.E.: showing bones and tiles in the latest occupation layer (p. 106)

a. Trench BI, looking N.E.: The timber-lined cellar of Period III (pp. 103 ff.)

PLATE XXXVI

b. The bronze jug (fig. 43, 143) in the Box (Pit 20) in the cellar floor

a. The timber-lined 'Box' (Pit 20) in the cellar floor, looking S.W. (p. 105)

PLATE XXXVII

a. Bones, tiles, and metal objects in the cellar (p. 105)

b. Iron objects on the cellar floor including the carpenter's plane (top right)

PLATE XXXVIII

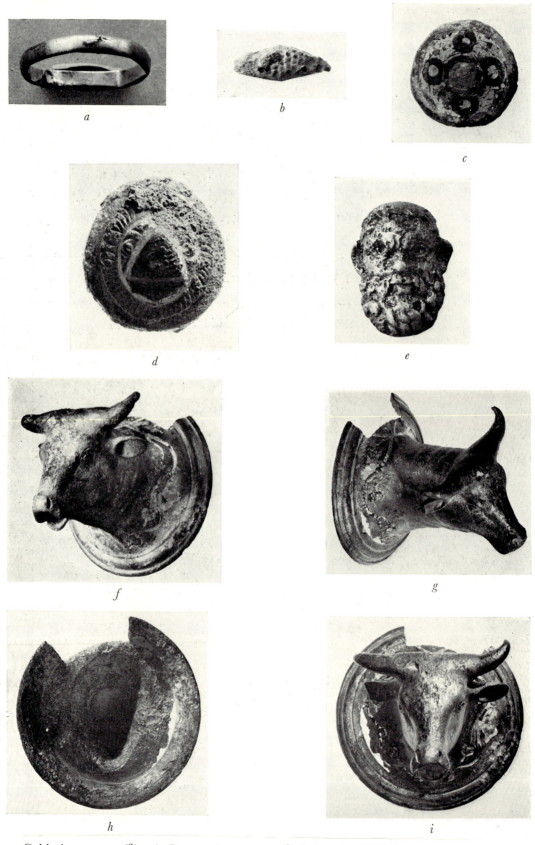

a. Gold ring, no. 25 ($\frac{2}{1}$)   *b.* Bronze ring, no. 29 ($\frac{2}{1}$) (*photo: R. Wilkins*)   *c.* Bronze enamelled stud, no. 97 ($\frac{2}{1}$) (*photo: R. Wilkins*)   *d.* Bronze mount, no. 108 ($\frac{2}{1}$) (*photo: R. Wilkins*)
e. Bronze mask, no. 140 ($\frac{1}{1}$)   *f.* Bronze spout with niello decoration, no. 142 (*c.* $\frac{1}{1}$)
g. Bronze spout, no. 142 ($\frac{1}{1}$) (*photo: R. Wilkins*)   *h.* Bronze spout, no. 142 ($\frac{1}{1}$) (*photo: R. Wilkins*)
i. Bronze spout, no. 142 ($\frac{1}{1}$) (*photo: R. Wilkins*)

PLATE XXXIX

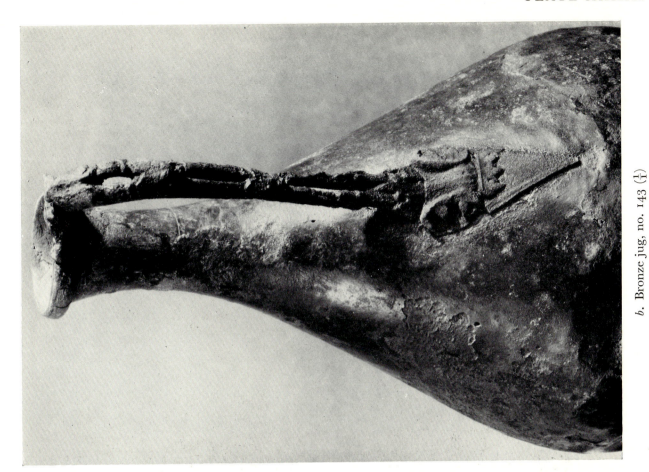

b. Bronze jug, no. 143 ($\frac{1}{1}$)

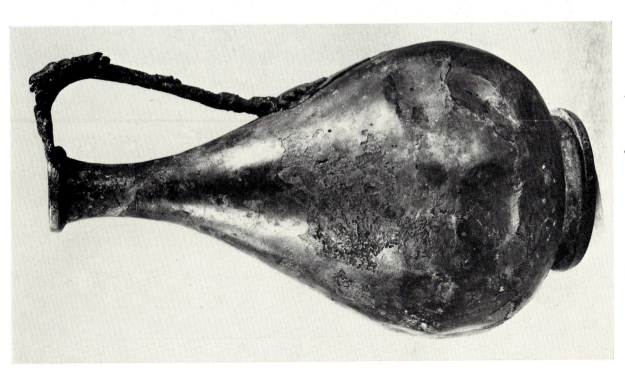

a. Bronze jug, no. 143 ($\frac{2}{3}$) (p. 132)

PLATE XLII

b. The Verulamium Venus

a. The Verulamium bronze Venus (no. 155, p. 140):
height *c.* 20 cm.

PLATE XLIII

b. The Verulamium Venus

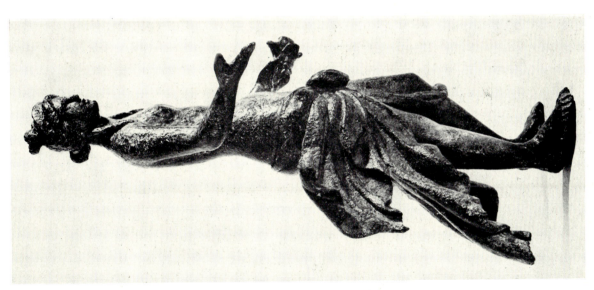

a. The Verulamium Venus (p. 140, no. 155)

PLATE XLIV

b. Plaque of iron, bronze, and lead (p. 138, no. 151) ($\frac{3}{4}$)

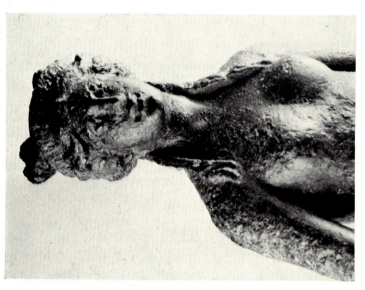

a. The Verulamium Venus: detail (c. $\frac{3}{2}$)

PLATE XLV

c. Bronze scrap from II B, Room 4 ($\frac{1}{1}$) (pp. 26, 42, 144, No. 171)
(photo: R. Wilkins)

a. Bundle of bronze strips ($\frac{1}{1}$) (p. 144, no. 172)
(photo: R. Wilkins)

b. Bronze scrap from II A, Room 20 ($\frac{1}{1}$) (p. 144, no. 170)
(photo: R. Wilkins)

PLATE XLVI

b. Lead object with stamps, bottom side (½) (p. 146, no. 184) *(photo: R. Wilkins)*

a. Lead object with stamps, top side (½) (p. 146, no. 184) *(photo: R. Wilkins)*

PLATE XLVII

a. Lead object with stamps, detail ($\frac{2}{1}$) (*photo: R. Wilkins*)

b. Selection of the 108 lead roundels ($\frac{1}{1}$) (p. 146, no. 185)

PLATE XLVIII

a. Polished bone dolphin, no. 210 ($\frac{2}{1}$) (p. 152)

b. Purbeck Marble plaque, no. 232 ($\frac{1}{2}$) (p. 156)

PLATE XLIX

b. Wooden box from the Fayûm, Egypt: length of box 26·5 cm.
(*photo: Ashmolean Museum*)

a. Pieces of wooden boxes and caskets from the Fayûm,
Egypt (p. 149) (*photo: Ashmolean Museum*)

PLATE L

a. Carpenter's plane of iron ($\frac{1}{3}$) (p. 166, no. 14)

b. Plasterer's float of iron (*c.* $\frac{1}{4}$) (p. 168, no. 18)

PLATE LI

b. Black samian cup,
detail ($\frac{1}{2}$)

a. Black samian cup ($\frac{1}{2}$) (p. 254, no. D112)

c. Rhenish beaker ($\frac{1}{2}$) (p. 348, no. 1114)

PLATE LII

a. Crucibles from II D, Room 55 (pp. 81, 366)

b. Crucible from Pit 7 ($\frac{1}{2}$)
(p. 365, no. 1)

PLATE LIII

a. Graffito no. 6 ($\frac{1}{2}$)
(p. 364)

b. Graffito no. 9 ($\frac{1}{2}$) (p. 364)

c. Amphora with dipinti ($\frac{3}{8}$) (cf. p. 266, no. 18)

PLATE LIV

No. 1   No. 2

No. 3

No. 4

Fragments of burnt daub from the Boudiccan fire (p. 161)
(scales: 1–3 ($\frac{1}{3}$), 4 (c. $\frac{1}{2}$))

PLATE LV

No. 5

No. 6

Fragments of burnt daub from the Antonine fire $(\frac{1}{3})$ (p. 161)

PLATE LVI

No. 7

No. 8

No. 9

Fragments of burnt daub from the Antonine fire ($\frac{1}{3}$) (p. 161)

PLATE LVII

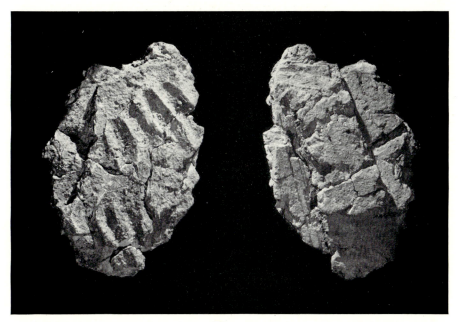

No. 10

No. 11

Fragments of burnt daub from the Antonine fire ($\frac{1}{3}$) (pp. 161 f.)

PLATE LVIII

No. 12

No. 13

Fragments of burnt daub from the Antonine fire ($\frac{1}{3}$) (p. 162)

PLATE LIX

No. 14

No. 15

Fragments of burnt daub from the Antonine fire ($\frac{1}{3}$) (p. 162)

PLATE LX

No. 16

No. 17

No. 18

Fragments of burnt daub (16, 17) and plaster (18) from the Antonine fire ($\frac{1}{3}$)
(p. 162)